Step-daughters of England

MANCHESTER
UNIVERSITY PRESS

Step-daughters of England

British women modernists and the national imaginary

JANE GARRITY

Manchester University Press

MANCHESTER AND NEW YORK

distributed exclusively in the USA by Palgrave

Copyright © Jane Garrity 2003

The right of Jane Garrity to be identified as the author of this work has been asserted by her in accordance with the Copyright, Designs and Patents Act 1988.

Published by Manchester University Press
Oxford Road, Manchester M13 9NR, UK
and Room 400, 175 Fifth Avenue, New York, NY 10010, USA
http://www.manchesteruniversitypress.co.uk

Distributed exclusively in the USA by
Palgrave, 175 Fifth Avenue, New York, NY 10010, USA

Distributed exclusively in Canada by
UBC Press, University of British Columbia, 2029 West Mall, Vancouver, BC, Canada V6T 1Z2

British Library Cataloguing-in-Publication Data
A catalogue record for this book is avalaible from the British Library

Library of Congress Cataloging-in-Publication Data applied for

ISBN 0 7190 6163 6 *hardback*
    0 7190 6164 4 *paperback*

First published 2003

11 10 09 08 07 06 05 04 03   10 9 8 7 6 5 4 3 2 1

Typeset in Caslon and Frutiger Condensed
by Koinonia Ltd, Manchester
Printed in Great Britain
by Bookcraft (Bath) Ltd, Midsomer Norton

For my mother,
Sophia (Toutoulis) Garrity,
and in memory of my father,
Charles Garrity (1928–99),
with gratitude and love

Contents

Acknowledgements

It is a pleasure, after all these years, to have the opportunity to thank those who have been instrumental to the completion of this project. This book began as a doctoral dissertation at the University of California, Berkeley, where I was extremely fortunate to work with three exceptional teachers: Elizabeth Abel, Susan Schweik, and Caren Kaplan. I am indebted in particular to Elizabeth for her continued support, intellectual encouragement, and critical eye, and especially for her friendship and nurturance of this project since its infancy. Her unflagging generosity and scrupulous reading of my work helped me to clarify my arguments and see what was often already there in encrypted form. Sue's enthusiasm for my inchoate early ideas regarding marginalized British women writers was a great inspiration and contributed centrally to my determination to pursue this topic. Caren's scholarship has been a model and an inspiration for my own. I am grateful for her useful advice and professional assistance in navigating academic life; she has remained the best academic cheerleader a girl could ever conjure. At Berkeley, my modernism dissertation group – Kate Brown, Cindy Franklin, Teresa Fulker, Christina Hauck, Leila May, and Irene Tucker – was a sustaining source of pleasure, interpersonal support, and intellectual rigor. It remains for me a model of what an intellectual community should approximate. This book has its origins in a bracing undergraduate seminar taught at Berkeley in 1980 by Diane Buczek; for stimulating my interest in Virginia Woolf, and for modeling the kind of teaching I now seek to emulate, I thank Diane most warmly.

Many thanks are due to friends and colleagues at the University of Colorado who generously provided expertise from their own fields – responding to an assortment of idiosyncratic queries – or read selected chapters of this book: Katherine Eggert, Jeremy Green, Bruce Holsinger, Kelly Hurley, Timothy Morton, Cathy Preston, Beth Robertson, Terry Rowden, Charlotte Sussman, Mark Winokur, and Sue Zemka. I am grateful to Anna Brickhouse for reading a draft of my Introduction at a critical stage and wielding her astonishing editorial skills. I owe special thanks to Suzanne Juhasz, who painstakingly read the entire manuscript and offered nuanced suggestions. Other colleagues at the University of Colorado were equally generous with their encouragement: Jeffrey DeShell, Sidney Goldfarb, Jill Heydt, Ann Kibbey, Mary Klages, Lee Krauth, Ed Rivers, Jeffrey Robinson, Elizabeth Sheffield, John Stevenson, and Eric White. I am grateful to the graduate students in my two seminars, "British women modernist prose writers" (1995) and "British modernism and nationalism" (1999); their helpful suggestions as fellow interlocutors and enthusiastic readers of noncanonical British fiction enabled me to further discern the overarching argument of this book. For their exemplary research skills, I thank Meghan Savage, Thérèse Migraine-George, Alison Perry, and the incomparable Lindsey Collins and Evalie Horner.

I have benefited from the commentary of several modernist scholars who read successive drafts or offered invaluable suggestions: Jessica Berman, Kristen Bluemel, Pamela Caughie, Laura Doan, Christina Hauck, Tamar Katz, Alison Light, Patricia Moran, Suzanne Raitt, Sonita Sarker, and Brenda Silver. I am grateful, in particular, to Alison, whose ground-breaking work on the interwar period helped to inspire this project. I value Tamar's friendship and collegial support not least of all for the fact that we both lived through the "Dorothy Richardson period" of our respective books at the same time. Special thanks are due to Tricia, whose friendship and modernist expertise since graduate school I've greatly appreciated. I thank Avril Maddrell for introducing me to interwar women geographers, and am grateful to Roslyn Reso Foy for helping me to sort out the strangeness that is Mary Butts. Susan Kingsley Kent's magical box of primary historical sources landed in my lap at an auspicious moment; without her generosity and willingness to respond to endless questions, this book would have been a diminished thing.

Old friends have sustained me over the many years that it has taken to complete this project. Although it is unlikely that most will ever read a word of this book, I am grateful for their love and continued interest in what must have seemed an arcane project: Valerie Anderson, Rebecca Biron, Sidney Boral, Nancy Bucka, Christa Christaki, Martha Ertman, Karen Graves, Sue Ann Mead, Judy Olsen, Liz Ozol, Colleen Paretty, Sue Petrakis, Kit Price, Kate Sher, Dena Schoen, Jean Savoia, Andy Steckle, Kathryn Stockton, Jane Whitley, and Michelle Warren. I am grateful to Linda Fitzgerald, my first intellectual friend, whose brilliance and stimulating conversation have inspired me since my years as an undergraduate. My lifelong friendship with Peggy Hall, whose fearlessness and appetite for adventure are a joy, has always helped to keep me sane. Eve Cominos's big passions and kindness – and her incredible generosity in every way – have been invaluable. I owe special thanks to Laurel Holloway, for always showering me with letters, talismans, and medicinal emollients, and to Pauline Shaver, whose unstinting loyalty and promise of lodgement (both literal and spiritual) have been a great source of comfort. I am particularly grateful to Pamela Body, whose love of ritual and the unseen since childhood helps me to remember that there is life beyond academia. Mary Caraway's friendship and devotion have been sustaining in every way, and Cindy Weinstein's intellectual voracity, solidity, and ability to make me laugh have remained an ongoing source of pleasure since our International House days. I am tremendously grateful to Catherine Rubenstein, for her compassion, and Catherine Ratcliffe, for her fabulous sense of humor; both have been unflinchingly steadfast friends, and models of integrity, over the years.

Since graduate school I have relied on Mary Pat Brady, Cindy Franklin, Laura Green, Leila May, Lori Merish, Frann Michel, Judith Rosen, and Kerry Walk, whose far-flung friendships I have come to treasure and whose generosity of spirit helped me to complete this book. Despite the geographical distance between us, Irene Tucker continues to offer sustenance and encouragement through long-distance phone calls that always reaffirm for me the splendid virtue of old friend-ships. I am especially indebted to Kate McCullough, who not only provided astute readings at critical junctures but has been a source of incalculable intellectual and emotional support. The Denver law girls – Christine Cimini, Jessica West, and Julie Nice – are that rare combination of brilliance and loyalty; for their inexplicable interest in this project and their unflinching advocacy, I thank them. I want too to express my gratitude to Donna Goldstein, Toni Rosato, Jeannie Quinn, and Polly Thistlewaite, whose companionship through many dinners helped to make the completion of this book a pleasure rather than a chore.

This project has benefited from the financial support of a National Endow-ment for the Humanities Summer Stipend (1997), which enabled me to conduct archival research on Mary Butts at the Bancroft Library, and a University of Colorado Graduate Committee on the Arts and Humanities Travel Grant (1997), which made possible my research at the British Library. A Summer Session Research Grant (1998), also from the University of Colorado, provided me with the time and funding to complete the primary research for this book. Those at Manchester University Press could not have been more helpful. I am indebted to the staff for their patience and kind support.

My most profound gratitude is to my family, which has nurtured and facili-tated my aspirations. I deeply regret that my father, Charles Garrity, did not live to see the completion of this project; its publication would have made him very proud. My father's resolute and myriad support and guidance continues to sustain me to this day, and it is because of him that I first learned to appreciate the pleasures of language. My debt to my mother, Sophia Garrity, cannot adequately be conveyed in words. She has fed me in countless ways. This book would not have been possible without her unalterable faith in my abilities and her unconditional love and encouragement. I am grateful to my brother, Tom Garrity, and my sister-in-law, Eunice Baek, who provided indispensable aid and goodwill through phone calls, reassurance, and mail-order treats. The thoughtfulness and encouragement of Bob and Alayne Jacobs have helped to fuel me throughout the writing process. I owe most of all to my partner and ally, Karen Jacobs, who has been a witness to this book from its earliest stages to its present incarnation. Karen's insight and sheer intelligence permeate this project – which would have been unimaginable without her shrewd eye, incomparable wit, and indefatigable scolding and caressing of every word. For her unwavering support, love, and confidence in me for fifteen years, I thank her with my entire self and with great affection.

An earlier version of Chapter 3 was published as "Encoding bi-location: Sylvia Townsend Warner and the erotics of dissimulation," in Karla Jay ed., *Lesbian Erotics* (New York and London: New York University Press, 1995), 241–68.

Introduction

Conquering new worlds –
women, modernism, and nationalism

A whole world is watching ... It would be a wonderful thing if it could be said that women's franchise had not only brought a new status to women throughout the Empire, but had helped members of all political parties at home to realise ... the uniting and knitting together of the hearts of all persons ... building "Jerusalem" in "England's green and pleasant land". (Duchess of Atholl, *Women and Politics*, 1931)

[A]s a woman, I have no country. As a woman I want no country. As a woman my country is the whole world. (Virginia Woolf, *Three Guineas*, 1938)

Women, Virginia Woolf argues in 1938, are still "step-daughter[s]" and "not full daughter[s] ... of England" because their civil and social rights are so curtailed in comparison to those of men.[1] Yet even the designation "step-daughters" is misleading: during the interwar period, British women were viewed primarily as mothers, not daughters, in the eyes of the State. Valued for their role as reproductive conduits, white Englishwomen's bodies were subjected to a variety of regulatory practices that sought to construct them, physically as well as spiritually, as potential mothers of the British race. Chiefly valued as national assets because they could bear healthy white citizens, these select Englishwomen would both stabilize the imaginary borders of the nation and contribute to the expansion of its empire.[2] Women's identification with nation was thus submerged in their identification with race, their status as citizens conflated with and compromised by the State's perception that their national role was first and foremost to be the guarantors of British racial stability. *Step-daughters of England: British Women Modernists and the National Imaginary* argues that this presumption of a sacred racial destiny necessarily complicates any attempt to speak exclusively about British women's role as national subjects during the interwar period. Drawing on the work of four central British modernists, from the canonical to the newly recovered, *Step-daughters of England* examines this female experience of nation between the wars, exploring novels that were produced during a period of crisis in Britain, roughly from 1915 to 1938, when questions about women's nationality status were subject to anxious scrutiny and debate. I focus specifically on the experimental novel as an exemplary site through which both the hegemony of and critical resistance to national identity formation are staged. The writers I examine – Dorothy Richardson, Sylvia Townsend Warner, Mary Butts, and Virginia Woolf – exhibit contradictory responses to the ubiquitous maternal and racial link to national identification, one which positions the female body as central to the maintenance of the nation, and, crucially, to the empire as well. Although the women in this study are, in general, overtly critical of imperialism, aligning it with masculinity and the espousal of loyalty to a contaminated Englishness, they nonetheless remain invested in an idea of nation that is inextricably tied up in conceptions of the female body which in turn cannot be severed from their concept of empire.

Indeed, within the context of waning imperialism, ideas of *nation* and *empire* were imbricated in one another precisely through tropes of the female reproductive body, and were used interchangeably as terms in public discourse, particularly in relation to topics such as eugenics and racial hygiene. Britain's losses in the Anglo-Boer War at the turn of the century, accompanied by the perception that military recruits were physically degenerate and racially inferior, precipitated a wave of eugenic and pro-natalist propaganda that persisted into the interwar period and continued to identify women with child-bearing, evolutionary progress, and national purity. The white, middle-class, procreative female body was regarded as integral to the well-being of the nation and central to empire-building, key to conceptions of racial fitness and national stability. Although much anti-feminist backlash circulated in Britain during the interwar years, concomitant with this rhetoric was the pervasive view (held by pro- as well as anti-feminists) that women were the redemptive embodiment of the nation's civilizing values. Given the centrality of motherhood during this period, it is striking to note that of the four women foregrounded here only Mary Butts had a child (whom she roundly neglected). Eschewing literal motherhood, they instead position themselves as *daughters* of the nation, suggesting that this filial relation is a necessary precondition of citizenship for women. Yet precisely because the ideology of motherhood was understood to be a national imperative, British women modernists still had to negotiate this conceptual impasse in their attempts to situate themselves as national subjects. Although Richardson, Warner, Butts, and Woolf often balk at the supposition that the reproductive female body legitimizes women's participation in national life, each nevertheless taps in to the correlative presumption that women are morally superior beings by trading on the idea of women's national responsibility and simultaneously alluding to the fact that Britain is already expressly gendered as a 'feminine' national body. British women modernists remain uneasily tied to such dominant discourses of national belonging and imperial redemption, plagued by fierce emotions and irrational desires that inform their sacred loyalties to place and betray their varied unconscious attachments to England.[3] Like many interwar Britons, these women were arguably seduced by the proliferation of mass cultural materials (such as books, magazine articles, and radio programs) that idealized English life and heritage and associated national character with ancient pastoral virtue that linked the countryside with authentic Englishness. Throughout their work we find traces of the vicissitudes of national desire and longing, even in that of Woolf and Warner – of the four, the most overtly critical of nationalism and the project of empire. Seeking continually both to disavow and to reify their English-ness, these women adopt a series of complex, ambivalent, and experimental literary strategies of identification and disidentification in locating themselves as national subjects. As Susan remarks in the first draft of Woolf's *The Waves*, simultaneously distancing herself from her country and confessing her ardent national attachment: "It was merely England ... I should never be myself anywhere else."[4]

The writers examined here pursue these varied experimental strategies by fabricating literary compensations for the political agency they lack in real life, trading on the familiar British trope of geographical expansiveness and conquest. Reinscribing the rhetoric of empire even as they resist it, they deploy spatial and territorial metaphors to carve a place for themselves within the national imaginary. Woolf captures the seductiveness of this project from a literary perspective, equating aesthetic mastery with the spatialization of identity, when she imagines "rows of books – territories conquered ... Before one can be a poet ... one must stand on a pinnacle...and survey the world."[5] Is such metaphorical colonization of literary space inevitably a form of imperialization, or is it possible to interpret the modernist mapping of simulacral space in less coercive terms? Woolf herself begins to open up this question regarding the ethical status of "our psychological geo-graphy" when she urges contemporary reviewers to abandon convention and actively seek out new literary terrain in terms which stress the fantasy of exploration: "Could [you] not," she rhetorically asks critics, "sometimes turn around and, shading [your] eyes in the manner of Robinson Crusoe on the desert island, look into the future and trace on its mist the faint lines of the land which some day perhaps we may reach?"[6] Like Crusoe, who lands on a seemingly deserted island and claims it without violence, Woolf's imaginary critic replicates the outcome of imperial expansion and settlement, but conspicuously without struggle or blood-shed. Indulging in a kind of utopian colonialism, Woolf conveys how fundamentally the mythologizing of place and the idea of conquest have shaped the formation of English identity and narrative. In so doing, she reveals the imaginative effects of empire on English literature – "are not enterprise and exploration a part of Shakespeare?" – even though she elsewhere ridicules novels which senselessly "celebrate the glories of the English Empire."[7] Woolf's bifurcated response, both repulsed by the jingoism of empire and seduced by the irreducible centrality of the narrative of conquest, exemplifies the conflicted position of the interwar British woman writer: rhetorically invested in mapping psychic and literary geographies while seeking to divest herself of the legacy of violence implicit in reterritorialization.

Because these imperial tropes – expansiveness, exploration, discovery, mapping, usurpation, appropriation – are so culturally pervasive, so imbricated in popular idioms of the period, modernist women invariably recapitulate them in their attempt to re-imagine themselves as full citizens, as legitimate and agency-wielding daughters rather than as subjugated mothers of England whose identities should be subordinated to their existing or future children. While not all spatial metaphors are necessarily imperialist, British women's relation to imagined geographies arguably derives from their particular historical experience as inheritors of the legacy of colonial Englishness at a moment of transition: prior to the onset of decolonization but long after the apogee of imperial strength. British women's fantasies of space often appropriate the cultural logic of empire, the conceptual (and literal) mapping so central to the constitution of English national identity, revealing their own political desires as enmeshed in a colonial legacy in which cartographic knowledge and boundary-making is always a transaction of power.[8] Indeed, their concept of territory is especially vexed, not only because their bodies were literally circumscribed by cultural prohibitions, but because those same bodies simultaneously functioned, metaphorically, as figures for the domestic and colonial landscape. We see a vivid example of the enduring appeal of an imperial identity in Winifred Holtby's *South Riding* (1936), where the heroine's survey of the English landscape exposes her vested interest in empire as a language of power. Contemplating her position as the headmistress of a Yorkshire girl's school, Sarah Burton re-imagines herself as a "commander inspecting territory ... [who] believed in fighting ... all roads led to her Rome ... [she] could conquer everything."[9] As she visualizes her "battlefield" (48), Sarah identifies with, and is legitimized by, the history of British colonial experience even though her actual authority as an unmarried schoolteacher is severely limited.

Doubly positioned as both racialized mothers and symbols for the motherland, women's bodies were subject to competing national interests: as mothers, their bodies were disciplined and regulated (by laws, sexual science, cultural conventions); but, as figures symbolic of British territory, their bodies were expansive, limitless, and aligned with acquisitiveness. In both cases the female body, though permeable and unstable, is associated with racial superiority and loyalty to a *civilizing* mission, notions that these writers at times repudiate and at other times exploit. Like the Little Englanders who opposed the expansion of empire during the interwar period yet maintained a belief in the country's moral superiority, the women writers in this study espouse a privately realized patriotism and focus their attentions on the homefront − even as foreign geographies and imperial imagery frequently shape their understanding of Englishness.[10] Ideologically, these authors can be said to occupy the position between those espousing insularity and those advocating the expansion of empire, both of which maintained a belief in the English as cultivators of civilized values. If the literal female body was continually subject to dominant legal, medical, and scientific discourses and practices, the women writers in this study work to dissociate it from its cultural limitations while retaining its national significance: displacing it, representing it as absence, regendering it, recoding its sexuality, or expressing it through synecdoche. Their physical erasures of the body register their desire to utilize the female body as the basis for new, varied, narratives of national belonging in which femininity, female agency, and English definitions of selfhood figure prominently.

Such narratives complexly intersect with other key cultural phenomena arising out of the process of modernization: women's participation in urbanization, the war effort, the sex-reform movement, new marital ideals, public discourse on homosexuality, debates about birth control and eugenics, the emergence of film, psychoanalysis, and the rise of feminism and mass culture. Methodologically, this project reads literary texts through the lens of material culture, building upon earlier work that situates women as central subjects of modernity who are implicated in regimes of power even when their domestic realm masquerades as a space that resides outside of politics or culture.[11] Each chapter foregrounds a range of cultural developments that coincided with the rise of modernism, such as emerging visual technologies, the revival of British neo-medievalism, ethnographic work on primitive mysticism, and nostalgia for English ruralism. This book tracks how various female (or feminized) protagonists engage with these discourses as national subjects, becoming the vehicles for the very national identity that excludes them in the political and social spheres. In foregrounding texts that both destabilize and reify – sometimes simultaneously – dominant accounts of women's role as guardians of the race, I demonstrate how 'England' emerges as a very different nation, one that challenges the critical assumption that the narrative of Englishness has been articulated only through an ideology of empire that valorizes male heroes, soldiers, and rulers. *Step-daughters of England* attempts to address the question of what happens to our concept of English citizenship in the modernist period when the female experience of national identity is seen as paradigmatic rather than marginal. What alternatives emerge against the dominant view that sees women's claims to nationhood as dependent upon, or mediated through, their relation to male citizens?

The three sections which follow attempt to answer these questions by fore-grounding British women's relation to modernism and nationalism; the enduring imaginative appeal of colonial tropes in the interwar period; and the gendered, as well as racialized, implications of territorial inscription.

Female modernism and national identity

For all the recently published work on eighteenth- and nineteenth-century women writers and their engagement with the discourse of nation, no book has as yet looked at British women modernists in relation to one another, or examined the diverse ways in which the category of *Englishness* is inflected by gender.[12] *Step-daughters of England* works to redress this startling omission.[13] The book begins with the assumption that the categories of *gender* and *national identity* are inseparable, and, furthermore, that they must be considered jointly in analyses of the possible meanings of experimental novelistic form. I focus on Richardson, Warner, Butts, and Woolf not simply because each highlights different key issues with respect to modernism and English national identity, but, more crucially, because each of them portrays the female body as a site for recasting the nation as a whole. Excluded from the primary focus of this study are modernists such as Jean Rhys and Katherine Mansfield who, as colonial subjects, inhabit hybrid identities and do not share the same cultural mythology of England as do the other four authors. Also excluded are writers such as Rose Macaulay and Rosamond Lehman, for, despite their popular appeal, their novels are not what I would classify as experimental. My project seeks to draw attention to the narrative experiments of British women modernists not in order to suggest that formal innovation is distinctively 'feminine' or more authentically liberatory than realism, nor to claim that non-experimental novels evade the topic of nationalism. Rather, I argue that their experiments with form bear directly on the question of national affiliation, and should be understood as a central way that such affiliation is negotiated.

Indeed, this book differs most importantly from earlier work on female modernism by showing how women's investment in formal experimentation is nationally inflected: configurations of 'the feminine,' I argue, are not only discur-sively and historically constructed, but are shaped by broader national concerns. Yet this project does not argue for a monolithic understanding of experimental form. Each chapter foregrounds a different model of experimental writing by historically situating the texts under discussion and showing how formal innovation is, in every case, tied to broader cultural discourses that employ the figure of 'woman' as a site for reconfiguring the nation. At the same time that this project rejects an essentialist understanding of feminine inscription – what Olive Moore, writing in 1934, presciently calls "that warm menstrous flow of womanly prose" – it recognizes that canonical modernism has frequently involved a renunciation of the feminine, a view that the writers considered here strongly resist.[14] While Richardson, Warner, Butts, and Woolf do register the problematic nature of the body, they do not replicate the male modernist "anorexic logic" wherein creativity is predicated on the expurgation of female flesh.[15] They displace female corporeality, in other words, without either recapitulating the cultural valuations that privilege masculinity, or suggesting that the work of civilization requires a withdrawal from the feminine. Instead, they show how the material inscriptions of the female body testify to the cultural devaluation *and* the redemptive possibility of femininity. What the disparate narratives under consideration here share, then, is a reliance on *the feminine* as an imaginative axis which organizes categories of race, sexuality, class, and national identity in distinctive but mutually resonant ways. I have chosen novels that all thematically foreground women's relation to territory as the basis upon which national identity is established, for whether it is the city (Richardson) or the countryside (Warner, Butts, and Woolf), it is always a love of England that sustains the core idea of national belonging and cultural redemption.[16]

Useful to this formulation of national affiliation is Pericles Lewis's recent argument that many modernists envisioned themselves as "redeemer[s] of the nation"; and he demonstrates how modernist formal experimentation, far from eschewing realism's concern with politics, repeatedly probes "the desire to tap into a national unconscious."[17] Yet whereas, for Lewis, only male modernists envision the reawakening of national consciousness as a primary concern, this book seeks to show how British women modernists similarly evinced a desire to redeem national culture, albeit not by situating men as paradigmatic subjects or makers of history. Speaking broadly, I argue that one of the motives for women's modernist experimentation is to refashion England into a feminized Paradise, one that recalls the contention of the Duchess of Atholl, the first Conservative woman to hold a ministerial position in the House of Commons, that women must construct a new "'Jerusalem' in 'England's green and pleasant land'" – a revisionary fantasy which dates back to the sixteenth century.[18] In this paradigm, it is women modernists who are constituted as the elect, as Mary Haweis, addressing a group of women writers in 1894, put it: "In women's hands – women's writers' hands – lies the regeneration of the world." Moreover, this imaginative remapping depends upon a notion of female citizenship that stands outside of existing political structures, but nonetheless regards contact with England's "green and pleasant land" as the basis upon which women's national identity – and larger cultural renewal – is made possible. It is no coincidence that three of the four authors examined here represent an intimate connection with the rural as fundamental to notions of Englishness, for the countryside was widely viewed as central to interwar conceptions of citizenship.

Yet while an "essentially territorial nationalism," to borrow Paul Gilbert's phrase, can be understood as the conceptual locus that mobilizes each author's affiliation with nation, the imaginative expression of that sense of belonging to a bounded territory is neither formally homogeneous nor thematically fixed. Experimentalism, I argue, facilitates this cultural work, for underlying British women's rejection of literary realism is their simultaneous repudiation of the political reality of women's exclusion from the nation state. If we accept Fredric Jameson's premise that "the production of aesthetic or narrative form is to be seen as an ideological act in its own right, with the function of inventing imaginary or formal 'solutions' to unresolvable social contradictions," then we can begin to understand the complicated ways in which gender and genre are integrally constitutive of national identity for Richardson, Warner, Butts, and Woolf.[19]

Each author deploys experimental techniques to capture this regendering of the national imaginary in ways that intersect with and shape her particular conception of territorial nationalism and somatic inscription. For example, in *Pilgrimage*, Richardson abandons narrative conventions such as linearity and causality, incorporating multiple climaxes and syntactic ruptures to map Miriam Henderson's body onto the imperial metropolis, London; in so doing, she not only colonizes the city as a heretofore unrealized homoerotic and feminized space, but uses the technique of rupture literally to disrupt received nationalist discourse. In *Lolly Willowes*, Warner similarly uses displacement to signal the claiming of homoerotic territory, but, rather than by exploding syntax or utilizing fragmentary nonlinear form, she revolts against confining linguistic structures by playing with binary oppositions. Warner relentlessly undermines hierarchies – such as normal–abnormal, male–female, nature–culture – by encoding her narrative with double meanings, aligning Lolly Willowes's inverted body with the soil, a move that plays upon the symbolic geography of the countryside as a *natural* female province. In *The Taverner Novels*, Butts also experiments with double meanings as she relies upon the conjunction of femininity and a rural ideal. Yet her narrative is not reducible to the cause-and-effect logic of heterosexual masquerade that governs Warner's text. Rather, Butts violates temporal and spatial verisimilitude by juxtaposing free indirect speech and first-person narration with omniscient points of view, creating a disconcerting linguistic collage that draws upon mythic structures to claim the female body as a metaphysical signifier for the English landscape. Mary Butts also shows how radical experiments with form may be put in the service of reactionary politics: her novels reflect a conservative perspective on female moral superiority that relies upon a belief in bloodlines and the transcendent value of genetics. In Woolf's *The Waves*, an emphasis on sound, rhythm, and repetition, as well as an absence of sequential logic, combines with the novel's ensemble of formally indistinguishable voices to draw attention to unconscious structures in order to unleash – arguably on a national scale – that which has been repressed by dominant culture. By formally erasing speech differentiation, Woolf privileges a "certain homogeneity of character" that, according to historian J.A. Hobson, is a psychical precondition to national life.[20] While Woolf does not fetishize racial purity as Butts does, she too values feminized "primitive impulses" as the source for the reawakening of national consciousness. Through these narrative innovations, Woolf celebrates the metaphorical colonization of masculine space through the feminization of the imperialist figure of Percival, associating his body with the English garden of Elvedon in order to show how the discourse of geographical conquest underpins the meaning of national belonging. The thematic results of these varied experiments, then, are not intrinsically radical or liberatory where women's relation to nationalism is concerned; nor do they express a unified ideology. Rather, they exist in a complex and strikingly variable (complicit, oppositional, ironic) relation to the experimental methods that fuel each narrative.

By juxtaposing both canonical and noncanonical texts, and by contextualizing these novels within broader cultural discourses, this book seeks to show that no monolithic or definitive concept of "the nation" is applicable to all women, though the category of *the feminine* provides each author with a conceptual model for imagining a universalized national identity.[21] Although the female body has functioned historically as an emblem of British national unity – England is conventionally figured as the feminine Britannia – legally and politically speaking, women have consistently been written out of the script of Englishness.[22] As Elizabeth Langland has argued, it is the discourse of heroic masculinity, with its vision of imperial destiny, that has been most central to the construction of myths of English nationhood.[23] But even this masculinist tradition is complicated in the interwar period. Alison Light's work on the privatization of national life after 1919 has demonstrated the degree to which masculinity and ideas of the nation were feminized during the Little Englandism of the interwar period, when a new rhetoric of domestic nationality was in circulation.[24] An editorial published in the *Englishwoman* in 1919 speaks directly to this phenomenon, in which the home was regarded as the cornerstone of civilization: "Those who maintain the Home uphold the Nation."[25] The modernist authors I examine here grapple with these competing concepts of nation and nationality, registering the domestication of the idea of imperial power by appropriating and dramatically revising the association of Englishness with specifically masculine virtues. Drawing on the conventional allegorical depiction of the female body as a metonym for the nation, these writers complicate the anthropomorphic model by deliberately subverting the convention of the "male penetration" of passive, feminized space.[26]

By positioning themselves as active explorers of the unknown world, Richardson, Warner, Butts, and Woolf also reconceptualize the territorial imperatives of nationhood, fabricating their own adult version of children's "colonization games" in which little girls functioned as intrepid "discoverers – Stanleys, Livingstones" of new territories.[27] The gendering of this process of discovery is key, for as women writers displace well-worn imperial tropes onto the homeland, they transform what it means to map out and carve up imaginative space. We see a prime example of this in Vita Sackville-West's *All Passion Spent* (1931), where Edith Slane, a spinster who never strays from her native England, fantasizes about her brother's collection of "globes, compasses, [and] astrolabes," magical objects which conjure for her "[a] romantic ... vast dark world where nothing was charted on the maps but regions of danger and uncertainty."[28] Throughout *Step-daughters*, then, my focus is not on women's literal global reach but on their appropriation of national and imperial discourses of power, an appropriation whose material consequences are unpredictable, variable, and debatable. Although I don't mean to elide the discourses of nationalism and imperialism with material practices *per se*, I am interested in tracking how dominant ideologies infiltrate – sometimes self-consciously and sometimes unwittingly – language, meaning, and symbolic representations, including the novels these women were able to write. As elements of nationalist discourse themselves, their novels may well have exerted some limited forms of influence, even though none of them had a direct hand in the operation of British rule. Indeed, none ever traveled to a colonial outpost; nor did any replicate the exoticized adventures of such contemporaries as Freya Stark (who traveled extensively in Asia, Egypt, and the Middle East), or Gertrude Bell (whose knowledge of Iraq and Persia led to her being drafted as a British intelligence agent in Cairo). But all evinced an interest in the exploration of unmapped territory, and, significantly, *England itself* is the space they imaginatively explored and colonized during a period when much mass cultural attention was lavished on encouraging British travelers to return to the homeland, "the heart of the Empire."[29]

This project of *domestic colonization* recalls the late nineteenth-century social schemes to establish "colonies at home" in the impoverished spaces of "Darkest England," a plan of moral regeneration intended to eradicate urban blight.[30] But for women modernists, the motives for domestication and regeneration are more complex, spanning Richardson's use of the female invert to redefine the exemplary metropolitan citizen and Butts's employment of the spiritualized female aristocrat to redraw the boundaries of membership in a national community. Although Woolf may have been partly right when she observed that women are categorically absolved from any responsibility in the furtherance of empire – "you have never introduced a barbarous race to the blessings of civilization" – many interwar women actively supported imperial ambitions.[31] In noting the ways in which these modernists' domestic explorations resonate with Britain's imperial projects, again I do not seek to reduce women's appropriation of tropes of exploration and conquest to a simple imperial will-to-power, or to suggest that discourse magically translates into practice in any simple way. However, I am suggesting that the image of an Englishwoman who "casts out her mind to imagine an empty land," or is "irresistibly drawn to gaze upon an imaginary map," is ideologically fraught and intimately linked to dominant ideologies of geographical knowledge and imperial vision.

Although nationalism and imperialism are *not* identical, the women in this study often use the terms and concepts *nation* and *empire* interchangeably, expressing anti-national and anti-imperial sentiment even as they aspire to national belonging. For example, Rebecca West, despite her critique of British nationalism, describes the empire in 1928 as "a political necessity, and a glorious one."[32] By the end of the 1930s she is more overtly critical of imperialism, yet she still affirms her identification with Englishness: "My national faith is valid."[33] In 1922 Woolf "thank[s] God for [her] British blood," but by 1927 protests: "can't you see that nationality is over?"[34] How are we to understand the ambivalence and equivocation of interwar women writers, for whom national and imperial identities were intertwined? It should be read, first of all, within the wider context of what Leonard Woolf calls "the savagely nationalistic" post-First World War period, when many intellectuals regarded nationalism either negatively or with suspicion.[35] J.A. Hobson, a key early theorist of imperialism, provides in *Imperialism: A Study* (1902) another useful context for understanding this equivocation through his distinction between "genuine" (4) nationalism – which has to do with common language, collective sentiment, loyalty, and pride for one's nation – and the high-expansionist imperialism of the late nineteenth century. Hobson argues that the latter is an autocratic "perversion" (9) of the former because it is based upon mindless territorial acquisition and economic exploitation. This is a distinction that, on a conscious level and to varying degrees, can be said to be shared by each of the four women foregrounded here. While Hobson denounces forcible seizure of territory as a "grotesque monster" (126), he does not regard all forms of territorial acquisition as anathema. Hobson's advocacy of "sane" imperialism (246) – the belief that "wholesome colonial connection" is possible in places such as Canada, where "free white democracies" (125) flourish – still relies upon expansionism and is predicated on the paternalistic and racist assumption that white Britons must have power over subject peoples by securing the "safety," "progress," and "civilization" (232) of "savages and 'lower races'" (124) in the protectorates and dependencies. This characterization is crucial because it reveals the conservative underpinnings of a seemingly *progressive* outlook, simultaneously exposing the imaginative appeal that *good* geographical expansionism and the promise of a "natural overflow of nationality" (5) holds. In the British women modernists I examine here, a similar attraction to the notion of an uncontaminated "true British nationalism" (362) is seen: a similar contempt for the siege mentality of conquest intertwined with a fantasy of benevolent expansionism and international cooperation; and a similar conservatism that distinguishes the colonizers from the colonized and leaves intact the sanctity of the idea of nation.

Influential to my understanding of the conjunction of space, national identity, and literary form has been Edward Said's contention that British modernism was fueled by a desire to compensate for a loss of imperial control. His account of the relations between narrative and empire identifies a convergence between Britain's geographical scope and its universalizing cultural discourses, characterizing territorial expansionism – and the consequent erosion of Britain's imperial confidence – as a precedent to the peculiarly spatialized language of modernist representation: "When you can no longer assume that Britannia will rule the waves forever, you have to reconceive reality as something that can be held together by you the artist ... Spatiality becomes, ironically, the characteristic of an aesthetic rather than of political domination."[36] While Said's work provides a crucial context for understanding the cultural underpinnings of the spatial preoccupations of British women modernists, it sheds little light on the specifically gendered dynamics of that representation. Nor does it consider British women's unique position relative to imperialism: not only in collusion with but *detached from* the political aspirations of empire, in so far as they were not full citizens in the imperial nation state. Also important to my understanding of the narrative implications of territorial expansionism has been Fredric Jameson's account of British modernism in his essay "Modernism and Imperialism" (1990), which emphasizes the aesthetic function and centrality of "spatial representation" and "spatial perception" in his discussion of the connection between modernism and imperialism.[37] Useful as Jameson's contention is that the forms and structures of modernism result in a "new spatial language" governed by a movement toward an "unrepresentable totality," he pays greater attention to style and formal innovation than to content as he tracks instances of "cognitive mapping" (58). Moreover, his problematic assertion that imperialism almost never figures in the content of modernist works ignores the connections between form and content that I track throughout this book. Like Said, Jameson disregards the ways in which the imaginative appropriation of "great imperial space" (64) is both historically *and* sexually specific. As I seek to show, British women's imaginative appropriation of space must be grasped within the context of culturally marked sexual difference. Jameson's close attention to novels that thematically oppose empire yet formally affirm it provides a productive frame-work for considering British women modernists' complicated relation to "imperial structures of feeling and aesthetics."[38] To date, few critics have considered how women modernists' form is an outcome of their desire to locate themselves within national culture, even though several have recognized that the idea of nation is forged through narrative.[39]

Step-daughters of England both draws upon and interrogates several founda-tional assumptions about nationhood and national form. Most importantly, it takes up Benedict Anderson's widely cited claim regarding the invented nature of nationalism and its relation in particular to the novel, while exploring what Anne McClintock has argued is the largely ignored gendering of the national imaginary.[40] At the same time, this study seeks to widen our understanding of the relationship between nationhood and narrative, a relation that scholars have, thus far, pursued most successfully in the traditional realist novel (or in texts authored by male modernists).[41] Modernism, produced by writers who circulated between national spaces, is conventionally regarded as a literature of mobility, fragmentation, and disruption. Precisely because modernist cultural production often enacts (not only thematically but structurally) the ideas of physical and psychical dislocation, it has seemed implicitly opposed to the master narratives of empire and nation that highlight "a progressive temporality, a linear cartography, and a unified European subject."[42] Traditional national narratives, as critics such as Anderson have charac-terized them, attempt to establish an authoritative connection between cohesive identity, historical linearity, and cultural destiny, elements that are seemingly opposed to modernism's formal and thematic interrogation of Western progress, reason, temporality and subjectivity. Yet all of the writers in this study produce fiction that formally engages in some way with modernist innovation while thematically coalescing around a concern with women's relation to English national identity. In short, this book questions the polarization of nation and modernism, and proposes that modernist fiction written in England *by women* provides an ideal place to investigate their intersection, for what we see foregrounded, repeatedly, is the conjunction of narrative experiment with the representation of women's insis-tence upon national inclusion.

Step-daughters of England stresses the fictiveness of nationalism, but departs from Anderson's claim that the nation is always conceived as a deep, horizontal comradeship among men, as it similarly diverges from George Mosse's argument that nationalism always legitimizes the dominance of men over women.[43] Whereas

Anderson and Mosse view nationalism as a form of homosocial bonding among male citizens, I understand it as a far less unified field, although British women's claims of nationalism still reveal their complicity with Eurocentric notions of imagined community. To borrow from Partha Chatterjee, their imaginations "remain forever colonized."[44] This is not to say that British women are incapable of oppositional responses, but only that their discursive agency is circumscribed and, moreover, that those culturally marked discourses shape their attempts to champion women's emancipatory aims. For Richardson, Warner, Butts, and Woolf, 'imagining the nation' has to do with the articulation of a specifically female experience of modernity, an articulation whose formally self-conscious and experimental features are imbricated both in the discourse of femininity and the language of empire. Crucial here is Antoinette Burton's contention "that the nation is not only *not* antecedent to empire, but that as both a symbolic and a material site the nation ... has no originary moment, no fixity outside of the various discourses of which it is itself an effect."[45] By foregrounding modernist women's distinctive relations to British imperial culture, I reveal the ways in which each writer's own location on the grid of Englishness shapes both the form and content of her attempts to forge a new narrative of England, one that both critiques and expresses nostalgic desire for women's right to an imperial inheritance.

Of course, numerous male writers of the interwar period had complex and subtle understandings of both nation and gender. Conrad, D.H. Lawrence, Ford Maddox Ford, even Wyndham Lewis, all challenge hegemonic notions of nation. While male modernist responses to nation fall outside of the parameters of this project, my omission of them here is not intended to oppose straw men to progressive women. Indeed, Viscountess Rhondda, the editor of the only feminist magazine of the interwar period, herself notes in 1937 the ways that male writers have perceived the gender bias lodged within nationalist debates when she lauds Aldous Huxley's scathing critique of the hypermasculinity of nationalism in *Beyond the Mexique Bay* (1934), maintaining that it was the best analysis published to date.[46] There, Huxley regards the conflict in Central America as a microcosm of the national tensions at work in Europe, attacking the hypermasculinity of nationalism by linking it to the discourse of sexual pathology. Although Huxley ignores women's relationship to nation, he provides a trenchant critique of how militant nationalism produces male violence.[47] In Lawrence's *Women in Love* (1920) we see a similar contempt for mass-produced nationalist hysteria, and a similar interest in the links between sexuality and nation. Yet, while Lawrence repeatedly critiques English nationalism, he still relies upon conventional tropes of exploration and conquest to depict his characters' search for new erotic paradigms. However, in contrast to British women modernists, who also exhibit nostalgia for the exploration of unmapped territory, Lawrence represents men as exemplary citizens of this "new universe."[48] Despite the fact that both male and female characters in *Women in Love* voice desire for "unbounded" (86) spaces and a "new world" (438) beyond English parochialism, women's desire for spaciousness in the novel is circumscribed and constrained by masculine prerogatives. For women such as Ursula and Hermione, access to untrammeled territory is contingent on male volition and desire. Ultimately in Lawrence's novel, women's material and imaginative navigation of blank spaces leads only to a discovery of the "Blessed Isl[e]" (438) of the male body. In contrast, the female authored texts I examine throughout this book do not conjoin a critique of nation with either the absorption or elision of femininity, nor do they fetishize – as does, for example, Conrad in a 1924 essay on geographical knowledge – the era of heroic exploration when "adventurous and devoted men" traversed the globe.[49] Rather, by foregrounding femininity, British women modernists invite us to re-appraise the sterile conjunction of masculinity, nationalism, and spatial trespass in order to open up a space for the fictional representation and recognition of women's politicized desires.

My understanding of the relation between the public realm and the privatized subjectivities of British women has been influenced by recent post-Habermasian studies which expose the limits of a binaristic understanding of gendered space.[50] Over the course of the last two decades the ideology of separate spheres – the notion that men and women inhabit completely different social terrain – has been subjected to rigorous critique. Rather than celebrating women's realm as removed from the world of politics, such critics have argued for the interdependence of the public and private spheres, showing how femininity cannot unproblematically be relegated to a private domain.[51] My project builds upon that work and pays special attention to Amy Kaplan's argument that domesticity is not removed from the world of politics and culture but is deeply implicated in its relation to nationalism and imperialism.[52] While this book registers that gender cannot easily be mapped onto the separate-spheres model, it simultaneously privileges modernist novels by *women*, a move that perhaps appears guilty of re-inscribing gender polarity. Although attentive to the polarizing danger of relegating women's texts to a *separate-sphere* category, I am also acutely aware that most of the British writers I discuss throughout this book are either critically neglected or seriously devalued. Despite the feminist literary recovery efforts that have been in place since the late 1970s, British female modernists remain, with the exception of Woolf, "even at this moment almost unclassified."[53] This project seeks to recuperate British women writers from their present position of marginality, not in order to privilege gender at the expense of nationality, race, class, and sexuality, but to expose the interconnectedness of these terms while showing how these writers undo the binary logic of public and private through their gendering of the national imaginary.

Mapping gendered space: reterritorializing the motherland

The chapters which follow seek to answer Susan Stanford Friedman's recent challenge to feminist critics to move beyond the cultural narratives of gender in order to focus on "the new geography of identity," a model that privileges the historically embedded meanings of space and emphasizes the fluid interaction of race, class, sexuality, and national origin.[54] While critics such as Susan Meyer and Deirdre David have shown that the work of Victorian women writers reflects both ambivalence and complexity in relation to imperialist ideology, little attention has been paid to how British women modernists identify with, repudiate, and interrogate the legacy of empire. The reasons for this, I suggest, are multiple, and stem in part from the misperception that British imperial dominance had ended by 1914, and therefore no longer exerted the same kind of rhetorical or ideological influence on interwar-years' writers. Recent re-assessments of British imperial history during the interwar years provide an invaluable corrective to the widely held view that the First World War marked the decline of a confident and expansive imperial policy and the beginning of decolonization.[55] Territorial expansionism did not come to a halt with the Edwardian era: indeed, at its zenith in the 1920s, the British empire held territorial possessions (colonies, dominions, and protectorates) on all five continents, covering about one-quarter of the globe and comprising a population of some 400 million individuals.[56] It is true, of course, that the economic resources at Britain's disposal were not as abundant as they had been before the First World War, but the country's position in relation to its European rivals remained strong; although the USA emerged as a potential rival after that war, it was only with the outbreak of the Second World War that Britain became financially dependent on the USA.[57] The Versailles Peace Treaty of 1919 consolidated the "principle of nationality" in the remapping of Europe, confirming Britain as the world's supreme imperial power while legitimizing the nation's white trusteeship over "completely helpless" and backward "primitive peoples."[58] As Barbara Bush writes: "British imperialism was extended, and 'Anglo-Saxonism' was strengthened through the white, imperial diaspora which was energetically promoted after the First World War."[59]

The distinction between Britain's "white" and "tropical" empires was a key feature of cultural imperialism both at home and in the colonial context, reinforcing strict racial boundaries and confirming white prestige and power.[60] Although official imperial propaganda had to some extent been discredited in England after 1918, popular cultural elements such as advertising and the cinema continued to be suffused with the ideology of imperialism throughout the interwar period. For example, to mark the coronation of George VI in 1937, Selfridges department store transformed itself into a spectacular imperial monument, complete with allegorical figures representing the various colonies and dominions.[61] Imperial sentiment was given prominence in the 1920s and 1930s through Boy Scout and Girl Guide pamphlets, children's books, and the jingoism of military valor; the marketing of imperial products and the continued celebration of Empire Day and Mafeking Night into the 1930s; public interest in the Empire Exhibition at Wembley (in 1924) and the Empire Games (first held in 1924); and the Imperial Institute's dissemination of ethnographic films, during the 1930s, that projected an image of British imperial and racial superiority.[62] If one accepts the argument that Britain was in decline as an imperial power after the First World War, then these cultural elements can be read as a form of "imperialist nostalgia," evidence of interwar anxiety about the loss of hegemonic power.[63] Yet it is also important to remember that, after the global depression that began in 1929, "Britain was the only true power of consequence in the 1930s."[64] Thus while displays of imperial strength may be interpreted as nostalgic forays into fantasy, throughout the interwar years Britain continued to regulate its worldwide network of empire that extended over 12.1 million square miles – even though post-war imperialism was more diffuse, unstable, and complex than in the pre-1914 period.[65] The idea that "Empire might be the salvation of Britain through protectionism and exploitation of tropical territories" faded after 1919, but was resurrected again both in 1929 and in 1945, during periods of depression and war.[66] Decolonization, it is crucial to realize, did not even begin until after the end of the Second World War, even though from the early 1920s members of the Labour Party regarded colonial self-government as a desirable objective.[67] In what follows I aim to demonstrate more particularly through literary examples why the pervasiveness of imperialism as an ideological feature of modern British culture must be considered as a factor in British women's engagement with spatial metaphors, territorialism, border crossing, and the assumption that femininity – in particular, the female body – functions as an agent of civilization.

We can see such strategies of bodily re-invention and their resonances with imperial tropes in the work of the English writer and feminist Winifred Holtby, whose laudatory characterization of Woolf, published in 1932, invokes the language of geography and navigation to position the author as a fearless explorer, narratively probing the uncharted terrain of female subjectivity:

> When she wrote of women, she wrote of a generation as adventurous in its exploration of experience as the Elizabethan men had been in their exploration of the globe. The women whom Mrs. Woolf knew were exploring the professional world, the political world, the world of business, discovering that they themselves had legs as well as wombs, brains as well as nerves, reason as well as sensibility; their Americas lay within themselves, and altered the map as profoundly as any added by Cabot or Columbus. Like Raleigh, they founded their new colonies; like Drake, they combined national service with privateering.[68]

By situating Woolf alongside Raleigh and Columbus, Holtby unwittingly aligns her with the violence of imperialism; one might infer that the author's narrative experiments – her profound alteration of the "map" of literary history – constitute a form of neo-colonialism.[69] While Holtby, like Woolf, was overtly critical of imperial ideology, here she nonetheless inscribes imperial tropes that equate the modern woman's quest for self-knowledge with the discovery of "new colonies" on the unknown "globe" that stands both for the world of the professions and the territory of her own body and psyche. Woolf herself, writing in 1929, argues "[f]or the first time this dark country [of femininity] is beginning to be explored in fiction," similarly deploying the imperial *topos* of travel to signal the exploration of female subjectivity and sexuality.[70] Like several of her modernist contemporaries who indulged in primitivist appropriation, Woolf's reference to the "dark country" of femininity – even if her intention is ironic – aligns it with racial otherness and unknowability, an equation that recalls Freud's own use of the "dark continent" trope to signify female sexuality.[71] Although Woolf, like Freud, never refers directly to Africa, her language inevitably recalls the British empire's infiltration of the "dark continent" during the late nineteenth and early twentieth centuries.[72] We see this trace disclosed both in Woolf's exuberant embrace of the rhetoric of territorial expansionism in the oft-cited epigram, above – "as a woman, I have no country ... my country is the whole world" (*TG*, 109) – and in Holtby's enthusiastic claim that modern women are founding "new colonies" in the name of "national service." Both remarks, uttered during the 1930s, allude to the construction of England as a world power, a result of its unique imperial status, even though neither woman would have identified herself as participating in the dissemination of a British worldview or espousing cultural and racial superiority. On the contrary, Holtby was an uncompromising anti-fascist who lectured for the League of Nations Union and agitated for the welfare of black South Africans from 1926 onward, while Woolf insists that women must fight fascism by divesting themselves of "patriotism" (*TG*, 81) and ridding themselves of the "pride of nationality" (80).[73] At the same time, Woolf acknowledges that "still some obstinate emotion remains, some love of England" that, however "irrational," will induce her to "give to England first what she desires of peace and freedom for the whole world" (109). Similarly, Holtby denounces militarism and nationalism yet confesses that she too harbors some vestigial patriotic sentiment, an "instinctive homage of the senses" that is aroused by public displays of national fervor.[74] This ambivalence speaks to the unconscious component of national identification, recalling Anderson's assertion that "nations inspire love."[75]

For both Holtby and Woolf, femininity is imaginatively constructed as a space that is untrammeled and subject to seizure; in other words, it is a geographical sphere that is inconceivable outside the discursive parameters of the British empire. But femininity is also imbued with agency, for Woolf's idea of feminine appro-priation of new territories extends beyond the self and has the capacity to eradicate difference, "to overflow boundaries and make unity out of multiplicity" (*TG*, 143). Although in *The Years* (1937) Woolf critiques the fascist implications of such a model, deriding the notion of a culturally and racially homogeneous globe – "all one jelly, one mass … a rice pudding world, a white counterpane world" – in *Three Guineas*, published just a year later, the idea of unity is compelling and serves as the basis for the moral improvement of the nation.[76] What makes the prospect of a unifying consciousness not only palatable but culturally necessary is its alignment with women's moral authority. This linkage between women, nation, and the world is not exclusive to Woolf, but was a common formulation among interwar-years' British feminists who maintained that women's redemptive influence was integral both to the maintenance of empire and to the moral governance of the globe. Like Holtby, who aligns female agency with the colonization of new space, Woolf theorizes that women belong everywhere: defined by their global mobility, the female construction of "one world" (*TG*, 142) imaginatively transgresses terri-torial borders as it disrupts conventional gender boundaries.[77] In doing so, Woolf assumes an inherently redemptive power and collective identity for women, regard-less of race or of class privilege, whose fundamental aim is to transform the national body politic and "create a civilized society" (*TG*, 113).[78] Woolf's remarks exemplify the perspective that is shared, although modified, by Richardson, Warner, and Butts, all of whom seek full inclusion in the nation by trading on the rhetoric of national responsibility. Holtby's assertion that women's "Americas lay within themselves" invokes the globalizing ambitions of empire building yet positions Englishwomen as self-colonizers, throwing off the yoke of "sex-inferiority" and "striding forward to conquer new worlds" – on and through the body – in the name of feminism.[79]

This metaphorization of America as an internalized feminized space, full of imaginative possibility, anticipates Woolf's own representation, in her essay

"America, which I have never seen," of an allegorical female figure, "Imagination," who travels from England to America and reveals a nation of uncharted potential (technological innovation, speed, modernity) which contrasts sharply with the staid parochialism of "the English, marooned on their island."[80] Woolf's fantasies about America during the 1930s, when the USA presented a serious challenge to British imperial hegemony, provide a window on to America's broader standing in the English imagination of the period. Again, although Britain's political determination to retain her global stature was undiminished during the interwar period, its economic reach was curtailed: after the First World War, Britain no longer had sufficient capital to fuel the world economy.[81] As a result, there was a permanent shift in the balance of world power, a shift that produced substantial English anxiety about the decline of empire. Both Holtby's and Woolf's invocations of America are symptomatic of this tension. Woolf's exuberant exclamation – "*America is the most interesting thing in the world today*" ("America," 56) – arguably has less to do with her admiration of Americans *per se* than with her fascination with America's originary status as a "primeval country" (58) that transcends national specificity and incorporates "all cultures, of all civilizations" (59) – language which suggests a contrast with the homogeneity of English culture. Yet Woolf's apparent embrace of America's unique ability to embody simultaneously "the past ... [as well as] the future" (59) camouflages the fact that the prototype of cultural diversity is England herself. Through her allegorical female figure Imagination, Woolf discovers Englishness in America by re-imagining the new world as an "ancient English village" whose occupants sing songs from the time of Shakespeare while conjuring the atmosphere of "the England of Charles the First ... Stratford-upon-Avon ... an Elizabethan cottage" (59). When Imagination visits a library, she sees its doors open to reveal not American books but "Shakespeare's folios, Ben Johnson's manuscripts, [and] Keats' love letters blazing in the light of an American sun" (59). In an interesting move that one might call reverse colonization, then, both Woolf and Holtby look to America as a space of imaginative possibility for the English-woman. By appropriating the imagery of colonialism for the purposes of female liberation, these writers show how civilizing tropes can function as a kind of compensatory political discourse for women who are otherwise denied political power.

The lingering trace of imperial tropes is symptomatic, Simon Gikandi argues, "of the incomplete project of colonialism" during the period of modernist activity, when we can observe the "enforcement of colonial categories in their moment of disappearance."[82] Domestic space is thus not separate from the space of empire, but exists in complicitous relation to it. We see evidence of this in an early short story by Woolf, "The Mark on the Wall," which anticipates many of the concerns of this project in its intertwining of the feminine usurpation of space with the interrogation of what constitutes civilization. Here, Woolf's implicitly female narrator privileges the practice of thinking "spaciously," meditating on an ambiguous object as she imagines a "spacious world" where one's consciousness would be free to wander unimpeded.[83] This uninhabited sphere is associated with the primitive – what she elsewhere calls "the dark places of psychology" – for here once dwelled "witches and hermits who crouched in caves and in woods brewing herbs, interrogating shrew-mice and writing down the language of the stars" (81).[84] Woolf's imagined geography conjures an uncolonized universe, situating the female artist-cum-narrator as the conqueror of a new globe that provides limitless mobility and access, yet which enables her to feel "rooted in the centre of the world" (81). While this language recalls early twentieth-century geographical representations of England as "the central ... land of the world," the story ultimately subverts the assumption that civilization is aligned with "masculine ... standard[s]" (80) and governance.[85] On the contrary, by repeatedly calling into question the masculine prerogative of "worshipping solidity" (80), the narrator dislodges objects from their referentiality, utility, and historical context, insinuating that precisely because "nothing is known" (81), anything is possible. It is into this space of perspectival indeterminacy that Woolf's narrator intervenes, suggesting that because "the masculine point of view" (80) has sanctioned a restrictive and circumscribed realm – has made a "world not to be lived in" (79) – women must claim new territory "all over the world" (83). In Woolf's story this transgression of conventional borders and the ability to "slip easily from one thing to another, without any sense of hostility, or obstacle" (79), are aligned with femininity; as location, the feminine recognizes no national frontier and functions as the basis for a global reconstruction of how "our civilisation" (78) is both mapped and perceived. Woolf's pacifist model for a civilized world stresses the freedom of displacement and the pleasures of unimpeded circulation, yet her understanding of reterritorialization arguably relies upon spatial metaphors that cannot escape colonial discourse. While one may be tempted to read Woolf's short story as a parody of domination, such an interpretation would ignore the ways in which her fantasy of transparent space is implicated within colonial paradigms and overlaps with universalist feminist claims during this period.

A word must be said here about Woolf's status relative to the other authors in this study, as well as her presence in this Introduction, since she enjoys a position of privilege that speaks both to her ascendancy in the academy today and to the fact that during her lifetime she was promoted and marketed as *the* female modernist celebrity.[86] To the extent that Woolf's current popularity and canonical stature have eclipsed those of all of her female modernist peers in Britain, one might argue that her rise represents a historical moment of territorialization, a moment that can be traced back to the interwar period. We can hear resistance to Woolf's usurpation of literary space in the voices of some of her contemporaries, who register objections to the hegemony of what one fan, writing in 1927, calls "the Virginia Woolf school."[87] Mary Butts, perhaps irritated that the Hogarth Press had rejected one of her novels or simply annoyed with Woolf's highbrow celebrity status, writes to Ezra Pound in 1934: "all this Virginia Wolf [*sic*] worship. Not my totem." Richardson bridles at the "unpleasant ... tributes to women writers of the Woolf period," maintaining that she and Woolf "are alien to each other."[88] Similarly, Olive Moore, a scandalously under-read experimentalist, critiques Woolf's ascendancy and her condemnation of interlopers like herself: "*Example of how a verdict is obtained in the English Literary Courts. Mrs. Woolf in a literary weekly reviews the books of newcomers, and finds neither interest nor distinction*" (389). Certainly Woolf was a formidable presence – the only woman writer in England during this period who ran her own press (Hogarth) and was thus able to self-publish outside of market considerations; was associated with an influential literary group (Bloomsbury) that was engaged in self-promotion; and had a caretaker (Leonard) who, both during her lifetime and after her death, worked diligently to establish her lasting reputation.[89] One wonders how different the map of British modernism would have looked had Woolf organized a literary salon for women, or had actively solicited and published the work of writers such as Butts, Moore, Jean Rhys, Una Marson, or Anna Kavan. One wonders, additionally, what might have transpired on Britain's literary front if Woolf had involved herself in the system of patronage that was foundational to the institutional structure of male modernism.[90] Instead, despite her exhortation that women "write all kinds of books" (*ROO*, 109), and despite the eleven Hogarth Press publications on women, Woolf herself never made a point of publishing female writers – even though she viewed herself, as she jocularly notes, as the "Queen Victoria" of the British publishing world.[91] Indeed, she expressed contempt for many of her female peers – exhibiting what Richardson calls the "feminine cruelty" of a "successful lady novelist" – while harboring an acute sense of her own cultural capital and cultivating "the prevailing Bloomsbury ethos of individualism."[92] If Woolf's competitiveness and disparagement of (in particular) best-selling female authors are inseparable from her anxiety surrounding her own popularity and the economic basis of her literary production, it is also true that, while she reviewed books by women throughout her career, she never used her considerable influence to further the careers of struggling British women novelists.[93]

My intention in sketching Woolf's institutional and popular ascendancy is not to castigate her, or even to provide a corrective to the extremes of critical hagiography; rather, I'm offering one lens through which we can begin to understand the relative obscurity of the other authors in this study. Relevant to this issue of marginalization is the fact that, in addition to lacking a professional outlet such as the Hogarth Press, or a familial and artistic infrastructure such as Bloomsbury, the writers I examine never conceived of themselves, communally, as members of a movement. There was no organized group of women literary practitioners in Britain during the period of high-modernist activity comparable with the female expatriate communities in Paris; nor did the women I consider ever work in concert by sharing work or offering one another editorial direction.[94] This material absence speaks to a crucial ideological issue that Woolf herself raises in *A Room of One's Own*: namely, how is a national literature both created and transmitted, and what is its relation to gender? In *A Room*, Woolf argues that "masterpieces are not single and solitary births" but are "the outcome of many years of thinking in common, of thinking by *the body of the people*" (65) [emphasis mine]. Woolf suggests, in other words, that what a writer requires is some kind of larger cohesive national identification, even though she elsewhere argues that literature is "not cut up into nations" but is "common ground" that welcomes cultural trespass.[95] In contrast to this utopian transnational view of literary production, *A Room* engages with the difficulties of what it means to be a woman writer within a constraining national tradition. Tacitly acknowledging that women cannot write if they are severed from the idea of a national culture, Woolf delineates a genealogy of female authorship that is nationally bounded: Jane Austen is indebted to Fanny Burney, while George Eliot is indebted to Eliza Carter, and they are all indebted to Aphra Behn, their

literary foremother. In making this argument Woolf demonstrates that her conception of the "mass" behind the "single voice" (65) has as much to do with national
consciousness as with gender. Although it does not explicitly invoke the rhetoric of
nationhood, Woolf's matrilineal remapping of literary history – "we think back
through our mothers if we are women" (76) – conveys that some sense of solidarity
or belief in a common national culture is a precondition for writing. It also suggests
that the mothers she imagines are necessarily Englishwomen.

One reason why such nationalist underpinnings have gone largely unnoticed is
that British historical work on what Barbara Caine calls "the imperial consciousness of interwar feminists" is still in a nascent stage; indeed, "the whole interwar
period [has] only recently come to be recognized."[96] It is thus not surprising, given
this historical absence, that literary critics would be inattentive to the importance of
the British imperial context for the development of both middle-class feminism
and female modernism. This has arguably contributed to the critical tendency to
privilege British women writers' interrogation of gender hierarchies while leaving
unexamined how the rhetoric of female individualism intersects with the construction of a nationalistic individualism. Yet, Woolf's ideological assumptions have
serious implications for how she, like Richardson, Warner, and Butts, seeks admission for women as full citizens in the nation state. British women's fictional
narratives convey, in Woolf's words, "not only that novelists own a country, but
that all who dwell in it are their subjects."[97] In staking a claim to unrealized
geographies, these authors seek to expand the borders of what Woolf gleefully calls
"that curious thing, the map of the world in one's mind."[98] Woolf herself, with
Leonard's help, bound and titled two maps of the village surrounding their English
country home, in Rodmell, in 1931; but her real preoccupation was with imagined
places she had never seen: "I should like to die with a complete map of the world in
my head."[99] Importantly, while this "non-real space" is grounded in the material
conditions of early twentieth-century modernity, it is also distinct from the
masculinized world of empirical reality; Woolf's conviction that "civilisation means
awareness" underscores the conceptual nature of this narrative remapping, a
reterritorialization that is constructed through the encoding of sexual difference.[100]
It is extremely useful, in attempting to visualize this alternate feminized sphere, to
consider Mina Loy's poem, "Lunar Baedeker", as well as her late-1920s decorative
lampshades of illuminated globes, both produced during the period in which
British women were urged to be avid map readers.[101] The poem's title evokes the
standard reliable guide familiar to European travelers – the Baedeker – with its
reassuring format and elaborate maps. Loy's poem, in contrast, attempts to chart
the landscape of the imagination: "Delirious Avenues/ lit/ with the chandelier souls/
of infusoria."[102] Like "Lunar Baedeker", which is a kind of guide to the modernist
mindscape, Loy's illuminated globes – delicate hand-made lighting fixtures which
she called *mappemondes* (world maps) and *globes célestes* (celestial globes) – attempt
to give material shape to imagined geographies.[103] Aestheticized household objects,
Loy's lamps are associated with the interior space of the feminine, yet conceptually
extend far beyond the boundaries of the domestic, incorporating, to borrow from
H.D., the territory of the "unrecorded" for which "we have no map."[104] Such concep-
tualizations of space do not see "home" as a retreat from the world, but rather

envision it as a global expansion into the public sphere of the feminized space of domesticity.[105] This is a move that will be seen repeated, in culturally specific ways, in the following chapters, and it is also a paradigm that speaks directly to how these writers use the notion of "home" as a metaphor for the nation.[106] Loy's lamps can be read as cartographies of desire that speak to a fundamental question this book explores: how do female modernists negotiate in their fiction the constraints and material demands of women's worlds while simultaneously seeking to chart symbolic landscapes?

Richardson, Warner, Butts, and Woolf seek to map new territory by con-joining the concerns of the domestic realm with the desire for an autonomous national culture, where conjuring imaginary maps can be understood as a political act. Useful here is Anderson's observation that the map is a form of representation deeply imbricated in power relations; he offers the example of the British colonial mapping of space, in which pink–red dye was used to signal conquered territories (*Imagined Communities*, 175). Detached from their geographical context, colonial states were thus transformed into pure signs of Britain's imperial mission, becoming "new possessions" through imagery that evoked blood and "penetrated deep into the popular imagination" (174). We see evidence of the map's links with rapaciousness and war during the interwar period in Britain's map-selling boom, which was fueled by public anxiety surrounding the rise of militarism.[107] The prominent geographer Vaughan Cornish intended that his book *A Geography of Imperial Defence* (1922) be read by both the military specialist and the layman, for "Imperial Military Geography" was "eminently a Citizen's Subject."[108] Indeed, the geography textbook series that British schoolchildren studied during the interwar years, *The Conquest Geographies*, featured maps that represented a decidedly Anglocentric perspective on global dominance and control.[109] Warner's heroine Lolly Willowes provides a compelling response to the map's association with violence when, after moving to the English countryside, she throws away her map and embraces an alternative cartography that rejects masculinist framings of space. Her act may be seen as an implicit challenge to such views as archaeologist O.G.S. Crawford's, that women "do not as a rule take to the geographical way of thinking."[110] Like Warner, the other three authors considered here privilege female reconfigurations of space as a way to recreate the imagined community of nation. In contrast to Rhys's Sasha Jensen, who longs to acquire a "book like a flat green meadow [with] sheep feeding in it" but is forced to purchase a collection that reminds her of the colonial legacy of domination – "stories on the white-slave traffic" (*Good Morning, Midnight*, 132) – the Englishwomen foregrounded in this study are alienated neither from the plot of conquest nor from the ideology of rural England. Indeed, Woolf's confession that the "holiness" and "beauty of England ... feeds me, rests me, satisfies me, as nothing else" captures the period's dominant view, articulated by Prime Minister Stanley Baldwin, that rural England is constitutive of English identity: "England is the country, and the country is England."[111] In demonstrating their attachment to territory, British women's rhetorical strategies invert the dynamic of female passivity and male action that has been "imprinted deeply upon the racial imagination" of the British.[112]

The racialized female body and imaginary geographies

The interwar period was one of increased immigration, when definitions of *Englishness* and *Britishness* were particularly blurred, a conjunction that has consequences for understanding how female modernists configure the racialized female body. The creation of Britain through England's absorption of Wales (1536), Scotland (1707), and Ireland (1801), necessitated England's sacrifice of part of its national particularity; thus, with the development of the idea of *Britain*, something of Englishness had to be abandoned.[113] And yet, as Philip Dodd observes, Englishness remained the dominant national identity: the cultural life of the rest of Britain "could have no meaning other than in its satellite relationship with the cultural life of England."[114] Stephen Haseler has argued that although the "Empire was a decidedly *British* affair," it was the ideology of Englishness that "created the Empire – which guided the civil servants, top military and clergy who later *ran* the global enterprise."[115] The terms "English" and "British," according to Jane Mackay and Pat Thane, are often used interchangeably in the period under consideration; like other modern British historians, these two tend to reproduce the elision, arguing that "English writers, then as now, were inclined to use 'British' and 'English' interchangeably ... and to assume Englishness as a norm."[116] We can see a prime example of this in feminist Cicely Hamilton's 1926 article in *Time and Tide*, entitled "The Abolition of England," which decries the postwar "disappearance" of England and critiques "the title of Britain" as misguided. Hamilton proposes that the inhabitants of the British empire should properly be called "English," a suggestion that provokes a Scottish reader to respond: "Miss Hamilton's article may appeal to an Englishwoman, but from a Scotswoman's point of view it is meaningless ... let us, the inhabitants of the British Isles, present a united front and be British."[117] Meanwhile, the idea of an equal and cohesive Britain was compromised by the English investment in the belief in Anglo-Saxon racial supremacy, a belief which reached its peak in the two decades preceding the First World War. A good example of this can be seen in late nineteenth-century British scientific discourse about race, which promulgated the view that the Irish were primitive or semi-civilized "white negroes."[118] Common during this period was the deployment of the term "race" to signal not just skin color but also ethnic and cultural differences, so that the perceived Otherness of not only the Irish, but the Welsh and the Scots was central to the construction of English national identity.[119] Useful here is the contention that Englishness is consolidated precisely through that which it claims to exclude, so that the subject's encounter with "spaces of alterity"[120] actually underwrites and produces English national identity.

By the interwar period, English feelings of Anglo-Saxon racial superiority had not dissipated; indeed, the mutually reinforcing discourses of race and empire were, as I show, enthusiastically embraced by feminists.[121] Importantly, the term "British" itself, as Raphael Samuel observes, "derives its legitimacy from the expansion of the nation-state."[122] The move to present a united "British" front was a tactic that interwar feminists adopted, yet while the women's movement itself encompassed activists from England, Ireland, Scotland, and Wales, it often privileged "Englishness" as its core value and attributed to it the so-called best qualities of the Anglo-

Saxon race.[123] This view is exemplified by the well-known English gynecologist Mary Scharlieb, who enthuses: "It is of the deepest significance that the words 'health' and 'holiness' come from the same Anglo-Saxon root ... The safety of the race, the stability of nations," depend upon this recognition.[124] Although Scharlieb here appears to be making a linguistic point, the term Anglo-Saxon is implicated in dominant ideas of racial hierarchy. Julia Bush helps us to understand this when she observes that "[a]mong the significant meanings attached to 'race' by the Edwardians was a gradual elision of racial and national identities. 'Anglo-Saxons' were assumed to be British, and indeed usually English."[125] Scharlieb's nationalistic fervor is echoed by Cicely Hamilton (also in "The Abolition of England"), who predicts that "England and the English will emerge from oblivion and once more take their place among the nations." It is crucial to recognize that the word "race," when applied to women in early twentieth-century Britain, invariably had imperial connotations and functioned as a synonym for "nation." Although it is true that "race" during this period also signified the "human race," the term's inescapable biological implication inevitably suggests women's racial responsibility as mothers. But the connections between race and nation remain complex: Mackay and Thane argue that because women's reproductive role identified them "not with nation but with race," the Englishwoman was "believed to possess transnational qualities" that superseded the category of nationality.[126] This argument regarding the presumed transnational character of Englishwomen is problematical, for it disregards the extent to which the rhetoric that positions women as primordial mothers is in fact deeply enmeshed in the discourse of both race and nation. We can trace this conflation back to Frances Swiney, who maintains in her influential feminist tract *The Awakening of Women* (1899) that "mothers everywhere" must elevate the "whole human race," yet argues that it is Englishwomen's "racial, national, and personal duty" to inculcate "racial pride" and keep the "great Anglo-Saxon nation ... pure and undefiled."[127] Such beliefs did not suddenly evaporate with the interwar era, though this kind of crudely hyperbolic rhetoric was often softened or camouflaged. When the Duchess of Atholl referred in 1931 to "the tremendous responsibilities resting on this country as the Motherland of a world-wide Empire," she described a sense of responsibility that was felt by many British women.[128] The four authors I examine share with many of their British feminist contemporaries an investment in the powerful and enduring myth that women have a unique national responsibility, one that is fueled by globalizing rhetoric and by fantasies of territorialization such as that of the virgin land, or what Sylvia Townsend Warner calls the delight of voyaging "through an unknown country to an unknown destination."[129]

Importantly, the women foregrounded in this study were all born during the height of the British empire (Richardson in 1873, Woolf in 1882, Butts in 1890, Warner in 1893), and each grew up within the infrastructure of Englishness. To the extent that each of these authors shares something of Woolf's desire that "commoners, outsiders" – meaning white women – trespass on the terrain of literary history and "make that country our own country," such appropriation can be interpreted as a form of racialized and imperializing femininity.[130] Recent theoretical work on the analysis of whiteness can help us to understand the seeming transparency of Englishwomen's identification with white positionings, exposing how whiteness masquerades as universal and often operates as a synonym for Englishness.[131] For example, Radclyffe Hall aligns maternal beauty with the "white smell" of the English landscape; Vita Sackille-West describes the hand of an English lady in Calcutta as being "as white as the muslin"; Mary Butts repeatedly fetishizes the intersection of whiteness, the land, and femininity; and one of Warner's landed heroines gazes at the "chalk-white" countryside and observes: "Like me, exactly ... I am glad to resemble them."[132]

In examining how whiteness underwrites the subjectivities of Englishwomen, one must be attentive to how the longing to transgress spatial boundaries intersects with particular class formations. Rita Felski has observed that the "nostalgic yearning for an indeterminate 'elsewhere' is ... a foundational trope within the modern itself," provoking the question: what is the difference between "nowhere" and "elsewhere," and what is its relation to modernist women's class-inflected national desires?[133] Although all four authors enact some form of territorialism in their bodily inscriptions of femininity, they neither inhabit nor align themselves with identical class positions in regard to English topography. For example, Butts's love of the English countryside as the space that offers a refuge from the assaults of urban modernity hinges upon her distrust of the ability of anyone other than a rural native (like herself) to manage the scenery of England. Although she regards the land as a national spiritual resource, Butts vehemently opposes the democratic access both of workers from industrial cities and of suburbanites. This anti-democratic posture privileges the Englishwoman's blood-right to territory, to the exclusion of all non-indigenous peoples – particularly those who are perceived as racially Other. Warner, in contrast, was a middle-class city dweller who saw the miserable reality of poverty behind the rural idyll and worked for the rights of farm laborers, helping to create educational and cultural programs to enliven the demoralized village of East Chaldon, her adopted home.[134] While each of these four women has a different relation to the English locale, each identified herself as a British national during a period when the United Kingdom was regarded as an extension of England.[135] As a result, their experience of cultural liminality is not at odds – as it is for someone like Rhys (who was born to a Welsh father and Creole mother and was raised as a colonial subject in Dominica) with the construction of an imperial self whose deployment of expansionist discourse is able to authorize a certain kind of autonomy and sovereignty. We see a salient example of this in Richardson's *Pilgrimage*, where Miriam Henderson's feelings of expansiveness trade on the rhetoric of imperial conquest and demonstrate the centrality of female embodiment: "liberated and expanding to the whole range of her being ... tingling to the spread of London all about her, herself one with it, feeling her life glow outwards, north, south, east, and west, to all its margins."[136] Miriam's territorialism is imaginary, but it is nonetheless ideologically powerful and contrasts sharply with Anna Morgan's reflection on her London life in Rhys's *Voyage in the Dark* (1934), which conveys the oppressiveness and homogenizing effect of colonizing tropes: "the same ... the same – all alike ... the streets going north, east, south, west, all exactly the same."[137]

The homogeneity that Rhys registers as oppressive is actually a distinctive value for Richardson, Woolf, Butts, and Warner, recalling Paul Gilbert's observation that "the presumed right to cultural homogeneity" (123) is commonly taken to be constitutive of membership in a national community. Like all of the writers in this study, Woolf subtly reworks the conventional fusion of the national and the feminine by positioning women as active agents of what we might call "cultural nationalism."[138] In doing so, she conveys a kind of tribalism that exposes her belief that women must repossess the idea of a nation, a position we see reflected in her argument that a creative genius arises only under favorable national conditions: "[How can] the great geniuses of history ... [spring] from a people stinted of education and held in subjection, as for example the Irish or the Jews?"[139] By aligning women with the "foreigner" Woolf claims them as the nation's Other, but in doing so, she does not destabilize the category of normative Englishness. This is a gesture repeated, albeit with differing emphases, by Richardson, Warner, and Butts. Eve Kosofsky Sedgwick's observation that "there exists for nations, as for genders ... no single kind of 'other' ... to which all can by the same structuration be definitionally opposed," is useful in understanding how female alterity may be situated relative to other contenders.[140] The following chapters highlight this instability, showing not only women's alignment with, but their opposition to, diverse categories of Otherness by foregrounding each novel's distinct understanding of national belonging. Thus, for example, Richardson parallels woman with the figure of the Jew in order to lament her national exclusion, while Butts portrays the Jew as a racial contaminant that sharply contrasts with the purity, and consequent national entitlement, of the Englishwoman. While Otherness is configured differently by each author, all share something of Woolf's belief that women are nothing more than "foreigners" (*TG*, 108) in England. This contention elides the very real distinctions (racial, economic, linguistic, and so forth) between the native and the immigrant, at the same time as it speaks both to the psychic subjugation that British women feel and to the estrangement and alterity that Julia Kristeva, in her work on nationalism, has argued is constitutive of identity: "foreignness is within us: we are our own foreigners, we are divided."[141]

The dichotomy of difference and sameness that white Englishwomen play with contrasts sharply with the way Otherness is configured by colonial British women. In a 1927 journal entry, Katherine Mansfield discusses the geraniums in her garden in terms that reveal a central difference between "native" and colonial female subjects: "But why should they make me feel a stranger? Why should they ask me every time I go near: 'And what are you doing in a London garden?' They burn with arrogance and pride. And *I am the little Colonial* walking in the London garden patch – allowed to look, perhaps, but not to linger."[142] For Mansfield, everything in her suburban London neighborhood, even the tidy English geraniums, accuse her of foreignness.[143] In contrast, the cultural alienation that Richardson, Warner, Butts, and Woolf experience is rarely expressed as a repudiation of English territory; rather, for them, English space – be it the countryside or the city – is fueled by visions of regeneration and appropriation. Such topophilic fantasies of territorial increase – the sheer pleasure of "so much space" – also stand in marked distinction to the sentiment expressed by one of Rhys's characters, whose geographical displacement marks not freedom but perpetual severance from home: "I often wonder who I am and where is my country."[144] For the colonial subject,

Englishness authorizes not the pleasure of spaciousness but a suffocating confinement: "England ... [is] 'a very nice place ... so long as you don't suffer from claustrophobia."[145] For writers such as Rhys and Una Marson, the Jamaican poet, such claustrophobia and loss of identity is directly linked to British racism and imperialism. Marson captures this racial and topographical estrangement from the heart of empire:

> Little brown girl,
> Why do you wander alone
> About the streets
> Of the great city
> Of London?
> [...]
> And the folks are all white –
> White, white, white,
> And they seem all the same.[146]

Marson reminds us that *race*, for Englishwomen, is always aligned with the materiality of whiteness. One way to understand the territorial implications of this is through geographer Marion Newbigin's observation, in her 1917 essay "Race and Nationality," that the meaning of the term "race" derives not only from heredity, but from communal habitation: if people occupy a particular environment, then "the species is said to run into *geographical races*." While Newbigin balks at the "one-race–one-nation theory" proposed by some of her contemporaries, she none-theless argues that race and geography are intertwined, each playing a crucial role in "what makes a nation."[147] Although Newbigin's concept of "geographical race" is never directly invoked by Richardson, Warner, Butts, or Woolf, it can help us to think about the complexities at work in determining each woman's relationship to nationality, race, and territory. To be sure, British women's disregard for boundary markers is expressed in contradictory and conflictual ways, but their celebration of imagined spaces is invariably undergirded by Anglocentric ideologies of femininity and domesticity.

British women's metaphorical mapping of space can be read as an attempt to recast their actual marginality and displacement by constructing an alternative *women's sphere* that conjoins female agency, mobility, and national expansion. Thus, for example, Sylvia Townsend Warner, recalling Holtby's reference to the new world, in a love letter addresses her lifelong partner Valentine Ackland as "my America! my new-found land."[148] Though both women are English, Warner expresses her desire for the body of the other through the conventional British trope of exploration and colonization, illustrating Woolf's contention that America "was not merely a land on the map, but symbolised the unknown territories of the soul."[149] Mary Butts, who identified herself as profoundly English, refers to her French lover, Mireille Havat, in terms that foreground the pair's national dis-similarity: "It is as if the life and sap of France enters me with Mireille in my arms."[150] Similarly, Radclyffe Hall, another politically conservative Englishwoman, foregrounds her beloved's national difference, referring to Eugenia Souline, a White Russian émigré, as her "darling Russian–Chink," whom she urges: "please adopt my heart as your country."[151] Woolf, in recalling the relationship between her sister Stella and a suitor, remarks that relationships between the sexes "were carried on as relations between countries ... with ambassadors, and treaties," trying to forestall "a state of war."[152] While these disparate examples are all autobiographical, they presage the fictional preoccupations with nation and with the mapping of female bodies that are so important to Englishwomen between the wars. These articulations also stand in marked contrast to the exilic sentiment voiced by one of Jean Rhys's characters: "I have no pride – no pride, no name, no face, no country. I don't belong anywhere."[153] Rhys here exposes the fallacy of the freedom of displacement, showing how the valuation of travel depends upon a sense of rootedness to place.

That Richardson, Warner, Butts, and Woolf demonstrate an interest in both literal and conceptual mapping is arguably a material consequence of their particular relationship to British space, in which, historically, national identity has derived from one's relationship to territory. These writers equate female embodiment with the land, not in order to authorize masculine control over it, but to align themselves with *the* interwar definition of citizenship as a consequence of one's birthplace, not of parentage. In this way, they betray yet another investment in the ideology of Englishness: namely, the belief that power derives from territorial control. Each seeks to establish national affiliation through imaginative recourse to the *ius soli*, the notion that national identity derives from "the law of the soil," one's place of birth. Yet while Britishness was equated with territory, women's territorial identification ended abruptly upon marriage to a foreigner, when their nationality rights were effectively suspended. However, even to claim that women had territorial rights is questionable, for the rule of primogeniture – the common law that allowed women to inherit land only if they had no brothers – survived in England until 1925, when the Administration of Estates Act equalized male and female inheritance.[154] Despite this law and several post-suffrage changes in the devolution of property, a married British woman was still legally required to take the domicile of her husband even if she was living in a different place.[155] The law of the *ius soli* did not change until 1981, when there was a legal shift from an inheritance of place to an inheritance of race (parentage); yet this paradigmatic shift from *place* to *race* is problematized by the fact that, for British women of the time, there was always an elision of racial and national identities.[156] Moreover, as women subject to marital expatriation, they were never fully integrated with the imagined collectivity of British citizens that one's birth-right allegedly conferred. For women, the law of the soil was not absolute, even though the empire was symbolically feminized through imagery that depended heavily on maternal tropes. Britannia may have ruled the waves, thus "enabling the motherland to keep in constant touch with her daughter states in other lands" through "the bond of common blood," but British women themselves were denied the full rights of imperial citizenship.[157]

One of the central means these writers use to position themselves at the center of national culture is to link the visual with territory and to imbue the gaze with redemptive agency. Dissociating vision from its conventional association with male scopophilic pleasure, they align feminine spectatorship with redemptive power and convey that this gaze is essential to civilization because it can function as a vehicle for spiritual and moral uplift.[158] In deploying the language of visual exploration in the context of moral regeneration at home, they ultimately defamiliarize the domestic landscape.[159] For Richardson and Butts, in particular, the central metaphor for female nation-building is perception, for the eye fosters an identification with territory that at times depends upon a national–imperial worldview. We can see an exemplary illustration of this in Cicely Hamilton, whose argument that the female gaze functions as a vehicle for national redemption borrows from the vocabulary of Britain's civilizing enterprise. In discussing British women's role as peacekeepers of the world, Hamilton argues that women's "power of vision" is crucial to the moral improvement of society, linking this gaze to "the salvation of the race": "the quality most lacking in the race and whereof it stands most in need is *imagination*."[160] Like Benedict Anderson, who regards the nation not as a predetermined product of a certain set of societal conditions but as an imagined community, Hamilton proposes that Britain can be imagined into existence – but through a specifically *female* visualizing practice. My chapters on Richardson and Butts highlight how the privileging of female visuality coincides with the Englishwoman's racialized "gaze of entitlement."[161]

Although women in Britain were deemed mentally incapable of creating "imperialist geography" – and as a result were denied membership of the Royal Geographical Society until 1913 – British women's use of spatial metaphors imaginatively refuses such marginalization by claiming mastery through their own feminized spatial knowledge.[162] Their awareness of the relation between visualization and territorial expansionism echoes a founding assumption of the burgeoning discipline of British geography. Halford Mackinder, a prominent member of the Royal Geographical Society, sought to legitimize geographical inquiry by linking it with nationalism, arguing that "to see with the mind's eye … and then to prolong it by an effort of imagination … is of the very essence of geographical power."[163] While Richardson and Butts would not see themselves reflected in Mackinder's rhetoric because it privileges only men, they do nonetheless privilege feminine visualization as *the* means through which British territory is remapped. This focus on visual perception and the land also recalls the interwar period's preoccupation with what David Matless calls geographical citizenship, the preservationist ethos of proper conduct in nature.[164] Like rural preservationist Clough Williams-Ellis, who argued in 1928 that the "good citizen" is someone who "train[s] his eyes" in the "habit of observation" in order to "prophesy and proselytize and do something for England," British women modernists privilege women's perceptual capacity as a national spiritual resource.[165] Thus, while not all the writers in this study are preoccupied with women's specifically biological role as racial conduits, each imagines women's spiritual guardianship as central to the regeneration of the body politic, rendering femininity as fundamental to nation-building.

When, in relation to the representation of literature, Woolf asks "are not all Arts her tributaries, all sciences her continents and the globe itself but a painted ball in the enclosure of her arms?", she reflects the Englishwoman's all-encompassing sense that the world is her possession.[166] This image of literature as a feminized geographical space, a giant female body that both is, and embraces, the entire globe, suggests two important things: one, that women are potent rhetorical agents for national expansion; and, two, that space, gender, and location are central to the concerns of literary production. The four writers I consider in the chapters that follow evince the desire to construct new worlds by re-imagining the nation as a body that is propelled by female intervention. In doing so, they domesticate and place into the hands of women the responsibility for England's reawakening of national consciousness. This project recalls the evocative image of Katherine Hilberry, in *Night and Day* (1919), who "held in her hands for one brief moment the globe which we spend our lives in trying to shape, round, whole, and entire from the confusion of chaos."[167] As the Englishwomen in this book attempt to chart new literary territory, they redraw the map of the world by situating women as subjects, not objects, of historical processes. By miniaturizing and domesticating the globe, Woolf's image suggests, women are able to shape and control their own destinies, even though that agency is still rendered, typically, through tropes that evoke the imperial act of discovery.

Step-daughters of England seeks to understand the rhetorical implications of this colonization by examining how British women's experimental narratives engender national identity, and, conversely, how women's complex national identification engenders narrative. But, before turning to sustained analyses of individual writers, I continue, in the next chapter, to historically situate British women's interwar fiction by showing how the contexts of nationality law, the social construction of femininity, and the discourse of maternalist imperialism made an impact on British women's fantasies of cultural agency. Because the female body is already both a site of social inscription and a metonym for the nation, British women writers are able to refashion it as the basis for a new paradigm of national belonging in which feminine agency is key. And that, as Woolf puts it, "is a sight that has never been seen since the world began" (*ROO*, 84).

Notes

1 Virginia Woolf, *Three Guineas* (New York: Harcourt Brace, 1966), 14; hereafter cited in the text as *TG*.

2 When I refer to British women hereafter, I mean to signal the select group of upper-middle-class Englishwomen who comprised the national ideal implicitly addressed by the discourses of the period. This shorthand is meant to streamline discussion, but not to homogenize the many differences among real women living in Britain during the interwar period. In addition, I use the term "lesbian" advisedly, even though modernist women themselves deployed the term, since it was not often used during the interwar period. In using "lesbian" interchangeably with "invert" and "sapphist," my goal is to avoid the clinical tinge of the former and the class bias associated with the latter.

3 J.H. Grainger observes that patriotism arises from intense emotions and "sacred loyalties ... [which] are beyond analysis." See *Patriotisms: Britain 1900–1939* (London: Routledge & Kegan Paul, 1986), 5. Another way to understand women's bifurcated response to the nation is through Ernest Renan's argument that nationality is ultimately a "spiritual principle" that consistently evokes violent passions and irrational desires. See "What is a nation?" in Homi K. Bhabha ed. *Nation and Narration* (London and New York: Routledge, 1990), 19.

4 Virginia Woolf, *The Waves: The Two Holograph Drafts*, transcribed and ed. J.W. Graham (London: Hogarth Press, 1976), 184.

5 *The Letters of Virginia Woolf*, ed. Nigel Nicolson, 6 vols. (London: Hogarth Press, 1975–80), Vol. 4: 276.

6 Virginia Woolf, "David Copperfield," *Collected Essays*, 4 vols. (London: Hogarth Press and

New York: Harcourt Brace Jovanovich, 1966–7), Vol. 1 (1967): 193. Virginia Woolf, "The narrow bridge of art," *Granite and Rainbow: Essays* (New York: Harcourt Brace & Co., 1958), 11.

7 Virginia Woolf, "Sir Walter Raleigh," *The Essays of Virginia Woolf*, ed. Anne Olivier Bell (London: Hogarth Press, 1988), Vol. 3: *1919–1924*: 91. Virginia Woolf, "Mr. Bennett and Mrs. Brown" in S.P. Rosenbaum ed. *A Bloomsbury Group Reader* (Oxford, and Cambridge, MA: Blackwell, 1993), 238.

8 See J.B. Harley, "Maps, knowledge, and power" in D. Cosgrove and S. Daniels eds. *The Iconography of Landscape: Essays on the Symbolic Representation, Design and Use of Past Environments* (Cambridge: Cambridge University Press, 1998), 277–312.

9 Winifred Holtby, *South Riding* (London: Virago, 1988 [1936]), 48; hereafter cited in the text.

10 For a discussion of Little Englandism, see Grainger, *Patriotisms*, 10 and 154; also Richard Gott, "Little Englanders" in Raphael Samuel ed. *Patriotism: The Making and Unmaking of British National Identity*, Vol. 1: *History and Politics* (London and New York: Routledge), 90–102.

11 See Nancy Armstrong, *Desire and Domestic Fiction: A Political History of the Novel* (Oxford: Oxford University Press, 1987).

12 See, for example: Elizabeth Eger, Charlotte Grant, Clíona Ó Gallchoir, and Penny Warburton eds. *Women, Writing and the Public Sphere 1700–1830* (Cambridge: Cambridge University Press, 2001); Catherine Hall, *Civilising Subjects: Colony and Metropole in the English Imagination, 1830–1867* (Chicago, IL, and London: University of Chicago Press, 2002); Angela Keane, *Women Writers and the English Nation in the 1790s* (Cambridge: Cambridge University Press, 2001); Devoney Looser, *British Women Writers and the Writing of History, 1670–1820* (Johns Hopkins University Press, 2000); Deirdre David, *Rule Britannia: Women, Empire, and Victorian Writing* (Ithaca, NY, and London: Cornell University Press, 1995); Inderpal Grewel, *Home and Harem: Nation, Gender, Empire, and the Cultures of Travel* (Durham, NC, and London: Duke University Press, 1996); Reina Lewis, *Gendering Orientalism: Race, Femininity, and Representation* (London and New York: Routledge, 1996); Anne McClintock, *Imperial Leather: Race, Gender, and Sexuality in the Colonial Contest* (New York: Routledge, 1995); Billie Melman, *Women's Orients: English Women and the Middle East, 1718–1918* (Ann Arbor: University of Michigan Press, 1995); Susan Meyer, *Imperialism at Home: Race and Victorian Women's Fiction* (Ithaca, NY, and London: Cornell University Press, 1996); Vron Ware, *Beyond the Pale: White Women, Racism, and History* (New York: Verso, 1992).

13 To date, the only literary historical accounts of writing by women in Britain between the wars are the following: Nicola Beauman, *A Very Great Profession: The Woman's Novel 1914–39* (London: Virago, 1983); Margaret Crosland, *Beyond the Lighthouse: English Women Novelists in the Twentieth Century* (New York: Taplinger, 1981); Maroula Joannou, *"Ladies, Please Don't Smash These Windows": Women's Writing, Feminist Consciousness and Social Change 1918–38* (Oxford and Providence, RI: Berg, 1995); Sydney Janet Kaplan, *Feminine Consciousness in the Modern British Novel* (Urbana and Chicago, IL: University of Illinois Press, 1975); Alison Light, *Forever England: Femininity, Literature and Conservatism between the Wars* (London and New York: Routledge, 1991); Elaine Showalter, *A Literature of Their Own: British Women Novelists from Brontë to Lessing* (Princeton, NJ: Princeton University Press, 1977). Margaret Lawrence's *We Write As Women* (London: Joseph, 1937), is now outdated, but remains a useful overview of important writers of the period. Even though the 1990s witnessed the publication of more than one anthology on British women writers, the institutional marginalization of interwar authors continues. Among these volumes the allegedly comprehensive *An Encyclopedia of British Women Writers*, edited by Paul and June Schlueter (New Brunswick, NJ: Rutgers University Press, 1998), notably contains no entries for Mary Butts, Olive Moore, or Una Marson.

14 Olive Moore, *Collected Writings* (Elmwood Park, IL: Dalkey Archive Press, 1992), 388; hereafter cited in the text.

15 Leslie Heywood, *Dedication to Hunger: The Anorexic Aesthetic in Modern Culture* (Berkeley: University of California Press, 1996), 65.

16 Paul Gilbert discusses the significance of "an essentially territorial nationalism" in *The Philosophy of Nationalism* (Boulder, CO: Westview,1998), 98.

17 Pericles Lewis, *Modernism, Nationalism, and the Novel* (Cambridge: Cambridge University Press, 2000), 2, 7.

18 Duchess of Atholl, *Women and Politics* (London: Philip Allan, 1931), 178. Christopher Hill discusses representations of England as the new Israel, "the chosen nation," in *Milton and the English Revolution* (Harmondsworth: Penguin, 1979), 280–1. Blake's reference to "England's green and pleasant land" was invoked frequently throughout the interwar period, not only by politicians and rural preservationists but by women who sought to intertwine women's civic and racial responsibility. See also Mrs. Halbot, "Pro patria," *The Conservative Woman* (June, 1921): 10.

19 Mary Haweis, *Words to Women: Addresses and Essays*, quoted by Joanne Winning, *The Pilgrimage of Dorothy Richardson* (Madison: University of Wisconsin Press, 2000), 187 n. 28. Fredric Jameson, *The Political Unconscious: Narrative As a Socially Symbolic Act* (Ithaca, NY: Cornell University Press, 1981), 79.

20 J.A. Hobson, *Imperialism: A Study* (London: George Allen & Unwin, 1938 [1902]), 165; hereafter cited in the text.

21 While the idea of a modernist *canon* has been the subject of much controversy and debate, I would argue that the terms "canonical" and "non-canonical" are still useful – not because critics have failed to consider gender in their accounts of modernism, but rather because institutional legitimacy still continues to elude women writers such as Mary Butts.

22 Instead of celebrating the martial qualities of Britannia, the writers I examine register the distortion that occurs when women are transformed into mythic national symbols. In *Orlando*, for example, Woolf caricatures Britannia's Amazonian links to imperial power, depicting her as a monumental "female figure clothed in flowing white" whose stance, surrounded by her amulets of "globes, [and] maps," resembles a "gigantic coat of arms": *Orlando* (New York: Harcourt Brace & Company, 1956), 232. Although women are key to the idea of national progress, Britannia herself is shot through with allegorical meaning that has historically been associated with masculine mastery of the nation-as-female. See Madge Dresser's "Britannia" in Raphael Samuel ed. *Patriotism: The Making and Unmaking of British National Identity*, Vol. 3: *National Fictions* (London and New York: Routledge, 1989): 26–49; and Maria Warner's *Monuments and Maidens: The Allegory of the Female Form* (New York: Atheneum, 1985).

23 Elizabeth Langland, "Nation and nationality: Queen Victoria in the developing narrative of Englishness" in Margaret Homans and Adrienne Munich eds. *Remaking Queen Victoria* (New York and London: Cambridge University Press, 1997), 13–32. See also Philip Dodd, "Englishness and the national culture" in Robert Colls and Philip Dodd eds. *Englishness: Politics and Culture 1880–1920* (London: Croom Helm, 1986); Jonathan Rutherford, *Forever England: Reflections on Masculinity and Empire* (London: Lawrence & Wishart, 1997).

24 Alison Light, *Forever England: Femininity, Literature and Conservatism between the Wars* (London and New York: Routledge, 1991). Deirdre Lynch's phrase "domestic nationality" occurs in her essay, "At home with Jane Austen" in Deirdre Lynch and William B. Warner eds. *Cultural Institutions of the Novel* (Durham, NC, and London: Duke University Press, 1996), 168–9.

25 M. Lowndes, "Domestic service," *The Englishwoman*, 123 (March, 1919). See also "A Woman's Place," *The Englishwoman*, 123 (March, 1919). Rosemary Marangoly George argues that "[i]magining a home is as political an act as is imagining a nation": *The Politics of Home: Postcolonial Relocations and Twentieth-Century Fiction* (Cambridge: Cambridge University Press, 1996), 6.

26 Anne McClintock, "Family feuds, gender, nationalism and the family," *Feminist Review*, 44 (1993): 62. See also: "'No longer in a future heaven': gender, race and nationalism" in Anne McClintock, Aamir Mufti, and Ella Shohat eds. *Dangerous Liaisons: Gender, Nation, and Postcolonial Perspectives* (Minneapolis: University of Minnesota Press, 1997), 89–112; McClintock, *Imperial Leather: Race, Gender, and Sexuality in the Colonial Contest*. (New York: Routledge, 1995).

27 T. Ploszjska, "Down to earth? Geography fieldwork in English schools, 1870–1944,"
    Environment and Planning D: Society and Space, 1 (1998): 760–1 and 764.
28 Vita Sackville-West, *All Passion Spent* (London: Virago, 1983 [1931]), 27.
29 W. Percy, *The Empire Comes Home* (London: William Collins, 1937), 25.
30 Felix Driver, *Geography Militant: Cultures of Exploration and Empire* (Oxford: Blackwell,
    2001), 170–98.
31 Virginia Woolf, *A Room of One's Own* (New York: Harcourt Brace, 1981), 112; hereafter cited
    as *ROO* in the text. See Julia Bush, *Edwardian Ladies and Imperial Power* (London: Leicester
    University Press, 2000); Antoinette Burton, *Burdens of History: British Feminists, Indian
    Women, and Imperial Culture, 1865–1915* (Chapel Hill: University of North Carolina Press,
    1994); Nupur Chaudhuri and Margaret Strobel eds. *Western Women and Imperialism:
    Complicity and Resistance* (Bloomington: Indiana University Press, 1992). For a discussion of
    Woolf's colonial heritage, see Jane Marcus, *Virginia Woolf and the Languages of Patriarchy*
    (Bloomington: Indiana University Press, 1987).
32 Rebecca West, *The Strange Necessity: Essays and Reviews* (London: Jonathan Cape, 1928), 142.
33 Rebecca West, *Black Lamb and Grey Falcon: A Journey through Yugoslavia* (New York:
    Penguin, 1994 [1941]), 1060. Elizabeth Maslen discusses West's shifting attitude toward
    nationalism and imperialism in *Political and Social Issues in British Women's Fiction, 1928–1968*
    (New York: Palgrave, 2001), 105–6.
34 Woolf, *The Letters of Virginia Woolf*, ed. Nigel Nicolson, 6 vols. (London: Hogarth Press,
    1975–80), Vol. 2: 572; *The Diary of Virginia Woolf*, ed. Anne Olivier Bell, 5 vols. (London:
    Hogarth Press, 1977–84), Vol. 3: 145.
35 Leonard Woolf, *Downhill All the Way: An Autobiography of the Years 1919 to 1939* (New York:
    Harcourt Brace Jovanovich, 1967), 185. Frank Furedi maintians that, by the early part of the
    twentieth century, "[n]ationalism was identified as the main cause of conflict and war from
    the Balkans to Central and Western Europe": *The New Ideology of Imperialism: Renewing the
    Moral Imperative* (London and Boulder, CO: Pluto Press, 1994), 41–2.
36 Edward Said, *Culture and Imperialism* (London: Chatto & Windus, 1992), 189–90.
37 Fredric Jameson, "Modernism and imperialism," *Nationalism, Colonialism and Literature*
    (Minneapolis: University of Minnesota Press, 1990), 53; hereafter cited in the text.
38 Laura Chrisman, "Imperial space, imperial place: theories of empire and culture in Fredric
    Jameson, Edward Said and Gayatri Spivak," *New Formations*, 34 (1998): 68.
39 Studies of modernism published in the last decade have generated increasing interest in the
    relation between modernity, femininity, and literary form, but most of these books have
    focused on single authors or have been comparative studies crossing national borders. This
    focus, in my view, has occurred at the expense of looking closely at the heterogeneous range
    of British women writers engaged in modernist practices. Recuperative projects that fore-
    ground a historical–biographical approach include Shari Benstock, *Women of the Left Bank:
    Paris, 1900–1940* (Austin: University of Texas, 1986); Gillian Hanscombe and Virginia L.
    Smyers, *Writing for Their Lives: The Modernist Women 1910–1940* (Boston, MA: North-
    eastern University Press, 1987); and Bonnie Kime Scott ed. *The Gender of Modernism: A
    Critical Anthology* (Bloomington and Indianapolis: Indiana University Press, 1990). Sandra
    M. Gilbert and Susan Gubar's three-volume study on women and modernism is also
    recuperative, but the authors' methodology is primarily thematic, focused upon the "plot of
    sexual battle" between the sexes (1988: 5). Although rich in historical and sociological detail,
    this totalizing approach tends to ignore the important differences between female modernists.
    See *No Man's Land: The Place of the Woman Writer in the Twentieth Century* (New Haven,
    CT: Yale University Press), Vol. 1: *The War of the Words* (1988); Vol. 2: *Sexchanges* (1989); Vol.
    3: *Letters from the Front* (1994). Other important books that discuss women's centrality to
    modernism include: Suzanne Clark, *Sentimental Modernism: Women Writers and the Revolu-
    tion of the Word* (Bloomington: Indiana University Press, 1991); Marianne DeKoven, *Rich
    and Strange: Gender, History, Modernism* (Princeton, NJ: Princeton University Press, 1991);
    Rachel Blau DuPlessis, *Writing Beyond the Ending: Narrative Strategies of Twentieth-Century
    Women Writers* (Bloomington: Indiana University Press, 1985); Ellen G. Friedman and
    Miriam Fuchs, *Breaking the Sequence: Women's Experimental Fiction* (Princeton, NJ: Princeton

University Press, 1989); Tamar Katz, *Impressionist Subjects: Gender, Interiority, and Modernist Fiction in England* (Urbana and Chicago, IL: University of Illinois Press, 2000); Bonnie Kime Scott, *Refiguring Modernism* (Bloomington: Indiana University Press, 1995), 2 vols.

40 Benedict Anderson, *Imagined Communities: Reflections on the Origin and Spread of Nationalism* (London and New York: Verso, 1983); hereafter cited in the text. The fictiveness of British nationalism and imperialism, as Patrick Brantlinger observes, has been discussed by a number of critics in the 1980s and 1990s. See *Fictions of State: Culture and Credit in Britain 1694–1994* (Ithaca, NY, and London: Cornell University Press, 1996). Anthony Easthope offers a critical overview of critics who, since Anderson, have promulgated the view that the nation is an imaginary construct, arguing that greater attention must be paid to the materialist underpinning of national culture: *Englishness and National Culture* (London and New York: Routledge, 1999). Other recent theorizations of nationalism that ignore or marginalize gender include: Ernest Gellner, *Nations and Nationalism* (Oxford: Blackwell, 1983); Liah Greenfield, *Nationalism: Five Roads to Modernity* (Cambridge, MA: Harvard University Press, 1992); Eric Hobsbawm, *Nations and Nationalism since 1780* (Cambridge: Cambridge University Press, 1990); Anthony Smith, *Nations and Nationalism in a Global Era* (Cambridge: Polity Press, 1995). Notable exceptions to this trend, in addition to McClintock, include: Partha Chatterjee, *The Nation and Its Fragments: Colonial and Postcolonial Histories* (Princeton, NJ: Princeton University Press, 1993); Julia Kristeva, *Nations Without Nationalism* (New York: Columbia University Press, 1993); Nira Yuval-Davis, *Gender and Nation* (London and Thousand Oaks, CA: Sage, 1997). See also Vincent J. Chang, *Joyce, Race, and Empire* (Cambridge: Cambridge University Press, 1995); Con Coroneos, *Space, Conrad, and Modernity* (Oxford: Oxford University Press, 2002); Emer Nolan, *James Joyce and Nationalism* (London and New York: Routledge, 1995).

41 Like Anderson, Timothy Brennon, for example, privileges the traditional novel and remarks that the development of European nationalism is concomitant with its rise, arguing that the nation is, above all, a discursive, novelistic formation: see "The national longing for form" in Homi K. Bhabha ed. *Nation and Narration* (London and New York: Routledge, 1990), 49.

42 Simon Gikandi, *Maps of Englishness: Writing Identity in the Culture of Colonialism* (New York: Columbia University Press, 1996), 161 (hereafter cited in the text). I am grateful to Tamar Katz for helping me to formulate my ideas about the relation between modernist form and nationalism. For an analysis of the relationship between British imperialism and modernism, see Howard J. Booth and Nigel Rigby eds. *Modernism and Empire* (Manchester and New York: Manchester University Press, 2000).

43 See Anderson, *Imagined Communities*, 7. George L. Mosse, *Nationalism and Sexuality: Middle-Class Morality and Sexual Norms in Modern Europe* (Madison: University of Wisconsin Press, 1985), 67.

44 Chatterjee, *The Nation and Its Fragments*, 5.

45 Antoinette Burton, "Who needs the nation? Interrogating 'British' history" in Catherine Hall ed. *Cultures of Empire: Colonizers in Britain and the Empire in the Nineteenth and Twentieth Centuries* (New York: Routledge, 2000), 141.

46 Viscountess Rhondda, *Notes on the Way* (London: Macmillan, 1937), 153–4. Margaret Haig (known as Viscountess Rhondda) was a wealthy former suffragette and businesswoman who edited *Time and Tide*, the only woman-run, political, literary, and artistic magazine to be accepted into the world of reputable periodicals in England during the early twentieth century.

47 Aldous Huxley, *Beyond the Mexique Bay* (New York and London: Harper & Brothers, 1934), esp. 68, 81, 88, 90.

48 D.H. Lawrence, *Women in Love* (New York: Penguin, 1987), 312; hereafter cited in the text.

49 Joseph Conrad, "Geography and some explorers" (1924), reprinted in *Last Essays*, ed. R. Curle (London, 1926), 3.

50 For a critique of Jürgen Habermas's work on the historical emergence of a private-public distinction, see Nancy Frazer, "What's critical about critical theory?" and "Rethinking the public sphere: a contribution to the critique of actually existing democracy" in Bruce Robbins ed. *The Phantom Public Sphere* (Minneapolis: University of Minnesota Press, 1993), 1–32.

51 For an overview of this critique, see Cathy Davidson's introduction, "No more separate spheres!" *American Literature*, 70. 3 (1998): 443–63.

52 Amy Kaplan, "Manifest domesticity," *American Literature*, 70. 3 (1998): 581–606.

53 Woolf herself makes this remark about British professional women in *A Room* (85).

54 Susan Stanford Friedman, *Mappings: Feminism and the Cultural Geographies of Encounter* (Princeton, NJ: Princeton University Press, 1998), 29.

55 See Barbara Bush, *Imperialism, Race and Resistance: Africa and Britain, 1919–1945* (London and New York: Routledge, 1999), 3–4; See also Barbara Caine, *English Feminism 1780–1980* (Oxford: Oxford University Press, 1997).

56 See B. Porter, *The Lion's Share: A Short History of British Imperialism 1850–1983* (London: Longman, 1984).

57 P.J. Cain and A.G. Hopkins, *British Imperialism 1688–2000* (London: Longman, 2002), 405–8.

58 Marion I. Newbigin, *Aftermath: A Geographical Study of the Peace Terms* (Edinburgh: W. & A.K. Johnson, 1920), 6. Leonard Woolf, *Imperialism and Civilization* (New York: Harcourt Brace, 1928), 101 and 109.

59 Bush, *Imperialism, Race and Resistance*, 24–5.

60 *Ibid.*, 4–8.

61 Felix Driver and David Gilbert, "Heart of empire? Landscape, space and performance in imperial London," *Environment and Planning D: Society and Space*, 16 (1998): 23.

62 See for example: John M. Mackenzie, *Imperialism and Popular Culture* (Manchester: Manchester University Press, 1987), 165–85; Bush, *Imperialism, Race and Resistance*, 24–5; Stephen Constantine, "'Bringing the empire alive': The Empire Marketing Board and imperial propaganda, 1926–33" in John M. Mackenzie ed. *Imperialism and Popular Culture* (Manchester: Manchester University Press, 1987), 192–3; P.J. Cain and A.G. Hopkins, *British Imperialism: Crisis and Deconstruction, 1919–1990* (London: Longman, 1993). Mafeking was a small town in South Africa where British troops were besieged for seven months in 1899–1900. Mafeking Night was first celebrated in London on May 18, 1900, when delirious crowds took to the streets to celebrate the relief of the besieged town during the Boer War. Caroline E. Playne provides a compelling account of Englishwomen's "atavistic" response to Mafeking Night, when many wore brooches with portraits of Baden Powell and espoused an unforeseen nationalistic fervor. See *The Pre-War Mind in Britain: An Historical Review* (London: Allen & Unwin, 1928), 193–4 and 198.

63 Renato Rosaldo, "Imperialist nostalgia," *Representations*, 26 (spring, 1989): 108.

64 Cain and Hopkins, *British Imperialism 1688–2000*, 407. Cain and Hopkins stress the enduring vitality of British imperialism after the First World War: see Ch. 16.

65 Eric Hobsbawm notes that, by the late nineteenth century, the United Kingdom controlled roughly a quarter to one-third of the land surface of the globe, referring to London as "the switchboard" of the world: *The Age of Empire 1875–1914* (New York: Vintage, 1989), 74 and 51.

66 W. Roger Louis, "Introduction" to Judith M. Brown and W. Roger Louis eds. *The Oxford History of the British Empire*, 4 vols. (Oxford and New York: Oxford University Press, 1999), Vol. 4: *The Twentieth Century*: 12. Of course, not everyone was pro-empire. For a discussion of anti-imperialist sentiment in Britain during the interwar period, see Stephen Howe, *Anticolonialism in British Politics: The Left and the End of Empire, 1918–1964* (Oxford: Clarendon Press, 1993).

67 See Howe, *Anticolonialism*.

68 Winifred Holtby, *Virginia Woolf: A Critical Memoir* (Chicago, IL: Academy Press Ltd., 1978), 90–1. All of the explorers named by Holtby either conquered, or wanted to conquer, America. Woolf regards America as a space of uncharted imaginative possibility. To the extent that Americans lack "the richness of an old civilization" like England's, their position is analogous to that of women: "Women writers have to meet many of the same problems that beset Americans. They too are conscious of their own peculiarities as a sex." See "American fiction" in *The Moment and Other Essays* (San Diego, CA: Harcourt Brace, 1947), 121 and 116. Woolf's antidote to the problem of acute self-consciousness in "American fiction" is national amnesia – the writer should "forget that he is an American" (116) – a

solution that parallels her view, in *A Room*, that women must write without consciousness of their sex. If women are *de facto* Americans to the extent that they are in some way unmarked by history and tradition, then they too should arguably divest themselves of their nationality. Ultimately, Woolf privileges the Englishwoman's worldview: "the more I see of that [American] race, the more I thank God for my British blood": *Letters*, Vol. 2: 572.

69 Woolf's review "Sir Walter Raleigh" links Renaissance literature to imperial travel, seeing the two as similarly invested in enterprise and exploration. She writes: "The navigator and the explorer made their voyage by ship instead of by the mind, but over Hakluyt's pages broods the very same lustre of the imagination." Richard Hakluyt had been a geographer who actively promoted English colonization and published *Hakluyt's Collection of the Early Voyages, Travels and Discoveries of the English Nation*, which Woolf owned. In her 1925 essay, "The Elizabethan lumber room," Woolf refers to Hakluyt's texts as "magnificent volumes" (53) which remind the reader "how the soil of England had been enriched by the discoveries of travellers in the past" (55). Woolf's tone in this essay shifts between admiration and repudiation, just as in "Sir Walter Raleigh" she assumes an equivocal stance toward her subject. Woolf frequently invokes Renaissance imagery of globes and references to 'new worlds' in her work to signal imaginative expansiveness.

70 Virginia Woolf, "Women and fiction" in Michele Barrett ed. *Women and Writing* (New York: Harcourt Brace, 1979), 50. One might also consider Patrick Brantlinger's argument that all "representation may be inherently imperialistic, because it seems always to involve an attempt to 'master' some aspect of the external world": *Fictions of State: Culture and Credit in Britain 1694–1994* (Ithaca, NY, and London: Cornell University Press, 1996), 8.

71 Of course, the infiltration of the "dark continent" was not confined to Britain, but was a European venture. Mary Ann Doane links Freud's use of the phrase "dark continent" to nineteenth-century colonialist discourse, utilizing it to show how psychoanalytically informed feminist theory has largely neglected to register the geographic location of this trope. Doane argues that this neglect is symptomatic of a larger problem: the hierarchizing of sexual difference over racial difference. See "Dark continents: epistemologies of racial and sexual difference in psychoanalysis and the cinema," in *Femmes Fatales* (New York and London: Routledge, 1991), 209–48. Jean Walton engages with Doane's argument and provides a fuller historicized account of how psychoanalytic feminist theory has elided race. See "Re-placing race in (white) psychoanalytic discourse" in Elizabeth Abel, Barbara Christian, and Helene Moglen eds. *Female Subjects in Black and White: Race, Psychoanalysis, Feminism* (Berkeley: University of California Press, 1997), 223–51.

72 Barbara Bush discusses Africa's role in sustaining a strong "imperial consciousness" in interwar Britons in *Imperialism, Race and Resistance*, Ch. 1. Patrick Brantlinger examines the dark continent trope in "Victorians and Africans: the genealogy of the myth of the dark continent," *Critical Inquiry*, 12. 1 (autumn, 1985). For an account of Britain's imperial interests in Africa, see Daniel Bivona's *British Imperial Literature, 1870–1940: Writing and the Administration of Empire* (Cambridge: Cambridge University Press, 1998). Annie E. Coombes examines the image of Africa prevalent in the British popular imagination from 1890 to 1913. See *Reinventing Africa: Museums, Material Culture and Popular Imagination in Late Victorian and Edwardian England* (New Haven, CT, and London: Yale University Press, 1994).

73 Marion Shaw discusses Holtby's politics in "Winifred Holtby and the peace movement between the wars" in Wayne K. Chapman and Janet M. Manson eds. *Women in the Milieu of Leonard and Virginia Woolf: Peace, Politics, and Education* (New York: Pace University Press, 1998), 111–24. Barbara Bush examines Holtby's involvement with the Workers Union in South Africa, her support of the "Friends of Africa" league in London, and her crucial role as a hostess of "interracial salons." Despite her earnest liberalism, Holtby held deeply ingrained prejudices and betrayed signs of covert racism. See Bush, *Imperialism, Race and Resistance*, 183, 213–15, and throughout.

74 In *Women and a Changing Civilization* (London: John Lane–Bodley Head, 1934), 103, Holtby writes: "I hate war. I think military values pernicious. I believe that the world would be healthier if all military pageants were abolished. Yet I cannot hear a band playing in the street, or see the kilts of a Highland regiment swing to the march of men, or watch a general

ride to review his regiment, without a lift of the heart and an instinctive homage of the senses." Elsewhere, in a *Time and Tide* article on King George V's Jubilee celebrations, Holtby argues for the importance of royalty and public displays of national sentiment – despite her critique of the State's use of "barbarous" military imagery: "Notes on the way," *Time and Tide* (May 4, 1935): 647–8.

75 Anderson, *Imagined Communities*, 141. Eric Hobsbawm's reference to "civic religion" recalls Anderson's observation that emotionalism informs one's relation to the nation. See *Nations and Nationalism since 1780: Programme, Myth, Reality* (Cambridge: Cambridge University Press, 1990). 85. Anthony Easthope discusses the unconscious structure of national identity in *Englishness and National Culture*.

76 Virginia Woolf, *The Years* (New York: Harcourt Brace, 1965), 410; hereafter cited in the text. This passage is spoken through the consciousness of North Pargiter: "not marching in step after leaders, in herds, groups, societies … Not black shirts, green shirts, red shirts – always posing in the public eye … Why not down barriers and simplify? … To keep the emblems and tokens of North Pargiter … but at the same time to spread out, make a new ripple in human consciousness …" (410). This is evidence of North's desire to eradicate nationalities and political ideologies (the black shirts of the fascists, the red of the communists) that lead to conflict and war. By 1936, Sir Oswald Mosley's black-shirted British Union of Fascists' members were marching through London's predominantly Jewish east end. North fears that a unified globe would result in a homogeneous world – another version of totalitarianism. Despite North's ambitions, he ultimately cannot see outside of his own cultural and national context. Woolf demonstrates how his consciousness is governed by imperial imagery: "He felt that he had been in the middle of a jungle; in the heart of darkness; cutting his way towards the light …" (411).

77 I am building here upon Caren Kaplan's work on the politics of location, which interrogates Woolf's universalizing gestures and argues that her "modernist concern with space and location" depends upon metaphors that imaginatively recapitulate "the expansion and contraction of colonial worlds": *Questions of Travel: Postmodern Discourses of Displacement* (Durham, NC, and London: Duke University Press, 1996), 161.

78 It is true that Woolf's focus in *Three Guineas* is on "the daughters of educated men," and true also that she acknowledges women of the working class, but her rhetoric of collectivity works against this particularization. Of course, Woolf's overt argument here is vehemently anti-imperialist. We see this in several spots, as in the moment when, in contemplating what should be taught in her experimental college, Woolf satirically writes: "Not the arts of dominating other people; not the arts of ruling, of killing, of acquiring land and capital. They require too many overhead expenses" (34).

79 For Holtby's reference to conquering "new worlds," see *Women and a Changing Civilization*, 98.

80 Virginia Woolf, "America, which I have never seen," *The Dublin Review*, 5 (winter, 2001–2): 56; hereafter cited in the text. This essay was first published in *Hearst's International* (combined with *Cosmopolitan*) in April 1938. For another interpretation of Woolf's essay, see Andrew McNeillie, "Virginia Woolf's America," *The Dublin Review*, 5 (winter, 2001–2): 41–55.

81 Cain and Hopkins, *British Imperialism 1688–2000*, 449–53.

82 Simon Gikandi, *Maps of Englishness*, 9.

83 Virginia Woolf, "The mark on the wall," *The Complete Shorter Fiction of Virginia Woolf*, ed. Susan Dick (New York: Harcourt Brace, 1985), 79, 81; hereafter cited in the text.

84 Woolf, "Modern Fiction," *Essays*, Vol. 4: 162.

85 H.J. Mackinder, *Britain and the British Seas* (Oxford: Clarendon Press, 1902), 1, quoted by Christ GoGwilt in "The geographical image: imperialism, anarchism, and the hypothesis of culture in the formation of geopolitics," *Modernism/Modernity*, 5. 3 (1998): 56. GoGwilt discusses Mackinder's nationalism through the geographer's use of maps, showing how he depicts "a whole history of geographic representation from classical antiquity to the present, in which the position of Britain shifts from the periphery to the center of the world" (57).

86 Brenda Silver tracks the construction of Woolf's "star power" and historicizes her iconic status, helping to explain, in part, why the other writers I examine never enjoyed comparable

literary success. See *Virginia Woolf Icon* (Chicago, IL, and London: University of Chicago Press, 1999).

87 Humbert Wolfe, "Turning over new leaves," *Vogue* (September 21, 1927).

88 Nathalie Blondel, *Mary Butts: Scenes from the Life* (Kingston, NY: McPherson & Co., 1998), 359. Richardson's remark about the "Woolf period" occurs in a 1937 letter in *Windows on Modernism: Selected Letters of Dorothy Richardson*, ed. Gloria G. Fromm (Athens and London: University of Georgia Press, 1995), 332.

89 Establishing the Hogarth Press was undeniably crucial to Woolf's development as a writer; as she herself observes, in 1925: "I'm the only woman in England free to write what I like": *Diary*, Vol. 3: 43. Regina Marler demonstrates how Leonard carefully cultivated his wife's public image after her death, exerting judicious control over her posthumous reputation. See *Bloomsbury Pie: The Making of the Bloomsbury Boom* (New York: Henry Holt & Co., 1997).

90 Lawrence Rainey discusses the system of patronage (though not in relation to Woolf) in *Institutions of Modernism: Literary Elites and Public Culture* (New Haven, CT, and London: Yale University Press, 1998). Although *A Room* carefully outlines the importance for women of "the great art of making money" (21), Woolf herself never facilitated the marketability of female artists in a manner comparable to someone like Pound, who actively promoted the literary careers of men such as Eliot, Lewis, and Joyce. Among the authors I examine, only Dorothy Richardson had a patron (Bryher) who contributed financially to her work; however, Richardson – like Butts, Warner, and Woolf – still had to work in journalism in order to pay the bills.

91 Woolf, *Letters*, Vol. 4: 403. H.H. Willis Jr. discusses the bearing of Woolf's commitment to feminist causes on the eleven Hogarth publications on women, which included Willa Muir's *Women: An Inquiry* (1925), Viscountess Rhondda's *Leisured Women* (1928), Margaret Llewelyn Davies's *Life As We Have Known It* (1931), and Ray Strachey's *Our Freedom and its Results* (1936). While these examples are impressive, Woolf's actual engagement with the world of feminist politics was limited. See Willis, *Leonard and Virginia Woolf as Publishers: The Hogarth Press 1917–1941* (Charlottesville, VA, and London: University Press of Virginia, 1992), especially 244–51. Although Woolf expressed a utopian vision in which women would publish books on "travel and adventure, and research and scholarship, and history and biography, and criticism and philosophy and science" (*ROO*, 109), she herself never utilized the means of production to solicit and produce a female body of literature that would reflect this range.

92 See Richardson, *Windows on Modernism*, 151. Bridgett Elliott and Jo-Ann Wallace, *Women Artists and Writers: Modernist (Im)positionings* (London and New York: Routledge, 1994), 64.Despite Woolf's pose of disinterest, she was deeply invested in the literary marketplace. The following excerpt, from a 1931 letter, exposes this: "That copy of The Waves I sent you was the last – this is a boast – of the first edition ... so if you keep it very carefully in brown paper ... [in] ten years or so it may be worth [ten shillings and four-and-a-half pence]. This is advice to you as a book collector": *Letters*, Vol. 4: 409.

93 Laura Marcus argues that Woolf's competitiveness was genre-specific, focusing on other prose-writers and novelists. See "Virginia Woolf and the Hogarth Press" in Ian Willison ed. *Modernist Writers and the Marketplace* (London: Macmillan, 1996), 132. Despite Woolf's competitive nature, the Hogarth Press did publish such writers as Gertrude Stein, Nancy Cunard, Laura Riding, Melanie Klein, and Vita Sackville-West.

94 See Benstock, *Women of the Left Bank: Paris, 1900–1940*, 33. Although Richardson, Warner, Butts, and Woolf never worked communally, their paths did intersect and they did refer to one another in letters and diary entries.

95 Virginia Woolf, "The leaning tower," *Collected Essays* (London: Hogarth Press, 1966), Vol. 2: 181. In this essay Woolf echoes the genealogical model of authorship she proposes in *A Room*: "Books descend from books as families descend from families. Some descend from Jane Austen; others from Dickens" (163).

96 Caine, *English Feminism 1780–1980*, 219 and 173. We see several examples of imperial consciousness in Vera Brittain's 1928 book, *Women's Work in Modern England* (London: Noel Douglas). A staunch advocate of women's rights, Brittain also supported the importance of imperial citizenship for women. See e.g. 33, 34, 150, 152–3, 177.

97 Woolf, "Literary geography," *Essays*, Vol. 1: 32.

98 *The Diary of Virginia Woolf*, Vol. 3, ed. Anne Olivier Bell (London: Hogarth Press, 1980): 147. At times Woolf associates maps with male aggression – see e.g. *Mrs. Dalloway* (New York: Harcourt Brace & Co., 1925), 89 – but she also displays great interest in the symbolic value of maps, particularly for women who seek access to unknown territory: see e.g. *Night and Day* (New York: Penguin, 1922), 471. David Matless shows how the map functioned as a key document in the construction of the "geographer–citizen" during the interwar years in England, instructing people in the art of "proper perspective" and teaching them respect for what rural preservationists called "distinctly English observations." See *Landscape and Englishness* (London: Reaktion Books, 1998), esp. 75–80. Woolf herself was an avid map reader, but arguably would have resisted the suggestion that map-reading is a form of social-inscription. However, her interest in cartography, open-air leisure, and the English landscape is in many ways consistent with what Matless calls "geographical citizenship" (78). After Woolf acquired a car in 1927, she recorded that one of the things she liked about driving was "lighting accidentally, like a voyager ... upon scenes ... [that] went on precisely so in Cromwell's time." *Diary*, Vol. 3: 153. Woolf here regards the landscape as a palimpsest of English prehistory, much like other motorists and hikers who, during the interwar years, embraced the field of popular archaeology through outdoor leisure and perceived the English countryside to be a spiritual resource.

99 Leonard and Virginia Woolf's collection of forty-nine maps is now at the Washington State University Library. Maps 2 and 3 – of Rodmell and surrounding areas – were bound and titled by Virginia, with annotations by Leonard. For access to this collection, go to: www.wsulibs.wsu.edu/holland/masc/finders/woolfmapfa.htm. Woolf's statement appears in a letter to Clive Bell, where she expresses envy for those who travel outside of Europe and laments: "But shall I ever see a naked savage?" See *Letters*, Vol. 4: 294. One wonders what image Woolf contemplated when she refers to the map of the world in her head, for certainly available to her would have been the popular Imperial Federation Map of the World, which was produced at the end of the nineteenth century to promote imperial unity. James R. Ryan discusses this map's role in promulgating global geography from a British perspective in *Picturing Empire: Photography and the Visualization of the British Empire* (Chicago, IL: University of Chicago Press, 1997), 20–1.

100 Woolf, "A sketch of the past," *Moments of Being*, ed. Jeanne Schulkind (New York: Harcourt Brace & Co., 1985), 146. Gillian Rose discusses the distinction between real and non-real space within geographical discourse, showing how the latter is culturally aligned with femininity. See "As if the mirrors had bled: masculine dwelling, masculinist theory, and feminist masquerade" in Nancy Duncan ed. *Body Space: Destabilizing Geographies of Gender and Sexuality* (London and NY: Routledge, 1996), 58–9.

101 One can see a good example of this in British *Vogue*'s "Summer days *en automobile*" (early June, 1919), which depicts the "Necessary Map" as a fashion accessory: "A map is, of course, one of the most essential accessories to any tour, and the time has passed when women find the traced hieroglyphics of a road hard to follow ... puzzling out a route is ... stimulating these days to most feminine minds ... So let your riding outfit include a map!"

102 Mina Loy, *The Lost Lunar Baedeker*, ed. Roger L. Conover (New York: Noonday Press, 1996), 81.

103 My information about Loy's lampshades, and their relation to the poetry, comes from Carolyn Burke's terrific biography, *Becoming Modern: The Life of Mina Loy* (Berkeley and Los Angeles: University of California Press, 1996), 342–3.

104 Like Loy, H.D. in *Trilogy* (New York: New Directions, 1973), 59, expresses interest in navigating an imagined landscape: "*we are voyagers, discoverers/ of the not-known,/ the unrecorded;/ we have no map*" (italics in the original).

105 Kaplan reads this expansion of "home" from the domestic to the public sphere as one of the "hallmarks of contemporary Euro-American feminist practice" (161). Much recent work by feminist geographers and literary critics has addressed the relation between gender and space, particularly in relation to the concept of home. See, for example: Alison Blunt and Gillian Rose eds. *Writing Women and Space: Colonial and Postcolonial Geographies* (New York

and London: Guilford Press, 1994); Nancy Duncan, *Body Space: Destabilizing Geographies of Gender and Sexuality* (London and New York: Routledge, 1996); Margaret R. Higonnet and Joan Templeton, *Reconfigured Spheres: Feminist Explorations of Literary Space* (Amherst: University of Massachusetts Press, 1994); Linda McDowell and Joanne P. Sharp, *Space, Gender, Knowledge: Feminist Readings* (New York: Arnold–Hodder Headline, 1997); Doreen Massey, *Space, Place, and Gender* (Minneapolis: University of Minnesota Press, 1994); Gillian Rose, *Feminism and Geography: The Limits of Geographical Knowledge* (Minneapolis: University of Minnesota Press, 1993).

106 In addition to celestial globes, Mina Loy constructed lamps that featured depictions of ancient ships and war boats, suggestive images that situate the navigational inside the domestic realm and recall Holtby's claim that modern women now inhabit the places formerly occupied by Drake, Cabot, Columbus, and Raleigh. Loy's decorative lamp shades can be read as "metaphors of mobile space extending over the reaches of the planet," yet they are also objects whose production was motivated by the need for capital. Tyrus Miller, *Late Modernism: Politics, Fiction, and the Arts Between the World Wars* (Berkeley and Los Angeles: University of California Press, 1999), 213.

107 Holly G. Henry, "Nebulous networks: Virginia Woolf and popular astronomy," Dissertation Abstracts International (May, 1999), 108–20.

108 Vaughn Cornish, *A Geography of Imperial Defence* (London, 1922), quoted by David Matless in "Seeing England with Morton and Cornish: travel writing and a quest for order" in Mike Hiffernan and Pyrs Gruffudd eds. *A Land Fit for Heroes: Essays in the Human Geography of Inter-War Britain*, Occasional Paper 14 (Loughborough: Loughborough University, Department of Geography, 1988), 115.

109 Teresa Ploszajska, *Geographical Education, Empire and Citizenship: Geographical Teaching and Learning in English Schools, 1870–1944* (Liverpool: University of Liverpool, Department of Environmental and Biological Studies, 1999), Ch. 5.

110 O.G.S. Crawford, *Said and Done: The Autobiography of an Archaeologist* (London, 1955), 74, quoted by Matless in *Landscape and Englishness*, 69.

111 Jean Rhys, *Good Morning, Midnight* (New York: W.W. Norton, 1986). Woolf, *Diary*, Vol. 4: 124. Baldwin's statement appears in *On England* (1926), reprinted in *Writing and Englishness*, 101.

112 Holtby, *Women and a Changing Civilization*, 98. Paul Rich tracks the evolving meaning of the word "race" which, until the 1930s, had generally been synonymous with "nation." See *Race and Empire in British Politics* (Cambridge and New York: Cambridge University Press, 1986).

113 See Easthope, *Englishness and National Culture*, 26–27. Keith Robbins distinguishes between British and English nationalism in *Great Britain: Identities, Institutions and the Idea of Britishness* (Harlow: Longman, 1998). My characterization of the creation of Great Britain is necessarily condensed and does not do justice to the complex histories of these individual nations. For example, despite England's forced integration of the Highlands, the Scots were active in the imperial project at all levels throughout the empire.

114 Philip Dodd, "Englishness and the national culture," 12.

115 Stephen Haseler, *The English Tribe: Identity, Nation and Europe* (New York: St. Martin's Press, 1996), 37.

116 Jane Mackay and Pat Thane, "The Englishwoman" in Colls and Dodd eds. *Englishness: Politics and Culture 1880–1920*, 209.

117 Cicely Hamilton, "The abolition of England," *Time and Tide* (September 3, 1926). The letter from the anonymous Scotswoman who replies to Hamilton's article appears in the November 12, 1926, issue of *Time and Tide*. For a discussion of the conundrum of Britishness versus Englishness, see David McCrone, *The Sociology of Nationalism* (London and New York: Routledge, 1998).

118 For a discussion of the English stereotyping of the Irish as backward, simian, and feminized, see Vincent J. Cheng's *Joyce, Race, and Empire* (Cambridge: Cambridge University Press, 1995), Ch. 2. McClintock also discusses the English preoccupation with the Irish as racially Other in *Imperial Leather*, Ch. 1.

119 For an elaboration of the relation of race to nationalism, see Eric Hobsbawn's *Nations and*

Nationalism Since 1780: Programme, Myth, Reality (Cambridge: Cambridge University Press, 1990), 36. David McCrone discusses the relation of subordinate 'ethnicities' to dominant culture, showing how the concept of a unified national identity requires the coexistence of a marginalized Other (e.g. English–Scottish). See *The Sociology of Nationalism*, Ch. 2.

120 Gikandi, *Maps of Englishness*, 44.

121 Barbara Bush demonstrates the extent to which the Victorian hierarchy of race was still strongly ingrained in British consciousness during the interwar period: *Imperialism, Race, and Resistance*, Ch. 1.

122 Raphael Samuel ed. *Patriotism: The Making and Unmaking of British National Identity* (London and New York: Routledge, 1989), Vol. 1: *History and Politics*: xii. David Armitage argues that the constitutive elements of Great Britain are military conquest, racial subjugation, economic exploitation, and territorial expansion: *The Ideological Origins of the British Empire* (Cambridge: Cambridge University Press, 2000).

123 Antoinette Burton, *Burdens of History: British Feminists, Indian Women, and Imperial Culture, 1865–1915* (Chapel Hill: University of North Carolina Press, 1994), 5–6.

124 Mary Scharlieb, *What It Means to Marry* (London: Cassell & Co., 1914), 89, 127. Although Scharlieb makes these remarks in 1914, they are consistent with her views throughout the interwar period.

125 Julia Bush, *Edwardian Ladies and Imperial Power* (London: Leicester University Press, 2000), 106.

126 Mackay and Thane, "The Englishwoman," 191–2.

127 Frances Swiney, *The Awakening of Women* (London: William Reeves, 1899), 256 and 121. For a discussion of Swiney's influence, see Rita Felski, *The Gender of Modernity* (Cambridge, MA: Harvard University Press), Ch. 6.

128 Duchess of Atholl, *Women and Politics*, 2.

129 *I'll Stand by You: The Letters of Sylvia Townsend Warner and Valentine Ackland*, ed. Susanna Pinney (London: Pimlico, 1998), 24.

130 Woolf, "The leaning tower," *The Collected Essays* (London: Hogarth Press, 1966), Vol. 2: 181.

131 These books are important contributions to the growing body of materials interrogating whiteness: Mike Hill, *Whiteness: A Critical Reader* (New York and London: New York University Press, 1997); Ruth Frankenberg, *White Women, Race Matters: The Social Construction of Whiteness* (Minneapolis: University of Minnesota Press, 1993); Ruth Frankenberg ed. *Displacing Whiteness: Essays in Social and Cultural Criticism* (Durham, NC, and London: Duke University Press, 1997).

132 See Radclyffe Hall, *The Well of Loneliness* (New York: Anchor, 1990), 32; Vita Sackville-West, *All Passion Spent* (London: Virago, 1983), 224; Sylvia Townsend Warner, *Summer Will Show* (New York and London: Penguin, 1987), 9–10. This remark, uttered by Sophia Willoughby as she observes the landscape surrounding her Dorset estate, illustrates the constitutive link between rural England and English national identity. We see this vividly echoed by Sackville-West in her poem "The Garden": "So do I say of England: I do love her/ She is my shape, her shape my very shape." Quoted by Suzanne Raitt, *Vita and Virginia: The Work and Friendship of Vita Sackville-West and Virginia Woolf* (Oxford: Clarendon Press, 1993), 41.

133 Felski, *Gender of Modernity*, 31.

134 Patrick Wright gives an overview of Warner's and Ackland's political commitment to communism in East Chaldon during the 1930s, discussing both women's anti-bucolic writings during this period. See *The Village That Died for England: The Strange Story of Tyneham* (London: Vintage, 1996), 136–49.

135 See McCrone, *The Sociology of Nationalism*, 37.

136 Dorothy Richardson, *Pilgrimage*, 4 vols. (London: Virago, 1979), Vol. 3: 272–3.

137 Jean Rhys, *Voyage in the Dark* (New York and London: W.W. Norton, 1982), 103.

138 Gilbert, *Philosophy of Nationalism*, 123, 122.

139 From Woolf's response to Desmond MacCarthy who, as "Affable Hawk," published an article in *The New Statesman* upholding Arnold Bennett's view that women are intellectually inferior to men. Woolf's protest "The intellectual status of women" appears in *Diary*, Vol. 2:

339–42. Woolf argues that "a great creative mind" requires freedom of mobility and experience, both of which have been denied women. Her suggestion that "[p]erhaps in Lesbos, but never since, have these conditions been the lot of women" (341) again conveys that creativity is predicated on the idea of national cohesiveness. Woolf herself does not invoke the language of the tribe, but her preoccupation with sameness recalls the remarks of imperial statesman Karl Pearson, who asserted that the "nation could survive only if it were an efficient homogeneous whole." Pearson invokes the notion of "tribal conscience" to convey that the individual must be subordinated to the group. Quoted by Grainger in *Patriotisms: Britain 1900–1939*, 184.

140 Eve Kosofsky Sedgwick, "Nationalisms and sexualities: as opposed to what?" *Tendencies* (Durham, NC: Duke University Press, 1993), 150.

141 Julia Kristeva, *Strangers to Ourselves* (New York: Columbia University Press, 1991), 181. Stephen Constantine discusses the migration of peoples of colonized countries into imperial territories outside their homelands, as well as into Britain, during the interwar period. See "Migrants and settlers," in *The Oxford History of the British Empire*, Vol. 4: *The Twentieth Century*, 163–87. For a comprehensive history of the migration of Asian, African, and Caribbean peoples into Britain, see Peter Fryer, *Staying Power: The History of Black People in Britain* (London: Pluto Press, 1984).

142 From *The Journal of Katherine Mansfield*, ed. John Middleton Murry (New York: Ecco Press, 1983), 108.

143 Angela Woollacott discusses Australian women's complex identities as both colonized subjects of empire and as colonizers of Aboriginal people. See *To Try Her Fortune in London: Australian Women, Colonialism, and Modernity* (Oxford: Oxford University Press, 2001).

144 For the reference to "so much space," see Woolf, *The Waves*, 284. Jean Rhys, *Wide Sargasso Sea* (New York: W.W. Norton, 1992), 102.

145 Rhys, *Voyage in the Dark*, 81.

146 Una Marson, *Towards the Stars* (Bickley: University of London Press, 1945), 52.

147 Newbigin, "Race and nationality," *The Geographical Journal*, 1. 5 (1917): 318, 321, and 326. See also Newbigin's "The origin and maintenance of diversity in man," *The Geographical Review*, 6 (July–December, 1918): 411–20.

148 From Warner, *I'll Stand by You*, 24. While Warner's lesbophilic association of her lover's body with America resignifies the correlation between imperial expansionism and masculinity, what remains unchallenged is the notion of a British imperial identity.

149 Woolf, "The Elizabethan lumber room," *Collected Essays*, Vol. 1: 56.

150 Blondel, *Mary Butts: Scenes from the Life*, 201.

151 From *Your John: The Love Letters of Radclyffe Hall*, ed. Joanne Glasgow (New York and London: New York University Press, 1997), 43 and 68.

152 Woolf, "A sketch of the past," 99. Throughout this piece Woolf invokes the discourse of tourism and metaphors of mapping to characterize the dynamics of the domestic. See 99, 104–5, 147.

153 Rhys, *Good Morning, Midnight*, 44.

154 See Amy Louise Erickson, *Women and Property in Early Modern England* (London and New York: Routledge, 1993), 26, and 61–78. We can see an example of the significant social and psychological implications of the Administration of Estates Act in an unsigned editorial in *Time and Tide* (January 1, 1926): "Men and women under the new law rank equally as inheritors ... The inequalities which have hitherto existed ... have been swept into the limbo of other legal injustices and anachronisms." In *Orlando* Woolf satirizes discriminatory inheritance laws (see 168 and 255).

155 Erna Reiss, "Changes in law" in Ray Strachey ed. *Our Freedom and Its Results* (London: Hogarth Press, 1936), 102. The Law of Property Act of 1922 improved the position of women whose husbands had died intestate by decreeing that "a husband and wife will inherit equally the property of the other, and that the share of a mother will be the same as that of a father." The 1925 Administration of Estates Act similarly dealt with the devolution of property on intestacy, materially changing the position of women under English law by abolishing all of the old forms of inheritance. Importantly, this Act abolished the distinction between sons

and daughters who were now, on intestacy, able to inherit in equal shares. See Reiss, *ibid.*, 93–4.

156   Ian Baucom, *Out of Place: Englishness, Empire, and the Locations of Identity* (Princeton, NJ: Princeton University Press, 1999), 8.

157   Bush, *Edwardian Ladies and Imperial Power*, 2.

158   Halford Mackinder, whose prolific writings on the teaching of geography from an imperial point of view were widely disseminated, championed visual imagery as the means of furthering geographical knowledge. Crucially, he considered the geographical gaze to be specific to white European men. See Ploszajska, *Geographical Education, Empire and Citizenship*, Ch. 5.

159   British women implicitly challenge Joseph Conrad's lament that, because the era of true exploration has been superseded by global tourism, "[n]othing obviously strange remains for our eyes now": "Travel" (1923), reprinted in *Last Essays*, ed. R. Curle (Garden City, NY: Doubleday, Page, & Co., 1926), 121–34.

160   Cicley Hamilton, "The Women's Congress and the peace problem," *The Englishwoman*, 140 (August, 1920). Emphasis added.

161   Michelle Cliff, "Virginia Woolf and the imperial gaze: a glance askance" in Mark Hussey and Vara Neverow eds. *Virginia Woolf: Emerging Perspectives: Selected Papers from the Third Annual Conference on Virginia Woolf* (New York: Pace University Press, 1994), 95.

162   Gillian Rose, *Feminism and Geography*, 9.

163   H.J. Mackinder, *The Development of Geographical Teaching Out of Nature-Study* (London: George Philip, 1908), 7; quoted by Christ GoGwilt, "The geographical image," 56.

164   David Matless, "'The art of right living': landscape and citizenship, 1918–1939" in Steve Pile and Nigel Thrift eds. *Mapping the Subject: Geographies of Cultural Transformation* (London and New York: Routledge, 1995), 93–122.

165   Clough Williams-Ellis, *England and the Octopus* (London: Geoffrey Bles, 1928), 96.

166   Woolf, *Letters*, Vol.1: 282.

167   Virginia Woolf, *Night and Day* (New York: Penguin, 1992), 428. Jeffrey Brotton discusses the powerful iconography of the globe as "an abiding symbol of imperial authority," in "Terrestrial globalism: mapping the globe in early modern Europe" in Denis Cosgrove ed. *Mappings* (London: Reaktion Books, 1999), 81. See also Denis Cosgrove, *Apollo's Eye: A Cartographic Genealogy of the Earth in the Western Imagination* (Baltimore, MD, and London: Johns Hopkins University Press, 2001).

1

Domesticating the empire:
British womanhood and national culture

Childlessness cannot kill the maternal in a true woman ... The maternal instinct only needs enlarging to be the most effective power of modern times. The maternal woman, in the work of the State, as in her private home, will diffuse sanity and serenity into the difficult details of legislation. (Edith Lees Ellis, *The New Horizon in Love and Life*, 1921)

Domestic labour...is a necessary part of civilisation ... Upon the foundation of the well-ordered home is built the health, the happiness, the prosperity, and the very life of our race. (M. Lowndes, *The Englishwoman*, March 1919)

These epigraphs, like so much British feminist propaganda of the interwar period, envision the privatized feminine sphere of the domestic as central to national culture; within this pervasive paradigm women are upheld as national saviors, their ameliorative influence portrayed as central to the preservation of the imperial body politic. We see a similar refrain in "Pro patria," published in *The Conservative Woman* in 1921, where a Mrs. Halbot enthusiastically writes: "Now that our women have been given the Parliamentary vote, a new spirit has been born which will raise the whole tone of political life."[1] While the belief that women occupied the sacred center of national culture was widespread among British feminists in the early decades of the twentieth century, the post-suffrage legislative evidence does not support the view that female politicians themselves constituted a redemptive and constructive force. Although by the late 1920s between twenty and thirty women had been elected to Parliament, this number, which did not increase during the interwar period, had no significant impact on the policies that directly affected women's lives. According to Patricia Hollis, women MPs were "party MPs first ... constituency MPs ... second, and women MPs only third."[2] What this means, in effect, is that because women elected to office refused to be ghettoized in "women's issues," and because they accepted the male account of what policy issues mattered most, no wide-scale feminist reforms accompanied women's entry into parliamentary politics. Nor did the female electorate vote as a bloc.[3] Nevertheless, throughout the interwar period we see evidence of the belief that "woman is the homemaker" of England, and as such must be encouraged to discharge her duty as a global citizen, bringing "civilisation" to her "beloved Empire."[4] One concrete reason for this expansion of the local to the global may lie in the fact that some British women had (based on property qualifications) secured the local government vote some fifty years prior to obtaining the parliamentary vote in 1918.[5] Hollis observes that women's interest in local government was initially motivated by philanthropy – the desire to grapple with problems such as unclean milk, impure water, urban squalor, and infant mortality. If we accept Hollis's argument that women regarded local government as an apprenticeship for national politics, then to what extent did women's "morally authoritarian" impulse to exert control over the local thus perhaps authorize women's global reach?[6] The answer is equivocal. We can see a prime example of this dynamic in Winifred Holtby's *South Riding* (1936), where the heroine longs for "a great co-operative commonwealth of free people, all over the world," yet focuses her reform efforts on the girls in her small rural community, where "[l]ocal government was an epitome of national government."[7] British women's perception of the global is informed by their awareness of the growing dimensions of the empire's reach, even when they question the effectiveness of that project. Symptomatically, while Richardson, Warner, Butts, and Woolf express varying responses to the principle of women's national responsibility, none puts her faith in parliamentary reforms. All of these writers register a gap between their subordinate status as female citizens and their desire to resist the State's repression of their cultural agency, reminding us of Jean Rhys's line: "everybody knows England isn't a woman's country."[8] Putting Richardson, Warner, Butts, and Woolf into conversation with other British women writers and activists who similarly sought to remap the empire by championing femininity, this chapter explores how vexed the conceptual and the material realities of the female body were for British women, providing a historical basis for understanding why they imaginatively circumvent it.

In the sections which follow, I discuss the sociopolitical contexts British women inhabited during the interwar period, foregrounding their shifting relation to the category of nationality and showing how anti-feminist sentiments were fueled by collective anxiety about women's role as national subjects. I also explore the cultural devaluation of femininity and the problematic nature of female embodiment and sexuality, asking: how was the female body regarded by medical experts as well as by legislation, popular culture, and feminist propaganda, and what role did the constructed nature of whiteness play in this equation? Finally, I turn to the ways in which British women both challenged and sanctioned the legal and medical status quo by examining the racialized discourse of maternalist imperialism, interrogating how they negotiated competing discourses of femininity as they sought to capitalize on their role as civilizing agents. If, as Cain and Hopkins argue, imperialism was spearheaded by "gentlemanly elites" who sought to inculcate "gentility ... [and] the high ideals of honour and duty" as they promoted expansionist forces of investment, then it may also be possible to see British women as co-conspirators in the quest for civility as an aspect of their belief in the regenerative potential of femininity and its capacity to revitalize national life.[9] Could women, in other words, have borrowed from this dominant male model and subverted it by intertwining an idealized understanding of their own gendered role within empire with a sense of mission and the liberal British desire to "reshape the world in her own image"?[10]

The following sections seek to answer that central question and are intended to be read complementarily; although necessarily less than exhaustive, these perspectives, when read against one another, cumulatively reveal some of the key issues and contradictions of what it meant to be a female citizen during the interwar period. This examination of the constricted sociocultural context of women's lives provides a material and historical rationale for understanding why the idea of "vast empty spaces" and their imaginary reconfiguration was so compelling to interwar-years' British women.[11]

Female citizenship in modern Britain: national limbo

I begin by considering the sociopolitical context of British women during the interwar period, for in order to understand the gendered implications of the meta-phorical mapping of imaginary space, one needs first to comprehend the various ways in which women were excluded from direct action as national citizens. As many have observed, British women were politically situated in radically different ways than men. To take only a few examples from the sphere of law: Parliament passed the Representation of the People Act in 1918, granting the vote to women aged 30 years and over – largely in appreciation of their war efforts – but the remaining 5.5 million women over the age of 21 were not enfranchised until 1928.[12] Under the terms of the Act, only women who were local government electors or who were the wives of local government electors were enfranchised, a qualification that tied the majority of women's rights to their marital status.[13] Even with the power of the vote, women were still denied full legal agency and economic inde-pendence during the interwar period: although they won the right to earn and spend, women were barred, for example, from the armed forces, the diplomatic and consular branches of the Civil Service, the Church of England, and the Stock Exchange.[14] According to Ray Strachey, a prominent interwar feminist, by 1934 women workers made 75–80 percent of the money that men earned for doing the same work, while their chances of promotion were small.[15] Women were forbidden from working at night, a provision, instituted allegedly for women's safety, that resulted in their exclusion from jobs which required night-time activity – such as the newspaper trade.[16] In 1937, Cambridge still refused women students the status of members of the university, denying those who had passed the same examinations as men the right to put "B.A." after their names or participate in the governance of the university.[17] Although by 1934 the provincial medical schools were open equally to men and women, albeit with annual quotas for female students, nearly all of the London schools were closed to women. Women were especially subject to discri-mination because of the special marriage bar, which dictated that women relinquish their occupations upon marriage; introduced in the early 1920s, this prohibition remained in force for several decades despite legal challenges from feminists. Although this remained a controversial policy, two professions – the Civil Service and teaching – strictly enforced the bar through state regulation.[18] Many forms of legislation underscored the disparate treatment of married and unmarried women; for example, the National Health Insurance Act of 1933 sharply penalized married women by reducing the benefits to which they were entitled if they became ill or disabled.[19] A wife was subject to special income tax restrictions, and had no legal redress if her husband, no matter how wealthy, left her destitute at his death.

Arguably the most salient evidence that British women were not accepted as full members of the political community during this period is the fact that they had no fixed nationality. Woolf's prime example of women's inferior status is the fact that women changed their nationality upon marriage. Like many other feminists, Woolf condemns the discrimination against married women in the public sphere: "As for 'Mrs.,' it is a contaminated word; an obscene word" (*TG*, 93).[20] Historically, the constraints on women's citizenship have derived, above all, from their loss of this entitlement upon marriage to an alien.[21] A woman's political relation to the nation was thus submerged as a social relation to a man.

We see a prime fictional example of this in Rebecca West's 1922 novel *The Judge*, in which Richard Yaverland says to Ellen Melville, the young suffragette he impregnates but does not marry: "One doesn't think of you as belonging to any country."[22] This moment of cultural erasure is framed in terms of national difference – Richard is an Englishman, whereas Ellen is a Scot – but it speaks more generally to the contingent nature of all British women's national status during this period. The novel offers an exemplary critique of the widespread view that the majority of British women wanted to assume their husband's nationality.[23] Inhabiting, in Richard's eyes, a kind of nationless limbo, Ellen is in fact heavily identified with the countryside of Scotland, even though she longs for escape. An impoverished typist, Ellen becomes sick at the sight of maps (19) because they signal travel impossibility, and she resents Richard's "kingly progress through the world" (133) – he's a munitions expert with ties to South America and Spain – because it underscores her obscurity and fixity. West's novel forges a congruence between the female body and the landscape, demonstrating how Richard's exploitation and infantilization of foreign lands parallels his treatment of Ellen, who figures in his imagination as an uncolonized space for him to explore, strip bare, and dominate. Although obsessed with the possibility of travel, Ellen is doomed to "no adventures other than love" (33). Like the "silly subalterns" (88) of Spain who wallow in a state of "national decay" (84) and are portrayed as beastly savages, frozen in a moment of uncivilized prehistory, women "stood on the edge of the primeval swamps and called the men down from the highlands of civilization" (71). Both "primitive peoples" and women, in short, had "been prevented … from growing up" (37). Ellen, in particular, is lodged in some remote period that is a kind of arrested development, in which "it seemed at the sight of her as if time had turned back again and earth rolled unstained by history" (79). Both temporally and spatially nowhere, Ellen is attractive to Richard precisely because she appears to be removed from history and has no connection to place. His explorations become focused on her virginal body, an inexhaustible ground on which to indulge his imperialistic urges. West uses the language of scientific discourse to characterize Richard's desire for a woman who "would be an endless research … so that one could observe her reactions and find out her properties" (71). By alleging that she belongs to "no country," Richard invents a fantasy of transparency that enables him to regard her as the uncolonized, ripe for appropriation, at the same time that the evacuation of her British citizenship alludes to the larger problem of women's nationality.

West's novel offers a striking example of what it meant for women during the interwar years to be stripped of nationality rights and relegated to non-citizen status. Although in *The Judge* Ellen Melville neither marries nor, as a Scot who is in love with an Englishman, is subject to an involuntary loss of British citizenship, her hypothetical statelessness illustrates women's precarious relation to nationality: any British woman was vulnerable to the possibility of statelessness if she married a foreigner whose country (such as America) did not immediately naturalize her.[24] The novel's invocation of *the foreign*, moreover, recalls the British feminist concern with international and imperial questions during this period, particularly with respect to the problematical nationality of married women. As Barbara Caine has shown, British women sought international treaties to override the legislation which discriminated against married women within their national borders.[25] It was not until 1948, with the passage of the British Nationality Act, that women were allowed to retain their nationality upon marriage (whereas men had always been viewed by the State as full citizens regardless of their marital status). Yet even with this law, the subordination of women was not eradicated, for children still obtained their nationality through their fathers, not their mothers, again demonstrating the extent to which women's status as national citizens was mediated by their social relation to men. The design of the British passport makes this clear: introduced during the First World War as a security measure, the passport was differently distributed according to sex and was used to reinforce "homogeneous Englishness" among Britain's citizenry.[26] In the interwar passport document, "the bearer" is categorically assumed to be a heterosexual male. The passport asks the bearer to fill in his profession, place and date of birth, domicile, height, hair and eye color, as well as any "special peculiarities," a category that enabled passport officials to offer racialized descriptions "resonant with phrenological and physiognomic implications" that could be used to delimit the nation by controlling the influx of "aliens."[27] Beside these descriptive categories is a space for the bearer's "wife," demonstrating that the passport was inextricably linked to the normalization of sexual as well as racial categories and symbolically conveying that the mobility of women was contingent upon their relation to male citizens. Similarly, under the space for "photograph of bearer" there is a box entitled, simply, "Wife," again subordinating a married woman's citizenship status to that of her husband. Women were not prevented *per se* from being the primary holder of the passport, but there was never a document issued by the State that assumed the "bearer" to be a woman. It thus comes as no surprise to find British women playing with the disciplinary meaning of the passport. For example, Richardson calls attention to the restrictiveness of the document, writing that money is the "only passport" (*Pilgrimage*, 3: 287) of consequence to the impoverished Englishwomen. Later, she subverts its meaning entirely by utilizing the passport as a sign for female sexual transgression, characterizing her heroine's homoerotic love for another woman as "her only passport to eternity" (*Pilgrimage*, 4: 580). Both examples reappropriate the passport from its governmental dominance of individual lives, challenging the notion that women should be made to swear allegiance to a nation that does not recognize them as full citizens.

The interwar years witnessed much feminist activity on this contentious issue of female citizenship, even though, as several historians have demonstrated, the women's movement was deeply divided as to its aims and objectives. Although, as Harold Smith has suggested, after the vote was secured, British feminists seemed poised for a significant reformation of society during the 1920s, by 1930 feminism seemed much less of a threat to traditional structures.[28] Caine contrasts mid-Victorian feminists with their interwar counterparts, arguing that the former were considerably more visible and more controversial in their demands for equal representation. She shows how the various conflicts that divided interwar feminists stemmed from the fact that women could no longer rally around a single issue (i.e. suffrage), and were now faced with crucial and problematical questions that centered on "the nature of women's citizenship."[29] Further complicating the considerable difficulty of this endeavor was the fact that the postwar period in Britain was plagued by powerful anti-feminist sentiment and reaction. A salient example of this appears in Caroline Playne's *The Neuroses of the Nations* (1925), which argues that the suffragettes' methods were "thoroughly neurotic" and "typical of the irritability shown by mass-minds."[30] The ideological battles waged by women during this era of political backlash fell into what British historians have identified as two main camps, advocating "old" versus "new" feminism: the proponents of old or "equal rights" feminism, such as Six Point Group member Winifred Holtby, who stressed the importance of women being regarded as "humans" rather than sexual beings and emphasized the common humanity of men and women; and new feminists, who foregrounded sexual difference and argued that women had completely separate interests from men when it came to family life, employment, and politics.[31] Eleanor Rathbone, elected president of the National Union of Societies for Equal Citizenship (NUSEC) in 1919, spoke for the needs of new feminists when she argued for reforms particular to women's concerns, especially those involving the welfare of wives and mothers.

For all their differences, the writers I examine in *Step-daughters of England* share something of Rathbone's belief that women hold a set of values and have a perspective distinct from those of male citizens. Like the other authors in this study, Woolf ascribes to the feminine an inherently redemptive function, locating it at the center of a new cultural paradigm that contests and circumvents male definitions of national affiliation but does not altogether turn its back on the republic. Woolf's own position, articulated in both *A Room* (1929) and the more lacerating *Three Guineas* (1938), repeatedly calls attention to the disparity that results from the social construction of gender: "though we look at the same things, we see them differently" (*TG*, 5). While Woolf does make claims for the desirability of a universal human mind in *A Room*, she ultimately feminizes the idea of androgyny; her materialist argument, both here and in *Three Guineas*, undermines the idea's spurious idealism.[32] Much more persuasive is her contention that the sexes inhabit distinct cultural microcosms: "There are two worlds in the life of the nation, the world of men and the world of women" (*TG*, 53). Woolf uses this aphorism to denounce the fascist promulgation of innate gender difference, drawing parallels between Hitler's two-gender world and its counterpart in England. Although Woolf is deeply critical of the domestic ideology that naturalizes the maintenance of these two spheres, her text also acknowledges the liberatory aspect, for women, of "remain[ing] uncontaminated" (*TG*, 83) by masculine culture. Woolf's argument that differences in "sex and education" (*TG*, 103) situate women outside of the public mainstream simultaneously privileges them as model citizens, much more "civilized human beings" (*TG*, 75) than their male counterparts. While I am not attempting here to minimize Woolf's denunciation of fascism or her very real fear that civilization was under siege, I am interested in investigating, to borrow Caren Kaplan's language, under what conditions the "claiming of a world space for women" is a benevolent gesture or "a form of feminist cultural imperialism."[33] The belief of Western feminists such as Woolf in the superiority of European culture is a crucial factor in the fashioning of their feminist consciousness. We can see a salient example of this in Woolf's primitivist caricature of English masculinity in *Three Guineas*, where she depicts the "monstrous male" as a "savage with feathers [who] goes through mystic rites," flaunting his "power and domination" (105). Here, Woolf stages gender conflict as an ethnographic encounter, proclaiming the monstrosity of Englishmen by suggesting that non-Western norms of rationality and behavior – "the primitive," in short – are at the root of female subjugation. Within this polarized construct, women are civilized exemplars. Woolf's query "But the educated man's sister – what does 'patriotism' mean to her?" (*TG*, 18) interrogates the nature of patriotism but re-invests it with what *A Room* calls "that extremely complex force of femininity" (87). While it would be a mistake to equate Richardson's, Warner's, Butts's, and Woolf's concepts of femininity, what is true is that each of them adheres to the view propounded by English feminist Maude Royden in *The Englishwoman* in 1920: "this coming age must be the 'woman's age' in some more real sense than the rather sentimental idea of old-fashioned 'woman-liness', or we are indeed confronted with the suicide … [of] Western civilisation."[34] Anticipating Woolf's globalizing rhetoric in *Three Guineas* by eighteen years, Royden similarly aligns men with destructiveness and war, arguing that civilization is "largely the work of women." Yet, whereas Royden seeks to work for reforms from within the established political system – her larger target is the exclusionary tactics of the League of Nations which, in 1919, had excluded women's rights from its draft of treaties – Woolf advocates an uncompromising separatism through her Society of Outsiders. Both camps, however, despite their tactics, share the belief that "women are the keepers of the world's conscience."[35]

And yet the novels I consider do not attempt to suture the gap between public and private by celebrating women in Parliament or agitating for the passage of constitutional amendments. Much like Woolf in *Three Guineas*, they propose extra-legislative solutions to women's disenfranchisement: "they wanted, like Antigone, not to break the laws, but to find the law" (138). That law, however, is not subject to the constraints of existing politics, but finds its inspiration in what Jane Harrison calls the power of "woman, the primeval Lawgiver."[36] Yet this seemingly trans-historical feminism is in fact deeply entrenched in British cultural values. For example, Woolf's embrace of internationalism in *Three Guineas* arguably parallels – in spirit, if not in practice – the attempts of interwar feminists who worked closely with the League of Nations and agitated for the worldwide removal of all legal distinctions based upon sex, especially the acceptance of the Equal Nationality Treaty.[37] Although Woolf repudiates the concept of national identity for women, declaring that "the law of England denies us, and let us hope will long continue to deny us, the full stigma of nationality" (*TG*, 82), her repeated attention to this issue arguably underscores its centrality. The growing global interest in nationality issues

during this period, as Candice Lewis Bredbenner has observed, induced the League
of Nations to organize the Hague Conference on the Codification of International
Law in 1930 to discuss the international problem of women's maritally induced
expatriation, statelessness, and dual citizenship. Read within this context, Woolf's
declaration, "as a woman, I have no country," takes on wider relevance for the
writers discussed here, offering both evidence of anger toward the State and the
legal ground upon which to authorize a sense of global entitlement.

By the time that Woolf published *Three Guineas* the feminist investment in the
League of Nations had markedly declined, but the imperialist view that British
women represented the reconstructive potential of civilization had not been abandoned by feminists. Indeed, in the 1930s, the NUSEC expanded its program to
"assist women throughout the British Empire," particularly addressing the issue of
organized prostitution in Hong Kong and Malaya; Eleanor Rathbone, elected to
Parliament in 1929, focused her attention on India, where she worked to liberate
women by putting a stop to child marriage and venereal disease.[38] Although critical
of the importation of Western values, Saroj Nalini, the most influential feminist in
India during the interwar years, modeled reforms in her own nation on the
"democratic progress" of "the more advanced" women's organizations in England.
While Nalini argued that Indian women were responsible for their own emancipation, she worked closely with British feminists and, like both Rathbone and
Woolf, believed that "the influence of the women of all nations ... [could] change
the face of the world."[39] Yet for many British women, the emancipationist arguments
of Indian women were authorized by imperial values. Thus, for example, those who
attended the 1927 Conference on Mother India did so because they believed that
the "responsibility" for social reforms rested primarily with British women, who were
urged to utilize "every means in their power" to work for "the social amelioration of
India."[40] The idea that colonial women existed in an enslaved state, awaiting the
intervention of British imperial reform, was also the operating assumption of the
Duchess of Atholl. While Atholl never espoused feminist rhetoric, she did take up
a number of feminist causes during the 1920s and 1930s, working alongside Eleanor
Rathbone to outlaw female circumcision in parts of Africa under British control.[41]
A part of this effort was Lady Joan Grigg's work for maternal welfare in Kenya,
where, as she recounted in letters to *The Times* in 1927, young native women await
"enlightenment from women of our own, higher civilization": "This is women's
side of Empire-building!"[42] Of course, not all British women were ethnocentric
proponents of imperialism. Kumari Jayawardena demonstrates how several British
women activists, dissidents in their own culture, were pioneers in socialist and anti-
imperialist movements abroad.[43] British women's attitudes toward their non-
Western counterparts were complex, motivated by sympathy for and identification
with women's global oppression as well as an unyielding belief in what Maude
Royden, writing in 1918, called "the duty of white women towards the backward
native races in the Overseas Domininions and Dependencies of the Empire."[44]
Woolf addresses none of these issues in *Three Guineas*. Yet, like other feminists, she
too imagines an international context in which women, as a civilizing force, will
transgress national borders in the name of "freedom" (*TG*, 143), disseminating the
feminine values of the "private figure" into the "public world" (142–3). As Helena

Swanwick, a feminist pacifist, put it in 1938, the year that *Three Guineas* was published: "[women] are, collectively, indispensable and ... it is their duty to use their *selective* power to save the race."[45]

Richardson, Butts, and Warner tacitly concur with Woolf's declaration to male citizens that women have "no wish to be 'English' on the same terms that you yourself are 'English'" (*TG*, 101). This is an implied critique of the binary divisions between the public and the private and the natural and the civilized that excluded women from the governance of the State, but it is not an abdication of women's purported moral responsibility to Britain. Winifred Holtby's ambivalence captures the equivocal nature of British women's national identification during the interwar period. In her influential *Women and a Changing Civilization* (1934), Holtby denounces nationalism, particularly German nationalism, even though she else-where invokes, as we saw in the Introduction, imperial tropes to characterize women's writing. Holtby offers a sustained attack on Germany's "insistence upon racial solidarity, instinctive unity, [and] 'blood-thought,'" which she regards as a "revolt against reason which has affected the intellectual life of the entire Western World" (158). Like Woolf, Holtby self-consciously sees the "revived enthusiasm for Nationalism" as a sign of the "contempt for democracy" (159); also like Woolf, she identifies the perpetrators of nationalist violence as men whose investment in "jingoism and military values" necessarily excludes women: "The nation is defended as a traditional, instinctive unit, something to which men feel themselves bound by blood and history ... Its appeal is to the emotion rather than the intellect" (163). Of course, Holtby's critique excludes the perspective of women such as Radclyffe Hall or Mary Butts, who, like the men Holtby condemns, similarly uphold the primacy of "blood and history."[46] She herself appears to acknowledge the limits of her paradigm when she writes: "Nationalism itself might be a neutral influence upon the position of women. Indeed, in some countries it has acted as an *additional impetus to their emancipation*" (163, emphasis added). From structural foundations such as these evolved complex national affiliations and fictional responses to the dominant ideologies of the nation state.

Several of the central questions that both Holtby and Woolf probe speak directly to the preoccupations of my larger project: What is women's relation to British culture? Why should women adhere to male definitions of citizenship? How can women utilize their marginality to create new cultural paradigms? In order to begin to answer these questions it is useful briefly to consider Richardson's, Warner's, Butts's and Woolf's political affiliation and social engagement during the interwar period. Stated broadly, they occupied diverse but overlapping political positions.

As a middle-class woman in London, Dorothy Richardson worked in a series of low-end jobs, supported the suffragette cause, and attended meetings of the Fabian Society, where topics such as free love, state-supported motherhood, and eugenics were debated. Richardson's political views were shifting and complex: despite her socialist leanings, she had Tory sympathies. The best epithet for her may be Tory–anarchist. She wrote for avant-garde journals and befriended a number of revolutionaries, anarchists, and Eastern European Jews – despite her anti-Semitism. Toward the end of her life, Richardson retreated into Quakerism because it eschewed the tyranny of the group and privileged the individual.

Sylvia Townsend Warner, in contrast, embraced communism and was, through-out the 1930s, deeply involved in the local politics of West Chaldon, attending Labour Party meetings, agitating for trades unionism, and organizing a bonfire to protest the monarchy. Warner wrote for the *Left Review* and was sent to Brussels in 1936 as a member of the British delegation to the International Peace Congress. Despite the British Government's policy of non-intervention during the Spanish Civil War, she made a humanitarian visit to Barcelona. Deeply irreverent on a variety of fronts, Warner believed that anarchism "ought to be the political theory of heaven."[47]

Mary Butts can be described as an arch anti-anarchist. An anti-Semite and royalist sympathizer, she donned a black armband when George V died and was demoralized by the abdication of Edward VIII, in 1936. Although during the war she had worked for the National Council Against Conscription, she did not support the Labour Party and was never a democrat. By the 1930s she came to see commun-ism as the "supreme enemy" of individual and spiritual values. Cumulatively, these traits can be read as proto-fascist.[48] Butts's conversion to Roman Catholicism capped her final repudiation of the world of politics and science, and she ended her life maintaining that Darwin's theory of natural selection was a fabricated fiction.

Unlike Butts, Woolf was an irreligious anti-fascist and anti-royalist who, despite her marriage to a Jew, still harbored anti-Semitic sentiments and in many ways aligned herself with the dominant ideas and values of the English upper class. Woolf's political engagement has often been remarked upon by critics: she worked with the Women's Cooperative Guild, criticized establishment recognition, and refused both honorary degrees from universities and national titles such as the Dame of the British Empire. And yet her class privilege complicates the meaning of these activist gestures. A good example of this is Woolf's problematical Intro-duction to a collection of working-class women's memoirs published in 1931. There, she admires the "sculpturesque quality" of the working-class female body, yet maintains that "it is much better to be a lady; ladies desire Mozart and Einstein – that is they desire things that are ends, not things that are means."[49] Ultimately, Woolf's ideological commitment was to the anti-utilitarian values promulgated by the Bloomsbury Group, which fetishized "the thing in itself" – that is, pure form – above and beyond its utility.[50] To borrow E.M. Forster's language, Woolf arguably believed not in "an aristocracy of power" but in "an aristocracy of the sensitive."[51]

These characterizations are not exhaustive, nor do they provide a precise road map for a reading of the fiction. Such biographical signposts do, however, fore-ground the fact that these writers, although all British, occupied extremely diverse locations in terms of class and political affiliation – despite those locations' inability to fully capture the internal contradictions and complexities of each writer. Mary Butts highlights such complexity: although she held extremely conservative values, she can simultaneously be classified as a feminist. Like some of her contemporaries, Butts published several reviews in the progressive feminist weekly *Time and Tide*, but none of her contributions addressed overtly political concerns. In 1922, Butts was showcased in an article entitled "Unpleasant court cases" which speaks directly to one of the most pressing feminist issues of her day: the status of women jurors. During the 1920s the NUSEC worked diligently for passage of the Women Jurors

Bill, a proposal that sought to invalidate the discriminatory practice by which a judge could either declare that a jury would consist only of men or dismiss a woman juror because of the nature of the evidence.[52] Butts herself was called to be a juror in the case of Nelson *v*. Moir, a case of slander in which the plaintiff, Nelson, claimed that the defendant, James Moir, a heavyweight boxer, had accused him of committing "an act of indecency" with the defendant's son. Because the case would involve "evidence of the most unsavoury kind," the three women on the jury were requested to recuse themselves, an option that Butts and one other woman refused.[53] Interviewed by the *Pall Mall Gazette*, Butts argued that "it does not at all follow that because a woman knows and hears many of the unpleasant facts of life, she is thereby coarsened ... women ... are quite capable of forming a reasoned judgment on the facts ... [and] are now taking a continually increasing part in public life." Butts maintains that women must not abrogate their voice in matters that are labeled "unseemly," arguing that they only stultify themselves and defeat the very ends for which they are allegedly working. She goes on to suggest, moreover, that "women will add a fresh point of view" to the legal system, for in cases of "child assault women jurors would act in a very valuable capacity."[54] The tactic Butts uses here was echoed by Jane Harrison, who similarly maintained that the *feminine* point of view is desperately needed to protect the rights of women and children: "Let no one think that the English Bench is a place unfit for a lady."[55] Yet Butts's ideas of female citizenship are elsewhere revealed to be anti-feminist, as her remark that it would be a "pleasure to be raped" by Wyndham Lewis vividly attests.[56] Such contradictions are the rule and demonstrate the complexities of the female citizen during the interwar period.

Negotiating "the return to femininity": the problem of the female body

Mary Butts's concern with the woman juror highlights the much larger problem that informs public and legal discourse during this period: the devaluation of femininity and the difficulty of assimilating, to borrow Teresa de Lauretis's phrase, "the female-sexed or the female-embodied social subject."[57] The judicial attempt to dismiss the female juror stems from the age-old assumption that women's temperamental volatility compromised their ability to assume the full responsibility of citizenship. Widespread belief in the profound disjunction between female citizenship and women's corporeality was expressed through the fear that a somatically based, volatile, female emotionality would import hysteria into politics. This section examines prominent representations of the female body during the interwar period, showing how difficult it was for women to reconcile the concepts of citizenship and corporeality during the conservative postwar backlash against feminist progress. In order to highlight how female flesh was perceived as an impediment, I focus first on a story by Woolf that parodies the incompatibility of female corporeality and politics, and shows how dominant cultural discourses contribute both to the devaluation and fetishization of femininity. To a much greater extent than was the case with their male peers, modernist women's presentation of the self, as Tim Armstrong argues, was conditioned by an awareness of the body's visibility, a visibility that is predicated upon a masculine aesthetic in which women are objectified.

Female modernists both participate in and satirize this aesthetic of manufactured beauty, at times using the body "as a means of performing modernity … disrupting its gendered assumptions."[58] Yet even when gender is critiqued, racial and national boundaries remain largely in place. In seeking a collective identity, British women at times simultaneously scapegoat and enter into a common identification with those they designate as culturally Other, but such identification rarely destabilizes the fundamental assumption of Western superiority. This section demonstrates how the racialized depiction of the female body is linked to the longing for cultural homogeneity, showing how the British woman is identified with whiteness in both mass cultural and fictional idioms of the period.

A prime example of the problem the body poses for women who seek to enter the public sphere is seen in a short story by Woolf entitled "A society," published in 1920 but set on the eve of war, in 1914. The story was composed during a period when social purity groups such as the National Vigilance Association (NVA) sought to regulate female sexuality by arguing that chastity was a woman's patriotic duty.[59] While Woolf never refers directly to the NVA, "A society" does satirize the presumption – as she puts it in *Orlando* – that "the whole edifice of female government is based on that foundation stone; chastity is their jewel."[60] The story's playful political stance anticipates the strategic use of the discourse of chastity in both *A Room* and *Three Guineas*. Whereas *A Room* equates female agency with a loss of chastity, and *Three Guineas* urges a figurative chastity for women who seek to enter the professions, "A society" takes chastity more lightly than the later works, incorporating sexuality and reproduction into its attempt to secure a place for women in public culture.[61] In this irreverent piece a group of Englishwomen found a subversive women's club, "a society for asking questions," and simultaneously take a vow of chastity in order to determine whether centuries of female reproduction have ultimately produced a valuable culture. As one character shrewdly asks: "We have populated the world. They have civilised it. But … what prevents us from judging the results?"[62] In questioning whether women "are justified in continuing the human race" (125), Woolf arguably alludes to the discourse of racial health and purity that circulated widely among feminists during this period.[63] While she ridicules the notion that it is women's duty and destiny to be mothers of the race, Woolf shrewdly registers the ideological import of equating child-bearing with national responsibility. The story parodies the idea that the function of maternity is to "safeguard the nation's health" by populating "the British Empire" (124, 126). By taking a vow of chastity, Woolf's characters by implication challenge prevalent sexological models which maintained that sexual activity with men was crucial to a woman's physical and mental health.[64] Indeed, it is precisely their sexual withdrawal from men that facilitates their infiltration of a series of male bastions in order to determine whether male culture is worth preserving. At Oxbridge, Castalia disguises herself as a charwoman in order to access the professors' rooms without suspicion; she discovers Professor Hobkin's life's work, a "queer looking" (122) edition of Sappho's poetry with accompanying commentary that occludes any reference to homoeroticism. Castalia conveys this indirectly, remarking that the book is "a defense of Sappho's chastity" that engages in a scholarly debate regarding "the use of some implement which looked to me for all the world like a hairpin" (122). This curious object is in fact a medical tool used to check the hymen's intactness, a reading that is substantiated by another character's speculation that Professor Hobkin is probably not a classicist at all, but "a gynaecologist" (122). By ridiculing the male fetishization of female chastity and virginity, as well as the male gaze's inability to register lesbian eroticism, Woolf conveys the absurdity of imposing male sexological models on female sexuality. The result is the dismantling of chastity as an ideal model, an aim further demonstrated when Castalia, branding herself "impure" (123) because she has become pregnant, is nominated to be the group's president. Here, the story inverts its earlier embrace of celibacy, calling into question its tacit alignment with the sexological conviction, shared by many feminists, that in the sublimation of sex "lay the potential for civilization's salvation."[65]

"A society" registers the ideological shifts that surrounded the issue of female chastity, and in its refusal to condemn extra-marital sex it reminds us of the radical call for sexual activity and pleasure outside of marriage advocated by British feminists such as Dora Russell and Stella Browne. The story's iconoclasm does not end there. Another character, Judith, proposes a measure for "dispensing with prostitutes and fertilising virgins by Act of Parliament" (124), a position that recalls Mina Loy's own call for the "unconditional surgical destruction of virginity through-out the female population at puberty" in her 1914 "Feminist manifesto." Like Loy, who maintains that fetishized virginity is "the principal instrument of [woman's] subjugation," Woolf's short story denounces female virtue as a "ficti-tious value" and a "man made bogey."[66] In "A society" Judith goes on to sketch out her plan to implement her "fertilization" program by erecting booths at "Tube stations and other public resorts, which, upon payment of a small fee, would safeguard the nation's health, accommodate its sons, and relieve its daughters" (124). While not as radical as Loy's surgical procedure, which completely extricates virginity from male control, Judith's plan would dispense with prostitution while ensuring a sexual outlet for men; at the same time, it would demystify virginity by making the defloration of young women a perfunctory procedure. In addition, Judith contrives a method of "preserving in sealed tubes the germs of future Lord Chancellors" or artists (124), thereby enabling women to bypass compulsory heterosexuality by impregnating themselves through artificial insemination.[67] Although "A society" parodies sexological labels, it simultaneously imagines a world in which women become, in effect, not only sexologists but policy-makers and popularizers of a new idiom of the female body.

In the end, however, "A society" serves only to illustrate that women's corporeality is at war with their desire to penetrate the public sphere. The society for asking questions opens with a paean to men, but concludes that women's "belief in man's intellect is the greatest fallacy of them all" (129), a revelation that materializes only with the story's shift to the postwar period. What the women ultimately realize is their own complicity in the social construction of gender. Woolf alludes to the exigencies of the war, dramatically upsetting the perception that gender differences are inherent, but the women in the story are unable to utilize this insight to alter the status quo. Their phantasmic scheme to "devise a method by which men may bear children" (129) exposes their realization that female reproduction reinforces the ideology of separate spheres, even though that ideology – with women's participation in the war effort and their entry, however circumscribed, into the professions – is no longer securely in place. The story ends in a stalemate: the women register the limits of the female body, but they propose no solution as to how women might circumvent those limits to intervene effectively in culture. The story's final frame encapsulates this impotence: the group elects Castalia's young daughter to be president of the society in the future, and the girl promptly bursts into tears. With that inconclusive ending Woolf leaves suspended the problem of women's embodied existence and its relation to the public sphere, pessimistically suggesting that the body's corporeal excess is incompatible with female agency beyond the domestic.

The historical and legal contexts in which Woolf composed "A society" make clear why she was preoccupied with bodily discourse. The depiction of the body as a material obstacle in this story speaks to a much larger preoccupation during the interwar period with the nature of female sexuality, and the contested meaning of the female body in public discourse. Woolf's story raises a secondary question: what are the political consequences of claiming equality with men while simultaneously agitating for reforms that address the distinctiveness of *women's* issues? The feminist campaigns for sex reform in Britain addressed a range of diverse topics – such as birth control, eugenics, sexual pleasure, and social purity – that privileged the female body as the ground upon which social policy could conceivably be enacted. But because the feminist positions on these issues were ideologically conflicted, aligned with conservative as well as radical strands of thought, there was no sexual campaign that united all women. Yet, while there was no consensus as to the meaning of women's sexuality, there was considerable legal attention paid to the distinctiveness of women's bodies. As feminist historians have observed, the 1920s witnessed several legislative advances that sought to eradicate discriminatory social practices by passing laws that were of particular concern to women: the Criminal Law Amendment Act of 1922 raised the age of consent for girls from 12 to 16; the Matrimonial Causes Act of 1923 enabled wives to sue for divorce on the basis of adultery (a right that men had acquired in 1857); the Guardianship of Infants Act of 1925 gave wives equal rights and responsibilities with respect to the protection of their children; the Infanticide Act of 1922 maintained that a woman who willfully caused the death of an infant before she had fully recovered from its birth was held to be guilty, not of murder, but of infanticide, which was not punishable by death.[68] Yet as Barbara Caine observes, this impressive program of legislation served largely to enhance motherhood, thereby reinforcing the view that maternity is a woman's primary role and preserving traditional notions of sexual difference. The conservatism of feminism after the Great War, as Susan Kingsley Kent has argued, pursued a program that "championed rather than challenged the prevailing ideas about masculinity and femininity that appeared in the literature of psychoanalysis and sexology."[69] By the late 1920s, with the onset of the Depression, the spate of legis- lative reforms that addressed feminist issues came to an end. We see evidence of the postwar backlash against women in Cicely Hamilton's warning against "the danger of a return to femininity" in the pages of *Time and Tide* (1927), by which she means a return to conservatism. Here, she refers to the "hard-won liberties" that women gained through their participation in the war effort, yet claims that the return to peace has been accompanied by the repression of women's independence. Hamilton sees this retrogression most vividly in the semiotics of clothing, arguing that women's return to "dress of the flowing or crinoline species" hampers their movements, condemning them to a dependence on "the sex whose muscles and breathing apparatus are not hampered by the fashion of their clothes."[70]

Many women writers of the interwar period attacked this "return to femininity" through influential theoretical works – such as Woolf's *A Room of One's Own* (1929) and Holtby's *Women and a Changing Civilization* (1934) – that addressed the psychological bases of women's cultural oppression, yet their critiques did not insulate them from its effects. For example, although Holtby was a talented journalist and dedicated activist, she was also seriously pained by her belief that she was not conventionally pretty and her body was "gawky and weird."[71] Yet despite being plagued by "the horrid facts of [her] physique," Holtby continued to interrogate the conventions of femininity: "We do not know how much of what we usually describe as 'feminine characteristics' are really 'masculine', and how much 'masculinity' is common to both sexes."[72] As sexologists discussed the "psychical peculiarities" and narcissistic tendencies of "mature femininity," insisting that women long to be "feminine, specifically feminine and exclusively feminine," critics such as Holtby sought to show how the notion of a female "inferiority complex" was in fact derived from men's conception of what women should be – particularly their fetishization of "womenly women."[73] While women writers scrutinized how the social construction of gender subordinated femininity and, as Rebecca West put it, "handicapped [women] as heavily as possible in every conceivable way," they simultaneously found themselves both trapped and seduced by the dictates of beauty culture.[74] It is perhaps unsurprising to note therefore that female modernists at times relished the pleasure of being pampered – or what Elizabeth Bowen, in a 1936 *Vogue* article, called the joy of self-indulgence, "moments … [which] make us inhabit a heroic, innocent world."[75] For example, Richardson writes to Bryher about the benefits of daily massage, remarking that "a face-lift at the proper intervals" might, like psychoanalysis, "carry anyone over in a crisis." Warner sits in a London hair salon with her head wrapped in "an Egyptian bag," composing a love letter to Valentine about the joys of bisexuality.[76] Woolf condemns mass culture but still makes small forays into the world of female commodity culture: she shops, has her hair shingled, gets her ears pierced, and admits that she "will rise to powder, but not to rouge."[77] While Lady Rhondda, in the pages of *Time and Tide*, railed against the monthly glossies for staging the "semi-conscious day dream of a large number of young women … to be kept in gorgeous luxury by a rich husband," authors such as Richardson, Warner, Woolf, Vita Sackville-West, and Edith Sitwell reappropriated these venues by publishing articles in periodicals such as *Vogue*, *Good Housekeeping*, and *Eve*.[78] At the same time, British women's fiction during this period repeatedly draws attention to pejorative notions of feminized mass culture, depicting women as both marketplace consumers and products of consumption. For example, *Mrs. Dalloway* foregrounds the postwar emphasis on the conventions of femininity through the reactions of Peter Walsh, who notices that young women now routinely can be spotted promiscuously "taking out a stick of rouge, or a powder-puff and making up in public" (71). Here, the public performance of femininity –

"the delicious and apparently universal habit of paint" (71) – functions as a representational marker of a masculine ideal, rather than a reflection of female desire.

Heterosexually conceived notions of female beauty in the interwar period linked the Englishwoman, crucially, to whiteness. Despite a token embrace of exoticism throughout these years, British *Vogue*, the magazine in which Richardson, Warner, and Woolf all appeared, repeatedly conveyed that the complexion of the English beauty was a composite of "lovely roses and whites." Even the average Englishwoman required whitening products to achieve the classical "English rose" appearance. As *Vogue* put it, "normal skin" may be "white as milk," but it still requires "the coquetry of powder" to achieve "unblemished artifice." Ads for creams and potions such as "Kemolite" – the "radio-active properties" of which were purported to stimulate the skin – promised to eliminate facial wrinkles and discolorations, while plastic surgery, readers were assured, could reconstruct an "obstinately Hibernian or Semitic" nose and transform the racialized Englishwoman into a "Grecian" beauty.[79] In *To the Lighthouse*, Mrs. Ramsay's beauty reflects this Aryan ideal: "Greek, straight, blue-eyed" (29). Butts's heroine, Scylla, a modern English goddess, is described as having skin the color of the "the moon's palette," with white shoulders and blonde "moon-fair hair."[80] In *Pilgrimage*, the heroine reimagines herself as a German beauty – "I *am* German-looking to-day, pinky red, and yellow hair" (1: 150–1) – but this momentary identification does not destabilize her English essence. Despite the anti-German sentiment that circulated in England during the post-First World War period – when British beauty salons displayed placards bearing such slogans as "Is your hairdresser English? If not – why not?" – Richardson does not deem Miriam's Germanic blondness as unpatriotic.[81] Instead, Miriam's Aryan wholesomeness arguably reminds us that even the British royal family harbored German roots.[82] Moreover, her Germanophilia may be indebted to the fact that, during this period, school textbooks and popular histories regularly maintained that the English and the Germans were racially intertwined, sharing the same Anglo-Saxon ancestry.[83] In order to understand such references, one needs to situate them within several larger contexts: the intensified British consciousness of racial types, spurred by scientific theories of Anglo-Saxon supremacy; ethnographic inquiry into the "savagery" of non-European peoples; ambivalence toward the public display of African artifacts; and heightened restrictions on the immigration of racial "undesirables."[84] In relation specifically to beauty culture, this was an era in which mass-market advertisers promoted exoticism but stressed the link between whiteness and refinement, celebrating skin-whitening products as a sign of English purity. Beauty features and ads invited Englishwomen to embrace non-European standards of beauty, but these posed no real threat of cultural assimilation for this was merely a craze that targeted a white female audience obsessed with the joys of consumer tourism. Thus, Englishwomen could adopt the fashionable "Oriental dress" and simultaneously deplore the "shapeless black *chadar*" that Persian women were forced to wear. *Vogue*, in particular, encouraged such traversing of borders, but repeatedly reminded women of the need to police racial boundaries in the home.[85] The magazine constructed an image of the Englishwoman that asserted her ascendancy in a normative hierarchy, equating her with moral superiority, racial supremacy, class privilege, and progressive ideals – all elements circulating in both feminist discourse and women's novels during this period. Although the authors I examine exhibit varying degrees of class and racial self-consciousness, each registers, even if she does not exploit, British beauty culture's identification of whiteness with civilization.

Woolf makes the argument that women are intrinsically repelled by the male impulse for global acquisition, claiming that women have no interest in marking territory or flaunting their ownership of "a dog … a piece of land or a man with curly black hair" (*ROO*, 50). Within this imperial equation colonial subjects and property become interchangeable commodities, similarly devalued as objects that are ripe for seizure by men who are "childishly intent upon scoring the floor of the earth with chalk marks" (*TG*, 105). In contrast, Woolf self-righteously argues, women lack the European male "instinct" for possession. Exposing the internal contradictions of her position, she notes: "It is one of the great advantages of being a woman that one can pass even a very fine negress without wishing to make an Englishwoman of her" (*ROO*, 50). Although some critics have maintained that this reference to "a very fine negress" must be read ironically, I would argue that the passage exposes the author's racial blindspot, her difficulty in thinking outside polarized notions of the primitive and the civilized. Woolf's prejudice is not an isolated incident, for we can find references throughout her work to "the untutored taste of negresses," the "seductive" and "passionate" quality of the "negress," and the "yearning, sad" faces of "negresses" who looked "like chimpanzees brought out of their cocoanut groves."[86] One is struck here by the extraordinary durability of racial stereotypes, reminding us that pseudo-scientific studies of racial types survived in Britain into the 1940s – despite the fact that the black population in Britain can be traced to the sixteenth century.[87] As Jane Marcus observes, furthermore, "'negress' carries no national identity and 'Englishwoman' carries no racial identity," a lacuna that reveals how, for Woolf, the figure of the Englishwoman is normatively defined as white.[88] Such covert racism betrays a deep-seated belief in homogeneous English-ness. We can see this reflected in the remarks of the British Prime Minister Stanley Baldwin who, speaking "On England and the West," praises "the English stock" and celebrates the manifold achievements "of that great English race."[89] Woolf's racism is rarely so conspicuous, but her inability to align "even a very fine negress" with England is deeply problematical, given the interwar presence of blacks such as Una Marson, who was active in British movements for colonial independence, and the deliberate migrations of colonial peoples to the United Kingdom.[90] Woolf never met Una Marson, but as a Londoner she would have been exposed to the growing presence of immigrants from Asia and Africa during the interwar period, when imperial subjects traveled to and resided in Britain in great numbers.[91]

An unselfconscious belief in British racial privilege and purity informs the work of each of the writers examined here, a phenomenon that is consistent with Frank Furedi's argument that "racist thinking" in Britain was largely unquestioned until after the Second World War.[92] Laura Talibi echoes this observation, remarking that in the "1920s and 1930s imperial racial categories and racial subordination were reconstituted on British soil."[93] This is not evidence that modernist women writers were themselves racist, but it does help us to contextualize the racialized language that appears throughout their work. Even Warner, the most politically progressive author I foreground in this study, encodes racial stereotypes while critiquing conventional English perceptions of the Other. In *Summer Will Show* (1936), Sophia Willoughby, the daughter of landed gentry in Dorset, registers "the hooked nose" and "large full-lipped mouth" of the Jewish face, yet still falls in love with the "grotesque" body of Minna Lemuel, "a Jewess, one of a race who can divine gold even in the rock." Elsewhere, Sophia contemplates the arrival of her illegitimate nephew, Caspar, a "little blackamoor" from the West Indies whose exoticized "woolly negro" head recalls the British fetish for what *Vogue* calls "the blackamoor in art and decoration." *Vogue* laments the fact that modern Englishwomen must content themselves with representations of the blackamoor, whereas Victorian ladies owned "real ones" whom they could outfit in brocades, "hanging them with jewels." Warner never exploits Caspar to that degree, but the unassimilability of his "actual black body" alludes to this larger cultural context.[94] Although in certain ways blackness and Jewishness stand in for the suppressed Otherness of lesbianism in Warner's novel, the interrelated images of difference demonstrate how much "Englishwoman" connotes whiteness and how fundamental the Other is to the consolidation of English national identity.

That British women are a product of multiple identifications, often regarding themselves as marginalized, is reflected in their responses to the contradictory cultural messages of mass culture, a space in which the white female body figures prominently. In many texts we find female characters who are positioned as mass-market consumers, reading magazines likely to have been filled with cosmetic ads and columns on beauty aids and advice. In *The Well of Loneliness*, Mary desultorily reads the *Tatler* and the *Sketch*, staring at images of "self-satisfied people" (368) as her lover Stephen ignores her. Stephen herself spends considerable time and money shopping in the fashionable West End, acquiring *crepe de Chine* pajamas, and pots of cuticle cream (186) – in other words, luxurious objects and grooming aids that were marketed to the fashionable elite, people who presumably subscribed to the magazines Mary consumes. In *The Judge*, Rebecca West critiques the fact that magazines promised women personal transformation, yet she also registers the influence that mass-produced images of femininity have on female conceptions of the self. Ellen Melville fantasizes about winning a "girls' magazine competition" (18) while Marion Yaverland, her would-be mother-in-law, behaves "like an old mother in an advertisement ... [for] Mackintosh's toffee" (384). In Elizabeth Bowen's *The Death of the Heart*, the adolescent Portia sits reading an issue of *Woman and Beauty* even though she functions as a destabilizing figure in the lethal story of heterosexual convention. What these disparate images convey is the impact of commodity culture on modernist women's perceptions of normative femininity, and their awareness that the art of beautification is tied to broad cultural concerns over female sexual mores and social roles.

Although, as Billie Melman has shown, the interwar era saw a flourishing of mass-market magazines, films, and novels of escapist and fantasy fiction – all of which engaged the topic of feminine sexuality and were aimed at a predominantly female audience – there remained a profound well of female sexual ignorance (particularly regarding the mechanics of getting pregnant) during and after this period.[95] A good illustration of this occurs in Warner's novel *The True Heart* (1929), where the lower-class virgin Sukey Bond enjoys an awkward kiss with a would-be suitor, the village "idiot," and consequently fears that she is pregnant. Although lower-class white women were thought to exude a primitive sexuality that aligned them with black women, Sukey herself knows nothing of sexuality, even though she is repeatedly assumed by some to be sexually profligate.[96] And yet Warner exploits the racial implications of Sukey's presumed sexual excess by staging a scene in which she meditates on an engraving of Queen Victoria giving "a Negro, a heathen obviously" (163), a gift of the Bible, only to substitute her abject body for his own: "the Negro was not there; in his place, kneeling at the foot of the throne, was Sukey Bond" (176). Warner satirizes Sukey's "natural" (163) admiration for subjugation by titling this foundational image of imperial interpellation "The True Secret of England's Greatness" (162).[97] At the same time, the text participates in the Englishwoman's fantasy that her cultural disempowerment is equivalent to and commensurate with that of "good negroes" (41). What this example crystallizes is not only British women's racial blindspot, but their divided loyalties: critical of empire, yet often disseminators of its moral principles.

Of course, publishing in a women's magazine or dramatizing female interest in a monthly glossy is not necessarily an endorsement of mainstream beauty culture, but it does speak to the impact of visual technologies – particularly the standard-ization of female appearance – on women's everyday lives. We see a salient example of this in *Good Morning, Midnight* (1939), in which Rhys critiques the cultural importance of self-image through the character of Sasha Jensen. As Sasha reads about breast implants, Rhys parodies magazine advice to women: "Do not delude yourselves. Nothing is easy. But there is hope (turn to page 5), and yet more hope (turn to page 9) …" (62). This scene occurs in a beauty salon as Sasha is having her dark hair dyed blonde, a "transformative act" (63) that is directly linked to her desire to pass as an upper-class Englishwoman. At the same time, by having Sasha succomb to peroxide, Rhys reminds us of the novel's larger preoccupation with the links between fascism and social violence against women, for the promotion of blondness during the 1930s was part of the larger worship of Aryan culture.[98] The most pronounced example of femininity as masquerade occurs in the novel's final pages, where a drunken Sasha hallucinates a grotesque futurist image of female artifice: as she overhears a hum of voices repeating "femmes, femmes, femmes," she envisions "an enormous machine, made of white steel … [with] innumerable flexible arms … At the end of each arm is an eye, the eyelashes stiff with mascara" (187). One can read this racialized image ("white steel") as evidence of Rhys's fear and condemnation of feminized mass culture, particularly the visual objectification of the female body. In addition, one can read it as a sign of Rhys's acknowledge-ment that women are complicit in their own commodification, for the steel arms of this enormous mechanized female body wave themselves in accompaniment to music they recognize and mimic. The emphatically feminized prosthetic limbs that support a proliferation of mascara-caked eyes brilliantly convey both the activity of looking and the desire to be the thing observed; in this way, the eyes suggest female spectatorship as well as feminine narcissism. Rhys's image captures the plurality of narcissistic positions and identifications of the female body, a plurality that is marked by ambivalence. This artificial image of commodified femininity arguably attests to the colonial outsider's repudiation of the "English rose" standard of cosmetic beauty, even as Sasha strives to be "devastatingly English" (73). Like Rhys, Olive Moore sees femininity as a masquerade that cripples the "pretty woman" who is "lost ... without a mirror," for even women who deliberately assume a feminine posture in order to disrupt masculinist constructions of gender are, in the end, forcibly re-inscribed as objects of male desire, unable to control their performance.[99]

Such characterizations anticipate Joan Riviere's 1929 argument about the performative nature of femininity, and they speak to the larger preoccupations of the modernists I examine, each of whom concurs with the observation that womanliness functions culturally as a mask that can be worn or removed.[100] We can see a fascinating example of Mary Butts's equivocal response to the hyperbolizing of femininity in one of her journal entries for 1927, where she writes from the perspective of a female *flâneur*, strolling around a giant Parisian department store, "the Bazaar." In this holy shrine where beauty is "encouraged ... [and] ugliness corrected or concealed," Butts lovingly gazes upon the seductive display of archetypal female products, beautifully displayed:

> On glass shelves stand the scents in their hierarchies. The middle-shelf is enclosed, a glass box ... precious bottles of d'Orsay and Chanel ... Humble bottles accompany them ... proper for a working girl ... in the rear stand the cologne-waters and skin waters, colours for the lips, the cheeks, and lids of the eyes, the face-powders, the body-powders and the soaps. This is the glass pyramid which is really and strictly an altar – to Our Lady, Our Lady of All Beauty, to Aphrodite Pandemos – all men's Aphrodite.[101]

This description of commodities segregated by class access conveys desire as well as alienation, for in the end the Bazaar appears to be nothing more than a masculine fantasy: "all men's Aphrodite." One here recalls Butts's reference to "the beauty business" as a "too concentrated food" (11) in her 1928 novel *Armed With Madness*, a characterization which parodies the idea that female self-display is bound to the act of consumption. Laura Doan describes the way Englishwomen "performed" modernity during the 1920s through their adoption of masculine fashion. Providing a corrective to earlier analyses that read boyish attire as an unequivocal sign of lesbianism, Doan demonstrates how the cultural shift to feminine dress in England was concomitant with Radclyffe Hall's 1928 obscenity trial.[102] The shifting meaning of the female body, Doan reminds us, is inextricably linked to national context as well as to material culture. Plastically malleable, the body is a surface that can be manipulated and controlled also for Mina Loy. In her 1919 pamphlet "Auto-facial-construction," she proposes a model of facial revitalization through which the individual can reconstruct his or her own face in order to "enhance ... beauty, instead of attempting to disguise" the complexion.[103] Loy's embrace of "beauty culture" (165) aims for a restoration of some kind of youthful authenticity – she claims the objective of her technique is to make us "look like ourselves" (165) – but her patrons can "become masters of their facial destiny" (165) only through her intervention. By advertising her services to teach people how to manipulate their skull and cranium back to its "original form" (165), Loy exposes her awareness that the body is not a "natural resource" but a constructed surface needing to be artificially "mastered" (166).

Loy's idea that the corporeal is something to be mastered acknowledges that the body is a medium of culture, a locus of social control – a fact that interwar feminists exploited in their attempt to regulate two contentious areas of female sexuality, birth control and lesbianism, both of which were perceived as threats to national stability. Like Cicely Hamilton, who cautions against a return to femininity in her focus on the shifting meaning of clothing in the pre- and postwar periods, Loy exposes the historical mutability of the female body and speaks to what Denise Riley, following Foucault, has described as the body's status as a malleable "concept," imprinted by history: "The body becomes visible *as* a body, and *as* a female body, only under some particular gaze – including that of politics."[104] We see this reflected in feminist discourses of the period, which trained a politicized and medicalized gaze upon the female body and argued that the regulating of women's sexuality was a national problem. A prime example of this alleged national crisis was the issue of birth control, which deeply divided interwar feminists. The conflicts centered on such questions as whether the value and importance of birth control lies, as socialist Stella Browne believed, in "its *self-determining* significance for women ... [its] social and sexual freedom," or, as many others argued, in the production of healthy offspring for the State.[105] Even though by the mid-1920s most feminist organizations supported birth control, the vast majority insisted that it should be made available only to married women.[106] A similarly conservative twist can be seen in the feminist dissemination of advice on sexual activity and companionate marriage. While Marie Stopes's best-seller *Married Love* (1918) popularized an ideal of sexual pleasure for women, the book promoted an exclusively heterosexual model of desire which conforms to sexological prescriptions.[107] Thus, many of the developments which were seen as marking women's freedom did little to undermine prevailing sexual hierarchies, particularly compulsory heterosexuality. Indeed, Stopes herself, in propounding the joys of clitoral stimulation and female orgasm, simultaneously condemns lesbian eroticism as "unnatural," arguing that "women can only *play* with each other and *cannot* in the very nature of things have natural union or supply each other with the seminal and prostatic secretions which they ought to have, and crave for unconsciously."[108] The period's emphasis on women's sexual pleasure within marriage served to undermine the status of single women, who were already seen as a problem because of their significant surplus after the Great War's depletion of young men, and render lesbianism invisible.

The most pronounced example of the invisibility of lesbian desire can be traced to 1921, when female homosexuality was almost criminalized by Parliament; the bill failed to pass because those who opposed it argued that making lesbianism illegal would only spread the offense by giving "cases of gross indecency between women" excessive publicity.[109] The alleged danger of this, Sheila Jeffreys observes, was that husbands would "lose their wives to the 'wiles' of the lesbian," and it would in effect destroy the civilization of the British empire by forcing the nation's "race to decline."[110] We see further evidence of this eugenic anxiety throughout feminist and anti-feminist discourses of the interwar period, even though actual references to female homosexuality were largely avoided by the mainstream press.[111] Arabella Kenealy, in *Feminism and Sex Extinction* (1920), warned that dangerously "masculinized" women who were biologically "incapable of parenthood" would precipitate a national crisis of "Race-suicide."[112] The view that spinsters and lesbians would contribute to racial decline is further illustrated by Charlotte Haldane, the author of *Motherhood and Its Enemies* (1927), who maintained that "a definitely homosexual type of spinster ... may do an enormous amount of harm" to the nation's health, specifically to those "normal women" who are "destined to carry on the race."[113] Although some pro-spinster arguments were in circulation, these largely recapitulated existing models of imperial femininity. Thus, psychologist Esther Harding maintained in 1933 that the single woman had a critical role to play in a world that was seriously deficient in "specifically feminine values"; the spinster could be of cultural and racial importance "not only [to] the individual but [to] our whole civilisation."[114] Such arguments, however, did little to eradicate the increasing association of spinsterhood with lesbianism. This was in part a reaction to the widespread perception that, because of declining fertility rates and women's demands for access to male educational and professional enclaves, masculinity was at risk. Without distinct male and female roles, social commentators argued, British culture would become increasingly emasculated and feminized. Central to this fear was the lesbian herself, whose female body was thought to be marked by a recognizable mannishness, and therefore, to invert sexual norms that were associated with Englishness. Racial anxiety overlapped with homophobia to such a degree that, as Lucy Bland observes, lesbians were at one point labeled "non-patriotic, non-British, sexual perverts" and summarily denounced as "traitorous lovers of all things German" because of hysterical anti-German sentiment, due to the war, and the perception that sexology was a German export.[115]

We see a vivid example of this xenophobia even in Woolf's portrayal of the lesbian body in *Mrs. Dalloway*. The contrast between her depiction of the German Doris Kilman (originally "Kiehlman," we learn), the predatory lesbian tutor who Clarissa denounces as "some prehistoric monster, armoured for primeval warfare," and the English Clarissa herself, is telling.[116] While Miss Kilman's homoerotic desire for Clarissa's daughter, Elizabeth, is denigrated, Clarissa's homoerotic desire for Sally is redeemed for reasons that are inflected by both class and nationality. Clarissa's same-sex desire is neither tyrannical nor parasitical, as Kilman's is (in keeping with British stereotypes of Germans); nor is she linked like Kilman to prevalent sexological perceptions of the lesbian as a degenerate man-hater.[117] Instead, Clarissa's lesbianism is couched in the language of romantic friendship and largely escapes prevailing sexological condemnations of female inversion and lesbian perversion.[118] This asymmetry betrays not only historical changes in understandings of lesbianism, but more particularly, Woolf's nationalistic bias that the monstrous and vampiric lesbian simply is not English. Unlike the "unlovable" Miss Kilman, Woolf's butch lesbian figure in *Between the Acts*, Miss La Trobe, is neither consumed by self-hatred nor subjected to virulent condemnation; this is arguably because she is explicitly aligned with Englishness, despite her ambiguous national origins. Woolf never depicts La Trobe as atavistic or degenerate, though her body is described as "swarthy" and she is clearly not "altogether a lady": "Nature had somehow set her apart from her kind."[119] Such signifiers convey her deviancy, but do not mark her as repulsive. Unlike Miss Kilman, La Trobe's lesbianism is recuperable because she is a preserver of English cultural values. La Trobe's task, in staging an outline of England's history to an English audience, is to provoke, along with a critique of patriarchal violence, a respect and awe for the culturally enduring legacy of Englishness. Although her concept of national unity seeks to transcend nationalistic propaganda and sentiment, her play nonetheless is predicated on ideas of an ancestral English unity and community. Woolf thus aligns the provisionally English lesbian not with racial decline, but with the recuperation of civilization. To this extent, Woolf surprisingly echoes the views of eugenicist Edith Lees Ellis, who argued that inverts could mold the "higher ideals" of the nation by remaining "true to the laws of their own being and vision," thereby constructing "beautiful realities" that will be of "service for the world."[120] Of course, this utopian view did little to alter the widespread perception that the lesbian was a race apart in British culture, an unnatural being whose unreproductive body did not conform to the dominant ideal of women's procreativity. This idea may explain why, despite Miss La Trobe's affiliation with Englishness, characters speculate that she is not pure English, and wonder if she comes from the Channel Islands or has Russian blood. La Trobe's uncertain national and racial origins exemplify the degree to which lesbianism was figured as Other within British culture, even by a writer fundamentally sympathetic to lesbians.

Yet, while the view that lesbians and spinsters would contribute to racial decline through their refusal or inability to reproduce was a fear that was in general circulation, the State never intervened to outlaw this behavior (spinsters, however, were encouraged to emigrate to the Dominions, where they could allegedly fulfill their biological destinies and boost the increase of the British population overseas). In *Mrs. Dalloway*, we see evidence of Woolf's contempt for this plan through her portrayal of Lady Bruton, whose scheme encouraging young people to emigrate to Canada is a sign of her loss of "proportion."[121] Although, beginning in 1919, the government funded the Society for the Oversea Settlement of British Women, no similar program was ever established to deal with the unreproductive superfluity of the lesbian. In fact, "unnatural offences" were selectively punished by the State, predominantly targeting men. We see, for example, that with the passage of the Matrimonial Causes Act in 1923, wives could sue for divorce on the grounds of "an unnatural offence," whereas a husband could not. Philippa Strachey, in her *Memorandum on the Position of English Women in Relation to That of English Men* (1935), notes that certain "unnatural offences" were punishable in the case of both men and women, but she does not *name* them.[122] This refusal to acknowledge female homosexuality as an unnatural offense is consistent with the State's earlier decision not to criminalize lesbianism, and oddly parallels modernist women's circumspect treatment of this taboo subject. But whereas the State renders lesbianism invisible because it is regarded as unnatural, these writers renounce the dominant discourse on female homosexuality in order to extricate the lesbian body from its association with degeneracy and perversion, a fact perhaps in part attributable to each woman's bisexuality. Yet, in doing so, they often trade on prevalent constructions of English national identity in ways that compromise such progressive aims.

Thus, for example, Warner signals homoeroticism in *Summer Will Show* through imagery that conjures a fantasy of uncolonized space: fueled by love for Minna, Sophia could "do anything, go anywhere" (156); same-sex desire makes Sophia's mind roam "as one wanders through a new house" where the boundaries are still "unknown" (256); life with Minna makes Sophia feel like "something exactly fitted into its right station on the face of the globe" (226). Because lesbianism itself resembles a "new world emerging from chaos" (74) that remains as yet unnamed – that has "no place" (374), representationally speaking – Warner conveys it indirectly: Minna and Sophia share an "extraordinary colloquy" (157) on a pink sofa; Minna, clad in a purple velvet robe, "thoughtfully lick[s] the last oyster" (274) as the two women conspiratorially bond; Sophia watches Minna's reflection, candle-lit in bed, in a mirror, and her "whole being was ravaged with love and tenderness" (301). Yet underpinning such moments of intimacy is the taint of anti-Semitism. In an extraordinary moment of Jewish erasure, Sophia lies alongside Minna, "her body pressed against [her] body," and imagines "lying hard and authentic on the English acres" (251). Sophia's rumination on landscape is precipitated by "the spurting authentic ... blood" of Englishness, and coincides with her desire to "save" Minna, the "outcast" with a "hooked nose" whose "deathly body" groans like a "stricken animal's" (249–50). Lesbian representation, I'm arguing, is inextricable from its larger national context in which women are considered to be inherently redemptive. Richardson's and Warner's representations of female homoeroticism revise or subvert the stereotype of the mannish lesbian – they neither pathologize the English lesbian body, through recourse to sexological models, nor do they link that body to racial decline. Each, furthermore, calls normative heterosexuality into question by positioning the lesbian herself as a morally superior figure. In doing so, each privileges the lesbian body as a regenerative source, central to the British body politic. So prevalent is the notion that British women are the very embodiment of progressive civilization that even lesbians can be imagined as indispensable to national culture.

Seeking "the salvation of the race": maternalist imperialism

The moral panic that lesbianism engenders can be read as part of the larger discourse circulating in Britain during this period which focused upon the fear of "national decay" stemming from the declining fertility of the middle class and the perceived physical degeneration of its citizens.[123] On both counts women were singled out as the reproductive conduits through which the nation could be revitalized; that is, female national responsibility was rhetorically linked to women's racial responsibility and to the preservation of the species. As a full-page ad in *Vogue* put it: "On the safeguarding of women's health depends the future of our race."[124] Anna Davin has demonstrated how, by the turn of the century, child-rearing became a national duty for middle-class women, particularly because members of the working class were regarded as poor maternal models for an imperial race.[125] Antoinette Burton's work on the suffrage movement has shown how British feminists similarly appropriated the rhetoric of imperial motherhood, in part as a response to those who argued that female emancipation would enervate the race. When feminists adopted the eugenicist terms which spoke of women as mothers of the race, they simultaneously referred to women's evolutionary function (as reproductive conduits), and women's role as "mothers of a 'superior' race, be it white, Anglo-Saxon, or British."[126] For example, the Women's League of Health and Beauty, established in London in 1930, advocated exercise so that women would become physically fit maternal vessels; the organization's explicit aim was "racial health" through movement.[127] Feminists accepted their responsibility as racial mothers, but they strategically "utilized the burden of their particularly gendered responsibility to claim a specifically *female* authority in *imperial* government as well."[128] Burton's argument that the moral responsibilities inherent in motherhood legitimized women's participation in the imperial body politic describes the period up to 1915, but her observations have important relevance for the postwar years as well. A salient example of this is afforded by Jane Harrison, whose intellectual engagement with matriarchal prehistory coincides with her belief that women are *"more* racial" than men, and thus "may be of use for the whole body politic." Harrison's aspiration that women become "citizens of the world" hinges upon her conviction that national consciousness can be reshaped by this *"racial* conscience."[129] Interwar feminists continued to trade on the rhetoric of imperial responsibility to justify women's inclusion in the nation as full citizens, even though, as Brian Harrison observes, there was a pervasive correlation between anti-feminism and imperialism among the various political parties during this period.[130]

We see this invocation of imperial authority, particularly in women's use of the discourse of racial motherhood, as a way of legitimizing their access to birth control during the 1920s. This rhetoric was utilized by both conservative and more radical proponents of artificial contraception, many of whom ideologically concurred with an anonymous 1926 article in *Time and Tide*: "Woman has always known that it is her part to bear the greatest sufferings and inconveniences for the propagation of the race … that motherhood is her greatest salvation."[131] While Stella Browne, a pro-sex and pro-abortion socialist, would arguably have repudiated such senti-mentalizing claims, her refutation of "forced motherhood" still has recourse to a eugenicist paradigm: she maintains that "unwilling maternity and pregnancy" will result in irreparable "racial damage."[132] From a more conservative perspective a similar preoccupation with racial health may be seen to be expressed, albeit more vehemently, by Marie Stopes, whose interest lies less in procuring women's right to extra-marital sex than in foregrounding the link between a married woman's sexual enjoyment and the resultant healthy offspring. Although Stopes sought to make contraception available to all "highly civilized human beings" through her Mother's Clinics, she advocated that birth control would be of the "greatest racial and social value" to the working classes, "the lowest and most negligent strata of society," who repeatedly produce "low-grade or semi-feeble-minded puny infants."[133] Among the various contraceptive barriers advocated, Stopes especially urged the use of a cervical cap she named "the Pro Race," arguing that if such devices did not work for "undesirable mothers" then they should be sterilized by the State.[134] Such racial panic sounds extreme, but Stopes was by no means the only feminist who proposed sterilization or insisted on the eugenic aspects of reproductive control. Not all British feminists, of course, were proponents of racial motherhood. Winifred

Holtby maintains that "[m]aternal instinct as a political impulse has been greatly over-rated," arguing that because "fecundity is revered as a patriotic virtue" the world is moving dangerously toward "militant nationalism."[135] While Holtby critiques British society for neglecting to respect motherhood, declaring that "saccharine sentiment" substitutes for genuine governmental support of maternity-services, she denounces the "cult of the cradle" and its attendant racism.[136]

The work produced by British women modernists reflects varying responses to the charge that motherhood is women's racial responsibility. Although much feminist critical attention since the 1980s has been paid to the modernist engage-ment with maternal absence and maternal loss, and particularly to the psychoanalytic significance of the preoedipal mother, what has gone largely unnoticed is how those maternal paradigms intersect with an imperial discourse that enshrines women as "the salvation of the race."[137] Jean Rhys alludes to the racial hegemony of British motherhood in *Voyage in the Dark*, juxtaposing Anna Morgan's memory of being denounced as a "fair baboon" because of her West Indian roots with her meditation on an advertisement for "Biscuits Like Mother Makes, as Fresh in the Tropics as in the Motherland" (148–9). Rhys here satirizes both the imperial ethos of racial purity and the idea that England is the mother country of the empire, civilizing her daughters – colonial subjects – around the globe. In general, we see in women modernists a complex negotiation of the concept of "maternal imperialism," ranging from repudiation to ambivalence to endorsement.[138] At the very least, interwar British women writers register the linkage between motherhood and race, if only to satirize it, as does Woolf's narrator during the Victorian phase of *Orlando*: "The life of the average woman was a succession of childbirths ... Thus the British Empire came into existence" (229). Such relentless childbirth, coupled with women's economic dependence upon men, is perhaps what leads Woolf to endorse endowed motherhood, or state-supported family allowance, in *Three Guineas*, where she argues that the "mothers of educated men" (110) should be compensated for their labor because "the birth-rate is falling, in the very class where births are desirable – the educated class" (111).[139] Woolf's call to delimit the distribution of a maternal wage to society's "desirable" class aligns her with other British feminists who advocated "selective breeding"; although Woolf never utilizes such eugenicist vocabulary, her class bias and attention to the birth-rate bleeds invariably into the anxiety of those who agitated for the "improvement of racial stock."[140]

In marked contrast, we see evidence of the deprecation of racial motherhood in Olive Moore, who dramatizes women's refusal to equate motherhood with national responsibility. In Moore's extraordinary novel *Spleen* (1930), about an English-woman who goes into self-imposed exile in Italy after giving birth to a deformed child, the brooding heroine, Ruth, acknowledges that she has "no maternal sense," yet denies that she is "unnatural and not sane."[141] Although the novel engages the rhetoric of imperial responsibility – "a million mothers can found a nation" (227) – it simultaneously resists the propaganda of "mother-love and patriotism" (196), foregrounding a single mother who satirizes the sentimentalizing claim that "woman is but the eternal oven in which to bake the eternal bun" (128). Instead, Ruth chooses to model herself on Zeus, whose cerebral birth of Athena renders pregnancy obsolete: "I think I carry my womb in my forehead" (128). In *Spleen*, the mother's refusal to essentialize the body is both her "curse" (128) and her source of power – "Woman's thunderbolt" (132) – for in denaturalizing procreation Ruth exposes the fallacy that "all women are born mothers" (130). By renouncing her racial responsibility, Ruth turns her back on England and embraces a more transgressive, if imaginary, concept of affiliation, "beyond patriotism and nationality … colour, blood-tie, creed" (199). The ideological implications of this are clear: if Englishwomen abandon racial motherhood the empire will perish, for without the vaunted purity of blood-lines it would eventually become "impossible to define where races begin, end, and merge" (140). We see similar evidence of the contempt for the imperial sacredness of maternity in Mina Loy's long poem "Anglo-Mongrels and the Rose" (1923–25), which aligns the sexlessness of the Victorian mother (the "English Rose") with the decline of the British empire:

> Conservative Rose
> storage
> of British Empire-made pot-pourri
> of dry dead men.[142]

The rose that Loy describes is a shriveled body "of arrested impulses," whose blossoms cling to "the divine right of self assertion":

> Early English everlasting
> quadrate Rose
> paradox–Imperial
> trimmed with some travestied flesh
> tinted with bloodless duties dewed.

Loy's maternal rose is a paradox because its imperial pedigree showcases modesty and purity, yet indulges in "mystic incest with its ancestry."

Where Loy's poem can be read as an indictment of the late-Victorian imperial mother, Woolf's representation of a similar maternal type in *To the Lighthouse* is characterized by much greater ambivalence. Woolf often uses imperialist language to critique the maternal sovereignty of Mrs. Ramsay, who is described as regal and magisterial, a "tyrannical, domineering, masterful" figure who constantly interferes in the domestic arrangements of others, in short, "making people do what she wished" (56–7). Woolf uses the discourse of territorial expansionism to describe Mrs. Ramsay in her private self-reflective moments as "a wedge-shaped core of darkness," thus both critiquing her imperiousness and celebrating her sense of limitless possibility. Embodying the appropriative impulses of empire, Mrs. Ramsay's civilizing mission is focused on the family, where she tries to squelch the "infidel ideas" (6) of her rebellious daughters and to insist that women "[m]arry, marry!" (174), arguably a sign of her investment in race preservation. One of the best examples of this is her crusade against the "iniquity of the English dairy system" (103). This was a period in which the redistribution of the population to the cities created a demand for milk far removed from its source; as a result, milk was subjected to contamination and infection, propelling British health officials to herald milk consumption as an issue of "national importance."[143] Mrs. Ramsay's desire to construct a "model dairy" (58) and make the trafficking in "illegal" milk

(58) a crime implicitly speaks to this fear that drinking tainted milk would result in racial degeneration. Herself an Anglo-Saxon mother of eight who relishes reproduction, Mrs. Ramsay's campaign for pure milk recalls the rhetoric of eugenicists who sought to end the propagation of the defective. Indeed, her imperiousness resembles a colonizing force, for it is through her intervention that the "barbarity" of the domestic "was tamed, the reign of chaos subdued" (47). Although Tansley complains that "[w]omen made civilization impossible" (85), Woolf's portrayal suggests the opposite, that "the progress of civilization depends" not on "great men" (43) but on a collectivity of great mothers, whose pure milk would ensure the purity of future Britons. While Mrs. Ramsay is, of course, critiqued by various characters and ironized by Woolf for her myopia – she literally has "short-sighted eyes" (71) – she is the catalyst for Lily's final vision and remains the text's sacred centerpiece. Like a secular missionary intent upon "coherence ... [and] stability" (105), the maternal body restores order and is a "universal law" (50) unto itself, even though it ultimately cannot subdue the Orientalized figure of Lily Briscoe, whose "Chinese eyes" (91) signal a resistance to the tyranny of the British mother's nationalist and domestic sphere.

Whereas some authors (such as Moore, Loy, and Woolf) seek to convey the cost of women's association with a maternally inflected national–imperial identity, others write not to resist the idealized mother or to destabilize gender roles, but to advance an imperialist ideology of race motherhood. We see evidence of this perspective in *The Well of Loneliness* (1928), where Radclyffe Hall invokes the discourse of racial motherhood to make a case for the lesbian's national inclusion, recalling Edith Lees Ellis's plea that the invert has "special powers of work in the eugenics field of spiritual parenthood," a concept that is "a manifestation of Nature's finest vibrations of the body."[144] Stephen Gordon's intense bodily identification with "the soil and fruitfulness of Morton" (108), her rural English home, is cast in terms of racial purity and is a genetic signifier of her hereditary entitlement to England. Published just two years after the formation of the Council for the Preservation of Rural England, in 1926, *The Well* dramatizes how, although Stephen's neighbors recoil from her strangeness, they cannot reject her because "her blood was theirs also ... they were one in their blood" (108). *The Well of Loneliness* is complicated on the issue of Stephen's fertility–sterility and relation to nature. On the one hand, Stephen's affair with Mary is completely naturalized, despite the novel's acknowledgement that their lovemaking is non-procreative.[145] The novel vacillates between pathologizing the lesbian body as "monstrous ... [and] sterile" (187), and making a case for its naturalness by aligning it with "the fruitfulness" (108) of the English earth. Even in instances where Hall invokes the discourse of the natural to normalize lesbian sexuality, she still conveys the stigma of inversion (299). Although irreparably "marked and blemished" (301), the lesbian body, Hall insists, is a product of nature, albeit "the most normal abnormal" thing (351): "Nature was trying to do her bit; inverts were being born in increasing numbers" (406). At another point in the text, however, Hall appears to align herself with those who would argue that inversion is an aberration: "in such relationships as Mary's and Stephen's, Nature must pay for experimenting ... A drop too little of the male in the lover, and mighty indeed will be the wastage. And yet there are cases – and Stephen's was one – in which the male will emerge triumphant" (338). Nature, so it seems, is capable of making mistakes (e.g. by producing a butch who is too femme), but Stephen is not such a creature. Thus the novel retains its reliance on Nature as proof of the lesbian's "right to [her] existence" (437), even though the meaning of "the natural" shifts in different contexts.

The rhetoric of blood-lines that ties Stephen to the English land is directly linked to her representation as a maternal savior, despite her overt masculinity, and is what fuels her identification with English nationalism.[146] We see this in Stephen's infantilization of Mary, upon whom she gazes "with the eyes of a mother" (328), and we observe it in her relation to her writing, where she is depicted as a "creator" whose books draw "life and strength" from her generative body: "Like infants they had sucked at her breasts of inspiration, and drawn from them blood" (214).[147] In this novel the lesbian body does not represent reproductive failure, but rather procreative fecundity and racial purity through authorship: the "miracle of blood, the giver of life, the purifier" (214) that aligns Stephen with the fertility of Morton (and enables her to publish a novel about nature called *The Furrow*) positions her as the biological inheritor of a national culture from which she cannot legitimately be displaced. That Stephen is the embodiment of the lesbian's racial responsibility is evident in the final frame, where Hall fully exploits the equation between maternity and race preservation. On these critical final two pages, during what appears to be an hallucinatory (or perhaps visionary) scene in which Stephen conjures a room full of homosexual bodies – both living and dead – who call her by name and demand her intervention, the language suggests that Stephen metaphorically gives birth. Her body experiences "burning rockets of pain" which "tea[r] her to pieces" as her "barren womb" becomes "fruitful," aching with its "sterile burden" of "helpless children." As this mass of "the yet unborn" clamor "for their right to salvation," Stephen hears a voice that sounds "like a gathering together of great waters," making her entire body "throb," shaking "her very entrails" until she staggers and falls. Whereas earlier Stephen's "miracle of blood" had given birth to her novel, on the last page her "great final expiation" (214), or contraction, appears poised to give birth to a new generation of inverts (436–7). The ending's juxtaposition of Christian iconography and reproductive discourse positions Stephen as a maternal savior whose mediating function is to be the 'mother of the race' for homosexuals.

What fuels this fantasy of lesbian procreation, I'm arguing, is nothing less than the contention, voiced by Dora Montefiore in 1920, that "woman is and remains the human race."[148] Montefiore captures the desire for equal citizenship rights, utilizing the discourse of domesticity to claim women's share in "public duties and responsibilities": "we women, as Home-makers, claim the right to legislate and to administer laws in order that the harmful influences to the race, which are at present settled on a purely androcentric basis, may be removed." Hall makes no overt demand for legislative reform, but, by aligning the lesbian body with – to borrow Monetfiore's phrase – "Nature's great reproductive aims," by implication she endorses Britain's national and racial ideals.

The argument made by gynecologist Mary Scharlieb, that Britain "need[s] the unmarried women as well as the married to be the spiritual mothers of the race," positions women globally as national guardians, yet the rhetoric that enshrines women as racial saviors rests upon a paradox.[149] While women's racial responsibility as mothers situates them as conduits to civilization, the female body itself was perceived to be aligned with nature and therefore inimical to the concerns of empire. The pervasive naturalization of women, and the importance of this construction to the dichotomizing of gender, is captured by Havelock Ellis at the turn of the century: "[W]omen are for men the embodiments of the restful responsiveness of Nature. To every man ... the women whom he loves is as the Earth."[150] Such essentializing of woman in the name of nature raged on through the early decades of the twentieth century, becoming the ground upon which women were excluded from public culture. So typical was this equation that political leaders, such as Prime Minister Herbert Asquith, routinely ascribed fixed biological essences to women. Speaking in the 1920s, Asquith maintained that "sexual differences were indelible bequests of Nature," arguing that women's physiological uniqueness made them unfit to enter public life. Asquith's objections were based on "menstruation ... the declining birthrate, hysteria, invalidism, pregnancies" – in other words, the basic workings of the female body, whose excesses were regarded as evidence of women's "ineptness at contributing to the governing of the Empire."[151] Asquith's view that women are, in effect, the uncivilized aligns him with Freud's argument, in *Civilization and Its Discontents* (1930), that women are incommensurable with, and even opposed to, culture: "Women soon come into opposition to civilization and display their retarding and restraining influence ... The work of civilization has become increasingly the business of men."[152] The construction of woman's evolutionary nature as primitive, uncivilized, and atavistic is consistent with the modernist alignment of the primitive with both European femininity and the colonized, a familiar trope that, as Marianna Torgovnick argues, stems from repulsion as well as the countervailing impulse to idealize the Other.[153]

Of course, Freud's observations are entirely at odds with those of many interwar feminists, who also presumed women's affinity with nature, but believed that it was the basis of civilization: "Nature has ordained that the female should play by far the most important part in the life of the race."[154] Whereas a "distinguished" physician of the Ethnological Society, in a paper on comparative anatomy entitled "The female mind," insisted in 1927 that women were "mentally inferior" to men because their brains on average weighed five-and-half ounces less, British women argued that "education, training and environment" are the real causes of "the apparent differences" between the sexes.[155] Yet while women contested such anthropometric determinations of female intelligence and behavior, they did not abandon altogether a belief in the essential properties of femininity. Thus, where "The female mind" maintained that once women became mothers they "lost all incentive to further culture," British women fervently argued that the maternal body was a powerful and ameliorative instrument, indispensable to culture and "the mainstay of nations."[156] Although the scientific comparison of women and "lower races" (a term that included "primitives," "savages," and "negroes") was widespread throughout the late nineteenth and early twentieth centuries, women implicitly repudiated this equation by showcasing their white, middle-class, Anglo-Saxon bodies as necessary to the evolutionary development of the race.[157] British women rejected the cultural authority of medical science, but they simultaneously exploited gender ideologies that were already in place by using the female body to justify their political and economic inclusion. For that reason, one might call them strategic essentialists who selectively highlighted women's anatomical difference when it was politically efficacious and repudiated sexual classifications of the female body that supported women's disenfranchisement from the nation state. The contradictions inherent in women's alleged alliance with, but superiority to, nature resulted in their simultaneous confirmation and transgression of social codes. Eleanor Rathbone illustrates how British women's rhetoric of civilized emancipation was pervaded by the assumption of racial difference between themselves and men and women of other races and classes; she denounces men as uncivilized savages, arguing that they suffer from what she calls "The Turk Complex" – that is, tyrannical and violent impulses toward women. By arguing that "the hidden Turk" lurks in the average Englishman, Rathbone unleashes the stereotypical English arrogance toward the Orient, implicitly suggesting that Englishwomen are a colonized and sexually subjugated race while failing to register how she herself is an agent of Orientalism.[158] Such moments effectively expose the racism and ethnocentrism that exist at the heart of British feminism, demonstrating how women's emancipatory rhetoric often reinforced colonialist perceptions of white superiority.

Conveying the fundamental belief that women are "the salvation of [our] country," Dr. Mary Scharlieb, writing in 1923, urges women and young girls to recapture their "national faith": "womanly power will call forth a fresh increase in [our] hereditary sense of duty ... women collectively will work out the salvation of our Empire as St. Joan of Arc individually saved France."[159] What is important here is the assumption of imperial supremacy, hereditarian access, and female superiority, a conjunction that will be central to my chapter on Woolf, which similarly engages the alignment of militarism, salvation, and femininity. For Scharlieb, as for many others, civilization depends upon the redemptive intervention of femininity, a power whose alignment with nature serves only to underscore women's legitimacy as imperial citizens. Such women repudiated the view upheld by male political journalists, such as G. K. Chesterton, who acknowledged women's "civilising influence" yet insisted that it is precisely because women are "so much purer, nobler, finer and more sensitive than men that they should never be allowed to soil their white hands in the world's dirty work."[160] Feminists accepted the designation of moral guardians of the nation, but argued that women's "white hands" have a place in British politics. If women are genetically destined to be the saviors of the British race, then on what grounds can they be denied the prerogatives of citizenship? The writers I examine variously register that feminine and masculine are respectively coded as primitive and civilized, but they often invert the hierarchy. To that extent they echo Jane Harrison, who posits a primordial past dominated by nature, the non-rational, and the preeminence of the maternal – ideas that are informed by Anglocentrism. Like other British feminists who disavow patriotism yet confess to some nationalistic fervor, Harrison writes: "I hate the Empire; it stands to me for all that is tedious and pernicious ... But when I search the hidden depths of my heart, I find there the most narrow and local of parochialisms. I am intensely proud of being a Yorkshire woman."[161] Each of the authors I consider exhibits traces of this Anglocentric pride, and each concurs with those British feminists who argued that nothing less than a new standard of human value would accompany women's infiltration of the public sphere.

Rebecca West's *Harriet Hume: A London Fantasy* (1929), explores this continuity between women's essentialized femininity and their moral responsibility to the nation. Harriet's mystical qualities and creative alignment with nature situate her in opposition to Arnold Condorex's world of imperial concerns; as an expert in Far Eastern affairs, he dismisses her as being entirely beyond politics, "[p]rattling not too intelligently about India and elephants and Nabobs' jewels."[162] Yet like other British feminists who argued that women occupy the very heart of civilization, West presents Harriet as a figure whose intuitive sensibility and sympathy for leaves and flowers challenge the masculine construct of "the real world" (32). Harriet is the embodiment of some elusive "principle" (93) that recalls the liberal feminist focus on women's essentialized redemptive "power" (57). West leaves in place women's traditional association with nature, but she uses it to interrogate the male claim to imperial dominance. Through Harriet's uncanny influence, Arnold experiences "monstrous doubt" (63) about the meaning of his life: "Would he … be advancing the cause of the British Empire, of civilization …?" (71). Femininity, in short, serves to model for men the pedagogical value of being "loyal to nature" (55), a loyalty that negates the elements that enable the masculinized world to cohere: manipulation, fraud, and racist domination. By aligning Harriet with "some value beyond [her] seeming" that is indelibly tied to the feminized concepts of "truth" and "justice" (93), West inverts the perceived hierarchy between men and civilization, on the one hand, and women and nature, on the other. Here, it is the latter conjunction that is upheld as the truly *civilized* components of culture, a paradigm that will be echoed by Warner and Butts. And yet while the novel celebrates Harriet's embrace of a different moral register, it ends on an ambivalent note regarding women's marginalization from the domain of imperial politics. In the couple's final encounter, we find Harriet upholding the value of British imperialism: "What was the use of me being so innocent in this g-g-garden … I was … impotent … you performed many worthy achievements that enabled our species to establish itself on this globe" (266–7). By capitulating at this moment, Harriet accedes to the value of empire and acknowledges that female agency is "impotent" in the public sphere, even though, within the confines of her garden world, her creativity and artful vision proves to be all-powerful. West's novel ends on a bifurcated note, registering women's cultural superiority as well as their powerlessness to alter the status quo, recalling the stalemate of Woolf's "A society," which similarly ends by admitting women's political impotence. Harriet's final disclosure – "I must put my house in order" (179) – seems deprived of the larger political resonance it has for other British feminists, for whom the home functions as a microcosm of the nation.

The alignment in *Harriet Hume* of women, nature, and civilization presumes women's exclusion from the political system and fails to register the, admittedly small, impact made by women in electoral terms. Yet this novel, like so much feminist propaganda of the period, still imagines that women alone can preserve the British empire from self-destruction. Although Harriet herself is not a mother, her essentialized relationship to nature, and the novel's presentation of her as instrumental to Arnold's moral uplift, imbues her with the same kind of maternal responsibility toward British culture that ardent propagandists argued was integral to women's character. Although West's novel never stages women's quest to govern, Harriet provides a compelling argument for women's political equality.

A similar allusion to women's maternal responsibility may be seen in another unlikely venue, Woolf's "The Plumage Bill," published in the feminist *Woman's Leader* in 1920. This essay invokes maternal discourse to address a controversial parliamentary bill that attempted (and failed) to prohibit the importation of exotic plumes, which were widely used in women's fashions. Woolf's essay is framed as a response to H. W. Massingham, an editor of the *Nation*, who was an active opponent of the bill and wrote a column on the issue. Massingham focused on women as the perpetrators of plumage crime, condemning their selfish practice of wearing outlandish egret feathers that are themselves the product of child-bearing birds, because "[i]t is in the nesting season that the plumes are brightest."[163] Ironically, he observes, the birds "have to be shot in parenthood for child-bearing women to flaunt the symbols of it" (241). Woolf's essay is a scathing critique of Massingham's attack on child-bearing women for not "raising the moral currency of civilisation" (244). It juxtaposes an image of the beautiful yet petulant English-woman of child-bearing age who shops on Regent Street for the perfect "lemon-coloured egret" (242), with the gruesome killing of the "fantastically lovely" birds who inhabit an undisclosed "blazing South American landscape" (242). Painting a tortuous picture of how the feathers are violently extracted, Woolf describes how the parent bird is tightly held by one anonymous hand while "another hand pierces the eyeballs with a feather" (242). Although women reap the benefits of this slaughter, it is men who are condemned as perpetrators of abomination: egrets are "killed by men, starved by men, and tortured by men" (242) alone. Her rhetorical query "But what do men care?" (243) is a denunciation of the Members of Parliament who neglected to pass the Plumage Bill, but it is also an implicit exoneration of women, whom she refuses to hold responsible for the plumage trade. Instead, Woolf links the enslavement of Englishwomen and the captivity of South American birds, seeing both as the victims of male violence, a move that effectively erases cultural and geographical differences as it proclaims the innocence of white women. In a letter that was later published in the *Woman's Leader*, Woolf further addresses Massingham's "injustice to women" (243), clarifying, with language that sarcastically echoes his own, that her method of "raising the moral currency of civilised nations" (245) is to defend women from spurious charges. Yet what is clear from Woolf's essay is her belief that women constitute a redemptive force, even though she never goes so far as to equate motherhood with patriotism. "The Plumage Bill" nonetheless alludes to women's maternal authority and suggests that the dissemination of women's moral influence can alter the course of world politics.

The chapters that follow demonstrate how four modernists, in strikingly divergent ways, seek to disseminate women's moral influence by producing cultural fictions that help to secure British women's place in the national imaginary. Although in certain ways these women perceive themselves as inhabiting a "strange no-man's land" (*TLH*, 84) where national affiliation is concerned, they simultaneously trade on the civilizing authority that their national identity confers.

Although, as we have seen, the concept and material reality of citizenship was, for British women, extremely vexed, Richardson, Warner, Butts, and Woolf do not represent women as outside culture or outside history. On the contrary, each imaginatively constructs a fictional "supplement to history" (*ROO*, 45) *within* the rubric of Englishness. We can see this exemplified in *To the Lighthouse*, where Cam's mind wanders unimpeded, conjuring "shapes of a world not realized but turning in their darkness, catching here and there, a spark of light" (189). Although Woolf does not imbue Cam with an overt national consciousness, the girl's image of a new globe moving out of darkness into light suggests that the foundational presumption of *Englishness* is already in place. That Cam is a girl who seeks "adventure and escape" as she gazes at an island and fantasizes about her "place in the universe" (189) only underscores the alliance between femininity and spatial trespass that, for British women modernists, was so indispensable to their location of women in culture. Although Woolf's claim that "[a] writer's country is a territory within his own brain" (35) appears unmarked by gender or national identification, her preoccupations elsewhere suggest that this imaginative landscape is tied precisely to England, just as the question of space is bound up with the question of woman.[164]

Notes

1 Mrs. Halbot, "Pro patria," *The Conservative Woman* (June, 1921): 10. For an analysis of British women's role in the Conservative Party, see G.E. Maguire, *Conservative Women: A History of Women and the Conservative Party, 1847–1997* (Oxford: St. Anthony's College, 1998).
2 Patricia Hollis, *Ladies Elect: Women in English Local Government 1865–1914* (Oxford: Clarendon Press, 1987), 470. It is not a coincidence that the first female MP was Nancy Astor, an attractive American millionaire socialite – and mother of six – who inherited the Conservative seat of her father-in-law, Viscount Astor, in 1919. Lady Astor was never a declared feminist but supported controversial issues such as birth control and equal pay. See Karen J. Musolf, *From Plymouth to Parliament: A Rhetorical History of Nancy Astor's 1919 Campaign* (New York: St. Martin's Press, 1999). Ray Strachey offers an overview of women's candidature, explaining the obstacles that women of all parties encountered when they ran for local and national seats previously occupied by men. See "Changes in public life" in Ray Strachey ed. *Our Freedom and Its Results* (London: Hogarth Press, 1936).
3 Martin Pugh discusses women's enfranchisement in British politics, arguing that during the 1920s and 1930s women voters made a significant impact on domestic issues such as widow's pensions and housing, in addition to international campaigns for peace and disarmament. See *Women and the Women's Movement in Britain 1914–1959* (New York: Paragon House, 1993), Ch. 5.
4 Halbot, "Pro patria," 10.
5 Hollis, *Ladies Elect*, vii. Unmarried women ratepayers were the first to obtain the local government vote (p. 7)
6 *Ibid.*, viii.
7 Winifred Holtby, *South Riding* (London: Virago, 1988 [1936]), 421 and 3.
8 Jean Rhys, *Good Morning, Midnight* (New York: W.W. Norton, 1986), 157. Of course, as a colonial subject Rhys speaks from a very different position from that of Richardson, Warner, Butts, and Woolf, but her writing often demonstrates a similar preoccupation with gender construction, male violence, and the dominant ideology of Englishness.
9 P.J. Cain and A.G. Hopkins, *British Imperialism 1688–2000* (London: Longman, 2002), 56–7.
10 *Ibid.*, 57.

11 Virginia Woolf, "A sketch of the past" in Jeanne Schulkind ed. *Moments of Being* (New York: Harcourt Brace & Co., 1985), 78.

12 It is worth noting that in 1914 Britian did not have full manhood suffrage. The second Reform Act of 1867 gave the vote to borough householders; the 1884 Act brought the total electorate to over 5 million. The excluded 40 percent of adult males were enfranchised in 1918, introducing the potential power of the working-class vote. The Equal Franchise Act of 1928 gave women the vote on the same terms as men.

13 Pugh, *Women's Movement in Britain*, 34.

14 Virginia Woolf, *Three Guineas*, 12. See also Vera Brittain's *Women's Work in Modern Britain* (London: Noel Douglas, 1928), 119 and, 123.

15 Ray Strachey, *Careers and Openings for Women: A Survey of Women's Employment and a Guide for Those Seeking Work* (London: Faber & Faber, 1934), 69.

16 For discussion of the 1920 Employment of Women, Young Persons, and Children Act, see Brittain, *Women's Work in Modern Britain*, 15–16.

17 Cambridge did not admit women to undergraduate courses until 1948. Oxford granted women admission to degrees in 1920, but withheld from them the right to take degrees in divinity and instituted quotas on the number of female students allowed to matriculate at the women's colleges. See Vera Brittain, *The Women at Oxford: A Fragment of History* (London: Harrap, 1960), 172.

18 Brittain, *Women's Work in Modern Britain*, 66–7. In order to enter the Civil Service, a woman candidate had to be unmarried or a widow. The marriage bar in the Civil Service was not lifted until 1946; in teaching, the bar was abolished by the Education Act of 1944.

19 Strachey, *Careers and Openings*, 58–9.

20 Twelve years earlier, Vera Brittain had written about the difficulties she encountered in retaining her maiden name after marriage in "Married women and surname," *Time and Tide* (January 15, 1926).

21 See Erna Reiss, "Changes in law," in Strachey ed. *Our Freedom and Its Results*, 79–116; also Reiss's earlier *Rights and Duties of Englishwomen* (Manchester: Sherratt & Hughes, 1934), Ch. 7. Pat Thane discusses the question of women's national status in Billie Melman ed. *Borderlines: Genders and Identities in War and Peace 1870–1930* (New York and London: Routledge, 1998), 29–45.

22 Rebecca West, *The Judge* (London: Virago, 1993 [1922]), 98; hereafter cited in the text.

23 Ernest J. Schuster, "The effect of marriage on nationality," *International Law Association*, I. 2 (1923): 9–51, especially 28 and 17.

24 See Candice Lewis Bredbenner, *A Nationality of Her Own: Women, Marriage, and the Law of Citizenship* (Berkeley: University of California Press, 1998).

25 See the section "Feminism and internationalism" in Barbara Caine's *English Feminism 1780–1980* (Oxford: Oxford University Press, 1997), especially 217.

26 Lesley Higgins and Marie-Christine Leps, "'Passport, please': legal, literary, and critical fictions of identity," *College Literature*, 25. 1 (1998): 100–1.

27 *Ibid.*, 100. I examined six of Rebecca West's passports, those issued in 1924, 1938, 1948, 1958, 1968, and 1978. In each case West's photographic image appears in the category "photograph of bearer," while the category for "wife" is either left blank or is cancelled. The space for "special peculiarities" is either left blank or is occupied by the word "none." It is only in 1978 that the categories of the document change from "bearer" and "wife" to "bearer" and "spouse." West's passports are housed in the McFarlin Library at the University of Tulsa.

28 Harold L. Smith, "British feminism in the 1920s," *British Feminism in the Twentieth Century* (Amherst: University of Massachusetts Press, 1990), 47–65.

29 Caine, *English Feminism*, 175.

30 Caroline Elizabeth Playne, *The Neuroses of the Nations* (London: George Allen & Unwin, 1925), 47.

31 See Caine, *English Feminism*, 184–90. Holtby, commenting in *Time and Tide* (August 6, 1926), insists upon the fundamental similarity of the sexes.

32 See Elizabeth Abel, *Virginia Woolf and the Fictions of Psychoanalysis* (Chicago, IL: University of Chicago Press, 1989), 89.

33 Caren Kaplan, *Questions of Travel: Postmodern Discourses of Displacement* (Durham, NC, and London: Duke University Press, 1996), 162.

34 Maude Royden, "Women and the League of Nations," *The Englishwoman*, 134 (February, 1920).

35 Mary Agnes Hamilton, "Changes in social life" in Strachey ed. *Our Freedom and Its Results*, 273.

36 Jane Harrison, *Alpha and Omega* (London: Sidgwick & Jackson, 1915), 132.

37 For a discussion of the international women's movement during the early 1930s, see Arnold Whittick, *Woman into Citizen* (Santa Barbara, CA: Athenaeum Publishing, 1979).

38 From *The Woman's Leader* (6 April, 1930), quoted by Caine, *English Feminism*, 221.

39 G.S. Dutt, *A Woman of India: The Life of Saroj Nalini* (London: Hogarth Press, 1929).

40 From the minutes of the executive committee meeting of the National Union for Equal Citizenship, November 22, 1927 (archived at the Fawcett Library, London). The goals of this group were to abolish "the evil" of child marriage, reduce maternal and child mortality, improve health and education in India, and raise the "depressed classes."

41 For a discussion of the Duchess of Atholl's role in Parliament, see Maguire's *Conservative Women*, 87–9.

42 As cited by A. Susan Williams, *Ladies of Influence: Women of the Elite in Interwar Britain* (London: Allen Lane–Penguin, 2000), 93 and 92.

43 Kumari Jayawardena, *Feminism and Nationalism in the Third World* (London: Zed Books, 1986), 20–1.

44 As quoted by Angela Woollacott, *To Try Her Fortune in London: Australian Women, Colonialism, and Modernity* (Oxford: Oxford University Press, 2001), 136. For a discussion of British feminists' perception of the leadership role of Western feminism, see Charlotte Weber, "Unveiling Scheherazade: Feminist Orientalism in the International Alliance of Women, 1911–1950," *Feminist Studies*, 27. 1 (2001): 125–57.

45 H.M. Swanwick, *The Roots of Peace* (London: Jonathan Cape, 1938), 192 (emphasis mine).

46 See *Your John: The Love Letters of Radclyffe Hall*, ed. Joanne Glasgow (New York and London: New York University Press, 1997), 142.

47 Claire Harman, *Sylvia Townsend Warner: A Biography* (London: Chatto & Windus, 1989), 156.

48 Natalie Blondel, *Mary Butts: Scenes from the Life* (New York: McPherson & Co., 1998), 349. I do not mean here to suggest that Butts was ever a member of Oswald Mosley's British Union of Fascists, though she does to an extent "pass the test of the fascist minimum" laid out by Julie V. Gottlieb in her "[m]onarchist, anti-Semitic, anti-alien … radically conservative … [and] chauvinistically nationalistic" leanings: *Feminine Fascism: Women in Britain's Fascist Movement, 1923–1945* (London and New York: I.B. Tauris, 2000), 34. It makes the most sense to situate Butts within the wider context of modernism's engagement with fascism – its xenophobia, virulent anti-Semitism, and racism – even though she vehemently rejected the macho ethos of militarism and technology.

49 Woolf, "Introductory letter" in Margaret Llewelyn Davies ed. *Life As We Have Known It* (New York: Norton, 1975), xxxvi.

50 Clive Bell, "The metaphysical hypothesis," *Art* (New York: Capricorn Books, 1958), 45. See also Bell's contempt for utilitarianism in *Civilisation: An Essay* (New York: Harcourt Brace & Co., 1928), 169, 179, 195, and 213.

51 E.M. Forster, "What I believe" in S.P. Rosenbaum ed. *A Bloomsbury Group Reader* (Oxford and Cambridge, MA: Blackwell, 1993), 170.

52 See Philippa Strachey *Memorandum on the Position of English Women in Relation to That of English Men* (London: National Society for Women's Service, 1935), 8–9.

53 Blondel discusses the case in her biography *Mary Butts*, 123–4.

54 Mary Butts, quoted in "Unpleasant court cases," *Pall Mall Gazette* (December 20, 1922). Like Butts, Vera Brittain argues against the dismissal of women jurors on the grounds that certain cases are "unsuitable" for them, maintaining, in Butts's words, that: "Women who have anything to do with the life of the country must maintain their civic sense." Brittain notes, in *Women's Work in Modern Bitain* (75), that while in 1911 there were no English women in the

legal profession, by 1921 the Census reported twenty barristers and seventeen solicitors. And yet, according to Philippa Strachey, women solicitors employed by the government received less pay than male solicitors and were required to resign upon marriage. See her *Memorandum*, 18.

55 Jane Harrison, *Reminiscences of a Student's Life* (London: Hogarth Press, 1925), 31–4.

56 Blondel, *Mary Butts*, 70.

57 Teresa De Lauretis, "Upping the anti [*sic*] in feminist theory" in Marianne Hirsch and Evelyn Fox Keller eds. *Conflicts in Feminism* (New York: Routledge, 1990), 267.

58 Tim Armstrong, *Modernism, Technology and the Body* (Cambridge: Cambridge University Press, 1998), 114.

59 Celia Marshik discusses this point in "Publication and 'public women': prostitution and censorship in three novels by Virginia Woolf," *Modern Fiction Studies*, 45. 4 (1999): 865–6.

60 Virginia Woolf, *Orlando* (New York: Harcourt Brace & Co., 1956), 154.

61 For a discussion of the relation between chastity and female writing, see Patricia Moran, "'The flaw in the centre': writing as hymenal rupture in Virginia Woolf's work," *Tulsa Studies in Women's Literature*, 17. 1 (1998): 101–21.

62 Virginia Woolf, "A Society," *The Complete Shorter Fiction of Virginia Woolf*, ed. Susan Dick (New York: Harcourt Brace, 1985), 119; hereafter cited in the text.

63 In discussing the difficulties of women's work and the potential motherhood of women, Ray Strachey writes: "The physical burden of continuing the race lies upon women; and whatever else they may individually do … it colours all thoughts about them": *Careers and Openings for Women*, 48.

64 Sheila Jeffreys, "Spinsterhood and celibacy" in *The Spinster and Her Enemies: Feminism and Sexuality 1880–1930* (London: Pandora, 1985), 95.

65 Susan Kingsley Kent, *Making Peace: The Reconstruction of Gender in Interwar Britain* (Princeton, NJ: Princeton University Press, 1993), 129.

66 Mina Loy, "Feminist manifesto," *The Lost Lunar Baedeker*, ed. Roger L. Conover (New York: Noonday Press, 1996), 154–5. Loy equates her call for the surgical destruction of virginity on demand with female sexual emancipation, but her proposition reads as much less radical when one realizes that the procedure was actually carried out by some doctors in order to facilitate marital intercourse. Marie Stopes, who did not endorse the practice, describes this medicalized "preparation for marriage": "in their surgeries [physicians] stretch the hymen or lance it, and then fit the bride before marriage with some contraceptive device." See *Marriage in My Time* (London: Rich & Cowan, 1935), 80–1.

67 For a discussion of the debates surrounding the notion of technologized reproduction during the 1920s, see Susan Merril Squier's *Babies in Bottles: Twentieth-Century Visions of Reproductive Technology* (New Brunswick, NJ: Rutgers University Press, 1994).

68 For reference to these Acts, see Philippa Strachey's *Memorandum*.

69 Susan Kingsley Kent, "Gender reconstruction after the First World War" in Harold L. Smith ed. *British Feminism in the Twentieth Century* (Amherst: University of Massachusetts Press, 1990), 66.

70 Cicely Hamilton, "The return to femininity," *Time and Tide* (August 12, 1927).

71 Deborah Gorham, *Vera Brittain: A Feminist Life* (Oxford: Blackwell, 1996), 166.

72 Winifred Holtby, *Women and a Changing Civilization* (London: John Lane–Bodley Head, 1934), 192. Holtby goes on to link her discussion of the cultural construction of gender with a critique of compulsory heterosexuality, arguing: "We do not even know – though we theorise and penalise with ferocious confidence – whether the 'normal' sexual relationship is homo- or bi- or heterosexual" (*ibid.*).

73 See Sigmund Freud, "Femininity," *New Introductory Lectures on Psychoanalysis* (New York: Norton, 1965 [1933]), 90. Th. H. Van De Velde, *Sex Hostility in Marriage* (London: William Heinemann, 1931), 99. Holtby, *Women and a Changing Civilization*, 97 and 118.

74 Rebecca West, "Equal pay for men and women teachers," *Time and Tide* (February 9, 1923), 147.

75 Elizabeth Bowen, "H2o," *Vogue* (July 8, 1936).

76 Dorothy Richardson, *Windows on Modernism: Selected Letters of Dorothy Richardson*, ed. Gloria

G. Fromm (Athens and London: University of Georgia Press, 1995), 290; *I'll Stand by You: The Letters of Sylvia Townsend Warner and Valentine Ackland*, ed. Susanna Pinney (London: Pimlico, 1998), 40.

77 Woolf, *Letters*, Vol. 3: 403.

78 Lady Rhondda, "Woman's place VI," *Time and Tide* (December 9, 1927).

79 See Anon., "Paint and powder," *Vogue* (late January, 1921); Anon., "On her dressing table," *Vogue* (early November, 1922; and early August, 1923); Sydney Tremayne, "A career for women: being beautiful," *Vogue* (early September, 1923). Sander L. Gilman discusses the racialized implications of plastic surgery in *Creating Beauty to Cure the Soul* (Durham, NC, and London: Duke University Press, 1998).

80 Mary Butts, *The Taverner Novels* (Kingston, NY: McPherson & Co., 1992), 4 and 145.

81 Caroline Cox, *Good Hair Days: A History of British Hairstyling* (London: Quartet Books, 1999), 72.

82 See Alison Wier, *Britain's Royal Families: The Complete Genealogy* (London: Bodley Head, 1989), 317.

83 Stephen J. Heathorn, *For Home, Country, and Race: Constructing Gender, Class, and Englishness in the Elementary School, 1880–1914* (Toronto: University of Toronto Press, 2000).

84 For an overview of the dominant versions of Englishness during this period, see Judy Giles and Tim Middleton eds. *Writing Englishness 1900–1950: An Introductory Sourcebook on National Identity* (New York: Routledge, 1995). For an examination of the ethnic and racial implications of the period's engagement with ethnographic materials, see Elazar Barkan and Ronald Bush eds. *Prehistories of the Future: The Primitivist Project and the Culture of Modernism* (Stanford, CA: Stanford University Press, 1995). For a discussion of the British ambivalence toward African art, see Marianna Torgovnick, *Gone Primitive: Savage Intellects, Modern Lives* (Chicago, IL, and London: University of Chicago Press, 1990). For a discussion of the restriction on "undesirable aliens" in Britain, see Lesley Higgins and Marie-Christine Leps, "'Passport, please,'" 101.

85 See *Vogue*, "When the world begins to fly" (early March, 1920); Jay Marston, "My cook was an African," *Vogue* (August 19, 1936).

86 See Woolf, *Roger Fry: A Biography* (London: Hogarth Press, 1940), 152; *Orlando*, 258; *Letters*, Vol. 3: 285; *Diary*, Vol. 4: 349.

87 See Gretchen Gerzina, *Black London: Life Before Emancipation* (New Brunswick, NJ: Rutgers University Press, 1995), and Ron Ramdin, *Reimagining Britain: Five Hundred Years of Black and Asian History* (London: Pluto Press, 1999).

88 Jane Marcus, "Registering objections: grounding feminist alibis" in Margaret R. Higonnet and Joan Templeton eds. *Reconfigured Spheres: Feminist Explorations of Literary Space* (Amherst: University of Massachusetts Press, 1994), 174.

89 As reprinted in Giles and Middleton eds. *Writing Englishness 1900–1950*, 98, 102.

90 See Delia Jarrett-Macauley, *The Life of Una Marson, 1905–65* (Manchester: Manchester University Press, 1998); Antoinette Burton, *At the Heart of Empire: Indians and the Colonial Encounter in Late-Victorian Britain* (Berkeley: University of California Press, 1998).

91 See, for example: Peter Fryer, *Staying Power: The History of Black People in Britain* (London: Pluto Press, 1984); Gretchen Gerzina, *Black London: Life Before Emancipation* (New Brunswick, NJ: Rutgers University Press, 1995); Norma Myers, *Reconstructing the Black Past: Blacks in Britain c. 1780–1830* (London: Frank Cass, 1996); Ron Ramdin, *Reimagining Britain: Five Hundred Years of Black and Asian History* (London: Pluto Press, 1999); Laura Tabili, *"We Ask for British Justice": Workers and Racial Difference in Late Imperial Britain* (Ithaca, NY: Cornell University Press, 1994); Rozina Vishram, *Ayahs, Lascars and Princes: The History of Indians in Britain, 1700–1947* (London: Pluto Press, 1986); James Walvin, *England, Slaves and Freedom* (Basingstoke: Macmillan, 1986).

92 Frank Furedi, *The Silent War: Imperialism and the Changing Perception of Race* (New Brunswick, NJ: Rutgers University Press, 1998), 6.

93 Tabili, *"We Ask for British Justice,"* 1.

94 Sylvia Townsend Warner, *Summer Will Show* (New York and London: Penguin, 1987), 37,

79, 123, 212, 299, 227; hereafter cited in the text. See Ruby Ross Wood, "Blackamoors come back into fashion," *Vogue* (May 17, 1933).

95 Billie Melman, *Women and the Popular Imagination in the Twenties: Flappers and Nymphs* (New York: St. Martin's Press, 1988), 1–12.

96 Sylvia Townsend Warner, *The True Heart* (New York: Viking Press), 43 and 68; hereafter cited in the text. Lucy Bland, *Banishing the Beast: Sexuality and the Early Feminists* (New York: New Press, 1995), 73–6.

97 Warner alludes here to the painting by Thomas Jones Barker entitled the *Secret of England's Greatness (Queen Victoria Presenting a Bible)*, dated 1861.

98 Mary Lou Emery discusses fascism and the Second World War in *Jean Rhys at "World's End": Novels of Colonial and Sexual Exile* (Austin: Univeristy of Texas Press, 1990). Cox, *Good Hair Days*, 160.

99 Olive Moore, *Collected Writings* (Elmwood Park, IL: Dalkey Archive Press, 1992), 291.

100 Joan Riviere, "Womanliness as a masquerade" in Victor Burgin, James Donald, and Cora Kaplan eds. *Formations of Fantasy* (New York and London: Routledge, 1986), 35–44.

101 Mary Butts, journal entry, Paris, May 2, 1927.

102 Laura Doan, *Fashioning Sapphism: The Origins of a Modern English Lesbian Culture* (New York: Columbia University Press, 2001), 95–125.

103 Mina Loy, *The Lost Lunar Baedeker*, ed. Roger L. Conover (New York: Noonday Press, 1996), 166; hereafter cited in the text.

104 Denise Riley, *"Am I That Name?" Feminism and the Category of "Women" in History* (Minneapolis: University of Minnesota Press, 1988), 104–6.

105 F.W. Stella Browne, "The feminine aspect of birth control" in Raymond Pierpoint ed. *Report of the Fifth International New-Malthusian and Birth Control Conference* (London: Heinemann, 1922), 40.

106 See Simon Szreter, *Fertility, Class and Gender in Britain, 1860–1940* (Cambridge University Press, 1996), 577.

107 For a discussion of Stopes's popularity, see Jeffrey Weeks, *Sex, Politics and Society: The Regulation of Sexuality Since 1800* (New York: Longman, 1981), 188. Sheila Jeffreys discusses Stopes's promotion of compulsory heterosexuality in *The Spinster and Her Enemies: Feminism and Sexuality 1880–1930* (London: Pandora, 1985), 119–21, 157–8.

108 Marie Stopes, *Enduring Passion* (1928), as quoted by Lesley A. Hall, "Uniting science and sensibility: Marie Stopes and the narratives of marriage in the 1920s" in Angela Ingram and Daphne Patai eds. *Rediscovering Forgotten Radicals: British Women Writers, 1889–1939* (Chapel Hill: University of North Carolina Press, 1993), 122.

109 See Laura Doan, "'Acts of female indecency': sexology's intervention in legislating lesbianism" in Lucy Bland and Laura Doan eds. *Sexology in Culture: Labelling Bodies and Desires* (Chicago, IL: University of Chicago Press, 1998).

110 Jeffreys, *The Spinster and Her Enemies*, 114.

111 See Alison Oram, "Repressed and thwarted, or bearer of the new world? The spinster in interwar feminist discourses," *Women's History Review*, 1. 3 (1992).

112 Arabella Kenealy, *Feminism and Sex Extinction* (London: Unwin, 1920), 246 and 263.

113 Charlotte Haldane, *Motherhood and Its Enemies* (London: Chatto & Windus, 1927), 153, 155, 159, 156.

114 Esther Harding, *The Way of All Women: A Psychological Interpretation* (London: Longman, 1933), 87.

115 Lucy Bland, "Trial by sexology? Maud Allan, *Salome* and the 'cult of the clitoris' case" in Bland and Doan eds. *Sexology in Culture: Labelling Bodies and Desires*, 192–3.

116 Woolf, *Mrs. Dalloway*, 126.

117 Playne, *The Neuroses of the Nations*, 55. See also Playne's *The Pre-War Mind in Britain: An Historical Review* (London: George Allen & Unwin, 1928), which contains a chapter on anti-German sentiment in England.

118 Eileen Barrett, "Unmasking lesbian passion: the inverted world of *Mrs. Dalloway*" in Eileen Barrett and Patricia Cramer eds. *Virginia Woolf: Lesbian Readings* (New York and London: New York University Press, 1997), 146–64.

119 Woolf, *Between the Acts* (New York: Harcourt Brace, 1969), 58 and 211.

120 Edith Lees Ellis, "Eugenics and spiritual parenthood," *The New Horizon in Love and Life* (London: A. & C. Black, 1921), 68–9.

121 For the references to Lady Bruton's emigration plan, see *Mrs. Dalloway*, 108–9. Janice Gothard discusses the demographic argument that single women constituted an 'excess' in Britain during the interwar period; see "The healthy, wholesome British domestic girl: single female migration and the Empire Settlement Act, 1922–1930" in Stephen Constantine ed. *Emigrants and Empire: British Settlement in the Dominions between the Wars* (Manchester: Manchester University Press, 1990), 72–95.

122 Homosexuality was punishable in the case of men (though a boy under 14 could not be prosecuted), but *not* in the case of women. See Strachey's *Memorandum*, 11 and 14.

123 See Szreter, *Fertility, Class and Gender in Britain, 1860–1940*.

124 From an ad for "Kruschen's Habit" in *Vogue* (late March, 1918).

125 Anna Davin, "Imperialism and motherhood," *History Workshop: A Journal of Socialist Historians*, 5 (spring, 1978): 16 and 10. See also Jane Lewis, *The Politics of Motherhood: Child and Maternal Welfare in England, 1900–1939* (London: Croom Helm, 1980); Ellen Ross, *Love and Toil: Motherhood in Outcast London, 1870–1918* (New York: Oxford University Press, 1993).

126 Bland, "Trial by sexology?" 231.

127 Jill Julius Matthews, "They had such a lot of fun: the Women's League of Health and Beauty," *History Workshop: A Journal of Socialist and Feminist Historians*, 30 (autumn, 1990): 25.

128 See Antoinette Burton, *Burdens of History: British Feminists, Indian Women, and Imperial Culture, 1865–1915* (Chapel Hill: University of North Carolina Press, 1994); also Nupur Chaudhuri and Margaret Strobel eds. *Western Women and Imperialism: Complicity and Resistance* (Bloomington and Indianapolis: Indiana University Press, 1992), 50–1.

129 Harrison, *Alpha and Omega*, 134 and 242 [original emphasis].

130 Brian Harrison, *Separate Spheres: The Opposition to Women's Suffrage in Britain* (New York: Holmes & Meier, 1978), 231 and 75.

131 Anon., "The biological study of women," *Time and Tide* (September 24, 1926).

132 Stella Browne, "The right to abortion" in Norman Haire ed. *World League for Sexual Reform, Proceedings of the Third Congress* (London: Kegan Paul, 1930), 180–1.

133 See Stopes's *Married Love* (London: Trafalgar Square, 1918), 116; *Wise Parenthood* (London: Trafalgar Square, 1918), 38 and 37.

134 Stopes, *Wise Parenthood*, 36 and 38. Although eugenicists lobbied to legalize sterilization in Britain during the 1930s, no such law was ever passed by Parliament.

135 Holtby, *Women and a Changing Civilization*, 165–6.

136 *Ibid.*, 168.

137 Cicley Hamilton, "The Women's Congress and the peace problem," *The Englishwoman*, 140 (August, 1920). An exception to the general neglect of the intersection between maternity and imperialism is Laura Doyle's *Bordering on the Body: The Racial Matrix of Modern Fiction and Culture* (New York: Oxford University Press, 1994). The work on modernist women writers and motherhood is voluminous. Two recent examples include: Marylu Hill, *Mothering Modernity: Feminism, Modernism, and the Maternal Muse* (New York: Garland, 1999), and Heather Ingram, *Women's Fiction between the Wars: Mothers, Daughters and Writing* (New York: St. Martin's Press, 1998). Primarily, the work that has been published on women writers and the maternal has been grounded in either psychoanalytic or French feminist theory. See, for example: Shirley Nelson Garner, Claire Kahane, and Madelon Sprengnether eds. *The (M)other Tongue: Feminist Essays in Psychoanalytic Interpretation* (Ithaca, NY: Cornell University Press, 1985); Marianne Hirsch, *The Mother/Daughter Plot: Narrative, Psychoanalysis, Feminism* (Bloomington: Indiana University Press, 1989); Margaret Homans, *Bearing the Word: Language and Female Experience in Nineteenth-Century Women's Writing* (Chicago, IL: University of Chicago Press, 1986); Madelon Sprengnether, *The Spectral Mother: Freud, Feminism, and Psychoanalysis* (Ithaca, NY: Cornell University Press, 1990).

138 For a discussion of "maternal imperialism," see Barbara N. Ramusack, "Cultural missionaries, maternal imperialists, feminist allies: British women activists in India, 1865–1945" in

Chaudhuri and Strobel eds. *Western Women and Imperialism: Complicity and Resistance*, 119–36.

139 When Woolf asks "Is the work of a mother ... worth nothing to the nation in solid cash?" (54), it is crucial to recognize that she is talking only about a slice of the population. Several other British feminists expressed the need for a family endowment during this period. Eleanor Rathbone, in *The Disinherited Family: A Plea for the Endowment of the Family* (London: Edward Arnold, 1924), supported this measure, which she eventually saw come into effect with the Family Allowances Bill of 1945.

140 Haldane, *Motherhood and Its Enemies*, 320.

141 Moore, *Collected Writings*, 126.

142 For a discussion of "Anglo-Mongrels," see Carolyn Burke, *Becoming Modern: The Life of Mina Loy* (Berkeley and Los Angeles: University of California Press, 1996), 350–1.

143 Megumi Kato, "The milk problem in *To the Lighthouse*," *Virginia Woolf Miscellany*, 50 (1997): 5.

144 Ellis, *The New Horizon in Love and Life*, 69.

145 Stephen and Mary's relationship is consummated not in England, but in Orotava on the Canary Island of Tenerife, an edenic space with a "glory peculiar to Africa" (307) that Hall exoticizes through primitivist discourse that works to further naturalize lesbian desire. Orotava is a displacement of the lesbian's racial Otherness, where the two lovers are "obsessed by a kind of primitive urge towards all manner of procreation" (305). Sarah E. Chinn discusses the importance of Tenerife to lesbian sexuality in "'Something primitive and age-old as nature herself': lesbian sexuality and the permission of the exotic" in Laura Doan and Jay Prosser eds. *Palatable Poison: Critical Perspectives on "The Well of Loneliness"* (New York: Columbia University Press, 2001), 300–15.

146 Margot Gayle Backus discusses the connections between inversion, race, and nationality in "Sexual orientation in the (post)imperial nation: Celticism and inversion theory in Radclyffe Hall's *Well of Loneliness*," *Tulsa Studies in Women's Literature*, 15. 2 (autumn, 1996): 253–66.

147 The use of the mother–daughter dyad is a familiar trope in lesbian theory, perhaps attributable to Freud's view that lesbianism marked a woman's failure to progress beyond a preoedipal attachment to the mother. Marylu Hill devotes a chapter to Stephen Gordon's relation to maternity, but does not discuss the novel's engagement with the discourse of race motherhood or nature. See *Mothering Modernity: Feminism, Modernism, and the Maternal Muse*.

148 Dora B. Montefiore, *Race Motherhood* (London, 1920).

149 Mary Scharlieb, *The Claims of the Coming Generation* (London: Kegan Paul, 1923), 126.

150 Havelock Ellis, *Man and Woman: A Study of Secondary Sexual Characteristics* (London: Walter Scott, 1894), 461.

151 Herbert Asquith, quoted by Brian Harrison, *Separate Spheres*, 229.

152 Sigmund Freud, *Civilization and Its Discontents* (New York: W.W. Norton, 1961), 50–1.

153 Marianna Torgovnick, *Primitive Passions: Men, Women, and the Quest for Ecstasy* (New York: Alfred A. Knopf, 1997), 10.

154 From a letter by Margaret E. Hill to the editor of *The Freewoman: A Weekly Feminist Review* (November 30, 1911). Like Francis Swiney, who published *The Cosmic Procession; or, the Feminine Principle in Evolution* in 1906, many interwar feminists who presume women's affinity with nature do so on the grounds of female superiority.

155 From "The female mind!" *The Vote* (January 28, 1927): 30.

156 Lees Ellis, *The New Horizon in Love and Life*, 125.

157 See Lucy Bland, "Trial by sexology," 73–6.

158 Rathbone, *The Disinherited Family*, 268–74. See also Billie Melman, *Women's Orients: English Women and the Middle-East, 1718–1918: Sexuality, Religion, and Work* (Ann Arbor: University of Michigan Press, 1992).

159 Scharlieb, "The moral training of young girls," *The Claims of the Coming Generation*. This reference to Joan of Arc recalls her earlier incarnation as the patron saint of the suffragette movement, often appearing in full armor on the cover of *The Suffragette*, the organ of the militant Women's Social and Political Union.

160 G.K. Chesterton, quoted by Holtby in *Women and a Changing Civilization*, 105.
161 Harrison, *Reminiscences of a Student's Life*, 11.
162 Rebecca West, *Harriet Hume: A London Fantasy* (London: Virago, 1980 [1929]), 65; hereafter cited in the text.
163 Virginia Woolf, "The Plumage Bill," *Essays*, Vol. 3: 242; hereafter cited in the text.
164 Virginia Woolf, "Literary geography," *Essays*, Vol 1: 35.

2

"Neither English nor civilized": Dorothy Richardson's spectatrix and the feminine crusade for global intervention

And so here we all are. All over London, all over England, all over the world. (Dorothy Richardson, "The increasing congregation," 1927)

You shall not group me anywhere. I am everywhere. (Miriam Henderson in Dorothy Richardson's *Pilgrimage*, 2: 307)

Winifred Bryher's laudatory 1931 review of one "novel–chapter"[1] of Dorothy Richardson's epic modernist narrative *Pilgrimage* focuses upon what she argues is the book's overall filmic potential. Bryher's observation that *Pilgrimage*, as a film, would be "the real English film for which so many are waiting" is somewhat startling for contemporary readers who contemplate the marathon spectatorial possibilities inherent in translating the author's thirteen-volume serial novel to the big screen.[2] Richardson praises Bryher for "emphasizing the aspect no one else has spotted," yet it is unclear whether "aspect" refers to the text's formal strategies or its identification as an "English" product.[3] Although Richardson herself never ventured into film making, between 1927 and 1931 she was a frequent contributor to the avant-garde film magazine *Close Up*, the collaborative effort of Bryher, her husband Kenneth Macpherson, and H.D.. *Close Up* was the first English-language film periodical; its stated purpose was the promotion of film as an emancipatory educational, social, political, and artistic medium. Although the journal was vigorously international in scope, a frequent topic that reappears throughout *Close Up*'s pages is the problematic issue of defining a British national cinema.[4] The volume in which Bryher's review of *Pilgrimage* appears also contains an article, "Be British," which laments that "there has not yet been an English film," arguing that English movies lack technical innovation, audience engagement, and are devoid of "spirit, national or of any other kind."[5] Although Bryher's contention, several pages later, that *Pilgrimage* perfectly "express[es] ... the English spirit" does not frame itself as a response to the "Be British" essay, it does address several of the complaints raised by that essay and similarly acknowledges that no film of the period has yet captured the national characteristics of the English. Bryher upholds *Pilgrimage* as the quintessentially "English" text, highlighting the novel's experimentalism, its collaborative demands, and its status as an exemplary ethnographic document of the period. Like a movie, Bryher observes, Richardson's novel unfolds as a narrative montage in which multiple images are juxtaposed to "revolve before the eyes as we read" in order to create "an actual sense of movement" for the reader.[6] At the same time, the novel functions as a documentary – "the best history yet written" – of England's shift, between 1893 and 1912, from the Victorian to the modern age, read from the perspective of the years 1912–46.[7] While *Pilgrimage* has never been made into a movie, Bryher's suggestive remarks unintentionally underscore a crucial, if unexplored, dynamic at work in Richardson's text: the author's attempt to deploy an experimental narrative technique that would simulate a cinematic experience for the reader and the novel's engagement with the problem, for women, of Englishness – a dynamic which must be understood from a historical viewpoint.

This chapter relates Richardson's film criticism to her serial novel *Pilgrimage*, outlining the continuity of the visual themes and preoccupations that link them. I begin by considering the relation between Richardson's novelistic form and Englishness, showing how Miriam Henderson's visual consciousness is portrayed as central to the redemption of the national body politic. Richardson depicts her protagonist, Miriam, as a kind of living movie camera who optically perceives and renders England. The visual in this novel is crucial, because it is the literal and metaphorical means through which Miriam registers her movement through space: as she circulates through a variety of concrete material spaces within London, Miriam simultaneously experiences an "irrevocable expansion of her consciousness" (3: 45) that is correlated specifically with visual perception.[8] Although the novel's abundant spatial metaphors anchor her to specific locales, ultimately what *Pilgrimage* privileges is Miriam's topographical journey through imaginative space. As she walks through London "the streets ... arranged themselves in her mind ... making a neat map" (4: 155), illustrating Miriam's pivotal role in restructuring the world by fusing the division between public and private spaces. As she psychically maps her surroundings, Miriam appropriates and takes possession of new territory, moving "on and on towards unknown space" (3: 85).[9] This spatial appropriation, I argue, is precisely what authorizes her status as a universalized subject of empire. Although Miriam's subjectivity is both a national and international construct, and is the product of myriad oscillations between sexual and social categories, what the novel ultimately values is not incessant mobility, but stillness; not internationalism, but Englishness. Paradoxically, Miriam's endless wanderings lead her to the discovery of contemplative space: "Of course, there is actually no such thing as travel ... There is nothing but a *Voyage autour de ma Chambre ... even in a tour du monde*" (4: 167).

This notion that traveling the world is co-extensive with traveling round one's homeland captures a defining feature of Miriam's consciousness: her identification of Englishness with that which is homogeneous, interchangeable, and everywhere the same. In *Pilgrimage* national identity is constructed through the refraction of the Other's gaze, although, as Miriam's relationship with Michael Shatov, a Jew, makes clear, the Englishwoman must not subordinate her 'pure' English gaze to the totalizing racial vision of another. Within this paradigm in which cultural sameness is highly prized, it is Miriam's *homoerotic* gaze – both imperial and subversive – that ultimately promulgates a British worldview. Richardson posits a mystical relationship between Miriam and the nation, celebrating women's *civilizing* cultural vision by constructing a feminized London as its chief homoerotic object. As the city claims

Miriam as its rightful heir – "[be] a citizen of my kingdom" (3: 246) – she taps into England's national unconscious, radically revising the terms of women's national affiliation. Significantly, as Miriam imaginatively rejects the social constraints that have historically impeded women's role as national citizens, Richardson simultaneously abandons the assumptions that underlie literary realism – such as narrative omniscience, linearity, and objectivity. The most pronounced formal consequence of this radical restructuring is the novel's search for a pictorial language that might capture Richardson's desire for a common language, one able to fuel a reawakening of national consciousness. She locates this language not in conventional discourse, which she associates with masculinity and monocular vision, but in the *image*, which is the province of the female spectator and is linked with multi-perspectivalism, silence, and the homoerotic. By standing metonymically for England, Miriam both reconfigures the nation, recasting it as a space of liminality, androgyny, homoeroticism, and the sacred, and simultaneously upholds its core cultural value of homogeneity, and the imperial vision with which it is linked: "She sat ... surrounded by images of the things that had made her; not hers, England's, but which she represented ... [and] had been born with her" (3: 319).

Novelistic form and national consciousness

Today, despite renewed interest in Richardson's film criticism and novel, as well as the publication of a volume of her letters and the re-issuing of Gloria Fromm's biography,[10] *Pilgrimage*'s status within the academy remains precarious, at best. While literary critics have certainly been successful at making a case for the correlation between the sequenced novel, the origins of modernism, and feminist aesthetics, *Pilgrimage* remains today a book that is largely unread.[11] The reasons for this are varied, but arguably have much to do with Richardson's uncanonical status, her novel's protracted length (over 2,100 pages), its limited availability, the general impression that the text is primarily autobiographical, and the misperception that this is a boring big book in which "nothing happens" and "nothing is important."[12] This last objection might seem ungrounded, given the novel's attention to historical specifics, but it speaks to the proliferation of seemingly random descriptive detail that is endlessly registered by Miriam's elastic consciousness. Richardson herself, in a 1921 letter, admits that it may be difficult for certain readers to tolerate the relentlessness of Miriam's point of view, recognizing that some people will want "to shake & smack her nearly all the time."[13] The presumption that nothing of significance happens in *Pilgrimage* underscores what several critics have observed to be Richardson's deliberate refusal to impose an authoritative meaning on her text. As a result, the aesthetic experience of *Pilgrimage* is often arduous, violating the reader's expectations on multiple levels: characters often speak for several pages before they're introduced; typically, the relationship between individuals is only implied; the author repeatedly delays revealing vital information about characters that would help ground her readers in the text (e.g., the death of Miriam's sister Eve is revealed a year after the event); some details are never disclosed (the circumstances surrounding Miriam's miscarriage, or her mother's suicide). Moreover, as critics have observed, Richardson frequently abandons punctuation: she often utilizes intricately claused sentences, ellipsis, and sentence fragments; she changes from one tense to another within a single paragraph and indiscriminately shifts from first- to third-person pronouns. This plotless text lacks transitions within chapters and creates significant temporal gaps between books (such as the unexplained three years between *Interim* and *Deadlock*).[14] The novel repeatedly stalls chronology in still subtler ways as Miriam moves seamlessly between memory and the present moment. Richardson's mega-novel never builds to a climactic revelation – exemplified by the fact that Miriam's eventual consummation of her love affair with Hypo Wilson (in volume 6) is decidedly uneventful – nor does it lead to any interpretive closure. Richardson herself, fully registering the resistant nature of her narrative, joked that literary historians will relegate her book to the annals of "Martyrdom of a Worst Seller."[15]

Early feminist critics of the novel adeptly argued that Richardson's deliberate refusal to participate in narrative conventions should be understood as her desire to subvert the romantic courtship plot of her nineteenth-century predecessors. For these critics, Richardson's "stream of consciousness" technique is both a critique of the realist novel and an attempt to capture the psychology of women.[16] Most recently, critics have read Richardson's experimentalism through the lens of French feminist theories of language and the body, on the grounds that *Pilgrimage*'s "nonlinear, polyphonic, open-ended" structure constitutes "a way of writing the feminine."[17] Richardson's identification of her work (in her Foreword) with "feminine prose" underscores her interest in exploring the link between gender and the ideological significance of form, but it has also unwittingly situated her as the precursor of contemporary feminist theorists who argue for the existence of specifically feminine languages. Although there are indeed correspondences that can be drawn between the form of *Pilgrimage* and the narrative features of *écriture féminine*, the considerable critical focus on the novel's purportedly inherent feminine aesthetic has occurred at the expense of looking at how Richardson also problematizes the category of femininity.[18] Moreover, such an approach neglects the ways in which femininity itself intersects with larger national, racial, and imperial aims. I wish here to extend the parameters of the discussion and to consider to what extent Richardson's narrative reformulations, as well as her investment in female subjectivity, are informed by her Anglocentrism, her engagement with the operations of cinema, and her privileging of female homoeroticism.

In order to answer these interrelated questions, I consider first the relation between *Pilgrimage*'s seeming formlessness and the allegation that "nothing happens." In doing so, I seek to establish a link between the novel's narrative structure, its representation of Miriam's subjectivity – "going on and on" – and her belief in the notion of a collective national consciousness.[19] Frequently in *Pilgrimage* Richardson foregrounds Miriam's interpretive acts to signal a point of correspondence with her own textual practices: "Miriam's mind leapt from incident to incident, weaving all into a general impression"; "[t]he disconnected narrative was flowing again" (2: 306, 340). Such moments work both to describe Miriam's localized activity and to characterize the reader's own collaborative relation to the text. Miriam's ironic observation, "What is the novel? I don't care for novels ... They seem to be an endless fuss about nothing" (3: 45), acknowledges the criticism leveled against

Pilgrimage but invites readers to adopt a metacritical vantage point. During one revealing scene, Miriam sits in a café reading Ibsen's *Brand*: "It was all the *same*. You might as well begin at the end ... You are in the strangeness of Norway – and then there are people saying things that might be said anywhere" (2: 382–3). Miriam's focus here on the interchangeability of Ibsen's narrative – "all the *same*" – parallels in certain ways the reader's relation to Richardson's aesthetic, in which, according to Woolf, from page to page "[t]hings look pretty much the same as ever."[20] What Woolf arguably means by this, and what I mean to suggest by citing Woolf, is that there is a kind of uniformity and surface quality to the novel's profusion of encyclopedic detail. Miriam's observations of daily life may be acute, but she deliberately neglects to subordinate and hierarchize the flood of information that filters through her consciousness. As a result, although she encounters over 600 people and travels a varied geographical and psychical territory throughout the thirteen books of *Pilgrimage*, there is a something discernibly anti-developmental about her journey that may be characterized as the postponement of meaning.[21] *Pilgrimage*'s fluidity arguably reflects Richardson's belief that one should be able to read the pages of a novel in any order – something that she encouraged readers to do with her own text.[22]

One recognizes a point of correspondence between Richardson's encouragement that readers begin her novel at any point and the title of her film columns – "Continuous performance" – which refers to the back-to-back screening of films enabling viewers to enter and leave the cinema at will. And yet the question remains: why did Richardson endorse these practices of narrative equivalence and circularity? To interpret this textual phenomenon as a result of Richardson's search for new *feminine* forms is inadequate because it does not account for the relation between her novel's structure and its thematic content. Richardson's interest in systems of narrative equivalence arguably has to do with her larger commitment to a vision of communal subjectivity, suggested, for example, when Richardson blurs the boundary between the autonomy of Miriam's inner world and what her heroine at one point refers to as "communal consciousness" (4: 334). *Pilgrimage*'s resolute attention to detail and specificity are ultimately subordinated to an idea of universalism, in which Miriam imagines a "common vision" (4: 621) to undergird all manner of individual difference. To return to the Ibsen example: what is striking about this scene is its double movement, in which Miriam registers the shock of national particularity – "You are in the strangeness of Norway" – yet immediately disavows any Norwegian uniqueness, claiming that people there say things "that might be said anywhere." This moment of cultural conflation and "discursive homogenization" – to borrow Chandra Talpade Mohanty's phrase[23] – is replayed several times throughout *Pilgrimage* as Miriam argues that beneath all cultural and racial differences "[e]verybody is the same really, inside, under all circumstances" (3: 146). Because the narrative dynamics of *Pilgrimage* emphasize process rather than destination, inclusivity and integration over expulsion, the book may be said to stage the author's democratic – albeit naïve – impulse to include almost everything in the world. Yet Miriam's English gaze remains the center of this novelistic universe.

Richardson's characterization of Miriam, "[p]oised between the competing interests of many worlds" (2: 71), suggests the relational nature of her heroine's subjectivity, underscoring the significance of symbolic space as a crucial marker of identity. Miriam's self-disclosure, "I'm something new – a kind of different world" (1: 260), speaks directly to what I argue is Richardson's attempt to map the body of a woman onto the body of the nation, representing the female appropriation of space as a resistance to the diverse territorial boundaries that have historically impeded women's mobility. The central means by which Richardson accomplishes this is through the optical metaphors that situate Miriam's "wandering eyes" (3: 488) as the cultural vantage point from which she reconceptualizes the world by, in effect, feminizing it. What conceptions of location inform Richardson's representation of female vision? While her engagement with vision seeks to inaugurate a globally discerning feminist ethics, it is simultaneously complicit, however unwittingly, in the tactics of feminist cultural imperialism. To the extent that Richardson's well-intentioned universalism reproduces, in Mohanty's words, " the authorizing signature of western humanist discourse" (197), she occupies the position of "benevolent missionary." Richardson's utopian aims are predicated upon the desire to claim "the whole world for her home," a desire in which Miriam's homogenizing gaze not only redeems but appropriates.[24] We see evidence of Richardson's belief that Western women function as global agents of enculturation in a 1917 essay, written as the First World War raged, in which the author rhetorically domesticates the public sphere and identifies Englishwomen as cultural workers who go about "doing the world's housekeeping in the world."[25] In *Pilgrimage*, Richardson further legitimizes a feminine point of view as a world-wide historical force and an extension of Britain's civilizing mission by giving free rein to Miriam's optical appropriations.

Miriam's growth in consciousness, then, is cast in overtly visual terms: by the end of the novel she surveys "all that her eyes had made her own" (4: 414) – a gesture that here, as elsewhere, is steeped in the rhetoric of British territorial expansionism. Ultimately, by exploring Richardson's "geographics of identity," I intend to examine how the spatialized representation of female consciousness as a self-enclosed globe leads Miriam not toward greater inclusion of difference or an embrace of the Other but, rather, into "neutral territory" (4: 634), a final realm which is based upon cultural and racial homogeneity.[26] In order to fully understand the novel's emphasis on spectatorship and its idealized transcending of cultural, national, and racial specificity, it is necessary to focus, first, on Richardson's film columns, which offer a clear articulation of her position on these interrelated issues. This chapter will demonstrate the multiple links between Richardson's theorizing of silent film and her characterization of Miriam, arguing that the novel's preoccupation with vision and its endorsement of silence are ultimately linked to Miriam's lesbianism and her English national identity. Although vision is rooted in the spatial home of the female body – operating in, on, and through it – Miriam's visual knowledge is ultimately conceived in terms that privilege *invisibility*, a universal subjectivity that is predicated upon a *homoeroticized* corporeal absence. Miriam's final vision is achieved only by sacrificing the sexualized body and cultural specificity, and is contingent upon asserting a woman's sense of imperial duty.

Spectatorship as appropriation: creating "world citizens"

Recently, critics such as Susan Gevirtz and Carol Watts have given increased attention to the relationship between Richardson's film theory, her work on gendered spectatorship, and her representation of female experience in *Pilgrimage*.[27] As these critics observe, the cinema provided Richardson with a spatialized model of femininity; that is, *Pilgrimage* draws an implied parallel between Miriam's shifting perspective, which resembles the roving eye of a camera, and the reader's unstable position. Gevirtz, in particular, highlights the usefulness of Richardson's film articles for understanding the parallel forms of gender identification in visual and textual narratives, but her analysis largely neglects the complex ways in which racial, racist, and colonial discourses are also inscribed through Richardson's privileging of femininity. This section seeks to broaden the analytical base by considering the question of spectatorship and gender in Richardson alongside issues of ethnicity, sexuality, class, race, and empire. What still needs to be explored are Richardson's cultural blindspots, what Rebecca Egger refers to as the author's "desire to efface various kinds of difference" in her cinematic writings, although *Pilgrimage* may ultimately be more interested in subsuming difference than in effacing it.[28]

Richardson's film column appeared in *Close Up* from 1927 to 1933 – the entire duration of the journal – and consisted in a series of twenty-three articles, twenty of which were titled "Continuous performance." *Close Up* did not put forward a carefully defined theoretical agenda, but entertained what Anne Friedberg calls a variety of "film-theoretical models, many of them contradictory."[29] The publication's articles reflect the aesthetic, social, and political concerns raised by the new medium of cinema, focusing less on movie reviews *per se* than on the conceptual and philosophical problems that surround the issue of spectatorship. *Close Up* grappled with the topics of, for example, censorship, the pedagogical value of film, the relationship between film and psychoanalysis, and the limitations of sound. To an extent Richardson's articles – which rarely mention specific films – are consistent with the theoretical bent of the magazine. Rachel Low confirms that despite *Close Up*'s small circulation, the journal was historically significant, exhibiting considerable influence on film-making and scriptwriting practices even though the publication's importance is often overlooked in contemporary standard histories of cinema.[30] The reason for this, according to Friedberg, was the journal's international focus, its refusal to "insist on a nationalistic categorization of [film] history and production."[31] *Close Up* featured a series of correspondents from around the globe – Paris, London, Berlin, Geneva, Hollywood, New York, Moscow, and Vienna – focusing on international cooperation rather than attempting to foreground the idea of a national cinema. Yet, despite this interest in internationalism, *Close Up* was indisputably "an English project … continually stern with England."[32] The journal was both extremely critical of the British film industry, which in the 1920s was generally perceived to be producing mediocre work, and also deeply invested in what Kenneth Macpherson, writing in March 1929, called the cinephile's desire to help "build the English cinema to a position of triumph equal to the Russian."[33] Although the weekly film audience, estimated at 7–8 million prior to 1914, measured about 20 million in 1927, it is important to recognize that the majority of those people – primarily the working and lower-middle classes – were viewing not British but American productions.[34] During *Close Up*'s tenure the cinema was still regarded by many as a low-grade art form, "a drug" that catered to the masses who eagerly consumed Hollywood features in order to escape the tedium of their daily lives.[35] *Close Up*'s anti-Hollywood stance had to do both with the journal's disdain for American popular culture and with its recognition that the economy of the British film industry was adversely affected by the predominance of American films after the First World War. Perhaps, in consequence, *Close Up* understood itself to be not only the vanguard in the campaign to establish film as a legitimate artistic medium – "voices crying in the wilderness of a filmless England" – but the main artery for the revitalization of British "race consciousness" in the cinema.[36]

In order to fully appreciate Richardson's film columns it is necessary to situate her within this larger cinematic context, in which *Close Up*'s commitment to internationalism, its interest in promoting Englishness, and its self-perception as an avant-garde subculture of the world's most influential medium are all elements that feature prominently in her own work.[37] Equally critical to an understanding of Richardson's theorizations about film is the journal's ideological struggle to legitimize the cinema as not only a national but a universal art form. The importance of the idea of a "universal cinema" cannot be over-estimated: it is a foundational concept of *Close Up*'s ideological mission – "internationalism is the aim" – and the basis of Richardson's own enthusiastic embrace of the cinema as *the* primary source of "universal hospitality" among nations, forging greater cultural awareness, in her words, "of alien people and alien ways."[38] What constitutes "the alien" for Richardson requires greater elaboration, but let it suffice, momentarily, to say that the author's idealization of "the socializing influence of the cinema" is dependent upon polarized Western notions of the "primitive" and the "civilized."[39] Central to Richardson's columns – which range in subject matter from the problem of censorship to the use of captions, the architectural style of movie theatres, and the disadvantage of "talkies" – is her underlying belief in the enculturating value of silent film. Most often, she argues for the cinema as an unlimited vehicle for enlarging the personal, social, and aesthetic consciousness of those who attend – working-class mothers and businessmen, as well as children. Richardson sees the cinema as both a unifying and a democratizing medium, for in contrast to the theater, which she dismisses for being too elitist, movies are affordable and therefore allegedly cut across class, gender, and race stratifications.[40] She deems the theater, moreover, to be too invasive, for there the actors perform *at* rather than *with* with the audience, in contrast to the cinema which requires a collaborative effort, compelling "the co-operation of the creative consciousness of the audience."[41] This emphasis on the audience's active participation is the most crucial aspect of Richardson's theorizations about silent film. The cinema is "something for collective seeing," an ostensibly social art form the context of which is nonetheless extremely intimate, "a small ceremonial prepared for a group."[42]

For Richardson, the experience of watching a film is almost alchemical, producing "a new dimension of consciousness" in the spectator; it is thus not surprising to find that the author often utilizes the language of religion – in particular, Christian iconography– to convey the transformative potential of the cinema.[43] Film-going is analogized as a "pilgrimage" of the "faithful," for whom the film provides a kind of visual "miracle," awakening the audience's "imaginative power" and transporting them to a more expansive experiential realm.[44] Richardson reconceptualizes the spectator's relationship to the cinema as a sacramental moment, while the film itself is invested with the symbolic power of the Eucharist: the film provides spiritual nourishment – "miraculous food to feed our souls" – to the "congregation" which, gathered in the "nave" of the "little bethel," is visually stirred to "feelings of common humanity" through their participation in this ritual.[45] Sounding much like an evangelical minister in search of communicants, the author declares: "Let us by all means confess our faith ... in Art as ... a way of salvation."[46] Richardson's messianic ardor leads her to insist that "[t]he screen should dominate" the audience, a fact that speaks to her conviction that the cinematic space is sacred, the screen itself a kind of altar that must at all times confront its spectators, but the phrasing here – "should dominate" – also reveals a more coercive cinematic subtext. Although Richardson regards film as an impartial medium, celebrating its "freedom from any ulterior motive," at the same time she argues that the cinema has a very specific social function: nothing less than the "re-education of humanity."[47] While all spectators can benefit equally from an exposure to film, the results of which can best be summarized as escape, enlargement, and enculturation, certain demographic groups seem more susceptible to improvement than others. Richardson makes specific reference to "weary women of all classes," for whom the "merciful darkness" of the cinema is a "refuge" from the demands of the outside world. This insulated image recalls another essay in which Richardson recounts visiting a movie theater in a working-class neighborhood of north London, where she is surprised to discover that the audience – on a weekday – is composed almost entirely of mothers with young children, again "figures of weariness at rest."[48] For Richardson the movie theater is both "a sanctuary" and "an escape," the film itself a transitional "balm" through which the audience is "stilled to forgetfulness of itself as an audience."[49] For the duration of the film these working-class women are able to experience a kind of temporary amnesia, so that they transcend their constricted lives and "forget" that they are socially situated subjects, limited in terms of gender as well as material circumstance.[50] Rebecca Egger refers to this phenomenon as Richardson's investment in "cinematic forgetfulness," seeing it as a result of the author's desire to occlude and efface various kinds of difference.[51] While mothers are singled out as a group particularly susceptible to the film's restorative effects, Richardson identifies others – uneducated children, slum-dwellers, village inhabitants – for whom the cinema has an overtly pedagogical, more than a merely reparative, function.

Given this educative ambition, the question is: what kind of ideological work are Richardson's film columns doing? It is crucial to recognize the degree to which the author's idealization of film, and her interest in visual aesthetics, intersects with larger sociological concerns. Richardson hails film-going for its purgative potential, but she legitimizes this enthusiasm by invoking the rhetoric of Christian evangelism; in doing so, she justifies the cinema's moral superiority and affirms its righteousness as "a civilizing agent," "immeasurably more powerful" than any other cultural medium.[52] Richardson also ascribes to film a distinctly imperial function –

"of bringing light into darkness" – although she does not self-consciously align herself with this agenda.[53] And yet, she does position herself as an agent of salvation. The language she utilizes to describe film's social and cultural contribution is also class-marked and resonates with the discourse of England's imperial mission. In her 1928 article, "The cinema in the slums," Richardson denounces the State's oppression of "labourers of all ages and both sexes available for exploitation in the basements supporting the British empire"; she sees this vast population living in "a state of mental and moral constriction … paralyzed by circumstance" and held hostage to various missionary influences.[54]

Richardson distances herself from these intrusive elements, which she believes are tainted by self-interest and the motive for profit, despite her borrowing from missionary rhetoric to convey the salvific aspect of film elsewhere. Instead, she turns to silent film as the answer to her desire for cultural salvation. To the extent that silent film requires the active collaboration of the viewer in order for meaning to be conveyed, Richardson does not regard it as a form of propaganda. Yet she refers to the impact of silent film on the viewer as "civilization working unawares," deploying the vocabulary of conversion to argue that film can reach even "undesirable types" who harbor "the passions of the jungle," elevating and expanding their "cramped consciousness" until they are, in effect, born again, inhabiting "new lives."[55] While Richardson's celebration of film as a value-free medium hinges upon a universalistic impulse, her missionary zeal targets the lower classes and is at times indistinguishable from colonial discourse as well as the classist and racist ideologies of empire.[56] Film-going is a "[t]raining in taste," a cultural "elevator" that induces people to seek out "positive cultural activities" which are evidently class inflected; ideally, exposure to silent film, in particular, stimulates receptivity, producing an audience that is much more capable of appreciating the objects in a museum or gallery than were "their pictureless predecessors."[57]

During the period in which Richardson was publishing her articles in *Close Up*, discussion within the film industry focused on the educational as well as patriotic role of film, with an eye to its "capacity to create a national ideology."[58] An "imperial world view remained the central ideology" of interwar popular culture, especially in the films produced during the 1920s and 1930s.[59] The British Empire Film Institute was established in 1926 with the specific aim of promoting a public interest in British films that would disseminate an imperial ideology throughout the world.[60] A year later, in December 1927 – the year that *Close Up* was launched – the Cinematograph Films Act, which was designed to enforce a quota on the number of British films required to be shown on British screens, was passed by Parliament.[61] Although *Close Up* was contemptuous of this legislation, arguing that the Act sacrificed quality to quantity, the film journal was similarly preoccupied, as we have seen, with the establishing of a *British* cinema.[62] Certainly, *Close Up* was critical of the notion of empire films spreading wholesome imperial sentiment, but it nevertheless sought to draw attention to and to promote a specifically British aesthetic worthy of the "extraordinary nation" at the same time as it cultivated an international market.[63] During the period in which Richardson espoused this view, British documentary film-makers were creating propagandist films that demonstrated the work of imperial officials in "spreading civilization" to the colonies.[64] The Empire

Marketing Board, which, like the Film Institute, was formed in 1926 with the aim
of disseminating imperial ideology to a mass audience, readily embraced film to
advertise the virtues of empire and to encourage the consumption of empire
products. A recurrent theme in the propaganda produced by the Board was that
citizens of the empire – both at home and overseas – constituted a single community
propelled by cooperation, not exploitation, a message that implicitly denied the
official imposition of a dominant imperial ideology on subordinate groups.[65] While
Richardson's film columns do not invoke an overtly nationalist agenda, one sees
various links between her view of film as a civilizing medium and England's larger
investment in disseminating imperial values through the distribution of British
films. While I am not suggesting that Richardson was a fervent empire loyalist, I
am arguing that her views on the cinema must be read within this larger imperial
context, in which film's potential as a cross-cultural propagandistic medium was
perceived to be enormous. There is an ironic congruence between Richardson's
assertion that film facilitates a "world-wide conversation" among spectators and the
views of Stephen Tallents, the secretary of the Empire Marketing Board, who, in
advocating for a "world-wide projection" of English characteristics, declared that
"the greatest agent of international communication at the moment is unquestion-
ably the cinema."[66] Tallents reveals his conservatism when he lists the subjects he
finds appropriate for worldwide distribution, for example: the monarchy, Parliament,
English literature (Dickens, Shakespeare), the British Navy, and English sports.
These institutions, overwhelmingly patriarchal, are among the many elements of
empire that Richardson critiques in *Pilgrimage*, but, like Tallents, she still readily
embraces the international potential of the cinema.

Richardson differs from Tallents, however, in that she imagines a global
dialogue the ideological dimension of which is *feminine*. Her belief that film is an
agent of social growth which enables spectators to become, as she puts it, "world
citizens" – that is, potential collaborators in a global cross-cultural conversation –
hinges upon the privileging of silent over "talking" film, and the equation of that
silence with femininity.[67] Writing in 1931, Richardson laments the increasing
unpredictability and fragmentation of modern society: there is "change all over the
world, and a dim sense that nobody knows with any certainty [anymore] ... about
the universe of which his world is a part."[68] As Richardson sees it, the cinema has
contributed largely to this problem, in that, more than any other element of
modernity film has produced a profound shift in mental climate, but the cinema is,
paradoxically, also regarded as the antidote to this modern quandary. The beauty of
this new medium, as the author perceives it, is that it exposes people to "the breath
of otherness" by "getting [them] into communication with the unknown," introducing them to alien cultures until they "become for a while citizens of a world
whose every face is that of a stranger."[69] Richardson betrays no anxiety here about
internationalization, instead idealizing the prospect of different social groups
coming into contact through their participation in mass culture. What is also true,
however, is that Richardson distinguishes between *films* and *movies*, seeing the two
as "contrasted territories" that are geographically segregated and class-inflected: the
highbrow connoisseur of film is "aesthetically adult," while the "citizen of the lower
world" – the consumer of commercial movies – has "infantile tastes."[70] Richardson

ultimately sides with the aesthete who, as "rightly dogmatic," professes: "Art by all means. Let us live and die in and for it."[71]

If Richardson regards film as a democratizing medium and a celebration of diversity despite the fact that the classes rarely mixed at the cinema, like British colonialism itself she too analogizes film-going as a kind of colonization of space – "a world in the making" – through which spectators become "full citizens of the spirit, free from the tyranny of circumstance and always and everywhere perfectly at home."[72] This spatialized image of being "at home" anywhere recurs throughout Richardson's film columns, underscoring the cinema's pervasiveness as a cultural tool – "the film educating Everyman, making him at home in a new world" – and betraying her perhaps unconscious identification with British imperial ideology.[73] Sounding much like a spokeswoman for the achievements of empire, Richardson celebrates the cinematic transmission of culture in language suggestive of colonial expansionism: "And so here we all are. All over London, all over England, all over the world."[74] Yet, whereas literal colonization displaces, violates, and enslaves actual people, Richardson's metaphorical colonization does the opposite: it purports to rescue and liberate individuals from their formerly shackled state. Film-going is associated with mobility and the dissolution of boundaries, an experience bestowing on the spectator "the gift of expansion" – a sense of unrestricted passage – through which one enters uncharted territory, "a new dimension of consciousness."[75] Richardson celebrates this appropriative gaze – "there is no limit to vision" – equating it with the colonization of space, the discovery and presentation of "resources whose extent is unknown" to viewers who trespass freely, embarking without violence upon "new world[s]."[76] Although it is difficult to read Richardson's description of the cinematic experience without registering the degree to which her language of expansion, limitlessness, unknown resources, and the new world resonates with the greater context of British imperial history, her imaginative deployment of it shifts the ground on which she stands. Hers is a fundamentally revisionary project that may be indebted to imperialism for its metaphorical basis, but seeks to recast it as a trope of inclusivity rather than conquest.

While Richardson does not selfconsciously invoke imperial nostalgia, what appears indisputable is the extent to which the language she relies upon to characterize her experience of the cinema is steeped in both colonial and Christian missionary discourse. If, as Richardson argues, film is the most potent civilizing influence in modernity, then as a film critic she is the medium's self-appointed civilizing agent. While Richardson does not see this as coercive, simply by identifying silent film as a civilizing force, and by equating it with femininity, the author unwittingly aligns herself with what Antoinette Burton describes as the position of British middle-class feminists: representing themselves as "agents of salvation" in a worldwide movement for "global sisterhood" by equating female emancipation with Britain's imperial mission.[77] In the film columns, in particular, Richardson privileges a model of spectatorship that is selfconsciously feminine, though not necessarily aligned with the position of the female spectator. In a 1932 essay entitled "The film gone male," Richardson valorizes silent film as "essentially feminine" because, without the distraction of any authoritative verbal text, the audience is left on its own to decipher and make sense of the overall narrative.[78]

Despite the popular embrace of the talkie (the first sound feature shown in London was in 1928), Richardson remained opposed to any cinematic sound other than musical accompaniment, arguing that because silent film privileges only one sense – vision – it requires the viewer to concentrate on the images projected on the screen until "a sufficient rousing of his collaborating creative consciousness" is achieved.[79] In contrast, the intrusion of sound invites passivity and involves the delineation of a didactic point of view, something Richardson opposed; as a result, she labels the talkie a "medium of propaganda," claiming that it fulfills a "masculine destiny."[80] By chastising the female spectator who takes up a "masculine" position, Richardson seems to de-essentialize gendered viewing positions. And yet there is sufficient evidence (in both the film columns and *Pilgrimage*) to suggest that, while Richardson's theory of spectatorship is not dependent upon bodies *per se*, for her it is women who are the more susceptible to "feminine" modes of perception; as such, they are singled out as potential vehicles of enculturation. As "humanity's silent half," women talk – may even "chatter incessantly" – but they lack men's "absolute faith in speech as a medium of communication."[81] Richardson suggests a homology between silent film and female silence: like silent film, which is distinguished by its undecidability – "its quality of being nowhere and everywhere" – women are equated with mobility and instability, being at once "anywhere and everywhere."[82]

What is striking about Richardson's characterization of space, then, is the centrality of gender to its geographical construction. By utilizing the language of infiltration – anywhere and everywhere – to describe spectatorship as a distinctly feminine practice, Richardson participates in what feminist geographers have called the production of "imperial notions of transparent space."[83] Richardson presumes that in film "the world can be apprehended as it really is" and that there can be "unmediated access to the truth of objects": in characterizing silent film as boundless, Richardson perpetuates a notion of transparent space that denies all frontiers and "tends toward homogeneity, toward a denial of difference."[84] This is most vividly reflected in Richardson's assumption that the international language of silent film is politically neutral, unmarked by cultural variance; as Bryher put it, silent films "offered a single language across Europe."[85] Yet Richardson's own language betrays how situated are her views of spectatorship: toward the end of "The film gone male," Richardson invokes the vocabulary of conquest – using terms such as "battle-ground," "rival ideologies," "civil war," "advantage," and "weapons" – to describe the conflict between silent and audible film, ultimately suggesting that, despite the ability of sound to "sway an audience in whatever direction," silent film will prevail because "[it] is the unconquerable, unchangeable eternal feminine. Influential." Whereas masculinity is disparaged as propaganda, femininity is aligned with an influence held somehow to be uncoercive. Yet the image that Richardson constructs – of a monumental "unconquerable" feminine essence – re-introduces the idea of militancy, if only to divest it of any conflict. The immediate conse-quences of these issues for a reading of *Pilgrimage* consist not just in identifying Richardson's cultural blindspots but in exploring the implications of her mapping of the feminine gaze onto transparent space. Whereas Egger argues that Richardson's conception of femininity is ultimately "outside the reaches of language and analysis," I suggest that the author's essentialist stance must be read precisely within a British context and its imbrication within the ideology of imperial expansion.To be sure, Richardson's argument that silent film functions as a universal discourse can be read as an index of her desire to break down national borders and promote cross-cultural identification, but such a perspective obscures her defining contradictions. Richardson praises silent film for "its freedom from the restrictions of language," seeing it as "more nearly universal" than other forms of communication because it can incorporate "the originality of each race unhampered by the veil of trans-lation."[86] From that perspective it appears as though Richardson's celebration of universal access genuinely values diversity. The reality, however, is very different, for when confronted with racial particularity in the first all-black sound film, *Hearts in Dixie* (1929), Richardson's response is violent opposition – an opposition framed as a response to synchronized sound, but which exposes her ideologically charged preconceptions about race. Richardson's review appears in a special issue of *Close Up* devoted to an analysis of race in the cinema, and is one of several articles that both reflect white self-consciousness concerning filmic reproductions of black stereotypes and perpetuate English racial attitudes toward blacks.[87] Richardson begins her review of *Hearts in Dixie* by acknowledging her bias – "clasping our prejudices" – an admission that works also to characterize her confrontation with the black body: "the simulacrum of a tall sad gentleman who, with voice … gave us, on behalf of the Negro race, a verbose paraphrase of Shylock's specification of the claims for the Jew to be considered human. He vanished, and here were the cotton-fields: sambos and mammies at work, piccaninnies at play – film, restored to its senses by music."[88] By likening the negro to the Jew, Richardson seeks to make a larger claim about the nature of racial inclusivity, but because her essay hinges ultimately on the erasure of black speech and the expression of dominant Anglo-Saxon racial ideas of the period, it cannot sustain this argument.[89] Richardson's description of the "Negro-bass" as "slow, enunciatory, monstrous … perfectly unintelligible," speaks to the poor quality of sound film at the time, but it also reveals what Egger has astutely described as the author's refusal to make any sense of this belabored speech.[90] Where Richardson disparages black speech for its low audibility, she is enthusiastic about the "lush chorus of Negro-laughter" which she deems "the noble partner of silent film."[91] By dismissing black speech and by celebrating the black body only when it is in motion, Richardson participates in what Donald Bogle has termed "blackface fixation," the desire for the black body to conform to classifications of racial types.[92] We see this reflected in Richardson's celebration of "Negro-dancing, of bodies whose disforming western garb could not conceal the tiger-like flow of muscles," and in her conviction that *Hearts in Dixie* is "deeply moving" only when the performers are "acting, moving, walking, singing, dancing, living … But the certainty of intermittent dialogue ruined the whole."[93] Richardson's response to racial particularity here suggests the limits of her univer-salist ideals.

No doubt, Richardson would resist a reading her of work as racially coded, for like Kenneth Macpherson, who upholds silent film as a source of "inter-racial goodwill," Richardson similarly believes that soundlessness provides all spectators – regardless of race – with a "universal language."[94] But, as Egger perceptively argues, "Richardson's high-art, silent, feminine … might properly be coded white," foregrounding the degree to which "notions of technological and racial purity are thoroughly conflated" in her work.[95] Richardson's insistence that "it is impossible both to hear and to see ... at one and the same moment" effectively silences the black body, relegating it to the realm beyond signification, and thus exposing the limits of her spectatorial paradigm.[96] That the author codes silent film as feminine and white does not confine sound to being an exclusively black signifier, despite its links to primitivist notions of the black body. Indeed, as "The film gone male" makes clear, the critique of synchronized sound is launched overtly as an attack on *gender*, not race. But ultimately, the desire to create global citizens through cinematic exposure hinges not on the incorporation of difference but on its marginalization; to that extent, Richardson's preference for silent film recalls the British feminist conviction that oppression of women is universal, transcending national and racial boundaries, even though this insistence – as feminist historians have amply shown – is based on ideas of racial segregation and purity. Beneath Richardson's abstract call for a universal conversation among film-goers is a similar investment in racial and cultural homogeneity, a desire that at times expresses itself coercively: "By whatever means, the aim is to unify."[97] Richardson's conception of spectatorship as a collaboration between the conscious and the unconscious has profound implications for the re-education of the body politic, but the actual transmission of cultural knowledge occurs at the level of the individual. Like colonialism itself, film-going is imagined to be a process of enculturation, a means through which spectators "[l]earn that we are infinitesimal parts of a vast whole."[98] The cultural trajectory that the author envisages moves from the consciousness of a single person – in *Pilgrimage*, this will be Miriam – to encompass the collectivity: "the everlasting WE who is to accomplish all this remains amidst all change and growth a single individual."[99]

Richardson describes the individual's education as a process of optical defamiliarization and amplification that bears directly on a reading of Miriam's role in *Pilgrimage*. Just as film functions as "a mirror for the customary ... restoring its essential quality," defamiliarizing the spectator's habitual world through "enforced detachment," rendering him a "disinterested observer" of his everyday context, Richardson privileges defamiliarization in the novel.[100] Richardson's image of the mirror and her focus upon the individual suggests Miriam herself, whose gaze similarly functions in the novel as a "mirror-focus"; but there, the process of mirroring is homoeroticized as it defamiliarizes all it surveys and makes newly visible that which had "grown too near and too familiar" to readers of heterosexual romance.[101] In the film columns, Richardson maintains that only through a refining of the visual register – the "elevation of the observer to ... perfect contemplation" – can one experience a "world transformed."[102] Richardson never defines the object of this contemplation, choosing instead to posit that one's attainment of the contemplative state hinges upon a shift in perspective. For Richardson, it is this perspectival shift which is the source of all growth in consciousness – and the means by which the individual, existentially displaced because of the rise of new technologies, is able to make personal use of them by locating herself in this unfamiliar universe. In *Pilgrimage* it is Miriam herself who is the embodiment of this new world – *the* "observing centre" – whose gaze attempts to counter and resist the encroachment of others, particularly men and foreigners, who seek to intrude upon its territorial expanse.[103] For Miriam, "contemplation is adventure into discovery," a visual process through which the self can conveniently "forget" its location and, like the film viewer, at once "be everywhere" (4: 657). Richardson upholds Miriam's gaze as a cultural model, investing it with uninhibited access to unexplored territories in order to suggest that femininity can infiltrate all spaces and function as the basis for a new social organization. Undeterred by the colonizing implications of Miriam's free-floating gaze, Richardson suggests, a shift in national consciousness begins, in short, with the expansion of a single woman's scopic field.

Privileging liminality: Miriam's shifting gaze

Given Richardson's tremendous investment in the cinema's transformative potential, it is perhaps perplexing to learn that Miriam never goes to the cinema. Although she takes in various other cultural events in London – she visits the British Museum, watches Shakespeare, attends a Wagner opera, views photography – Miriam never experiences the collaborative sensation of watching a silent film, even though the novel's time-frame (1893–1912) coincided with the birth of cinema in 1895. The reason for this is complicated, and has to do in part with the fact that when the novel opens Miriam is only 17, barely beyond adolescence, and therefore would have been subject to the pervasive social resistance to the idea of children attending the cinema. As Annette Kuhn has described, the cultural anxieties regarding the effects of cinema-going on children during this period were tremendous, focusing in particular upon the fear of sexual assaults in or near the cinema, the dread of contagion within an enclosed space, and the risk of eyestrain as well as other physical damage allegedly caused by film viewing.[104] For a young and inexperienced Englishwoman like Miriam, a dark cinema would have been perceived as a space of danger, even though she wanders freely throughout London by both day and night. While the question of vulnerability is certainly an issue, it does not adequately explain why Richardson would not have depicted Miriam's initial encounter with this new medium, particularly when she exposes her to other forms of visual culture. This omission becomes explicable once we realize that the novel itself is modeled on filmic experience. Richardson's narrative technique – in particular, the length and elasticity of her sentences – has, first of all, a discernibly filmic quality: rather than unfolding in a linear manner, the writing is spatial and synchronous.[105] Frequently, the author calls attention to this cinematic quality by thematizing it, so that, for example, the landscape becomes "a picture sliding away" (4: 21), or Miriam's memories unfold "like a transparent film" (4: 141). Miriam's "screened gaze" (3: 421) constantly oscillates between subject and audience, character and reader, in ways that upset conventional syntax, linearity, and closure; like silent film, moreover, the narrative is unintelligible without the collaborative effort of the reader. Richardson repeatedly calls attention to Miriam's shifting perspective – "her eyes roaming from thing to thing" (2: 68) – in order to amplify the novel's emphasis on questions of cinematic perception.

But, more fundamentally, Richardson never represents her as a film-goer because Miriam herself usurps the function of the camera, operating as a kind of living lens through which all things are filtered. Like an optical device, Miriam's gaze reflects "that strange concentration that made one see things" (2: 262). *Pilgrimage* is filled with references to Miriam's roving eyes, which often function as a kind of independent apparatus or appendage. At one point, Miriam appears to operate an optical pulley: she "drew her eyes from watching the room ... Moving about unseeing, she broke up the shape of her room and blurred its features" (3: 320). Seeming to have both weight and the quality of a zoom lens, Miriam's orbs appear palpable – "she brought her eyes back" (3: 209) – resembling a visual instrument that projects from the body. Elsewhere, Miriam's gaze seems disembodied, working almost autonomously: "There were other eyes looking at it. They were inside her ... dragging her away" (2: 109). Even Miriam's body resembles a cinematic apparatus, a permeable surface through which "some source of light within her" (2: 392) emanates, while her "eyelids were transparent ... light filtering through" (2: 231) as it does from a movie projector. Richardson often distinguishes between Miriam's gaze and the "inner channels of her eyes" (2: 318), suggesting that within her is another source of perception: a kind of Emersonian transparent eyeball that is not subject to the constraints of the physical body.[106] The text analogizes the expansion of Miriam's visual field and the development of her identity, and mirroring images are frequently utilized to signal the young woman's coming to consciousness: "She hunted out her handglass and consulted her unknown eyes ... brown; not grey ... her unknown self" (3: 337). The reference to eyes here suggests an undeveloped subjectivity – a diffuse rather than unitary sense of self – which is amplified when Richardson shifts from first- to third-person pronouns to convey Miriam's sense of visual detachment: "I always forget that I am visible. She called in her eyes" (3: 71). That Richardson characterizes Miriam as a "blind spectator" (3: 384), or a woman whose eyes are both "seeing and unseeing" (4: 21), speaks to her heroine's conceptual limitations and exposes the ironic distance between author and character that so many readers seek to conflate. A telling detail is that Miriam has "severe myopic astigmatism" (1: 129), a nearsightedness requiring her use of glasses – or risking the loss of half her vision. Miriam's condition is material evidence of her frequent obtuseness and lack of foresight, made explicit when she pauses to read a billboard for "Eye Treatment" (1: 195). Yet where Miriam's myopia can be read as mere short-sightedness, her astigmatism – an aberration of the lens that results in multiple points of focus– is indicative of her ceaseless mobility and her refusal to be fixed. To that extent, Miriam's glasses can be said to signify not a "deficiency in seeing but an active looking."[107] Richardson's use of cinematic discourse provides a language for Miriam's emerging selfconsciousness, giving shape to her nascent identity during a historical period in which one of the great social and political concerns was women's struggle to change their conditions and definition.

Within the imaginative structure of the novel, in which the upper-class British male represents the prototypical citizen, Miriam suffers from two fixed disqualifications for full citizenship: her femininity, and her working-class status. That Miriam "seemed to be looking with a hundred eyes, multitudinously, seeing each thing from several points at once" (3: 324), suggests not just the eye of a camera but a woman whose social location has been in flux since her father's bankruptcy forced her into an uncertain lower-class job market. *Pilgrimage* reveals the centrality of the visual to Miriam's exploration of gender, class, and national affiliation, depicting a parallel between her perpetually shifting gaze and an equivocal relation to these categories. Given her distance from *ideal* Englishness, Miriam must imaginatively resituate her cultural marginality to qualify herself as a legitimate British citizen. Although the last thing that one might expect is for Miriam to find this solution in lesbianism (which, as another stigmatized social identity, would appear to be merely an additional disqualification for ideal citizenship), this is precisely what *Pilgrimage* proposes. As I show in the sections which follow, Richardson accomplishes this unlikely retooling of homosexuality as the mechanism for Miriam's national inclusion in two ways. First, she minimizes the disqualifying aspects of lesbianism by never fully embodying it, and thereby avoiding its stigma. Second, she maximizes two aspects of lesbian identity that were prominent during the period – the idea of sameness underlying woman-to-woman erotic bonds, and the notion of the lesbian as border crosser – each of which resonates with her collectivist and internationalist vision. Together, these two dimensions allow Richardson to craft the homoerotic as the imaginative basis for her larger ideal of a homogenized collectivity of citizens. To be sure, Richardson begins by attempting to redefine femininity broadly as a model of ideal citizenship on the grounds of its opposition to the monomania associated with masculinity. But her turn toward lesbians suggests that the limits placed upon heterosexual women undermine their success as border crossers. By contrast, to the extent that homosexuality is tied up with the notion of national indeterminacy in the novel, lesbian subjectivity can be said to constitute its own meta-nation. As I will show, however, Richardson's apparently progressive aspirations for the lesbian as the exemplary British citizen are mitigated by the simultaneously conservative discourse she employs to represent that figure. Significantly, Miriam herself gazes not only with the eyes of a border-crossing "stranger" (1: 180), but also "with English eyes" (2: 426) that underscore her role as visual ethnographer, documenting the meaning of the Englishwoman's experience of modernity. Female spectatorship is crucial to Miriam's quest for self-legitimacy, for it is linked to the higher currency of the imagination and it enables her to circumvent the pathologizing discourse that inheres to lesbian embodiment.

The first example we have that demonstrates this constellation is Miriam's position as a quasi-governess in Hannover, where she threatens the established order by exposing her homosexual potential in visual terms. Like the Victorian governess, Miriam is a figure of contradiction, occupying the boundary between the gentlewoman and the working-class servant.[108] Richardson both exploits and subverts the association between the governess and female promiscuity, portraying the sexually inexperienced Miriam – the supposed guardian of class and sexual order – as a figure who seeks to destabilize heterosexuality. To the extent that Richardson represents Miriam's desire for other women in terms of a scopophilic longing, she would appear to problematize Terry Castle's argument that lesbianism "may be sensed but never *seen*."[109] This will be further complicated later, but here, circulating within the homosocial world of women and young girls at the Waldstrasse school, Miriam fixes her gaze upon the group: "[she] met eye after eye – how beautiful they all were … her eyes came back unembarrassed" (1: 140). Miriam's frank observation gives rise to her first homoerotic twinges when she is attracted to a student, Ulrica:

"[She] fed upon the outlines of her head ... wished she could ... gaze undisturbed into the eyes" (1: 97). Later, during charades, Miriam encourages Ulrica to join the game "[j]ust to have her to look at" (1: 108), casting her as Juliet in Shakespeare's balcony scene, while she herself takes on the role of Romeo – gazing up at her beloved.[110] The scenes with Ulrica are crucial because they establish Miriam's erotic possibility via saturated visual encounters, countering the pervasive critical assumption that because she expresses no heterosexual desire she is an asexual figure. At one point Ulrica reads a poem aloud, her voice so "rich and full and liquid" that it shakes Miriam's body, filling the room with "despairing ululation." Miriam hears no words, only sound, and wishes that "the eyes could be raised ... to hers and that she could go and put her hands about the beautiful head ... and say ... 'I will stay with you always'" (1: 99). This representation of Miriam's sexual susceptibility to Ulrica as a form of mirroring presages her later infatuation with Amabel and Jean, both of whom function as sapphic signifiers and are, as we shall see, similarly linked with vision (as the means through which sexual sameness is conveyed) and a signifying practice that is outside of conventional discourse.

Miriam's self-masculinization as Romeo is not an isolated incident, but is variously replayed throughout the narrative as she oscillates between the two genders. Although consistently attracted to women, Miriam is at the same time highly critical of them, and, despite her rebellion against patriarchal conventions, it is men with whom she most clearly identifies. Richardson identifies Miriam's gender mobility, as expressed in her intellectual pursuits, as a consequence of her "masculine mind" (3: 236) – but it is also a result of her critique of the social construction of femininity. Richardson's representation of femininity as spectacle anticipates Joan Riviere's argument that the masquerade of womanliness is constituted through a hyperbolizing of the trappings of femininity.[111] We see a good example of this in the scene where Miriam observes a strange photograph of an Englishwoman in Grecian drapery. The woman's head is thrown back, her eyes stare up into the sky, and the inscription beneath the image reads "Inspiration." What this staged photograph conveys to Miriam is the performative nature of femininity: "She was not a woman, she was a *woman* ... men liked actresses" (1: 400). Miriam reads women's preoccupation with beauty to be a result of external regulation of the female body, identifying men as "complacent idiots" (2: 106) because they insist on making women, as the photograph testifies, into spectacles, "object[s] of romantic veneration" (2: 389). While women may appear to be focused on self-modification, Richardson suggests, it is only because men regulate the practice of femininity by demanding the masquerade. Miriam's observation that women never speak "what they thought or felt, but always things that sounded like quotations from men" (2: 251) casts women in the ventriloquizing role of female impersonator, pleasing men visually and sexually through the pursuit of a feminine ideal. Donna Haraway's argument that "[v]ision is *always* a question of the power to see" because the Western eye has often been insistent on "having mirrors for a conquering self," provides one way of understanding the violence implicit in men's visualizing practices in *Pilgrimage*.[112]

A second, equally important, moment that elaborates this relation between femininity and spectacle is the scene in which Miriam, with Mr. Hancock, attends a lecture at the Royal Institute on the new photographic technique of Daguerre. As

Miriam's thoughts shift back and forth between the images she perceives and Mr. Hancock's observation of a young woman in the audience, the text forges an association between female spectatorship and a critique of the social construction of femininity. Just as the lights are beginning to dim, Mr. Hancock admires an attractive woman who Miriam immediately identifies as a walking endorsement of femininity: "[it] was just an effect, a deliberate 'charming' ... advertising effect" (2: 105). Unable to reproduce this homogenized visual image, Miriam feels both critical and inadequate; her thoughts shift back and forth between the woman singled out by Mr. Hancock and Daguerre – the process through which sunlight is refracted and broken up to create filmy black-and-white images on glass. Through a series of multiple voyeuristic displacements – Miriam watches her employer watch the woman in the audience who watches the screen – Miriam's thoughts about this woman focus upon her self-imposition as spectacle, deliberately imposing herself on the scene: such "'women will talk shamelessly at a concert or an opera, and chatter on a mountain top in the presence of a magnificent panorama'" (2: 106). Miriam's remark here recalls Richardson's commentary in *Close Up* in which she critiques the female viewer on the grounds that she utilizes her spectatorial position to foreground her own subjectivity, rather than allowing the art to dominate.[113] But, whereas in the film column Richardson masculinizes the female spectator who seeks to foreground her subjectivity, in the novel it is men who are blamed for making spectacles of women, "treat[ing] them as works of art" and forcing them to *exhibit* their bodies (2: 106), while women remain vigilant observers of themselves. As Miriam's thoughts drift back to the images of Daguerre, she overhears Mr. Hancock praise the wonderful scientific achievement being projected onto the screen, musing that "there was something else ... there, that he did not see" (2: 107).

Miriam's observation here that women see things which elude male spectators is invoked throughout *Pilgrimage* in terms that explicitly critique masculine perception – "the blindness in men ... about women" (3: 256). Her focus upon men's limited visual range – "man is a badly made machine ... an oculist could improve upon [his] human eye" (2: 408) – suggests that, in order for women to *see* more clearly, they must radically separate themselves from "the clumsy masculine machinery of observation" (4: 315). This belief is reflected in the scene in which Miriam's expansive appreciation of the rich-colored images contrasts sharply with Mr. Hancock's partial perspective. For her, the colorful shapes provide a springboard to think about "something one sometimes *saw* when it wasn't there" (2: 107). The problem with men, in other words, is that they perceive only what's before them, whereas "[w]omen *see* things when they are not there. That's creativeness" (3: 259). The assertion that women see the relationship between things – "the relations of things which don't change, more than things which are always changing" (3: 259) – recalls Richardson's remarks about female spectatorship in "The film gone male," in which women are similarly praised for their "awareness of being, as distinct from man's awareness of becoming."[114] Like Richardson, Miriam is critical of men's focus upon "becoming" rather than "being," that is, their inability to live in the present: "Men ... never *are*. They only make or do ... That would explain their *ambition*" (3: 280–1). In the film article, it is femininity that is lauded for its ability to evoke what Richardson calls "the changeless being at the heart of all becoming."[115]

While this comment may sound somewhat cryptic and mysterious to contemporary ears, when read alongside *Pilgrimage*, what emerges is a portrait of femininity that privileges an alternative system of knowledge, one based not on totalization and single vision – which Miriam aligns with masculinity – but on multidimensional viewing. Miriam's reference to the Daguerre images as "brilliant unearthly pictures" (2: 108) situates her as a visionary who sees into another dimension, a role that she will embrace more fully when she becomes erotically involved with Jean and also joins a Quaker community. What Miriam offers is a radically different perspective, one that privileges a split and contradictory self, and urges new ways of looking at the world; as she herself says to Michael, as part of her critique of masculine sight: "It's no good looking, with no matter *what* eyes, if you look in the wrong place" (3: 256). By interweaving Miriam's thoughts on Daguerre with her critique of the social construction of femininity, Richardson forges an association between the new technologies of vision (such as photography and the cinema) and the hope for transformative knowledge embodied in the female spectator. Importantly, Miriam revises her earlier characterization of the woman in the audience at the Daguerre presentation as the one who chatters at the top of a mountain to privilege precisely that panoramic capacity of the female spectator; women "were like people who had climbed a hill and were eagerly intent on what they could see on the other side" (2: 354).

Richardson does not so much define what's on the other side of the mountain as critique what's already in full view; for Miriam, what that means is compulsory heterosexuality, as well as various other "masculine systems of thought" (4: 378) which have impeded women historically. Miriam's criticism of the domestic life as the "troglodyte life" (4: 488), through which "millions of women [are] serving life sentences" (4: 454) as hostesses to husbands and fathers, singles out women as the "enforcers of … the dictum that women exist in order to please men."[116] The real project of *Pilgrimage*, however, is not to vilify women but to expose the systemic and crippling effects of patriarchy as it has infiltrated all areas of existence – particularly science, language, art, and religion. Richardson is careful to situate Miriam's violent reaction to men – "[they] ought to be horsewhipped" (1: 423) – within the larger framework of late nineteenth- and early twentieth-century discourses on female inferiority, providing a window into the obstacles that British women faced while situating themselves as citizens in the period. A prime example of this is when Miriam looks up the entry on "Woman" in the encyclopedia, uncovering a range of misogynistic sexological preconceptions (2: 220).[117] Miriam's dismissal of scientific inquiry as "[c]enturies of unopposed masculine gossip about the universe" (3: 367) speaks to her view that male objectivity is an optical illusion, a kind of "maiming aperture" (2: 316), with direct consequences for the cultural interpretation of the female body. Miriam's observation of Hypo captures the partiality of male sight succinctly: his "filmy sightless grey [eyes] – fixed always on the … mass of obstructive mannish knowledge, always on *science*" (3: 354). What Miriam calls "man's massive unconsciousness" (3: 459) is perhaps best conveyed in an image that unintentionally invokes this one-dimensional perspective, that of the "amoebae, awful determined unconscious … octopuses … frightful things with one eye, tentacles, poison-sacs" (2: 317). This grotesque image conjoins the monocularity of men's perspective with the danger latent in their objectification of both women and the world. It is thus not surprising to find Miriam later reflecting on the oppressiveness of the male gaze: "Men … looking out at women … with one unvarying eye … no escape from its horrible blindness" (3: 208). Miriam's remark about the one-eyed creatures – "They were civilization" – suggests that this monstrousness is both pervasive and endemic to masculine British culture, for the poisoned-sac octopus recalls her earlier conclusion: "Life is poisoned, for women, at the very source" (2: 222).

Cosmopolis, Englishness, and the Jews: the crisis of national affiliation

In a characteristically dialectical gesture, Richardson problematizes the idea of civilization: it is portrayed, on the one hand, as toxic because it is masculine and, on the other hand, as redemptive because of its link with the interior life of women. Importantly, this gendered bi-polarity is sustained through visual means: the edifices of masculine civilization are visible to the eye, whereas feminine civilization can be accessed only through internalized modes of perception. Women occupy both physical and figurative space (as opposed to the exclusively physical spaces reserved for men), a privileged position of simultaneity that is formally enacted through the doubleness of Richardson's spatial metaphors. For example, as Miriam sits in her London bedroom and listens to music, she experiences one of her "expansive moments" (2: 282) in which time and space contract: the music "came far back amongst the generations where everything was different; telling you that they were the same" (2: 301). This elastic yet static moment is notable for its representation of both temporal simultaneity and historical compression, leading one to ask: if distinct historical periods are merely interchangeable, then what does this say about cultural and racial difference? Miriam's notion of civilization as a cross-cultural, transhistorical continuum seems at odds with the novel's obsessive attention to historical specificity, yet it is precisely in encountering local difference, *Pilgrimage* suggests, that an essential homogeneity is revealed. This notion of a synchronous, collective, cultural identity – what Miriam calls the "astonishingness of … find[ing] the same world … in someone else" (4: 333) – exposes her Anglocentrism, for it aligns her with the principle of Englishness that fueled imperial rule: people distant from one another in space (and, of course, culture) may be subsumed under an emphatically British conception of their potential commonalities.[118] Richardson herself exposes the coercive terms that inform this imperative of uniformity when she represents London, the imperium, as a boundless space that has the "power to evoke the continuous moment that was always and everywhere the same" (4: 176). The novel's engagement with the ideas of collectivity and simultaneity, then, are rhetorically undergirded by the globalizing imperatives of empire, recalling the silent-film articles in which Richardson equates the desirability of international exchange with the promotion of cultural homogeneity.

Yet *Pilgrimage* does not promote a simplistic model of community; on the contrary, the novel sustains a dialectical relation between Miriam's collaborative and oppositional responses to the idea of national belonging, a tension that arises specifically from her culturally liminal position as Englishwoman. Miriam fetishizes the idea of a common culture, but not the homogeneous nation that has been conceived by men. Rather, her fantasy of a transcendent subjectivity that exists beyond race, nation, and creed enshrines the values of femininity even as it recapitulates English notions of sameness. Thus, Miriam is able simultaneously to insist upon the transcendence of nationality and to recapitulate, rhetorically, the outward spatial expansion that marks her as singularly English. We see this in Miriam's desire for "a single world holding all the possible variations of everything at once" (2: 93), for that vision of global unity is problematized by her inability, finally, to incorporate those whom she regards as racially other. The Jews are the paradigmatic Other for Miriam in this text, for they both threaten to destabilize her Englishness at the same time as they enable her to consolidate her English self against their alterity. A salient example of Miriam's bifurcated attitude toward global unity, and the gendered implications of that equivocation, occurs in her thoughts on cosmopolitanism. As Miriam meditates on the word "cosmopolis," she imagines a map of Europe in which London, Paris, and Berlin are conjoined: "All over the globe ... people who read and thought, making a network of unanimous culture" (2: 342). Initially comforted by this image of transnational exchange in which distinct cultures "arrived independently at the same conclusions in different languages," Miriam embraces a more critical view when she maintains that it would be through "the world of science [that] they communicated with each other" (2: 343). Thus, she distances herself from this idea of a single masculinized culture, concluding that if the world were to become "all one piece" it would be a disaster, resulting in a form of cultural imperialism in which English would inevitably displace all foreign languages: "Anglo-Saxon supremacy. 'England and America together could rule the world'" (2: 342). Miriam's feelings vacillate between security – comfort at the thought of this linguistic domination, thinking that it would be "like a police station ... wonderful to belong to the race whose language was spoken, all over the world" – and a dreadful sense of loss at the prospect of a cultural assimilation in which every foreigner would simply have to "become English" (2: 343–4). As Miriam is exposed to class and regional differences, she appears to gravitate toward the more inclusive perspective: "when people discuss the possibility of English becoming a world speech, I always wonder which English they have in mind" (4: 164). However, she does not uphold this view in the balance of the text.

Despite Richardson's critique of the conventions of the English language on the grounds that it functions as a form of British cultural imperialism and is a reflection of masculine discourse – "To write books, knowing all about style, would be to become like a man" (2: 131) – Miriam's boastfulness about Anglo-Saxon supremacy is not altogether invalidated by the novel. She at times functions as a self-appointed arbiter of linguistic standards, upholding "the right pronunciation" (1: 378) even when it implicates the English themselves as cultural imperialists. In a conversation with Mr. Lintoff – a Russian revolutionary and college friend of Michael – Miriam recoils at the thought of Cockney or London–Essex accents permeating English culture. Her insistence that "deformed speech is increasing" is a critique of the English who allow their own language to be cannibalized, but it is also an attack on "unapprehensive foreigners" such as Michael and Lintoff who, oblivious to the insidious effects of "the horror," would allow all sorts of linguistic mutilations to be disseminated by the masses (3: 318–9).[119] In effect, Miriam's response suggests that the racial and cultural purity of authentic English is being defiled by the infiltration of foreigners. It is telling that Miriam's insistence "there *is* a cosmopolis" (2: 343) is framed as a response to Bernard Mendizabal, "[a] *Jew*" (2: 434), whom she dismisses as "another of those foreigners who care for nothing in England but practising English" (2: 343). As this small detail demonstrates, it is the moments in which Miriam feels threatened by opposing cultural voices that she most vehemently defends English and expresses deeply embedded notions of British superiority. While the tension between assimilation and segregation is sustained throughout much of *Pilgrimage*, Miriam's investment in cosmopolis as a cultural model that touts the "sympathy between races" (2: 344) is ultimately at odds with the text's representation of her repudiation of cultural difference. Although Miriam's interest in cosmopolitanism is what attracts her to Jewishness, which represents the possibility of international culture beyond national borders, her nationalist sympathies cannot imagine such a culture outside of the terms of British imperialism itself.

Whereas in the film columns what is most highly valued is cultural homo-geneity and the transcending of nationality, what Miriam *seems* to promote in *Pilgrimage* is a visually inflected notion of cultural diversity. Even when visual metaphors do not appear to be significant, as in Miriam's dialogue about cosmo-politanism, the centrality of the image is still invoked through her moments of cognitive mapping – what she calls her "love" of "filling … empty space … by imagining [herself] going on and on through it, endless space" (2: 93). Such instances of spatial appropriation must be read within the wider context of Miriam's search for the meaning of nationhood – "What is England? What do the qualities mean?" (3: 113) – for her boundary crossing is ultimately inseparable from her quest to legitimize the perspective of the white middle-class British woman, disenfranchised by the State until women's full suffrage was achieved in 1928, some time after the novel's closing context of 1912. Although Miriam is dismissive about the (relative) merits of the vote because she sees the system as a masculine construct, at the same time she assumes the role of moral (rather than legal) guardian of the race: "Keeping an eye on injustices" (3: 492) done to women. Simultaneously, however, Miriam's contempt for Englishwomen and her ambivalent relation to her own Englishness complicate her identification with the nation, and express themselves, too, in ambivalence toward other cultures, particularly the Jews. We see, for example, that when Miriam is in Germany and surrounded by a populace who look very much like she does, she feels at liberty to critique England and distance herself from the parochialism of "the English way" (1: 335). Miriam even upholds German women as superior to Englishwomen, regarding them as less constrained and less self-conscious, so that when Fräulein Pfaff remarks "'I think you have something of the German in you'" (1: 155), Miriam receives it as a compliment: "I *am* German-looking to-day, pinky red, and yellow hair" (1: 150–1). This fluid understanding of national identity, in which the self constructs itself through the gaze of another – what Richardson elsewhere calls Miriam's admission of "her identity, seeing herself as she was being seen" (4: 32) – is possible only when there is no real threat of cultural assimilation. In Hannover, Miriam is able both to critique English culture and to celebrate "wonderful Germany" (1: 66) precisely because the Germans do not seem, as do the Jews, to be racially other.

What *Pilgrimage* illustrates through its representation of Miriam is the degree to which "her English heredity" (3: 151) is relational and unstable. We see this reflected in Miriam's response to Mendizabal, whose romantic interest in her creates a scandal at the boarding house, where Mrs. Bailey fears that Miriam's association with a Jew will tarnish her reputation and ruin her chances of marrying Dr. Von Heber, a Canadian. Although Miriam expresses no interest in becoming Von Heber's wife, his nationality contrasts sharply with Mendizabal's outcast status – the "wicked fast little foreigner" (2: 395) – and throws Miriam's Englishness into relief. As she walks to meet Mendizabal for dinner at Ruscino's, a continental café heavily coded as an illicit space, Miriam imagines herself "bearing within her in secret unfathomable abundance the gift of ideal old-English rose and white gracious adorable womanhood given her by Dr. Heber" (2: 393). Despite her earlier critique of the "awfulness of Englishwomen" (1: 336), Miriam here embraces the role of English lady: Von Heber's position as a colonial subject situates him as a stand-in for the Englishman, reassuring her of her national and racial privilege. But what is equally important is Mendizabal's Jewishness, against which Miriam constructs herself. At Ruscino's, surrounded by a non-British clientele, Miriam feels like an interloper, a foreigner, who filters the experience through an English lens, observing "a spectacle she could not witness without contamination" (2: 394). The most marked example of this "contamination" is Miriam's relationship with Michael Shatov, a brilliant Russian Jewish émigré to whom she gives tuition in English. Although Miriam admires Michael's "encyclopedic Jewish mind" (3: 295), she ultimately finds him inassimilable, "completely foreign, a mind from an unknown world" (3: 113). For Miriam, this socialist Zionist harbors a "hidden flaw" (3: 193), which is to say, "the unmanageable burden of his Jewishness" (3: 305).

To the extent that Richardson reproduces deeply embedded stereotypes of the Jew, bound up with notions of degeneration and infection, she shares with several of her modernist contemporaries the fear of Semitic "contamination."[120] We see, for example, evidence of Miriam's anti-Semitism even before she encounters Michael – such as in the scene at Wordsworth House, when she refers to the "clever watchful eyes of the cheating little Jewess" (1: 353), or the moment at the dental surgery when she refers to a patient as "'jolly kike'" in response to her employer's question "'Kike?'" (2: 69). The text rarely registers such moments as racial slurs, and instead represents the difference between Jew and non-Jew as "something essential … that could not be shelved" (3: 262). Miriam's rejection of Michael hinges ultimately on this essentialized view of the unassimilability of his racial otherness, for despite the odd moments in which she re-imagines him as a Frenchman – thus reconstructing him as a tolerable suitor – he remains for her the "disreputable foreigner" (3: 55), the Jewish Other whose difference cannot be absorbed. The only moment in the text in which Michael's presence is completely "shorn of its alien quality" (3: 217) is the scene in which he and Miriam visit a dank London teashop and observe a black man at a nearby table. Richardson's use of primitivist discourse to describe this "snorting and devouring" figure is consistent with her racist treatment of the black body in her film columns. Here, Miriam sits paralyzed, "frozen, appalled by the presence of the negro," experiencing an oppressive sense of "contamination. It *was* contamination. The man's presence was an outrage" (3: 217).[121] For a brief moment Michael's Jewishness is no longer a pollutant, for Miriam displaces his Otherness on to the black body and aligns Michael with her Englishness, reconstructing him as both white and European: "He was an Englishman in the fact that he and she could *not* sit eating in the neighborhood of this marshy jungle" (3: 217). That the racial identity of the Jew is not a stable category is evidenced, too, by an earlier moment, when Miriam and Michael visit a German restaurant in London's east end. When Michael discloses to her that nearly all the patrons are Jews, Miriam's shock is framed as a racialized response: "'Jews? But they are nearly all *fair!*'" (3: 127). Even though Michael corrects her misconception, assuring her that many Jews are fair, Miriam dismisses the information; as a result, she re-appraises the room and on second glance registers that nearly all the people there are dark. Richardson's move here is consistent with her day's racialized representations of Jews, with what Bryan Cheyette calls the "ambivalent positioning of 'the Jew' in terms of a racialized 'black-ness'."[122] At the same time that Miriam positions the Jew as black, she still manages to invoke an anti-Semitic slur: "But there were no hooked noses; no one in the least like Shylock. What *were* Jews? ... Why did the idea cast a chill ...?" (3: 127).[123]

   Jacqueline Rose provides a useful historical context for a reading of the figure of Michael Shatov, demonstrating that one of the most pressing concerns in England during the period in which his relationship with Miriam transpires (1900–5) was the question of the place of the Jews within English culture.[124] Richardson engages with this debate by pitting Michael against Miriam, staging a series of conversations in which he defends Jewish separatism, predicting that England will have its anti-Semitic movement, while she upholds an assimilationist model, believing in the English tolerance of the Jews. Miriam's arguments against Zionism are grounded in her naïve belief that "'England can assimilate anything'" (2: 167), ironically, despite her own inability to incorporate Michael's otherness. The only way in which Miriam can conceptualize Michael as a potential mate is through his Anglicization: "Not again could she suffer his nearness, until the foreigner in him, dipped every day more deeply into the well of English feeling, should be changed" (3: 197). Yet the problem, as Miriam perceives it, is that Michael's Jewish parti-cularity ultimately contradicts the possibility of his incorporation. Michael himself acknowledges this racial prejudice when he asserts that British "Jews [are] not Englishmen" (3: 167). Homi Bhabha's argument about the "double vision" of racial discourse is useful for an understanding of Miriam's attitude toward Michael: despite her desire to assimilate him into British culture, he remains for her precariously on the borders of empire – "to be Anglicized ... is *emphatically* not to be English."[125] Michael's conviction that "'[n]o nation can assimilate the Jew'" (3: 167) speaks to his belief in cultural separateness, but it also – unwittingly – reproduces the ideology of racial exclusion that, as Miriam's response reflects, was deeply entrenched in British culture.[126] To the extent that Miriam's expulsion of Michael hinges ultimately on her perception that "the foreigner of foreigners is the perfectly alien Jew" (3: 376) she functions as a kind of embodiment of Englishness, insisting on Jewish unassimilability. We see this amplified in Miriam's visit with Mrs. Bergstein, an

Englishwoman who has married a Jew, to discuss intermarriage. As Miriam rings the bell to the Bergsteins' home, she feels a surge of nationalism: "she was *England*, a link in the world-wide being of England and the English life" (3: 224). Again constructing herself against Jewishness, Miriam here identifies with a country that she elsewhere disparages, while once inside the home, where the matter of Jewish conversion is discussed, Miriam identifies with Mrs. Bergstein, seeing the two of them as mutual "outcasts" from the "warm magic circle of English life" (3: 228). Significantly, after Miriam's departure from Mrs. Bergstein's home, her anxieties about Michael and intermarriage are expressed as a racialized fear of isolationism: when she envisages herself alone with him, "the troubled darkness … would return," reminding her of the "world's condemnation" and propelling her toward the "darkest centre" (3: 229) – away from the light that is England.

Just as Miriam's perception of Michael's Jewishness is variable and contingent, her identification as a national subject is both fluid and unstable, even in instances where she seems to embody the role of micro-nation. Rose's suggestion that Miriam's characterization as "distanced, alien, estranged in herself" positions her as "something … of a Jew" makes a certain sense, particularly if we consider that both the Jew and the woman function as cultural outsiders in the text, and that Miriam is a Jewish name.[127] To be sure, the conventional association of the figure of the Jew with homelessness and wandering speaks to Miriam's own displaced position, in which she is essentially nowhere at home. Yet this identification of Miriam as a Jew minimizes her anti-Semitism, especially her contempt for Jewish women (3: 221), and neglects the ample textual evidence that Miriam is a "mass of British prejudice" (3: 253).[128] At the same time, Rose's observation shrewdly exposes Richardson's unarticulated assumption about modernity in *Pilgrimage*: "Supra-national or micro-national, what is crucial is that in neither case does the Jew (or woman) *belong*."[129] Cheyette sees Richardson's simultaneous attraction to and repulsion by the figure of the Jew as replicating the depiction of several of her male imperialist counter-parts, reading the scene in which Miriam displaces her antipathy for Michael's Jewishness on to the contaminating black body as a prime example of the bourgeois woman's identification with "the potentially 'liberating' Other."[130] As Cheyette points out, the scene with the black man occurs in the context of a longer and charged discussion between Miriam and Michael concerning the role of women in society. Miriam's irritation with Michael's claim to be a feminist, and her resentment of his view that women are inferior beings, reaches an apex in the teashop scene when – in the "awful presence" of the black man – she articulates her "best, most liberating words" (3: 219) to Michael: that they are fundamentally dissimilar, occupy different worlds, and are incapable of communication. The "monstrous" and "crude male" body here has a mediating function, facilitating what had up to now been largely repressed in Miriam: "he had helped her," despite "his blind unconscious[ness]" (3: 219). This scene is crucial both in its representation of Miriam's appropriation of the Other as a conduit for liberatory speech and in its staging of her divestiture of Michael's "alien qualities," demonstrating the instability and contextual nature of her identification with and differentiation of herself from the figure of the Jew. However, Cheyette's argument that Miriam's displacement enables her to trans-form Michael, not only from Jew to non-Jew but "from being black to being white and, by extension, from being male to female,"[131] elides a crucial distinction that Richardson sustains between masculinity and femininity. While Miriam clearly re-invents Michael as an Englishman, her feminization of him – often referring to him as childlike, delicate, and little – is superseded by her repudiation of his relentless masculinity. While the Anglo-Jewish debate is played out in miniature through the couple's dialogues, Miriam's resistance to Michael is not only a rejection of his alternate world of Zionists and Russian revolutionaries, but a condemnation of his masculine privilege.

The novel's preoccupation with vision, particularly the "horrible blindness" (3: 208) of the male perspective, is recapitulated in Miriam's response to Michael: his obsession with Jewish racial destiny is dismissed as his inability, quite literally, to perceive the individual. Miriam's conclusion that she and Michael "'are living in two utterly different worlds'" (3: 219) is grounded in their most critical area of divergence: his investment in an ideology of racial exclusion – in his words, "'I ... [am] one who believes in the *race*'" – and her insistence that "'the race is nothing without individuals'" (3: 150). Although this appears to be a rather paradoxical position for Miriam to uphold, given her inability to see *him* as anything other than a representative Jew, it is consistent with her refusal elsewhere to align herself with any special-interest group or cause, and is, moreover, another reflection of her liberal humanist commitment to the sovereignty of the individual. Michael's "unseeing gaze" (3: 242) stems from his perception of Miriam as merely an embodi-ment of her country, a "proud English possession" (3: 291) to be consumed. Despite his ambivalence toward the British, Michael trades on the patriarchal construction of woman as "English spectacle" (3: 292). Miriam herself fully registers the national dimension of this heterosexual fantasy: "All her meaning for him was her English heredity, a thing she seemed to think the finest luck in the world ... That was it; he gave her her nationality" (3: 151). This reference to nationality has a double meaning, for on the one hand, under British law, Miriam would in effect become a Russian citizen were she to marry Michael. On the other hand, the reference to Michael "giving her her nationality" also speaks to what we have seen to be Miriam's con-solidation of an English self against the threat of Jewish encroachment. Although Miriam does reflect upon the fraudulence of this perspective, thinking that "just sitting there basking in being English ... was too easy" (3: 151), we see repeated evidence that national identity is constructed through the refraction of the other's gaze, whether that look is based on identification or on established racial difference. Thus, in Michael's presence, Miriam's "inexorable Englishness" (3: 292) is amplified, while her gaze functions as a projection screen for his own misidentification: "*I am a Jew ... It is your eyes. I must see them always ... I am even willing to renounce my Judaism*" (3: 228).

Consistent with the novel's preoccupation with spectatorship, Miriam's rejec-tion of Michael is framed as a repudiation of his point of view: her "shifting visions" (3: 304) clash irreconcilably with his monocular perspective on Jewish destiny. As a result, Miriam's disentanglement from the relationship is expressed as a refusal to subordinate her gaze to his visualization of a Zionist future: "no longer trying to see with his eyes, while still hoarding, as a contrasting amplification of her own visions, much that he had given her" (3: 255). Even Michael's offer to renounce his Judaism

is not enough for Miriam, who remains unable to incorporate his "alien unaccep-
tables" (4: 416), her blanket term for his unassimilability, which includes a vital area
of contention: her inability to fathom herself as the mother of Jewish children.
Rose's argument that the opposition between assimilation and Zionism in the
novel is "overlaid with the proto-feminist opposition between the individual and
the race" situates Miriam in relation to the eugenicist theory of motherhood which
stressed the importance of fertility for the future of the British race.[132] Rose reads
Miriam's reproductive refusal – "'I *couldn't* have Jewish children'" (3: 260) – as a
rejection of a eugenics that is steeped in the language of anti-Semitism, and to the
extent that the rhetoric of eugenics invokes the notion of racial destiny, the
equation makes sense. But there is a crucial difference here as well: Miriam's
rejection of racial motherhood[133] is not a repudiation of the *British* ideal of national
responsibility, but a refusal of *Jewish* race preservation, a concept she associates
with death, not regeneration. Thus Miriam perceives Michael's obsession with "the
race" as "an endless succession of people made in God's image, all dead or dying" (4:
155), while his own countenance resembles an unseeing "Jewish death-mask" (4:
288) because of his plea, informed by the ideas of Theodor Herzl, for anti-
assimilationist Zionism. Miriam's belief that having children with Michael is a
dead-end, that it would only shelve "the problem, leaving it for the next generation
to solve" (3: 262), does not however occlude her interest in reproducing British
citizens.

   This is not to say that Miriam is a rabid eugenicist, but only that her repudiation of Michael's notion of racial destiny should not be read as a rejection of
maternity altogether. It is instructive to contrast her refusal of the position of Jewish
mother with the scene in which she writes a "joyous message" (4: 280) to Hypo
about her pregnancy with their child. Miriam refers to her conception as a "strange
blissful intensity of … vibrating particles," claiming that there are no words to
describe the "miracle" and "mystery" (4: 280) within her body. Miriam's awe and
contentment are attributable to her recognition that, with Hypo, she would be
reproducing a British citizen – not the "beady eye[d]" (4: 294) offspring of a Jew.
Hypo Wilson, as critics have observed, is a fictionalization of Richardson's real-life
lover, H.G. Wells: like Wells, Wilson is a rationalist who advocates scientific
socialism, practices free love, and believes that reproduction is a woman's duty –
essential to the racial health of the nation.[134] Miriam composes her pregnancy letter
to Hypo in 1907, just one year before the formation of the British Eugenics Education Society, a vast assemblage of groups worried about the reproductive habits of
Englishwomen. Although the text itself makes no reference to this organization,
Miriam and Hypo frequent Lycurgan socialist meetings – Richardson's fictionalization of the Fabian Society – an organization that overtly allied itself with
eugenicist ideology.[135] Reflecting on her role as a Lycurgan, Miriam utilizes the
language of territorial expansionism to characterize the aims of this "small exclusive
group" to grow – and to make "a new world" (3: 286).

   To be sure, Miriam sometimes expresses anti-eugenicist arguments: "'I don't
care a button for the race, and I'd rather kill myself than serve its purposes'" (3: 152).
Yet these words, uttered to Michael, do not account for her rapture at the prospect
of producing Hypo's child (4: 282). It would be misleading, however, to suggest that

Miriam is ultimately transformed by her brief pregnancy. The text's oblique reference to her miscarriage as a "recently restored freedom" (4: 309) fully registers the cost of child-rearing, underscoring her contempt for the male relegation of women to stereotypical roles. Miriam associates the ideology of racial motherhood with masculinist thinking, critiquing the assumption that child-rearing is a matter of imperial importance: "The hand that rocks the cradle rocks the world? What world? What race? Men … .Nothing but men; for ever" (2: 220). Although Miriam recoils from the view that women are only reproductive conduits, her repudiation of motherhood is not formulated in terms that reject Michael's ideas altogether: her insistence that "[t]he race is nothing without individuals" (3: 150) leaves unchallenged the notion that racial typologies exist, revealing the fluid and contradictory nature of her claims. To the extent that Miriam's investment in the race has to do with the preservation of "her inexorable Englishness" (3: 292), she implicitly aligns herself with middle-class British feminists who upheld the belief in white racial and cultural superiority. Indeed, Michael's description of her as "pure-Tory" (3: 151) suggests that she holds conservative principles. Similarly, Hypo, despite Miriam's protestations, remarks upon her identification with an imperializing and xenophobic Englishness: "You're Britannia, you know. The British Constitution … You've no *idea* how British you are'" (3: 253).

To the extent that Miriam's gaze creates a radical restructuring of spatial and temporal relations, colonizing intersubjective territories that are not her own, this observation makes sense. At the same time, however, because Miriam is a woman, her status as a citizen and her relation to the national interest is inherently problematical. We see this reflected in Miriam's outburst:

> [T]he English were "the leading race" … "the Anglo-Saxon peoples … could govern the destinies of the world." *What* world? … millions and millions of child-births … colonial women would keep it all going … abominable … for women. (2: 252).

This passage is significant for its overt association of colonialism with masculinity: although women are complicit in the ideological work of empire, their collaboration and sense of imperial responsibility is compelled through patriarchy. Miriam here distances herself, along with all women, from "the sacred responsibilities of motherhood" (2: 221), yet her racialized language to distinguish between Anglo-Saxon and indigenous women exposes her assumption that female colonial subjects cannot regulate their sexuality: "even if civilized women stop the colonials … primitive races would go on. It is a nightmare" (2: 220–1). Richardson masculinizes "civilization" and absolves women from any responsibility for the promotion or maintenance of imperial rule – "Women do not need civilization. It is apt to bore them" (3: 219) – but she also refers to women who resist masculine co-optation as inherently "civilized." In a characteristic double movement, Richardson associates civilization both with distortion and authenticity: the civilization of the "outside world" is gendered male, while the "real inside civilization" (3: 218–19) is feminized, located outside the politics of the public sphere, and, importantly, is not susceptible to conventional vision. Through Miriam's mediation, Richardson proposes a kind of feminist reform that positions women as redemptive figures of national culture, a move that privileges both Englishness and, as we shall see, the homoerotic.

Colonizing homoerotic space: the embrace of invisibility

Remarkably, given the novel's preoccupation with heterosexual relations and progeny, Richardson identifies sapphism as the source of female moral superiority and the rejuvenation of the British nation. Such a reading requires the acknowledgement that Miriam herself is a lesbian, an imaginative solution that Richardson makes possible by trading on the relationship between the national body politic and the female body.[136] It is not only, as Kristin Bluemel has proposed, that it is more meaningful to refer to Miriam as a lesbian, but that the privileging of female homoeroticism bears directly on the text's spatialized preoccupation with vision, where it functions to facilitate Miriam's accession to alien territory. Miriam's homoerotic gaze cuts in two gender directions and suggests ambivalence. On the one hand, it challenges conventional psychoanalytical interpretations which align female spectatorship with masculinity, for as a woman she mediates between desire for and identification with other women in the text. But, on the other hand, Miriam's libidinal investment in looking frequently resembles what Laura Mulvey calls the female spectator's phantasy of masculinization, an appropriation of the male viewer's active position: "I'm as much a man as a woman. That's why I can't help seeing things'" (3: 221).

An example of this deliberate spectatorial pleasure occurs during Miriam's visit to Ruscino's, where, as bearer of the look, she is "there as … a free man of the world … a connoisseur of women" (2: 394). Despite Miriam's sustained critique of patriarchal epistemological systems, she repeatedly identifies with masculinity: her succinct self-definition "I am a man" (3: 282) crystallizes her investment in male privilege, but it also speaks to her voyeuristic interest in seeing women as objects of desire. Elsewhere, however, Miriam expresses a fear of masculinization: "'Perhaps I can't stand women because I'm a sort of horrid man'" (1: 404). Although the novel insists on a gendered dualism, once again Miriam's mobile positioning invites a much more complex and covert understanding of the subject's relation to identification and desire. Miriam is indeed a misogynist, but her most explicit sexual longing is directed toward other women. As Lynette Felber argues, Miriam deconstructs the binary opposition between male and female, between activity and passivity, for although she identifies with men she privileges receptivity – which is clearly aligned with femininity in the novel.[137] Hypo calls Miriam "'a paradox'" (3: 351), providing a useful way of understanding her as a bifurcated being, split between conflicting desires and irreconcilable impulses. The text characterizes her as "a special category" (4: 325), a "strange self" which longs to "discover the secret of its nature" (3: 141), designations that speak directly to the problem of lesbian representation. Richardson's structural realignment of desire in *Pilgrimage* poses a challenge to what Marilyn Farwell calls "the lesbian subject's non-narratibility," for although Miriam experiences her body as an "unknown possession" (4: 150) awaiting discovery, the text simultaneously stages her self-discovery – consciousness of "her own world" (4: 106) – through homoeroticism.[138]

In contrast to Sarah Schuyler, who argues that "Miriam thinks with a straight mind; for her, sex *is* gender," I suggest that Richardson denaturalizes the supposed congruence between sex and gender by forging an asymmetrical relation between the two.[139] Miriam poses a challenge to the structure of the binary opposition by assuming the position of "the third sex," a term coined by sexologist Karl Heinrich Ulrichs to characterize the indeterminate status of the invert. But whereas Ulrichs utilized the phrase in arguing that homosexual men "harbored a female soul in a male body," Richardson invokes third- and indeterminate sex notions to represent a woman's internalized masculine nature.[140] The third-born of four girls, Miriam is neither masculine nor feminine, but both to varying degrees, enabling us to read this coalescence – as does Joanne Winning – as "a marker of lesbian sexuality."[141] Hence we see her constantly shifting between the two poles, "going to and fro between two temperaments" (3: 245), in effect enacting Havelock Ellis's observation that female homosexuality is the abnormal disruption of gender boundaries. The language that Richardson utilizes to characterize Miriam's mobility suggests that she not only struggles against the culturally constructed meanings attached to femininity, but that she embraces the rhetoric of inversion as a way of defining herself: "Within me ... the *third* child, the longed-for son, the two natures, equally matched, mingle and fight ... Feeling so identified with both, she could not imagine either of them set aside" (3: 250). The text here formally enacts Miriam's internal split, shifting between first- and third-person pronouns to describe her conflicted sense that "her life would be the battlefield of her two natures" (3: 250). Although she acknowledges the structure of a binary opposition, Miriam's embrace of her "three separate selves" (3: 383) subverts the notion of gender dimorphism. Her identification as a third term situates her within the discourse of inversion, a move that necessarily undermines both Michael's and Hypo's insistence upon a heterosexual imperative. We see this resistance reflected in Miriam's conversation with Dr. Densley, a suitor who denigrates women's intellectual pursuits; as Miriam simulates attentiveness, she simultaneously retreats into herself, "where she found, *like a third person looking on* and listening ... some part of herself ... eager to discuss the situation ... with herself alone" (4: 378; emphasis mine). Rather than pointing to Miriam's solipsistic inclination, this reference to an internalized third self – what we might rightly call her "third eye" – demonstrates the links between spectatorship and sexuality.[142] Her remark, "I am something between a man and a woman, looking both ways" (2: 187), captures her liminality and illustrates the centrality of vision to her mobile positioning.

Joan Riviere's classic argument that the display of femininity hides an unconscious masculinity speaks to Miriam's position in *Pilgrimage*: like Riviere's intellectual woman who wears womanliness "as a mask" in order to pass in a male-dominated world, Miriam too "identifies herself with the father" and then "uses the masculinity she thus obtains by *putting it at the service of the mother*."[143] Anticipating Riviere, for whom the origin of homosexuality is located in childhood, Richardson conveys Miriam's homosexuality through her identification with masculine signi-fiers and her eroticized relation to her mother. The text colludes in this linkage by representing Miriam as a girl whose aspirations position her as a boy: "'I am my mother's son'" (3: 220). A vivid example of her transgressive role as usurper of male prerogatives occurs during a scene in which she smokes a cigarette in front of her scandalized mother. Miriam feels that "she had embarked on her first real flirtation ... [lighting] a cigarette with downcast lids and a wicked smile, throwing a triumphant possessive glance at her mother as it drew" (1: 474). This reference to smoking recalls another incident in the novel that similarly alludes to Miriam's coded lesbianism: she furtively reads Ouida's *Under Two Flags* (1: 285), an "evil book" (1: 281) that features the unconventional tomboy heroine Cigarette. Although Richardson makes no explicit reference to the fact that "tommy" was popular slang for sapphic women, the novel draws our attention to this possibility by staging Miriam's late-night reading as an illicit activity: her murmur "Ouida, Ouida ... I want bad things – strong bad things" (1: 286) underscores this interpretation.[144] The possessive glance that Miriam directs toward her mother as she smokes situates her in the position of the beloved, a flirtatious move that is repeated when she makes Mrs. Henderson "blush" as she thinks to herself "it's I who am your husband. Why have I not been with you all your life?" (1: 456).[145] Although Miriam is not always so masculinized in relation to her female lovers, Amabel and Jean, the very fact that she aligns herself with masculinity here (as elsewhere) works to code her as a lesbian. Whereas the male assumption of privilege in the novel results in a paternalistic "laying down [of] the law" (1: 460), Miriam's repudiation of femininity and her identification with the father undo the dynamics of masculine authority. Rather than read Miriam's oscillation between masculinity and femininity as indicative of her confused sexuality, I would argue that this vacillation itself marks her as sexually deviant.

The novel's representation of Miriam's uniqueness – she is "[s]omething that has not existed before" (3: 282) – revises the pathological rhetoric of inversion yet still relies upon language that is replete with homosexual connotations to convey her commingling of genders: "there seem to be two. A waiting self to welcome me. It can't be wrong to exist" (3: 282). Miriam's concern with her right to exist can be read as an allusion to the fact that, during this period, sexual relations between women were not criminalized because lesbianism did not fall under the sodomy statute. Precisely because Miriam never articulates her inversion in the same way that Stephen Gordon does in *The Well of Loneliness*, she circumvents the pathologizing of the lesbian body that plagues Hall's heroine. And yet several factors invite a comparison between Miriam and Stephen: Miriam's 'masculinity'; her embrace of the category of third term; the repeated references to her frightfully oversized yet "secret hands" (1: 283); and her sense that, in forging her identity, she "must leave behind uncreated lives" (3: 508).[146] Although Miriam evinces butch leanings – claiming that she'll never marry and at 30 will cut off her long hair and wear divided skirts (2: 149) – perhaps most compelling are her frequent references to secrecy and her perception that, within her, there exists a kind of sacrosanct space, utterly separate from her socialized self, that marks her as different: "something else that was her own ... keeping her apart" (1: 467). The novel frequently invokes this enigmatic internalized space – Miriam's sense that she harbors "[s]omething that was not touched" (1: 425) – associating it with inviolability and invisibility. Sounding much like a closeted invert, Miriam inhabits a "secret world" (1: 402) through which the "innermost part" of herself predominates against "all her other selves" (2: 312). Her self-characterization: "'I am not what I seem, am ... a wolf in sheep's clothing'" (4: 516), draws attention to her duplicity. One scene in particular stands out for its suggestiveness regarding Miriam's "unknown self" (3:

337): as she wanders the streets of London her gaze settles on a female vagrant, stooped over the gutter, exposing a reddened scalp covered with wart-like knobs. Miriam is both horrified and captivated by this squalid figure, whom she refers to as "Familiar. Forgotten" (3: 288). While one may want to dismiss this old woman as merely an embodiment of the city's dark underside, Miriam's strong identificatory response exposes the inadequacy of such an interpretation. Her words suggest a subliminal meaning, inviting us to read the woman as a homosexual signifier, an embodied projection of her own abject self: "Unimaginable horror ... Revealed. Welcome ... naked recognition ... It was herself ... Her beloved hated secret self" (3: 288–9). Miriam's experience here is both liberating and oppressive, for although she registers this encounter with the grotesque female body as a moment of recognition, she simultaneously retreats "unrevealed" from the figure's bodily excess, resigned to maintain the "screen" which obscures "what she was in the depths of her being" (3: 289). The scene with the vagrant woman attests to the monstrosity and unspeakable nature of same-sex love, for without identifying Miriam as a lesbian Richardson still manages to convey the social threat of same-sex desire.

Yet it would be entirely misleading to say that *Pilgrimage* is preoccupied with the lesbian body as grotesque, excessive, and a figure for abjection. Predominantly, the novel stages lesbian desire visually, in a way that resonates strikingly with the depiction of female spectatorship and its relation to silent film in the *Close Up* columns. Through an invocation of the language of visuality, Richardson represents lesbianism as a utopian ideal and a vehicle for freedom from constrictive gender norms and compulsory heterosexuality. But because the embodiment of lesbian desire still functions, as the scene with the old woman testifies, as a cultural taboo, same-sex desire between women is possible only in mediated form. Ultimately, what that mediation of lesbian desire privileges is invisibility, not ostensibility, a move that stages Miriam's retreat from the social realm as the basis for the dismantlement of compulsory heterosexuality. Richardson relies on an idea of sameness, what Toni McNaron calls "sexual likeness," to signal the presence of lesbianism, moving the term beyond its association with narcissism by privileging both an eroticized and an identificatory relation between women.[147] In doing so, she foregrounds the sexual implications of spectatorship, but only intermittently. The novel cannot sustain the embodied possibility of lesbian desire outside the parameters of heterosexuality. Just as the mother–daughter dyad is triangulated by the father, so too is Miriam's relationship with Amabel mediated by Hypo, with whom she pursues an affair during her involvement with the "strange girl" (4: 188). We see this amplified in the scene where Miriam appropriates Amabel's gaze in order to disrupt the moment of heterosexual consummation: as she prepares to have sex with Hypo, she sees herself "[w]ith the eyes of Amabel, and with her own eyes opened by Amabel," and regards her own body – the "velvety gleaming of her flesh" – as an "object of desire" (4: 230). Allowing for the simultaneity of similarity and difference, Richardson stages Miriam's attraction to Amabel in terms of both narcissism and desire: the sexualized relation between the two women is specularly realized, conveyed through language that registers the homoerotic pleasures of looking. Miriam first encounters Amabel at a Lycurgan meeting, and is captivated by her eyes (4: 175), a fascination with the visual repeated when Amabel kneels beside Miriam and the women flirtatiously embark on what Richardson terms "an unknown quest" (4: 188). Turning her face toward Miriam, who surveys her countenance in full light, Amabel teases: "'It's like a peach. Say it, say it.'" Miriam responds in the affirmative and gazes into Amabel's "eyes … as into a mirror," admiring "the girl's open appreciation of her own beauty" (4: 188).

The question of which woman is being a narcissist here is not easy to answer, for both participate in the pleasures of self-observation, a pleasure that is realized only through the vehicle of the other woman's gaze.[148] Richardson thus appears to conflate the distinction between identification and desire, allowing both women to occupy fluid gender positions because neither here assumes the scopophilic dominance conventionally associated with masculinity. As the scene unfolds, the women continue to communicate through both physical and visual gestures; Amabel's hands stretch toward Miriam, who "read[s] in the girl's eyes the reflection of her own motionless yielding" (4: 190), illustrating the reciprocity of the gaze wherein both women are positioned as desiring subjects as well as objects of desire. It is difficult to distinguish in this scene the pursuer from the pursued, or the feminine from the masculine position, for both women appear to oscillate between these gendered extremes. We see this in Miriam's affirmation of her homoerotic love for Amabel, which is again represented as an experience of reciprocal specularity: "seeing with the same eyes at the same moment" (4: 242). Here, Miriam confirms: "Life with Amabel … Nothing could be better … not even the shared being of a man and a woman … could be deeper or more wonderful than this being together " (4: 242). It is here also that Miriam fantasizes about their shared longing to escape a social gathering in order to go to bed, to "get away and lie side by side in the darkness" (4: 243). Such evidence makes it difficult to understand how the presence of lesbian desire in *Pilgrimage* has gone undetected. But, even among the critics who have commented on the homoerotic charge between Miriam and Amabel, no one has noticed the role that national identity plays in their relationship. From the outset, concerns with nationality overlay and infuse the women's sexual relation. As Amabel kneels beside Miriam, she is shocked to discover that such intimacy is possible with an Englishwoman, while Amabel's Frenchness arouses Miriam's "repudiation of the foreign quality of her intelligence" (4: 189).

National differences between the two women mitigate their homoeroticized identification, revealing the importance of Englishness to Miriam's conception of lesbian identification. Yet unlike Miriam's male lovers, Michael and Hypo, for whom national identity is a fixed and stable category, Amabel's nationality – like Miriam's own – is both mutable and contingent upon contextual demands. Despite Amabel's apparent Frenchness, it is difficult to ascertain precisely what her nationality is. Miriam's complicated account of Amabel's national affiliation underscores this undecidability:

> In speaking with Frenchwomen her voice grows devout and, because she is more Celtic than English, being partly Irish and partly Welsh, and *has no sense of nationality,* she became French … Her disapproval of English people is both Irish and French. In any social difficulty the Frenchwoman comes to the front. But intimately, she is Irish. Yet her brogue is as inaccurate as her French. (4: 242; emphasis mine)

Amabel is a cultural hybrid, a complex composite of several nationalities, but she is ultimately characterized by "her absence of national consciousness" (4: 292). This detail is important in two respects. First, in contrast to Miriam's involvement with men, the relationship with Amabel poses less threat to her status as an English-woman and still helps to bring it into relief. Second, and equally significant, is that Amabel's national mobility arguably operates as a signifier for her lesbianism; in other words, like lesbianism itself, whose embodiment functions as a kind of absence in the text, Amabel's nationality is conveyed both through the proliferation of signs and through their conspicuous absence. The conflation of these identity categories suggests a complicitous relationship between homosexuality and the sort of feminized Englishness the novel seeks to endorse, for ultimately it is the "spiritual compass" (4: 579) of same-sex desire that teaches Miriam the value of foreign invasion – "to accept incursions without evasion or resentment" (4: 575) – a model that originates in the idea of imperial possession.

Although Amabel's nationality remains indeterminate, Miriam intermittently reconstructs her as British, a gesture that is symptomatic of her appropriative desire to integrate all others into an imagined collectivity of sameness. When Amabel expresses anxiety about the prospect of meeting Hypo, wondering what kind of pose to assume, Miriam advises: "don't be French ... Be Irish," urging her to act like a performer in a play (4: 314). Miriam contributes to Amabel's propensity for striking "plastic poses" (4: 191), despite her critique of this behavior elsewhere, by communicating that she is simply "too French" (4: 278). Thus, in preparation for the meeting with Hypo, Amabel transforms herself – specifically *for* Miriam – into an English spectacle, donning a gown of English design in place of her French frock, and projecting the "graciousness of the kind of Englishwoman" (4: 311–12) whom Miriam elsewhere denigrates. The anxiety that Miriam projects onto Hypo is specifically a spectatorial fear of homosexual exposure; she imagines his faulty eyes working like a "hidden camera" (4: 315) to reveal their "'intense, over-personal feminine friendship'" (4: 315). In assenting to Amabel's cosmetic change, Miriam foregrounds their sameness at the same time as she betrays her prejudice in favor of Englishwomen. Because lesbian desire in *Pilgrimage* is conveyed only through the conflation of identificatory and erotic impulses, Amabel's metamorphosis is repre-sented as a kind of narcissistic triumph: "They gazed at each other ... rejoicing together over an achieved masterpiece" (4: 312). The scene suggests a reciprocal relation between Englishness and the lesbian gaze, a relation that is further solidi-fied by Amabel's identification with militant suffrage activity.

By representing Amabel as a suffragette who sees women as facilitators of the "world's housekeeping" (4: 351), Richardson invokes the imperialist ambitions of British feminists who saw themselves as civilizing agents of both the nation and the world. In the novel this mission is trivialized, not because Richardson disputes that women are the embodiment of progressive civilization, but because Amabel herself is not a worthy candidate for the role of national savior. Miriam imagines the militant suffragette sitting in her prison cell reading Browning's poem about scandal, *The Ring and the Book*, vacillating between the contradictory poses of "defiant law-breaker" and beloved coquette: "Babinka poised on the edge of her bed in pale delphinium-blue kimono, retrospectively rapturous" (4: 349). Miriam's sexualized description of the prison in which Amabel and other suffrage agitators are housed as a "Black Hole of Calcutta" (4: 370) pits English civilization against foreign contaminants, testifying to the barbarity of non-British cultures and suggesting Miriam's complicity in the British feminist objectification of women of the East.[149] Although it is Amabel who (despite her national mobility) is positioned as a British suffragette in the novel, we see no evidence of her own culturally determined views of non-Western women. This is perhaps because Amabel herself, even though she is aligned with Western feminism, is positioned as a kind of Other in the text, an "unlocated, half-foreign being" (4: 292) whose racialization as Welsh and Irish, in particular, signals her marginality. At the same time, Amabel's beauty and alleged commitment to the British cause elevate her to the status of national "symbol," a role that foregrounds her investment in her own image, "worthy of throngs of spectators" (4: 345). Richardson expresses her ambivalence toward feminism in her caricatured portrayal of Amabel's militancy: her political motives are suspect precisely because they appear staged, inconsistent, and compelled by self-interest.

To Miriam, Amabel is both a "stranger" and "better known and more beloved than any one on earth" (4: 351), a woman whose excess of femininity marks her as a "marionette" (4: 357–8) at the same time as "every aspect, every word and movement" (4: 242) of her being produces pleasure. It is precisely those contradictions that speak to Amabel's role as homosexual signifier. If, as Elizabeth Meese has proposed, we privilege "the lesbian" as a sign of "strategic undecidability," then it becomes possible to read Amabel's inconsistency, her national mobility, her self-constructedness, her hyperfemininity, and her transgression of conventional gender boundaries as figures for lesbian signification.[150] As Miriam herself attests: "Incongruities amuse her" (4: 244). Arguably the clearest evidence that Amabel's undecidability is a figure for lesbianism occurs in the two scenes in which Miriam attempts to decipher her beloved's handwriting. In both cases, the text forges a connection between language and femininity that is punctuated with the trace of national difference. In the first instance, Miriam sits down "unobserved" at her bureau, prepared to indulge in unimpeded ruminations about her sense of freedom as a Londoner. As she notices a mirror on the wall behind her, she pauses to "exchange over her shoulder a smile of congratulations with her reflected image" (4: 196). This moment of solipsistic self-regard, however, is interrupted when Miriam observes a scrawl of cloudy letters across the glass, which she slowly deciphers as: "*I love you*" (4: 196). The mirror in this scene again functions as a surface that amplifies – through refraction – homoeroticized identification. Although Amabel is not invoked by name, Miriam attributes the message to her through a chain of signifiers, the most elaborate of which is her reference to an "unaccountable presence … [a] strange apparition" (4: 196) that silently witnesses her attempt to decode the soapy writing on the mirror. Miriam spies a "shadowy semblance" pass through the room, the figure of a girl surreptitiously moving back and forth, "unEnglishly" (4: 197). This characterization is important in several respects. First, Richardson's invocation of spectral metaphors recalls Terry Castle's argument that lesbian representation has historically been associated with disembodiment. This provides one way of locating Amabel, whose ghostly presence arouses Miriam's passion – the chapter ends with reference to her "swift blush" (4: 197) – at the same time as it insists upon the derealization of lesbian desire. Second, Miriam's gaze – "looking out through the eyes of her body" (4: 196) at the other woman – conveys an image of eroticized tactility, in which sight is figured as a kind of caress. This representation complicates Irigaray's argument that because vision is aligned with masculinity women reject looking in favor of touch. In contrast, Richardson privileges the female body as the source of visuality, eroding the distinction between the visual and the tactile and recalling Merleau-Ponty's theory of the embodied gaze as a model for intersubjectivity.[151] Richardson's reference to Amabel's spectral presence, moving about "unEnglishly," links female homoeroticism with the subversion of British decorum, drawing attention to the relation between sexuality and national difference only to reconstitute her, moments later, as indisputably English.

Richardson addresses the sexual implications of vision in a second scene that similarly relies upon the spectator's interpretive capacity, recalling her emphasis in the *Close Up* columns on the viewer's cinematic collaboration. Here, Miriam strains to decode a letter from Amabel: "Queer staccato pen-strokes, sloping at various angles, with disjointed curves set between ... Gaps ... Letters and words to be put together by the eye as it went along" (4: 214). Like a silent film that is punctuated with captions, Amabel's enigmatic text requires the collaborative effort of the reader: literary interpretation is dependent on the mediation of Miriam's gaze, so that words are only "set together by her eye, to their proper meaning" (4: 215). Also like a cinematic text, Amabel's written script has the pictorial quality of celluloid: "Each letter ... was a picture, framed in the surrounding space" (4: 215). That this text is feminized is evident from Miriam's use of the body of the woman as a trope for the textual body: "Each word, each letter, was Amabel, was one of the many poses of her body, upright ... elegant ... [with] embellishing curves" (4: 215). Lynette Felber persuasively argues that Amabel's writing – fluid, filled with gaps, and reminiscent of the sensuality of a woman's body – is a model for *écriture féminine*, but her analysis neglects the centrality of vision in Miriam's explication of this female authored text.[152] In contrast, I argue that Amabel's "queer" missive privileges the relation between vision and tactility, for it is only through the mediation of Miriam's gaze that language becomes associated with the lesbian body, "call[ing] her directly to the girl herself, making her, and not the letter, the medium of expression" (4: 215). Like lesbianism, which is mediated in the text, the letter's meaning is produced only through the interpretive gaze of the woman who actively looks, for "no single word showed its meaning directly" (4: 215). Whereas male signification is associated with transparency, with an unproblematized belief in semantic intelligibility, moving "from *word* to *word*" (3: 278), female linguistic practice is characterized by disjunction, defamiliarization, and the gap between signifier and signified; as Jean Radford astutely argues, it is the "visual effect of the signifiers not their meanings" which engages Miriam.[153] It thus comes as no surprise that Miriam's contempt for masculine writing, particularly her disparagement of linearity and climax, is conveyed in terms that ridicule the ejaculatory nature of male sexuality: "Bang, bang, bang, on they go, these men's books, like an L.C.C. tram" (4: 239). In contrast, Miriam's scrutiny of Amabel's letter recalls Meese's eroticized account of reading lesbian inscription: "I approach the white body of the page – stroke its surface as I would your skin."[154] Miriam ascertains that the translation of

Amabel's letter – like her body, "a balance of angles and curves" (4: 216) – will require several hours of attention, suggesting that the interpretive act is a form of lovemaking, focused on the body of the beloved.

Yet Miriam's affirmation of Amabel's text is not idealized, nor is it celebrated as an essentialized expression of *écriture féminine*. Like Amabel herself, the letter is marked by its status as artifice, "elegant as a decorative plant," the individual letters of which appear to reflect the various habitual "poses" (4: 215–6) of Amabel's synthetic femininity. By acknowledging the link between Amabel's character and its relation to textuality, Miriam suggests that lesbian representation is defined by semantic indeterminacy: "the letter itself seemed quite as much to express the impossibility as the possibility of exchange" (4: 215). The description of Amabel's text as a pictorial language – Miriam refers to the individual letters as "a picture, a hieroglyph" (4: 216) – positions the body of the woman as a kind of cinematic spectacle, recalling Mary Ann Doane's observation that "the hieroglyphic, like the woman, harbors a mystery, an inaccessible though desirable otherness."[155] By regarding Amabel's letter as a cinematic language, Miriam removes it from the *proper* system of representation, suggesting that in order to *read* the lesbian body one must abandon altogether the realm of conventional signification; instead, what is privileged is the materiality of the signifier and its relation to vision. Imbricated in this visual discourse that links lesbian sexuality and spectatorship are critical references to national difference, the most pronounced of which is Amabel's question: "'Isn't – E-g-y-p-t – a beautiful word?'" (4: 216). Miriam initially regards the inscription and sound of "Egypt" as the ugliest word in the English language, the most unassimilable and impossible to beautify; but when she transposes the word from a linguistic to a visual register, focusing on its pictorial quality, it is so defamiliarized that she finds it "[b]eautiful, yes … [in] all its associations" (4: 216). It is no accident that the word-choice here is *Egypt*, for this selection literalizes Miriam's interest in the hieroglyphic and reflects Richardson's Orientalist view of the East as the locus of mystery and exoticism.

Richardson here participates in the period's representation of Egypt as a site of gender fluidity and subversive sexuality.[156] For Richardson, "Egypt" marks the spot of lesbian erotic possibility, as is evidenced by Miriam's conflation of the letter-as-hieroglyph scene – "[l]ike words traced on the mirror" (4: 216) – with the earlier episode in which Amabel's enigmatic "twirly … moist" (4: 196) lettering on glass had conveyed homoerotic love. Like lesbianism itself, the word "Egypt" is a hieroglyph because it privileges and makes possible "something [Miriam] could not see" (4: 216). Nevertheless, it is through the gaze that Miriam gains access to this invisible realm, in which she and Amabel experience "the mysterious interplay of their two beings" (4: 217). The linguistic instability of the hieroglyph is recapitulated in the ambiguous national positioning of the letter-writer: initially, Miriam regards Amabel's literary "pose" as that of a Frenchwoman, then determines that the letter is "more English than French," only to decide that the document is "altogether English" (4: 216). Just as the word "Egypt" shifts in its associations from ugly to beautiful, so too is Amabel reconstructed – from foreigner to Englishwoman. By deeming the letter an indisputable English product, Miriam betrays her Anglocentrism and simultaneously foregrounds her investment in their sexual sameness.

But Miriam and Amabel do not end up living in connubial bliss. Because lesbianism requires some form of mediation in *Pilgrimage*, an embodied same-sex dyad is impossible within its parameters. But it is precisely through the text's investment in triangulation that Miriam is able to sustain her desire for Amabel; she is the one who self-consciously orchestrates her beloved's marriage to Michael, an action that clearly seeks to delimit Amabel's future sapphic liaisons. It is no coincidence that during the sacrificial moment in which Miriam urges Amabel to marry she does so "without any meeting of eyes" but with the sense that "an invisible third" (4: 294) term hovers in the space between them. Without the presence of a mirroring surface, lesbian sexuality is demonstrably occluded. Despite Michael's "horror of assimilated Jewesses," Amabel is the perfect partner because her nationality is so indeterminate that she is able to adopt Jewish orthodoxy (4: 294). Although their marriage results in disaster, depoliticizing Amabel and domesticating her to such a degree that, for the first time, she is not an "audience for her own performance" (4: 604), the union is advantageous for Miriam in two crucial respects: by arranging the marriage of the foreign woman to a Jew, she maintains her national purity and also successfully resists procreative sex. In doing so, the Englishwoman remains an uncontaminated vessel, polluted neither by the threat of cultural assimilation nor by compulsory heterosexuality. Even Amabel's last-minute request that the two women run away together before the wedding is unthinkable to Miriam, for what she privileges is a homoerotic fantasy that retains the inviolability of the individual; Miriam's words here echo her earlier pronouncement that life with Amabel equaled perfection: "Completeness of being. Side by side, silent, with *the whole universe between us, within us*, in a way no man and woman ... can ever have" (4: 545; emphasis mine). Miriam both embodies unexplored territory and is herself the explorer of an alternative landscape: "a new self and a new world" (3: 454). This heretofore unrealized concept of the self is complexly gendered and privileges sexual liminality, autonomy, and the appropriation of transparent space. While the mapping of this utopian world is realized only through the deployment of a homoerotic gaze, Miriam's sense of boundlessness – "When I open my eyes ... I see ... worlds and worlds" (3: 478) – is undergirded by Anglo-centric assumptions of spatial conquest.

Richardson invites us to read the characterization of Miriam, "abroad in a strange land" (3: 454), in terms of her visual colonization of homoerotic space, an imagined geographical location that collapses the distinction between public and private and is completely self-contained: "There is no need to go out into the world. Everything is there ... the world is added" (3: 67). This "magic enclosure" (4: 286) is a space that exists exclusively within individual women, and has the potential to erupt between women when they are alone together; importantly, this space privileges silence, precisely the kind of "wordless communication" (4: 244) that prevailed between Miriam and Amabel. Miriam's characterization of this feminized space calls attention to unconscious processes, suggesting a link between the female unconscious and sexuality: "there is a moment in meeting a woman, any woman, the first moment, before speech, when everything becomes new ... speech becomes superfluous, even with women who have not consciously realized [this]" (3: 280). Miriam equates her new relationship with Amabel with the creation of an untrammeled universe: "'This is the birthday of the world'" (4: 243). Like lesbianism itself, this new world is not visible, but is nonetheless based upon specularity: Miriam summons it with her "mind's eye" (4: 266). A kind of internalized geographical region, this new location is characterized in language – "the inner vastness of space … inner expansibility of space" (4: 307) – that invokes an image of colonial mapping. Importantly, Miriam bases her visual understanding of this new world on the same eradication of cultural difference and insistence upon homogeneity that she celebrated in her discussion of silent film: "I can see that new world in all sorts of ways. But it must also be the *same world*, to be real to me. It's finding the *same world* in another person that moves you to your roots. The *same world* in two people, in twenty people, in a *nation*'" (4: 333; emphasis mine). To the extent that sameness is foundational to lesbian identity, one might argue that lesbianism itself represents the prototype for this global vision; Miriam's goal, ultimately, is "to lose the weight of individuality and keep its essence, its queer power of being one with every one alive" (3: 496). What this "queer power" of incorporation requires, in other words, is the retention of homoerotic possibility without the burden of individualized – or embodied – experience. Yet this "new world" clearly reproduces, imaginatively, the ideology of imperialist expansion, particularly the way in which Miriam's notion of a universal subjectivity is predicated on exclusion: "Her world was uninvaded" (2: 442). Miriam's desire to absorb and consolidate different worlds in order to demarcate "the same world" is a mark of her Englishness, as is her focus on London – the imperial center – as *the* idealized homoerotic space. Like femininity, which is associated with both moral superiority and the unconscious, Miriam identifies England as a country that is "[m]arked among the nations, for unconscious qualities" (3: 113), suggesting a link between female sexuality and national responsibility that recalls the unconscious effects of silent film.

London: the invisible body

The most compelling textual link between sexuality and nationality is Richardson's representation of London as a giant female body – expansive, spacious, and diffuse – pulsating with life and erotic possibility. Despite Miriam's overt preoccupation with individuality, she is incapable of committing herself to any single person; rather, she identifies with and gives herself over to "London, her beloved territory" (4: 267), a space that is both feminized and homoeroticized, and also emblematic as the heart of empire. For Miriam, the city offers the greatest potential for the exploration of her unstable, unknown self; indeed, we find numerous parallels between the coded way in which Miriam marks herself as a lesbian and the language she utilizes to describe her urban existence: "the London life was sacred and secret" (2: 89). Significantly, in the city she is "not a woman … [but] a Londoner" (2: 266), a characterization that highlights her status as a third term, outside the binary opposition of male and female. Miriam's remark, "[a]nother self, in London" (2: 349), suggests that sexuality is not a matter of essence, but a question of location. The city enables her to inhabit "the enviable life of a stranger" (3: 88), a sense of anonymity that is defined by its liminality: her home occupies "the borderland of the part of London she had found for herself … to live, in freedom, hidden" (2: 29).

A space that provides liberation as well as concealment, "London's magic circle" is the ideal hiding-place for the modern lesbian, allowing her the "[f]reedom ... [to circulate] unobserved" (4: 196). Miriam's incessant urban wandering induces a "strange familiar state" of being (3: 106), an oxymoronic description that alludes to the lesbian as an uncanny figure; like Miriam, London "held a secret" (4: 363) – that is to say, both privilege the homoerotic.

Although Miriam feasts upon the city's sights with her roving gaze, she herself remains invisible, her sexuality hidden by the glorious anonymity of the city: "her untouched self here, free, unseen ... the strong world of London all round her" (2: 76).[157] The language that Miriam uses to characterize "the beloved pavement" of London (3: 288) recalls her obsession with Amabel: she turns her face toward the city's light "as towards the contemplative gaze of a lover" (4: 309), and the city mirrors back and amplifies her desire. Richardson frequently anthropomorphizes the city as a woman who directs her gaze to Miriam alone: the "voice of London" (4: 544) whispers to her; the "secret" trees lining the urban streets "looked into the depths of her [being]" (4: 413); and the "low, sweet English air" (4: 214) is "the best lover" (4: 539), its embrace "touching her all over, as if she were unclothed" (4: 149). As she strolls uninhibited through the city streets at twilight, Miriam reflects upon "the secret life" that London guarantees; her description of sunset – the "rosy gold was deepening and spreading" (2: 405) – evokes an image of orgasmic pleasure, in which the city-as-woman welcomes the "freshness pouring through the streets" (2: 406). Paradoxically, because it is as much abstract as material, London allows Miriam to experience her homoerotic pleasure in an unmediated manner, a forbidden pleasure that was impossible with Amabel.

What is compelling about this voluptuous representation of London is that lesbianism is not associated with foreign soil, but is explicitly aligned with English-ness, and, by extension, with empire.[158] By positing London as her lover, Miriam preserves her sense of the inviolability of the individual, while simultaneously implicating herself in the regime of imperial power: "It is only by remaining free that one can have the whole world round one all the time" (3: 20). Richardson's privileging of Miriam's homoerotic urban gaze can be read as an inversion of the conventional trope that aligns urban anonymity with male spectatorship.[159] In *Pilgrimage*, it is "the lesbian *flâneur*" who strolls unaccompanied through the city streets, gazing at "all that her eyes had made their own" (4: 415).[160] Richardson transforms the classic high modernist city of fragmentation and estrangement, reconstructing it as a domain that reflects not only a female but a lesbian vision of urban life.[161] Whereas canonical modernist writers, as Radford observes, often align the city with masculinity – depicting it as a kind of wasteland of the soul – Richardson figures an alternative London, a "mighty lover" (3: 272) which provides Miriam with gainful employment, but, more importantly, with an endless source of emotional sustenance and erotic pleasure.[162] *Pilgrimage* seeks to track how the process of urbanization reorganizes a woman's visual field, and is inseparable from questions of national identity. As Hypo tells her: "'you are a Londoner, you know, Miriam, in your *bones*'" (4: 169). Although, as an Englishwoman, Miriam has limited civil rights, her national identity draws on the idea that Englishness is coterminous with terri-tory: "Euston Road, beloved of my soul, my own country, my native heath" (2: 256).

Miriam develops a kind of imperial gaze, intent on staking out new territory as an exercise of woman's moral and racial authority: she "thanked heaven she was English" (4: 126). London holds out the possibility of an egalitarian feminist environment, then, but at the cost of positioning the lesbian herself as a proponent of colonial expansionism:

> No one in the world would oust this mighty lover, always receiving her back without words, engulfing and leaving her untouched, liberated and expanding to the whole range of her being … tingling to the spread of London all about her, herself one with it, feeling her life glow outwards, north, south, east, and west. (3: 272–3).

Miriam's sensual experience of boundlessness is the source of her liberation, but it is precisely this sense of entitlement – her language here conflates an image of orgasmic satisfaction and imperial invasion – that exposes her Anglocentrism. The privileging of silence and disembodiment recalls the satisfaction that Miriam felt with Amabel, but the city fosters an identification with Englishness that Amabel could not reproduce. Like other Britons who regarded London as the nucleus of the world, Miriam celebrates living "in the heart of London; secure from all the world that was not London, flying through space, swinging along on a planet spread with continents – Londoners" (2: 77). Ultimately, the city is a contradictory site, revealing Miriam's complicated relation to her own nationality and class position. Thus, on a walk through the West End, Miriam's gaze registers the rich accumulation of products culled from foreign lands as she identifies with the center of imperial security: "I am part of the dense smooth clean paving stone … The pavement of heaven" (1: 416).[163] Although the description of her body – "She was vast" (1: 417) – suggests her collusion with the rhetoric and objectives of empire, Richardson points out that Miriam can afford to buy only the smallest quantity of notepaper and a single pencil. Not lost on the reader is the gap between Miriam's sense of entitlement – "all hers, unlimited" (2: 30) – and the reality of her impoverished existence as a low-paid laborer. Richardson uses London both to critique the material condition of women's lives and to convey the identificatory power of the imperial center, for despite her socially marginal position, Miriam still reconstitutes the city as a utopian, homoerotic, sacred space.

While Richardson's interest in the operations of gendered spectatorship provides her with a spatialized model with which to explore the issue of one woman's shifting location in early twentieth-century England, what the novel comes to celebrate is not movement, ironically, but stability: "The power of London to obliterate personal affairs depended upon unlimited freedom to be still" (3: 188) – to be contemplative. This may seem counterintuitive, given the striking mobility of Miriam's gaze, but it is consistent with other reversals in the book's final chapters. Despite Miriam's engagement with London's social and cultural heterogeneity – her encounters with diverse races, religions, and nationalities – what she ultimately values is the city's potential to level all forms of difference. Like silent film, London has a homogenizing effect: "the lovely, strange, unconscious life of London … holding the secret of the fellowship of its inhabitants … [to] achieve communal consciousness" (4: 334). The "secret" of London's "unconscious," like woman's own, has to do with tapping into the homoerotic, but Miriam's final movement in the novel supersedes her earlier preoccupation with individuality. The reference to "communal consciousness" is key to understanding Miriam's shift away from London, the Lycurgans, social commitment, and the body, toward the impersonal and mystical path represented by the Quakers and, most importantly, by her final lover, Jean. Although Richardson's use of cinematic techniques enabled her to defamiliarize the urban landscape by affirming her heroine's perspective, what the author finally celebrates is not the visual economy of film but Miriam's "mind's eye" (4: 266). Richardson conveys this in a way that resonates strikingly with the concerns of the *Close Up* columns – in particular, her privileging of silence, homogeneity, and the feminine – demonstrating the novel's continued, if fraught, engagement with specularity. Miriam's move away from the city to Dimple Hill, a Quaker farm in Sussex, signals a rejection of the social constraints of sexuality: she argues that "sex-love dies unless it grows, for both partners, towards universal love" (4: 645). But the move is not a repudiation of romantic entanglement altogether. Rather, through her embrace of the enigmatic and diffuse Jean, Miriam successfully contains her homoerotic impulses by banishing the threat of embodiment. Jean is not so much a woman as a source of identification and a projection screen for Miriam's desire for sameness: "To return to Jean is to find oneself at an unchanging center" (4: 566). Like a living mirror whose function is to facilitate Miriam's coming to consciousness, when Jean speaks Miriam hears her own voice, and when she converses she is aware of Jean influencing her speech (4: 570). Whereas her "treasure" (4: 240), Amabel, had to be abandoned because she was not only individualized, but foreign and embodied, Jean can be embraced because she provides an imaginary means of suturing the self–Other divide: "If only I could remain always in possession of my whole self, something of Jean-in-me would operate" (4: 612). Here, Miriam has transcended her earlier problem with the body by internalizing her lesbian desire. Jean enables Miriam to escape the vulnerabilities of embodiment, facilitating her retreat into a hermetic and narcissistic realm that privileges the homoerotics of the mirror but evades the problem of lesbian sexuality: "she and I together, because we were together ... she for me, I for her" (4: 573).

What initially attracts Miriam to Jean, as was the case with Amabel, are her prominent blue eyes (4: 574). Their relationship is forged through specular moments of intersubjective communion: "Our relief and unspoken delight expressed themselves in smiles, observed rather than exchanged" (4: 566). Yet while Jean enables Miriam to pursue the anonymity of communal subjectivity, the relationship is not asexual. On the contrary, Miriam refers to their "schoolgirl joy in illicit exchange" (4: 565), recalling Ulrica's remark that the Catholics are right to separate within their orders "those who grow too happy in each other" (4: 612) – lesbians like themselves. Arguably the most provocative evidence that their relationship is homoerotic is Jean's pet name for Miriam: "Dick" (4: 576). That Jean selects an endearment is in itself not remarkable. The novel has a proliferation of names that are attached to Miriam's character, testifying to her mobility: Mimmy, Mim, Mariamne, Mirry, Miriorama, Miriametta, Mira, Miretta, and Mirissima. But all of these derivatives of Miriam, synonyms for 'mirror,' read as feminine appellations. In contrast, "Dickie" (4: 576) is distinguished by its manliness. One way to read this is as evidence that Richardson seeks to mark Miriam as "the phallic girl," to borrow Chris Straayer's phrase, and re-introduce the idea of her heroine's "masculinity complex" and "deviance" during a point in the novel which appears to privilege the transcending of gender distinctions.[164] While this may seem to be an anachronistic reading, the *OED* reminds us that "dick" has been used as slang for the penis since 1891. Miriam's relationship with Jean coincides with her involvement with the Quakers, a group she values because it emphasizes "a common vision, rather than man and woman" (4: 621). By christening Miriam "Dick," Richardson reminds her readers that there is no transcending of the sex binary, only its destabilizing. Statements such as "I see what you mean, Dick," or "Dick, with you it's different" (4: 586) provide playful commentary on the issue of lesbian invisibility and difference, at the same time as they comically allude to the absent phallus. Jean enables Miriam to escape physical passion, but not without invoking the sensate body. Through her, Miriam effectively conjoins her need to resist the corporeal with her desire for the commingling of self and other; we see this in the meditative utterance, which resembles a sexual release: "Jean. Jean. Jean. My clue to the nature of reality" (4: 612). To the extent that Jean functions as a lesbian signifier, like Amabel and London, she too provides a "clue" to Miriam's concealed interiority.

It is significant that Jean's kissing of Miriam – the only one – occurs within the context of a conversation about civilization and village life which recalls Richardson's remarks in "The cinema in Arcady." Like Richardson, Jean questions the assumption that the yokel lacks a "reverence for civilization" (4: 568), by implication aligning herself with the author's view that rural inhabitants can become world citizens. Whereas in the film columns Richardson privileges the cinema as the vehicle for this transformation, in the novel she presents Jean herself as the feminizing source and instrument of civilization. Richardson's valorization of silent film as an essentially feminine vehicle for enculturation is literalized in Miriam's relationship with Jean, where the language used to characterize their desire – "our intermittent silences … were fragments of a shared eternity" (4: 567) – is strikingly reminiscent of the *Close Up* columns. Like a spectator at a silent film, Miriam watches her beloved and relishes their "common silence" (4: 564); elsewhere, she experiences a "sense of being stranded in a vacuum whose sole light was the certainty of Jean's immortal love" (4: 584). At times, the women together appear to be positioned before a cinematic screen: "we contemplated whatever had been summoned to stand before us" (4: 567). Jean combines the erotic pleasure of Amabel with the expansiveness, impersonality, and stillness of London. Precisely like these two previous lovers, Jean facilitates the joy of disembodied affection: she "knows that *nothing* can be clutched or held" (4: 575). Miriam's remark that Jean's love "was her own passport to eternity" (4: 580) is a curious locution, given that her nationality, unlike Miriam's other lovers', is not a prominent feature. Jean's Scottish ancestry, and her association with Vaud, in Switzerland, positions her as another lesbian border crosser, though it is precisely her muted national specificity that further aligns her with the homogenizing effects of silent film. Jean is less the citizen of a particular nation than she is a representative of world citizenship. Not bound to the particulars of any single nationality or region, Jean represents unlimited access to unseen worlds: "I should follow her path, the path to freedom"

(4: 612). This territorialization, a kind of virtual border crossing, recalls imperial notions of transparent space. Jean herself is not site-specific, but Miriam associates her with the ideas of geographical rootedness and centrality, reminding the reader of London itself, the nucleus of the world: "With Jean, for me, friendship reaches its centre. All future friendships will group themselves around that occupied place" (4: 613). Although throughout the text Miriam has been the incessant traveler, through the mediation of Jean she ultimately retreats into an internalized, seemingly apolitical, yet spatially expansive realm: "'There's more space within, than without'" (4: 168).

Ultimately, what Jean represents is the specular colonization of lesbian space, an ideologically charged move that, paradoxically, privileges invisibility. In turning away from the world of external stimuli toward her "inward eye" (4: 293), Miriam proposes a radical reorganization of the conventional distinction between a public male realm and private female space.[165] Her embrace of the Quaker's foundational "belief in the universality of the inner light" presupposes the erosion of public and private spheres; what Miriam ultimately advocates is the permeability of gender and spatial boundaries through the assumption that "the world is home and home is the world … in other words, the inner is able without obstruction to flow out and realize itself in the outer."[166] Richardson's admiration of Quaker women is based on their lack of a notion of the particularized home or isolated woman cut off from social responsibility in the world. In language that is strikingly reminiscent of her notion that women provide "the world's housekeeping" (3: 351), Richardson praises Quaker women for bringing female values into the public sphere, "cleansing and ventilating … the life of the whole society."[167] The reference here to social cleansing at once recalls the salvific effects of the cinema, and a more menacing vision of racial purity: like silent film, women disseminate a unique civilizing function – "universal hospitality."[168] This premise is crucial to an understanding of Richardson's positioning of Miriam as the embodiment of a "new world" (3: 354) and a proponent of Hypo's view – "Women *ought* to be reformers. Keeping the peace and making the world habitable is eminently their job" (4: 334). While it appears as though Miriam retreats from the world of political agency and social commitment into a cerebral and isolated sphere, it is precisely that withdrawal that facilitates her enlargement of consciousness and its concomitant cultural dissemination. Like the Quakers, who Richardson regards as a microcosm of society, Miriam represents an alternative social possibility, based on "the renewed moral visibility of woman," which she regards as "the only real culture."[169] Although Miriam upholds the Quakers as a group whose values transcend the gender binary, their emphasis on silence and communal experience clearly positions them, ideologically, as proponents of the feminization of culture. By giving free rein to Miriam's "inward eye considering her many aspects" (4: 315), Richardson conveys that the construction of a new global order is dependent on women's moral agency and their visual conquest of masculine territory. This new world order rejects phallocentric discourse – "we all live under a Metaphorocrasy … I'm giving up thinking in words" (4: 607) – and privileges, instead, a homoerotic language of visuality. At the same time, although it seems counterintuitive given the text's relentless focus on Miriam's visual apprehension of the world, what *Pilgrimage* finally embraces is the invisibility of women's spectatorial fantasy. At the end of the novel, as Miriam is poised to write, she tries to retain concentration in order "to see, without looking, everything within her range of vision" (4: 618). In *Pilgrimage*, the feminization of England hinges upon women's visual conquest – "seeing everything simultaneously" (3: 393) – an optical infiltration that seeks nothing less than a re-awakening of national consciousness.

Notes

1 The time-frame of Richardson's novel is 1893–1912, but the text itself (the first eleven volumes) was published between 1915 and 1935. In 1938 these "novel–chapters" were collected in a four-volume edition, the twelfth title was added, and Richardson included also the oft-cited Foreword to her novel. The thirteenth and final volume, *March Moonlight*, was published posthumously in 1967, when the collected editions (in four volumes) of *Pilgrimage* were reprinted (in London, by Dent, and in New York, by Knopf). The thirteen titles, collected in four volumes, were reprinted by the Popular Library (1976) and Virago (1979). My citations refer to the Virago 1979 reprint, as follows: Vol. 1: *Pointed Roofs* (1915), *Backwater* (1916), and *Honeycomb* (1917); Vol. 2: *The Tunnel* (1919), and *Interim* (1919); Vol. 3: *Deadlock* (1921), *Revolving Lights* (1923), and *The Trap* (1925); Vol. 4: *Oberland* (1927), *Dawn's Left Hand* (1931), *Clear Horizon* (1935), *Dimple Hill* (1938), and *March Moonlight* (1967).

2 Winifred Bryher, "Dawn's Left Hand," *Close Up*, 8. 4 (1931): 338.

3 *Windows on Modernism: Selected Letters of Dorothy Richardson*, ed. Gloria G. Fromm (Athens and London: University of Georgia Press, 1995), 231.

4 See Anne Friedberg's dissertation "Writing about cinema: *Close Up* 1927–1933" (New York University, 1983).

5 Dan Birt, "Be British," *Close Up*, 8. 4 (1931): 284–6. Birt uses uses the terms "British" and "English" interchangeably. Andrew Higson discusses the British "fear of denationalization" in *Waving the Flag: Constructing a National Cinema in Britain* (Oxford: Clarendon Press, 1995), 18–22.

6 Bryher, "Dawn's Left Hand," 338.

7 *Ibid.*, 337.

8 For a more extensive discussion of modernism's relation to visuality, see Karen Jacobs, *The Eye's Mind: Literary Modernism and Visual Culture* (Ithaca and London: Cornell University Press, 2001).

9 Elizabeth Bronfen provides a fascinating analysis of the importance of spatial metaphors in *Pilgrimage*, but her study largely neglects the historical dimension of this topic: *Dorothy Richardson's Art of Memory: Space, Identity, Text* (Manchester: Manchester University Press, 1999).

10 Gloria Fromm, *Dorothy Richardson: A Biography* (Athens: University of Georgia Press, 1994).

11 Jean Radford, "Coming to terms: Dorothy Richardson, modernism and women" in Peter Brooker ed. *Modernism/Postmodernism* (London and New York: Longman, 1992), 98.

12 Bryher, "Dawn's Left Hand," 338. Virginia Woolf, "Romance and the heart," *Essays*, Vol. 3: 367.

13 Richardson, *Windows on Modernism*, 52.

14 *Pilgrimage*'s chronology follows Miriam's development from her eighteenth to her forty-second year, but the novel–chapters are not divided equally between those twenty-four years; thus, for example, *Pointed Roofs* covers five months, while *Interim* consists of fragments of only a few days, and *Deadlock* covers almost two years. George H. Thomson provides readers with the first chronology and index to characters in *A Reader's Guide: Dorothy Richardson's "Pilgrimage"* (Greensboro, NC: ELT Press, 1996).

15 Richardson, *Windows on Modernism*, 251.

16 Several critics have noted that Richardson found Sinclair's phrase – borrowed from William James – distasteful; it seems therefore particularly unfortunate that "stream of consciousness"

appears to be Richardson's only lasting epithet. For Richardson's "bewildering" response to the label, see "Novels" in Bonnie Kime Scott ed. *The Gender of Modernism: A Critical Anthology* (Bloomington and Indianapolis: Indiana University Press), 432.

17   Ellen G. Friedman and Miriam Fuchs, *Breaking the Sequence: Women's Experimental Fiction* (Princeton, NJ: Princeton University Press, 1989), 3–4. See also Jean Radford, *Dorothy Richardson* (Bloomington and Indianapolis: Indiana University Press, 1991); Lynette Felber, *Gender and Genre in Novels Without End: The British Roman Fleuve* (Gainesville, FL: University of Florida Press, 1995).

18   Tamar Katz beautifully complicates the category of femininity, linking it to the problem of interiority and narrative form in *"Pilgrimage: a woman's place," Impressionist Subjects: Gender, Interiority, and Modernist Fiction in England* (Urbana and Chicago, IL: University of Illinois Press, 2000), 138–68.

19   May Sinclair, "The novels of Dorothy Richardson" in Bonnie Kime Scott ed. *The Gender of Modernism*, 444.

20   Woolf, "The tunnel," *Essays*, Vol. 3: 11.

21   See Felber, *Gender and Genre in Novels Without End*, 101.

22   Richardson certainly recognized that her novel's form would impede its commercial viability. At one point in the novel Miriam denounces narrative conventions as a commercial ruse: "If [the book] was finished and the interest gone when you know who married who, what was the good of reading at all? It was a sort of trick, a sell" (1: 384).

23   Chandra Talpade Mohanty, "Under Western eyes: feminist scholarship and colonial discourses" in Patrick Williams and Laura Chrisman eds. *Colonial Discourses and Post-Colonial Theory: A Reader* (New York: Columbia University Press, 1994), 198; hereafter cited in the text.

24   Richardson, "The reality of feminism" in Bonnie Kime Scott ed. *The Gender of Modernism*, 407.

25   *Ibid.*, 402.

26   Susan Stanford Friedman, "'Beyond' gynocriticism and gynesis: the geographics of identity and the future of feminist criticism," *Tulsa Studies in Women's Literature*, 15. 1 (1996): 13.

27   For analyses of *Pilgrimage*'s filmic aspects see: Rebecca Egger, "Deaf ears and dark continents: Dorothy Richardson's cinematic epistemology," *Camera Obscura: A Journal of Feminism and Film Theory*, 30 (May 1992): 4–33; Susan Gevirtz, *Narrative's Journey: The Fiction and Film Writing of Dorothy Richardson* (New York: Peter Lang, 1996); Stephen Heath, "Writing for silence: Dorothy Richardson and the novel" in Sue Kappeler and Norman Bryson eds. *Teaching the Text* (New York: Routledge, 1983); Paul Watson, "'Siamese twins': the verbal and the visual in Dorothy Richardson's *Pilgrimage*," *Trivium*, 18 (May, 1983): 73–85; Carol Watts, *Dorothy Richardson* (Plymouth: Northcote House, 1995), 58–82.

28   Egger, "Deaf ears and dark continents," 10.

29   Friedberg, "Writing about cinema," 5 and 23.

30   Rachel Low, *The History of the British Film, 1918–1929* (London: George Allen & Unwin, 1971), 22.

31   Friedberg, "Writing about cinema," 20. The international context of *Close Up*'s production echoes the journal's conceptual interest in transgressing national borders: the magazine was edited in Territet, Switzerland, printed in France (until 1928) and England, and distributed in Paris, Berlin, London, New York, and Los Angeles.

32   Harry Alan Potamkin, "The cinema in Great Britain" (1930), quoted in Friedberg, "Writing about cinema," 212.

33   Kenneth Macpherson, "As is," *Close Up*, 4. 3 (1929): 9. For an analysis of the impact of national identity on the British film industry during the 1920s, see Kenneth Bamford, *Distorted Images: British National Identity and Film in the 1920s* (New York: St. Martin's Press, 1998). Although the target audience for *Close Up* was the serious cinephile interested in avant-garde films, Macpherson maintained a respect for the commercial viability of mainstream cinema, maintaining that "really good art IS commercial, and the mob has a curious nose for what is good – that is, what is *real.*" See *Close Up*, 1. 1 (1927): 9.

34 For information about British audience attendance, see Rachel Low, *History of the British Film*, 46–7. Harry Alan Potamkin epitomizes the English attitude toward the American infiltration of British film culture: "We are suffering from too much America!" See "The English cinema," *Close Up*, 4. 3 (1929): 20. Philip Corrigan recounts that, as early as 1925, 95 percent of the films shown in Britain were Hollywood products: "Film entertainment as ideology and pleasure: a preliminary approach to a history of audiences" in James Curran and Vincent Porter eds. *British Cinema History* (London: Weidenfeld & Nicolson, 1982), 26.

35 Richardson, "Pictures and films," *Close Up*, 4. 1 (1929): 56–7.

36 Richardson equates the editors of *Close Up* with prophets in "Almost persuaded," *Close Up*, 4. 5 (1929): 33. Macpherson argues that one of the great values of film is that it encourages cross-cultural awareness, but this insight ultimately consolidates a British idea of "race consciousness." See "As is," *Close Up*, 1. 3 (1927): 15.

37 Amelia Defries's article "Criticism from within," *Close Up*, 1. 3 (1927), expresses considerable anxiety about cultural assimilation, proposing as a solution that England establish a "national experimental workshop" (p. 54) to train potential filmmakers. While this "National School and Training College of the Cinema" (55) would be open to all nationalities, it would resist "foreign domination" (p. 54) – especially the influence of Hollywood – by creating a pedagogical context that would espouse an explicitly nationalistic (i.e., English) point of view. Such a university never materialized, but Defries's perspective, that to allow the continued infiltration of foreign influence on the British cinema would be to "stamp the whole of the next generation with something unworthy, *something which degenerates a race!*" (54), was variously echoed and supported by several *Close Up* contributors. For Kenneth Macpherson's arguments for an English school of cinematography, see "As is," *Close Up*, 4. 3 (1929): 7–8.

38 Macpherson, "As is," *Close Up*, 5. 2 (1929): 85. Richardson, "The increasing congregation," *Close Up*, 1. 6 (1927): 64. Richardson, "This spoon-fed generation?" *Close Up*, 8. 4 (1931): 307.

39 Richardson, "The cinema in Arcady," *Close Up*, 3. 1 (1928): 53.

40 Richardson, "There's no place like home," *Close Up*, 1. 4 (1927): 46.

41 For an analysis of the British cinema as a "democratic" medium, see Asa Briggs, *Mass Entertainment: The Origins of a Modern Industry* (Adelaide: Griffin Press, 1960), 18.

42 Richardson, "Almost persuaded," 34.

43 Richardson, "This spoon-fed generation?" 307.

44 Richardson, "There's no place like home," 44–7. "This spoon-fed generation?" 307.

45 Richardson, "There's no place like home," 45, 44, 47. Richardson's analogy between cinemas and churches is echoed by Rachel Low, who confirms that some critics "referred to the cinema in 1919 as the Church's 'legitimate competitor in moulding the character of the nation'": *History of the British Film*, 16.

46 Richardson, "The thoroughly popular film," *Close Up*, 2. 4 (1928): 48.

47 Richardson, "The cinema in the slums," *Close Up*, 2. 5 (1928): 60; Richardson, "Narcissus," *Close Up*, 8. 3 (1931): 183.

48 Richardson, "Continuous performance," *Close Up*, 1. 1 (1927): 35. Stephen G. Jones observes that an important part of cinema audiences were composed of working-class women: *Workers at Play: A Social and Economic History of Leisure 1918–1939* (London: Routledge, 1986), 60.

49 Richardson, "Continuous performance," *Close Up*, 1. 1 (1927): 36.

50 Richardson, "The cinema in Arcady," 55; 57.

51 Egger, "Deaf ears and dark continents," 8–10. Egger's reading of Richardson's "technology of forgetfulness" is based on a psychoanalytical understanding of the subject. Where Egger sees Richardson's work on spectatorship primarily in terms of psychical conflict and ambivalence, I seek to foreground the intersection between spectatorship and national identity.

52 Richardson, "The increasing congregation," *Close Up*, 1. 6 (1927): 64–5; Richardson, "The cinema in the slums," 60.

53 Richardson, "The cinema in the slums," *Close Up*, 2. 5 (1928): 60.

54 *Ibid.*, 62.

55 *Ibid.*, 59, 62, 61, 62.

56 *Ibid.*, 61.

57 Richardson, "Films for children," *Close Up*, 3. 2 (1928): 22. Richardson, "This spoon-fed generation?" 307–8.
58 John M. MacKenzie, *Propaganda and Empire: The Manipulation of British Public Opinion, 1880–1960* (Manchester: Manchester University Press, 1984), 76.
59 *Ibid.*, 76–7. The idea of British film propaganda was taken up at the Imperial Conference of 1926, which resolved to increase the number of films of imperial value. This desire was furthered by the Empire Marketing Board (established in 1926), which publicized the marketing of empire products.
60 Low, *The History of the British Film*, 35.
61 For a discussion of the quota legislation of 1927, see *ibid.*, 91–8 and 309–10; Friedberg, "Writing about cinema," 218–20.
62 Elizabeth Madox Roberts captures the journal's scorn for the Quota Act: "Oh dear, oh dear, these Brrrrrrr-itish Films, these wonderful major-generals and people with wholesome ideals!" See "Comment and review," *Close Up*, 1. 3 (1927): 66–7.
63 Macpherson, "As is," *Close Up*, 4. 3 (1929): 5.
64 MacKenzie, *Propaganda and Empire*, 87. One of the most overtly propagandist films of the period, *Men of Africa*, was made for the Colonial Office in 1939 to demonstrate the beneficent influence of the white man in Africa. See also Rosaleen Smith, "Movies and mandarins: the official film and British colonial Africa," in Curran and Porter eds. *British Cinema History*, 129–43.
65 Stephen Constantine, "'Bringing the empire alive': the Empire Marketing Board and imperial propaganda, 1926–1933" in John M. Mackenzie ed. *Imperialism and Popular Culture* (Manchester: Manchester University Press, 1986), 218.
66 Richardson, "The cinema in Arcady," 57. Stephen G. Tallents, *The Projection of England* (London: Faber & Faber, 1932), 22 and 12. See also Jeffrey Richards, "'Patriotism with profit': British imperial cinema in the 1930s" in Curran and Porter eds. *British Cinema History*, 245–56.
67 Richardson, "The cinema in Arcady," 57.
68 Richardson, "This spoon-fed generation?" 306.
69 Richardson,"The cinema in Arcady," 55, 57, 55.
70 Richardson, "The thoroughly popular film," 46–7.
71 *Ibid.*, 48.
72 Richardson, "The increasing congregation," 65; "There's no place like home," 44. Richardson's characterization of this imagined audience as "members of a family" recalls the rhetoric of the Empire Marketing Board, which envisioned a new world of inter-imperial relations based on the international cooperation of a global family. See "The cinema in Arcady," 55; "This spoon-fed generation?" 307. Jeffrey Richards discusses the social hierarchy of cinemas among different neighborhoods: *The Age of the Dream Palace: Cinema and Society in Britain 1930–1939* (London and New York: Routledge, 1984), 17.
73 Richardson, "There's no place like home," 46; "This spoon-fed generation?" 306.
74 Richardson, "The increasing congregation," 63.
75 Richardson, "This spoon-fed generation?" 307.
76 Richardson, "There's no place like home," 46. "The cinema in Arcady," 56.
77 See Antoinette Burton, "The feminist quest for identity: British imperial suffragism and 'global sisterhood,' 1900–1915," *Journal of Women's History*, 3. 2 (1991): 48 and 61. Barbara N. Ramusack employs the term "cultural missionary" to describe the activity of British women who "preached the gospel of women's uplift based on models evolved in Britain": "Cultural missionaries, maternal imperialists, feminist allies: British women activists in India, 1865–1945" in Nupur Chaudhuri and Margaret Strobel eds. *Western Women and Imperialism: Complicity and Resistance* (Bloomington and Indianapolis: Indiana University Press, 1992), 120. Antoinette Burton illustrates how British feminists "relied heavily on Christian principles to justify the notion of female moral superiority … link[ing] the two together to affirm the special righteousness of the British civilizing mission": *Burdens of History: British Feminists, Indian Women, and Imperial Culture, 1865–1915* (Chapel Hill and London: University of North Carolina Press, 1994), 42–3 and 60.
78 "The film gone male," *Close Up*, 9. 1 (1932): 37. Richardson here denounces sound and regards

the "direct giving of information in captions" as "the mark of a weak film," though she elsewhere claims that "the right caption at the right moment is invisible." See "Captions," *Close Up*, 1. 3 (1927): 55; "Dialogue in Dixie," *Close Up*, 5. 3 (1929): 217. Although she repeatedly argues that sound is a barrier to intimacy, she does makes some concessions: see "A thousand pities," *Close Up*, 1. 4 (1927): 62 and 64.

79 See Richards, *The Age of the Dream Palace*, 11. Richardson, "A tear for Lycidas," *Close Up*, 7. 3 (1930): 199. Although the cinema attracted a steadily increasing audience in Britain from its inception until the end of the First World War, from 1918 attendance fluctuated wildly until there was a definite slump in 1926. People did not start pouring into cinemas again until the development of the "talkie," and from 1929 onwards attendance steadily increased in Britain, by 1939 reaching a weekly total of 23 million.

80 Richardson, "The film gone male," 38. Richardson's bias is consistent with the opinion of many other *Close Up* writers who condemn the introduction of sound. See, for example, Ernest Betts, "Why 'talkies' are unsound," *Close Up*, 4. 4 (1929): 22–4.

81 Richardson, "The film gone male," 36.

82 *Ibid.*, 37 and 36.

83 Alison Blunt and Gillian Rose, *Writing Women and Space: Colonial and Postcolonial Geographies* (New York and London: Guilford Press, 1994), 8.

84 *Ibid.*, 5–6.

85 Quoted by Jayne E. Marek, *Women Editing Modernism: "Little" Magazines and Literary History* (Louisville: University of Kentucky Press, 1995), 124.

86 Richardson, "Films for children," *Close Up*, 3. 2 (1928): 24.

87 Kenneth Macpherson, for example, acknowledges the limitations of English audiences – "Our idea of the negro is as negroid as Al Jolson" – arguing that because "the white man is always going to portray the negro as he likes to see him," blacks should develop their own cinema so that the "negro [will become] an observer of himself." Yet like several other reviewers, Macpherson maintains a belief in racial "essence," demonstrating how primitivist definitions of race prevail even in instances that purport to celebrate the achievements of "negro art." This is evidenced by Harry A. Potamkin, who argues: the "negro is plastically interesting when he is most negroid … He should be black so that the sweat may glisten the more … He should be woolly, tall, broad-nosed and deep voiced. The moaning should be drawn from a source in the vocal experience of the negro, the medicine doctor's dance." See Macpherson, "As is," *Close Up*, 5. 2 (1929): 89–90 and 85. Harry A. Potamkin, "The Aframerican cinema," *Close Up*, 5. 2 (1929): 109 and 114–15.

88 Richardson, "Dialogue in Dixie," 213. For a historicized discussion of *Hearts in Dixie*, see Peter Noble, *The Negro in Films* (London: Skelton Robinson), 50–1; also Donald Bogle, *Toms, Coons, Mulattoes, Mammies, and Bucks: An Interpretive History of Blacks in American Films* (New York: Continuum, 1992).

89 For an account of the development of English racial attitudes, see Paul B. Rich, *Race and Empire in British Politics* (Cambridge and New York: Cambridge University Press, 1986).

90 Richardson, "Dialogue in Dixie," 214.

91 *Ibid.*

92 Bogle, *Toms, Coons, Mulattoes*, 27.

93 Richardson, "Dialogue in Dixie," 214–15.

94 Macpherson, "As is," *Close Up*, 1. 3 (1927): 5.

95 Egger, "Deaf ears and dark continents," 20 and 19.

96 Richardson, "A tear for Lycidas," 199. Despite the anti-sound bias of *Close Up*, several critics, such as the African-American writer Geraldyn Dismond, praise the talkie for making audible "the fact that all Negroes can sing and dance." See "The negro actor and the American movies," *Close Up*, 5. 2 (1929): 94.

97 Richardson, "Musical accompaniment," *Close Up*, 1. 2 (1927): 61.

98 Richardson, "Narcissus," *Close Up*, 8. 3 (1931): 183.

99 *Ibid.*

100 *Ibid.*

101 *Ibid.*

102 *Ibid.*, 185 and 183.

103 *Ibid.*, 185.

104 Annette Kuhn, *Cinema, Censorship, and Sexuality, 1909–1925* (London and New York: Routledge, 1988), 120–1. These are the precisely the kinds of issues that Richardson, among others, attempted to counter in *Close Up*.

105 See Steven G. Kellman, "The cinematic novel: tracking a concept," *Modern Fiction Studies*, 33. 3 (1987).

106 George H. Thompson documents the numerous references and allusions to Ralph Waldo Emerson throughout the novel, arguing that he was a deeply influential philosophical source for Richardson: *Notes on "Pilgrimage": Dorothy Richardson Annotated* (Greensboro, NC: ELT Press, 1999).

107 Mary Ann Doane, *The Sexual Subject: A Screen Reader in Sexuality* (London and New York: Routledge, 1992), 236.

108 Mary Poovey, *Uneven Developments: The Ideological Work of Gender in Mid-Victorian England* (Chicago, IL: University of Chicago Press, 1988), 127–8.

109 Terry Castle, *The Apparitional Lesbian: Female Homosexuality and Modern Culture* (New York: Columbia University Press, 1993), 45. For a discussion of the single female teacher and her relation to homosexuality, see Alison Oram, "'Embittered, sexless or homosexual': attacks on spinster teachers 1918–39," *Not a Passing Phase: Reclaiming Lesbians in History 1840– 1985* (London: Women's Press, 1989), 99–118. Ulrica's name invokes the groundbreaking German sexologist Karl Heinrich Ulrichs, who maintained that homosexuality was natural. He argued that homosexuals constituted a third sex: lesbians embodied a male soul, while homosexual men were thought to have internalized a female disposition. See Hubert Kennedy, "Kark Heinrich Ulrichs: first theorist of homosexuality" in Vernon A. Rosario ed. *Science and Homosexualities* (New York: Routledge, 1997).

110 In "The school friendships of girls," Havelock Ellis discusses the homoerotic "flame" between young girls that "proceeds exactly like a love-relationship": *Psychology of Sex* (New York: Random House, 1936), 368–84.

111 Joan Riviere, "Womanliness as a masquerade" in Victor Burgin, James Donald and Cora Kaplan eds. *Formations of Fantasy* (New York and London: Routledge, 1986), 35–44.

112 Donna Haraway, "The persistence of vision" in Katie Conboy, Nadia Medina and Sarah Stanbury eds. *Writing on the Body: Female Embodiment and Feminist Theory* (New York: Columbia University Press, 1997), 287–8.

113 Richardson, "Continuous performance VIII [article untitled]," *Close Up*, 2. 3 (1928): 51–5.

114 Richardson, "The film gone male," 37.

115 *Ibid.*

116 Sarah Schuyler, "Double-dealing fictions," *Genders*, 9 (fall, 1990): 82.

117 Joanne Winning offers an extended reading of this passage, situating it within scientific discourses of the period: *The Pilgrimage of Dorothy Richardson* (Madison: University of Wisconsin Press, 2000), 53–9.

118 For a discussion of this phenomenon see Ian Baucom, *Out of Place: Englishness, Empire, and Locations of Identity* (Princeton, NJ: Princeton University Press).

119 For a discussion of how regional and class-based linguistic differences are related to national identity, see Joanna Bourke, *Working-Class Cultures in Britain, 1890–1960* (London and New York: Routledge, 1994).

120 See Bryan Cheyette ed. *Between "Race" and Culture: Representations of "the Jew" in English and American Literature* (Stanford, CA: Stanford University Press, 1996).

121 This is not the only time in *Pilgrimage* when Miriam remarks on blackness. On a trip to Brighton she observes a group of "nigger minstrels," maintaining that it "spoilt them when one knew that they belonged to small London music-halls, and had wives and families" (1: 319). In other words, what Miriam objects to is imbuing blackness with subjectivity. "Nigger minstrels" were popular at English seaside resorts during the second half of the nineteenth century. See B. Pertwee, *Promenades and Pierrots: One Hundred Years of Seaside Entertainment* (Devon: Westbridge Books, 1979). For a discussion of the black presence in England see Folarin Shyllon's contribution to Jagdish S. Gundara and Ian Duffield eds. *Essays on the*

History of Blacks in Britain: From Roman Times to the Mid-Twentieth Century (Aldershot: Ashgate Publishing Limited, 1992); Edward Scobie, *Black Britannia: A History of Blacks in Britain* (Chicago, IL: Johnson, 1972).

122 Cheyette ed. *Between "Race" and Culture*, 10–11. See also Cheyette's essay, "Neither black nor white: the figure of 'the Jew' in imperial British literature" in Tamar Garb and Linda Nochlin eds. *The Jew in the Text: Modernity and the Politics of Identity* (London: Thames & Hudson, 1995), and Sander Gilman, *Difference and Pathology: Stereotypes of Sexuality, Race, and Madness* (Ithaca, NY: Cornell University Press, 1985).

123 Michael Ragussis discusses the position which Shylock occupies in the English imagination in *Figures of Conversion: "The Jewish Question" and English National Identity* (Durham, NC, and London: Duke University Press, 1995), 58–60. Miriam attends a performance of *The Merchant of Venice*, where she announces that Shakespeare's genius is evidenced by the way in which "he makes you sympathize even with Shylock ... the wiley Jew" (2: 187–8). This scene is also notable for Miriam's speculation about the relation between Portia and Nerissa, which suggests a homoerotic subtext.

124 Jacqueline Rose, "Dorothy Richardson and 'the Jew'" in Bryan Cheyette ed. *Between "Race" and Culture*, 118.

125 Homi Bhabha, "Of mimicry and man: the ambivalence of colonial discourse," *October*, 28 (1984): 126–8.

126 David Feldman examines the figure of "the Jew" in British culture during this period in "Jews in London, 1880–1940" in Raphael Samuel ed. *Patriotism: The Making and Unmaking of British National Identity* (London and New York: Routledge, 1989), Vol. 2: *Minorities and Outsiders*.

127 Jacqueline Rose, "Dorothy Richardson and 'the Jew,'" 125 and 118.

128 For an analysis of the links between anti-Semitism and misogyny, see Andrea Freud Loewenstein, *Loathsome Jews and Engulfing Women: Metaphors of Projection in the Works of Wyndham Lewis, Charles Williams, and Graham Greene* (New York and London: New York University Press, 1993).

129 Jacqueline Rose, "Dorothy Richardson and 'the Jew,'"117.

130 Cheyette, "Neither black nor white," 39.

131 *Ibid.*, 40.

132 Rose, "Dorothy Richardson and 'the Jew,'" 124.

133 Anna Davin demonstrates how during the early 1900s (when Miriam's affair with Hypo transpires) the birthrate was a matter of "national importance" in England; the influential propaganda of eugenics emphasized that "good motherhood was an essential component in [the] ideology of racial health and purity." See Anna Davin, "Imperialism and motherhood," *History Workshop: A Journal of Socialist Historians*, 5 (spring, 1978): 10 and 12. Unlike Richardson herself, who was an advocate of "endowed motherhood" – the demand that mothers, because they contribute to the good of society by producing future citizens, should be financially remunerated – Miriam never discloses her views about this socialist program. Yet as a member of the Lycurgan Women's Group, Miriam is likely to have encountered several lectures and conversations about why it was a mother's national duty to rear healthy members of an imperial race. For a discussion of Richardson's role as a defender of "endowed motherhood," see Gloria Fromm, *Dorothy Richardson: A Biography*, 47, 39, and 53.

134 For an account of H.G. Wells's attitude toward the sexes, see Anne B. Simpson's "Architects of the erotic: H.G. Wells's 'new women'" in Carroll M. Kaplan and Anne B. Simpson eds. *Seeing Double: Revisiting Edwardian and Modernist Literature* (New York: St. Martin's Press, 1996), 39–55.

135 Maroon Arrive Asian, Jr., *The Rhetoric of Eugenics in Anglo-American Thought* (Athens, GA, and London: University of Georgia Press, 1996), 37.

136 Most critical studies of Richardson either ignore or marginalize the novel's engagement with lesbianism. Kristin Bluemel's groundbreaking work is a notable exception: "Missing sex in Dorothy Richardson's *Pilgrimage*," *English Literature in Transition, 1880–1920*, 39. 1 (1996): 20–38; and *Experimenting on the Borders of Modernism: Dorothy Richardson's "Pilgrimage"* (Athens and London: University of Georgia Press, 1997). Most recently, Joanne Winning

has argued compellingly that an embedded lesbian subtext runs throughout *Pilgrimage*. Winning pays historically nuanced attention to Richardson's attempts to articulate a language for lesbian desire and identity, but she does not address the novel's linking of sexuality and Englishness: *The Pilgrimage of Dorothy Richardson*.

137 Felber, "Dorothy Richardson's *Pilgrimage*," p. 82.

138 Marilyn R. Farwell, *Heterosexual Plots and Lesbian Narratives* (New York and London: New York University Press, 1996), 16.

139 Schuyler, "Double-dealing fictions," 84.

140 Theo van der Meer, "Sodomy and the pursuit of a third sex in the early modern period," in Gilbert Herdt ed. *Third Sex, Third Gender: Beyond Sexual Dimorphism in Culture and History* (New York: Zone Books, 1994), 137. Richardson's representation of the inverted woman is not primarily preoccupied – as are several sexologists – with the masculinized *body*. Miriam refuses to be constrained by her anatomical sex, but her status as a masculinized female is primarily based on psychological, rather than physical, characteristics. Edward Carpenter's description of the lesbian as a figure who is marked not by bodily characteristics but by an "inner ... masculine [nature]" is useful for an understanding of Miriam's inversion: *Love's Coming of Age: A Series of Papers on the Relations of the Sexes* (New York and London: Mitchell Kennerly, 1922), 138. For a look at the early twentieth-century lesbian response to Carpenter's work, see Emily Hamer, *Britannia's Glory: A History of Twentieth-Century Lesbians* (London: Cassell, 1996), 15–39.

141 Winning, *The Pilgrimage of Dorothy Richardson*, 85. Joanne Winning also discusses Miriam's hands as a marker of her lesbian sexuality, demonstrating how Miriam's oscillation between gender identities is informed by psychoanalytic understandings of female homosexuality that were contemporary with the writing of *Pilgrimage*. Winning also demonstrates how Richardson's novel is in dialogue with *The Well of Loneliness*. See *The Pilgrimage of Dorothy Richardson*, 78–9 and 108–14.

142 Fatimah Tobing Rony's reading of the internalized "third eye" is suggestive for an understanding of Miriam's position as lesbian: *The Third Eye: Race, Cinema, and Ethnographic Spectacle* (Durham, NC, and London: Duke University Press, 1996).

143 Joan Riviere, "Womanliness as a masquerade," 41. Because Riviere speaks more directly to Miriam's role as a professional woman who harbors a wish for masculinity, I focus here on her analysis rather than on Freud's equally relevant discussion of women's "masculinity complex" in "The psychogenesis of a case of homosexuality in a woman" (1920), *Collected Papers: Volume 2*, ed. Ernest Jones (New York: Basic Books, 1959), 202–31.

144 For a discussion of the historical usage of the term "tommy," see Randolph Trumback, "London's sapphists: from three sexes to four genders in the making of modern culture" in Gilbert Herdt ed. *Third Sex, Third Gender: Beyond Sexual Dimorphism in Culture and History* (New York: Zone Books, 1994), 133.

145 Jean Radford discusses the psychoanalytic implications of Miriam's identification with her mother in *Dorothy Richardson*, 86–105. Joanne Winning demonstrates how Miriam's desire for her mother, and subsequent mother-substitutes, are a marker of her lesbianism: *The Pilgrimage of Dorothy Richardson*, Ch. 3.

146 In *Pilgrimage*, much is made of Miriam's "enormous arm and ... hand frightful in its size" (3: 194), grotesque signifiers of her sexual difference (1: 283). That hands and arms stand in for more explicitly sexual parts of the lesbian body is echoed in *Mrs. Dalloway*, where Woolf draws attention to Miss Kilman's predatory "large hand" (131) which longs to possess Elizabeth (132). Miss Kilman's cannibalistic desire is synecdochially displaced on to her mechanical grasping hand. Havelock Ellis writes about the peculiarities of the lesbian arm in *Studies in the Psychology of Sex* (New York: Random House, 1940), Vol. 1: 229. Joanne Winning also discusses Miriam's hands as a marker of her lesbian sexuality: *The Pilgrimage of Dorothy Richardson*, 78–9.

147 Toni A.H. McNaron, "Mirrors and likeness: a lesbian aesthetic in the making" in Susan J. Wolfe and Julia Penelope eds. *Sexual Practice, Textual Theory: Lesbian Cultural Criticism* (Cambridge, MA, and Oxford: Blackwell, 1993), 291–306. Marilyn R. Farwell also invokes the notion of "sameness" to characterize lesbian narrative space. See *Heterosexual Plots*.

148 In *On Narcissism* (1914), Freud links narcissism and homosexuality: *The Standard Edition of the Complete Psychological Works of Sigmund Freud*, Vol. 14 (London: Hogarth Press–Institute of Psychoanalysis, 1957).

149 Antoinette Burton, *Burdens of History*, 94.

150 Elizabeth Meese *(Sem)erotics: Theorizing Lesbian Writing* (New York: New York University Press, 1992), 12.

151 Luce Irigaray equates male ocularcentrism with the oppressiveness of male sexuality, identifying both as vehicles for female objectification in *Speculum of the Other Woman* (Ithaca, NY: Cornell University Press, 1985), 145.

152 Felber, "Dorothy Richardson's *Pilgrimage*," 79; 87.

153 Radford, *Dorothy Richardson*, 131.

154 Meese, *(Sem)erotics*, 19.

155 Doane, *The Sexual Subject*, 228.

156 See Sandra M. Gilbert and Susan Gubar, *No Man's Land: The Place of the Woman Writer in the Twentieth Century* (New Haven, CT: Yale University Press, 1988), Vol. 2: *Sexchanges*: 26–39.

157 Richardson's characterization here is consistent with Judith Walkowitz's argument that the undefined status of female homosexuality afforded lesbians a much greater degree of urban safety than their male counterparts: *City of Dreadful Delight: Narratives of Sexual Danger in Late-Victorian London* (Chicago, IL: University of Chicago Press, 1992), 6 and 284.

158 For a discussion of the relevance of foreign locations to the British woman's expression of lesbian love, see Louise A. DeSalvo, "Every woman is an island: Vita Sackville-West, the image of the city, and the pastoral idyll" in Susan Merrill Squier ed. *Women Writers and the City: Essays in Feminist Literary Criticism* (Knoxville: University of Tennessee Press, 1984), 97–113.

159 See Elizabeth Wilson, *The Sphinx in the City: Urban Life, the Control of Disorder, and Women* (Berkeley: University of California Press, 1991), 26–46.

160 Sally Munt, "The lesbian *flâneur*" in David Bell and Gill Valentine eds. *Mapping Desire: Geographies of Sexualities* (London and New York: Routledge, 1995), 114–25.

161 Susan M. Squier has written extensively about how female modernists have experienced and written about the city in ways that diverge from that of their male contemporaries. See *Virginia Woolf and London: The Sexual Politics of the City* (Chapel Hill and London: University of North Carolina Press, 1985); and *Women Writers and the City*.

162 Radford, *Dorothy Richardson*, 62–5. Radford also argues that Richardson utilizes London to represent the mind and the body of a woman, but she reads the city as a maternalized space.

163 According to Erica D. Rappaport, by 1909 the West End was a center of commercial leisure for middle-class and working-class women: *Shopping for Pleasure: Women in the Making of London's West End* (Princeton, NJ: Princeton University Press, 2000).

164 Chris Straayer, *Deviant Eyes, Deviant Bodies: Sexual Re-Orientations in Film and Video* (New York: Columbia University Press, 1996), 140.

165 Heidi J. Nast and Audrey Kobayashi discuss the historical shift from a Cartesian model of vision, in which an interiorized and disembodied "mind's eye" is privileged, to a contemporary model of "physiological optics" in which the subject is "simultaneously everywhere and nowhere." Miriam seems to fall somewhere in between these two extremes, as what she comes to embrace at the end of *Pilgrimage* is an interiorized mind's eye that both escapes the confines of the body and is omnipresent: Heidi J. Nast and Audrey Kobayashi, "Re-corporealizing vision" in Nancy Duncan ed. *Bodyspace: Destabilizing Geographies of Gender and Sexuality* (London and New York: Routledge, 1996), 76 and 79.

166 Richardson, *The Quakers Past and Present* (London: Constable, 1914), 72 and 79.

167 *Ibid.*, 79.

168 Richardson, "The increasing congregation," 64. This spatialized sense of boundlessness recalls Richardson's essay "Leadership in marriage" in which she remarks that the "essential characteristic of the womanly woman … [is] being all over the place and in all camps at once," an ability that accounts for her role as global "peacemaker": "Leadership in marriage," *The New Adelphi*, 2. 4 (1929): 347.

169 Richardson, "Women and the future" in Bonnie Kime Scott ed. *The Gender of Modernism*, 411.

3

Encoding bi-location:
Sylvia Townsend Warner and the
primitive erotics of sapphic dissimulation

Among the drawbacks in the lot of the unmarried woman must be reckoned the injuries to character and failures of development which may be caused by unfulfilled desires ... This, of course, would account for dryness, hardness, want of sympathy, and also for the loss of feminine grace ... incompleteness ... an incessant aching longing for the fulfilment of that primary feminine instinct ... children. (Mary Scharlieb, *The Bachelor Woman and Her Problems*, 1929)

The marriage may be said to be consummated when the male organ passes through the hymen and enters the vagina of the woman ... if the usual and natural position is used the male organ enters in the correct anatomical position ... the woman to be lying on her back ... If after a year or so the woman does not begin to take part with her husband in [sexual] unions, then she is probably an abnormal person and it would have been better for her to remain a spinster. (Isabel Emslie Hutton, *The Hygiene of Marriage*, 1923)

These statements capture several fundamental assumptions that inform much sexological discourse of the interwar period in Britain: single women are "unfulfilled" and "incomplete" beings; normative heterosexuality (the missionary position) is what is considered "natural" for women; spinsters are "hard," "dry," and unfeminine; women who exhibit a disinclination for heterosexual sex are definitely "abnormal." As is the case in these two sexological tracts, female same-sex desire is rarely presented in the mainstream or feminist press as a conceivable *alternative* to heterosexuality; nor is it ever referred to without circumspection or the taint of pathology. A salient example of this appears in a book review of *The Well of Loneliness*, entitled "The vulgarity of lesbianism," which appeared in *The New Statesman* in 1928. Here, the reviewer, Cyril Connolly, denounces the "widespread social phenomenon ... [of] professional man-hating," nostalgically reflecting on the prewar days when the lesbian was categorized as a simple "psychopath."[1] Now, in these confusing gender-bending "post-war days of boy–girls and girl–boys," the average Briton must repeatedly confront the "vulgarity" and "social disease" of lesbianism, as well as the "intrinsic dreariness of the Sapphic theme" in modern novels. The fundamental basis of Connolly's contempt for "lesbian love" stems from his perception that female homosexuality offers "no restraints" on female sexuality, a horrifying prospect for a culture in which women's knowledge of their own sexual pleasure was severely circumscribed and policed. During this period, mere familiarity with the meaning of the word "clitoris" was suspect and opened one to charges of lesbian perversion.[2] Even Dr. Isabel Emslie Hutton's marriage manual, which purported to teach women about the mechanics of heterosexual sex, makes no mention of the clitoris by its name, referring to it as a "very sensitive" organ that "*probably* has much to do with sexual stimuli." Hutton urges women to familiarize themselves with their vaginas, in order to facilitate intercourse for the husband, but she also assures women that they "need not be introspective about it or even examine it" themselves.[3] Female sexual arousal was imaginable, but only within the parameters of reproductive sex.

Lesbian seduction was something to be feared and repudiated by straight women. Although "passionate friendships" between women are at times acknowledged, these relationships, as Dr. Mary Scharlieb argues, can attain a "singular beauty" only if there is no "practical outcome" and only if one partner is considerably older – more "motherly" – than the other, otherwise such exclusive unions are "dangerous" and "wholly bad."[4] The intimation here that only the maternal can *save* a lesbian relationship is consistent with the mass of interwar propaganda that fetishized the moral guardianship of the mother as integral to the nation's health, but Scharlieb's remarks unwittingly align her with Freud's argument that lesbian desire marked a woman's failure to progress beyond a preoedipal attachment to the mother. Although Scharlieb makes no reference to the lesbian's presumed "masculinity complex," she does reproduce the dominant ideology that motherhood is a woman's natural destiny by her insistence that the singular "motive in the case of the unmarried woman must be the welfare of the race."[5] Like Edith Lees Ellis, who earlier argued that inverts can "diminish unfitness and increase racial possibilities" by working for the greater national good, Scharlieb understands the spinster's (and implicitly, the lesbian's) responsibility in terms of a kind of spiritual guardianship that will further the racial stability of the nation.[6] Even though, as we saw in chapter 1, the British lesbian herself is perceived to be racially Other, efforts to recuperate her (in her guise as spinster) routinely invoke the rhetoric of service and focus on her responsibility to the State. We see this dynamic at work in Radclyffe Hall's short story "Miss Ogilvy finds herself" (1934), in which the "very odd" female invert finds satisfaction and meaning during the war doing "excellent work for the nation" in London, where others of "her kind" similarly assert "their right to serve" their country.[7] This representation of the invert's national identification directly contrasts with the view, articulated by the controversial eugenicist Anthony Ludovici in 1925, that "thousands of bitter or subnormal [single] women" with "thwarted or deficient passions" are interfering with the "normal functioning" of the nation's health.[8] Because a "nation ultimately becomes the image of its values" (8), Britain must not tolerate the "bodily defects" (9) of the spinster: these "bungled and the botched" (106) women contribute only to the "debilitation of the national physique" (11). Ludovici's howl of moral indignation at the prospect that unmated women could have fulfilling emotional lives culminates in an oblique critique of lesbians, those women "whose bodies are so conspicuously inferior in passion and equipment" that they will remain forever indifferent to men through "sheer physiological apathy" (37).

Given the intensity of such hysteria, it comes as little surprise to learn that *The Well of Loneliness* was denounced by Sir Chartres Biron, the chief magistrate who prosecuted the obscenity case, as a book that contains accounts of women indulging in "actual physical acts" and "unnatural vices" which are "described in the most *alluring* terms." Echoing Cyril Connolly's anxiety that female same-sex desire offers no restraints on physical passion, Biron condemns Hall's novel on the grounds that lesbianism may offer women extraordinary "contentment and *pleasure*."⁹ The real crime, from a male perspective, is that lesbianism makes heterosexuality superfluous and drives women to "unnatural" erotic acts which evade male surveillance and control. Even though straight women were routinely taught to believe that "sex and sex-feeling and passion are unwomanly and base," the romantic notion of hetero- sexual desire was still firmly entrenched in British culture.¹⁰ Sylvia Townsend Warner registers the national implications of this normative ideal when she laments the fate of the single woman: "Being kept by a husband is of national importance enough. But to be feme sole [*sic*], and self-supporting, that hands you over, no more claim to consideration than a biscuit."¹¹ Where Radclyffe Hall had erroneously assumed that the condemnation of her lesbian characters was not merely an attack on her "but upon the women of the British Empire," Warner registers more fully the degree to which the unmarried woman is marginal to national life, despite attempts by social critics such as Scharleib and Ellis to recuperate her, a fact succinctly conveyed by the word popularly used to describe the superfluity of the spinster: "surplus."¹² Yet, like Hall, Warner is interested in the plight of the lesbian, in particular how her gender and sexuality intersect with *nation*. Unlike *The Well*, which was successfully prosecuted for obscenity in 1928 (despite its conspicuous omission of sex and its celebration of English nationalism), none of Sylvia Townsend Warner's texts that engage the conjunction of homo- eroticism and Englishness were ever censored or denounced as notorious, a difference which suggests that fantasy and circumspection are more culturally palatable than conventional realism.

To ask why Warner's novels were not spurned is to ask, in other words, what role modernist form has played in the British representation of lesbian subjectivity and desire. In contrast to Radclyffe Hall, who embraced sexological categories and relied on a – comparatively – more traditional realism to convey the trials of the female invert, Warner resists collusion with existing models of "deviant" sexuality and elects, instead, to employ an individualized discourse of inversion that relies on elements of fantasy, evasion, dissimulation, and displacement. That is, she avoids the problem of notoriety associated with Hall's realism by creating fantastic prota- gonists who rebel, escape, disrupt time and space, and construct their own originary myth of the homoerotic, one that revises ascendant notions of degeneracy while retaining sexology's attribution of primitive passions and impulses to the congenital invert. Warner's depictions of homoeroticism in two of her 1920s' novels, *Mr. Fortune's Maggot* (1927) and *Lolly Willowes* (1926), are deeply imbricated in a trope of inversion – a series of narrative reversals that upset the *proper*, or *usual*, order and signal the presence of same-sex desire – illustrating the complex interdependence of homosexual tendencies and sexological discourse even as its literary marking resists pathological manifestations of homoerotic desire. While sexual inversion, as

Jay Prosser has pointed out, is not synonymous with homosexuality, but is "a broad transgendered condition of which same-sex desire [is] but one symptom," my contention in this chapter is precisely that Warner plays with the discourse of inversion in order to signal same-sex desire.[13] Warner depicts homosexuality as an anomaly, but like Havelock Ellis and Edward Carpenter, she also regards the invert as a part of nature. In doing so, her representation of inversion often intersects with profoundly English notions of *the natural*, such as the idea that rural England is constitutive of national identity, exposing her use of nationalism to integrate the lesbian with national ideals. In naturalizing inversion and linking it with distinctly English forms of culture and English notions of space, Warner affirms the values of sexual autonomy *and* Englishness – even as she overtly critiques the conjunction of nationalism and imperialism. Warner's representations of the homoerotic resonate with national meaning in such a way that inversion becomes the province of the English nation.

In order to appreciate Warner's alignment of the invert with the natural, it is crucial to understand her perspective on English territory and contextualize her views within the larger interwar preoccupation with the countryside. While Warner's involvement in land issues (specifically, her agitation for the rights of rural inhabitants) did not come about until the 1930s, the essays she produced on this topic productively inform my understanding of the novels she published during the 1920s, when the issue of rural preservation and the association of Englishness with indigenous rural values were in circulation. In her 1939 article "The way by which I have come" Warner discusses her relation to the English countryside and recounts her move to East Chaldon (in 1930) where, because she and her lover, Valentine Ackland, employed servants, they were dismissed as "gentry" and were "mistrusted by [their] earthy" neighbors.[14] Warner critiques English pastoralism as "a grim and melancholy thing" (478), yet like other Britons she still regards "a plot of earth, clean, and well dug" as life's "deepest gratification" (483). Her contempt for the "falsification of [rural] values" (481) interestingly echoes the sentiments of such preservationists as Clough Williams-Ellis who, in *England and the Octopus* (1928), denounces the "false standards and values" of English people who have no conception that the beauty of England is "worth preserving."[15] Warner despised the Council for the Preservation of Rural England because of the group's hypocrisy – its members were appalled by the appearance of pink bungalows in the countryside yet ignored the plight of rural workers – though she too was contemptuous of urban "week-enders" who exploited the countryside for leisure.[16] Warner sought to protect her beloved East Chaldon – a favorite of "bohemian Bloomsbury and elegant London society" – from the tourist onslaught, but unlike her contemporary Mary Butts, who shared her disdain for urban trippers, Warner did not believe that rural inhabitants had a predestined right to land.[17] Rather, she imagined a communist future of collectivized farms in East Chaldon to which anyone who worked the land had rights of access.[18] Yet, like the more conservative Butts, Warner upholds "the soil" as "the essential thing," even though she maintains that her topophilia transcends national particularity. Deploying the global rhetoric of international cooperation, Warner maintains that one must look beyond "the decay" in Britain to the agricultural problems in "other countries, other continents" (485–6). In urging England to look beyond itself to the agricultural problems elsewhere, she recapitulates the particu-larity of location she claims to disavow. That is, it is an English conception of space that arguably authorizes Warner's universalizing gesture, in which she implicitly positions herself as a citizen of the world, investing her cultural authority elsewhere. This chapter demonstrates the links between this concept of expansiveness, sapphic modernism, and what national affiliation means for the interwar lesbian whose metaphorical mapping of space is suffused with both progressive ideas regarding culture and politics and the conventional notion that cultural purity resides in English geography.

Before delving into *Lolly Willowes*, I glance at *Mr. Fortune's Maggot*, for I read these two fantasy novels as companion pieces, preoccupied with similar structural and thematic concerns. *Mr. Fortune's Maggot*, about a middle-aged English missionary who travels to the South Sea in order to convert the heathen, crystallizes several of the issues that engage this chapter: the function of the primitive and its relation to homosexuality; the association of nature with same-sex desire; the feminization of Englishness; and the centrality of the trope of inversion. Like *Lolly Willowes*, this later text escaped censorship, even though its representation of homosexuality is more overt. Where one critic describes *Mr. Fortune's Maggot* as a novel of "major importance to gay male literature," I argue that this quirkily experi-mental text belongs within the canon of modernist lesbian literature.[19] Historically, lesbian authors have often assumed male narrative personae in order to write about female same-sex desire from a skewed perspective (Mary Renault, Marguerite Yourcenar, and Willa Cather are prime examples of this).[20] In Warner's novel the two main characters, the English missionary Timothy Fortune and Lueli, the young Polynesian boy he hopes to convert, exemplify such an adaptation of male figures to mask lesbian themes. These figures are nevertheless legible as *female* because of the ways they are overtly feminized, a characterization that speaks not only to the convention of homosexual coding but also to the modernist infantilizing of the native Other. Fortune is described as "housewifely" – he both sews and bakes – and has a temperament that is "mild as ... mothers' milk"; identifying with Sappho, he eschews the offer of native girls and remains so infatuated with Lueli that he longs to "ravish" him.[21] Lueli is a British fantasy of native compliance: he is girlish, eager to please, a docile "coquette" (20) who flaunts his "maidenly demeanour" (29). Warner self-consciously deploys primitivist discourse to portray Lueli; yet, by imbuing him with no interiority, no point of view, she reinscribes the very prelogical mentality of the *savage* that she sets out to critique.[22] Lueli remains the exotic Other: he is indolent, childish, inscrutable and fickle, does not know right from wrong, is incapable of abstracted thought, and "like a dog ... beg[s] for more" (66) when Mr. Fortune plays his harmonium. A feminine spectacle, Lueli exists so that the Englishman can have "a good stare at him" (37), and, indeed, there is an extended scene in which Fortune scrutinizes Lueli's anatomy with the precision of an evolutionary scientist, making note of his somatic differences and determining that he is a racial exemplar of "the true Polynesian type" (21). Although the novel by implication positions itself in opposition to the cultural authority of such allegedly objective scientific methods, it is nonetheless often complicit in reproducing the very stereotypes it seeks to disavow. Warner's text positions itself as a critique of imperialism; yet, like other modernist novels, it exhibits a kind of imperial nostalgia for a primitive Edenic existence outside of English culture. In locating her queer couple in an idyllic and permissive setting, one congenial to homosexuality, Warner repeatedly trades on racialized notions of the uncivilized Other despite her attempt to expose the worst excesses of modernist primitivism.[23]

Mr. Fortune's Maggot turns on a series of inverted binaries – "a turning of the tables" (90) as the novel puts it – that signal the presence of the homoerotic and crystallize what I'm calling the trope of inversion. Timothy Fortune and Lueli are not merely gay men but are feminized figures of lesbian displacement. As a missionary Mr. Fortune is obsessed with "the work of conversion" (24); he arrives on Fanua with the declared aim of proselytizing by proclaiming the gospel, and his initial exposure to the island is described through conventional imperial imagery of penetration and conquest. Fortune marvels at "having discovered" (12) this native landscape, and gazes at the eroticized foliage – which drips, ripens, and is "thick with taboos" (32) – like a new world explorer "looking at it for the first time" (9). Filled with a "sense of ownership" (10), Fortune enacts the foundational gesture of colonialism: he marks his territory by renaming Lueli "Theodore," which means God's gift.[24] This artless yet deluded missionary believes that fireworks could function as an agent of conversion (59), but this detail merely presages the fact that it is Fortune, and not Lueli, who ultimately *converts* through the mediation of a volcanic earthquake. What he converts to is a realization that Christianity and British imperialism are mutually constitutive, a "European conspiracy ... which rounds up the negro into an empire and tricks him of his patrimony" (140). This is the most serious inversion, but there are several others throughout the narrative that subvert Mr. Fortune's sense of the expected order: he is so unnerved by Lueli's nakedness that he sews him a white garment, only to conclude that clothing is an "improper spectacle" (83); he sets out to teach the natives about "dominant" Western ways, but he is the one who happily feels "dependent" (92) when Lueli teaches him how to swim; he believes that Lueli will "be saved" (176) through abstract mathematical concepts, yet Lueli is the "rescuer" (129) who prevents him from drowning during the earthquake. In this novel it is the would-be proselyte who saves the converter, the native who enlightens the missionary. Although Fortune repeatedly attacks the unholiness of idol worship, it is he who fashions a hand-made idol for his beloved, "bringing Lueli a god" (226) that is also an emblem of love. Mr. Fortune critiques his own possessive gaze – "Lueli [had] become like his idol" (118) – but his liberation from the self-serving and violent politics of British imperialism does not coincide with the relinquishing of polarized notions of the primitive and the civilized. On the contrary, Fortune's transgression into native culture marks his descent into a primordial space of homoerotic abandon that is replete with modernist conceptions of savage promiscuity.

In the end, Timothy Fortune goes native. He loses his faith in Christianity, stops wearing Western dress, abandons Western conceptions of time, and dons a feathered head-dress. Although initially he fears the termination of his "last link with European civilisation" when his watch stops (142), he ultimately comes to relish living outside of time and history – just like the other natives.[25] Warner's characterization of Fortune recalls Bronislaw Malinowski's argument that "the primitive mind" is "the human mind as we find it universally," but this anti-evolutionist presumption masks the European belief that primitive culture is inherently *backward*, a fixture of Western thought that Warner exploits.[26] Havelock Ellis wrote the Preface to the 1929 edition of Malinowski's *The Sexual Life of Savages*, perpetuating the idea that primitive peoples are libidinous, childlike, irrational, and inherently dangerous – all elements, again, that Warner borrows in her representation of Fortune's Polynesian sex odyssey.[27] The earthquake which facilitates Fortune's transformation is an eroticized interlude that simulates a sexual encounter: it shakes and rocks him and Lueli "as though they were being tossed in a blanket" (121), their arms linked around one another's bodies. Also at the scene of the quake is Mr. Fortune's fallen harmonium, which lies in devastation on the ground with "its scorched ivory keys strewed round about it like teeth fallen from a monstrous head" (137). This Medusa image is repeated later, after Fortune decides to leave Fanua forever. As he gazes into the feminized crater of the volcano, Warner writes:

> By night the spectacle might have had a sort of Medusa's head beauty, for ever wakeful and writhing and dangerous; but in the light of day it was all sordid and despairing ... What he had seen was something older than the earth; but vestigial, and to the horror of the sun ... degenerate. (218)

In both instances the Medusa image is used to signal the homoerotic, for her ancient castrating visage is a reminder that here queerness is not only feminized but is a source of cultural fear.[28] The clearest example of this occurs when Mr. Fortune initially objects to being oiled by Lueli because he believes that it is an "effeminate" (93) practice, only to justify it on medicinal grounds and rewrite it as "nothing but what was manly" (95). Although Fortune disavows the pleasure – "he assured himself [this] was not oiling" – he nonetheless revels in his "effeminacy" (94) and again subordinates his body to Lueli's tutelage.

The words Warner uses to characterize Mr. Fortune's observation of the volcanic crater – dangerous, sordid, vestigial, degenerate – are all terms that link homosexuality to the primitive, recalling Edward Carpenter's argument that the "intermediate type" is "widespread ... among ... primitive peoples and civilisations."[29] By geographically distancing Timothy Fortune from England and locating him in the imaginary space of a South Sea island, Warner projects sexual freedom on to the native landscape. The ex-missionary's lament – "Why can't I be natural?" (197) – makes little sense, given his triumph over conventions of morality, but it exposes the relative constraint of homosexuality within a British context. Similarly, Fortune's confession – "'I loved him' ... Not with what is accounted a criminal love" (192) – is legible only within an imperial realm where homosexuality is criminalized and prosecuted. Warner comically draws attention to the release of sexual impulses within primitive culture: Lueli's idol has a length of two feet, but "it was not obscene" (77), and Mr. Fortune languishes in bed, surrounded by bananas "neatly arranged [by Lueli] to encircle him as sausages" (37). In this text the phallus is a joke, a ludicrous appendage that Fortune "couldn't always control" and which signifies his "wandering from the straight path" (71).[30] Both moments underscore the sexual license that is antithetical to British reserve, accessible only outside the parameters of empire. This is made clear by the end of the novel, when Timothy Fortune decides to leave the island without Lueli. Despite his claim that "distinctions of nationality scarcely exist" (231), Fortune's "odd ways" (232) cannot ultimately be assimilated within Polynesian culture; conversely, the non-Western sexual practices of the native cannot coexist with "straight and tidy" (246) Englishness. Where *Mr. Fortune's Maggot* geographically displaces the homoerotic on to a foreign locale, *Lolly Willowes* seeks to appropriate the primitive, and link it to homosexuality, within a British context.

The section that follows helps us to understand why Warner's attempt to expand the boundaries of the normal were necessarily covert in this earlier novel, which situates the lesbian within the habits and practices of a more repressive English society. Here, it is not Polynesia that functions as a liberating Other: it is the English countryside itself that harbors a zone free of the constraints and encumbrances of same-sex taboos.

The question of sapphic modernism

In 1959, when Virginia Woolf's reputation as a writer was flagging, Warner delivered a lecture entitled "Women as writers" which revived interest in Woolf by creating intertextual dialogue with Woolf's then-forgotten essay *A Room of One's Own*.[31] Woolf's observation that women writers experience a "splitting off of consciousness" (101) – an ability to be simultaneously inside and outside of culture – is playfully echoed by Warner, who similarly invokes an image of women's dual positionality:

> Women as writers are obstinate and sly ... There is, for instance, bi-location. It is well known that a woman can be two places at once ... She can practise a mental bi-location also ... Her mind is so extensive that it can simultaneously follow a train of thought, remember what it was she had to tell the electrician, answer the telephone, keep an eye on the time, and not forget about the potatoes.[32]

While Warner's characterization of the woman writer as "sly" and capable of "bi-location" can be read as a description of Woolf's equivocal strategy in *A Room*, I suggest that these remarks – privileging duplicity and couching subversiveness within the realm of domestic familiarity – also have particular resonance for Warner's own fictional tactics. Her eccentric prose, which in one critic's words is always "pull[ing] the carpet from under the reader's feet,"[33] both obscures and reveals what I see as Warner's interest in encoding a lesbian thematic. Of course, Woolf's canonical status has never been more certain than it is today, while Warner's literary placement within the tradition of women's twentieth-century writing – despite her past prominence – is tenuous, at best. An author with prodigious imaginative scope, Warner's work includes nine books of poetry, seven novels, ten volumes of short stories, a translation of Proust, a biography of T.H. White, and many essays and reviews. One might argue, as does Warner's biographer Claire Harman, that the author's name eludes recognition precisely because her oeuvre is so tremendously varied and, as a result, difficult to categorize. Jane Marcus speculates similarly that Warner's exile from the canon has to do with the multiple genres in which she worked, but she also argues that Warner's neglect is due in large measure to the fact that she was both a lesbian and an active member of the British Communist Party.[34] While Warner's political writings on the Spanish Civil War have recently begun to be reassessed, her contribution to the development of both modernism and lesbian literary history remains undertheorized.[35]

Warner's obscurity may indeed be linked to her involvement with Marxism and her passion for women, but I would add that her marginalization – in particular her exclusion from studies of literary modernism – has at least as much to do with her narrative style itself, which consistently employs the props of traditional storytelling. Warner never "broke the sentence" in any discernibly Woolfian sense: she never attempted to rupture or reconfigure prevailing linguistic structures. Instead, her desire, as Marcus recognizes, was to deconstruct "fundamental belief systems" through her use of elegant and witty, if seemingly conventional, English prose.[36] Although several of Warner's most important texts appeared between 1925 and 1948, she is rarely categorized as a 'modernist' – even in studies which attempt to identify a predominantly sapphic aesthetic – presumably because her poetry and fiction are seen as formally conservative. Because the dominant critical discourse on modernism has tended to fetishize formal experimentation, readers today who encounter Warner for the first time are likely to assume, as does her biographer Wendy Mulford, that the author was completely unaffected by "the currents of modernism ... [of] the twenties and thirties."[37] Yet, how are we to reconcile Mulford's dismissal of modernist influence with the claim of an earlier critic, Glen Cavaliero, that Warner was, in fact, "at heart a modernist"?[38] The problem exposed by Warner's indeterminacy, it seems to me, is less about the dilemma of categorization as it is about the limitations of our conceptual understanding of modernism itself. Celeste Schenck's analysis of modernism's devaluation of conventional form, and her interrogation of the degree to which we, as feminist critics, have colluded in the marginalizing of women writers who were not stylistically radical, provides us with a way of situating an unacknowledged modernist such as Warner.[39] Certainly, at the level of the sentence, Warner's prose never approaches the lyricism or linguistic complexity of Virginia Woolf or Djuna Barnes; nor does it reflect the kinds of stylistic innovations and syntactical transpositions that can be said to characterize Gertrude Stein's work. However, in terms of larger narrative structure Warner's fiction, far from conventional or conservative, frequently melds satirical fantasy, social realism, allegory, and literary allusion – always with a convoluted eye toward subversiveness. The cumulative effect of her individually accessible sentences is never one of transparency.[40] Thus, it is disconcerting to encounter critics who valorize her as a writer of "old-fashioned virtues," particularly in light of evidence which repeatedly suggests that, in terms of the representation of heterosexuality as a normative cultural and ideological model, "breaking taboos was her *forté*."[41]

To carve a place within the canon for Warner's previously marginalized texts will necessarily alter our notions of canonicity: it will involve a rethinking of not only how Warner's work might conform to the aesthetics of modernism, but of how the aesthetic itself is challenged by her inclusion – the inclusion of a lesbian writer. I qualify her admission in this way because it is my contention that a re-evaluation of Warner at this historical juncture is made possible by, perhaps even hinges upon, our ability to claim a lesbian specificity in conjunction with her work. Jane Marcus's identification of lesbianism as that which has most contributed to Warner's neglect underscores the general tendency in the critical evaluation of her work either to ignore or to minimize the prevalence of what Terry Castle has described as "the theme of homosexuality" in Warner's "brilliant and varied writings."[42] Despite the thematic recurrence of same-sex desire in Warner's fiction and poetry, almost never is she discussed as an author of lesbian fiction. What one finds repeatedly in introductions to her work are oblique or sanitized references to her lifelong "friendship" with the poet Valentine Ackland (her partner for almost forty years), or, as is the case with the 1987 Virago reprint of *Summer Will Show*, a complete dismissal of the implications and representation of lesbian desire in the text itself.[43] One recent critic, even as he acknowledges the evident homoeroticism in one of Warner's early novels, cautions readers not to allow their knowledge of what he circumspectly terms Warner's "domestic situation" color their evaluation of her work, claiming that "the specifically sexual should not be over-stressed."[44] While this confusion of fictional content with biography is troubling because it boarders on essentialism, I suggest that the assessment of Warner's work has suffered not from essentialist readings but from a reluctance to recognize that lesbian representation figures in her writings at all.

While one can question whether Warner's own sexuality should have any bearing on the critical evaluation of her work, I think one needs simultaneously to interrogate the implications of invisibility, and consider how such erasure might function to ensure – or, conversely, disallow – certain textual readings. Much recent work in lesbian literary theory has focused upon the text's latent content – upon what is not named but rather may be inferred – as a way of extracting a lesbian reading that is, oftentimes, not immediately apparent. The influence of poststructuralism on lesbian theory, as Sally Munt has recognized, reflects this desire to read between the lines in order strategically to "inhabi[t] the text of dominant heterosexuality" and at the same time "undo it, undermine it, and construct our own destabilizing readings."[45] By suggesting that a book requires a different set of interpretive conventions, we recognize that the inscription of what we might call a lesbian aesthetic often necessitates a particular deconstructive process. Elizabeth Meese's provocative claim that "lesbian" is "a word written in invisible ink"[46] not only understands that the representation of lesbian desire has historically been subject to the imposition of cultural restraints, but suggests that lesbianism – as narrative practice – can be defined, for certain writers, as a kind of conspiratorial inscription. For if the word "lesbian" is at times, as Meese intimates, a kind of disappearing hieroglyphic, readable and yet necessarily disguised, then the question arises: on what historical and cultural conditions does its visibility depend? It is here that Warner's theorization of "bi-location" is particularly salient, for the use of doubleness as a textual strategy is not only relevant to Warner's own authorial tactics in *Lolly Willowes*, but is applicable to our experience of reading this deceptively straightforward text. Warner repeatedly draws attention to her own duplicitous intentions by explicitly thematizing the role of *the double* in her novel, both through the juxtaposition of unlikely pairings and by making overt reference to the protagonist, Lolly's divided self. In utilizing Warner's term "bi-location," I wish to emphasize what I identify as the novel's two trajectories: its overt portrayal of a single middle-aged woman's psychic evolution, and its more covert, allusive, mapping of a sapphic subtext through its depiction of this independent spinster's mutation into witch. To borrow from Willa Cather's biographer Sharon O'Brien, who asks rhetorically – regarding Cather's encoding of lesbian passion through the use of a male persona – "When is a male character not a male character?" – I would similarly inquire, concerning Warner: when is a witch not a witch?[47] The answer, it may be argued, is when the witch is a lesbian. But to arrive at such a reading requires what O'Brian, among others, has observed, namely that the sign of lesbian presence is frequently detectable only through deflection, through that which is subtle, symbolic, indirect, or covert – in short, lodged in textual places that expressly demand that we become adept at multilayered reading.

I aim to demonstrate that knowledge of Warner's sexuality, in conjunction with an understanding of the larger historical context of literary modernism, can enable an alternative and more provocative reading of Warner's best-selling first novel *Lolly Willowes*. Although published to wide critical and popular acclaim in 1926, *Lolly Willowes* is relatively unknown today. Robert Caserio, however, has recently argued that the novel "is a feminist manifesto deserving a place in the curriculum no less than Virginia Woolf's texts."[48] While Warner's novel in fact anticipates many of the issues Woolf raises in *A Room of One's Own* (published three years later), specifically the necessity for female privacy and autonomy, *Lolly Willowes* has all but disappeared from the curriculum while Woolf's essay enjoys a privileged position as one of the founding texts of modern feminist literary theory. Yet while the sapphic subtext of *A Room* has recently been addressed by critics, the lesbian implications of *Lolly Willowes* have gone completely unnoticed – even though both Woolf and Warner similarly deploy an aesthetics of indirectness to signal the presence of the homoerotic in their texts.[49] Warner's novel flouts literary conventions by combining narrative realism with satirical fantasy to tell the story of Lolly Willowes, a 47-year-old woman who is magically transformed from traditional spinster to self-empowered witch. While critics have rightly identified Lolly's retreat from marriage as a rejection of British patriarchal social values, and seen her psychic transformation as a sign of her refusal of conventional femininity, no one has attempted to read the figure of the spinster or the witch as a code for lesbianism, or analyzed the way in which Warner covertly maps lesbian desire by displacing it in the text. Despite the near consensus that recognizes in Warner a "quirky, individualistic" sensibility which relishes mischief and incongruity, critics persist in reading this novel – a valorization of witchcraft – literally.[50] Lolly's celibacy is repeatedly celebrated as the result of her self-induced autonomy, but is never contemplated as signifying an alternative sexuality; her spinsterhood is consistently read as asexual – that is, within the context of a heterosexual norm – rather than as a challenge to the boundaries of what constitutes the sexual.[51] Such critical interpretations embody certain heterosexual assumptions about female desire, at the same time as they work to eclipse and foreclose variant readings of Lolly's character.

I intend to shift the contextual focus by situating Warner's novel within a different narrative space – one that problematizes the author's relationship to representation – in order to highlight what I see to be the text's undisclosed, yet central, homoerotic focus. One might say my objective here is a creative *misreading* of what critics have presumed is the novel's heterosexual imperative: in Bonnie Zimmerman's words, a "perverse reading," a strategic lesbian–feminist appropriation of the text.[52] By foregrounding Warner's slyness, her eye for strangeness and her devotion to irreverence, I aim to demonstrate how her novel can most accurately be described in terms of its artful refusal, in essence, to play it straight with readers.

The conspicuous absence of any clear reference to female homosexuality in *Lolly Willowes* is not a strategy unique to Warner, but is characteristic of much of the modernist writing that was produced by her British and American lesbian contemporaries. By historically situating Warner's novel within the diverse context of what Shari Benstock has defined as sapphic modernism, we can begin to postulate a relation between Warner's sexual orientation and her interest in literary masquerade. Benstock, in her attempt to specify a lesbian tradition of modernist writing, distinguishes between women whose work was formally traditional, yet whose subject matter was overtly sapphic (e.g., Radclyffe Hall's *Well of Loneliness*), and those women "who filtered the lesbian content of their writing through the screen of presumably heterosexual subject matter or behind experimental literary styles" (e.g. Virginia Woolf, Gertrude Stein, H.D.).[53] Warner's novel oscillates between these two extremes to the extent that her language, while formally accessible and seemingly transparent, disguises an alternative – homoerotic – narrative. In this respect, Warner's lesbian modernist aesthetic is aligned more with Willa Cather's and Nella Larsen's than it is with those of Woolf, Stein, or Djuna Barnes, writers whose interest in a lesbian thematic is inextricable from their radical innovations in syntax and style. In contrast, both Cather and Larsen, like Warner, were busy producing writing in the 1920s and 1930s that appears conservative by high modernist standards, but whose surface simplicity belies an undercurrent of thematic complexity that encodes homoerotic desire.[54] Warner's representation of lesbianism cannot easily be subsumed within Patricia Juliana Smith's recent theorization of "authorial lesbian panic," which argues that women writers often create compelling or dangerous female characters only to destroy them "so that the narrative ideologies of institutional heterosexuality may be fulfilled."[55] Indeed, Warner's lesbian functions not as a pretext for the re-assertion of heterosexuality but as a figure of disruption who delegitimizes the courtship plot even as she herself inhabits a homoeroticized narrative space that, by implication, defines the lesbian as a non-narratable subject. Lolly Willowes's eroticized relation to nature deflects suspicion from her own same-sex desire, though homosexuality itself remains unnamed, discernible only to those who are attuned to reading for a lesbian subtext. In Warner's novel, "lesbian narrative space" exceeds our conventional understanding of discursive and narrative boundaries; Warner's representation attests to the fact that while the discursively constructed lesbian is historically variable, she always re-orders crucial narrative elements and requires new forms of representation.[56] In this way, the "formal radicalism" of *Lolly Willowes*, as John Lucas astutely observes, "is *intrinsically political*."[57] My approach juxtaposes literary with historical evidence in order to attend to "the inexplicable presence of the thing not named"[58] – in other words, the suggestion and intimation of the homoerotic.

It is important to remember that *Lolly Willowes* was published during a transitional period in England when, despite the reconfiguration of sex-roles, obscenity laws were used to censor the portrayal of "'immoral' sexual themes" – and lesbianism was invariably one of the most prominent casualties of the postwar public censure of *perverse* behavior and desire.[59] Given this homophobic climate of repression, it comes as no surprise that Warner's representation of lesbianism in *Lolly Willowes* would have more in common with *Orlando*'s sapphic blend of fantasy and truth – which, notably, escaped public censure in 1928 – than with Radclyffe Hall's starkly realistic lesbian novel, immediately banned that same year. The hermeneutical problem in Warner's work has to do with locating the homoerotic, an identification which requires that we read with a kind of double vision, with attention to more than one story concurrently. By situating Warner alongside the modernists Cather and Larsen, I am suggesting that she employs a similar strategy of concealment and disclosure, for *Lolly Willowes* tacitly invites us to read the narrative mindful of the author's literary interest in the doubling and subterfuge of "bi-location," what she elsewhere calls her "love of opaque honesty and transparent cunning."[60] A central device that illuminates this dialectic between what is named and what is not, between what is visible and what remains unseen, is Lolly's spinsterhood. The novel's fantasy element operates as a seductive ploy, creating the illusory sense that Warner's fanciful spinster–witch is dissociated from historical or social concerns. While critics have maintained that *Lolly Willowes* "ignore[s] history,"[61] I intend to demonstrate instead how this novel, punctuated throughout with historical dates, is in fact deeply embedded in the politics and culture of early twentieth-century England.

Julie Abraham's recent formulation of the relation between lesbian modernism and history does not account fully for Warner's subversive use of historical narrative. Abraham argues that lesbian experimentalists developed "more complex accounts of history" than those who were producing formally conventional work, narratives that were likely to reflect a "more conservative" understanding of history.[62] Although Warner's style appears "conventional" by Abraham's standards, her use of history is not politically conservative: like her more formally disruptive peers, Warner too selfconsciously constructs "alternative histories" for the lesbian subject through her own literary experimentalism.[63] The novel's alignment of spinsterhood with lesbianism and witchcraft needs to be situated within the larger historical context in which homosexuality and primitive mysticism were regarded as mutually constitutive, and "inverts" were thought by some to be spiritually in advance of their species. Edward Carpenter, in *Intermediate Types Among Primitive Folk: A Study in Social Evolution* (1914), argues that homosexuals have long been linked with "female wizards, or witches," a congruence that speaks to sexology's attribution of moral and intellectual superiority to the invert: "it is certain that among primitive folk the prophet, the priest, the wizard, and the witch-doctor largely unite their functions, and are … naturally [associated with] homosexuality."[64] Carpenter sees inversion as a transhistorical, cross-cultural, phenomenon linked with divination, a primitivist attribution that speaks to the larger English preoccupation with ethnographic materials and peoples.[65] As a lesbian witch, Lolly arguably signals such an evolutionary advance: she is aligned with primitive impulses – albeit sanitized English ones – and is able to see beyond the confines of her culture. Carpenter's connecting of the homoerotic nature of "primitive folk" with matriarchy speaks further to Warner's novel, which stages its heroine's escape into a community of English witches as an ultimate liberation from compulsory heterosexuality; those rites, as Carpenter notes, would likely have incorporated the "religious symbols of the Mother-goddess and her cult."[66] While *Lolly Willowes* does not involve maternal sacrifice *per se*, it does represent its heroine's unleashing of sexual pleasure in a homoeroticized English space that plays with conventional witchcraft imagery of brooms and familiars.

The odd woman as double

Lolly Willowes opens with the death of Lolly's father, Everard, and her subsequent expulsion from the Willowes's family home, a country estate the name of which, Lady Place, literalizes its affinity with the feminine and represents for her a kind of idyllic state in which the pressure to conform to a heterosexual model is all but absent. The novel relates in flashback the autonomy Lolly enjoys at Lady Place, where she exhibits no interest in any potential male suitors, and instead immerses herself in what the text indicates are subversive pursuits for a woman: brewing beer – a family passion formerly enjoyed only by male members – growing medicinal herbs, and devouring books on philosophy, demonology, and botany.[67] In particular, it is Lolly's voracious and unrestricted appetite for *unfeminine* books – "Locke on the Understanding or Glanvil on Witches" (24) – that signals her nonconformity, and unsettles the "neighbouring mammas [who] considered her ignorant" because of her unfamiliarity with the books on conduct that "*their* daughters" (24) were reading. Owen Davies observes that literate witches were thought to enhance their powers through the written word; such books and manuscripts were believed to be dangerous signifiers of nonconformity, indicators that the witch was immersed in evil-doings.[68] Warner suggests that it is precisely the absence of a maternal presence (Mrs. Willowes dies early in the novel) that most emphatically enables Lolly to disregard the dictates of female conformity and pursue alternative interests. This is not to suggest, however, that gender distinctions are not enforced at Lady Place, for the novel details the various ways in which Lolly's childhood reflects the late nineteenth-century preoccupation with femininity as a protected sanctum. The text repeatedly associates heterosexuality with entrapment and confinement, at the same time as it illustrates how Lolly manages to circumvent her early socialization. Everard's gift to his newborn daughter is a little string of evenly matched pearls, which "exactly fitted the baby's neck" and annually would be extended "until it encircled the neck of a grown-up young woman at her first ball" (12–13), a noose image which presages the sense of strangulation Lolly later experiences as a single woman in London. The mock-chivalric childhood scene in which her two elder brothers, Henry and James, tie her to a tree in order later to rescue their "captive princess" (15) – only to be endlessly distracted from her predicament – similarly prefigures Lolly's feelings of captivity, entrapment, and neglect when, at 28, she becomes an "inmate" (3) of a masculine protectorate.

As a single woman with older brothers, Lolly has no hopes of inheriting Lady Place once her father dies, and instead is immediately absorbed into her eldest brother Henry's household in London; this process of commodification – she felt "as if she were a piece of property" (7) – signals her paternalistic initiation into the world of separate spheres and indelibly marks her as a "redundant" woman.[69] Henry's family is a microcosm of the novel's larger portrait of patriarchal privilege within British society, in which the Willowes's conservatism and entrenched "old-fashioned ways" (7) are Lolly's greatest impediment to any kind of self-determination or autonomy. The text equates the family's domestic mirroring of Britain's imperialist enterprise – relatives hoard "accumulations of prosperity" (90), amassing foreign treasures from their trips to the West Indies, the Sudan, and India – with the colonization of the female body. Lolly's aunt, Emmy, returns from a trip to India preoccupied with her aging niece's single status – "Why isn't she married already?" – and insists to Everard that a trip to the colonies would improve the young woman's marital prospects: "You must let me give her a season in India" (27). This comment recalls the remarks of Anthony Ludovici who, bemoaning the 4 million "surplus women" in England in 1921, urges the nation to send this "formidable army" of spinsters to the dominions.[70] Warner's linking of heterosexuality and imperialism alludes to this practice of government-sponsored emigration for single British women, but it also signals her awareness that women were often complicit in the ideology of imperial rule.[71] It is perhaps curious that Warner aligns Aunt Emmy – who clearly believes that India "might prove to be to [Lolly's] advantage" (28) – with the government's position that regards odd women as a social problem, for she, like Lolly herself, had never married. By implicating the Aunt Emmy figure, Warner complicates her portrayal of the single woman, suggesting that spinsters too are capable of collusion with the State's regulation of heterosexual desire. At the same time, the textual evidence illustrates that Lolly and her aunt have much in common: as single unemployed women, they occupy parallel positions of superfluity. But despite her passing interest in Emmy's travel stories, Lolly consistently refuses her aunt's invitations to go to India, thereby distinguishing herself from "the Willowes way of life" (11), that is to say, the family's tacit support of colonial domination. While Aunt Emmy intends her romantic tales of "Indian life … mangoes … porters who carried Mem Sahibs … parrots flying through the jungle, ayahs with rubies in their nostrils" (28–9) as a harmless enticement to marriage, the novel aligns this British appropriation of the non-Western with the imperial intervention in domestic life.[72] Emmy's exoticized (and feminized) image of India is a Western fantasy of European expansion, in which, as the novel puts it, her narrative "beckoned [to Lolly] like … dark arms tinkling with bangles of soft gold" (29).

Whenever the text deploys colonial rhetoric it does so in order to illustrate that the "price of Empire" (90) entails the inevitable suppression of female liberty. However, the novel's invocation of feminist reform at times colludes with Anglo-centric conceptions of womanhood as a subject race: as Lolly critiques empire, she simultaneously appropriates the role of colonized Other. A clear example of this is seen immediately following Lolly's transformation into a witch, when she joyfully reflects on her triumph over "her tyrants" – the nuclear family – and re-imagines herself as a freed black slave who does "a derisive dance on the north bank of the Ohio" (152). This moment recalls the scene in Warner's *The True Heart* where Sukey

Bond identifies herself with the enslaved "good Negro," again demonstrating how the Englishwoman understands her cultural disempowerment as equivalent to that of other colonized peoples everywhere. Of course, Lolly's dance – that "slavish remnant" (152) of the past – is merely a vehicle for establishing her own feminist authority. Warner fails to recognize that her racial appropriation elides different historical legacies, conflating nineteenth-century America with twentieth-century England in order to foreground a critique of gender which hinges upon the perception that white women inhabit a colonial and subordinate role within British culture. Lolly's quest for female emancipation, in other words, is unimaginable outside of the scope of middle-class British feminism, in which women freely borrowed from the discourse of slavery to further their own ideological ends. Yet within the context of the family, Lolly's subordination and powerlessness are part of the natural order of things, a justification for British patriarchy. One of the clearest examples of the surveillance and circumscription of the single woman's self-sufficiency occurs immediately following the death of Lolly's father, when the family's antidote to her bereavement is to "put her to bed" and consequently make her feel "like an unhappy child" (44). The precise gesture of putting the daughter to bed recurs in the novel, but the family's infantilizing of Lolly, its insistence on the patriarchal status quo, is present at almost every juncture. Henry's wife, Caroline, dutifully "blink[s] her wider views in obedience to his prejudices" and "minister[s] to his imperiousness" (55), while as a couple they embody the tyranny of heterosexual privilege; Warner parodies this by depicting them as an unassailable fortress – "Henry was like a wall, and Caroline's breasts were like towers" (82) – for they function as the self-appointed arbiters of Lolly's matrimonial prospects.

The novel indicates that Lolly's subjugation is due in part to her own lack of consciousness about the possibilities of self-emancipation – an unawareness that, as will be seen, is directly linked with her latent homosexuality. Although some of her contemporaries are already challenging social and sexual conventions in 1902, Lolly, nearing 30, is not yet prepared to "take up something artistic or emancipated" (6) when her father dies. The generous inheritance Everard leaves her – "five hundred a year" (6), exactly the sum that Woolf stipulates is necessary in *A Room* – is not immediately used to forge an independent existence. Yet Lolly's psychical evolution eventually undermines the binary operations of gender in the text. Through her, Warner examines women's internalizing of societal expectations regarding normative models of female behavior and illustrates how the single woman's assault on the conventions of femininity is inextricably bound up with the political upheavals of the British suffrage movement. The novel's historical parameters cover a period in England when feminism and lesbianism were not only highly visible but frequently linked in order to discredit the suffragist cause. As Elaine Showalter observes: "The popular image of the odd woman conflated elements of the lesbian, the angular spinster, and the hysterical feminist."[73] Lolly's status as a spinster is the text's most blatant indicator that she is not all she appears to be, for despite its virginal connotations *spinster* is not at all a fixed or stable category. We know from historical sources that several pre-First World War feminists in England were choosing to have no sexual relations with men as a form of protest against the oppression of women, publicly maintaining that society "could only be improved ... [with] a large class of celibate women."[74] In the period immediately following the war, unmarried women were fighting back against the prejudices which created difficulties for them in finding a livelihood, a social life, and relationships outside of marriage. Some women were deliberately choosing to remain single and were articulating their decision in political terms. As feminist historians have pointed out, many of those identified as spinsters loved women and were involved in passionate, even perhaps sexual, relationships with members of their own sex.[75] Although these women did not always identify themselves as lesbian, either because to do so would have been seen as invalidating their cause or because they did not identify with "lesbian" as defined by the medical discourse of the sexologists, the spinster was by her very existence, in Sheila Jeffreys's words, "a living reproach to men."[76] Because single women defied sexual classification, they were pathologized as deviants: they "threatened the social organization of society, and undermined the concept of separate spheres that guaranteed patriarchal hegemony."[77] Havelock Ellis, in his study of female inversion, classifies as "homosexual" precisely those forms of behavior for which spinster–feminists were criticized by the anti-feminists; accusations of lesbianism could effectively stigmatize and subvert women's attempts at emancipation.[78] Despite Ellis's sexually progressive view that the female invert is a *natural* anomaly, he nonetheless stigmatizes her – a move that is perhaps symptomatic of the pervasive misogyny that surrounded the single woman who "refuse[d] to hand herself over as a vessel to the race."[79]

Sheila Jeffreys argues that it is important to realize that "[a]ny attack on the spinster is inevitably an attack on the lesbian," a cultural equivalence that is perhaps overstated yet nonetheless conveys the degree to which spinsterhood was perceived as pathological.[80] By the time Warner was writing *Lolly Willowes*, in the 1920s, the visibility of the spinster – specifically, the liminality of her status – was unmistakable: her appearances in the press and the novel ensured that the spinster, with all of her homosexual connotations, was a part of public discourse, subject to speculation. A salient example of this is found in Margaret Lawrence's *We Write As Women* (1937), a strange hybrid of literary criticism and psychobiography in which she speculates that "an extraordinary number of successful women are implicitly, if not actually Lesbian," and goes on to suggest that "the whole feminist enterprise ... is to a large extent the result of a sudden subconscious determination on the part of the Lesbian population to assert itself."[81] Lawrence draws a clear connection between spinsterhood and homosexuality, maintaining that "a sense of sex bitterness" often results in "the development of Lesbianism in women."[82] Although some feminist doctors and psychiatrists, as Alison Oram observes, engaged in a sustained critique of the "frustrated spinster" model, there was never any organized feminist response that attempted to formulate a politics of spinsterhood or to incorporate into public debate the increased association of spinsterhood with lesbianism.[83] Winifred Holtby effectively captures the perceived deviance of the unmarried woman when she writes:

> Today, there is a far worse crime than promiscuity; it is chastity. On all sides the unmarried woman today is surrounded by doubts cast not only upon her attractiveness or her common sense, but upon her decency, her normality, even her sanity.[84]

While *Lolly Willowes* never engages specifically with these interwar debates, the text contains several passing references to the controversy over women's sexual and social autonomy, and Warner's use of the spinster category in 1926, I would argue, is itself an implied signal of Lolly's double valence. At one point the text suggestively introduces the legal term *feme couverte*, which refers to a married woman, and then ultimately subverts its association by demonstrating that it is actually the spinster, *feme sole* (6), who is "covered over." Warner uses the language of concealment to mark the body of the single woman, expressly associating her with the idea of dissimulation, of veiling. It is lesbianism, the text intimates, that Lolly's spinsterhood disguises, and works to camouflage. From the novel's opening pages we are aware that Lolly is not like most women, a perception that is reinforced throughout the text by references to her oddness, her tendency, for example, to interrupt a staid dinner party by asking one of the guests, a man her family hopes will marry her, if he is a "were-wolf" (58). Warner frequently employs the word "odd," or suggestions of "queerness," in describing Lolly: we learn, for example, that her clothes "smelt so queerly" (18), that she relishes telling "odd jokes" (98), gathering "strange herbs" (67), "behaving ... oddly" (220), and probing "the strange places of [her] mind" (79). Increasingly, Lolly's eye gravitates toward the deviant, the "odd thing" (129). Terry Castle has argued that a "subterranean 'lesbian' meaning may be present in *odd* and its derivatives," for while the terms "homosexual" and "lesbian" are relatively new, there have "always been other words ... for pointing to the lover of women."[85] Warner's text plays on these associations, repeatedly offering the reader codes and clues regarding Lolly's indeterminate status. Thus, by the end of the novel Lolly remarks that one of the great advantages of associating with witches is that "they do not mind if you are a little odd" (250), a revelation that, it will be seen, has everything to do with the unleashing of her own repressed homoerotic longings.

At a young age Lolly evinces what Warner suggestively terms a "temperamental indifference to the need of getting married," an aversion, the narrative suggests, that is further exacerbated by her close companionship with her father (26). While Lolly's intimacy with him is never pathologized, this identification with her father is a sign of her disdain for girlish trappings, for anything that might domesticate or "subdu[e her] into young-ladyhood" (18). Warner subverts the expectation that "a young woman's normal inclination [is] towards young men" (26) by illustrating Lolly's contentment with her father, who, despite his own traditional notions regarding gender, does not impede his daughter's rejection of the conventions of femininity.[86] Thus, "[a]s innocently as the unconcerned Laura might have done, *but did not*, he waited for the ideal wooer," although he too repeatedly expresses relief when "budding suitors [are] nipped in their bud" (28; emphasis added). This suggestion of castration is consistent with other imagery in the text that aligns heterosexuality not merely with impotence but with death. Prospective husbands are referred to as "likely undertakers" (56), while Lolly visualizes one of her potential mates as a cannibal, hunched over "upon all-fours with a lamb" – presumably herself – "dangling from his mouth" (59). Henry's wife, Caroline, is the novel's clearest example of the deadening effects of marriage: at one point she describes the orderliness of her undergarments as "graveclothes ... folded in the tomb" (52). Elsewhere, at an anesthetizing family gathering, Lolly observes her sister-in-law

Sibyl as one who "exchanged her former look of a pretty ferret for this refined and waxen mask," a face preparing "for the last look of death" (91). Given the repeated evidence which envisions heterosexual union as a kind of living death, it comes as no surprise that Lolly would reject her family's efforts to transform her into yet another "memorial urn" (91). Yet, at the same time, the novel's suggestion that Lolly's resistance to marriage stems also from her "*temperamental indifference*," a predisposition which "her upbringing had only furthered" (26; emphasis added), anticipates Warner's amplification of Lolly's instinctual lesbian identification. For Lolly, "her father ... [and] Lady Place" (29) represent alternatives to the pressures of heterosexual conformity, alternatives which pave the way for her eventual substitution of the homoerotic "graces of the countryside" for London (78).

One way the text schematizes gender distinctions is through the contrast between the country, which is feminized throughout, and the city, which is aligned with masculinity and mechanization, and is portrayed as "fundamentally unnatural."[87] However, despite this seemingly neat dichotomy, the novel also problematizes the notion of what constitutes *the natural* through its representation of Lolly, whose refusal of the conventions of heterosexuality repeatedly threaten her family's idea of normative behavior. The neighbors' greatest fear when Lolly is a child is that "she might grow up eccentric," a suspicion that is subsequently realized when she rejects all male suitors and, aged 47, leaves her brother Henry's home. Warner's characterization of Lolly as "eccentric" invokes Teresa de Lauretis's theorization of the lesbian as an "eccentric subject," that is, situated in a space that is excessive to, rather than contained by, "the sociocultural institution of heterosexuality."[88] Lolly's feminine disidentification propels her to demand her inherited income from Henry, who without her knowledge has mishandled the bulk of her capital by transferring it, in 1920, to the "Ethiopian Development Syndicate" (105), a speculative investment in a part of the world where Britain's "dream of tropical wealth" flourished during the late nineteenth and early twentieth centuries.[89] Warner's selection of Ethiopia alludes to Britain's increased commercial and political involvement in Africa during the interwar period, illustrating Henry's colonial impulses and demonstrating the clear linkage between masculine empire-building and the domestication of women.[90] Henry tells Lolly, in 1921, that her stocks "will rise again the moment we have a Conservative Government" (105), an allusion to the coalition government of Prime Minister Lloyd George, which was rapidly losing ground.[91] Lolly herself never engages directly with what Henry derisively calls "all this socialist talk" (105), but she does understand her freedom from the constraints of the nuclear family as an escape from the material accumulations of Henry and Caroline's capitalist existence. The emancipationist rhetoric Lolly addresses to Henry anticipates Woolf's pronouncement in *A Room*: "Nothing is impracticable for a single, middle-aged woman with an income of her own" (104), and after procuring her inheritance, Lolly establishes her own cottage in a village called Great Mop – a comic allusion to the folklore of the witch's broom (17). The observation of feminist critics that the broomstick functions as "an emblem of female potency" is evident in Warner's text which, it will be seen, links Great Mop with Lolly's expanded eroticism.[92]

The various descriptions of Lolly as "a little odd" (251) hinge on what the text identifies as her subversive impulses: her bibliophilia, her obsession with "unseasonable" (80) flowers – an addiction the family terms "naughty ... [and] reckless" (81), her furtive consumption of French desserts (79), and, above all, her transgressive expeditions to the Chilterns, the land of witchcraft. The tension between what Lolly appears to be in public, under her family's guardianship, and who she is in private, when she slips undetected to wander the countryside alone, is exemplified by the unstable position her name occupies in the text. Depending on the speaker and the context, she is either Lolly or Laura, a nominal split which recapitulates the feelings of duplicity she experiences in London, and underscores Warner's interest in thematizing the double. Born Laura Erminia Willowes, when she "went to London she left Laura behind, and entered into a state of Aunt Lolly" (61), becoming, in effect, "two persons, each different," each embodying divergent, seemingly irreconcilable, aspects of Lolly's character (62). Significantly, although "[e]veryone spoke of her as Aunt Lolly, till in the course of time she had almost forgotten her baptismal name" (60), Everard refuses to be complicit in this erasure of her identity: he "never spoke of his daughter but as Laura" (61), thus illustrating once again his alliance with what, for Lolly, is a more authentic representation of the self. Yet Warner also calls into question this perception of authenticity by repeatedly pointing to Lolly's doubleness, the tension – even once she becomes a witch and reclaims her given name, Laura – between "her old self" (154) and the new. The text critiques the assumption that Lolly had renounced so much of herself in leaving Lady Place that "it seemed natural to relinquish her name also" (61) by defamiliarizing the concept of the natural. Through Lolly, Warner interrogates the cultural boundary of what constitutes normative behavior by illustrating that a woman's birth-name is not, as Lolly's family supposes, "a thing out of common speech" (61). The problematical position that *naming* occupies in the text, the numerous references to the Lolly–Laura bifurcation, is a gauge of the author's recognition that women have historically been exiled from linguistic self-definition. At the same time, the focus on duality reflects Warner's larger preoccupation with her character's split subjectivity – the friction between her conscious and unconscious selves.

The text aligns Lolly's homoerotic impulses with the unconscious; at the same time it situates her transformation into a witch within a larger historical framework. Although Lolly's internal stirrings are a considerable impetus, equally important to her metamorphosis is the centrality of the war, and the concomitant crisis in gender roles it precipitates. It is ultimately the interrelation between internal and external stimuli that propels Lolly to leave her brother Henry's home and eventually recuperate the part of herself that has been suppressed – "Laura [who] was put away" (62) – through domestication and socialization. Robert Caserio's observation that Warner's work exhibits a "fidelity to historical concreteness," at the same time as her fiction "attempts to dissolve realism," is an astute assessment of what Warner seeks to do with *Lolly Willowes*; however, his contention that the novel's fantasy element obscures that which is "politically and historically immediate" works against what I see as Warner's interest in historicizing Lolly's conversion.[93] The novel's several key historical dates and references localize and situate what *appears* to be Lolly's purely arbitrary magical mutation into a witch. We learn that she is born into a conservative family in 1874, a period in Britain in which, according to historian Susan Kingsley Kent, the battle for women's suffrage was at a standstill.[94] By the time Lolly is relegated to Henry's home this doldrum stage of reform is still in effect, as is evidenced by her own unawareness that "[e]ven in 1902 there were some forward spirits" (7) – women who are already politicized – working for emancipation. In 1905 Lolly's brother James dies unexpectedly, and as a result Lady Place is let. According to Kingsley Kent, that year was a turning point for the proponents of women's suffrage, signaling an increase in feminist fervor, although Lolly herself never exhibits signs of militancy. Even so, 1905 is still a critical year for Lolly because it marks her loss of a feminine ideal, Lady Place, which represents for her both intellectual freedom and sexual autonomy. Her adherence to these principles aligns her with the suffragette cause, although she is not yet a self-conscious feminist. Lolly has not lived at Lady Place for several years, yet it still occupies for her a kind of mythic, primordial status; because the effect of this feminized space is more psychic than material, Warner employs the language of repression to describe Lolly's loss: "it seemed as though some familiar murmuring brook had suddenly gone underground" (64).

By the time the war breaks out the dissonance between Lolly's two selves is fully in play, but she remains initially a docile and complacent family member despite her intermittent transgressive wanderings to the Chilterns. Although the husband of her niece Fancy "was killed in December 1916" (69), provoking Fancy to leave her baby and go to France to drive motor lorries, "[t]he war had no such excitements for Laura" (70). As if compelled by some vague sense of patriotic duty, Lolly wraps parcels for the Front, but unlike Fancy, whose war fervor horrifies the restrained Willowes, Lolly remains largely disaffected and for the most part uninvolved in the war effort. She continues to do up parcels until "the eleventh day of November 1918," the end of the war and also the year in which women over 30 in England got the vote (primarily for their war work); but Lolly herself, now 44, does not register the political implications of female enfranchisement. Although Lolly never sentimentalizes the war, instead ridiculing the "cheap symbolism" of the recruiting posters she observes, she is nevertheless moved by the fact that "blood was being shed for her" (70). The social disorder provoked by the war initially appears to be inconsequential for Lolly's life, but the evidence suggests that, in fact, her feminist and erotic awakening is linked directly to her experience of the Great War. Sandra Gilbert and Susan Gubar have demonstrated how, for both heterosexual and homosexual British women, "the war's 'topsy–turvy' role reversals" brought about a "release of female libidinal energy."[95] While Lolly's erotic release has nothing to do with militarism *per se*, her first taste of freedom is nonetheless a consequence of the war's erosion of prescribed gender roles. It is only after the war that Lolly selfconsciously questions the Willowes's entrenched traditions, when, almost imperceptibly, she slowly shifts perspective: "she was conscious, more conscious than [Henry and Caroline], that the younger members of the family had somehow moved into new positions" (73). This ideological shift is captured by Warner's contemporary, Maude Royden, who observes that the war has created an unprecedented generational divide: "there was never so great a gulf as there is [now] between the generation to which I belong and those young people who are now

eighteen, nineteen, or twenty years of age."[96] Echoing Royden's perception that one
major consequence of war has been the destabilizing of custom and tradition, Lolly
begins for the first time to question the dominant views of sexual morality. Never
before had Lolly challenged the value of her family's "old and honourable symbols"
(73), traditions which generated and reproduced the Willowes's conservatism.
Once victory is declared in England, the family is intent on recuperating and re-
instating the paternalistic values of the past, for they "had done with war, whereas
[Lolly] had only shelved it" (73). What Lolly slowly registers is the reconfiguration
of sex roles that the war, and in particular the feminist attack on male privilege,
help to realize. The war is for her ultimately a catalyst through which, for the first
time, she sees her own subjugated life as an "anachronis[m]" (74), incompatible
with the independence of other single women.

Importantly, Lolly's independence begins with the secret purchase of a map.
Warner meticulously describes Lolly's selection of a guide-book to the Chilterns,
echoing the interwar fascination with topographical guides and country leisure:

> It was just what she wanted, for it was extremely plain and unperturbed. Beginning
> as early as possible with Geology, it passed to Flora and Fauna, Watersheds,
> Ecclesiastical Foundations and Local Government. After that came a list of all the
> towns and villages, shortly described in alphabetical order ... She unfolded the
> map. The woods were coloured green and the main roads red. There was a great
> deal of green (88–89).

This loving description of Lolly's guide to the English countryside is later under-
cut, however, when after her move to Great Mop (population 227) she does an "odd
thing" (129): she takes "her guide-book and map" (130) and deliberately throws both
down a disused well. Such a move situates Lolly in opposition to the mainstream
preservationist view that urged map-awareness and policed the hiker's appropriate
conduct in nature. The period's preoccupation with observation and orientation,
according to David Matless, aimed to produce an ideal "geographer–citizen" who
would gain respect for the landscape through surveying it. The key document of
geographical education was the map. Maps and the excursions to the countryside
they fostered not only indoctrinated citizens in the "proper perspective" but were
thought to purify them, and thus to consolidate their national identity.[97] As Matless
notes, the scene in which Lolly abandons her map and guide represents her
rejection of the masculinist bias of formal geography and signals her embrace of an
expressly feminized relation to the landscape.[98] By abandoning the products of
conventional cartography, Lolly repudiates the dominant geographical discourse
that privileged a male gaze and instead adopts an alternative spectatorship: one that
unleashes a subjective gaze which privileges that which is not visible – namely,
witchcraft and magic. Yet this subjective gaze is not a rejection of her cultural
identification as an English citizen. By moving to the Chilterns, a hidden hamlet in
Buckinghamshire whose territorial boundary markers survive from the Anglo-
Saxon period, Lolly consolidates her Englishness through identification with the
beauty of the landscape, a gesture that aligns her with interwar agronomists, rural
conservationists, and social historians who argued that the land was essential to the
spiritual life of contemporary Britons.[99] Lolly's reconfiguration of space privileges

both a *female* gaze, as Matless suggests, and a distinctly *homoerotic* one: her voyage into "unmapped" territory can be read as a metaphor for the way in which Warner re-imagines the community of the nation for the English lesbian.[100]

Locating the erotic

The turning point for Lolly, and the moment when the novel discernibly shifts from a realistic to a fantastic register – the point at which she "felt as though she had awoken ... from ... [a] slumber," only to find her familiars "unrecognizable" (90) – occurs in 1921, when Parliament refused to criminalize lesbianism. This was not for progressive reasons, but because the legislature feared an increase in lesbianism were it given publicity.[101] *Lolly Willowes* makes no overt reference to this parliamentary debate, but Warner's use of 1921 as the watershed year in Lolly's life, the point at which she experiences her pivotal erotic – and, as a result, political – awakening, suggests the author's interest in subverting the government's attempt to ensure the invisibility of Britain's lesbians. By staging Lolly's most charged and, I would argue, most homoerotic moment – her episode of "great longing" at the florist–greengrocer's (85) – during such a repressive period in England, Warner provides a corrective to the State's insistence that silence would render the lesbian invisible. At the same time, Warner counters the notoriety of the single woman as a sexual freak by depicting Lolly's moment of illumination, during the winter of 1921, as an experience of verdant lushness, bodily pleasure and renewal.[102] As Lolly wanders into the overcrowded florist–greengrocer's shop she harbors "no particular intention of extravagance" (83), but extravagance is precisely what happens once she finds herself inside the store – not in terms of consumption, but rather with respect to herself. That is, what Lolly experiences in the shop as she gazes with rapture at the abundance of flowers, vegetables, bottled fruits in syrup, home-made jams, baskets of eggs, trays of walnuts, chestnuts, and filberts – all heaped together in "countrified disorder" (84) – is her own lack of restraint, her own digression from moderation, from what her family views as the *proper* bounds of behavior for a woman. Standing in the midst of the shop's overgrown, earthy display, Lolly slips into a kind of sensual abandon in which she "forgot the whole of her London life," and instead imagines herself standing alone in an orchard, her feet implanted in the grass "as though she were a tree herself," her arms extended, "stretched up like branches" (84–5). Warner gives Lolly's inarticulate desire a somatic dimension in this scene, physicalizing her "great longing" by illustrating the way in which it "weigh[s] upon her like the load of ripened fruit upon a tree" (85). But because Lolly herself here *is* the tree, her limbs alive with ripeness and fruition, the description of her fingers eagerly "seeking the rounded ovals of the fruit," her hands "search[ing] among the leaves" (85), can be read only as a self-reflexive gesture, signaling her body's autoerotic reverie.[103] Not surprisingly, Warner tells us that Lolly "looked like a woman roused out of a fond dream" (86) when she is startled into wakefulness by a man's voice, for arousal is precisely what has developed in Lolly in the shop. The seemingly impulsive purchase she makes as she prepares to leave, a bunch of glorious chrysanthemums with huge "curled petals ... [a] deep garnet colour within and a tawny yellow without," is not at all arbitrary. Lolly's fixation with "their sleek flesh" and her "long[ing] for the moment when she might stroke her hand over those mop heads" (86) recapitulate her interest in erotic exploration and allude to Great Mop as the site of this pursuit. Warner here substitutes curled, fleshy petals for the female body, but her meaning is not obscured; Lolly's responsiveness, in short, "pleased her greatly" (84).

Significantly, this indulgence of "her sensations" has a liberatory effect, instilling in Lolly the conviction that escape from convention is possible, that she can leave London and create her own material reality out of "the country of her autumn imagination" (87) – in other words, out of the confluence of pleasure and nature. Warner's use of 1921 as the turning point for this conversion has additional import because it marks the publication of a book that was highly influential to Warner's text, Margaret Murray's *The Witch Cult in Western Europe*. Warner read the book when it first appeared, and after *Lolly Willowes* had been published she sent Murray a copy of her novel. The two women met soon afterward for lunch, and Warner, clearly entranced, records in a letter her impression of Murray's charisma: "I wish I were in her coven, perhaps I shall be."[104] Murray is the first feminist historian to counter the conventional wisdom, initially disseminated by the Catholic Church, that witches are the perpetrators of Satanic evil; her book explores the late medieval period in Great Britain to demonstrate that the witch cult was a highly developed pagan religion which Christianity was determined to eradicate. Murray replicates Frazer's model of fertility cults,[105] arguing that witchcraft was a form of nature worship that survived from pre-Christian paganism and was the original religion of the British Isles.[106] This focus on nature and English pre-history is crucial to an understanding of how Warner seeks to legitimize the spinster–lesbian's entitlement to the nation by associating her with indigenous English values. If rural England is constitutive of English identity, then Lolly's robust love of her "milky green" (151) and fragrant "pastoral landscape" (164) is a sure sign that she is marked by essentially English qualities. Murray notes that sexual rites played a role in the nature rituals of witchcraft, and her evidence suggests that participants engaged in sexual activity with members of the same as well as the opposite sex. Murray's influence on *Lolly Willowes* is evident in Warner's representation of the witch as an eroticized figure who is preoccupied with the English countryside; but Warner diverges from Murray's historical perspective by decontextualizing the witch, transporting her to the twentieth-century in order to politicize her as a feminist agent. We see evidence of the British rehabilitation of the witch as a liberatory outlaw figure in the work of Edith Lees Ellis, who claims her as a national icon: "As mystic, as witch, as conjurer, and as artist it is time [woman] unfurled her own flag and hoisted her own colours."[107]

Although less conspicuously nationalistic, Warner conflates the spinster and the witch because each similarly poses a threat to heterosexuality. Inquisitorial records report that witches were held accountable for obsessive sexual desire in men as well as male impotence, and in some cases "were also known for removing the male organ altogether."[108] While spinsters were not vilified for literal castration, the rise of the sexually independent woman created a crisis in masculinity, enabling men to accuse her, in effect, of emasculating England.[109] Both the spinster and the witch are dangerous precisely because each threatens the hegemony of male sexual privilege. Warner's text invokes this association by linking Lolly's feminist conversion with sexual inversion – an equation originally made by the sexologists, who claimed that female homosexuality was increasing because of feminism. Just one year after her electric moment in the greengrocer's, Lolly is transformed: "She, Laura Willowes, in England, in the year 1922, had entered into a compact with the Devil" (172), a compact, I argue, that has as its source a heretofore unacknowledged erotic basis. This was, importantly, a period of increased interest in the occult in Britain: magician and demonologist Aleister Crowley, for example, was conducting pagan rituals and sexual rites, declaring that he would "restore paganism in a purer form" to modern culture.[110] Warner never replicates Crowley's bestial orgies, but she does eroticize the body of the witch, linking it to the uncanny and to homoerotic desire. Critics have unproblematically accepted, and celebrated, the novel's explanation of Lolly's celibacy as the result of her fidelity to a feminist agenda, a fact underscored by Caserio's observation that Lolly is "so apparently fulfilled by herself, that her love appears to be of a paradoxically non-desiring kind."[111] This perspective originates in the text itself, where the Willowes's family repeatedly views Lolly as an asexual being, despite frequent attempts to marry her off, perpetually ensconced in a single bed for which "large linen sheets" (2) would be extraneous. The reading of Lolly as "old-maidishly" (227) non-desiring is persuasive only superficially, to the extent that she has no embodied lover, but it is misleading in light of her eroticized relation to nature, her passionate attachment to Great Mop, and particularly in terms of the repeated references to her enigmatic, indefinable, longing.

Underlying all of these attractions is Lolly's relation to her own body which, despite popular critical opinion, is not devoid of eros. While critics have argued that Lolly's self-possession "resists the erotic," that her rapture is analogous to that of "St. Teresa as the bride of Christ," I intend instead to demonstrate the ways in which Lolly's "recurrent autumnal fever" (78) – that is, her desire – destabilizes these suppositions.[112] She is said to be "without coquetry" (26), and, in terms of her resistance to the conventions of heterosexuality, this is largely true: – "[w]hat beauties of person she had were as unsweetened as her beauties of mind" (25); but this lack of affectation need not suggest that she is unconcerned with the body. As a young woman Lolly distracts herself from Caroline's talk of marriage by picking a red geranium and staining her wrist "with the juice of its crushed petals" (3), a cosmetic, if seemingly suicidal, gesture similar to her girlhood experience of "stain[ing] her pale cheeks" in order to gaze at her reflection (3). These details are not the signs of a woman unconcerned with physicality – though her impulses of adornment do not arise from a conventional interest in feminine allure – and indeed we see ample evidence of Lolly's susceptibility to corporeal pleasure. Because Lolly's attention to the somatic is never linked with an objective to incite male attention, critics have mistakenly read her body as a kind of blank slate, unmarked by desire. Warner contrasts the austerity and asceticism of Lolly's life in London, where bodily excess is realized through the once-weekly consumption of "extra trivialities such as sardines and celery" (51), with the gratification of the senses that Lolly repeatedly cultivates, alone, on her secret sojourns to the country. She subverts her family's practice of English thrift by allowing herself little indulgences of the body:

hidden packets of roasted chestnuts "taken home for bedroom eating"; the experimental purchase of "expensive soaps"; and the sumptuous pleasure she takes in eating "*marrons glacés*" (79). In particular, Lolly's attraction to French culture underscores her deviation from British propriety, as exemplified by the prominence in her new cottage of a classical print of the Empress Josephine, the consort of Napoleon, complete "with ruined temples, and volcanoes" (110); such an exhibit of wantonness would have been inconceivable in London. Such representation is consistent with other English lesbian uses of the foreign or exotic locale to signal female same-sex desire (we see this, for example, in Woolf's use of Constantinople as the site for Orlando's sex-change, and in Hall's staging of the consummation of Stephen's and Mary's love affair in Tenerife). We see that the splendidly colored lilies Lolly secretly procures come from Africa (81), a geographical space which, from an English perspective, is both exotic and inherently dangerous. One way in which Warner conveys Lolly's pleasure in the body, and which at the same time distinguishes her from the Willowes's Englishness, is by contrasting her version of domesticity with that of her great-great-aunt Salome. Unlike Salome who, as a "loyal subject" (8) to the crown, gained favor from King George III for her puff-pastry, Lolly's cookery is never that of a dutiful English housewife. Unconcerned with the predilections of "His Majesty's eating" (8), Lolly forms her current scones "into likenesses of the village people" (145), so that when the dough bakes their bodies swell, becoming malformed shapes. Although Lolly feels "slightly ashamed of her freak" because it "was unkind to play these tricks with her neighbour's bodies," her contrition does not prevent her from feeding the "strange shapes" (145) to Mr. Saunter, who without comment splits and butters them. Warner here situates Lolly in a very different relation to the empire from that of the compliant Salome, repositioning her not as loyal subject but, in effect, as a subversive queen, re-creating and transforming the body politic as it pleases her.

Lolly's intermittent indulgence of the senses is juxtaposed with multiple references to an insatiable *psychological* longing, a "groping after something that eluded her experience" (78). This slippery "something," I'm arguing, is Lolly's lesbianism, for the text offers us several suggestive "clue[s] to her disquiet" (78), disclosures that invite us to interpret Lolly's spinsterhood as a site not of lack but of contradiction, a space of instability which ultimately privileges the homoerotic. Warner creates a jarring contrast between Lolly's limited bodily "self-indulgences" (79) and her more elemental insatiability, demonstrating that while Lolly is indeed a body with inarticulate yearnings, both her limited experiential context and the cultural prohibition against same-sex desire inhibit her from identifying herself as lesbian. "What It was exactly, she would have found hard to say" (76), for Lolly lacks not only the social exposure that would facilitate self-recognition, but the language that would enable self-representation. However, at the same time as Warner intimates that lesbian identity is constructed, she appears to align herself with a more essentialist position; the text indicates that Lolly's unnameable longing is not empirical, but clearly prefigures her circumscribed experience, arising instead from "the strange places of the mind" (79). Embedded within the text are many references to Lolly's nebulous desire, her "ghost-like feeling" that is described as both "familiar" and "underground" (64), conjuring an image of her split subjectivity.

We see repeated examples of this doubleness in Lolly, instances where, "while her body" sits passively with Henry and Caroline, "her mind walked by lonely seaboards, in marshes and fens, or came at night to the edge of a wood" (77). Warner's portrayal of Lolly's psychical dissociation here invokes Teresa de Lauretis's description of the unconscious as a point of resistance, "*a resistance to* identification ... with femininity."[113] It is significant that Lolly "never imagined herself in these places by daylight" (77), because in psychoanalytical terms her wanderings arise from that subversive part of herself which "lurked in waste places, that was hinted at by the sound of water gurgling through deep channels" (78) – in other words, her lesbian subconscious. The language Warner uses to portray Lolly's state during these episodes – "day-dreaming ... almost a hallucination" (77) – suggests that lesbian resistance may not be directly accessible, but at the same time the novel demonstrates that the source of Lolly's feminist transformation is precisely such oppositional moments of semi-consciousness. Warner's description of Lolly's sensations as ghostly recalls Terry Castle's analysis of the literary lesbian as a spectral figure, historically dematerialized by Western culture, "as if vaporized by the forces of heterosexual propriety."[114] In order to see this immaterial figure, one must necessarily "focus on presence instead of absence, plentitude instead of scarcity."[115]

Castle's term, "apparitional," provides us with a way of characterizing Lolly's lesbianism, of situating her submerged unconscious longing – her groping for "something that was shadowy and menacing, and yet in some way congenial" (78) – within a sexual context. This elusive desire, her "scarcely knowing what it was that she knew" (172), is explicitly linked with several references to Lolly's "secret" – a word one might consider replete with homosexual connotation – which in turn is tied to her transformation into a witch, itself a category suggestive of lawlessness and subversiveness. Warner's reference to Lolly's "aptness for arousing ... a kind of ungodly hallowedness" (78) foreshadows her witchery at Great Mop, but it also underscores the author's interest in identifying Lolly with the incongruous, with the destabilizing of conventional juxtapositions. The most marked example of this unlikely coupling is, of course, Lolly herself, whose embodiment of the spinster–witch dualism both camouflages and exposes "her own secret" (78). Yet the revelation of this secret requires an intervention: it necessarily "wait[s] to be interpreted" (139) by the reader. *Lolly Willowes* contains various suggestive statements that invite us to read the text meta-critically, for the language of detection – clues, secrets, interpretation – invariably has as much to do with our hermeneutical experience as postmodern readers as it does with Lolly herself, who, like us, searches until "she had almost pounced on the clue ... to the secret country of her mind" (137). One of the most salient confirmations of Lolly's hidden identity is the evidence with which Warner marks her heroine's body from the outset. When Lolly becomes a witch it is "her flesh" that first accepts "the new order of things" (176), a readjustment that is prefigured by several earlier indications that perhaps witches are not made, but born.

Warner maps on to Lolly what we might call a *physiognomy of witchiness*, alluding not only to the notion that the bodies of suspected witches were unnaturally marked (by extra teats or spots from which familiars were thought to suck blood), but to the pervasive idea that the lesbian embodied Otherness: her features are "rather pointed" (25) from an early age, and over time she develops a "hook nose and ... sharp chin" (59) that become progressively more pronounced until they "were defined as sharply as the peaks of a holly leaf" (120). Lolly's "natural leaning" (234) toward witchcraft thus reads as equivalent to an undisclosed lesbianism. Claire Harman's observation that Warner's words often have a double or "second meaning" is evident in this novel, where the word "natural" is repeatedly used in conjunction with Lolly's metamorphosis to mark her lesbianism as normative.[116] Warner stresses that "it seemed most natural" (251) for Lolly to become a witch in order to illustrate the lesbian body's "dignity of natural behaviour" (249), for this was a time in England when both lesbians and spinsters were routinely regarded as sexual deviants. Although the text at one point refers to Lolly's transformation as "the moment of election," thus suggesting that her witchery is a choice, Warner maintains that "the true Laura ... was a witch by vocation" (178), again aligning herself with a more essentialist view of lesbian identity. Although the novel vacillates between contradictory claims regarding the construction of the lesbian subject, to the extent that Warner seeks to destigmatize the lesbian body, her text frequently upholds a notion of Lolly's innate difference. Thus, the evidence reveals that even in the old days at Lady Place the elusive "impulse had stirred in her" (178), a predilection that Warner sexualizes when she states that "unrealized, had Laura been carrying her talisman in her pocket" (178), a hidden eroticized space that synecdochially stands in for her female genitalia. Illustrative of this point is an additional veiled reference to Lolly's sexual organs, in which the "warmth between her knees" – literally, a kitten on her lap – figuratively signals her unmatched bodily "contentment" (176) as a witch. This cat, "her familiar," is significantly an emissary from Satan, a "sign of the bond between them" (173). One of the characteristic elements of the body of the witch is her ability to transform herself into other bodies, to shift shape, and to breach boundaries.[117] What the text repeatedly indicates is that spinster–lesbians, like witches, are spatially coextensive with a variety of objects and are frequently "under cover" (149).

The text is ultimately based on a series of substitutions – in Judith Butler's words, a "specific practice of dissimulation" – that point toward Lolly's lesbianism.[118] Butler's discussion of Willa Cather, in which she argues that "lesbian sexuality within [her] text is produced as a perpetual challenge to legibility," provides us with a cogent way of understanding Warner's own strategy in Lolly Willowes, where the workings of lesbian desire are never discursively immediate.[119] Rather, Warner constitutes the lesbian through a process of displacement and exchange. Nature, in particular, has a substitutive function in this novel, frequently standing in for the eroticized female body, as was seen earlier in the representation of Lolly as a ripening tree. Nature is a feminized presence throughout the text, described at one point as so "moist and swell[ing]" that Lolly languishes with "the contentment of the newly awakened" (186) in its pastoral lushness.[120] Yet this is not a landscape, from her perspective, that is subject to the co-opting and violence of a male gaze. At one point her nephew Titus, surveying the view at Great Mop, confesses that he "should like to stroke it" (162), a remark that sends a "cold shiver" through Lolly because his desire is synonymous with sexual violation. Lolly experiences Titus's love as a "horror" because it "was different in kind from hers," that is to say, based on a "possessive and masculine" (162) model of heterosexual desire, but what precisely constitutes her "kind" of love is left undisclosed. The only clue Warner offers is that, since Titus's arrival, "[Lolly] had not been allowed to love in her own way" (163), a suggestive though circumspect allusion to her homoerotic impulses. Titus is represented as a colonizer, a "usurping monarch" (160), who "loved the countryside as though it were a body" (162), a distinctly female body that, "[without] struggle" (163), he can appropriate at will. This representation captures the conventional gendering of the landscape as feminine, and recalls the preservationist assumption that the English countryside is a female body that requires male protection.[121] Titus is "burgeoned with projects" (161) to improve village life, a sign that the countryside is being eroded by masculine urban influence.

Warner draws a parallel between heterosexuality and imperialism, indicating that even though Lolly too relishes the landscape – the green meadows and hills were "hers ... all hers" (157) – she herself is allegedly not "in possession" (163) of its beauty. Although Warner later complicates this equation, here female spectatorship is not aligned with domination. Lolly's gaze repeatedly returns to "the landscape that she loved so jealously" (162), but her observation distances itself from Titus's masculine way of seeing. Where much preservationist literature sought to create observant citizens through proper spectatorship – guides instructed rural visitors on "*how* to see" – Warner subverts this model by privileging a woman's homoerotic gaze upon nature.[122] Rather than desiring to own the countryside, Lolly, who had relinquished everything to come to Great Mop, pursues a more reciprocal relation with the landscape, so that, for example, when Titus's "dynastic will" (227) encroaches on her solitude, the anthropomorphized countryside "withdrew itself further from her," the woods "hushed their talk," and the hills "locked up their thoughts" (164) whenever he is in her company. Spatially, Titus's presence transforms nature for Lolly, making her feel constricted and "enclosed ... as though [nature] were a room" (155) surrounded by "barriers" (157) from which she cannot break free. Yet when Titus is away, Lolly once again experiences the countryside as a boundless and liberating space: the winds release "exciting voices" (109) for her pleasure and the hills fold "themselves round her like the fingers of a hand" (129). This image suggests a woman's conspiratorial embrace, for nature, with her "rising undulations" (108), is always coded feminine. By casting nature as a woman's body that is "congenial to [Lolly's] spirit" (109) only when Titus is elsewhere, Warner illustrates the degree to which lesbian eroticism is dependent on the absence of masculine intervention. Warner states that Lolly had not chosen Great Mop in order "to concern herself with the hearts of men," and indeed we see that the revelation of "her own secret, if she had one" (129) hinges upon her circulation within what is clearly a feminized rural community – despite the appearance of men.[123]

The day on which Lolly first arrives, alone, at Great Mop, she is greeted by "unchastened gusts" – riotous, excessive weather that "would never be allowed in London" (109) – a sign that the seeming placidity of her new home conceals a potential for excitability and intemperance, or, what Lolly herself might call, "a great deal of pleasure" (148). Where Jane Marcus reads the countryside as a maternal presence, I see the operations of a lover, even when the language of maternity invades the narrative.[124] We see evidence of this during one of the novel's more enigmatic scenes, which occurs before Lolly's compact with Satan but after her initial discomfort with the villagers' strangeness has dissipated. One night, as Lolly takes a solitary walk into her familiar countryside, she hears a distant pulsation that inexplicably fills her with "an overwhelming terror" (136), the shrill sound of an ordinary goods train making its way up a steepening track. While her ears welcome the "different voices" of nature, this noise renders her "defenseless" and makes her feel "exposed" – even though, having lived in London, Lolly is surely accustomed to the sounds of mechanization. The reason why this particular train alarms her is complicated, for the moment is ultimately not about *this* train's noise, but rather has to do with Lolly's own coming to consciousness as a sexual being. The imagery moves in more than one direction, but what is clear from the outset is that the accelerating fear Lolly experiences when she hears the train is linked, in her mind, with the uncovering of her "secret" (137). The relentlessness of the train's "wicked sound" prompts Lolly to recollect an earlier experience in the goods yard at Paddington when, unexpectedly, "she had almost pounced on [her] clue" (137). The train functions as a vehicle for Lolly's self-revelation, never fully disclosed but only intimated, regarding her lesbian identity: for Lolly, the deafening shriek that permeates the countryside "expressed something eternally outcast and reprobated by man, stealthily trafficking by night" (136–7), an allusion to homosexual covertness. Warner here combines recognizable male and female sexual imagery – the train, obviously phallic, inches its way through the "dark clefts" (137) of the feminized landscape – but she also conflates these elements and destabilizes the opposition. In her representation of the train Warner intertwines ejaculatory and reproductive imagery, so that as the locomotive reaches the top of a cutting, just as Lolly seems about to grasp her secret, "with a shriek of delight it began to pour itself downhill" (138). The elusive clue here "slid through her hands again," suggesting a kind of failed orgasm, but the expulsive outburst stimulates a birth-fantasy in which she reconfigures the train as a maternal source. This confluence of sexual and maternal imagery is consistent with the perspective of several medical "experts" who acknowledged that the single woman had sexual drives and maternal instincts; but, in contrast to these doctors and psychiatrists, who argued that the spinster could only *sublimate* her desires through platonic female friendships or adoptive children, Warner shows how sexual pleasure asserts its own place in Lolly's autoerotic imaginary.[125] Lolly amusedly imagines the train as it "labour[s]" toward London, "loaded with cabbages" until, finally, in "due course," the vegetables would reach "their bourne" and "shed all their midnight devilry" in Henry and Caroline's pot. The play on the word "devilry" – the context evokes both *delivery* and *devil* – indicates that what is at stake here is nothing less than Lolly's subversive self-genesis. That this reverie has to do with the birth of her own outlaw self is underscored by a later reference to Satan's "nine months" (179) of inconspicuous surveillance, the span of her erotic gestation in Great Mop. The initial terror that precedes this sexualized delivery scene suggests that Lolly's self-creation, her lesbian awakening, will be neither conventional nor easily achieved, but by the end of this convoluted interlude she has clearly crossed an invisible threshold, for she experiences "an odd feeling of respect" (139) for what has transpired.

Although Lolly's secret remains elusive at this point, she longs to "yield herself" (136) to its logic and realizes that "Great Mop was the likeliest place to find it" (138). The geographical trip from London to the countryside coincides with her journey into her "secret" self; what follows in the text are various manifestations of the way in which she gives herself over to the inducements of the village. This giving over is twofold, with both a political and a sexual dimension. Even before Lolly pledges herself to Satan, her psychical evolution as a witch is apparent – "She was changed, and knew it" (152) – a shift that is expressed in overtly feminist terms. In recollecting her prior life in London, Lolly thinks about the oppressiveness of her family and concludes that there was "no question of forgiving them," allegedly because she does not have a "forgiving nature" (152). On further reflection, however, she draws a parallel between the imperial will of the family and that of society, seeing a relation between the tyranny of the domestic and the larger patriarchal sphere: "If she were to start forgiving she must needs forgive Society, the Law, the Church, the History of Europe, the Old Testament … the bank of England, Prostitution, the Architect of Apsley Terrace, and half a dozen other useful props of civilization" (152). Although obviously politicized here, Lolly's consciousness does not compel her to intervene and attempt to transform the social body, either through legislative or through any other direct feminist action; rather, she resolves, simply, to "forget them" (152). Critics have interpreted this effacement as Lolly's flight from reality, evidence of her political apathy; from that perspective, her retreat – into an ahistorical fantasy world of oblivion – illustrates the novel's "disjunction between feminist theory and concretely lived elaborations of the theory."[126] This interpretation, in my view, has a heterosexual bias, for it neglects to consider the political aspect of Lolly's nonintervention, ignoring the degree to which her feminism is inflected by her unarticulated lesbianism. The representation of Lolly's refusal to engage in political activism has to do with Warner's recognition that sexual difference complicates one's relation to the State, requiring alternative forms of intervention.

The pleasures of concealment

By the 1920s – and the text pointedly tells us that Lolly's compact with Satan occurs in 1922 – charges of lesbianism had become a common way in England to discredit feminist reformers; clearly that was not the decade, if one were lesbian, to anticipate social affirmation or political incorporation. Warner's treatment of lesbianism in this text invites comparison with Radclyffe Hall's short story "Miss Ogilvy finds herself," about a "queer" middle-aged spinster who returns to England at the end of the Great War, after performing heroically at the French Front, only to realize the impossibility of assimilating her "manly" self into English society. This story (written in 1926 but not published until 1934) about the quandary faced by the postwar homosexual woman veers from realism into fantasy when Miss Ogilvy leaves England and takes refuge on a remote island, where she discovers that she harbors the soul of a prehistoric Englishman. Like Lolly Willowes, Hall's story takes on mystical and fantastic qualities after the spinster has retreated from English society, but Warner's text, unlike "Miss Ogilvy," does not pathologize its heroine as a way of explaining her dissatisfaction with the limitations placed on a woman's life.[127] Neither is Lolly forced to die, as does Miss Ogilvy at the end of Hall's story –

ostensibly for the crime of autoerotic excess. But the two narratives are linked, despite these differences, through their racialized use of the primitive, an association that recalls Carpenter's linkage of homosexuality and primitive impulses. Hall's and Warner's use of primitivist discourse to signal their English characters' homosexuality does not destabilize those characters' whiteness or national identification. Thus, for example, in *The Well of Loneliness* Stephen Gordon is described as an atavistic "primitive thing" and Miss Ogilvy's body – "tattooed…[and] extremely hairy" – is aligned with the prehistoric Bronze Age of England, yet neither woman's racial transformation is understood to be at odds with Englishness.[128] Similarly, Lolly's body is physically marked as Other, yet her bewitchment locates her firmly within an English national context, a white and green space of which the folklore – witches were thought to favor the western peninsula of Cornwall – can be traced to medieval sources.[129]

As her body registers her sexual transformation, so too does she "try to readjust her spirit" (176), a psychical change expressed through a quintessentially English appropriation of space. Sitting in her room and gazing at nature, Lolly imagines herself surrounded by Stonehenge-like concentric circles: "hills encircled her like the rings of a fortification. This was her domain … They could not drive her out … nor shake her possession of the place she had chosen" (177). Like an imperial queen presiding over her spoils, Lolly expresses her lesbian–witch identity through the trope of conquest and acquisition. Her expansive gaze, although elsewhere applied in repudiating the idea of possession, here relishes its spectatorial breadth and consumption: "What man can stand on their summit and look beyond?" (177). Warner spatializes Lolly's "ruling power" (178) by describing her imagination as that which "assaulted her with dreams and intimations, calling her … out from the warm safe room to wander in darkened fields … through marshes and fens … along the outskirts of brooding woods" (178–9). Later, when Lolly fastens her gaze on Titus as though she were spying "from a telescope" (221), she revels in her spectatorial dominance: "There is an amusing sense of superiority in seeing and remaining unseen" (219). Here, as she voyeuristically watches the violent movements of Titus's spastic body – he has either been stung by wasps or is the victim of Satan's "gratuitous peep show" (222) – Lolly again surveys the landscape from a position of ascendance. By imbuing Lolly's gaze with agency, Warner inverts the convention of masculine spectatorial dominance and feminine visual passivity. The lesbian's emancipation, in other words, is concomitant with the visual colonization of new English space that is understood to reveal Lolly's *true* and authentic secret self. Although Warner is more circumspect about Lolly's lesbianism than is Hall about Miss Ogilvy's, the novel takes a more radical feminist stance by attributing Lolly's turmoil both to biology and to patriarchy. Reading Warner's novel alongside Hall's story clarifies why Lolly would choose to retreat from the homophobia of English society, and choose to rechannel her feminism by infiltrating what the evidence intimates is a lesbian community of witches in the English countryside. While it appears as though history drops out of the novel at this point, Warner's text still imaginatively retains it by rejecting the demonizing of lesbianism and creating an alternative space – literally, an English village – of female desire and autonomy that is truly radical.

Terry Castle's characterization of lesbian fiction as that which "exhibits, even as it masquerades as 'realistic' in surface detail, a strongly fantastical, allegorical, or utopian tendency," provides us with an invaluable model for understanding how *the historical* works in Warner's novel.[130] For this is a text which, for the most part, carefully flags its relation to history, so that it seems implausible that this dimension would – without cause or explanation – suddenly evaporate. By privileging the novel as a "lesbian fiction," one thing we gain is an alternative understanding of the historical, not as something linear and recognizable but rather as a recuperation of the forgotten and the hidden. Like Lolly, who repeatedly attempts to concretize Satan's elusiveness – "For a moment [she] thought that she had him ... the next, as though he had tricked himself out of her grasp" (250) – one of the problems the reader has is in situating the novel's fantasy element within a social context. If we concur that Lolly is a crypto-lesbian, then an unstated question of the novel is: whose history gets told? Lolly's admission to Satan – "I can't take warlocks so seriously, not as a class. It is we witches who count" (238) – can be read as a revisionist account of English history, emerging from her identification of Great Mop as not only a feminist haven of women's rights but a space in which same-sex desire is able to flourish. One might call Lolly a prototypical separatist, to the extent that her decision to live in Great Mop has a political basis: the language Warner uses to characterize the villagers' kinship is replete with homosexual connotations. For example, Lolly wields the rhetoric of inclusion when making an appeal on the group's behalf: "If they were different from other people, why shouldn't they be?" (131). Renowned for its eccentricity, Great Mop "had a name for being different from other places ... an out-of-the way place if ever there was one" (131). The equivalence of the witch's minority status with that of the lesbian is signaled when Lolly refers to the villagers' demeanor as "odd" – the same word Warner employs in relation to Lolly – and is conveyed through her identification with the community's difference: "She felt at one with them, an inhabitant like themselves" (131). Lolly's incorporation is acknowledged by nature, which homoerotically coos to her: "We will not let you go" (172). Later, at the witch's sabbath, Lolly observes that a "single mysterious impulse seemed to govern the group" (197), another oblique reference, I suggest, to the villagers' shared sexuality.

From historical accounts we know that one of the alleged "crimes" of witches, and for which they were persecuted, was that of engaging in homosexual sex, although the extent to which this actually occurred remains a matter for speculation. What *is* evident, however, is that the codification of witchcraft by Church authorities emphasized that the participants in ceremonial rites would "indulge in the most loathsome sensuality, having no regard to sex."[131] Although Warner is never explicit about sexual acts, her eroticized depiction of the "Witches' Sabbath" (199) is arguably based on these cultural associations. Despite Owen Davies's recent argument that the notion that witches met at Sabbaths "to perform obscene and perverted sexual acts" is likely erroneous, Warner pointedly borrows from this stereotypical imagery of folklore to signal Lolly's homosexuality.[132] It is as a witch that Lolly experiences her most emphatically lesbian moment when she attends the Sabbath, a frenzied affair of ecstatic dancing, during which time "a nameless excitement caught hold of her" (200). Warner's representation of the witches' fondness for dancing and late-night revelry correlates with archaic folk elements that associate the witch with the English countryside, associations that continued to circulate in rural areas until the 1930s.[133] By homoeroticizing this quintessentially English space, Warner restores to the lesbian a sense of cultural entitlement and national belonging. Lolly's most overtly eroticized interlude is dancing with "red-haired … half-naked" Emily (199), a witch whose physical proximity – they are described as whirling "fused together like two suns" (195) – Lolly clearly finds arousing. A strand of Emily's hair brushes across Lolly's face as they "danc[e] with a fervour that annihilated every misgiving," while the contact electrifies her body, making her "tingle" uncontrollably "from head to foot" (195). The sensuality of the moment, for Lolly, is unparalleled: "She shut her eyes and dived into obliviousness – with Emily for a partner she could dance until the gunpowder ran out of the heels of her boots" (196). This is not, I would venture, the response of a woman preoccupied with chastity, or one resistant to the allure of physical desire. But because the etiquette of a Sabbath requires constant circulation – "one rule only: to do nothing for long" (197) – Lolly is eventually left by Emily to be entertained by other dance partners, both male and female. While various people "please and excite" (201) her, nothing approximates the homoerotic pleasure she experiences with Emily, though this is not to say that Emily is the only woman Lolly finds compelling.

I read Warner's Satan as a feminized figure, a homosexual signifier whose "effeminate sorcery" recalls Edward Carpenter's characterization of the "cross-dressing" homosexual as a standard figure whose association with primitive rites, "religious or mystical," recurs throughout history both "among savages" and in "our modern civilised populations."[134] Lolly's attraction to this transgendered man, I'm suggesting, is further evidence of her repressed lesbian identification. Several critics have rightly interpreted Satan as Lolly's alter-ego, seeing him as a kind of double for her mysterious underside, but no one has aligned this subterfuge with sexuality or registered how Warner positions him as a lesbian mirror. When Lolly first encounters him at the Sabbath, he is disguised as a woman, so that our first impression of Satan is of a man in drag. Queer theorists have argued for a relation between the theatricality of drag and homosexuality, seeing the parodic and performative promotion of identity as a way of understanding the fictive foundation of sexuality.[135] If, in other words, the body straddles a variable gender boundary, then the seeming coherence between sex and gender is destabilized: drag is a vehicle that works to denaturalize heterosexuality. Warner's representation of Satan's artifice draws on Margaret Murray's historical account, in which she states that the "Devil was … generally a man, occasionally a woman" who appears "disguised out of recognition," but Warner complicates this model by constituting Satan against this binary.[136] The most salient aspect of Satan is his dissimulation, his gender play. Lolly initially believes that she sees the face of a "Chinaman" when he appears, and only in full light does she realize that Satan wears a lifeless mask that "was like the face of a very young girl," whose narrow eyes, slanting brows, and curved small mouth she finds entrancing (203). Warner's Orientalist rendering colludes with dominant British stereotypes of the Asian male as effeminate. This racialized portrayal further under-scores Lolly's attraction to Otherness, particularly in comparison to the Willowes's staid Englishness. As Satan transgresses the codes of masculinity, so too does Lolly break the codes of respectable femininity. By exoticizing Satan, Warner situates the homoerotic within a *foreign* body, a move that suggests the difficulty of incorporating the embodied reality of lesbianism within an English context. Through the mechanisms of repression and displacement, Warner codes Satan's camp performance as gay and simultaneously signals that Lolly's alter-ego embodies a deviant sexuality; however, that Satan is, however provisionally, a male is important because it mediates Lolly's lesbian identification. Lesbianism is never figured mimetically in this novel, so Satan could not in fact *be* a woman; instead, his transvestism merely enables him to look like one. Nevertheless, his feminine concealment appears somewhat redundant, for beneath Satan's masquerade what surfaces are the traces of a female physique: "Mincing like a girl," his "lithe body" approaches Lolly, and through his "imitation face" she observes "the hollow of [a] girlish throat" (203). The cracks in Satan's drag, rather than revealing a masculine body, seem to ground a female identity. Satan's bodily gestures are clearly an act – he purposely licks Lolly's cheek at one point, much to her annoyance – functioning as evidence of his duplicity. Warner writes that Satan comes to Lolly's side with "secretive and undulating movements" (203), echoing the language she employed earlier to describe the feminized landscape (as undulating) and Lolly's relation to Great Mop (where her secret resides). Lolly's observation that "a flicker of life" pulses through Satan's throat as though "a pearl necklace slid by under the skin" (203) invokes and subverts the earlier image of Lolly's pearl necklace as a sign of strangulation, for here Satan, miming the feminine, has seemingly ingested the offending object.

Warner feminizes Satan and pointedly alludes to Lolly's girlhood pearls in order to signal their affinity as doubles, for the most salient of their shared characteristics is their duplicity. Satan not only represents Lolly's own subversive alter-ego, the "dangerous" underside of the "typical genteel spinster" (242–3), but is himself a double, a split that recapitulates her Lolly–Laura duality. He appears to her both in his guise as the representative of the "Powers of Darkness" (205), at the Sabbath, and in his incarnation as the protective gamekeeper on the downs in gaiters and a corduroy coat, when she is in the countryside. Like Lolly herself, Satan is more than one thing: "inscrutable as ever" (205), his innocuous behavior repeatedly challenges her expectations concerning the demonic, much in the same way that Lolly's crypto-lesbianism destabilizes the reader's assumptions regarding her spinsterhood. For each, there is a disjunction between appearance and what Warner might call essence, a scission between Aunt Lolly and the "true Laura" (178), and, similarly, between the fraudulent and "the real Satan" (211). However, the novel ultimately adheres not to any single *truth* about identity, but rather demonstrates the way in which it is created through a performative process of disguise and disclosure. Warner utilizes spectatorial imagery in conjunction with both Lolly and Satan in order to convey this notion of the "hidden" (179) self, for, like duplicity, the problem of (in)visibility – of seeing and remaining unseen – speaks to the novel's interest in thematizing lesbian dissimulation. Each of them exhibits "an amusing sense of superiority" (219) through undetected observation, so that as Satan watches Lolly with "unseen eyes" (203) through the slits in his mask, elsewhere she herself "releas[es] her gaze" (221) on Titus while "remaining unseen" (219). For both of them, the visual pleasure here has less to do with voyeurism than it does with concealment, a motive for secrecy, I want to suggest, that extends beyond the specificity of the moment and has instead to do with homosexual discretion. Satan comments on the remarkableness of "how invisible one is" (233) in the countryside of Great Mop, for this is the realm of the clandestine, a fact alluded to by Lolly's claim that she is Satan's witch "in blindness" (244) – that is, through a process of deliberate dissimulation – a mode of observation which contrasts sharply with Titus's possessive and imperious gaze. Like Lolly, whose lesbian identity hinges on deception, Satan operates primarily through stealth and evasiveness. He circulates undercover around Great Mop, reconfiguring himself as a friendly game-keeper in order to mask his "satanic playfulness" (233) – "put[ting] on this shape that she might not fear him" (211). Although earlier Lolly had dismissed Satan as "an imposter, a charlatan" (211), by the end she recognizes his identity as that of a dissimulator, as one who "always hide[s]" (232) from detection.

For both Lolly and Satan, this proclivity for concealment is an index of their mutual duplicity, but, where "Laura" functions as the subversive underside of "Lolly," Satan fuels the defiance and subterfuge of Laura. Warner's representation of Satan as Lolly's double invokes Freud's notion of the uncanny as that which is both familiar–congenial and at the same time so terrifying that it is "concealed and kept out of sight."[137] According to Freud, the "quality of uncanniness can only come from the circumstance of the 'double' ... dating back to a very early mental stage"; in other words, the uncanny has to do with the repression of something familiar that "ought to have been kept concealed but which has nevertheless come to light."[138] This notion of the uncanny as that which has been estranged through a process of repression provides us with a way of understanding Lolly's relationship with Satan: "he had never been far off" (179), psychically speaking, because he is the trace of her lesbian identification. As Diane Purkiss shows in her psychoanalytic account of the witch, one source of the uncanny is an excess of female desire.[139]

Lolly contemplates the role the supernatural has played in her Chiltern life: "How she had come to Great Mop she could not say; whether it was of her own will, or whether ... Satan had [led] her by the hand into the flower-shop" (179) – the site of her erotic awakening. This ambivalence regarding the status of Lolly's volition speaks to Warner's interest in problematizing her heroine's sexuality, for does she become a witch by her own desire or according to Satan's intention? The novel ultimately suggests that the two are interchangeable, a fact underscored by the book's rarely cited full title: Lolly Willowes or the Loving Huntsman. It is telling that Warner uses "or" rather than "and" as her conjunction here, for it suggests a mirroring of the two characters; moreover, that she chooses to put "Lolly" and not "Laura" in her novel's title further elucidates her objective of concealment – of deflecting attention from her heroine's Otherness. Satan is Lolly's double to the extent that he represents her repressed lesbianism, for from the outset it is he who has been her stimulus, guiding her away from her role as London spinster and, with the "sweet persuasions" (179) of a lover, easing her into her subversive calling as a witch. Lolly even refers to him in conventionally romantic terms, seeing him as "a kind of black knight, wandering about and succouring decayed gentlewomen" (238); because she yields to her desire, Satan considers her his "conquest" (245). Although Freud locates one example of the uncanny in "magic and witchcraft," he never associated the prohibition against the familiar, the proximate, with homo-sexuality.[140] The novel, however, enables us to read the doubling of Satan and Lolly in terms of precisely that equation. Sue-Ellen Case's assertion that "[t]he queer is the taboo-breaker, the monstrous, the uncanny," has particular resonance for Warner's juxtaposition of the demonic and the domestic, for the connective between Satan and Lolly is sexual sameness.[141] Clearly a feminized figure, constituted through disguise, Satan approaches Lolly "[w]ith the gesture of a man who can never hold out against women" (233), or, stated differently, like a female lover.

If we read Satan as an uncanny figure for Lolly's lesbian unconscious – despite his strangeness, he "struck her as being familiar" (232) – then he can be said to make representable what the novel largely implies but, in effect, leaves out. By casting Lolly as a witch who pledges herself to Satan, Warner invokes the associations of female sexuality as dangerous and susceptible to demonic control; as Lolly puts it, "women … know they are dynamite" (241). The reference to Satan as "the loving huntsman" (179) underscores his affiliation with the erotic forces of nature for, throughout Lolly's residence at Great Mop, "all the time, whether couched in the woods or hunting among the hills, he drew closer" (179). At one point Satan's words – "Remember, Miss Willowes, that I shall always be very glad to help you" (209) – are echoed by nature's feminine voice, which murmurs consolingly "Remember, Miss Willowes … Remember" (210). The text's focus on recollection – "She remembered, and understood" (210) – has to do with Satan's role as the harbor of Lolly's vestigial memory, her instinctual, yet repressed, lesbian identification. The intimate conversation between the pair at the end of the novel recalls Warner's theorizing of bi-location, for the language can be read as a coded dialogue, between doubles, that itself has a double meaning. Satan's promise to Lolly – "You will always find me in the wood" (209) – positions him in the space of the homoerotic, an alignment that is later reiterated when he says to her: "Once a wood, always a wood" (234). That sentence, which appears twice within the same paragraph, is meaningful only if understood in terms of lesbian displacement, for what the text posits is an equivalence between the invariability of "the wood" and Lolly's sexuality. It is this context in which Lolly contemplates her own "natural leaning towards the Devil," ironically contrasting her deviance with the behavior of "respectable people like Henry and Caroline" (234). She identifies herself here with the prohibitive, with the persistently marginalized, "the other people, the people of Satan" (234). The text identifies patriarchy as the most oppressive force that lesbian eroticism has to contend with; Satan represents the only possibility of liberatory escape: "Custom, public opinion, law, church, and state – all would have shaken their massive heads against her plea, and sent her back to bondage" (223). Lolly prolongs their flirtatious repartee when she discloses: "I do believe you wanted me. Though really I don't know why you should" (235), and a "slightly malevolent smile" crosses the Devil's face. This momentary reticence has to do with the mute-ness of homosexual desire in the novel, and yet their coded dialogue continues as Satan asserts: "Well, you're a witch now," and Lolly concurs: "Yes … I really am, aren't I?" (236). That this conversation is constituted on the basis of substitution is made explicit when Lolly reflects on Satan's language, and thinks that "a deeper meaning lay beneath his words" (237). Here, as elsewhere, the subtext is not revealed, though the substitutability of lesbianism is implicit. Satan refers to her as "[i]rrevocably" (236) a witch, and Lolly agrees by maintaining that her vocation is "perfectly natural" (237). His admonition – "you will never escape me, for you can never wish to" – merely reiterates their collusion as complementary halves, for Satan's "indifferent ownership" (252) of Lolly contrasts with the novel's other examples of masculine possessiveness and male control of female desire. Her assent – "I shall never wish to escape you" (237) – is about preserving her own sexuality, for the denial of her alter-ego would mean the annihilation of her erotic self.

Only by reading the novel slant, through the trope of inversion, can we fully appreciate the extent to which Warner thematizes Lolly's homosexuality both by multiple examples of her "oddness" and by constructing sentences whose content subverts the expected order throughout her text. By this I mean the various places in which Warner posits the conceptual inversion of heterosexual paradigms through literal reversal. Thus, for example, as a young woman Lolly describes her "coming out" – the point at which she is to appear as a debutante – as an occasion that actually signals her "going-in" (19). Or elsewhere, toward the end of the text, when Lolly and Satan are engaged in dialogue, Warner inverts the biblical narrative by having Lolly – who earlier is referred to as "Eve" because of her "unladylike curiosity" – offer Satan the desired apple, which in this case leads not to expulsion but merely to friendship (134). Yet even the designation of Lolly as "Eve" is itself further inverted when Warner writes that Lolly "was like God," who, "after casting out the rebel angels ... use[d] Adam as an intermediate step" (143). Here, the conventional hierarchy of the creation story – the myth of heterosexual origin – is repeatedly scrambled, until it is Lolly, as a feminized God, who utilizes Adam's body as a means to the creation of Eve. The text frequently transposes the expected sequence, and upsets any presumption of certainty, particularly where heterosexuality is figured. At one point, Lolly's sister-in-law Caroline condescendingly refers to her as the "unused virgin," while maintaining that her own role as wife and mother is "emotionally plumper" (60) – even though she herself is depicted as an asexual "Mother Superior" (51). The text continually upsets this dichotomy by associating heterosexuality not with the generative but with images of death and confinement, while Lolly – the "barren spinster" – is associated with fruit and vegetation, images of ripeness and renewal. At her father's funeral, held in a botanical garden, Lolly dismisses the pastor's banalities about the inevitability of death and revises conventional logic by rejecting Christian dogma, yet at the same time asserting: "In the midst of death, we are in life" (40). It is through the accumulation of such moments of reversal that Warner's novel alludes to Lolly's *inversion* without precisely naming it for what it is. The text mentions at one point that Lolly's eyes are simultaneously "blind" and "clear sighted" (40), an impossible image that crystallizes what I observe to be the novel's interest in the juxtaposition of incongruities, its desire to subvert the reader's expectations regarding "normalcy." By interpreting Lolly's spinsterhood and her status as a witch as codes for lesbianism, all of the textual references to her strange demeanor, her penchant for the peculiar and the unorthodox, become newly legible.

Warner's novel radicalizes the model that "English witches ... define[d] by inversion the acceptable social role for women" by depicting the witch herself as a

figure for the invert.[142] Lolly's final – feminist – speech to Satan fuels the super-
stitious terror regarding witches – that they perverted women's *natural* roles of wife
and mother – for she aligns herself with the destabilizing of traditional gender
norms. What is compelling about Lolly's passionate oration is her vision of feminism as a covert practice, a move that anticipates Woolf's focus on indirectness as a
feminist strategy in *Three Guineas*. Lolly's colloquy with Satan, both intimate and
flirtatious, emphasizes their role as homosexual doubles. Satan responds to Lolly's
initial request – "if I am really a witch, treat me as such … Tell me about yourself" –
by requiring that she expose herself: "Tell me first what *you* think" (238). While it
appears here as though Satan is withholding, the pedagogical dynamic is actually
staged in order to facilitate Lolly's self-disclosure: "I encourage you to talk, not that
I may know all your thoughts, but that you may" (244). Satan's perceptions about
himself never deviate from Lolly's own, for as her alter-ego, "he did not know much
more … than she did herself" (249). What he enables is a kind of transference
through which her dark side is able to speak, with the tone and language again
anticipating Woolf's grievance in *Three Guineas*: "When I think of witches, I seem
to see all over England, all over Europe, women living and growing old …
unregarded … wives and sisters of respectable men … listening to men talking
together in the way that men talk and women listen" (239). Whereas Woolf's
proposal that women create a society of outsiders arises, arguably, from a socialist
impulse, Warner's interest in female separatism is motivated by a recognition that
lesbianism is incompatible with the conventional demand that women "settl[e]
down … [and] be passive" (240). Nonetheless, Lolly's feminist manifesto, by implication addressed to all women everywhere, looks forward to Woolf's own vision of
a feminized globe, even though Lolly's oration has special resonance for the
"subjection" (239) of the lesbian body. Warner's signifier for this body is a stick of
dynamite, awaiting the moment of ignition: "for so many, what can there be but
witchcraft?" (241). Warner conveys that beneath the spinster's appearance of conformity and dormancy lurks the dangerous, if latent, possibility of a lesbian explosion:
"Even if they never do anything with their witchcraft, they know it's there – ready!"
(241). The image of the witch's "cloak of darkness" (142) invokes the spinster–
lesbian's protective secrecy; for each, there is an investment in obfuscation. Darkness,
both literal and figurative, is an integral feature of Lolly's life: Satan's promise that
he will give her "the dangerous black night to stretch [her] wings in" (242) recalls
the earlier reference to him as a black knight, for only opacity makes possible
Lolly's erotic "independence" (250).

   We can read Satan's closing injunction – "Don't try to put me in your pocket"
(245) – as counsel against Lolly's proclivity for hiding her sexuality, but the novel
provides no avenue for its unmediated expression. Instead, it displaces Lolly's
homoeroticism on to the English countryside, a fact that is underscored by the
novel's attention to the vegetation upon which Satan's body had lain during their
colloquy. Lolly observes the imprint his body has left on the landscape in terms
which emphasize his coextensiveness with the natural: she registers the "rampion
flower … withering quite *naturally*" and thinks of her double, Satan, "inscrutable
… with the dignity of *natural* behavior" (249; emphasis mine). By intertwining the
landscape and Satan's "most natural" (251) body, Warner not only posits an

equivalence between homosexuality and nature but suggests an imaginary solution to the lesbian's cultural and national disenfranchisement. By representing Lolly's attachment to the soil of England as her primary identificatory focus – the novel ends with her mind "brood[ing] immovably over the landscape" (249) – Warner demonstrates how, above all, it is an attachment to territory on which one's national affiliation is based. By linking the discourse of "the natural" with witchcraft, Warner tacitly alludes both to Edward Carpenter's association of the primitive with homosexuality and to rural preservationists, such as Vaughan Cornish, who maintained that contact with the English countryside facilitated a "mystic state."[143] Women become witches, Lolly discloses, "to satisfy [their] passion for adventure" (242). That passion is predicated on a quintessentially English conception of spatial appropriation, one which stresses the spiritual culture of landscape.

Chapter 4 considers how Mary Butts takes up the equation of nature and Englishness, but revises it by aligning the mystical potential of the countryside with a more deeply conservative vision of women's national inclusion.

Notes

1 Cyril Connolly, "The vulgarity of lesbianism," *New Statesman* (August 25, 1928): 614. Connolly may be striving to be tongue-in-cheek, but his review nonetheless pathologizes lesbianism.

2 See Lucy Bland, "Trial by sexology? Maud Allan, *Salome* and the 'cult of the clitoris' case" in Lucy Bland and Laura Doan eds. *Sexology in Culture: Labelling Bodies and Desires* (Chicago, IL: University of Chicago Press, 1998), 183–98.

3 Dr. Isabel Emslie Hutton, *The Hygiene of Marriage* (London: Heinemann, 1923), 40–1 (my emphasis).

4 Mary Scharlieb, *The Bachelor Woman and Her Problems* (London: Williams & Norgate, 1929), 49 and 52–3. Freud discusses the lesbian's "masculinity complex" in "Femininity" (1933), in *New Introductory Lectures on Psychoanalysis* (New York: Norton, 1965).

5 Scharlieb, *Bachelor Woman*, 71.

6 Edith Lees Ellis, *The New Horizon in Love and Life* (London: A. & C. Black, 1921), 66.

7 Radclyffe Hall, "Miss Ogilvy Finds Herself" (1934), in Sandra M. Gilbert and Susan Gubar eds. *The Norton Anthology of Literature by Women* (New York, 1985), 1445 and 1447.

8 Anthony M. Ludovici, *Lysistrata or Woman's Future and Future Woman* (New York: E.P. Dutton & Co., 1925), 29 and 18; hereafter cited in the text.

9 Quoted by Diana Souhami in *The Trials of Radclyffe Hall* (London: Weidenfeld & Nicolson, 1998), 209 (emphasis added).

10 Maude Royden, *The Moral Standards of the Rising Generation* (London: League of the Church Militant, 1921), 7.

11 Sylvia Townsend Warner, *Letters*, ed. William Maxwell (New York: Viking, 1982), 84.

12 Souhami, *Trials of Radclyffe Hall*, 210.

13 Jay Prosser, *Second Skins: The Body Narratives of Transsexuality* (New York: Columbia University Press, 1998), 138.

14 Sylvia Townsend Warner, "The way by which I have come," *The Countryman* (July, 1939): 482; hereafter cited in the text.

15 Clough Williams-Ellis, *England and the Octopus* (London: Geoffrey Bles, 1928), 22 and 20. Warner later produced a travel guide to Somerset (London, 1949) in Williams-Ellis's "Visions of England" series.

16 Patrick Wright discusses Warner's anti-bucolic poetry and her political involvement in East Chaldon in *The Village That Died for England: The Strange Story of Tyneham* (London: Vintage, 1996), 146. Warner's partner, Valentine Ackland, published a short book on the misery of rural life entitled *Country Conditions* (London: Lawrence & Wishart, 1936).

17 Judith Stinton, *Chaldon Herring: The Powys Circle in a Dorset Village* (Suffolk: Boydell Press, 1988), 1. See also Claire Harman for a discussion of Warner's anti-tripper stance in *Sylvia Townsend Warner: A Biography* (London: Chatto & Windus, 1988), 151.

18 Maroula Joannou discusses Warner's involvement in the communist-led initiatives to democratize the countryside. See "Sylvia Townsend Warner in the 1930s" in Andy Croft ed. *A Weapon in the Struggle: The Cultural History of the Communist Party in Britain* (London: Pluto Press, 1998), 92–3.

19 See Eric Garber and Lyn Paleo eds. *Uranian Worlds: A Reader's Guide to Alternative Sexuality in Science Fiction and Fantasy* (Boston, MA: G.K. Hall & Co., 1983), 146–7. Warner refers to Mr. Fortune as "fatally sodomitic" in a 1926 letter to David Garnett: *Letters*, ed. William Maxwell (New York: Viking Press), 9.

20 Gay Wachman defines this phenomenon as "lesbian crosswriting," but she argues that *Mr. Fortune's Maggot* contains no lesbian subtext even though the novel fits into her conceptual paradigm: *Lesbian Empire: Radical Crosswriting in the Twenties* (New Brunswick, NJ: Rutgers University Press, 2001), 83–4.

21 Sylvia Townsend Warner, *Mr. Fortune's Maggot* (London: Virago, 1978 [1927]), 211, 45, 61 and 43; hereafter cited in the text.

22 There is one instance in the text when Warner gives us Lueli's point of view. This moment serves to underscore the perception we already have of him as lazy and indolent: "I love [Timothy Fortune], but, oh dear! what a responsibility he is … I don't want responsibilities" (197).

23 In contrast, Nigel Rigby reads Warner's representation of homosexuality as a critique of imperialism: "'Not a good place for deacons': the South Seas, sexuality and modernism in Sylvia Townsend Warner's *Mr. Fortune's Maggot*" in Howard J. Booth and Nigel Rigby eds. *Modernism and Empire* (Manchester: Manchester University Press, 2000), 224–48.

24 For an examination of the relation between missionary work and colonialism, see Barbara N. Ramusack, "Cultural missionaries, maternal imperialists, feminist allies: British women activists in India, 1865–1945" in Nupur Chaudhuri and Margaret Strobel eds. *Western Women and Imperialism: Complicity and Resistance* (Bloomington and Indianapolis: Indiana University Press, 1992); Kumari Jayawardena, *The White Woman's Other Burden: Western Women and South Asia during British Colonial Rule* (New York and London: Routledge, 1995); Margaret Strobel, *European Women and the Second British Empire* (Bloomington and Indianapolis: Indiana University Press, 1992). Warner recounts the genesis of her interest in the missionary theme in *Letters*, 10.

25 When Mr. Fortune's watch stops he concludes that "time is a convention" (142) and sets the hour arbitrarily. One of the West's fundamental conceptions of primitive peoples is that they exist outside of linear time, in a kind of continuous present. Warner ends her novel with a reference to Mr. Fortune's watch, for as he leaves Fanua and prepares for repatriation to Britain, this notion of timelessness "was lost for ever" (249). Virginia-Lee Webb's essay "Manipulated images: European photographs of Pacific peoples" includes several early twentieth-century photographs, taken by missionary George Brown, of Solomon Island inhabitants with clocks inserted in their ear lobes: in Elazar Barkan and Ronald Bush eds. *Prehistories of the Future: The Primitivist Project and the Culture of Modernism* (Stanford, CA: Stanford University Press, 1996), 175–201.

26 Bronislaw Malinowski, *Sex, Culture, and Myth* (New York: Harcourt Brace Jovanovich, 1962), 126.

27 Bronislaw Malinowski, *The Sexual Life of Savages: An Ethnographic Account of Courtship, Marriage, and Family Life among the Natives of the Trobriand Islands, British New Guinea* (New York: Harcourt Brace, 1929; reprinted 1987).

28 Marilyn R. Farwell discusses the "myth of the *vagina dentata*" in *Heterosexual Plots and Lesbian Narratives* (New York and London: New York University Press, 1996), 33.

29 Edward Carpenter, *Intermediate Types Among Primitive Folk: A Study of Social Evolution* (London: George Allen & Co., 1914), 11–12. Gay Wachman similarly reads *Mr. Fortune's Maggot* alongside Carpenter, but argues that Warner "presents the colonialist discourse of the 'primitive' ironically": *Lesbian Empire*, 92. In general, Wachman argues that Warner

maintains a much more radical opposition to imperial ideology than I would concede.

30 The context here is a music lesson, but the language suggests a homoerotic subtext: "Mr. Fortune's European harmonies queered the pitch ... Lueli's pipe obeyed some unscientific native scale ... He couldn't always control it ... his voice wandering from the straight path" (70–1). Useful to an understanding of this feminized scene is Elizabeth Wood's term "Sapphonics," which denotes a "mode of articulation, a way of describing a space of lesbian possibility, for a range of erotic and emotional relationships among women who sing and women who listen": *Queering the Pitch: The New Gay and Lesbian Musicology*, ed. Philip Brett, Elizabeth Wood, and Gary Thomas (New York: Routledge, 1994), 27. In her epigraph to the novel Warner glosses "maggot" as a "perverse fancy" (1), establishing the imaginative parameters of "deviancy" which the text goes on to embrace.

31 See Sylvia Townsend Warner, "Women as writers" in Bonnie Kime Scott ed. *The Gender of Modernism: A Critical Anthology* (Bloomington and Indianapolis: Indiana University Press, 1990), 538–46.

32 *Ibid.*, 540.

33 *Sylvia Townsend Warner: Collected Poems*, ed. Claire Harman (New York: Viking Press, 1982), xv.

34 See Marcus's introduction to Warner in *The Gender of Modernism*, 531–8, and her essay "Alibis and legends: the ethics of elsewhereness, gender and estrangement" in Mary Lynn Broe and Angela Ingram eds. *Women's Writing in Exile* (Chapel Hill and London: University of North Carolina Press, 1989).

35 See Barbara Brothers, "Through the 'pantry window': Sylvia Townsend Warner and the Spanish Civil War" in Frieda S. Brown, Malcolm A. Compitello, and Victor M. Howard eds. *Rewriting the Good Fight: Critical Essays on the Literature of the Spanish Civil War* (East Lansing: Michigan State University Press, 1989), 161–73; "Writing against the grain: Sylvia Townsend Warner and the Spanish Civil War" in Broe and Ingram eds. *Women's Writing in Exile*, 350–68.

36 Woolf, *A Room of One's Own*, 85; Marcus, "Alibis and legends," 285.

37 Wendy Mulford, *This Narrow Place: Sylvia Townsend Warner and Valentine Ackland: Life, Letters and Politics, 1930–1951* (London: Pandora, 1988), 46.

38 Glen Cavaliero, *Poetry National Review*, 8. 3 (1981): 45.

39 See Celeste M. Schenck, "Exiled by genre: modernism, canonicity, and the politics of exclusion" in Broe and Ingram eds. *Women's Writing in Exile*, 226–50.

40 That Warner's language appears conventional by high modernist standards does not imply that the author was unconcerned with issues of style and form. Trained as a musicologist – she was one of four editors of the monumental ten-volume study *Tudor Church Music* (1917–27) – all of Warner's language is "musical in nature," as Claire Harman recognizes, to the extent that it exhibits a "fine ear for cadences and the lyrical effects of language" as well as a "keen interest in form and structure": *A Biography*, 60 and 218. Gillian Beer argues that Warner's experiments are narratological rather than verbal, attributing this to her gifts as a musician: "Sylvia Townsend Warner: 'the centrifugal kick'" in Maroula Joannou ed. *Women Writers of the 1930s: Gender, Politics, History* (Edinburgh: Edinburgh University Press, 1999), 76–86.What we find throughout Warner's writing is a sustained attention to condensing the text, an interest in intellectual play, and the juxtaposition of incongruities.

41 Both statements appear in the special edition of the *Poetry National Review* 23 (1981), "Sylvia Townsend Warner, 1893–1978: a celebration," which was edited by Claire Harman. The first is from J. Lawrence Mitchell's, "The secret country of her mind: aspects of the novels of Sylvia Townsend Warner" (56); and the other from Harman's "Introduction" (31).

42 Terry Castle, *The Apparitional Lesbian: Female Homosexuality and Modern Culture* (New York: Columbia University Press, 1993), 74. See also Gillian Spraggs, "Exiled to home: the poetry of Sylvia Townsend Warner and Valentine Ackland" in Mark Lilly ed. *Lesbian and Gay Writing: An Anthology of Critical Essays* (Philadelphia: Temple University Press, 990).

43 Claire Harmon, "Introduction," *Summer Will Show* (London: Virago, 1987), viii.

44 Paul Binding, "Sylvia Townsend Warner and *Mr. Fortune's Maggot*," *Poetry National Review* 23 (special issue) (1981): 52.

45 Sally Munt, "Introduction" in Munt ed. *New Lesbian Criticism: Literary and Cultural Readings* (New York: Columbia University Press, 1992), xxiii.

46 Elizabeth A. Meese *(Sem)erotics: Theorizing Lesbian: Writing* (New York and London: New York University Press, 1992), 18.

47 Sharon O'Brien, "'The thing not named': Willa Cather as a lesbian writer" in Estelle B. Freedman, Barbara C. Gelpi, Susan L. Johnson, and Kathleen M. Weston eds. *The Lesbian Issues: Essays from Signs* (Chicago, IL, and London: University of Chicago Press, 1985), 87.

48 Robert L. Caserio, *The Novel in England, 1900–1950* (New York: Twayne, 1999), 254.

49 See Jane Marcus, "Sapphistry: narration as lesbian seduction in *A Room of One's Own*," *Virginia Woolf and the Languages of Patriarchy* (Bloomington and Indianapolis: Indiana University Press, 1987), 163–87; and also "Sapphistry: the Woolf and the well" in Karla Jay and Joanne Glasgow eds. *Lesbian Texts and Contexts* (New York: New York University Press, 1990), 164–79.

50 Claire Harman ed., "Introduction," *Poetry National Review* 23, (special issue) (1981): 30.

51 See, for example, Barbara Brothers, "Flying the nets at forty: *Lolly Willowes* as female bildungsroman" in Laura L. Doan ed. *Old Maids to Radical Spinsters: Unmarried Women in the Twentieth-Century Novel* (Urbana: University of Illinois Press, 1991), 195–212; Robert L. Caserio, "Celibate sisters-in-revolution: towards reading Sylvia Townsend Warner" in Joseph A. Boone and Michael Cadden eds. *Engendering Men: The Question of Male Feminist Criticism* (New York: Routledge, 1990), 254. Caserio extends his argument that Warner is a major writer in *The Novel in England*, 254–74; Jane Marcus, "A wilderness of one's own: feminist fantasy novels of the twenties: Rebecca West and Sylvia Townsend Warner" in Susan Merrill Squier ed. *Women Writers and the City* (Knoxville: University of Tennessee Press, 1984), 134–60.

52 Bonnie Zimmerman, "Perverse reading: the lesbian appropriation of literature" in Susan J. Wolfe and Julia Penelope eds. *Sexual Practice, Textual Theory: Lesbian Cultural Criticism* (Cambridge, MA, and Oxford: Blackwell, 1993), 139.

53 Shari Benstock, "Expatriate sapphic modernism" in Lisa Rado ed. *Rereading Modernism* (Austin: University of Texas Press, 1986), 185.

54 See, for example: Judith Butler, *Bodies that Matter: On the Discursive Limits of "Sex"* (New York: Routledge, 1993), Ch. 5; Judith Fetterley, "My Antonia, Jim Burden, and the dilemma of the lesbian writer" in Jay and Glasgow eds. *Lesbian Texts and Contexts: Radical Revisions*, 145–63; Sharon O'Brian, *Willa Cather: The Emerging Voice* (New York: Oxford University Press, 1987).

55 Patricia Juliana Smith, *Lesbian Panic: Homoeroticism in Modern British Women's Fiction* (New York: Columbia University Press, 1997), 10.

56 Marilyn R. Farwell, *Heterosexual Plots and Lesbian Narratives* (New York and London: New York University Press, 1996), 20–3.

57 John Lucas, *The Radical Twenties: Writing, Politics, Culture* (Nottingham: Five Leaves, 1997), 99 and 104–5.

58 Willa Cather, "The novel démeublé" in Kime Scott ed. *The Gender of Modernism*, 55.

59 Cate Haste, *Rules of Desire: Sex in Britain, World War I to the Present* (London: Chatto & Windus, 1992), 29.

60 Sylvia Townsend Warner, *I'll Stand by You: The Letters of Sylvia Townsend Warner and Valentine Ackland*, ed. Susanna Pinney (London: Pimlico, 1998), 43.

61 Mitchell, "The secret country of her mind," 55.

62 Julie Abraham, *Are Girls Necessary? Lesbian Writing and Modern Histories* (New York and London: Routledge, 1996), 32.

63 *Ibid.*, 35.

64 Carpenter, *Intermediate Types Among Primitive Folk*, 38 and 36.

65 Havelock Ellis and John Addington Symonds identify "homosexual practices" throughout the world and in every culture in *Sexual Inversion* (New York: Arno Press, 1975 [1897]), 1–24. See also *Studies in the Psychology of Sex*, Vol. 2: *Sexual Inversion* (New York: Random House, 1936), 1–64. In *Intermediate Types*, Carpenter similarly sees the development of "homosexual customs" as "world-wide and universal" (54). For a discussion of the English fascination with

the primitive, see Elazar Barkan and Ronald Bush eds. *Prehistories of the Future: The Primitivist Project and the Culture of Modernism* (Stanford, CA: Stanford University Press); Marianna Torgovnick, *Gone Savage: Savage Intellects, Modern Lives* (Chicago, IL, and London: University of Chicago Press, 1990).

66 Carpenter, *Intermediate Types*, 51 and 52.

67 Sylvia Townsend Warner, *Lolly Willowes or the Loving Huntsman* (Chicago, IL: Academy, 1978), 24; hereafter cited in the text.

68 Owen Davies, *Witchcraft, Magic and Culture, 1736–1951* (Manchester and New York: Manchester University Press, 1999), 180–1.

69 Cicely Hamilton, in her 1935 memoir, laments the feminist backlash against the single woman: "To-day … in the eyes of certain modern statesmen, women are not personalities … they are back at the secondary existence, counting only as 'normal' women, as wives and mothers of sons. An inevitable result of this return to the 'normal' will be a revival of the old contempt for the spinster": *Life Errant* (London: J.M. Dent & Sons, 1935), 251.

70 Ludovici, *Lysistrata*, 31.

71 For a discussion of this topic see: Janice Gothard, "The healthy, wholesome British domestic girl: single female migration and the Empire Settlement Act, 1922–1930" in Stephen Constantine ed. *Emigrants and Empire: British Settlement in the Dominions between the Wars* (Manchester: Manchester University Press, 1990); Sheila Jeffreys, *The Spinster and Her Enemies: Feminism and Sexuality 1880–1930* (London: Pandora Press, 1985); Rita S. Kranidis, *The Victorian Spinster and Colonial Emigration: Contested Subjects* (New York: St. Martin's Press, 1999).

72 Ann Laura Stoler discusses the ways in which gender inequalities were integral to the structure of colonial racism and imperial authority: "Carnal knowledge and imperial power: gender, race, and morality in colonial Asia" in Micaela di Leonardi ed. *Gender at the Crossroads of Knowledge: Feminist Anthropology in the Postmodern Era* (Berkeley: University of California Press, 1991), 51–101.

73 Elaine Showalter, *Sexual Anarchy: Gender and Culture at the* Fin de Siécle (New York, Viking Press, 1990), 23. We can see this view exemplified by Havelock Ellis in *Sexual Inversion*: "The modern movement of [women's] emancipation … has involved an increase in feminine criminality and in feminine insanity, which are being elevated towards the masculine standard. In connection with these we … find an increase in homosexuality" (99–100). Emily Hamer discusses the role of lesbians during the interwar period in *Britannia's Glory: A History of Twentieth-Century Lesbians* (London: Cassell, 1996).

74 Sheila Jefffreys, *The Spinster and Her Enemies: Feminism and Sexuality 1880–1930* (London: Pandora, 1985), 88.

75 Lillian Faderman discusses the link between lesbianism and feminism in *Surpassing the Love of Men: Romantic Friendship and Love between Women from the Renaissance to the Present* (New York: William Morrow, 1991), 332–40.

76 Sheila Jeffreys, *The Spinster and Her Enemies*, 92.

77 Susan Kingsley Kent, *Sex and Suffrage in Britain 1860–1914* (Princeton, NJ: Princeton University Press, 1987), 204.

78 For a fuller discussion of the anathematizing of the lesbian in the work of the sexologists, see Jeffreys, *The Spinster and Her Enemies*, 106.

79 Havelock Ellis, *Studies in the Psychology of Sex*, Vol. 2: *Sexual Inversion*; Margaret Lawrence, *We Write As Women* (London: Michael Joseph, 1937), 261.

80 Jeffreys, *The Spinster and Her Enemies*, 100. In addition to Jeffreys, Lillian Faderman, in *Surpassing the Love of Men* and in *Odd Girls and Twilight Lovers* (New York: Columbia University Press, 1991), discusses the relation between lesbianism and the spinster. Other critics who observe a similar linkage include: Lyndie Brimstone, "Towards a new cartography: Radclyffe Hall, Virginia Woolf and the workings of common land" in Elaine Hobby and Chris White eds. *What Lesbians Do in Books* (London: Women's Press, 1991), 86–108; Showalter, *Sexual Anarchy*; Carol Smith Rosenberg, "The new women as androgyne: social disorder and gender crisis, 1870–1936," *Disorderly Conduct: Visions of Gender in Victorian America* (New York and Oxford: Oxford University Press, 1985); Martha Vicinus, *Indepen-*

dent Women: Work and Community for Single Women, 1850–1920 (Chicago, IL and London: University of Chicago Press, 1985).

81 Lawrence, *We Write As Women*, 261.

82 *Ibid.*, 299.

83 Alison Oram, "Repressed and thwarted, or bearer of the new world? The spinster in inter-war feminist discourses," *Women's History Review*, 1. 3 (1992): 413–34.

84 Winifred Holtby, "Notes on the way," *Time and Tide* (May 4, 1935): 647. See also Holtby's section, "Are spinsters frustrated?" in *Women and a Changing Civilization* (London: John Lane, 1934), 125–33.

85 Terry Castle, *The Apparitional Lesbian*, 9–10. Similarly, Judith Butler discusses how, although at the time the word "queer" did not explicitly mean homosexual, "it did encompass an array of meanings associated with the deviation from normalcy which might well include the sexual": *Bodies That Matter*, 176.

86 While one might be tempted to read Lolly's identification with her father as a sign of the lesbian's masculinity complex, Warner's representation has little in common with the image of the mannish lesbian popularized by sexologists during the interwar years. Lolly's identification with her father signals her discomfort with conventional gender roles, but that does not invariably link her to the discourse of sexual pathology. A more useful way of thinking about Lolly's identification with masculinity is through Edward Carpenter's description of the invert as a kind of "diviner" or "prophet" who transcends conventional gender roles. See *Intermediate Types*, 62–3.

87 Brothers, "Flying the nets at forty," 197. Warner uses the language of technology to characterize Lolly's life in London, where she exists as "sort of an extra wheel ... part of the mechanism" (47) within the family unit. The impersonal and "automatic" aspect of this anaesthetizing dailiness is an implied critique of alienated labor and masculine hegemony.

88 Teresa de Lauretis, "Eccentric subjects: feminist theory and historical consciousness," *Feminist Studies*, 16. 1 (1990): 144 and 127.

89 Philip D. Curtin, *The Image of Africa: British Ideas and Action, 1780–1850* (Madison: University of Wisconsin Press, 1964), 60.

90 For an account of the English colonization of Africa, see Margaret Strobel's *European Women and the Second British Empire* (Bloomington and Indianapolis: Indiana University Press, 1992).

91 John Lucas situates the conversation within the historical context of Lloyd George's unstable government and the succession of strikes that plagued 1921. See *The Radical Twenties*, 102–4.

92 Leslie Wilson observes that the broomstick "stands as an expression of feisty exuberance and ferocity. Though it is often supposed to represent a fertility ritual conducted with a phallic object, the broomstick itself might in fact represent an enormously extended clitoris ... In either case, it is an emblem of female potency": "Broom, broom," *London Review of Books* (December 2, 1993): 26.

93 Caserio, *The Novel in England*, 255.

94 Kent, *Sex and Suffrage in Britain*, 184.

95 Sandra M. Gilbert and Susan Gubar, *No Man's Land: The Place of the Woman Writer in the Twentieth Century*. Vol. 2: *Sexchanges* (New Haven, CT: Yale University Press, 1989), 289.

96 Royden, *Moral Standards of the Rising Generation*, 3.

97 David Matless, *Landscape and Englishness* (London: Reaktion Books, 1998), 75–7. Warner recounts her love of maps in "The way by which I have come," 467.

98 Matless, *Landscape and Englishness*, 80. Although Lolly abandons her map, she still thinks about the landscape in relation to its cartographical outlines later in the text (220).

99 Michael Reed discusses the topography of the Chilterns in *The Landscape of Britain from the Beginnings to 1914* (Savage, MD: Barnes & Noble, 1990), 105 and 138. John Sheal documents how the land was seen as a common denominator in British national character: *Rural Conservation in Inter-War Britain* (Oxford: Clarendon, 1981).

100 For a discussion of lesbians and space, see Sally R. Munt, *Heroic Desire: Lesbian Identity and Cultural Space* (New York: New York University Press, 1998), Ch. 6.

101 For a lucid discussion of the British attempt to criminalize lesbian activity, see Laura Doan,

"'Acts of female indecency': sexology's intervention in legislating lesbianism" in Lucy Bland and Laura Doan eds. *Sexology in Culture: Labeling Bodies and Desires* (Chicago, IL: University of Chicago Press, 1998), 199–213.

102 Winifred Holtby succinctly captures the pervasive disdain for the spinster during the interwar period: "Today, there is a far worse crime than promiscuity: it is chastity. On all sides the unmarried woman today is surrounded by doubts cast not only upon her attractiveness or her common sense, but upon her decency, her normality, even her sanity. The popular Women's Magazines, short-story writers, lecturers and what not are conducting a campaign which might almost be called The Persecution of the Virgins": see "Notes on the way," *Time and Tide* (May 4, 1935): 647.

103 This is not the only time that Warner associates female autoeroticism with nature. In *The True Heart* (New York: Viking Press, 1929), Sukey Bond's most intense sexual relationship is not with a male partner, but with the English countryside (see 25 and 241). In each case, Sukey's autoeroticism depends on an idea of spatial appropriation and boundlessness that is quintessentially English.

104 Warner, *Letters*, 9. Claire Harman notes that, in addition to Murray's book, Warner was influenced by Pitcairn's *Criminal Trials of Scotland*, a text that highlights the erotics of witchcraft: Harman, *Biography*, 59.

105 James Frazer, *The Golden Bough: A Study in Magic and Religion* (New York and London: Penguin, 1996 [1922]).

106 Margaret Murray, *The Witch Cult in Western Europe* (London: Oxford University Press, 1921); see also her *The God of the Witches* (London: Oxford University Press, 1931). Diane Purkiss discusses Murray's role as an authority on witchcraft in *The Witch in History: Early Modern and Twentieth-Century Representations* (London and New York: Routledge, 1996), 36–7.

107 Edith Lees-Ellis, *The New Horizon in Love and Life* (London: A. & C. Black, 1921), 128. Recent critics who discuss the witch as a figure adopted by lesbian writers include: Bonnie Zimmerman, *The Safe Sea of Women: Lesbian Fiction 1969–1989* (Boston, MA: Beacon Press, 1989), 66–7; Castle, *The Apparitional Lesbian*, 62; Faderman, *Odd Girls*, 229.

108 Karen Jo Torjesen, *When Women Were Priests: Women's Leadership in the Early Church and the Scandal of Their Subordination in the Rise of Christianity* (San Francisco, CA: Harper, 1994), 230.

109 Various critics have documented how the British ideal of manliness was threatened by the feminist assault on conventional gender roles. See George Mosse, *Nationalism and Sexuality: Respectability and Abnormal Sexuality in Modern Europe* (New York: Howard Fertig, 1985).

110 John Symonds, *The Great Beast: The Life and Magick of Aleister Crowley* (London: Mayflower Books, 1973), 13.

111 Caserio, *The Novel in England*, 264. For a witty refutation of Caserios's reading of celibacy in Warner's work, see Castle, *The Apparitional Lesbian*, 252–3.

112 Caserio, *The Novel in England*, 273; Marcus, "A wilderness of one's own," 148.

113 de Lauretis, "Eccentric subjects," 126.

114 Castle, *The Apparitional Lesbian*, 7.

115 *Ibid.*, 19.

116 Harman, *Biography*, 219.

117 Purkiss, *The Witch in History*, Ch. 5.

118 Butler, *Bodies That Matter*, 145.

119 *Ibid.*

120 Lolly's passionate response to nature echoes Warner's own love for Chaldon. See Judith Stinton, *Chaldon Herring: The Powys Circle in a Dorset Village* (Suffolk: Boydell Press, 1988), 53. Although many of Warner's poems, such as "In This Midwinter," expose the misery of rural conditions, several combine an anti-idyllic perspective with an enraptured contemplation of the landscape. See, for example, *The Green Valley*, which praises the "holy ground" of England yet ends with the speaker's inability to access this picturesque landscape. Warner's "The Green Valley" appears in *Selected Poems* (New York: Viking Books, 1985), 33. Barbara Brothers discusses "In This Midwinter," a poem published in the *Left Review* in 1935, in "Through 'The Pantry Window': Sylvia Townsend Warner and the Spanish Civil War" in

Frieda S. Brown, Malcolm A. Compitello, and Victor M. Howard eds. *Rewriting the Good Fight: Critical Essays on the Literature of the Spanish Civil War* (East Lansing: Michigan State University Press, 1989), 161–73.

121 See David Matless, "Ordering the land: the 'preservation' of the English countryside, 1918–1939," Ph.D. thesis, University of Nottinhgam (1990), 239–40; and his *Landscape and Englishness*, 79–80.

122 See, for example, E. Vale, *See for Yourself: A Field-Book of Sight-Seeing* (London, 1933), quoted by Matless, *Landscape and Englishness*, 75.

123 Although the novel indicates that men do inhabit Great Mop, Warner curtails the possibility of any masculine influence by feminizing the entire community. Lolly forms a close friendship with Mr. Saunters, an effeminate man who "darned [socks] much better than she" (133), brings her baskets of eggs, and "mother[s] his chicks" (147) just like the fairy-tale "henwife" (149). Elsewhere, we see the effects of Great Mop's witchcraft on Titus, who inexplicably becomes engaged to Pandora even though "the real match was made between Pandora and Lady Place" (227), a detail that suggests the potency of the homoerotic.

124 Marcus, "A wilderness of one's own," 138.

125 Alison Oram, "Repressed and thwarted; or, bearer of the new world?" 419–20.

126 Caserio, *The Novel in England*, 264.

127 Miss Ogilvy, we learn, harbors a vestigial memory of her island life during the Bronze Age, when she was a young man in love with an adoring cavewoman. Like Lolly, she is a split subject: "[she] knew that she was herself ... yet she was not Miss Ogilvy at all" (1452). The site of Miss Ogilvy's transformation is a small island off the coast of Devon, "marked on her map by scarcely more than a dot" (1449) – a sign that lesbianism is spatially elsewhere. Yet the story's loving attention to found archeological artifacts on this island – "bronze arrowheads, pieces of ancient stone celts" (1451) – are material reminders that the lesbian is indelibly linked to English pre-history. Hall's representation of the love relationship is a deeply conventionalized heterosexual coupling, in which Miss Ogilvy is cast as "the strongest man in [the] tribe," his manliness idealized by a voluptuous native woman whose only function in the story is to signal her sexual availability. Despite the suggestion that Miss Ogilvy rapes her "small berry" (1454), Hall evidently intends this melodramatic coupling to be read as a love scene. The story ends immediately after this lesbian sex fantasy, the dead Miss Ogilvy being found the morning after, "sitting at the mouth of the cave ... with her hands thrust deep into her pockets" (1457). As is the case also with Warner, Hall's use here of the word "pocket" suggests the female genitals: what Miss Ogilvy appears to die from is masturbatory excess.

128 This statement is taken from *The Well of Loneliness*, where Angela Crosby's primitivist gaze regards Stephen's body as racially Other: "There was something rather terrible about her ... the strong line of the jaw, the square, massive brow, the eyebrows too wide and too thick for beauty; she was like some curious primitive thing conceived in a turbulent age of transition" (150). For the references to "Miss Ogilvy," see p. 1453.

129 Davies, *Witchcraft, Magic and Culture*, 185.

130 Castle, *The Apparitional Lesbian*, 88 and 90–1.

131 Carolyn Matalene, "Women as witches," *International Journal of Women's Studies*, 1. 6 (1978): 574. Randy P. Conner offers a less essentialist account of the close association between homosexuality and witchcraft in *Blossom of Bone: Reclaiming the Connection between Homoeroticism and the Sacred* (San Francisco, CA: Harper Collins, 1993). See also: Arthur Evans, *Witchcraft and the Gay Counterculture* (Boston, MA: Fag Rag Books, 1978); Anne Llewellyn Barstow, *Witchcraze: A New History of the European Witch Hunts* (San Francisco, CA: Pandora–HarperCollins, 1994).

132 Davies, *Witchcraft, Magic and Culture*, 186.

133 *Ibid.*, 173.

134 Carpenter, *Intermediate Types*, 40–2.

135 See, for example: Judith Butler, "Imitation and gender insubordination" in Diana Fuss ed. *Inside/Out: Lesbian Theories, Gay Theories* (New York and London: Routledge, 1991); and, in the same volume, Carole-Anne Tyler, "Boys will be girls: the politics of gay drag," 32–70.

136 Murray, *The Witch Cult in Western Europe*, 31.
137 Sigmund Freud, "The 'uncanny'" (1919), *Collected Papers* (New York: Basic Books, 1959), Vol. 4: 373.
138 *Ibid.*, 389 and 394.
139 Purkiss, *The Witch in History*, 77–82.
140 Freud, "The 'uncanny'," 396 and 398.
141 Sue-Ellen Case, "Tracking the vampire," *differences: A Journal of Feminist Cultural Studies*, 3. 2 (1991): 3
142 Matalene, "Women as witches."
143 Vaughn Cornish, *Scenery and the Sense of Sight* (Cambridge, 1935), quoted by David Matless, *Landscape and Englishness*, 85.

4

Mary Butts's England:
racial memory and the daughter's
mystical assertion of nationhood

The world, the intelligent world, whose beliefs and opinions filter down now to the mass of the people ... must either abandon their scepticism or stick to it ... For it is another war for which we are preparing, the Armageddon ... of ... our civilisation. (Mary Butts, "Bloomsbury," 1936)

When the last comes to the last, in the woman is the race. (Mary Butts, *The Crystal Cabinet*, 1936)

One of the most startling aspects of the initial response to Mary Butts's 1936 essay "Bloomsbury" is that this piece was initially rejected on the grounds that the Bloomsbury Group was not widely known in England.[1] This perspective seems hardly credible today, particularly given the fact that the Group's popularity can be traced to 1920, when the term "Bloomsbury" began to appear in mass circulation periodicals.[2] Butts's essay is overtly an evaluation of the Group's self-promotion and an attack on what she calls its members' hollow "transvaluation of all values" (42), referring to them as intellectual omnivores who, because they "taste everything" indiscriminately, "have rarely time to sit down to a long meal" (43). Butts's fascinating critique of the Group's complicity in its own commodification anticipates contemporary analyses of Bloomsbury's status as a modernist spectacle. At the same time, the essay exposes Butts's own authorial preoccupations: her disdain for popularity, commercialism, vulgarization, and all forms of imitation. Most fundamentally, "Bloomsbury" functions as a diatribe against Butts's most consistently vilified antagonist: the modern skeptic. The language she employs to discuss the Group's ideological positions —"synthetic" (37), "papier-mâché" (36), "copies" (37), "*essential fake*" (42) – stems from her conviction that the Group scorned a belief in the "absolute" (37) and instead embraced a relativist perspective, deifying the simulacrum: "things made of one substance pretending to be things made out of another" (36).[3] Butts here reveals her own aesthetic conservatism by fetishizing the alleged authenticity of the modernist artifact, by implication positioning herself as a crusader for the real, the natural, and the sacred. Butts's unique eyewitness account of Bloomsbury from the perspective – as she puts it – of one of "the other writers of England" (34) who was not a member of the Group's ephemeral "magic ring" (33) immediately invokes, by contrast, an image of Butts's own beloved Badbury Rings, the prehistoric stone concentric circles of her native Dorset that reappear throughout her fiction.[4]

The subtext informing Butts's critique in her "Bloomsbury" essay is her lifelong obsession with "the problem of sanctity" (43) in modernity, her belief that something "deeper than the purely rational mind" (39) exists, and is accessible to those who would reject commercial values and surrender themselves to the irrationality of "a supernatural order" (40).

For Butts, this embrace of irrationality is not linked with what she regarded as the "all pervading insufficiency" (39) of psychoanalysis, but is instead connected to a notion of ancestral memory that privileges Englishness, aristocratic continuity, spiritual mysticism, and, crucially, the conjunction of femininity and nature. The values that Butts extols in "Bloomsbury" are evident throughout her fiction and criticism, but nowhere is her attack on commercialism, vulgarity, and imitation more apparent than in her 1932 experimental novel *Death of Felicity Taverner*. Both there and in that novel's prequel *Armed With Madness* (1928) Butts attempts to contrast imitation and authenticity by pitting the contemporary urban wasteland against the presence of a rural–supernatural order. Like other modernists, Butts laments the cultural and economic dispossession of life in postwar Europe – "everywhere there was a sense of broken continuity" – looking to mythic structures and contemporary anthropology to help her re-order an England that appeared not only chaotic and faithless, but seduced by plasticity.[5] If the reference to Armageddon (in the epigraph with which this chapter begins) seems somewhat hyperbolic, it is because Butts believed that she was battling in a world in which both landscape and belief were being engulfed by the rationalizations of science, technology, and psycho-analysis, categories which she implicitly masculinizes and denounces as inauthentic. Within this paradigm Butts aligns women and nature with myth, and privileges them as authentic signifiers of Englishness, upholding them as generative saviors of a dying nation.

Butts is, however, involved with scientific and psychoanalytical discourses even as she attempts to disavow them. This ambivalence is vividly reflected in *Death of Felicity Taverner*, a psychoanalytically and scientifically resonant text that none-theless regards psychoanalysis and science as the enemies of English civilization, grounding national identification in familial ancestry and sacred geography. In "Bloomsbury" Butts poses a rhetorical question – "Who has sufficient belief? And in what?" (43) – which her novels had earlier probed and attempted to answer by privileging "english family life" and "the land" as the only things "that mattered."[6]

Butts attempts to order the chaos of modernity through recourse to mythic structures and an insistence on nature's curative effects, identifying two central female characters – Scylla in *Armed With Madness*, and Felicity in *Death of Felicity Taverner* – as the generative loci through whom postwar England can be renewed. Both novels, published during England's revival of medievalism, incorporate crucial elements from Arthurian legend as popularized by Jessie Weston's *From Ritual to Romance* (1920). Both novels depict the female protagonist as a kind of living Grail, a genealogical signifier of England's cultural mythology. At the same time, both texts also reflect the period's interest in the anthropological discoveries of Jane Ellen Harrison relating to primitive ritual and animism, nature cults, and matriarchal origins – particularly the belief that femininity carries a residue of the mystical and the pre-rational. Like Harrison, Butts's interest in the maternalized primitive is informed by her experience of the social change wrought by early twentieth-century feminism and the First World War. Although her novels problematize literal maternity, Butts's books simultaneously idealize the female body's procreative potential, depicting it as a fertile source of cultural renewal that suggests, in a manner evocative of early twentieth-century discourse on race and eugenics, that women alone contain the possibility for racial survival. Scylla and Felicity are *goddesses* who, like Cleopatra, another of Butts's biologically determined heroines, become "impregnated with a life that is not the common run of the blood," for each woman transcends the human while simultaneously functioning as a racially pure blood-link to England's past.[7] Butts actively incorporates Harrison's work on female archetypes, seeing Hellenism as sympathetic to English culture because its origins, like Englishness itself, are coded as racially pure. She embraces Harrison's writings on the primacy of Dionysian vegetation cults, translating them for an English audience by inflecting them with specifically English concerns, namely, the preservation of rural England. I contextualize both novels, along with Butts's two conservative pamphlets, *Warning to Hikers* and *Traps for Unbelievers* (both published in 1932), within this larger anthropological framework, demonstrating how each text privileges ancient ritual as a way in which to preserve nature from corruption. These texts, I argue, can be read as responses to England's interwar crisis in landscape, when preservationist discourse circulated widely in an attempt to heighten awareness about the nation's need to preserve the countryside from destruction. Butts suggests that modern culture must incorporate elements of ritual practice in order to save rural England from both urban encroachment and spiritual deprivation.

In conjoining elements from two separate national traditions (Hellenic myth and the Grail legend) in order to construct a new national narrative for England, Butts suggests two things: one, that women, through their metonymic relation to the land, have *natural* rights of inheritance to England; and, two, that the future of the nation depends on female cultural intervention. Although *Death of Felicity Taverner* was published during a period when women could, in principle, inherit land, the novel engages the issue of women's legal disinheritance by alluding to the rule of primogeniture, which was not rescinded in England until 1925.[8] Butts's concern with women's inheritance rights can be traced to her autobiography, *The Crystal Cabinet*, which focuses on her own disinheritance from the family home and property. Here, as elsewhere in Butts's *oeuvre*, the central question is: who shall inherit the house and, by extension, England? Rather than focus on women's relation to the law, Butts stresses the female body's continuity with the English countryside, grounding women's national identification in their natural role as the inheritors of a pastoral ideal and cultivators of indigenous values. While the use of the imagined female body as a trope for the landscape is not new, what is radical is Butts's refusal to equate the purity of the land with female asexuality. Through the characters of Scylla and Felicity, Butts links sexual excess with spirituality, drawing from Harrison's conviction that primitive ritual is a discharge of emotion and longing, an authentic re-enactment of emotion and not a form of imitation. Butts's eroticized representation of woman as Nature situates the female body as a signifier of authentic Englishness, suggesting that the natural can function as the basis for cultural transformation. By insisting that women's natural inheritance rights transcend man-made laws, Butts's imaginative reconstruction of England relies on a mystical assertion of nationhood that is both animistic and overtly feminized. In carving this new place for women, Butts posits a blood-based definition of the nation that claims divine descent and racial purity; or, as a character in *Cleopatra* puts it: "What is rotten in the body of the Republic should be cut out, that the whole may be saved" (287). In *Armed With Madness* that contaminant is the black homosexual, while in *Death of Felicity Taverner* the source of pollution is a Bolshevik Jew. Although Butts herself draws no firm parallels between the Jews, blackness, and homosexuality, this constellation has a historical basis, as Sander Gilman's work on the pathologizing of the Jewish body has shown, providing us with a frame through which to read Butts's racialized characterizations.[9]

The impact of race science, primitive mysticism, psychoanalysis, and topographical guides on Butts's work has thus far remained unexamined. Cumulatively, the following sections attempt to demonstrate how Butts's investment in transhistorical mythic structures is reformulated to privilege female agency. In doing so, Butts seeks to secure citizenship rights for women on the grounds that they have inherent, timeless, unbounded, and mystical rights as daughters of England. Implicitly distinguishing between the nation as a natural product and the State as a cultural construct, Butts suggests that women embody the authentic roots of English racial ancestry. Although seemingly progressive in her desire to insert women within the national narrative, Butts's use of the discourse of "the natural" is deeply problematical, informed by racist and anti-Semitic notions of Anglo-Saxon supremacy. In each novel, a daughter's claim on the nation is stabilized, and naturalized, through the alignment of Englishness with heterosexuality and cultural homogeneity. Butts's autobiographical views on female disinheritance in *The Crystal Cabinet* provide the basis for my understanding of the author's fictionalizing of women as the true citizens of England. Butts further privileges each daughter's ancestral access to English prehistory through her use of optical metaphors that illustrate women's role as particularly observant citizens, echoing the discourse of rural preservationists who privileged the agency of the eye in their tracts on nature worship. In Butts's work, women are aligned with numinous forces invisible to the human eye but which are linked to conservative and prescribed social ends.

"A profoundly English life": familial inheritance and the centrality of home

In order to appreciate how fundamentally cultural fantasies of nationhood inform Butts's work, we must first grasp how she used experimental form, and how she understood the intersection of gender and Englishness. Although frequently acknowledged to be a writer of genius, Butts's "odd, oblique, tortured vision of the world" exasperated several early critics, who claimed that the average reader would not be able to decipher her "unintelligible jargon."[10] Butts began her writing career with poetry, and the technical discipline involved in its practice clearly affected her novels and short stories: they are lyrical, saturated with visual imagery, and filled with unfamiliar syntax and disconnected scenes stitched into a single narrative.

Jascha Kessler observes that Butts's prose "tends toward the laconic, the succinct, the terse ... [and] she is often syntactically eccentric."[11] Butts's most formally innovative novel, *Armed With Madness* (1928), combines free indirect discourse, first-person interior monologues, and snatches of omniscient third-person narration. Here, as elsewhere, the text is punctuated by an astonishing range of materials, incorporating a pastiche of quotations of popular music (such as fragments of jazz lyrics), English literature, contemporary film, and anthropology. Early reviewers frequently compared her prose style to Mansfield and James (without the latter's involution) for the acuteness of her perception; others attempted to situate her sensibility alongside those of Lawrence and Eliot to describe her interest in quasi-mystical states that are dependent on some notion of "racial memory," and to characterize her devotion to "intellectual classicism."[12] Her use of those categories, in particular her invocation of the primitive and the sacred, is conveyed through stylistic innovations that simultaneously privilege a critique of both gender and sexuality. *Armed With Madness* and *Death of Felicity Taverner* abandon conventional structures and patterns of thought in order to depict homoeroticism, bisexuality, and female aggression. While early critics did not comment directly on these themes, perhaps because her novels' complexity obscured their detection, many regarded her books as scandalous experiments. One review published in 1928 carries the caption "Mary Butts's Book Tortures Reader," while another, from 1923, reads: "Books We'd Like to Burn."[13] The most succinct conveys its sentiment in one word: "Irritating."[14]

Although, in general, most of the early reviews are favorable, several critics concur that Butts's work is bewildering in its eccentricities; her authorial pen is at one point referred to as a "surgical instrument," ruthless, callous, and devoid of "normality."[15] This phallic metaphor is consistent with the assessment of several reviewers who find her objectionable on the grounds that she does not conform to a feminine standard; one critic refers to her as a "woman writer with maleness" in her approach, a characterization that helps to explain the vehement critique of her alleged vileness.[16] While many reviewers mention the difficulty of her experimental prose style, arguably the real source of outrage is Butts's subject matter which, despite the fact that her work was well-circulated during her lifetime, often provoked doctrinaire responses. Butts's short-story collection *Speed the Plough* (1923) was banned from public libraries on the basis of its "indecency" and "the absence [from the stories] of normality and health" because it contained an irreverent fictionalization of the Annunciation tradition and a "queer" depiction of a young soldier who is obsessed with women's dress fabrics.[17] If Butts did not condemn "unnatural" practices, she in effect condoned them by allowing such vices to circulate freely throughout her fiction. Her thematic preoccupations included: erotic desire (particularly male homosexuality), sexual violence, sadomasochism, blackmail, extortion, addiction, environmental disease, black magic, and the horrors of the nuclear family. The critics, both men and women, who condemn Butts's work do so on the grounds that it deviates – without censure – from sexual norms: her stories are dismissed as "promiscuous reading," are called abnormal, queer, perverse, are said to "smell of blood and filth," and to leave a "nasty" and "sticky" taste in one's mouth.[18] Even Virginia Woolf betrays a level of moral panic when she refers to

Butts as the "malignant" author of "indecent" books.[19] By equating the reading of Butts's fiction with the pursuit of pornographic interests, certain reviewers effectively lumped the author together with other controversial modernists (e.g., Lawrence, Joyce, Hall) whose work had been suppressed for obscenity. To be sure, Butts was writing and publishing at a time when sexuality, particularly homosexuality, could not be discussed in English books or in the English press.[20] What becomes clear, as one sifts through the early reviews of Butts's work, is that her marginalization has as least as much to do with her thematic preoccupations as it does with the fact that it is a woman who voices such opinions.[21]

While Butts's investment in the primitive is steeped in both Greek antiquity and British mythology, her understanding and application of these categories is deeply informed by her critique of the social construction of femininity in early twentieth-century England. Butts implicitly historicizes her interest in transhistorical notions of "spiritual reality" (CC, 134) by anchoring it in contemporary discourses about gender and Englishness. Her autobiographical memoir up to the age of 22, The Crystal Cabinet, provides a clear articulation of Butt's blood-based definition of the nation and her preoccupation with a daughter's relation to familial inheritance – a paradigm that is of central importance to the novels. Butts's preoccupation with disinheritance can be traced to the events recounted in this memoir: her own expulsion from her Dorset home, "Salterns," after her mother financially mismanaged her father's estate and named Mary's brother Tony as the sole heir and beneficiary. Here, as in Death of Felicity Taverner, Butts paints a devastating portrait of an evil mother who privileges (albeit through domination) her only son while rejecting and seeking to harm her daughter. The Crystal Cabinet is a tale largely of paradise lost, in which Salterns and its surroundings of Poole Harbour are recalled in their perfection. "It was a profoundly English life" (16), Butts writes of her childhood, though certainly not an average one. Salterns was a substantial estate, requiring a number of maids and coachmen to keep it running, and full of hallowed family objects that could be traced as far back as Elizabeth I, not to mention the thirty-four Blake paintings now hanging in the Tate. When her mother had them sold off at Sotheby's to pay death-duties, Butts equated their loss with familial erasure: "Now we're nothing" (CC, 316). Butts recalls: "from our ancestors we had inherited not land, but possessions ... a secret common to our blood" (12). These references to blood and secrecy are crucial to Butts's personal mythology, which rests on the belief that her family is inclined "to mysticism" through its unique "ability to live in two worlds at once ... in time and out of it" (13). The temporal and spatial simultaneity embodied in the ancestral home is associated with femininity and English prehistory, forming the cornerstone of Butts's symbolism. One way in which to understand this alternative perception is through Anne McClintock's concept of "anachronistic space,"[22] a trope that is similarly associated with women, irrationality, and the primitive. But whereas McClintock argues that this space is anterior to history and bereft of human agency, Butts constructs her own modernist version of anachronistic space by privileging female agency and situating women both in and outside of history.

Although Butts does not fetishize material objects' function or utility, she is obsessed with acquisition because she believes in the auratic value of beautiful things – their ability to legitimize the family's genealogical and geographical link to English territory. Butts endows commodities with a luminous ability to evoke memories as poignant traces of the past. This "possessiveness over beautiful things" (316) appears at times pathological: Butts at one point lashes out at her mother for selling the family silver, thereby allowing their cutlery, embossed with the family crest, to circulate promiscuously "loose about the world" (376). While the role that fetishistic objects play in Butts's life and fiction cannot be overestimated, this preoccupation is not merely about the joy of handling rare and delicate things. Rather, it has to do with Butts's conviction that objects resonate with ancestral meaning. Both this notion of what we might call "thingness" – what she elsewhere refers to as the beauty of the "thing-in-itself" – and the belief that such material objects can literally facilitate one's access to "unknown categories" form the basis of Butts's personal mythology and are central to her concept of cultural homogeneity.[23] Butts's belief that family history is embodied in things situates her squarely within the modernist preoccupation with "the ability of objects to evoke a different world."[24] In *The Crystal Cabinet* memories are conceived of as residing in tangible objects, but those physical markers are simultaneously capable of transporting one to another realm. It thus comes as little surprise to find that her record of a visit to Gertrude Stein in 1927 refers not to the women's conversation but only to Stein's *things*. In a later short story, Butts attacks Stein for what she calls the "mutilat[ion of] altar ornaments," her sense that the modernist fashion for converting religious icons into art objects was a form of sacrilege.[25] In *The Crystal Cabinet*, Butts implicitly distinguishes herself from this allegedly reckless modernist practice, recalling her own beloved objects and seeing them as living testaments – relics, really – of a heritage that is, already in the 1890s, being threatened by the process of suburbanization and industrialization. Eventually, we learn in the autobiography, Poole Harbour would be linked to urban sprawl – what she derisively called "the menace of the [human] Tide" (243). Butts experiences this influx of people as an all-out invasion, the unwelcome penetration of "a herd of jungle-swine" (243) that upsets the placid "balance of an old rural constituency" (245) in which the symbolic and metonymic power of objects was central. Of course, Butts's celebration of "a family, a race" (46), and their things, is dependent upon exclusionary and elitist notions of property, class, and genealogy: "Something in my blood and my training that came out of the very stuff of England, the fabric out of which her soul is made" (262).

Although Butts used the country house and its contents as a symbol of tradition throughout her work, she did not herself live a life of affluence. Exiled from Salterns, Butts seeks to replace legalistic or legislative access to cultural inheritance with a mystical ownership, one that crucially provides a racial link between the daughter and England's prehistory. Although Butts's celebration of her "Saxon sturdiness of blood" (*CC*, 199) appears concerned with preserving a past tradition-ally gendered masculine, it is the daughter whom she inserts into England's mythic narrative as she insists that an alternative way of seeing is required in order to access this realm. Spectatorship facilitates access to a realm of temporal simultaneity, in which modernity is part of the interconnectedness of all history: "we are spectators of a situation which is the mask for another situation … [in] a remote age … a world that is outside time" (*Ashe*, 44). Although literal vision plays a role in Butt's dualistic paradigm, what she ultimately privileges, like Richardson, is another mode of perception, accessible only "when you stopped seeing" (*CC*, 148). During her moment of transcendence on the Badbury Rings, where she undergoes a kind of cosmic initiation – "I saw more than I could tell" (267) – what Butts glimpses is this spatialized alterity: "a translation ... between the seen and the unseen" (266). These themes resonate loudly throughout the novels, revising the narrative of the daughter's disinheritance by privileging her access to nature and British mythological history. In doing so, Butts exercises control over Englishwomen's past as well as their future, naturalizing their role as the "fulfillment of ... the race that bred [them]" (39) and thereby situating them in a relation to the nation radically different from that which their legal standing and social position would allow.

"In the woman is the race": aestheticized eugenics and the feminizing of landscape

In order fully to register the gendered implications of the supernatural in *Armed With Madness* and *Felicity Taverner*, and their consequences for women's *racialized* status as national subjects, one must first understand the basis of the author's belief in the dual connection of race and nationality. Butts was deeply influenced by two historically contiguous phenomena: the interwar crisis regarding the English countryside, and the modernist engagement with ethnographical materials. Both nature and myth, I argue, are crucial to an understanding of these novels' racialized depictions of the nation as a genealogical space. Throughout Butts's work we see a preoccupation with the idea of English heredity, in which the identification of race and nation is rooted, quite literally, in the soil of a historical argument about the English constitution. The author's writings repeatedly draw upon the common association of the landscape and notions of English identity, but her vision of rural England is most particularly aligned with the preservationist discourse of the interwar period.[26] A ruralist vision of a specifically English culture reached its peak during these years, when a great movement to inhabit the outdoors made the countryside an accessible and popular site of leisure. This concept of leisure, however, was fueled by a sense of crisis precipitated by the Great War, when the idealized notion of a pastoral England was threatened by those fighting, and those being slaughtered, on the Western Front. Butts's work repeatedly refers to the shell-shock associated with the war, seeing in nature the hope for a spiritual reconstruction that is unattainable in the industrial squalor of urban cosmopolitan life. Nowhere in Butts's writings is this more evident than in her conservative pamphlet *Warning to Hikers*, which reflects the general preservationist mistrust of the ability of a democratic system to manage the scenery of England. In both *Warning to Hikers* and *Traps for Unbelievers* Butts is at pains to stress the transcendence of nature over any human moral system. Published the same year as *Felicity Taverner*, these two texts appear during Britain's interwar craze for hiking and rambling, cycling, physical fitness, and naturalism.[27] Read together, they provide a window on to the historical controversy that fuels the novels' – and the period's – nostalgic longing for a return to a predominantly rural English nation in which blood-lines and familial inheritance are aligned with the presence of a supernatural order.

David Matless's recent work on the crisis in postwar English landscape discourse documents the traditionalist posture of the broad preservation movement during the 1920s and 1930s, in which campaigns for modern ruralism intersected with the promotion of Englishness. Matless vividly documents how country leisure was both welcomed by preservationists and seen as an act of cultural trespass whenever "anti-citizens," individuals who belonged to "the 'vulgar' working class," attempted unauthorized encroachment.[28] Butts similarly attacks the urban industrial worker, utilizing the language of reproduction and disease throughout *Warning to Hikers* to heighten alarm about his infiltration; she propounds that these anti-citizens whom England has "been breeding for generations" are now "spread[ing] like a nest of sores" across the landscape.[29] Her demonizing of these "new barbarians" (*W*, 15) is ultimately a critique of the urban working class: "The enemy is the democratic enemy, in a country where people have lost their stations and like badly-trained children can neither keep to their own places nor respect other peoples" (6). Like Clough Williams-Ellis, the promoter of the message of the Council for the Preservation of Rural England, Butts expresses anger at the new mobility of this urban hiker, referring to him as ignorant, uncultivated, and utterly unobservant. Just four years prior to the publication of Butts's pamphlet, Williams-Ellis had produced a diatribe on the destruction of England, a "Devil's Dictionary" containing similar complaints that focused on the "criminal" tendencies of hikers whose "loudness," "vulgarity," and "shamness" were deemed unacceptable.[30] Both Butts and the preservationists couch their arguments in ideologically charged language, situating themselves as upholders of the morality of the landscape. Composed during the expansion of the railway system into the English countryside, *Warning to Hikers* cautions against the increasing use of "mechanical transport" (5) in nature, arguing that such easy access contributes only to the progressive ruin of the landscape.[31] Butts struggles to differentiate her own love of the land from the encroachment of urban dwellers who, unconscious of the sacred status of nature, perpetuate idolatry by worshipping at "green altars" (27) and deifying an artificial "cult of nature" (6). Butts sarcastically deploys the language of religion to attack the anti-citizenship of the urban working-class "barbarians," dismissing their interest in nature as a form of cultism; these people have duped themselves – through the bogus "sacramental act" of hiking – into believing that their actions transform them into "the likeness of the Ideal Citizen" (10). For her, such behavior constitutes nothing less than eucharistic sacrilege, in which the wayward initiates, through the act of cultural trespass, "eat and drink damnation to themselves" (33). In contrast, Butts celebrates the entitlement of the landed gentry, maintaining that "the upper classes ... and ... our aristocracy have never left the land" (16). The fundamental problem, as she sees it, is that "working-class boy[s] and girl[s]" (17) have become intoxicated with "the unnatural idea of equality" (12), thereby demanding access to the countryside.

Butts's idea of an inclusive England rests fundamentally upon the idea of exclusion: throughout *Warning to Hikers* the urban masses are figured as debased and intrusively antagonistic, threatening not only the countryside but "our whole civilisation" (12). The depiction of these bodies carelessly darting into nature, only to "withdraw like tentacles, [like] arms of a squid pulled in and wrapped again about its mass" (20), perfectly captures Butts's perception that these uninvited visitors to the wilderness constitute an unindividuated blob. The language Butts uses here, and specifically her vilification of the working-class body, is characteristic of the modernist tendency to dehumanize the masses. In *Warning to Hikers*, however, Butts attacks also the intellectual town dwellers, particularly the "'red' intellectuals" (23), or communists, who were agitating for access to the countryside during this period. As a virulent anti-communist, Butts would not have welcomed the mass trespass on the countryside organized by the communist British Workers' Sports Federation in 1932.[32] Although she does not directly address this politicized mass mobilization in her pamphlet, she consistently critiques the militancy of "the ubiquitous barbarian" (17) who is motivated by "the absurd idea of equality" (10). Yet, surprisingly, despite her elitism, Butts at one point appears to uphold the rights of the intellectual town dweller, portraying him as a "model for something which is pretty good" when he ventures into the countryside and doesn't litter, uproot wildflowers, seek a crowd, defile the landscape, or advocate for a country cinema. Nevertheless, Butts ultimately regards this "model" individual as inhuman, "an assemblage of correct parts … with something weak about the mainspring or ignition" (23). Just as she had earlier denounced working-class hikers as "people of fake sensibility" (17) who construct a "hideously fabricated world" (15) of leisure in the countryside, so she here deploys mechanistic metaphors to launch her critique of the intellectual. Thus, despite the man's apparent sensitivity to the landscape, his interest is deemed inauthentic; as is evident elsewhere in Butts's writings, the simulacrum is unincorporable because "the model, even the working model, [is] not the thing" (23). Such fabricated town dwellers enjoy the countryside, but they are fueled by a "[s]ynthetic fire" that can never comprehend the "extreme reality of the land" (24). Whereas much preservationist discourse on leisure and the countryside suggests that citizens, following certain educational practices, might generate themselves anew in nature, Butts appears adamantly opposed to this kind of democratic access – even if certain rules of action are laid down and enforced. Such an extremist position situates Butts to the right of most preservationists who maintained that contact with nature was a means by which a citizenry fit for the nation might be produced.

Where preservationists argue that good citizens can be created through proper contact with the countryside, Butts upholds the view that real citizens are born, not made – though she never explicitly makes this claim. At one point in *Warning* she mocks the notion that what drives the hikers out into the countryside is "a half-articulate wish in the soul of man to return to the earth" (18), concluding that what really drives people, other than advertising, is idle curiosity, or a desire for exercise, or the wish for a secret tryst. While in much preservationist discourse of the interwar period we find both a code and an ethos aimed at nothing less than a transformation of the citizen's English being, in Butts's pamphlet there is no analogous move which presents contact with nature as a form of *national health*. On the contrary, Butts appears suspicious of any claim that responsible walkers might benefit from the "civilizing" influence of the countryside. From her perspective, the defilement of nature would not have happened in the first place had "man not recently altered the *essential* character of his living arrangements" (24; emphasis added) by transgressing his urban border. So much of Butts's writing is concerned primarily with the notion of historical, cultural, and ancestral connections to *place*, seeing the advance of suburban housing, commercial developments, American advertising, and Hollywood cinema as elements of encroachment, signs that English authenticity, is being endangered. Where the ultimate aim of the open-air lobby, as Harvey Taylor argues, was to "assert for the majority of the population the right to make reasonable use of the countryside," Butts concludes that the urban trippers "[e]ither destroy what they find or are lost in it" (28), in effect desecrating the landscape by their mere presence.[33] Such individuals are "essentially not fitted" (29) to the land because it is not their birthright, but a place "where neither they nor their fathers were born" (33). These irritating interlopers have no understanding of "the essence of nature" (29), for within Butts's paradigm they have been denied the privileges of hereditary access. Butts celebrates the countryman's relation to the land because it is his "original" (15) nature, yet she simultaneously theorizes a kind of geographical mobility for him that is inaccessible to the urban inhabitant. Thus, whereas the naturalist can make forays into the city and return (allegedly) unpolluted – because "he has something ... which can never be lost" (29) – the urban dwellers are granted no such luxury of oscillation. The "city native" is barred from cultural transgressions, for the contamination that emanates from his urban habitat is understood to be endemic to his being, "corrupt[ing] the country-side" (30) upon contact. At the heart of *Warning to Hikers* is Butts's conviction that, in effect, England has compromised her soul because her people "have begun to breed a race outside ... the true nature of things" (33). As a result, the formerly "pure man" (31) of the countryside has become polluted, chronically and irrevocably diseased, "leaving a dirty little trail through [nature's] sanctuary" (35).

In her preservationist writings, Butts deploys the charged language of purity and race during a period in which eugenics discourse circulated among environmentalists who perceived a link between racial degeneration and urban life. Although the eugenics movement in England was at its peak around 1913, membership remained strong and fears surrounding the issue of social degeneracy persisted into the 1930s. British historians have traced the pervasive belief in England to an industrial, urban, and racial crisis in the late 1870s, when arguments about racial decay were linked to modern urbanism; this anxiety led, by the early 1900s, to a rash of back-to-the-land propaganda seeking to return men and women to rural communities in order for the nation to survive.[34] Alun Howkins observes that by the First World War, country people were regarded as "the essence of England," an integral part of the national ideology that defined Englishness in terms of the idealization of the land.[35] Butts clearly can be situated within this larger paradigm, particularly alongside preservationists such as R.G. Stapleton, who maintained that "there was a genetic resource at stake in agricultural rural England" because country inhabitants were believed to be genetically pure. Writing in 1935, Stapleton argued that the "British countryside in short carries in its population the genes, unsullied and uncontaminated, that maintain and perpetuate our national vigour and our national characteristics."[36] A decade earlier, in 1924, Vaughan Cornish had written a paper entitled "The geographical aspects of eugenics" exploring the links between environment and heredity, focusing on the outposts of empire, and arguing for the need to "maintain the increase of the White Race and to people our own empty lands."[37] While Butts does not overtly engage with the topic of colonial rule, her work similarly invests in the connection between British stock and racial segregation; obsessed with the whiteness of the English landscape, Butts's rapturous outpourings read as a kind of eugenicist aesthetic, or an aestheticized eugenics. In *The Crystal Cabinet* she associates what we might call energy fields ("other forces") with the "white, white and mighty" (25) cliffs of Dorset, while elsewhere she venerates the "absolute whiteness" of Thornsdale, speculating on its primeval origin: "England once began there."[38] By grouping the concepts of birthright and whiteness with that of England, and in turn by suggesting that these overlapping categories are grounded in the mystical, Butts conveys that the countryman embodies a collective destiny whose essential components are racial health and purity.[39]

It is crucial to register that these notions of racial inclusion and Englishness are dependent on a gendered understanding of the countryside, for which ideas about the land and about purity are expressly linked with femininity. Relevant and instructive here is the following sentiment articulated in Butts's memoir in the context of a discussion of her step-father's family: "When the last comes to the last, in the woman is the race" (*CC*, 171). Although Butts does not elaborate on the relationship between maternity and racial health, the rhetoric she invokes is all but identical to that of early twentieth-century eugenicists, who argued that mother-hood was a matter of national importance, crucial to the future of the race. While Butts's focus is not actual mothers, she personifies the countryside as female and repeatedly contrasts this depiction with the masculinized city to convey her general anxiety about national deterioration. To that extent, Butts echoes preservationists who similarly feminized the land and utilized the language of rape to attack the corrupting of the English countryside.[40] In *Warning to Hikers*, Butts uses the language of prostitution and female chastity to startle readers into awareness, depicting the human infiltration of the landscape as a "hideous … dirty … [and] vulgar story" whose defilement has compromised the immaculate "virgin earth" (5). The problem, as Butts anthropomorphically puts it, is that people do not "respect the modesty … of the beloved."[41] Although at one point Butts suggests that nature is hermaphro-ditic, referring to "that great daimon, who is masculine as well as feminine, father as well as mother" (31), she carefully circumscribes this ambivalence by insisting on nature's feminization, calling attention to "[t]he 'bosom' of Nature" and under-scoring that "'She' has a breast" (31) that is subject to molestation. This depiction recalls Cornish's 1932 description of "the swelling domes of the English plain" whose "mammary undulations," lamentably, are no longer being tenderly cared for by her citizens.[42] Like those who regarded the violation of the landscape as a brutal rape, Butts characterizes the corruption of the countryside as a kind of sadistic attack on the female body: "It is to-day as if the lovers of England … saw the beloved thrown down and bound and trampled on and wounded, called by dirty names and false names of adoration" (35). Not merely a perpetrator of disrespectful transgression, man is a rapist whose "baseness" assaults the unblemished body of England: "Nature lies like a hand open with the fingers loose for man to run about the palm; dig into [her] pure flesh and build a … sewer … of his contrivance" (35). The image of ravishment that Butts invokes suggests that nature is passive, but this section ends by re-imagining the countryside as an active agent, no longer subject to the unconscious torment of man, who "does not see, nor understand" that "latent" in her being is the potential for "universal catastrophe" (35). Butts apocalyptically warns readers that earthquakes, tidal waves – and worse – will await those who venture into nature unawares, thereby providing clear evidence of "nature's hint to 'hikers' to turn home again" (36). In Butts's paradigm it is the countryside-cum-rape-victim who ultimately triumphs through the destruction of all traces of the human. Nature tramples and consumes her exploiter by making "all his works no more than a fertilizer for [her] flesh" (35).

This intimation of nature's inherent threat situates the feminine in an adversarial relation to male authority; it also implies that the relationship between the individual and the natural is heterosexual. One sees this vividly in the allusions to the rape of the countryside, above; but it is evident also – at least initially – in Butts's depiction of prostitution. Here, she offers her own twist on the conventional narrative in which rural innocence leads inevitably to urban prostitution by displacing desire for women on to desire for the countryside, suggesting that the real source of "temptation" and "peril" (29) is now the eroticized body of nature. Butts begins with the well-worn stereotype: "It is a common assumption that the Girl Who Left Home was a country girl, and the wrong turning led straight to Piccadilly," and then speculates on a "new school of thought, in which the innocent town-girl leaves home and is exposed to all the terrors and temptations of the country-side" (29). Initially this parable is startling, because it appears to suggest that urban girls who venture into nature will become prostitutes; nowhere, however, does the author confirm this as a possible outcome. Rather, what her story seeks to convey is that because both men and women have prostituted England through indecent transgressions, they will invariably be "exposed to all the terrors and temptations of the country-side" (29). Thus, women are situated in a homo-erotically charged relation to nature, "tak[ing] liberties with her" (30) just like the men who insist that nature seduces them with the desire to exploit her natural resources. Butts jokes that this may be the "first city-myth" to circulate in country lore, adding that such a tale will inevitably become fodder for "Cinema" (29) hounds in search of a sentimental story. Beneath these disingenuous cracks, however, is Butts's consternation regarding the fact that both sexes have imperceptibly drifted from any awareness that "Nature is a divinity" (30) who requires reverence and unswerving devotion. Butts considers this anti-civic behavior, yet she incredibly maintains that the infidels should be denied the opportunity to make obeisance "inside the precinct of the sanctuary" that is nature, insisting that renewal is possible only in their own "breeding-place" (35) – presumably the industrial squalor she critiques elsewhere in the essay. Again implicitly aligning herself against preservationists who argued that the individual's contact with nature could produce a new citizenry, Butts refuses the facile equation of exposure to the landscape with the means to good citizenship. Her position, ultimately, is situated within a cultural paradox, for although the "health … of the soul" (31) is dependent on the recognition of nature's "potency" (31), intermittent visitors are actively denied access to this feminized realm. In *Warning* she is both critical of and complicit in the eroticizing of the countryside, cautioning that "even pure air is not a friendly thing … until it has passed into you so completely that you cease to notice it," then elaborating that when consciousness of this "pure" resource returns it will be like "the sight of a lover who has never gone away" (17). The deterministic implication here is that only the country native is capable of negotiating the capricious lover that is nature, for "unless he was born already" (9) into rural life the hiking enthusiast's explorations, despite allegedly good intentions, invariably prostitute the beloved. The working-class interloper, we realize, is implicitly masculinized as rapist.

Visuality, the unseen, and the national logic of "mana"

While Butts reveres the countryside as a source of spiritual renewal, she is simultaneously at pains to convey that danger lurks in the landscape, particularly for those who are not optically vigilant. Ultimately, the author's concern is with how feminine spectatorship produces observant citizens by giving them access to indigenous English values. David Matless's phrase "geographical citizenship" stresses the relationship between observation, orientation, and Englishness, providing us with a useful way of characterizing Butts's own interest in vision and national identity.[43] Within her schema, the individual's interaction with landscape is animated through his or her distinctively English faculty of observation; direct perception facilitates aesthetic pleasure, but it is valued primarily as a means to achieving a mystical state. In privileging the eye, Butts suggests that the rediscovery of authentic Englishness resides within the body, not outside it, even though it is only through that body's cautious exploration of nature that the moral geography of the nation is revealed. Although Butts at times casts the traditional rural community in nostalgic contrast to the individualistic urbanism of the present, she is simultaneously at pains to convey the danger inherent in nature, urging awe and obedience, or what she calls an "indifference [to] nature" (34). To the extent that Butts believes this "indifference" is integral to one's perception of the omnipresent "danger" (9, 28) that lurks in the countryside, she participates in the larger interwar yearning for the mystical aspect of landscape, or what Frank Trentman calls the revival of "pantheism as a popular creed."[44] Trentman reads pantheism as a reaction against urbanized and mechanized living, identifying transcendentalism – self-forgetfulness before nature, a belief in the therapeutic function of nature worship – as central tenets of this neo-Romantic movement. While Butts can be seen as part of the larger romanticizing of pre-industrial English culture, she is not, in the end, a neo-Romantic writer who simply idealizes the landscape. Rather, in seeking to convey the presence of the divine immanent in nature, she stresses the "slow and dangerous" (18) workings of the earth, linking acute awareness of this phenomenon both to Englishness and to sight.[45] As we've already witnessed in her account of visuality in *The Crystal Cabinet*, Butts's real "[p]reoccupation [is] with the 'unseen,'" yet it is only through direct contemplation of "the wild, enchanting, incalculable force in nature" (*T*, 9, 47) that spiritual revitalization is possible. We see ample evidence of this logic of moral regeneration in the plethora of topographical guides to the English countryside that promoted spiritual renewal in the form of a travel book.[46] During the interwar years country leisure was regularly represented as a pilgrimage, with nature portrayed as a shrine; Butts participates in this deification, as when she nostalgically recollects growing up at Salterns surrounded by nature, "the superb Liturgy which is the matchless inheritance of the English child" (*CC*, 55). Nature thus educates the nation in the appreciation of its geographical heritage. Butts focuses on the mystical aspects of nature, but repeatedly conjoins the related ideas of "danger" and "indifference" to caution outsiders that, although nature is "the sacred" (30), a divine source for spiritual renewal, it is also something to be feared by the uninitiated. The basis of this fundamental danger is a specularized femininity.

For both Butts and the social historian and naturalist G.M. Trevelyan, the well-trained eye functions as a revelatory organ, remaking the individual as an ideal citizen through environmental exposure. We see reflected in Butts's work evidence of Trevelyan's oft-quoted phrase: "Without vision the people perish, and without natural beauty the English people will perish in the spiritual sense."[47] Yet, in contrast to Trevelyan, whose concern is with the citizen's visual receptivity, Butts is more interested in how *nature* regards the individual. Thus, Butts attributes spectatorial agency to the feminized landscape, conjuring the pantheistic image of a giant female eyeball: "The earth has its eye open night and day, an infinite number of eyes. Utterly observant, utterly indifferent eyes" (*W*, 20). This characterization recalls the Wordsworthian emphasis on direct perception, but here it is not the observer but nature herself who contemplates the unnatural: the endless stream of people who infiltrate and pollute her system.[48] Butts displaces the conventional association of male subjectivity with visual agency on to the feminized landscape in order to convey that nature must retrain the nation's faulty perception. Where once nature "trained [man's] sight" (22), today English citizens are inattentive to nature's role as pedagogical "goddess" (30) and have, lamentably, lost the faculty of observation. Implicit in this notion of feminized spectatorship is a critique of the tradition that has functioned historically to assert masculine privilege. By casting nature as a vigilant and contemplative female eye, and by insisting on its specific embodiment, Butts wants the reader to register the violence that has been carried out in the name of casual observation. Her remark that "we are ... only beginning to see" aligns vision with responsibility, suggesting that "short-sighted" (*W*, 22) citizens must become answerable for what they perceive. The importance of visuality in *Warning to Hikers* recalls Butts's attention to spectatorship in *The Crystal Cabinet*, where "Butts-eyes" are similarly valued for their ability to see what isn't ordinarily detectable; in both cases what is ultimately privileged is access to a space of liminality linked specifically with femininity and English prehistory.

Like these texts, *Traps for Unbelievers* foregrounds the gendered links between vision and mysticism, but here Butts exhibits greater panic regarding the fear of racial contamination and the promiscuous importing of non-indigenous primitive practices into England. This 1932 companion piece to *Warning* is Butts's most serious attack on what she perceives to be the pervasiveness of the irreligious attitude. *Traps* argues that modern culture has erroneously given priority to human nature at the expense of the phenomenal world by formulating an anthropomorphic inter-pretation of existence which privileges science, psychoanalysis, and materialism.

Taking the "moral temperature" (6) of the nation, Butts concludes that humanity is out of balance, suffering an enormous and fundamental lack, because religion is now regarded as shameful or obscene (12). What is absent is "a very peculiar kind of awareness" which Butts locates in primitive mysticism and the occult; crucially, this "perception" (25) has been lost by people who have abandoned the countryside for the city. Attempting to describe this ineffable "primitive 'awareness'" (26), Butts can find only approximations: "It has something to do with a sense of the invisible, the non-existent in a scientific sense, relations between things of a different order: the moon and a stone, the sea and a piece of wood, women and fish" (25). As this seemingly idiosyncratic list makes clear, Butts regards femininity both as elemental and as linked to a space of radical alterity. Geographically distinct from the material world yet utterly informed by it, this "invisible" location's meaning can never adequately be conveyed by language. By marking the space as linguistically inarticulable, she suggests that this feminized "different order" marks the limits of articulation itself. Centrally preoccupied "with the unseen, with the whole complex of emotions we call the religious attitude" (9), *Traps* aligns itself with a feminine understanding of "religious experience" (34) which is, I will argue, circumscribed by Englishness.

To the extent that Butts correlates linguistic excess and femininity with the sacred, her views intersect with those of Jane Harrison. Butts was an avid reader of Harrison's work; her central book, *Themis* (1912), argued that "the Great Mother is prior to the masculine divinities" and viewed the rationalist–hierarchical thinking exalted by her colleague G.S. Frazer as a perspective that subjugated mysticism and pre-intellectual religious experience.[49] In prehistory, Harrison claimed, matriarchy prevailed as the originary historical epoch, using anthropological evidence to connect the Great Mother to Dionysus who, in Harrison's reading, is a liminal figure – in terms of gender – and is associated with mysticism, irrationality, women, and "a 'return to nature.'"[50] This configuration speaks to Butts's own preoccupations, which similarly link "pure primitive instinct" (*T*, 27) with nature, irrationality, and the feminine. Like several of her modernist contemporaries who were influenced by anthropological research into maternal prehistory, Butts envisions a primordial past that is clearly matriarchal, arguing that "when Nature ceases to be the Mother, the all nourisher" (*CC*, 15), spiritual sterility infiltrates culture.[51] Interest in maternal prehistory even captured preservationists such as Trevelyan, who upheld nature as "the mighty mother for ever and for ever reborn," and argued that this feminine source stimulated a "religious instinct in mankind older than any religion."[52]

In *Traps for Unbelievers* we see ample evidence of Harrison's influence: Butts's embrace of the concept of "magic objects" (26); her privileging of emotion and the significance of "pure primitive instinct" (27); and her identification of "mana" as the pervasive energy source which animates nature and human beings alike. For Harrison, an ardent feminist, religious expression was the outcome of emotion rather than intellect; she saw it as a "matter of deep conviction" to reject the "intellectual attempt to define the indefinable."[53] One is here reminded of a character in *Felicity Taverner* who similarly posits that the irrational contains a deeper truth than rationality: "You can get a first in Greats or fly around the crater of Vesuvius, but what you depend on for your private life is your degree in witch-doctoring" (178). Butts's reference to "witch-doctoring" speaks to another similarity with Harrison: her deployment of primitivist discourse to forge the connectedness of nature and femininity. In *Traps*, Butts characterizes her irreligious age as a "pathless jungle" (5), utilizing myth and ritual "as weapons against a history that, from a feminist perspective," seems to narrate only masculine subjectivity.[54] Butts theorizes an alternative to masculinist conceptions of "religious inheritance" (34) by privileging "personal map-making" (26) as a challenge to the primacy of the objectivity prized by historical discourse. This figures prominently in *Armed With Madness*, where Scylla challenges male historiography by writing a country "*historië*" (*AWM*, 299) whose focus on the everyday recalls economic historian Eileen Powers's work, published in the 1920s, on ordinary citizens.[55] While Butts is keenly aware of the ways in which women have historically been eclipsed, her critique of gender coexists with certain conceptual blind-spots: race and nationality are categories uninterrogated in her work. We see a trace of this in her invocation of the rhetoric of cartography; Butts's reference to "map-making" alludes to the period's obsession with topography, which in turn reflects the larger cultural interest in prehistory through those maps' depiction of essentially English archeological sites.[56] *Traps* does not overtly engage the issue of modern monuments to British prehistory, but it is fundamentally informed by the interlocking concepts of "primitive man" (26) and Englishness. Initially *Traps* appears unconcerned with the particularity of national identity, positioned as it is, overtly, as a cross-cultural and transhistorical lament over the demise of "the religious impulse" (11). In fact, however, this pamphlet is fixated on national specificity, fueled both by a fear of racial contamination and an underlying insistence on the preservation of racial purity.

This is most manifestly evident in Butts's racialized discussion of "mana," which she disingenuously characterizes as "the non-moral, beautiful, subtle energy in man and in everything else, on which the virtue of everything depends" (47). The description of mana as "non-moral" masks a fundamental aspect of this seemingly boundless and free-floating entity: its association with racial and national specificity. At first this seems counterintuitive because mana appears to be defined by its inclusivity – it is "the all-prevalent" (40) – yet at the same time this invisible protoplasmic substance is consistently understood in relation to the discrete category, as that which keeps everything and everybody "essentially intact" (40). To the extent that mana is aligned with what Butts calls "the dangers inherent in the law of kind" (44), it can be read as a fascistic tool that works to resist any form of intermingling.[57] In *The Crystal Cabinet* Butts elaborates this linkage between mana and "the law of kind" through her belief that objects resonate with ancestral meaning, "their life communicating itself as Chaucer says, 'accordynge to its kynde'" (156). In attempting to describe what mana *is*, in *Traps*, Butts again invokes Chaucer's notion of "the 'law of kind,'" that which makes "every object, animate and inanimate" (42), uniquely itself.[58] At its most basic level, mana is concerned with the essential "nature of things" (44). Thus, in relation to nationality, mana is what enables and maintains cultural specificity, that is, "the stress a nation lays on individualism and on its racial type, the Frenchness of a Frenchman, the nature proper to an Englishman, or [to] spanish, german, chinese" citizens; in each case, the preservation of racial types "comes from the same instinct," namely, "mana or 'virtus'" (41). At the same time, mana is paradoxically a kind of "profoundly primitive" spiritual essence that appears to be multicultural, ahistorical, and translinguistic, "made serviceable to man in every religion he has ever conceived" (44).

While mana evokes multiple interpretations and has the power to contain contraries, Butts's conception of mana appears to align itself with Freud's evolutionist premise that the primitive represents "a necessary stage of development through which every race has passed."[59] *Traps for Unbelievers* draws from such early twentieth-century ethnographic understandings of the primitive, but its thrust is anti-evolutionist. In contrast to Freud who, like Frazer, tries to account for the evolution of man's intellect from a primitive to a civilized consciousness, Butts aligns herself with Harrison's repudiation of civilization and ecstatic embrace of the "primitive state of mind."[60] We even see a remarkable moment of confluence in which Butts borrows directly from Harrison's work to demonstrate the continuity and universalizing impulses of the "primitive form" (*T*, 44) of worship. Butts's language in *Traps*: "'Holy, holy, holy,' sang our fathers, and felt better. What they were doing was very ancient magic" (32), is an allusion to Harrison's earlier pronouncement: "We still say 'Holy, Holy, Holy,' and in some mystic way feel the holier."[61] This figuring of the sacred through ritual is the central tenet of Harrison's theory: maintaining that only rituals have religious significance, Harrison seeks to comprehend the psychology and gestures of "the savage" because "we realize that our behaviour is based on instincts kindred to his."[62] We see evidence of Harrison's theorization of the primacy of ritual practice throughout Butts's work, yet on this issue *Traps* evinces contradictory perspectives. While Butts's brand of primitivism celebrates mana as "the raw thing" common to all cultures in every historical period, she simultaneously balks at modern appropriations of this ancient "essence" (44). A clear example of this occurs in her scathing account of an art enthusiast, "civilised in french atheism," who indiscriminately collects "african cult-images and mana-projections" (45). Butts recollects interrupting this man while he was making offerings of "pure wax, honey, semen and blood" (45) to his eclectic assortment of fetish objects. Butts is scandalized by this spectacle because the collector has no fundamental understanding of his "unique objects of belief" (45): he is guilty of culling "exotic and out of the way" (46) devotional ornaments for his own "cult[ish]" (46) pleasure.

The unspeakable crime that this French collector commits is what we might call aesthetic miscegenation, the wrenching of objects from their original habitat and their subsequent cultural deportation to alien territory.[63] Butts's critique is not focused on the imperialist implications of such practice, but on what she regards as the dangerous hybridization of English culture. We see, for example, that she vigorously maintains the distinction between the "terrible fetishes" used by "savage religion" (44) and the form of religious practice that is native to English culture; the implication throughout *Traps* is that the two must remain forever separate. Although Butts recognizes that modern appropriations of earlier forms of religious worship are at times executed in good faith, she ultimately regards such "'chic' cults" (50) as debased expressions of primitive ritual (47). The real problem, as Butts sees it, is that "theosophic transplantations" invariably violate cultural boundaries and transgress national borders, resulting in an unsavory multiracial mishmash: "The gods of Africa are not indigenous to France. (Any more than the vast religious structures of Asia are native to the soil of England or America)" (46). The insinuation that indigenous cultures should stay put comprises the crux of Butts's argument in *Traps*: the beauty of the ancient Greeks, as she nostalgically envisions it, is that "they knew their place" (46) and did not encroach elsewhere. Of course, this preoccupation with one's appropriate station in life recalls her account, in *Warning*, of the ideal urban dweller who never ventures into the countryside; in each case, what is resisted is "the heaping of races pell-mell into territories" (47) where they neither belong nor are welcomed. The linchpin of Butts's obsession with maintaining both geographical and conceptual boundaries is mana, that which is "common and proper" (40) to every person and thing. Fundamentally, "the law of kind in action" (42) that mana personifies seeks to maintain discrete boundaries both within and between individual things; in relation to nationality and race, "the concentration of mana" (45) forecloses the possibility of intermixture and results in fixity, homogeneity, indivisible borders, and insularity. As a fantasy of cultural purity, mana works to ensure the solidification of Englishness.

Butts's fear of the promiscuous intermingling of categories in *Traps* is so great that it results in her pervasive use of the language of infection to denounce the contemporary "orgy of mana, stripped of the morals and ... tabu" (51) that once made it serviceable to mankind. Thus, mana gone awry is metaphorized as a "malignant cancer" on the body of the nation, the infiltration of "something poisonous" (40) that pervades contemporary culture and signals a breach in that which should otherwise be intact. The suggestion throughout *Traps*, based on the evidence that links the language of disease with fears of racial degeneration, is that the most pervasive fear in England is cultural contamination, "the old fear of the unclean" (29). So pronounced is "the preoccupation with physical infection," according to Butts, that it has become a kind of mass hysteria in which "perfectly healthy" (29) young men rush home from cinemas (which were then regarded by critics as houses of infection) in order to fend off disease. Butts locates the sources of this psychosomatic preoccupation outside of England, seeing it as an infiltration primarily of the foreign, or what she calls "a transatlantic ... rite, in its irrational aspects" (29). Where ancient people performed rites to rid themselves of real "tribal curse[s]," today men and women neurotically seek out "disinfection[s]" (29) to cleanse themselves of imagined maladies. Butts seeks to demonstrate the degree to which contemporary culture has gone awry because it comprehends only convoluted notions of cleanliness and taboo. By abrogating one's responsibility to "the law of kind," and by violating the "well-proportioned mixing of man and nature," today's citizens are "conscious only of a chaos of unrelated objects" (18).

In short, it is the demonstrable lack of cultural homogeneity and the exposure to a riot of difference that threatens the individual's psychic stability. Devoid of religious scruple, such people wallow in despair, intoxication, and reckless behavior; most importantly, they are no longer motivated to cultivate a "perfected state of society" (16). The rhetoric here of perfection, coupled with Butts's earlier invocation of disease, alludes to late-Victorian theories of race and eugenics, in which the idea of the innate superiority of the white race was used to bolster the image of the British empire.[64] *Traps* never overtly relates its discussion of cleanliness and infection to the colonizing process, but it does touch upon the discourse of eugenics by juxtaposing, at one point, anxiety about sexual disease with the view upheld by proponents of chastity who insisted on sexual abstinence "for the sake of the race" (15). Butts borrows from the language of sexual contagion, which is steeped in notions of racial degeneration, and applies it to the topic of religion in order to signal her alarm that the English race is lapsing into spiritual degeneracy. The "new disease" (16) that concerns her is not sexually transmitted viruses *per se*, but the infectiousness of disbelief, which she links to scientific rationalism. The language and preoccupations here are very similar to those expressed in *Armed With Madness*, where characters lament the pervasiveness of a cultural "dis-ease" (9), and in *The Crystal Cabinet*, in which Butts argues that modern men and women are "paralysed and hypnotized, in the name of Science," seeing contemporary disbelief as "a Black Death of the spirit sweeping over post-war Europe" (133). According to Butts, "real recoveries are rare … [but] once recovered, [one] cannot take the infection again" (133).

Self-inoculation and recovery rest upon the acceptance of Butts's belief in a supernatural order, one that privileges nature, women, mana, and the restoration of the authenticity of nationally inflected mystical experience. In *Traps* Butts intimates that "the race will come to no harm" (16) if primitive awareness is rekindled, but the expression of this spiritual awareness must, crucially, respect England's national borders. Throughout Butts's work ritual practice is inseparable from the organicist search for English origins. Thus, for example, in Butts's memoir her thrilling moment of initiation occurs not in France or Sicily but in Dorset, a holy spot – or "temenos" – which gives rise to an associative meditation on ritual practice, "the right balance of mana and taboo," and their integral relation to "Roman Britain" (*CC*, 266).[65] Although Butts's thoughts on myth and ritual are informed by her exposure to classical literature, they are indelibly linked with Englishness, with the "racial memory, the animal memory," that mediates between the seen and unseen worlds.[66] In this way she is very similar to Harrison, who invokes ancient Greece to discuss ritual practice but attributes her perception of invisible forces to her York-shire heritage. Sounding much like Butts, Harrison localizes visionary experience by privileging her Yorkshire familiarity with unseen worlds: "The unseen is always haunting me, surging up behind the visible."[67] Integral to this visionary experience is a crucial point of intersection between the two women: their mutual refutation of the view that ritual practice is merely a form of imitation. Harrison defines commemorative ritual against *mimesis*, seeing it as an outpouring of emotion that results in "a *presentation*," not in mimicry: she argues that ritual is not enacted "for the sake of copying" an event, but for "the *emotion felt about* [it]."[68]

Butts, as we have already seen, is similarly opposed to all manifestations of the imitative and the copy; in *Traps* she bemoans the trend toward "abstractions," arguing that whereas "our ancestors used to personify, or … represent" moral qualities, today they are merely reproduced in "plastic" (12). Like Harrison, who privileges material reality over abstraction, Butts's notion of ritual re-enactment stresses authenticity and focuses on the collective rather than the private emotions of the individual.[69] Most fundamentally, ritual facilitates the release and circulation of mana, which in the novels is located in the Englishwoman's body. The novels, as the following sections will show, demonstrate the centrality of ritual practice, mapping the female body onto nature in order to disseminate notions of authentic Englishness into the national body politic. Although Butts's understanding of mysticism claims to be "above race," what we see in the fiction is a preoccupation with English articulations of the mystical that work to ensure the continued existence of the race.[70] For both Harrison and Butts, British prehistory functions as a "temenos" that informs their perceived loss of organic community; each, moreover, privileges femininity and its curative relation to a mystical network formed by the interdependence of animate and inanimate things. The objective of "this business of the unseen," as Butts puts it, is to "sense a design," or pattern, that is traceable to a pre-industrial English culture whose national ideal is rooted in an identification with a mythic past.[71] Integral to this previously unimagined prehistory is the racial heritage of the female body.

Tracking the Grail: fetishizing the biologized object in *Armed With Madness*

The central issues this chapter has addressed thus far – nationality and its relation to the familial home and talismanic objects, the link between nature and femininity, the unseen and primitive ritual – all coalesce in Butts's two most stylistically innovative and thematically ambitious novels, *Armed With Madness* and its sequel, *Death of Felicity Taverner*. *Armed With Madness* makes several references to internationalism: English, Russian, and French characters dance the Charleston in Paris as a "baby-faced negro rolled his drum" (107); Boris, the Russian, is referred to as a "tibetan idol" (108); Felix, the Englishman, experiences in Paris an "irish love of a spree" (112); and a "musician's chinese rotundity ... [is] contradicted by a chin cleft like a Caesar's" (107). While these references convey a certain dynamism regarding the cosmopolitan diversity of modernity, they also signal the gradual destruction of transcendent values and the loss of ancestral continuity. No longer rooted in an individual place or culture, itinerant citizens of the world are "[w]ithout faith" (*AWM*, 9). Butts's novels are populated by people who are culturally dispossessed, uprooted and crippled by the effects of war; within this faithless context, characters scramble to discover "a new value, a different way of apprehending everything" (*AWM*, 9). Both *Armed With Madness* and *Death of Felicity Taverner* attempt to evoke meaning by recuperating ancient archetypes, particularly those derived from Arthurian legend. Butts was deeply influenced by the period's widespread cultural interest in the Grail, and both these novels are quasi-*quest* texts that reflect her desire to rework the current anthropological idiom which embraced a revival of medievalism.[72] Like T.S. Eliot, Butts was inspired by Jessie Weston's *From Ritual to Romance* (1920), a study which claimed that the Grail myth derived from ecclesiastical literature as well as popular folktales. In her journal, Butts likens herself to Eliot, maintaining that they are "working on a parallel," although she remarks that he "is working on the Sanc Grail, on its negative side, the Waste Land," while she is attempting something entirely different.[73] In contrast to Eliot, who uses pessimistic Frazerian imagery of social disorder and natural decay, Butts draws on Weston's observation that the secret of the Grail is deeply imbricated in primitive "Nature cults" that are structured around fertility cycles of rebirth and resurrection.[74] Where Eliot's work is saturated with images of reproductive sterility, Butts's fiction dramatizes the procreative and regenerative aspects of the spiritual Grail quest, linking it to ritual practice, the cycles of nature, and – crucially – the female body.

In both *Armed With Madness* and *Felicity Taverner* the concept of the Grail haunts and organizes the narrative: each uses this paradigm of fertility as a framework for the characters' transcendent vision. The earlier text explicitly positions itself as a modern recapitulation of the Grail myth, referring to the Saxons and Romans (*AWM*, 16) and "Gawaine, the knight of the world" (43). *Armed With Madness* has two intertwined plot lines: a triangulated love affair (Picus–Scylla–Clarence), and the mystery surrounding a small jade cup originally fished from the bottom of a dried-up well. Throughout the novel this object vanishes and reappears, compelling the characters to assume the role of knightly figures who search fruitlessly for its whereabouts. While this might sound tiresome, what saves Butts's modernization of the story is her astringent style, by which she interjects topical references and irreverent engagement with conventionally taboo subjects such as interracial homoeroticism, bisexuality, and sadism. The story is set at Gault House, the country home of Scylla Taverner and her gay brother, Felix, who play host to Ross, a live-in boarder whom Felix befriended on the queer party circuit in Paris, and Carston, an American expatriate who fantasizes about an affair with Scylla. Scylla thwarts Carston's desire and has a fling with Picus, a neighbor who had been living with his black lover, Clarence. This in turn enrages Clarence, a shell-shocked artist, who seeks revenge on Scylla. This abbreviated plot does no justice to the novel's formal complexity, for, as Lawrence Rainey notes, recounting the story of *Armed With Madness* "is as useful as giving a narrative summary of *Ulysses*."[75] Within this disjunctive textual world of psychoanalytically charged images and erotic intrigue, Butts rewrites the search for the Holy Grail as a detective story, casting the object itself as an ash-tray, a spitting cup, a whiskey-and-soda glass – as a banal signifier, in other words, that disappears from one guest-room and turns up in another.

One is here reminded of Tzvetan Todorov's structuralist argument that "the Grail is nothing but the possibility of narrative," for Butts's text is organized around and fueled by this central object's hermeneutical undecidability.[76] The novel repeatedly calls attention to the indeterminacy of the cup; as one character exasperatedly comments, "it's anything or nothing" (44). The jade cup has no inherent meaning, then, but functions as a projection screen for the novel's characters, providing an occasion for "adventures which are like patterns of another adventure going on somewhere else all the time" (31). This is not, however, just any adventure, but is a mythical quest into England's indigenous past; as such, it is bound up with conservative notions of historical continuity that privilege the English as racial survivors of an heroic and chivalric age.[77] Relevant here is the fact that during the interwar period, the Grail was appropriated by some as a fetish object with fascist connotations. While Butts does not glamorize war, she *is* fixated on blood-lines and racial purity in ways that resonate with fascist rhetoric, and she identifies the Grail as an auratic genealogical signifier of English prehistory.[78] Butts depicts the search for English roots, in a world devoid of inherent values, as neither easy nor guaranteed; *Armed With Madness* instead stresses the frustration of meaning: "A piece of worn jade … the question mark to the question we can none of us answer" (137). Both conceptually and geographically "the thing was off the map" (53), yet the object nonetheless facilitates a kind of "pilgrimage" (81) into British prehistory that demonstrates to the characters how, beneath the foreground of modernity, "old patterns repeated themselves" (16). Harrison's work on the centrality of ritual practice informs the novel's preoccupation with the Grail; the text's investment in ritual, though steeped in Hellenic notions of collective re-enactment, represents a longing to return to an English pastoral ideal embodied in the myth of "mediaevalis[m]" (89).

Like *Felicity Taverner*, *Armed With Madness* privileges a female character who functions as the focal point of this collective quest and provides a generative link to the sanctity of ancestral land. The territory is so saturated with the idea of racial origin that it is "blood-bright" (41), "dripping … with [flowers] the colour of blood" (3) that iconographically signal the fleshly significance of genetic ties. It is through Scylla Taverner that Butts most explicitly hypostatizes the relation between legitimate ancestry and landscape, privileging the body of the woman through the logic of substitution. The novel echoes the position Butts upholds in *Traps*, suggesting that "[t]he wood and the woman might be interchangeable" (12); anticipating her cousin Felicity, Scylla is described as inseparable from the landscape, "translating" the natural world "into herself: into sea: into sky. Sky back again into wood, flesh and sea" (67–8). Butts's depiction of Scylla's reconstitution into the natural world recalls Marianna Torgovnick's argument that the modernist identification with landscape has to do with the "linkages between the female, the oceanic, and the primitive," yet her paradigm excludes female modernists on the grounds that they "do not feminize the land, but rather perceive it as beyond sex and gender, as a sign of the sacred, as a sublime portent of cosmic unities."[79] Such a view is complicated by Butts's clear use of the female body as a trope for the English landscape.

An anti-rationalist who is against the dominance of "the machine" (90), Scylla is the conduit through which the English citizen's contract with a pre-industrial pastoral ideal is realized: "Naked, the enormous space, the rough earth dressed her" (5). Consistent with the novel's preoccupation with medieval legend, Scylla is the "damsel of the Sanc-Grail" (44), but as a sexually experienced woman who is well-versed in "erotic conversation" (32), hers is only a "hypothetical virginity" (132). In this way, she is at once human and other-worldly, a living legend who testifies to the reality of an alternative world for the worthy initiate. Described as both a "witch and a bitch" (10), Scylla is thoroughly modern: she wears make-up (9) and powders her arms (114), sports green pointy shoes (33), loves luxurious objects (53), and is described as a "neurotic hussy" (77). Yet she simultaneously assumes mythic proportions: her brother Felix refers to her as the sort of woman "'who'd have mothered the house of Atreus'" (19), an allusion to the horrific Greek myth that features adultery, incest, infanticide, and cannibalism. Scylla's name also resonates with the image of the six-headed, female sea-monster from the *Odyssey* who devours passing seamen; insofar as this creature lives in a cave on the side of a cliff and has multiple heads with teeth, she is a kind of *vagina-dentata* figure. This scary constellation of associations conveys Scylla's mythic potency, but she is aligned primarily with the regenerative, a fact underscored by her comparison to the Norse mother goddess Iduna, the keeper of the golden apples of youth. Scylla is "the female spirit of life" (30), a kind of earth mother–goddess who has survived the ravages of war and now, catapulted into poverty and "know[ing] everything about being lost" (31), embodies England's potential for cultural renewal. Much of the egg imagery pervading the novel, imagery which is invested with this idea of regeneration, is directed toward her: she is characterized as "a different egg" (19), "a bird ... woman" (87) who "broods situations and they hatch" (20). As such, Scylla is a genealogical symbol of English racial survival, recalling Charlotte Haldane's observation, in 1927, that there is a "certain 'egginess' in the feminine make-up."[80]

Like the Grail itself, which is the novel's central focus, Scylla is elusive, the only woman in the group of five men, and therefore "a point for reflection" (15). Structurally, furthermore, the Grail and Scylla – "a living cup" (38) – occupy analogous positions: each is associated both with fertility and with the recuperation, in Weston's words, of "the Waste Land," and each facilitates a ritual re-enactment for the collective.[81] Where conventional markers of the Grail saga privilege masculinity, Butts insists on the dominance of a female archetype by making Scylla the symbolic locus of meaning. In this way, she reminds the reader of Harrison's contention that "above even Zeus the Father" stands the "Great Mother" who represents the "collective conscience."[82] Butts conjoins the traditions of ancient Greece and Arthurian legend in order to fabricate "something in England off the regulation road" (12), a new national narrative that privileges femininity in order to restore the authenticity of mystical experience through the dissemination of primitive ritualistic practice. This new English narrative, however, despite its proto-feminist leanings, simultaneously reflects deeply conservative assumptions regarding race and sexuality. *Armed With Madness*'s thematic radicalism is located in its suggestion that the female body and the Grail are equivalent conduits to an authentic English past, a move that situates women's agency as central to the nation's cultural regeneration; but underpinning the subversiveness of this substitu-tive logic is Butts's profound conservatism with respect to race, heterosexuality, and genetics. Her privileging of femininity and her focus on the centrality of space are attempts to demonstrate that women can intervene in the nation's historical and mythical narratives, yet the production of this new story fosters a xenophobia which resists the commingling of categories and leads ultimately to exclusionary notions of Englishness. The text's emphasis on modern England's links with a Saxon and Roman past recalls the late-nineteenth-century classification of racial types, through which scientists attempted to secure the racial origins of the English people as unambiguously light-skinned.[83] *Armed With Madness* collaborates in that ambition by racializing the ancient features of the landscape, such as the "white porcelain rings" (8) that Scylla encounters on a walk through the countryside. This attention to *whiteness* is amplified in Butts's representation of her characters, where the notion of racial stock provides a conduit to an English national past rooted in a pastoral ideal. All of the men – except Clarence, who is black (14) – have a skin color that is modeled on "the moon's palette" (14), while Scylla herself is described as eminently fair, birdlike, with "white shoulder[s]" and "rose feet" (153) and blonde "moon-fair hair" (145).

Through the depiction of Clarence, Butts exposes her belief that authentic Englishness is synonymous with racial purity and heterosexuality. Clarence's black-ness and homosexuality are central to an understanding of the quasi-crucifixion scene in which, jealous and angry over losing "his jewel" (87) Picus to Scylla, he ties her body to a clay statue of his lover and ritualistically flings arrows at her until she bleeds and then faints.[84] The language that describes this violent yet eroticized act highlights Scylla's status as spectacle, her body indistinguishable from the greenish clay statue pricked with white feathers that Clarence has molded: "[an arrow] ripped the skin on her shoulder and entered the clay" (145). This climactic moment is prefigured by an earlier scene in which Clarence obsessively draws Scylla on huge sheets of paper in charcoal, "obscenely and savagely contorted" (129), then pierces the "bodies of his paper martyrs" (130). Read within the context of Harrison's work on ritual, Clarence's actions arguably constitute a cathartic attempt to rid himself, and the larger community, of what he perceives to be Scylla's evil influence. Precisely because Clarence is an artist, one is tempted to read this scene as evidence of the affiliations between the mystical savage and the sensibility of the artist, a connection that Harrison forges when she argues that art (like ritual) arises out of an inchoate emotional impulse. If Clarence's actions are to be read as purgative, then Scylla must be regarded as a contaminant. Yet the novel does not endorse a reading of Scylla as offender, and instead upholds the view that Clarence himself is the deranged wrongdoer for seeking her expulsion. In this way, Clarence's actions recall Butts's observation in *Warning to Hikers* (31) that rites can stem from "the ill-health of the soul," for he appears "mad" (129) to many characters. If we read Clarence through the lens of psychiatric discourse on shell-shock sufferers – for he is a veteran of the Great War – his behavior can be read as an example of man's "degeneration to primitive states," what anthropologically informed doctors at the time regarded as "evidence that individual personality structure was a stratified system embodying stages of evolution."[85]

Clarence is repeatedly subject to primitivist constructions of racial identity: "it was always dark in that country" (25) of his mind and body; he is terrified of "a menace that walked hand in hand with night" (128); his entering of a room is juxtaposed with another character's memory of the lyrics to a "negro song" – "Bear Your Burden in the Heat of the Day" (51). Unabsorbed by the community, he is perpetually "rac[ing] away on that black heath" (65–6) of infinite despair. Clarence is irredeemable not just because he is homosexual and suffers from emasculating shell-shock, but because he is racially Other; his brutish treatment of Scylla further demonstrates that, as a black man and war victim, he is an embodiment of atavistic psychical structures.[86] The scene in which Clarence "cattle-ranched" (145) Scylla, repeatedly throwing sharpened arrows at her body, upholds the evolutionists' view that primitive peoples have no sense of moral conduct, behave irrationally, and are analogous to animals. His transgressive behavior also illustrates the clinical view, upheld by Richard Krafft-Ebing and Havelock Ellis, that there is a psychosexual link between sadomasochism and homosexuality. Where the other characters can participate in modern forms of ancient ritual and remain *civilized*, Clarence cannot; his indulgence in "race sadism" (153) suggests that he is too primitive and too black to transgress the boundary and return unscathed.

Butts presents Scylla as a martyr to the cause of racial purity and heterosexual procreativity; the substitutive logic of the novel dictates that she, as a living emblem of the Grail – and therefore a sign of fertility, rebirth, and "natural" regeneration – must displace the homosexual coupling of Clarence and Picus because it represents only reproductive failure. Clarence himself makes this explicit as he repeats to himself "'Introvert, introvert'" (129) – a displaced signifier for "invert" – as he rages against Scylla. Sexually speaking, Clarence "had put all his eggs" (however unlikely their fruition) in one basket, and now "had no more eggs to lay" (87). A "frustrated hen" (111), Clarence can never be the vehicle for an authentic connection with nature and English prehistory. He seems to exemplify Sander Gilman's observation that, while blackness historically has been associated with earthy sexuality, it is "not the fecund earth but the earth associated with death."[87] We see him lash out against both the Grail and Scylla in the taunt: "down the well, where the cup came," is the "[b]est place for you" (144), a revealing moment that brings together the novel's two stories (the love affair and the cup saga), again demonstrating the interchangeability of the woman and the cup. Importantly, the Grail–cup is a "reminder" (21) that behind the images of cultural deterioration and decay – precisely those images embodied by Clarence through his alignment with the non-procreative and the nightmare of war – "another truth" (25) exists, a truth that finds its inspiration in a heterosexually conceived notion of spiritual renewal that also privileges whiteness. It is no coincidence that the "business of the cup" is tied to the refrain "Lighten our Darkness" (138, 147), or that the concept of *enlightenment* is represented as a process of discoloration: "lighten us" (139). Butts also uses spatial imagery to underscore the importance of place in the construction of racialized and sexualized identity: geographically dislocated – exiled to a "deadly grey land" (65) – Clarence inhabits a liminal zone that offers no hope of organic wholeness or historical continuity. Both sexually and racially marginalized, he has no access to the "white" and "green road[s]" (10) that lead to Gault House. Without this sense of connection to a historically embedded English past, Clarence is outside of time: "History did not exist for him" (127). Not only psychically–geographically but temporally exiled from the national and racial insularity of "Hardy's country" (11), Clarence is propelled into a borderland of infinite suffering, inhabiting "a place where no sane man would live" (126). Clarence is unable to follow Scylla's prescription to "have faith" (70) because faith requires the veneration of a procreative process and an ancestral legacy that necessarily excludes him.[88] In contrast, Picus and Scylla – fecund symbols of England's racial survival – remain enveloped by the "true greenwood" and "chalk roads" (8) of their home country, luxuriating in the "green even under [their] feet" (162) which demonstrates that they are living testaments to the connection between English national identity and the land. In the end, the heterosexual couple appears in a state of connubial bliss – "playing at happy warriors" (159) – a characterization that conveys the curative effects of pagan ritual for those who are *"the same thing"* (58; emphasis added). This celebration of sameness is ironic, given the text's expulsion of male homosexuality, but it speaks to Butts's characteristic denunciation of ungenerative desire. Like Scylla herself, whose body provides a genealogical link to English prehistory, "the earth was a map of naked beauty" (72) to those who know how to interpret its topography.

Because the novel is a series of shifting erotic triangulations (Picus–Clarence–
Scylla; Scylla–Lydia–Philip; Carston–Picus–Scylla; Felix–Boris–Ross), it is difficult
to enshrine any dyad as definitively stable. And, yet, despite the text's acknowledgement of the fluidity of object choice, heterosexuality in the end is still privileged,
and naturalized, through its association with Scylla and her role as procreative earth
goddess. Although she herself participates in a homoerotic dalliance with Lydia,
Scylla's allegiance is to Picus and the community; ultimately, the novel endorses
heterosexuality as normative by linking Scylla's disruption of the Clarence and
Picus dyad to the novel's larger preoccupation with England's cultural survival.
Informing this paradigm is the unarticulated yet pervasive cultural assumption that
reproduction is central to England's national survival, and that maternity is
responsible for the production of future citizens.[89] The sexual imagery of the Grail–
cup, aligned with fertility, speaks directly to this concern, as does the novel's
invocation of the lance, which was initially used by Picus (who initiates the search)
to pierce the cup and haul it from the bottom of the well. Weston provides a
historical context through which to read these paired objects, but even the characters,
adept at playing "the Freud game" (137), see the "sexual symbolism" (20) at work
here: "[These] are sex symbols … the Lance, or Spear, representing the Male, the
Cup, or Vase, the Female, reproductive energy."[90] This association with reproductive vitality is somewhat complicated by Picus's homoerotically charged remark –
"It was Clarence's spear that started me [on the grail hunt]" (140) – but the moment
is subverted by the fact that he himself, like Scylla, is intimately connected to
mythic structures which are linked to the "natural" world and hence uphold the
symbol's heterosexual connotation.

Harrison's argument that the mythological figure of Picus is aligned with "mana"
provides extra-literary evidence that Picus, like Scylla, embodies a heterosexually
conceived notion of cultural survival.[91] In *Armed With Madness*, the concept of mana
resonates with what Butts regards as Chaucerian connotations of heterosexual
propriety inherent in the law of kinds. The concept is invoked three times in the
text: once by Ross, who alludes to the law of kinds by thinking of "the brickness of
a brick" (92); and twice by Scylla, whose remarks recall Butts's conservatism on the
issue elsewhere. Scylla's first reference to the law of kinds alludes to heterosexuality
by invoking the notion of gender opposition: "Chaucer who loved everything for
what it was. A sword for being a sword, or a horse. And they for what they were,
the 'gentle girls and boys'" (68). Her second reference merely reiterates the essence
of what mana is: "Each thing *accordynge to its kynde*" (69). Crucially, Scylla's two
observations immediately follow on the heels of her sexual encounter with Picus
under Gault Cliff, an interlude described as being "as much of a creation as any
growth in nature" (68). Cumulatively, these references naturalize heterosexuality
and suggest that anything other than the male–female dyad is a sacrilege. They also
further the perspective, upheld by Scylla, that the female body is the site of racial
survival (and of racial, if not sexual, purity), and that homosexuality must be
displaced in order for the natural to flourish.

Family tribalism and "race solidarity" in *Death of Felicity Taverner*

Although the formal innovation and astonishing thematic range of *Armed With Madness* situate it more firmly as a classically high modernist text, the view that *Death of Felicity Taverner* marks a turn toward conventional realism because of its linear narrative seriously underestimates this text's other experimental features.[92] The assumption of linearity is problematized both by the novel's absent center (Felicity is already dead when the novel opens) and its unmarked moves from omniscient third-person narration to first-person interior monologue. Moreover, when Boris Polteratsky from *Armed With Madness* reappears in *Felicity Taverner* to help resolve the mystery surrounding Felicity's death, the novel perceptibly shifts its register, moving from the plausibility of domestic realism to the realm of the purely mythical. The implications of this shift are evident only if one has read Harrison and recognizes Butts's incorporation of the classicist's work on primitive ritual. Yet, while *Felicity Taverner* reflects Butts's modernist engagement with British cultural anthropology, as well as her simultaneous disdain for, and use of, psycho-analytical insight, it also demonstrates her admiration for the detective novel, a conservative genre that was wildly popular during the interwar period.[93] Butts's novel is self-consciously constructed as a crime puzzle, an intellectual "detective story of high merit" (*DFT*, 221) in which the circumstances surrounding Felicity's death and the significance of her missing body are the preoccupying questions. Butts thematizes this through the references to "keys" and "tea-leaves" that recur throughout the novel. As in *Armed With Madness*, which is similarly fueled by a desire to relocate a central object that has been lost, *Felicity Taverner* is fundamentally about the search for a central absence which is severed from its indigenous place. In each case, the nucleus of the novel (a jade cup; Felicity) is coded as essentially English, providing the occasion for a narrative of quest that is really about the mythical search for English origins.

Like *Armed With Madness*, *Felicity Taverner* is structured as a nostalgic quest for "a thing that's been lost" (79), yet here the sacred object which "had been lost out of the world" (*AWM*, 79) is Felicity herself, a metonymic Grail to the extent that she is central, absent, mute, indeterminate, and a signifier of English national identity.[94] Both texts turn on a central mystery (the loss of a cup; the death of a young woman), and each incorporates Harrisonian elements of ancient ritual that are intertwined with references to both contemporary England and British pre-history. Importantly, both books rely on magic and mythic structures, and in each case, the text is shaped by Butts's conviction that "great mystical and magical experiences" cannot be conveyed directly, but "must be expressed by an indirection"; in the matter of the Grail, especially, an oblique "translation" is required.[95] Both novels accrue meaning through the logic of association and substitution; both operate in more than one historical and spatial register at once; and both represent the female body as a generative source and a collective unconscious through which authentic Englishness is channeled. In *Felicity Taverner*, Butts reprises themes that she had established in her first novel, *Ashe of Rings*, where a primordial under-standing of blood-lines is the key to its characters' sense of identity and affiliation: "blood is the life. Mix it and you mix souls" (*Ashe*, 151). Here, as elsewhere, English cultural roots arise from ancestral memories that are genetically based. As in *Ashe*, where a character who has married outside the clan introduces a pollutant – "our race has become impure" (109) – *Felicity Taverner* focuses upon the disastrous effects of marrying an outsider who is also a contaminant. Whereas in *Armed With Madness* the cultural fantasy of Englishness is dependent on the expulsion of the black homosexual, here the myth of purity requires the demonizing of the Jew. In both cases, as in Butts's first novel, the "tribal instincts" of the family provide a shelter from the encroachment of alien forces, a "[s]anctuary of [the] race" (*Ashe*, 149, 187) that is connected to the animism of the countryside.

Like *Armed With Madness*, *Felicity Taverner* engages with the question of how women can function as active producers and transmitters of national culture; in both cases Butts relies on the familiar trope of women and nature to make her point. In contrast to her male contemporaries, for whom the linkage of woman and nature served to denigrate women's mental capacities, Butts suggests that the *primitive* nature of women is so "exquisitely civilized" (*DFT*, 343) that they are ideal moral teachers of the nation, capable of navigating "international waters, not properly charted" (314) by the uninitiated. For Butts, women function as cultural disseminators of those elements of authentic Englishness that have been suppressed by urbanization, technolo_y, rationalism, and mechanization – mystical experience, primitive animism, and the creative value of purgative acts. Women may thus transform national consciousness by helping England to rediscover her rural roots and embrace her indigenous values. In *Felicity Taverner*, it is Felicity herself who is the locus of this primitive spirituality, the female principle through whom the text's various ideological struggles are played out and resolved. At the same time, the Taverner family functions as a microcosm of the nation, an embodiment of the past, yet with a significant twist: whereas English law during this period decreed that a woman's nationality should follow her husband's, Butts's novel implies that citizenship is a matter of blood-lines, not marriage. Thus, Felicity, despite her marriage to a Russian Jew, Nicholas Kralin, not only retains her English nationality but becomes a metaphoric figure of the nation, an embodiment of "the beauty of England" (285) through whom women's cultural inheritance is naturalized and ensured. In this way, Felicity both subverts English law and becomes the paradigmatic standard for a new model of national citizenship, one in which femininity functions as the basis for a fantasy of territorial appropriation. To the extent that Felicity is Butts's attempt to suture the gap between the primitive and contemporary culture, she functions as a metonym of the power of "the Sanc-Grail," a mediating navigational figure whose "appearance and disappearance" helps her family members "find their way" through "the Waste Land" (283) of modernity.

Butts's representation of the Taverner family in many ways complicates the paradigm that Anne McClintock identifies regarding Britain's national narrative, in which the family has traditionally functioned as a trope for the historical genesis of the nation while being itself devoid of any historical agency.[96] In contrast, *Felicity Taverner* represents the family itself as the source of historical agency. Its members serve as the embodiment of authentic English values to the extent that they cultivate a pastoral ideal and identify with the cultural roots of English resistance to industrialization. This is, of course, an extremely insular model of nationality, one that hinges on the idea of racial essence to convey that only select members of society have access to England's ancient and mythic legacy. Interestingly, Butts invokes primitivist discourse to convey the primordial roots of the Taverner clan, referring to them as country-bred people who, like their ancestors, make forays into the cities only for amenities and then return to their land "as head-hunters … to examine spoil, but never as though their home could be anywhere else" (299). The Taverners occupy the position of modern savages, participants in the act of "tribal hunting" (230) whose primary objective is the retention of English "race-solidarity" (272). Yet Butts invokes the discourse of the primitive not to construct the Taverners as non-white but rather to demonstrate the family's tribal loyalties and to essentialize their relation to the English countryside.

This genetic model is complicated by Julia Taverner, Felicity's evil mother, who threatens this idealization of the family because she conspires with the heinous Nicholas Kralin against her own daughter, offering him "a few Taverner scalps" (253) as appeasement. Butts's use of the vocabulary of the tribe ironically recalls Franz Fanon's warning as to the dangers posed to national unity when "the nation is passed over for the race, and the tribe is preferred to the state."[97] The Taverner family displays precisely this impulse toward insularity and a myopic concern with "the nation-breeding doings" of only a small "part of an english shire" (301), although Butts implies that it is just this insularity that enables the family's national roots to flourish, thrive, and withstand the onslaught of industrialization, suburbanization, and a variety of other social ills. Blood-lines are central to Butts's conception of nationhood, even though in this novel it is the Russian Boris Polteratsky who ultimately *saves* the Taverner family from destruction. Thus the homosexual character Boris is not expelled from the narrative because he functions as a conduit for Taverner family values. In contrast to Kralin, who, like Clarence, "has no known history behind him" (315), the Taverners are living testaments to an authentic past, breathing archives of what Butts elsewhere names "Country History."[98]

In *Felicity Taverner*, Scylla records and preserves this country history, drawing from a range of sources, both conventional and unorthodox, in order to "leave behind her the full chronicle of [the family's] part of England," from "histories of houses, histories of families, to memories that were like visions, to visions which seemed to have to do with memory" (300). To the extent that Scylla's book-in-progress elides the distinction between official and unofficial history, embracing investigations of the past that fall beyond the margins of historical records, she can be said to represent the modernist interest in foregrounding "subjectivity and perspectivalism at the root of historical knowledge."[99] By revising the conventions of historical narrative, Scylla tacitly questions the veracity of historical chronicles that record only public events represented by the lives of heroic men; in constructing a more elastic and inclusive understanding of "the historic imagination" (300), she creates a space for women, the obscure, domestic life, mystical experience, and memory, however much this seemingly inclusive agenda is mitigated by other forms of parochialism. In addition to oral histories, Scylla listens to the speech of "trees and stones and turf" (300), observing that embedded in the countryside are genealogical traces of the whole of human history: "she saw their land as an exfoliation, not happening in our kind of time, a becoming of the perfected" (300).

Scylla values the kind of double perception that combines the verifiable with the visionary represented elsewhere in Butts's work. Here, Scylla's access to England's phantasmatic "historie" (299) remains unexplained, for even she herself does "not know how she knew" (300) about the existence of temporal anomalies and alternative geographical spaces. Butts depicts Scylla as one of the gifted few, able to perceive the "speechless sight" (300) of things that appear not to be there. She thus continues her role as seer from *Armed With Madness*, and puts her awareness to work by devoting her life to her book project, chronicling the private history of the inhabitants who populate "the country of the Sanc Grail" (300). Herself both storyteller (168) and archivist, Scylla regards the family as the repository of national history, but she is not blind to the psychopathologies of that hereditary alliance. Despite the text's cynicism regarding the family's dysfunctionality – the Taverner coat of arms is notably an image of self-consumption: "a snake with its tale in its mouth" (200) – Butts still privileges the genetic family as that which contains and embodies England's authentic past. Even Julia Taverner, "the original bitch" (171), evinces a deep love for "this bit of England" (258) that envelops their home.

Experientially, the Taverners' mania for the countryside is located in the body, and they perceive the landscape as a kind of imprint, in which nature's "pattern was repeated in them, the stuff of a country made into man" (339). As Julia describes it, the earth is "strictly of their flesh" to the extent that "leaf and air and water had nourished their bodies" (258–9). This bleeding of the boundary between the body and the natural world will become even more apparent in the characterization of Felicity, but here it is important to register the biological component of "Taverner-land" (339). Butts's representation of the family as the privileged guardians of the countryside is congruent with much preservationist discourse of the period, which celebrated hereditary ownership: "An owner whose roots are very deep in the soil … knows much better than anybody else … [how] to treat [the countryside] in the future."[100] In Butts's novel, family ownership is repeatedly celebrated for just such aesthetic and economic attentiveness to nature. Defenders of the landed status quo, the Taverners occupy two homes that are centuries old and are located in "the most ancient part of the wood" (165); Scylla and Picus inhabit one, while the other belongs to the dead Felicity. These homes, and the "Sacred Wood" (340) that surrounds them, are the Taverners' "blood-link" (174) to the "old part of oldest England" (340), for their property has been held by the family over many generations. In Butts's novel, the Taverners are represented as ideal guardians of the countryside, members of the "great gentry" (196) of landowners who, because of a historical trajectory of change (suburbanization, urban encroachment, commercial exploitation), are forced to confront the disintegration of their estate. In *Felicity Taverner* this threat to the family's inheritance is personified by Kralin, the speculative capitalist who seeks to desecrate Felicity's home by turning it into his "personal nucleus" (249); he wants to purchase the surrounding land and construct a hotel, vacation bungalows, and a golf course on the family's sacred soil. Among Kralin's many crimes are his plans to advertise this development and blackmail the family into compliance by threatening to publish what he alleges to be Felicity's sexually explicit personal papers.

In touch with numinous forces that are invisible but linked to the natural world, Felicity appears repeatedly in the novel as a ghost who is the real link to an authentic England rooted in an idea of ancient and timeless continuity with the rural past. The figure of the ghost of the murdered Felicity recalls Harrison's discussion of primitive ritual, in which "blood, once shed on the earth, poisoned the earth," and required "purification for blood-guilt."[101] Butts locates the anger within the Taverner family rather than in Felicity who, as an apparition, radiates primarily sadness – her "ghost's eyes looked out under a frown" (321) – and signals her presence through mild disturbances in the natural world (323). In addition, Felicity's presence is strongly felt in her home, which is saturated with her traces and is "preoccupied with [her] passion and death" (181). As Scylla, Felix, and Boris discuss their memories of her, the room seemed to move "to some uncharted place," as sometimes "[h]appy lovers" imagine themselves visiting "countries which lie east of the sun, west of the moon" (181). The geographical metaphor here calls attention to fact that Felicity's life, and her lovemaking, occupy unexplored imaginative space, but brings to mind also England's role as colonizing power, exceeding all boundaries in its quest to subsume territories unknown. Butts uses the rhetoric of territorial expansionism to capture how Felicity negotiates both the material and the metaphysical worlds in order to destabilize the invisible border that separates the two. Not merely an Englishwoman but a national spirit, Felicity spatially exceeds all boundaries and generates a "perception not easy to discuss for lack of terms" (181). Unable to be contained by language, Felicity also cannot be explained through conventional historical markers. Recalling Scylla's role as historical chronicler, Felix remarks that "after history had been ransacked for analogies" to explain Felicity's otherworldliness, he had settled upon fiction, the image of "Alice running with the Red Queen on the squares" (181). Like Scylla's country history, Felicity's requires something beyond "research into a story in known terms" (181). By invoking Lewis Carroll, Felix suggests that in order to describe her one needs to privilege the elements of fiction, especially metaphor and analogy: "If a crystal became a white narcissus, you'd have something like her" (169). The metamorphic nature of this image recalls Felicity's inherent instability, at the same time as its racialized dimension underscores her role as signifier of English purity. As such, the purification of her land is dependent on the expulsion of impure elements that threaten the racial survival of her people. Either absent (through death) or present as an absence (as a ghost), Felicity can be read as a figure for the spirit of rural England; her cultural identity, like that of the nation, defines itself through the suppression of that which threatens to disrupt it: namely, the Jew, the "untraditional part of humanity" (314). In her incarnation as national landscape, Felicity exhibits the cultural roots of English resistance to industrialization and the strong nostalgic pull of pastoral idealism.

The question of Felicity's sexual experience, like the circumstances surrounding her death, comprise the two central mysteries that fuel the narrative. By conjoining them, Butts interrogates the construction of female sexuality and challenges male sexological models that regarded excessive female desire as aberrant – or equated its lack with normalcy.[102] To the extent that Felicity's sexuality cannot adequately be explained through recourse to existing sexological paradigms, she necessitates a new vocabulary of desire. As Scylla puts it: "When Felicity started an

affair, it was somehow outside the rules" (172). By overlapping the mystery surrounding Felicity's death with the enigmatic nature of her sexuality – was she virtuous?
shameful? chaste? filthy? – the novel suggests that the cultural understanding of
female desire is itself a lacuna, a profound mystery. But, unlike Freud, who links the
"riddle" of femininity to phallocentrism, Butts does not limit Felicity's sexuality by
circumscribing it within a phallic economy. Rather, the narrative equates feminine
sexuality with excess, a libidinal and linguistic surplus that cannot adequately be
explained through conventional language: "something had been left out, like some
secretion we haven't yet isolated or named" (168). Like her "torn and strewn
members" which are discovered along the side of a road and have to be "collected"
and "laid out," the narrative is "full of omissions" and gaps that present to the reader
a different "version of the truth" (168) regarding Felicity's body.

Like the Grail itself, which signifies and opens up the possibility of narrative,
Felicity's absence is the "occasion for a good story" (168) that fuels the other
characters' quest for meaning. Also like the Grail, Felicity's indeterminacy signals
to the reader that, narratively speaking, "the mould would be broken" (168) and that
one shouldn't seek conventional means to "get this story straight" (169). What we
learn about Felicity and her death at age 33, we gather in bits and pieces: when the
novel opens she has already been dead for four months (170); her body has been
cremated (168) and people speculate about the possibility of suicide (166) and murder
(184). Scylla, Picus, and Felix deduce that she was in good health but worried about
her bills (184), and hence fear that something abominable had happened to her
(192); they wonder what could have driven her into Kralin's ghastly arms and by
turns blame him, Felicity's mother, and the war for her untimely death (324). These
are the facts that surface, but they shed little light on the larger questions of *who*
Felicity is, or *why* she is so central. From Scylla we learn that she had exquisite
beauty and grace, traits that Picus also registers when he thinks about her "before
her mirror, just out of her bath" in her bedroom shrine which was "to serve beauty
and nothing else … like the best american advertisements" (197). Here we have an
image of Felicity as erotic spectacle, a representation consistent with what Laura
Mulvey calls the "to-be-looked-at-ness" of women, their traditional exhibitionist
role as objects that are simultaneously observed and displayed.[103] This focus on
spectacle is also reflected in Felix's observation that "it seemed as though great
houses had been built to display her" (169), and his later comment that her role was
"to adorn that bitch of a house" (182) because her mother held the purse strings.

Yet Felicity's iconic status is a paradox, for despite the many references to her
beauty and her preoccupation with self-adornment – her Lanvin dresses, bangles of
jade and crystal – she is no narcissist, but rather a feminine screen to national
consciousness. Scylla describes her cousin as "dis-interested and without pretension"
(169), whereas Felix characterizes her "choice of objects – of possessions" as "perfect"
but similarly devoid of attachment or self-interest (169). Butts's representation of
Felicity as "dis-interested" pointedly recalls her description of Nature in *Warning to
Hikers* as "indifferent," an intersection that will be explored momentarily. Here,
what it is important to register is Felicity's detachment from the material world,
even as she appears to be caught up in the trappings of femininity. Although she
eschews work (despite repeated references to her supposed poverty), Felicity does

have secure employment: "Her occupation was to be lovely and exquisite … to understand things and to love" (182) – in other words, to cultivate her stewardship of her class. Here the text equates her role as mannequin, hostess, and ambassador-of-goodwill with that of contemporary "saint" (169), yet Scylla reveals that this "adorable" creature "prayed to Mozart" (169), not to God. Although the text often utilizes theological discourse to characterize Felicity's "genius for love" (330), it is a highly charged and subversive depiction of devotion, one that foregrounds the desires of the body and links eroticism to the sacred. Scylla remarks that she had seen Felicity "with the same look that Saint Catherine of Siena had in ecstasy" (172), bringing to mind Bataille's account of the relation between mysticism and sensuality, and also invoking the image of Bernini's sculpture of Saint Teresa with her expression of orgasmic ecstasy. From Boris, we learn that Felicity "was a woman made for a particular kind of love, a love that … [r]ecognises no God with her for priestess" (188).

This reference to Felicity as the "priestess" of a Godless universe, and Boris's description of her as a "mystery" – something "outside our range … a woman who was a miracle" (170) – underscores her resemblance to Scylla and to realms beyond conventional perception. Each woman derives her potency from her sexuality, and each is something other than what she initially appears to be. Scylla captures Felicity's duplicity, and also alludes to her cousin's mythic stature, when she confides to Boris: "I've somehow got from you a double image of her. One like a cameo, cut delicately, and then another, a terrible duplicate, over life-size, Io, Hathor or some such divine simplification" (187). Like Scylla herself, who is an incarnation of both feminine perfection and female monstrosity, her cousin embodies the potential for both life and death; we get an additional glimpse into the "[o]ther Felicity" in the following account of her scary, and here castrating, underside: "Think if the crescent moon showed you its teeth" (171). Felicity occupies a position structurally similar to that of Scylla in that she mediates between past and present, and is entrusted with a dangerous "power" (189) she does not fully comprehend. Felicity, in other words, is like the Grail: she "came out of Paradise" and navigates the earth to assist "people who could not find their way [back] in" (180). Also like the Grail, she is characterized by indeterminacy: Felicity is described by turns as "distinctly chaste" (172) and "a scandalous piece" of work (183), "the chastest maid that breathed" (322) and an "erotic expert" (260). She is said to embody "disgraceful knowledge" (323) because, during her time in Paris, she purportedly indulged unrepentantly in love affairs with multiple male partners (192).

The allegations of Felicity's sexual deviance are couched in the discourse of psychoanalysis and are tied specifically to the neuroses of family life, which Butts describes, in a satisfying gardening metaphor, as "the forcing-bed for the Oedipus complex" (171). The novel's pervasive use of such terms as repression, sublimation, and analysis underscores Butts's familiarity with Freudian theory, yet its relation to such terms is complex and inconsistent. The novel generates examples that both conform to and violate psychoanalytical principles, but this is not merely a point-lessly inconsistent application of Freud's theory. Rather, Butts sets out to call into question these psychoanalytical paradigms even as she depends on the reader's familiarity with them. In relation to Felicity, for example, the traditional formulation of the Oedipus complex has only partial relevance. Although she is accused by her husband of suffering from an "Electra-complex" (294), we see no evidence of Felicity's incestuous desire for her father, who indeed materializes only in a passing reference (326). We do, to be sure, witness the erection of paternal law as universal and normative, but this is instituted by the mother, not the parent Freud identifies as central to the daughter's negotiation of the complex. On the other hand, consistent with the traditional narrative is the fact that the mother encourages Felicity's sexual repression.

Primarily, the novel marshals psychoanalytical rhetoric in order to critique sexological models that purport to be based on scientific truths but actually encode traditional male sexual privilege. Butts's critique of psychoanalysis helps her to develop an alternative standard for female sexuality, one that values women's erotic autonomy and strengthens their ties to the land, to English ancestry, and to the nation. Felix sets the tone for Butts's critique when he observes that British culture in general and the family in particular have become saturated with sexological concepts, creating: *"A generation that is learning to treat sex only too scientifically"* (293). Felicity is said to have had "an inferiority complex" (180), while her mother's irrational hatred of powerful and attractive young women is explained in terms of repressed jealousy: "Felicity's life was wholly composed of the excesses she would have liked to have enjoyed," for in contrast to her daughter she "had sacrificed her jus saturnalia to God" (189). Butts's depiction of Julia is a prime example of her slippery usage of psychoanalysis: the mother is denounced for preaching sexual restraint to Felicity, yet is simultaneously seen as a dupe of the very structures she purports to uphold. Thus, in one of the more extraordinary moments in the text, Adrian provides an explanatory model for his mother's behavior, pronouncing her a victim of the social construction of femininity and critiquing her for internalizing psychoanalytical structures (321–2). Nonetheless, Butts still deploys the rhetoric of psychoanalysis to pathologize Julia Taverner and explain her "dirty" (322) obsession with sexuality. As Adrian explains it, his mother drilled "shame" (326) into his young sister, telling Felicity "she was filthy, when she was clean" (324). Elsewhere he remarks that his mother was unable to recognize Felicity's exceptional "quality of purity" because of her own "abnormality" (323) and repressive "complex" (322). By pathologizing Julia though psychoanalysis, Butts discredits the mother in three important ways: she critiques her literal interference with the daughter's inheritance of the family home and property; she delegitimizes her attack on the daughter's sexuality; and, perhaps most importantly, she makes room for a model of female sexuality and inheritance not tied exclusively to reproduction. There is more than one paradox to be noted in Butts's use of psychoanalytical paradigms for these purposes: first, Butts herself employs the very discourse she broadly aims to discredit; and, second, her character Felicity winds up illustrating a psychoanalytical idea even more effectively than her mother. Felicity's very impulse to turn away from the mother may be understood, as it has been by many feminist psychoanalytical theorists, as a girl's response to her discovery that her mother – and all girls by extension – lack cultural privilege.

What is complicated about the text's invocation of the discourse of sexual purity is the simple fact that Felicity herself is neither chaste nor a virgin, even though she is associated with the word "sophrosyne" (313), a Greek term that has to do with prudence, discretion, and moderation – especially in terms of sexual desire. Although Felix insists that his cousin "was most men's friend and very few's lover" (169), what lingers through the accumulation of evidence is that Felicity was certainly non-monogamous and quite evidently uninterested in marital fidelity. Kralin recalls the many times his wife ran away from him, and his response focuses pointedly on her carnality: "What business had a woman's body, blood-driven engine for secretion and excretion, to play such tricks" (214). The insistence on Felicity's physicality coexists with the many references to her "virgin purity" and "saintly chastity" (323, 324), leaving the reader to supply the resolution of this apparent contradiction. The text directly addresses the tension between Felicity's alleged purity and the reality of her sexual experience in its crucial invocation of Milton's *Comus*. Adrian recollects being a child and playing "Comus" with his sister, only to have his mother insist that he cut several of the Elder Brother's best lines because she feared that "it might put ideas into Felicity's head" (323). The masque is about the overwhelming power of the chaste woman to resist all that threatens her, though it is an ambiguous text because the virgin Lady is so passionate in her defense of chastity that she appears excessive, rather than contained. Butts quotes selectively from the speech of the Elder Brother's in which he explains to the Younger Brother that chastity is a form of hidden strength. Here, he compares the Lady to both Diana and Minerva, who carries Medusa's head on her shield; we know that Freud reads the decapitated head of Medusa as a displaced sexual organ, an allusion that in turn recalls the novel's earlier reference to Felicity's teeth (and hence castrating underside). Butts also cites a few of the lines from the end of the Elder Brother's speech, in which he contrasts a dead chaste woman – who is borne to heaven by angels – with the dead lustful woman, whose soul resists leaving its body. Within Milton's context, a woman's ghost lingering on earth would signify her unchaste former life, a fact that Butts fully exploits by having Felicity appear as a ghost in the pages in which Adrian invokes *Comus* (323–4), and elsewhere. The intertextual implication here is clear: Butts wants to draw our attention to the fact that Felicity was never sexually innocent while on earth, even though the novel repeatedly circulates the discourse of sexual purity in conjunction with her representation.

Butts arguably deploys this rhetoric for two reasons: one, to critique the fetishizing of female chastity by giving us a heroine who refuses to embrace the normalization of asexuality; and, two, to revise the ways sexual cleanliness is attached to the discourse of racial purity. Butts seeks to recast the sexual female body as the conduit for English racial survival by discrediting the only female body normally allowed limited sexuality – the maternal. Much like eugenicists who argued that healthy maternal bodies were essential for racial health and purity, Butts seeks to rescript a healthy and pure sexuality for the woman who nurtures national culture. Although Felicity is not a mother *per se*, her body is a matter of national importance, integral to the maintenance of the racial stock and the continuation of rural England. Butts reminds us of this when Picus, registering Kralin's plot to commercialize the land, overhears the earth's lamentation: "A mourning somewhere in creation that the freshest earth there is should lose its maidenhood" (249). The earth's loss of virginity implies its infiltration by foreign contaminants. We see that Felicity is not so much a woman as a figure for the English countryside, a displaced signifier for the purity of the land: "the hills were her body laid-down, and 'Felicity' was said, over and over again, in each bud and leaf" (191). Harrison's characterization of the omnipotent earth mother as "Lady of the Wild Things" captures Felicity's role as virtual agricultural deity, with "[e]yelash of flowers and a shoot of ivy closing [her] eyes" (214).[104] Her body is not merely *like* nature, but is the archetype to which the natural world is likened; thus, "petals" are said to be as "soft as Felicity's skin" (302), rather than the inverse. Metaphorized as the landscape, Felicity is "the White Goddess" who is aligned with a kind of nostalgic racialized longing for the indigenous English values of the Taverner clan: "The death of Felicity Taverner ... behind it lay ... the attack on their bodies, nerves, roots, the essence of their make-up, in the attack on their land" (342).[105]

The feminizing of the countryside hinges on an essentialized understanding of the female body as the source of natural fecundity and racial regeneration. Within this context, Felicity's sexual excess can be read as a sign of her patriotic investment in the moral rewards of reproduction: she mates with many but paradoxically maintains her corporeal purity. At the same time, her embrace of sexuality recalls Harrison's characterization of Dionysus as a feminized "god of orgy and ecstasy."[106] Compared to Scylla, who can be viewed as a kind of demi-goddess of fertility, Felicity is arguably the chief godhead; Scylla is the bee-keeper (301), while Felicity inhabits the "[c]ell of a queen bee" (220). Like the queen bee who organizes the hive and is the locus of reproductive activity, Felicity is both structurally central and has a destined and *natural* function. These bee allusions invoke both Butts's totemic image, elsewhere, of the "Earth-Mother ... of the Hundred Breasts" whose nipples sprout a "Holy Bee shining on the tip of each breast," and Harrison's description of fertility worshippers who danced wildly "for hives to bring increase."[107] Simultaneously woman and hive, Felicity provides sustenance for her community: "always ... robbing some heavenly orchard and sharing the spoil" (169). Felicity's fertility, again, has important implications for national identity. When she was living in Paris, hungry French boys would flock to her, "and she would feed them, and climb some tree in Paradise and shake down a petal-storm" (183); the boys would leave with "a momentary enthusiasm for virtue," learning some "fine English" (183) in the process. Thus, the queen bee is not only a food source but an inculcator of national values. Because modern culture has "lost the habit of stating problems in moral terms" (297), Butts intervenes with a narrative that privileges the issue of morality, examining it through the lens of the Taverners' family history. Felicity is depicted as the genealogical locus of ancestral England, the absent center through whom the question of rightful inheritance is debated, attacked, and ultimately settled in favor of notions of "race-solidarity" (272), moral pastoralism, and the insularity of the English countryside.

England's "biologic pressure": the expulsion of the Jew and the daughter's genealogical inheritance

The Taverners' desire to preserve Felicity's name from desecration functions allegorically as a desire to save the land (282); the family's happiness is dependent upon the preservation of her memory, an act that is inseparable from their attempt to save the English countryside from destruction: "before and behind and overtowering her memory was the threat to the land" (303). Not merely a woman but a source of genealogical and national continuation, Felicity was "killed" because she became "more dangerous than she knew" (188); like Nature, she is capable of bringing untold devastation as well as generative renewal. In Butts's depiction of Felicity as a genetic signifier for England we see evidence of Harrison's view that female divinities preceded the male gods, for Butts presents her heroine as a woman–goddess whose instrumental role is to *heal* a nation that has been made *sick* by the invasion of foreign contaminants – in this case, a Jewish Bolshevik husband who seeks to exploit both his wife's memory and her sacred geography. When Kralin states that "Felicity is dead, and her land is to die too" (249), the Taverners recognize this threat as a second assault on their beloved: "the land. To them it is part of her – 'part of her body'" (330). Resonant in the Taverner's response is the preservationist concern that, because the English countryside is invariably cast as female, her body is being violated by those interlopers who have no respect for the landscape. Kralin is the personification of this brutal rapist, the "lusty bachelor" (211) who assaults his dead wife's body by violating and mutilating her earth. Butts describes Julia's betrayal of her daughter to Kralin as an instance of hereditary amnesia, in which she "forgot common blood" (263).

Kralin's proposed commercialization of the Taverners' land – the construction of bungalows, parking lots, shops, movie theaters, and petrol pumps – will clog the arteries of the "Sacred Wood" (359) with "greasy papers" (343), making it all but impossible for the earth "to cleanse itself" (343) again. Although the text focuses on the immediate danger Kralin poses to the English countryside, Butts represents him as a "force" so evil that he threatens the stability of "european civilization" (316) broadly. Ian Patterson discusses the development of postwar British anti-Semitism and its construction of "the myth of the Jewish–Bolshevik menace," providing a useful historical framework through which to read Butts's caricatured depiction of Kralin as "the slippery, oily, hypocritical Jewish businessman."[108] Kralin, the "Red Russian" (206), embodies everything that Butts finds abhorrent about the modern world: he is obsessed with financial gain, is aligned with inauthenticity and mechanistic science – he is "a fabricated man" (303) – and he works for industrial expansion. Butt's representation of Kralin's racial Otherness is consistent with Sander Gilman's characterization of those traits conventionally attributed to the Jew, particularly his mixed racial heritage, his preoccupation with sex, and his urbanism. Kralin is described as not "officially" having "jewish blood" (177) but is nonetheless called "the Jew-about town" (212). The ambiguity surrounding Kralin's racial make-up works to underscore, rather than displace, his racial impurity; as Gilman argues, being of mixed race and marrying a non-Jew only heightened the individual's Jewishness, operating as signifiers of racial degeneration.[109] In contrast to the Taverners, whose aristocratic roots can be traced through many generations, Kralin was brought to England on the wave of Russian emigration and is from the "under-tow of the world's tides" (314).¹¹⁰ Boris describes him as coming from the ranks of society associated with "crooks, cranks, [and] criminals": "People of mixed or exiles' up-bringing; of fallen, uncertain or bastard origin; or of no fixed caste or situation" (314). At the same time, as Patrick Wright observes, the novel "finds the racial enemy *within* its valued England, not at the far-flung peripheries of empire." In Scylla's words, Kralin "has precedent in England" (339).¹¹¹ Although Boris at one point calls attention to his Russian similarity with Kralin, acknowledging that they "were partly of the same race," he ultimately drops this claim of national common-ality by foregrounding Kralin's Jewish difference.

Butts's characterization of Kralin should be read within the context of the early twentieth-century scientific discourse of racial anti-Semitism, which attributed the Jew's difference not to religious practice but to eternal and immutable hereditary characteristics.¹¹² Through Kralin, we see further evidence of Butts's investment in the rhetoric of racial essence, which transcends any question of his national affilia-tion; thus, despite his Russian roots and his quasi-English assimilation, "Kralin is a Jew" (284) definitively, though he is "in no way effeminate" (241). Butts's disclaimer here recalls Otto Weininger's argument that "Judaism is saturated with femininity," and while the novel backs away from that thought it upholds several of Weininger's other pseudoscientific assumptions about gender and race.¹¹³ In particular, Kralin reflects Weininger's views that Jewish males are not really individuals, that they are morally deficient, have no coherent self, are irrational, ignoble, materialistic, and sexually obsessed – though devoid of authentic masculinity. Cumulatively, Wein-inger uses this evidence to prove the Jew's essential femininity: "the most manly Jew is more feminine than the least manly Aryan."¹¹⁴ Useful to an understanding of Butts's depiction of Kralin as both "in no way effeminate" and as an example of the feminized Jew is Ritchie Robertson's analysis of Weininger's simultaneous application of seemingly contradictory models of Jewish masculinity: the "surplus model," in which "the Jew has more sexuality than the gentile male" (though his sexuality is not under rational or ethical control), and the "deficient model," in which "the Jew has less sexuality."¹¹⁵ Kralin certainly appears to straddle both models, since he is absorbed by sexual matters and is "[a] voluptuous man who could not yield himself to pleasure" (241).¹¹⁶ Elsewhere, he is called a "eunuch of the kingdom of nothing's sake" (178). These allegations point to Kralin's sexual impotence, his stature as a partial man, even though he also harbors books on "the curiosities of sex" (240). Although he is allegedly unable to yield to pleasure, Kralin is sex obsessed: he brings his "harem" of "heavy-haunched and over breasted" (201) city women into Felicity's home, a detail that calls attention both to his prostitution of Felicity's private space and to Butts's classism – the women are poorly dressed, lower class, and, worst of all, come to the countryside from urban slums on rapid transit. Butts's portrayal of Kralin as "actually obscene" (231) illustrates Gilman's observation that the Jewish body functions as a sign for diseased sexuality and perversion.¹¹⁷ Kralin's gestures repeatedly demonstrate that his sexual drives are "of psychopathic origin" (231): in addition to desecrating Felicity's bedroom with vulgar "strangers" who are prone to "running amok" (201), he hangs "shocking pictures"

(232) on his dead wife's wall; he turns her "treasure" (230) – her house and land – into a "public lavatory" (229); and he threatens to open a cinema showing first-run sex films on the Taverners' property (265). Worst of all, he seeks to publish Felicity's private papers as "an erotic classic" (261), arguing that in "these days of psychoanalysis, it might be very widely read" (260).

As was the case with Julia Taverner, Kralin's investment in psychoanalytical paradigms is used as evidence of his depravity; both characters, for different reasons, are bent on Felicity's destruction and act in collusion against her. Butts's portrayal of Kralin incorporates more of her idiosyncratic use of Freudian theory. Whereas Freud reads sexual proclivities as "a product of universal rather than racial psychology," deriving degeneracy from environmental more than biological struc-tures, Butts grabs on to the concept of sexual degeneracy and uses it to mark Kralin as both racially Other and genetically deficient.[118] In contrast to Felicity, whose sexuality is associated with regeneration, creation, and renewal, "Kralin represented a new variety of man ... with aims that were essentially destructive", and he is characterized by inherent impotence and sterility: "No life. Un-Doing, Not-Making" (246). One can best read Butts's erratically applied combination of Weinigerian and Freudian sexology as part of her effort to discredit scientific discourse. Thus, we learn that Kralin is a "practising psychologist" (292) whose "interests were all cerebral" (240), a man who has "impeccable perverse taste" but has been "psycho-analysed out of any pleasure in anything" (178). Scylla refers to him as a "scientific pornographist" (177) who understands only "scientific publicity" (284), a fact that is demonstrated by his desire to exploit the commercial value of Felicity's papers, which, he alleges, "throw so many lights on the ultimate psychology of our behaviour" (261). Here, Butts implicates not only Kralin but the psychoanalytically saturated "British Public" (260) that will buy his pornographic volume.

In Butts's depiction of Kralin as both urban native and the source of sexual infection we see evidence of the belief that the locus of the Jew's diseased sexuality is the metropolis: because the Jew is an urban dweller he is associated with the disease which lurks within the confinement of the urban environment.[119] In contrast to the Taverners, whose land connects them firmly to "the streams of England, whose spring ... is the life-source of a people" (339), Kralin has no natural relation-ship to the landscape and is indeed himself a kind of inorganic substance, insensible to "the touch-difference between silk and stone, or glass and jade" (296). His exposure to the city has rendered his imagination excessively abstract (242), elevat-ing rationalist precision, excising emotion, and severing any understanding of rural ways and habits; instead, he brings into the country "abstractions of machinery, an abstract of the cerebral life of towns" (300). The novel pathologizes this obsession with abstraction, seeing it as a direct affront to the Taverners' love of the tangible, the living, and the concrete. In contrast to the family's "realities of the blood and the nerves and the senses," Kralin substitutes prosthetic compensations: "the chill, the purpose, the strength of a machine ... impure values" (300). A mechanical personification of destructive impulses, Kralin's body can be read as the locus of Butts's anxiety regarding the encroachment of technological modernity. Unlike Felicity, whose body is a site of authenticity, Kralin's physiology is a horrific composite of bio-mechanical impulses that blurs the conventional distinction between them. In the same way that Kralin's Jewishness confuses the traditional categories of race and nationality, the synthetic nature of his body – suturing the corporeal to the prosthetic – threatens the anti-technological and conservative strain of the Taverners' Englishness. The Taverners' anti-Semitism is intrinsic to their perception of their sacred geography; it is what animates their proprietorship: "in their own country, had been imposed on them the desires and purposes of Nick Kralin … [in] his evil they sensed something urban and mechanical" (302). Elsewhere, Butts concedes that machines are not always inherently evil because they are created by man and are hence "ultimately a work of nature" (302), but she insists that they become destructive when they have lost their *"proper use"* (302; emphasis added). Kralin is the paradigmatic example of the men who, no longer seeing the utilitarian purpose of the machine, blindly worships it as an "end in itself" (302).

The reference here to "proper use" returns us to the concept of mana, a substance that is crucially lacking in Kralin, whose terrible commingling of categories – is he Slav or Jew? hyper-masculinized or effeminate? synthetic or organic? – situates him in an antagonistic relation to Butts's fetishizing of "each according to its kind." Although Kralin appears to recognize what mana is, he is unable to subsume its properties. Following a brief reminiscence about Felicity, he invokes without naming the conceptual intactness of mana: "Ivy in growth is ivy, and lobster lobster, and man man" (214). Yet in the next sentence his allusion to mana devolves into an evolutionary nightmare, prompting a moment of introspection: "Lobster turns into man and man into lobster … Was he himself? He did not know" (214). Butts's demonstration here of the depths of Kralin's depravity – his sense "that there was no reason; no meaning to meaning" (214) – illustrates that he is a living example of the antithesis of mana. To the extent that his soul was "no more than one of a series of masks" (217), Kralin appears to embody Weininger's claim that the Jew represents an "absence of any fundamental relation to the thing-in-and-for itself."[120] Although Weininger does not use the word *mana*, his disparagement of the Jew as someone who "adapts himself to every circumstance and every race, becoming, like the parasite, a new creature in every host," aligns him with Butts, who is similarly horrified by cultural mutations and embraces mana as that which is organically stable and structurally integral to every living thing.[121] Bryan Cheyette's discussion of the "protean instability of 'the Jew' as a signifier" is a useful way to understand Kralin, whose indeterminacy situates him as a locus of "radical emptiness."[122] Felicity had called Kralin's nihilistic drive "the Grey Thing" (178), and there is considerable speculation in the novel that it was her exposure to this substance that killed her. Scylla says as much when she gives this greyness a foreign name, referring to it as "'Le Kralinism' … Like pockets of poisoned air, it is everywhere now" (225). By conjuring this poisonous "grey web" (226) that endlessly circulates throughout culture (179), and by associating it directly with Kralin, Butts accomplishes several things: she singles out the Jew as the pervasive source of infection; she tags him with a hue that is antithetical to the Taverners' love of green and white – Kralin is "blind to colours" (296); and she effectively racializes the Jew's body by insisting on its essential difference. His body carries the indelible signifiers of his racial Otherness, reminding the reader of Clarence, who is similarly associated with the color gray; Kralin's eyes, described as "two almonds of grey jelly" (215), recall Gilman's characterization of the inexplicable nature of the Jewish gaze, while the reference to him being "a connoisseur in bad smells" (296) links him to the mephitic odor that was one of the central markers of difference imputed to Jews.[123] The novel asks "What *was* Kralin?" (259), and responds by presenting him as a mana-less personification of "a new agony let loose in the world" (245).

The Taverners, by contrast, are aligned with mana and perform ablutions to purge the land of Jewish contamination: "A rite that was like a bath, a purification, a becoming mana again ... a taking-back, in a profound sense, into caste" (229). The references here to "becoming mana again" and retreating "into caste" are central to an understanding of Felicity's function as the repository of racial memory and her role as familial intermediary, helping to save her land and blood-line from contamination. We see the full implication of Scylla's beloved word *sophrosyne* here, which Harrison defines as that "which *saves* and is saved."[124] One way of understanding Felicity is as an embodiment of living mana, the conduit through which the Taverners are ensured the cultural homogeneity they crave. Like mana, which distributes to "each according to its kind," Felicity is a source of spiritual energy who "gave to each relation its appropriate love" (188). The idea of love is crucial, because it speaks directly to Felicity's role as sacrificial martyr, preventing her all but "extinct family" (213) from utter annihilation through the Jew's destruction of their land. Felicity is "a being endowed with Her mana" which champions civilization, claims divine descent, and is racially pure.[125] Mana circulates in both the body of Felicity and in the English landscape, connecting each to the divine; like Felicity herself, the Taverners' England is a plot of "flawless, clean and blessed, mana and tabu earth" (258) that requires the expulsion of foreign contaminants.

Through Kralin's diseased and soulless infiltration, the Taverners' green map had "nearly all gone red" (337), a bloody indicator of his colonizing impulses. This breach literalizes the novel's anxiety that the future health of the nation has been compromised and reveals, as did the preservationists, that England's evolutionary vitality was threatened by the environmental dangers of racial decay. Kralin is the ultimate contaminant, who, as Scylla ruefully puts it, "would sell the body of our land to the Jews" (346) for next to nothing. We see in Butts's derisive attitude toward Jewishness further evidence of her similarity to T.S. Eliot, who remarked in 1934 that "reasons of race and religion combine to make any large number of free-thinking Jews undesirable."[126] We also see parallels with Eliot's perspective on the interrelationship between race and landscape: the happiest lands, he remarks, are those in which "the landscape has been moulded by numerous generations of one race."[127] Boris succinctly conveys to the Taverners this logic of racial inclusion and exclusion, focusing upon the identificatory relation between the land and English-ness: "living here, nature repeats to you what you are yourselves ... but one that is outside you, outside this place, killed your cousin" (225). Through the Taverners, Butts seems to corroborate Jessie Weston's claim that contemporary nature worship arises, not from Judaism, but from "a heritage from the far-off past of the Aryan peoples."[128] This invocation of the Aryan recalls Weininger's insistence that what the "natural disposition" of the Jew lacks is the "Aryan respect for his ancestors," a generalization that arises from his contention that citizenship is "an un-Jewish thing" because, as rootless wanderers, Jews have no "true conception of the State."[129] Of course, in the novel Kralin is not censured for incivility toward his own ancestors, but for disrespecting the English ancestry of the Taverners. His marriage to Felicity, interchangeable with the land, is tantamount to an affront to England.

Felicity is the locus of this fantasy of national culture, even though she herself is not legally recognized as the lawful heir to her own Taverner estate. Butts implies a distinction between the nation as a natural entity and the State as the product of culture, suggesting that because women have a privileged relation to nature they are therefore a part of the hereditary immemorial rights of England – even though the State does not recognize them as such. Thus, while Felicity's beloved home "in point of law" (274) belongs to her brother Adrian, who had planned to trade it with his mother in exchange for the discharge of his fraudulent debts, the novel privileges the daughter's *natural* inheritance rights. This is reflected in the scene in which Boris, having snatched a loose page from Felicity's stolen journal, enables the reader to get a long-deferred glimpse of the content of her allegedly pornographic papers. Rather than an eroticized confessional outpouring, this single page of Felicity's writing demonstrates her preoccupation with parentage and genealogy: "Adrian and I are only half-brother and sister ... Half a brother, but a whole sister ... my History" (282). This moment literalizes the problem of rightful inheritance by calling attention to the fact that Adrian is not a lawful heir but an illegitimate son, something his mother later corroborates (287); it also suggests that the daughter's fiction is a way of rewriting history, providing a corrective to the dominant family narrative which stipulates that "in any country the position of the favourite son" (182) is primary. The only way to construe Felicity's private papers as pornographic would be on the grounds that her attempt to tell the truth about Adrian's illegitimacy constitutes gross misconduct, or that her desire to stake a biological claim for her own ancestral legitimacy is inappropriate; the novel supports neither option, and instead suggests that those who seek to malign Felicity's name are the true pornographers. Like Scylla's historical chronicles, Felicity's journal page subverts a reliance upon conventional markers of historical inclusion; although the daughter's claim on her estate is not legally binding, it is upheld as "wholly moral" (278) by those characters who seek justice for Felicity outside the law.

Earlier, Scylla and Felix had scoured their cousin's home for evidence of her personal papers, only to discover that Kralin had already stolen her effects. In contrast to his disrespect of Felicity's rightful inheritance, they seek to preserve "the memory of her ... to keep rather than to destroy" (221). In the course of their abortive detective work, Scylla and Felix unearth a hidden treasure of Felicity's cherished objects: a "jay-feather posy, a handful of red rose leaves ... a ring of grey jade ... a rouge pot ... an amber cigarette-holder ... carnelian beads ... " (222). This private assortment of feminine *things* can be read as commentary on the hidden nature of female subjectivity, which in the text is exacerbated by Felicity's indeterminacy and absence. The list also suggests that Kralin's violation of his wife's interior domestic space further brutalizes Felicity's body which, as metonymic signifier, functions as a figure for her house as well as for the land.

By acknowledging the legal implications of Felicity's disinheritance while insisting upon her inherent and mystical inheritance rights as a daughter of England, the text challenges a notion of proprietorship that privileges masculinity as it embraces an essentialized notion of citizenship that is transhistorical, mystical, and based on blood-lines. As an embodiment of this new model of Englishness, Felicity is aligned with Harrison's emphasis on emotion rather than intellect, on primitive animism and the experiential rather than rationality. The "race-tragedy" (277) of the Taverners, however, is that Kralin's Jewishness, his scientific rationalism, and his investment in abstraction threaten to destroy Felicity's *natural* inheritance rights, requiring the intervention of an intermediary who will help to secure her hereditarian claim. Remarkably, Boris, the gay White Russian exile, is this mediating figure, an improbable projection screen for the Taverners' indigenous values, and whose training, like their own, "had been to enjoy splendour" (306), and who, crucially, is an Anglophile. Boris likes "the english best of all races" (*AWM*, 135).

Butts's choice of a homosexual advocate for the Taverners against Kralin is fundamentally mysterious, given the text's otherwise fascistic ideas of pure citizenship, which should necessarily exclude foreign homosexuals. Beyond the biographical fact that Butts adored gay men, one might speculate that Boris is the national and sexual exception – a Russian homosexual – who proves the rule that white racial purity is of primary importance. Boris also parallels Felicity's non-procreative appeal to blood-lines – the "biologic pressure" (184) – as the basis for identifying with the English land. Like the Taverners themselves, Boris is a man "of breeding" (198) who is racially pure and who has been violently severed from his ancestral home; also like the Taverners, he blames Kralin for this dispossession (277), and regards the Jew as a symbol of national terror. During the thirteen years during which Boris had wandered around Europe as a refugee on a "pilgrimage to nowhere" (304), only his "pure blood" and "scrupulous … up-bringing had kept him alive" (311). A displaced aristocrat, Boris's itinerate "national spree" (310) had taken him from Petrograd to Odessa, through Constantinople and Marseilles before Felix had induced him to come to England. This period as a displaced person is described as in part a retreat from the horrific "memory-storm" (306) of life in pre-revolutionary Russia, and in part a sex odyssey – a cosmopolitan "saturnalia" (309) of fleeting encounters with beautiful Scottish and Turkish men. Like his gay predecessor (also named Boris) in *Imaginary Letters*, who is similarly of noble and hieratic descent, the Boris of *Felicity Taverner* is "as elusive as any female minx"; each Boris can be described as "a naughty boy" who is "capable of every perversion of sentiment," and both men appear to live by the motto "queens survive."[130] In the novel, Boris's erotic excesses and his transgression of sexual convention align him with Felicity. Even more importantly, like Felicity, Boris has access to alternative visionary geographical spaces – "*Born to see strange sights, Things invisible*" (224) – and straddles two worlds (in his case, Russia and England, in addition to the seen and unseen).

That Boris is a worthy facilitator stems not only from "the eastern-slav tincture in his blood" (198), which the Taverners read as evidence of his aristocratic virtue, but hinges on his willingness to uphold the family's conservative values. He seeks "an indefinite saturation in [their] life" (239) and is receptive to the family's pedagogical desire to educate him in "virtue" and offer "payment in Taverner values and standards" (305). Whereas the homosexual in *Armed With Madness* had to be eliminated because his presence threatened the novel's investment in reproduction, Boris is entrusted with a key narrative role because he respects the heterosexual imperative and does not allow his sexuality to impede the procreative process. This is made explicit by the reference to Scylla and Felix who, anxiously awaiting Boris's return from the fatal cave, feel as though "they were unborn organisms inside an egg" (360). The implication here is they will be reborn through Boris's intervention, for even though his body is not aligned with procreative power, he is a man who could "boil his own egg" (271) – in other words, is a redemptive figure whose actions facilitate nature's rebirth, the reproductive cycle necessary for England's regeneration. Boris's actions demonstrate that to be pro-Grail (as well as pro-egg) is to be an anti-Semite.

It is precisely this willingness to absorb the family's English values, to enter "inside [their] magic ring" (224), that makes him an attractive agent of Jewish destruction: "Race apart, class apart, tastes apart, *he was their own kind*" (225; emphasis added). Structurally, Boris's role is to mediate between two spheres in order to enact a kind of double "katharsis" (198): cleansing the Taverner's green world of Kralin, and thus ensuring the expulsion of anti-mana; and at the same time symbolically purging the Jew from his homeland. At the root of the Taverners' loyalty to Boris is their attraction to the "poet's quality in him" (233), an attribute that links him to his alter-ego in *Imaginary Letters* and aligns him with the family's devotion to mana and the "unknown categories" that defined Felicity.[131] Like "a god whose head faces two ways" (275), Boris is Butts's Janus-faced conflation of the historical and the mythical, the intermediary through whom she stages the importance of Harrisonian ritual to modernity and demonstrates the neccessity of incorporating purgative acts into English life. Not merely a man but a facilitator of primitive ritual, Boris willingly "play[s] a *role*" (350) in the Taverners' family drama, enabling them to experience a purging of emotion. Boris's receptivity to the "daimon" (277) who speaks to him – arguably a spiritualized figure for Felicity, whom he regards as his "guardian-angel" (277) – can be read as an allusion to Harrison's argument that ghosts from the underworld are feminine spirits who seek revenge; we see that Boris is propelled by what one might call female mythic potency: he is like "a little baby born by [Scylla's] wild anger" (351). Aligned against those like Kralin who rationalize religion and subjugate humanity to so-called higher intelligences, Boris's actions appear consonant with Harrison's observation that religious belief is "the outcome rather of emotion than of intellect."[132] Unlike Kralin, whose familiarity with psychoanalytical jargon is a sign of his moral and spiritual bankruptcy, Boris importantly knows nothing about "fashionable psychology" (246). Where Kralin is a purveyor of "obscene ikons" (348), Boris wears an ancient religious icon which his mother had given him as a kind of amulet. Although there is speculation that he had traded this jewel for cocaine (310), the object is still a sign of Boris's respect for "[g]ood mother-magic" (309). This gesture, read through Harrison's interpretive lens, underscores Boris's devotion to the Taverners' ethos, for "the worship of the Mother emphasizes the group, the race and its continuance."[133] In worshipping the mother, Boris pays homage to Felicity; at the same time, the Christian icon functions as a safeguard against the toxicity of the Jew.

Coded as an effeminate male because of his homosexuality, Boris is a "queer miracle" (336) who is receptive to female influence and helps to facilitate the enactment of an overtly feminized ritual. In order to put an end to Kralin's blackmail of the Taverners (his plot to return Felicity's private papers in exchange for sole ownership of her house and land), Boris concocts a plan to lure Kralin to a secluded cave that he alleges would be an ideal spot from which to generate a tourist industry. Kralin is predictably seduced by the prospect of commercial gain; he contemplates the possibility of motorboat excursions from the cave and fantasizes about a "faked story of its history" (356). This detail is crucial because it further pits Kralin's investment in dissimulation against the Taverners, "lovers of truth" (257) who "cannot endure imitations of anything" (301). Although Boris entices Kralin to the cave in order to murder him, it is the cave itself, a displaced signifier for Felicity, which enacts revenge through invagination. A figure for the female genitalia, the cave is both highly eroticized and racialized: it is described as a "very long, very dark cave, full of water up to the barrier" (356), the wet floor of which is paved with "round pebbles which were white, very pure white; and in the pools as pure a green" (356). Intertwining these Taverner colors swim "jelly-fish like red flowers" (356), imagery suggestive of labia and whose color alludes to the centrality of blood-lines. At the end of this "secret place" (353) is a light and a "blow hole" (356) through which water enters when the tide is high, filling the cave until it can hold no more and it bursts "in a spout of water and a voice that is like a bull" (357), an image of orgiastic revenge. This mention of a bull recalls Felicity's mythic stature and dark underside, her ability to castrate and wield unapprehended power. It is into this vaginal space that Boris brings Kralin, inviting him to gaze into the water in order to see the reflection of a drowned man. When Kralin stares down at his own image and claims to see "nothing" (357), Boris confirms that the reflection is accurate. Like a vampire that has neither a self nor a soul, Kralin is an embodiment of Weininger's claim that the "Jew is really nothing, because he believes in nothing"; with his death, Nature-cum-Felicity destroys not only Kralin, but his sterile philosophy of "Not-Being, Un-Meaning, Un-Doing" (242).[134] When Nature swallows Kralin whole and buries him within her "island tomb" (363), we see further evidence that Felicity's body is a source of death as well as regeneration. Afterward, Boris takes Kralin's keys and retrieves Felicity's papers from a private safe, ensuring that both her reputation and the Taverners' land will remain an unviolated and unsullied garden in which the best elements of British society may grow into an ideal nation.

Through Boris, Butts fictionalizes Harrison's view that ritual is "a re-presentation ... a re-doing," but "always with a practical end" – in this case, the re-instating of the daughter's inheritance rights to England.[135] With the elimination of the Jew, Nature reasserts herself, but Felicity needs Boris to help her execute what amounts to a racial cleansing of her land. Following Harrison, who argues that rituals purge personal passion of emotion and function as a collective experience for the public good, Butts positions Boris as the modern savage whose ritualistic murder of Kralin enables the Taverners' nationalistic and genetic legacy to endure. Yet, while Boris facilitates the deed, Felicity is clearly the director behind the drama that unfolds; her "passion and detachment" (169) are amplified in Nature which, "for all its utter detachment ... had its eye on him" (239). The mystical, if tyrannical, language of visuality here underscores Butts's attention to the links between femininity, land-scape, and perception, recalling both Scylla's characterization as passionate and detached (*AWM*, 169), and the description of nature's visual agency as disinterested. Butts's focus on the agency of the eye, and her desire to use the mystical for prescribed social ends, remind one of Harrison's conviction that abstract ideas arise only from the concrete. As Harrison puts it: "Without *per*ception there is no *con*ception."[136] For both women, ritual practice consists not in ratiocination but in the expression of pure emotion, direct perception, and human intervention. Despite Felicity's literal absence, her presence as a national spiritual resource is conveyed through optical displacement: "Nature's enormous, satiric eye" (201) is ultimately an imperial gaze, possessively overseeing her dominion and attending to the spiritual welfare of her endangered species.

With the sacrifice of Kralin, Englishness is secured and the family is re-instated as the dominant cultural paradigm, for through the circulation of Felicity's mana the nation and the Taverners restore themselves and their values: hereditary access to the land, racial purity, and ancestral continuity. The bodily disappearance of the Jew signals both the family's and Britain's postwar recovery, a recuperative move that is coincident with the fulfillment of the daughter's mystical and biological birthright to England. Like Scylla in *Armed With Madness*, Felicity's body must endure a ritualistic martyrdom: "It was as if it had been decided on that she was to be crucified" (226). The text repeatedly signals that Felicity is a contemporary martyr, criticizing those who "had not found her light" (190) and bemoaning the fact that "people kill what they do not like" (225). Drawing from both Christian and pagan traditions, Butts constructs Felicity as a thoroughly modern savior who, although oppressed by those who seek to "wound and torture and bleed her to death" (171), maintains the power she derives both from her racial ancestry and from her female sexuality: "She was on earth '*pour faire aimé l'amour*'" (180). Boris's remark that Felicity's love was "'as good as any art to her'" (188) recalls Harrison's observation that art and ritual are "well-nigh indistinguishable" because both arise from a common human impulse: "the intense, world-wide desire that the life of Nature which seemed dead should live again."[137] Through Felicity, the embodiment of mana and the moral agent of the nation's revival, Butts grounds a reformist vision that negates legal structures but nonetheless rests upon the idea of cultural reconstruction: "Human energy, the *mana* out of which great nations are born."[138]

Notes

1 Mary Butts, "Bloomsbury," *Modernism/Modernity*, 5. 2 (1998): 32; hereafter cited in the text. For a discussion of "Bloomsbury," see Nathalie Blondel's biography *Mary Butts: Scenes from the Life* (New York: McPherson & Co., 1998), 398–403.

2 Regina Marler, *Bloomsbury Pie: The Making of the Bloomsbury Boom* (New York: Henry Holt & Co., 1997). I discuss Bloomsbury's commercialism in "Selling culture to the 'civilized': Bloomsbury, *Vogue*, and the marketing of national identity," *Modernism/Modernity*, 6. 2 (1999): 29–58.

3 Butts's critique does not take into account Roger Fry's attack on commercial imitation and mechanical reproduction: "Prospectus for the Omega Workshops" in Christopher Reed ed.

A Roger Fry Reader (Chicago, IL, and London: University of Chicago Press, 1996), 198–200. Nor does her tirade recognize that she and Clive Bell actually share a belief in "that which lies behind the appearance of all things … the thing itself, the ultimate reality." See Bell's "The metaphysical hypothesis," *Art* (New York: Capricorn Books, 1958), 54.

4 For a discussion of the significance of these prehistoric rings in Butts's life and fiction, see Blondel, *Mary Butts*, 113 and 179. For Butts's own account of her moment of transcendence at the Badbury Rings in Dorset, see *The Crystal Cabinet: My Childhood at Salterns* (Boston, MA: Beacon Press, 1988), 264–6; hereafter cited in the text and abbreviated *CC*.

5 Mary Butts, *Armed With Madness* (1928), re-issued in *The Taverner Novels* (Kingston, NY: McPherson & Co., 1992), 9; hereafter cited in the text and abbreviated *AWM*.

6 Mary Butts, *Death of Felicity Taverner* (1932), re-issued in *The Taverner Novels* (Kingston, NY: McPherson & Co., 1992), 272 and 266; hereafter cited in the text and abbreviated *DFT*. Butts often employs the lower case when using nationalities as adjectives, such as "english family," "french papers." Like Olive Moore, who also does this, Butts is arguably interested in understating the significance of nationality even as she invokes it.

7 Mary Butts, *Scenes from the Life of Cleopatra*, reprinted in *The Classical Novels* (Kingston, NY: McPherson & Co., 1994), 220; hereafter cited in the text.

8 See Amy Louise Erickson, *Women and Property in Early Modern England* (London and New York: Routledge, 1993), 26 and 61–78.

9 Sander Gilman, *The Jew's Body* (New York: Routledge, 1991); *Difference and Pathology: Stereotypes of Sexuality, Race, and Madness* (Ithaca, NY: Cornell University Press, 1985).

10 From an anonymous review of *Armed With Madness* in the *Manchester Guardian*, June 15, 1928.

11 Jascha Kessler, "Mary Butts: lost … and found," *Kenyon Review*, 17. 3–4 (1995): 211.

12 Glenway Westcott, "The first book of Mary Butts," *The Dial* (September, 1923). Hugh Ross Williamson, "A writer's childhood: the testament of Mary Butts," *John O'London's Weekly*, June 11, 1937.

13 All of the early reviews of Butts's work referred to in this chapter can be found in the Mary Butts Miscellany collection at the Bancroft Library of the University of California at Berkeley. The two citations here are from an anonymous review of *Armed With Madness*, in the *Oklahoma City Times*, October 14, 1928, and in Frank Vernon's review of Butts's short-story collection *Speed the Plough*, in "Books we'd like to burn: writers' contorted view of morality," *John Bull* (April 28, 1923).

14 From a review of *Armed With Madness*, by E.L., in the *Liverpool Post*, May 16, 1928.

15 From "Literary surgery," a review of *Speed the Plough* in the *Liverpool Post*, April 11, 1923.

16 This assessment appeared in a review of her short-story collection *Several Occasions* in the *Yorkshire Post*, March 16, 1932.

17 From "Literary surgery."

18 For references to promiscuity in Butts's writing, see Marguerite Steen's review of *The Macedonian*, "The glory that was Greece," *Everyman* (March, 1933); Frank Vernon, "Books we'd like to burn," *John Bull* (April 25, 1923). The reference to "blood and filth" appears in "Literary surgery."

19 Woolf, *Letters*, Vol. 6: 138.

20 Edward de Grazia discusses the campaign against obscene literature and pornography in England in *Girls Lean Back Everywhere: The Law of Obscenity and the Assault on Genius* (New York: Random House, 1992).

21 After decades of neglect, Mary Butts seems – at last – to be enjoying some well-deserved, if posthumous, celebrity. Her manuscripts have finally found a home in the Beinecke Library at Yale. Roslyn Reso Foy has written the first monograph on the author's work, *Ritual, Myth, and Mysticism in the Work of Mary Butts: Between Feminism and Modernism* (Arkansas: University of Arkansas Press, 2000). Butts's short-story about Paris in the 1920s, "The master's last dancing," was published in *The New Yorker* (March 30, 1998): 109–13. Most recently, Butts made the cover of the *TLS*, accompanied by Laura Marcus's article "Mysterious Mary Butts," *Times Literary Supplement* (August 24, 2001): 3–4. Throughout this revival McPherson & Co. has been re-issuing all of Mary Butts's books in uniform

editions. For an overview of the author's career and work, see Jennifer Gariepy ed. "Mary Butts, 1890–1937," *Twentieth-Century Literary Criticism*, 77 (1988): 69–109.

22 Anne McClintock, *Imperial Leather: Race, Gender, and Sexuality in the Colonial Contest* (New York and London: Routledge, 1995), 30.

23 See Mary Butts, *Imaginary Letters*, reprinted in *Ashe of Rings and Other Writings* (Kingston, NY: McPherson & Co., 1998), 260–1; hereafter cited in the text and abbreviated as *Ashe*.

24 Allyson Booth, "Forgetful objects," *Postcards from the Trenches: Negotiating the Space between Modernism and the First World War* (New York and Oxford: Oxford University Press, 1996), 127.

25 See Blondel, *Mary Butts*, 181.

26 Alun Howkins, "The discovery of rural England" in Robert Colls and Philip Dodd eds. *Englishness: Politics and Culture 1880–1929* (London and New Hampshire: Croom Helm), 62–88.

27 See Harvey Taylor, *A Claim on the Countryside: A History of the British Outdoor Movement* (Edinburgh: Keele University Press, 1997), 226–72; Stephen G. Jones, *Workers at Play: A Social and Economic History of Leisure 1918–1939* (London: Routledge & Kegan Paul, 1986).

28 David Matless, *Landscape and Englishness* (London: Reaktion Books, 1998), 67.

29 Mary Butts, *Warning to Hikers* (London: Wishart & Co., 1932), 17 and 11; hereafter cited in the text and abbreviated *W*.

30 John Lowerson discusses Clough Williams-Ellis's complaints in *England and the Octopus* (1928). See Frank Gloversmith ed. *Class, Culture and Social Change: A New View of the 1930s* (Brighton: Harvester Press, 1980), 258–80.

31 Much to Butts's disdain, countryside leisure was pursued by a substantial section of the urban population during this period, a result of the increased provision of paid holidays and the improved transportation. See Harvey Taylor, *A Claim on the Countryside*, 236.

32 For a discussion of mass tresspass, see Michael Bunce, *The Countryside Ideal: Anglo-American Images of Landscape* (London and New York: Routledge, 1994), 179–82; Matless, *Landscape and Englishness*, 71–2.

33 Taylor, *A Claim on the Countryside*, 242.

34 Howkins, "The discovery of rural England," 65–7. Michael Bunce discusses the idealization of the countryside as an inevitable consequence of the urban–industrial revolution in England: *The Countryside Ideal*.

35 Howkins, "The discovery of rural England," 69.

36 R.G. Stapleton, as quoted in David Matless, "Ordering the land: the 'preservation' of the English countryside, 1918–1939," Ph.D. thesis, University of Nottinhgam, 1990, 227.

37 See Matless, "Ordering the land," 79.

38 Blondel, *Mary Butts*, 261. Throughout Butts's *oeuvre* there is repeated evidence of her preoccupation with whiteness. See e.g. *Ashe of Rings*, 139, 185–6, 188–9.

39 This rhetoric conjures associations of fascism, and indeed parallels have been drawn between the outdoor movements in Germany, where it was fostered by the Nazi government, and Britain. For a discussion of the parallels between the open-air movement in Britain and the Nazi ethos of physical fitness, see Ann Holt, "Hikers and ramblers: surviving a thirties' fashion," *International Journal of Sport* (May, 1987): 58–9. Helen Walker situates the British outdoor movement within the discourse of national health: "The popularization of the outdoor movement, 1900–1940," *British Journal of Sports History*, 2. 2 (1985): 140–53.

40 For a discussion of the preservationist appropriation of the language of rape, see Matless, "Ordering the land," 239–40.

41 From Mary Butts's review of *Week-Ends in England*, published in *The Bookman* (Christmas, 1933).

42 Vaughan Cornish, *The Scenery of England*, quoted in Matless, "Ordering the land," 239.

43 Matless, *Landscape and Englishness*, 78.

44 Frank Trentmann, "Civilization and its discontents: English neo-Romanticism and the transformation of anti-modernism in twentieth-century Western culture," *Journal of Contemporary History*, 29. 4 (1994): 588.

45 Butts, *Traps for Unbelievers* (London: Desmond Harmsworth, 1932), 26; hereafter cited in the text and abbreviated *T*.

46 Matless discusses popular mysticism and nature in *Landscape and Englishness*, 84–6. See also Matless's Ph.D. dissertation for a more elaborate analysis of the centrality of the discourse of pilgrimage: "Ordering the land," 312–19. There he discusses the most popular travel book of its time, *In Search of England* (1927), by H.V. Morton, which presents the search for "a common racial heritage" (315) as a kind of Arthurian quest.

47 G.M. Trevelyan, *Must England's Beauty Perish?* (1929), quoted in Matless, *Landscape and Englishness*, 84.

48 Matless discusses the influence of Wordsworth on preservationists such as Vaughan Cornish, who echoes the poet's focus on the eye's receptivity and its function as a vehicle for contemplative mysticism: "Ordering the land," 33–5. In *The Crystal Cabinet*, Butts identifies her childhood love of nature with Wordsworth (22), attributing her awareness that nature is "a live thing, eminently visible" (10) to the poet.

49 Jane Ellen Harrison, *Themis: A Study of the Social Origins of Greek Religion* (Cleveland, OH, and New York: World Publishing Co., 1927 [1912]), ix. Harrison's earlier text *Mythology* (1890) had claimed that a single Great Mother Goddess prefigured the many goddesses who made up the Greek pantheon. For analyses of Harrison's relation to modernism, see: Martha C. Carpentier, *Ritual, Myth, and the Modernist Text: The Influence of Jane Ellen Harrison on Joyce, Eliot, and Woolf* (Amsterdam: Gordon & Breach, 1998); Ruth Hoberman, *Gendering Classicism: The Ancient World in Twentieth-Century Women's Historical Fiction* (Albany: State University of New York Press, 1997); K.J. Phillips, "Jane Harrison and modernism," *Journal of Modern Literature*, 17. 4 (1991): 465–76; Marianna Torgovnick, "Discovering Jane Harrison" in Carola M. Kaplan and Anne B. Simpson eds. *Seeing Double: Edwardian and Modernist Literature* (New York: St. Martin's Press, 1996), 131–48.

50 For a discussion of the pre-eminence of the mother in Harrison's work, see Renate Schlesier, "Prolegomena to Jane Harrison's interpretation of ancient Greek religion" in William M. Calder ed. *The Cambridge Ritualists Reconsidered* (Atlanta, GA: Scholar's Press, 1991), 213–17.

51 Artifacts found by Schliemann and Evans on Crete suggested that ancient Minoan–Mycenaean civilization was matriarchal. In Harrison's view, this discovery unambiguously confirmed the existence of a matriarchal culture: *Reminiscences of a Student's Life* (London: Hogarth Press, 1925), 72.

52 Trevelyan, *Must England's Beauty Perish?*, quoted by Matless, "Ordering the land," 261.

53 Jane Harrison, *Alpha and Omega* (London: Sidgwick & Jackson, 1915), 205.

54 Hoberman, *Gendering Classicism*, 178.

55 See Eileen Power's *Medieval Women* (London: Methuen, 1924), and *Medieval People* (London: Methuen, 1924). Butts's gendered interest in medievalism may in fact be indebted to Power, who was the best-known medievalist of the interwar period. Maxine Berg discusses Power's pioneering attempts to uncover the role played by women in medieval society, demonstrating how, throughout her work, she collapsed the boundaries between literature and history: *A Woman in History: Eileen Power 1889–1940* (Cambridge: Cambridge University Press, 1996).

56 H.V. Morton provides an elegiac account of England that in many ways echoes Butts's own. He critiques the "unaccustomed eyes of the townsman" and invokes the discourse of disease, maintaining that "behind the English country is an economic and a social cancer": *In Search of England*, vii–xi, 187–90.

57 Jacques Derrida cites Lévi-Strauss's discussion of mana as the ultimate "floating signifier ... capable of becoming charged with any sort of symbolic content whatever": quoted by Marc Manganaro in *Myth, Rhetoric, and the Voice of Authority: A Critique of Frazer, Eliot, Frye, and Campbell* (New Haven, CT: Yale University Press, 1992), 84.

58 For a discussion of Butts's use of the term "mana," see Hoberman, *Gendering Classicism*, especially 51–2.

59 Freud, *Totem and Taboo*, trans. James Strachey (New York: Norton, 1950), 29.

60 Harrison, *Alpha and Omega*, 166. Despite Frazer's comparativist approach, his underlying objective in *The Golden Bough* was to trace human progress from savagery to civilization.

61 Harrison, *Alpha and Omega*, 160.

62 Harrison, *Ancient Art and Ritual* (New York: Henry Holt, and London: Williams & Norgate, 1913), 29.

63 I read this representation of the collector as a caricature of Roger Fry, for Butts invokes him by name within the context of her discussion of the primitive (44). By the time that *Traps* appeared in England, primitivism had already dominated the art scene and entered public discourse – thanks in large part to Fry's influential essays on African art. Like other modernists, Fry's praise for primitive artifacts was couched in assumptions about the superiority of Western culture; his view that African art is the product of peoples, but not "culture in our sense of the word," is a position that Butts arguably would have upheld. See Roger Fry, *Vision and Design* (London: Chatto & Windus, 1925), 103.

64 See, for example, Shearer West ed. *The Victorians and Race* (Aldershot: Scholar Press, 1996).

65 Butts spent several years in France, during which time she befriended the demonologist Aleister Crowley. In the summer of 1921 Butts traveled to Crowley's abbey in Sicily, where she participated in a number of strange, sometimes orgiastic, ceremonies that involved hashish, opium, cocaine, excrement, and the use of children in sexual rites. Blondel recounts this erratic period of Butts's life (*Mary Butts*, 102–4). Given these experiences, it is therefore startling to hear Butts critique the "desire to be primitive at all costs" (36) in *Traps*, where she sees such indulgences as a sign of cultural depravity. Here, she denounces the resolve to "scour the cults and ceremonies for traces of totem-worship and fetish, for cannibalism and human sacrifice, for orgies and black magic" (36), even though she herself had earlier participated in several of these practices. Perhaps Butts ultimately abandoned Crowley not because of his methods were unorthodox but because they were not indigenous to England.

66 Glenway Westcott, "The first book of Mary Butts," 282–4. He here refers to Butts as "English to the core."

67 Harrison, *Alpha and Omega*, 206.

68 Harrison, *Ancient Art and Ritual*, 25 and 44. In *Alpha and Omega* Harrison further links the idea of re-enactment to authenticity, characterizing the primitive state of mind as follows: "If a child is 'playing at lions', he does not *imitate* a lion ... he *becomes* one" (166). Harrison's focus on authenticity recalls Butts's own preoccupations, particularly her disdain for imitation in *The Crystal Cabinet*, where we find a passage about childhood play that is strikingly similar to Harrison's attention to primitive re-enactment in children: "Grown-up people say that children like to pretend that the things they love are alive. This is nonsense – they *are* alive ... Alive, not with a copy of their own life, but with the life, the *mana*, proper to the thing itself" (81).

69 In *Ancient Art and Ritual*, Harrison argues that it is not the personal emotions of primitive man that "become ritual, but those that are public, felt and expressed ... by the whole tribe or community" (49). Butts singles out Harrison and praises ritual practice in "Ghosties and ghoulies: uses of the supernatural in English fiction," *Ashe of Rings and Other Writings*, 363.

70 See Butts's review, "Vision of Asia," *The Bookman* (Christmas, 1932): 223–5. Elsewhere, she betrays her belief that mysticism is nationally inflected: "It is inevitable ... that each nation has its own Christ. The failure (for us) lies here, that the Russian Christ is not the English. (Who ... will give us again an English Christ?)": "A Russian prophet," *Time and Tide* (October 14, 1933).

71 Mary Butts quoted by Blondel, *Mary Butts*, 73.

72 Blondel discusses Butts's fascination with the Grail (*ibid.*, 54–5). Butts reviewed two books on this topic during the 1930s: see "The Sanc Grail," *The Bookman*, 84. 499 (1933): 72–4, where she writes that the Grail "is the very spring of our culture ... the matter of Britain *in excelsis*"; and "Parzival," *Time and Tide*, 17. 2 (1936): 57–8. In *The Crystal Cabinet* Butts praises the "real Grail, which was the most wonderful thing to think about in the world" (33).

73 See Butts's entry for September 1927 in "Selections from the journal" (edited by Robert H. Byington and Glen E. Morgan), *Art & Literature*, 7 (winter, 1965): 167–9.

74 Jesse L. Weston, *From Ritual to Romance* (Princeton, NJ: Princeton University Press, 1993 [1920]), 3.

75 Lawrence Rainey, "Good things: pederasty and jazz and opium and research," *London Review of Books* (July 16, 1998): 14–17.

76 Tzvetan Todorov, "The quest of narrative," *The Poetics of Prose* (Ithaca, NY: Cornell University Press, 1977), 139.

77 The revival of medievalism in England reflects a conservative strain that is indelibly linked to the desire to create ideals of "gentlemanly" behavior that re-inscribe patriarchy, hetero-sexuality, and nationalism. See Paul Rich, "The quest for Englishness," *History Today*, 37 (June, 1987): 25; and Mark Girouard, *The Return to Camelot: Chivalry and the English Gentleman* (New Haven, CT: Yale University Press, 1981).

78 Mary Baine Campbell discusses the popularity of Arthurian objects during the interwar period and demonstrates how they were appropriated by fascists obsessed by racial lineage: "Finding the Grail: fascist aesthetics and mysterious objects" in Debra N. Mancoff ed. *King Arthur's Modern Return* (New York: Garland, 1998), 213–25.

79 Marianna Torgovnick, *Primitive Passions: Men, Women, and the Quest for Ecstasy* (New York: Alfred A. Knopf, 1997), 40 and 86.

80 Charlotte Haldane, *Motherhood and Its Enemies* (London: Chatto & Windus, 1927), 10. For a discussion of the symbolic significance of the egg in British seasonal customs, see Ronald Hutton, *The Stations of the Sun: A History of the Ritual Year in Britain* (Oxford: Oxford University Press, 1996), 198–203.

81 Weston, *From Ritual to Romance*, 63.

82 Harrison, *Themis*, xxii, 539, and 487.

83 Paul Rich discusses how the search for national roots was bound up with attempts to produce a "science" of race: "The quest for Englishness," 26.

84 In the martyrdom scene Scylla, as a kind of feminized St. Sebastian figure, beatifically moves from "absolute contempt of Clarence" (145) to forgiveness, but she never incorporates him within her "magic ring" (159). Clarence's iconic transformation of Scylla into St. Sebastian further exposes his rage against heterosexuality, for that figure has since the nineteenth century functioned as the patron saint of homosexual men. See Richard A. Kaye, "'A splendid readiness for death': T.S. Eliot, the homosexual cult of St. Sebastian, and World War I," *Modernism/Modernity*, 6. 2 (1999): 107–34.

85 Henrika Kuklick, *The Savage Within: The Social History of British Anthropology, 1885–1945* (Cambridge: Cambridge University Press, 1991), 165.

86 Elaine Showalter discusses the emasculating consequences of shell-shock in *The Female Malady: Women, Madness, and English Culture, 1830–1980* (London: Virago, 1987), Ch. 7. See also Samuel Hynes's work on the Great War and British masculinity, in which he characterizes the increased exposure of male homosexuality in all ranks of the military as an "infection [that] had burst out" into English culture: *A War Imagined: The First World War and English Culture* (London: Bodley Head, 1990), 226.

87 Gilman, *Difference and Pathology*, 120.

88 A document extremely useful for showing the contradictory range of Butts's racial views is her review of Nancy Cunard's groundbreaking anthology *Negro* (1934). Butts regards that anthology with both admiration and skepticism, praising its range but critiquing Cunard for her allegedly one-dimensional portrayal of racial prejudice. In particular, while Butts acknowledges the terrible injustice of race prejudice, she simultaneously argues that the book displays "a want of judgement and proportion" (186) because it neglects to portray "the colonizing white races" (187) sympathetically. At its core, the review disavows English racism by calling for representations that will show how "the black man ... lead[s] a tolerable existence" (186). See Butts, review of *Negro*, *The Adelphi* (3rd series), 9. 1 (1934): 185–7.

89 See Mary Langlan and Bill Schwartz, *Crises in the British State 1880–1930* (London: Hutchison, 1985).

90 Weston, *From Ritual to Romance*, 75.

91 From Harrison, *Themis*, cited by Robin Blaser, "Here lies the woodpecker who was Zeus" in Christopher Wagstaff ed. *A Sacred Quest: The Life and Writings of Mary Butts* (Kingston, NY: McPherson & Co., 1995), 194.

92 Lawrence Rainey does a terrific job of demonstrating the stylistic range and cultural sources of *Armed With Madness*, but he underestimates the complexity of *Felicity Taverner* and fails to see the similarities between the two novels: "Good things: pederasty and jazz and opium and research."

93 For a discussion of the popularity of detective fiction during this period, see Alison Light,

England: Femininity, Literature, and Conservatism between the Wars (New York: Routledge, 1991), 62–112.

94 For a discussion of the links between the Grail and femininity, see: Sherlyn Abdoo, "Woman as Grail in T.S. Eliot's *The Waste Land*," *Centennial Review*, 28 (1984): 48–60; Susan Aronstein, "Rewriting Percival's sister: eucharistic vision and typological destiny in the *Queste del San Graal*," *Women's Studies*, 21. 2 (1992): 211–30; Donald L. Hoffman, "Percival's sister: Malory's 'rejected' masculinities," *Arthuriana*, 6. 4 (1996): 72–83; Rosalyn Rossignol, "The holiest vessel: maternal aspects of the Grail," *Arthuriana*, 5. 1 (1995): 52–61. Christine Poulson, *The Quest for the Grail: Arthurian Legend in British Art 1840–1920* (Manchester and New York: Manchester University Press, 1999).

95 From Butts's diary entry for August 8, 1935, quoted by Blondel, *Mary Butts*, 492, n. 169.

96 Anne McClintock, "No longer in a future heaven: gender, race, and nationalism" in Anne McClintock, Aamir Mufti, and Ella Shohat eds. *Dangerous Liaisons: Gender, Nation, and Postcolonial Perspectives* (Minneapolis: University of Minnesota Press, 1997), 91.

97 Franz Fanon, *The Wretched of the Earth* (New York: Grove Press, 1963), 148–9.

98 Mary Butts, "Green," *From Altar to Chimney-Piece* (Kingston, NY: McPherson & Co., 1992), 64.

99 Melba Cuddy Keane, "Virginia Woolf and the varieties of historicist experience" in Beth Carole Rosenberg and Jeanne Dubino eds. *Virginia Woolf and the Essay* (New York: St. Martin's Press, 1997), 59–77.

100 Ambercombie, *Town and Country Planning* (London: Thornton Butterworth, 1933), 199.

101 Harrison, *Religion of Ancient Greece* (London: Constable, 1921), 42 and 44.

102 See Sheila Jeffreys in *Women's History: Britain, 1850–1945* (New York: St. Martin's 1995), 193–216.

103 Laura Mulvey, "Visual pleasure and narrative cinema" in Constance Penley ed. *Feminism and Film Theory* (New York: Routledge, 1988), 62.

104 Harrison, *Prolegomena to the Study of Greek Religion* (Princeton, NJ: Princeton University Press, 1991), 271.

105 The metaphorizing of Felicity as landscape recalls Butts's characterization of her beloved Salterns as a violated female body (*CC*, 15). Robert Graves's discussion of "the White Goddess" calls to mind Felicity, particularly in his contention that this figure is associated with whiteness and is closely connected to ancient British and Greek religions. See *The White Goddess: A Historical Grammar of Poetic Myth* (New York: Creative Age Press, 1948), 10 and 44–54.

106 Harrison, *Religion of Ancient Greece*, 54.

107 Butts's reference to the Earth-Mother's breasts occurs in *Scenes from the Life of Cleopatra*, 326. For the reference to hives, see Harrison, *Epilegomena*, 8.

108 Ian Patterson, "'The plan behind the plan': Russians, Jews, and mythologies of change. The case of Mary Butts" in Bryan Cheyette and Laura Marcus eds. *Modernity, Culture, and "the Jew"* (Stanford, CA: Stanford University Press, 1998), 130.

109 Gilman, *The Jew's Body*, 174–5; see also 101–2.

110 For a discussion of Jewish immigration in England, see David Feldman and Gareth Stedman Jones eds. *Metropolis London: Histories and Representations Since 1800* (London and New York: Routledge, 1989), 78.

111 Patrick Wright, *On Living in an Old Country: The National Past in Contemporary Britain* (London: Verso, 1985), 126.

112 See Andrea Freud Loewenstein, *Loathsome Jews and Engulfing Women: Metaphors of Projection in the Works of Wyndham Lewis, Charles Williams, and Graham Greene* (New York: New York University Press, 1993), Ch. 1.

113 Otto Weininger, *Sex and Character* (New York and Chicago, IL: A.L. Burt, 1906), 306.

114 *Ibid.*

115 Ritchie Robertson, "Historicizing Weininger: the nineteenth-century German image of the feminized Jew" in Cheyette and Marcus eds. *Modernity, Culture, and "the Jew,"* 24.

116 Weininger, *Sex and Character*, 311.

117 Gilman, *The Jew's Body*, 80–1 and 96–7.

118 *Ibid.*, 145. See also Gilman's *Difference and Pathology: Stereotypes of Sexuality, Race, and Madness* (Ithaca, NY: Cornell University Press, 1985), 204–13.

119 Gilman, *The Jew's Body*, 31 and 97.

120 Weininger, *Sex and Character*, 324.

121 *Ibid.*, 320.

122 Bryan Cheyette, *Constructions of "the Jew" in English Literature and Society: Racial Representations, 1875–1945* (Cambridge: Cambridge University Press, 1993), 8.

123 See Gilman, *The Jew's Body*, 99–101; *Difference and Pathology*, 30–5. For references to the Jewish gaze, see *The Jew's Body*, 68–9; for references to the relation between olfactory qualities and Jewishness, see *Difference and Pathology*, 114.

124 Harrison, *Alpha and Omega*, 123.

125 Butts makes these observations about Cleopatra, but they are absolutely consistent with Felicity's representation. From *The Macedonian*, quoted by Hoberman in *Gendering Classicism*, 141.

126 T.S. Eliot, *After Strange Gods* (London: Faber, 1934), 20.

127 *Ibid.*, 17.

128 Weston, *From Ritual to Romance*, 29.

129 Weininger, *Sex and Character*, 308 and 307.

130 Butts, *Imaginary Letters*, 254, 258, 236, and 239.

131 *Ibid.*, 260.

132 Harrison, *Alpha and Omega*, 203.

133 Harrison, *Mythology* (New York: Longman, Green & Co., 1924), 63.

134 Weininger, *Sex and Character*, 321.

135 Harrison, *Ancient Art and Ritual*, 135.

136 *Ibid.*, 71.

137 *Ibid.*, 26.

138 Butts, *Scenes from the Life of Cleopatra*, 278.

Mapping "the body of our mother": national desire, imperial nostalgia, and language in Virginia Woolf

The history of nations is determined not on the battlefield but in the nursery, and the battalions which give lasting victory are the battalions of babies. The politics of the future will be domestic. (Caleb Saleeby, *Parenthood and Race Culture*, 1909)

The twisting babies ... The little bodies wriggled & turned & twisted, curiously mobile & restless ... these pinkish balls, were ... new born babies, tossed from the top of the waves ... And soon the beach was covered with their markings ... they were staggering across the sand, & leaving foot prints ... innumerable children, pulsating, bubbling walking everywhere. (*The Waves: The Two Holograph Drafts*, 1976)

Woolf's early story "The journal of Mistress Joan Martyn" (1906), about historian Rosamond Merridew's research "into the system of land tenure in mediaeval England," would appear to have little in common with *The Waves*.[1] Yet the tale's preoccupation with the gendering of both history and territory, and its engagement with the links between female authorship, English national identity, and maternal pre-eminence, prefigure what, I argue, are the central tenets of Woolf's experimental novel. In "The journal of Mistress Joan Martyn," Woolf privileges the "poor private voice" of women in order to destabilize the claims of universality made by male historians, foregrounding the gendered dimension of geographical perception through the "archaeological eye" of Rosamond Merridew.[2] Discredited by her peers for indulging in needless "digressions" that have nothing, allegedly, to do with the "history of the time," Merridew trains her gaze on the English landscape and unearths the fifteenth-century diary of Mistress Joan Martyn. This disjunctive and incomplete journal provides a unique narrative of the nation's citizenry, one that focuses not on male lineage and pedigree but, rather, on the matrilineal. Woolf's story chronicles one daughter's cultural history of the maternal, demonstrating not only that the mother is an integral part of England's social order – "She rules us all" (46) – but that the home is the cornerstone of the nation. Crucially in this narrative it is the mother who maintains and regulates territorial borders, inspiring her daughter "to hope that one day the same power may be [hers]" (46). As Joan prepares for her marriage and contemplates her acquisition of "great lands" (51), her mother expounds on "what she calls her theory of ownership," her belief that, for women, identity is coterminous with the usurpation of geographic space: "one is as the Ruler of a small island set in the midst of turbulent waters" (59). Utilizing the language of imperial domination, Joan's mother positions the daughter not only as the inheritor of a spacious "plot of ground" (59) in the leading colonizing nation of the globe, but as the creator of an entirely "new world," the feminized promise of "what the future may bring to England" (60). By claiming a world space in the name of Joan Martyn, this mother suggests that gender relations are embedded in the spatial organization of place. Joan repeatedly registers this, envisioning herself as the mistress of her own territorial and imaginative universe: her thoughts traverse "a wide space" and appear in her mind's eye "as solid globes of crystal; enclosing a round ball of coloured earth and air, in which tiny men and women laboured" (58).

Both "The journal" and *The Waves* recognize that the official historical register enables the evolution of a nation by constructing narrative accounts of what Ernest Renan calls "national memories" of a "heroic past" – the chronicle of wars, revolutions, and the "glory" of "great men."[3] Yet, importantly, both texts seek to undermine this concept of history by foregrounding the domestic, the everyday, and the familial in order to construct a new story of national belonging in which women are central. Each acknowledges that the nation comes into being imaginatively through story-telling, and each postulates that an alternative national fiction arises when femininity is no longer subordinated or devalued. In both texts, moreover, the public and the private emerge as intertwined geographical spaces which are presided over by maternal authority.

In particular, the resonant image of feminine consciousness creating world order has important implications for this chapter, which argues that *The Waves*, albeit in more encrypted fashion, exhibits a similar belief in the culturally redemptive potential of maternal intervention; or, as Joan puts it: "to see the whole of England thus solidly established ... I shall thank my mother" (60). Like "The journal," too, *The Waves* suggests that the world is negotiated spatially, that female authorship (through the depiction of Elvedon) is located at the sacred core of national culture, and that the maternal (embodied improbably by Percival) is *the* principle of order, central to the national–imperial enterprise. Ultimately, Woolf delineates two distinct forms of nationalism that are fused in Percival: one, a militaristic nationalism that is associated with fascism and the symbolic order (and which the novel explicitly repudiates); the other, a more authentic ancestral Englishness that is tied to the semiotic, the recuperation of the mother/land, and primitive ritual (which Woolf celebrates).

My interpretation of *The Waves* brings together several seemingly contradictory, yet historically interconnected, discourses: the early twentieth-century revival of neo-medievalism in England; the interwar interest in the spiritual culture of landscape; the British feminist view that racial motherhood constituted the highest form of national responsibility; and the modernist engagement with matriarchal prehistory and *primitive* practices. We see in "The journal" an alignment of the mother with Helen of Troy (47), a compression of the medieval body and ancient Greek culture that speaks directly to Percival's own dual association with Arthurian legend and what Jane Harrison describes as the Dionysian pre-phallic mother. At the same time, this chapter builds upon earlier Kristevan readings of *The Waves* by historicizing the text's allusions to the preoedipal mother and showing that the semiotic is not merely linguistically present, but is also embodied in Percival. Woolf's treatment of history as a palimpsest is most clearly reflected in the imperialist Percival, whose feminized body functions as a metonym for the nation and carries within it traces of that which has been culturally suppressed. In bringing together these various maternal discourses, I seek to demonstrate both that linguistic and cultural formations are inseparable, and that the novel's invocation of poetic language – its longing for the restoration of lost maternal unity – is complicit with cultural narratives that encode Englishness and racial primitivism. Woolf recognizes that national culture is reproduced through narrative, but she is ambivalent about the role that empire plays in the consolidation of national identity. Although her novel is critical of imperialism, it simultaneously encodes a communal fantasy of nationhood that reflects a form of "imperialist nostalgia."[4] Like "The journal of Mistress Joan Martyn", which problematizes women's imperial dream of ownership – Joan's fantasy of territorialism is upset by her realization that colonial commerce undergirds her mother's vision of a "new world" – The Waves conveys both the seductiveness and the cost of the imperial narrative to women's psyches. Relevant here is Simon Gikandi's observation that the concept of "empire" is what sustains "the core of a common British identity," and moreover, that this identity "depend[s] on imperial possession."[5] The Waves inscribes the narrative of empire through the colonization of Elvedon, a feminized space of English high culture inextricably linked to Percival. The context of British imperialism that underwrites Woolf's novel reminds us of Renan's warning that "in the creation of a nation … [u]nity is always effected by means of brutality" (11). In The Waves, Woolf creates unity through the feminine usurpation of male territory, but in doing so she inevitably reproduces the tactics of female cultural imperialism.

My reading also builds upon Jane Marcus's breakthrough argument according to which The Waves "reveals that the primal narrative of British culture is the (imperialist) quest," but crucially diverges from her claim that the novel sustains a consistent anti-imperialist critique.[6] Marcus's own analysis of the female characters acknowledges that white women are implicated in the colonial project, yet she curiously absolves Woolf herself from any complicity with nationalism or imperialism. I read Woolf's novel as evidence of her equivocal relation to these mutually sustaining categories, revealing simultaneous attraction to and repulsion by the narrative of empire. Gikandi's claim that "the crisis of Englishness … is symptomatic of the incomplete project of colonialism" provides a way of understanding Woolf's ambivalence, for although The Waves was composed before the onset of decolonization it arguably reflects "the persistence and enforcement of colonial categories in their moment of disappearance" (9). This chapter situates Woolf's novel at precisely that juncture of inscription and erasure, simultaneous movements that locate the text's concomitant critique and valorization of characters who struggle to construct a subjectivity and an access to language through imperial tropes. I argue that The Waves demonstrates Woolf's belief that language acquisition and fluency in the narrative of empire are intertwined and, moreover, that coming into consciousness as a British subject is inseparable from this story. Woolf's resistance to women's patriotism is counterbalanced by her view, articulated in Three Guineas, that a "pure, if irrational" attachment to nation is instilled in childhood, when "some love of England [is] dropped into a child's ears by the cawing of rooks in an elm tree, by the splash of waves on a beach, or by English voices murmuring nursery rhymes" (109). *The Waves* exploits this nostalgic and pastoral vision instilled in childhood by presenting six characters who, in effect, remain forever children, caught up in an obstinate love of the motherland through their adoration of Percival.[7]

Benedict Anderson's observation that "nothing connects us affectively to [nation] more than language" (145) speaks to *The Waves'* preoccupation with the vocabulary of kinship, yet the novel shows how one's access to, and deployment of, "his or her mother-tongue" (154) is inflected by gender. The fundamental problem, according to Woolf, is that women do not have equal access to the dominant discourse of the imperial center: culturally estranged from this sustaining master narrative, Susan, Jinny, and Rhoda are all, to varying degrees, linguistically nowhere. Rather, each embodies certain aspects of "imperial femininity," to borrow Gikandi's phrase, that reflect both complicity with and resistance to their prescribed cultural roles as mothers, erotic objects, and mirrors for nationalist propaganda. Woolf demonstrates how women are constructed as national subjects through the body, even though they themselves do not regulate the cultural inscriptions that are marked upon them. To the extent that *The Waves* seeks both to critique the master narrative of imperialism and to give women access to the very discourse that has, historically, excluded and marginalized them, the novel reflects Woolf's unstable interpellation by the ideological structures of empire. Elvedon, I argue, is Woolf's 'solution' to the problem of women's cultural confinement, a maternalized space that comes into being through recourse to an ancestral Englishness and is evidence that "the imperial myth still continues to have a sacred presence ... at 'home' in England."[8] Through a complex network of associations linking femininity to empire, Elvedon illustrates that the motif of conquest is still an enabling cultural script, one that situates women as active agents of colonization – not of the dominions, but of England itself, the imperial center.

Despite the novel's sustained interest in abstraction as it explores the relation between constituted subjectivity and unconscious impulses, readers know almost from the first pages that we are fixed somewhere within the class system of the British empire, rather than suspended in an immaterial otherworld. Yet, since the publication of *The Waves* in 1931, critics have regarded the novel as largely ahistorical and overtly non-political, choosing instead to read its highly experimental structure and stream of consciousness lyricism – what Woolf herself calls the text's "mystical poetical" quality – as exemplary of a certain high modernist aestheticism.[9] I show how Woolf's interest in the mystical is not ahistorical but is rather associated both with Jane Harrison's work on the emergence of mystical nature cults in Greece and with the British revival of Arthurian legend and an embrace of sacred spaces such as Stonehenge, associations which operate in *The Waves* as signifiers of English national identity.[10] The novel identifies nature as a national spiritual resource, linking the enculturated space of Elvedon with the primitive through a transmogrification that depends upon Percival's intervention. Woolf's understanding of English prehistory is imbricated in her complication of gender categories in the novel. *The Waves* also exposes the masculine bias at work in cultural institutions, demonstrating how literary and historical influence – what Louis calls the boys' "inherited traditions" – operates to enable, as well as implicate, male imperial privilege.[11] The view, maintained by some critics, that *The Waves* is "the least political" of Woolf's fiction, that this experimental narrative represents the author's retreat from an "interest in external reality," obfuscates what I argue is one of the novel's primary concerns: a desire to reveal the extent to which the ideology of the British ruling class, with its entrenched paternalism, its fetishizing of canonical texts, its emphasis on the formation of a national subjectivity, hinges upon both the complicity of women and the suppression of femininity.[12]

Few critics have acknowledged any significant differences among the male and female speakers in *The Waves*, and no one has fully registered the national implications of what Marcus disparagingly calls the six voices' "discursive infantilization" (146). Whereas Marcus reads Woolf's formal strategy as a representation of the effects of cultural hegemony, I see evidence also of a desire to blur the boundary between self and Other in order to re-imagine the novelistic space in which the nation is produced. These are contradictory projects, perhaps, but there is a complementarity between them in that each exposes the novel's dual aim: to critique dominant discourse and to capture, in Jinny's words, the "common fund of experience" (175). That is to say, by unifying and thus equalizing her narrative voices, Woolf creates the imaginative possibility of equal access to discourse among characters who occupy incommensurate social positions, even though, in reality, the social inequities that underpin such linguistic fluency never actually disappear. Yet, in the highly stylized world of the novel, Woolf disputes the idea that articulation is contingent on one's class, gender, or racial position by having her characters share a common idiom; formally, she delineates a universalist fantasy in which alliterative poetic utterances function as a kind of communal Englishness, dissolving distinctions between the six voices.[13] Hence, the diction of Louis, the colonial subject, is indistinguishable from that of Bernard, the character most invested in narrative control who fantasizes about assuming "command of the British Empire" (261). By privileging this formal equivalence among disparate characters, Woolf's novel calls into question the category of normative Englishness by incorporating that which has been marginalized (e.g. the voices of women and colonials). At the same time, one could argue that by stylistically foregrounding the "unifying influence" of the English language, *The Waves* unwittingly aligns itself with the conservative view, propounded by the Newbolt Committee on the institutionalization of English, that "the body politic" requires linguistic cohesiveness in order for the nation to function effectively.[14] I suggest that both interpretations are able to coexist in the contradictory world of this novel, and also that one effect of Woolf's use of elevated diction is to expose the gap between her female characters' linguistic fluency and their purported problematical relation to language. By utilizing a literary style that effectively democratizes each character's access to speech, Woolf critiques the assumption that language is the prerogative of a universal male citizen, even though, thematically, that is precisely the story which the novel tells. Importantly, by constructing six interconnected soliloquies among characters who remain discernibly childlike even as they purportedly function as adults, Woolf unintentionally aligns herself with the insight offered by Arthur Mee in *The Children's Encyclopedia*, that the "nation is a living body" in which "[e]ach of us is part of a great whole ... members of one another."[15] Mee's comparison of the nation with the bodies of living individuals speaks directly to the novel's investment not only in showing how the meaning of the nation resides in human geography, but in employing that communal body to reterritorialize the space in which the nation is constructed. Yet, whereas Mee claims that the nation is propelled and regulated by men, Woolf re-envisions the nation as a great living feminine creature. The discrepancy between the characters' linguistic fluency and their infantilism has to do precisely with their relation to, and identification with, this feminized maternal source in the text.

The six sections that follow attempt to demonstrate how *The Waves*, although critical of it, simultaneously acknowledges imperialism as a precondition for locating oneself in the national imaginary. The early sections historicize the novel's complex engagement with maternity as a signifier of the nation, drawing from the network of interrelated cultural discourses – psychoanalytical, anthropological, political, literary – that inform the depiction of Percival as the imperial 'mother' of the six children.[16] I foreground the linguistic implications of the maternal, laying the theoretical groundwork for the chapter's larger argument that Percival and each of the six are less *characters* than they are *positions in language*. In order to illustrate this argument I show how identity is configured by the group when Percival, the principle of national unity, is not explicitly invoked, suggesting that British subjectivity is constituted and legitimized by its relation to this absent referent. One can comprehend Percival's significance as a linguistic signifier only, I suggest, by understanding how the male and female speakers' facility with language is an aptitude that depends on a sense of national belonging and the consequent ability of each to articulate a discrete "I." It is crucial, furthermore, to register that the girls' limited and problematical relation to linguistic agency can be traced to their cultural estrangement and inability to master the narrative of empire. With the parameters of the six characters' identities thus established, the final sections refocus on Percival, whose dual role as chivalric hero–abject mother facilitates both English national unification and linguistic cohesiveness for the group.

This chapter argues that through Woolf's triangular maternal matrix – Percival, Bernard, and Elvedon – what *The Waves* ultimately calls for is the recovery of a repressed language, one drawn from the discourses of conquest and English pre-history, that would help to shape a feminizing of national space. Ultimately, it is only through Percival's mediation that Bernard is able to access the linguistic strata the novel endorses, through his primary identification with the flesh-made-word, what might be called the maternal semiotic. Resonant throughout the novel is Woolf's bifurcated response to Englishness: while she contends that she is "not in the least patriotic," she concedes a love for English literature that exposes her investment in national kinship: "Chaucer, Shakespeare and Dickens. It's my only patriotism."[17]

Locating maternal origins

While much feminist attention since the 1980s has been paid to what Marianne Hirsch calls modernist women's fictional "celebration of mothers," little consideration has been given to how those maternal paradigms intersect with the British ideology of racial motherhood.[18] An exception is Laura Doyle's work on the figure of the racialized mother in modern experimental fiction, which demonstrates the discursive and historical links between maternal plots and early twentieth-century race theory. I build upon Doyle's argument that "the race or group mother is the point of access to a group history and bodily grounded identity" by demonstrating how *The Waves'* racialized mother – Percival – both functions as the dominant cultural vehicle for the "fixing, ranking, and subduing [of] groups and bodies" and is the transgressive disembodied source that undoes the conventions of enculturation.[19] Percival's doubleness occupies the border between nature and culture, and can be traced to his dual role as the novel's martial hero and symbolic mother, a counter-intuitive move motivated by Woolf's desire to denaturalize the maternal while utilizing it as an exemplum of intersubjectivity – fostering what Kristeva calls motherhood's ability to inaugurate "new thinking about the human race" that privileges "otherness" and "the sacred."[20] *The Waves* reveals the period's engagement with maternal origins, an interest that can be traced to the late nineteenth-century excavations in Greece where archeological artifacts suggested the existence of ancient matriarchal cults. Ruth Hoberman has demonstrated the extent to which Woolf and other women writers were influenced by the intellectual climate in which Freud and Harrison were positing a primordial past dominated by femininity, nature, the irrational, and indeterminacy.[21] *The Waves* was published in 1931, the same year that Freud's "Female sexuality" appeared, the work in which he likens the early, preoedipal, phase in girls with the effect of the discovery, in another field, "of the Minoan–Mycenean civilization behind that of Greece."[22] Freud assigns to preculture (i.e., nature) the whole preoedipal period, but ultimately occludes its significance for female psychology, seeing "this first mother-attachment ... [as] so elusive ... so dim and shadowy, so hard to resuscitate, that it seemed as if it had undergone some specially inexorable repression."[23] We can historically situate Woolf's interest in maternal origins and plentitude, as Elizabeth Abel has shown, by looking at how her fictional texts parallel, as they simultaneously revise, the developmental narratives of psychoanalysis.[24] Freud alone, however, cannot account for Woolf's engagement with maternal paradigms in *The Waves* which in many ways correspond with the theories propounded by Jane Harrison. Like Freud, Harrison was intrigued by the idea of a Minoan–Mycenaean "Great Mother [who] is prior to the masculine divinities," yet she significantly diverges from him in her valuation of this maternal legacy.[25] For Harrison, the shift from matriarchy to patriarchy does not mark an inevitable movement toward civilization but signals, rather, the abandoning of group collectivity and an embrace of individualism. In Woolf's novel, we can see a similar disdain for rationality and a longing for what Harrison calls the desire "to restore by communion that complete unity" which has been lost through patriarchal enculturation.[26]

For both Harrison and Woolf, this lost "unity" can be traced to the organizing principle of the maternal. We see scattered throughout Woolf's letters evidence of her admiration for Harrison's "superb high thinking agnostic ways" and her interest in the classicist's "sapphism," tendencies which contributed to the denunciation of Harrison by some of her peers as a controversial scholar of "feminist propaganda."[27] Yet it is precisely Harrison's feminism, I argue, that attracted Woolf – in particular, her argument that women's "racial conscience" has pervaded the public sphere to such a degree that it "may be of use for the whole body politic."[28] Woolf's use of racialized discourse is rarely so bald, but throughout *The Waves* there is ample evidence of Harrison's influence: her focus on the importance of collectivity and ritual practice; her belief that rituals are of religious significance; her conviction that the irrational occupies an originary status and thus contains a deeper truth than rationality; her equation of the primitive and the child; and her use of Christian iconography in conjunction with her discussion of ancient Greek religion.[29] Harrison's work on the unmapped terrain of matriarchal prehistory and primitive practices resonates throughout Woolf's novel, but the application of Harrison's theories alone cannot capture the complexity of *The Waves'* engagement with maternal paradigms. One needs, in addition, to remember that during this period, British motherhood was regarded as a sacred national duty, an essential component in the preservation of the race. Woolf exploits this link between imperialism and motherhood by inscribing Percival into this ideological frame, a move that both denaturalizes maternity by aligning it with a male body and relies upon culturally encoded tropes that inevitably invoke racial motherhood. Through Percival, Woolf subversively echoes a conventional social script: maternal duty is the highest form of national responsibility. At the same time, by locating maternalism in the body of a chivalric hero whose name invokes the Grail quest, Woolf alludes surreptitiously to the holy vessel's association with what Emma Jung – in her work on the psychological dimension of the Grail legend – calls "the primal image of the mother."[30] Percival functions metaphorically as a kind of living Grail, providing the six characters with "nourishment, protection, and perfect union, all primal experiences arising from the original relationship with the mother."[31] Yet even the conjunction of maternalist imperialism with Harrison's work on the primitive structuration of the maternal does not account exhaustively for *The Waves'* focus on the linguistic implications of the maternal body. Relevant here, I argue, is Kristeva's metaphorizing of the semiotic as "maternal territory," a geographical depiction that associates linguistic belonging with one's relationship to, in Gillian Rose's words, "the inaccessible plenitude of Mother."[32] Woolf's novel reflects this "sense of nostalgia for this first and ultimate dwelling-place" of the maternal body.[33]

While both Woolf and Kristeva focus varyingly on the mother–child dyad obscured in Freud's (and Lacan's) work, Woolf's preoccupation with maternal origins in *The Waves* can be read as a radicalizing of Kristeva's theory to the extent that the novel attempts to represent the unrepresentable – the mother's body – and then link this body with women's and men's relation to signification. Whereas both Freud and Lacan can be said to theorize an oedipal model that insists on the abandoning of the mother, Kristeva attempts to reformulate the oedipal story so that the mother can claim a space within the symbolic system – if only as disruption. In contrast, Woolf seeks to carve an independent discursive place for the mother by imaginatively projecting the possibility of a mythic 'female symbolic' in *The Waves* through her depiction of the enigmatic, yet discernibly maternalized, space of Elvedon. Although it is true that Woolf's text illustrates how the constitution of femininity within patriarchy presents considerable obstacles to signification, the novel simultaneously subverts the assumption that women are necessarily estranged from language. On the one hand, the girls lack the capacity to form cohesive identities because of their linguistic difficulties; on the other, the novel suggests that unified selves are illusory. Although the boys' identities are represented as largely cohesive and thus conducive to language acquisition, they are each critiqued for lacking the girls' disability: diffuseness, permeability, a resistance toward singularity. The novel suggests that neither a "masculine" nor a "feminine" position is, in isolation, a viable linguistic solution; instead, Woolf's text illustrates the desirability of the speaking subject's heterogeneity.

In many ways, however, Woolf's depiction of constricted female possibility in *The Waves* parallels Kristeva's view that women are marginalized in relation to the symbolic, and thus estranged from linguistic agency.[34] For Kristeva, to recall, one's successful entry into language depends upon both the loss of the mother and an identification with the sociosymbolic paternal order – the realm of verbal communication, temporality, inhibitions, and taboos – even though, if one is a male writer, the maternal remains a vital source of preoedipal pleasure whose "reactivation ... recreates in his speech this pre-sentence-making disposition to rhythm, intonation, [and] nonsense; makes nonsense abound within sense."[35] Whereas men can acquire an enunciative position because, through the threat of castration, they sever their preoedipal identification with their mothers, women never fully enter language because they never experience a threat analogous to castration, and therefore never successfully sever their maternal tie. Unlike male authors, who can recover the mother through avant-garde writing, a woman writer's recuperation of the maternal will necessarily result in some form of psychosis or self-destructiveness, making her "ecstatic, nostalgic, or mad."[36] As Kristeva soberingly puts it: "[a] woman has nothing to laugh about when the paternal order falls."[37]

Kristeva's contention that unless a woman identifies with the symbolic order "she collapses into psychosis or suicide" is clearly reflected in *The Waves*, where (unified) identity, (male) gender, and (symbolic) language are at once inextricably connected *and* conspicuously unsettled throughout her text.[38] Woolf and Kristeva are similarly concerned with discourses that instigate a crisis in identity, that threaten the notion of a unified subject; for each of them the maternal functions as such a discourse. The critical difference is the way in which each of them imagines the representation of maternity. Kristeva's theorization of the recuperation of the maternal in language has to do solely with issues of formal innovation, and is unconcerned with the thematic content of the avant-garde text. But to discuss *The Waves* solely in structural terms, as a reflection of the dialectic between meaning and musicality, is not in itself an adequate assessment of what I see to be the novel's historically grounded thematic engagement with maternity – in particular, with its social and cultural implications for the woman writer. While the absence of literal mothers from *The Waves* is conspicuous, pervasive throughout the text is the group's shared obsession with the centrality of maternal loss, with what Kristeva terms "the desire to return to the archaic mother."[39] Neville's articulation of longing after the group's communal meal at Hampton Court – "we only wish [now] to rejoin the body of our mother from whom we have been severed" (233) – crystallizes what I argue to be the novel's preoccupation with the maternal body, and with the child's desire to "return to the origin."[40] For Kristeva, simply to know the mother is to allow semiotic activity to make its way into language through "rhythms, intonations, and echolalias of the mother–infant symbiosis," but this textual phenomenon is not at all dependent on the representation of a real maternal body.[41] Woolf's text, however, complicates Kristeva's model by displacing the functions of the maternal on to Percival. Kristeva's contention, following Lacan, that the mother is always considered phallic – to the extent that desire (within her psychoanalytical framework) is always conceptualized as desire for the phallus – is certainly problematical from a feminist perspective, but the epithet "phallic mother" is persuasive in terms of Percival's particular status as the source of all gratification.[42] And, yet, how could a male figure plausibly represent what many have argued is a necessarily essentialized female body within Kristeva's schema?

If we conceptualize the maternal body through its association with gratification and enculturation, straddling the border between nature and culture, we may begin to understand Percival's problematic status in *The Waves*, for he is arguably an embodiment of "split symbolization,"[43] a figure of abjection who confounds the boundary between self and Other, animal and human, whose "in-between" and "ambiguous" status ultimately "does not respect borders, positions, rules."[44] The "attraction and repulsion" inherent in Percival is paradoxically "what disturbs identity, system, order" on a national scale, for the abject is "precisely that which constitutes and opposes the self, whether of the individual or of the nation state."[45] This might seem to go against the grain of conventional readings, but it derives from Woolf's own contention that the modernist novel in women's hands will exploit the Englishwoman's new role as "responsible citizen" and "gadfly to the state" while foregrounding those seemingly negligible female tactics of "concealment and suppression" (*ROO*, 84–5).[46] Linden Peach's "cryptanalysis" – his method for excavating the concealed political and historical content of Woolf's 1930s fiction through attention to implicit meanings – assists us in exposing those novels' suppressed anxiety over the demise of empire.[47] Percival's meaning, I'm suggesting, requires a cryptographic approach, for critics have consistently read him too literally.[48] Like the maternal abject which, within Kristeva's schema, cannot be fully incorporated by the symbolic, Percival's alterity cannot adequately be accounted for by simply identifying him as an imperialist subject.[49] Instead, Percival should be read as the "strange fold" between culture and nature in that he fuses an ideological symbol of the British empire with a maternal function. This would not be the first time, we may recall, that Woolf attempts the seemingly incongruous juxtaposition of imperialism and maternity. In *To the Lighthouse*, Woolf compares Mrs. Ramsay to Victoria, the Imperial Queen, critiquing the legitimacy of maternal imperialism at the same time as she implicates herself in the discourse of racial motherhood.[50] To the extent that Mrs. Ramsay's moments of private self-reflection and will to domination (57) reveal an "imperial consciousness," she can be read as "*the* agent of civilization" in the novel.[51] Mrs. Ramsay and Percival have similar narrative functions of unifying disparate elements in the novel. Each is the locus of desire for other characters – in both cases that desire is thematized in specifically corporeal terms – and both are pivotal figures who are largely absent. In each novel, that absence is associated with linguistic disruption. Both, moreover, initiate a ceremonial ritual for a group that involves food, performing the mediating function of symbolically offering their bodies as a kind of cannibalistic sacrifice. But while in *To the Lighthouse*, Woolf uses the language of imperialism to censure and implicate the figure of the mother, in *The Waves* she can be said to map the body of the mother on to Percival in order to destabilize, and subvert, the imperialist figure.[52]

Yet Percival's meaning simultaneously exceeds any single interpretation. It is precisely this indeterminacy that enables us to read him as a figure for language in the novel. Percival is also the natural embodiment of an ancestral Englishness the maternal aspect of which has been repressed by culture, a phenomenon that recalls Renan's claim that national identity, like personhood, is engendered through amnesia. Precisely because "it is impossible to 'remember' the [originary] consciousness" of either childhood or the nation, one constructs enabling fictions in order to ground national identification: "Out of such oblivions ... spring narratives" (204).[53] In Woolf's novel, this imperative to narrate is carried out by Bernard but is facilitated by Percival, a character whose doubleness both reminds readers of England's association with empire and enables them to disavow it. Woolf herself, in a different context, captures the sense of what Homi Bhabha calls "nationalist pedagogy" when she admonishes her fellow Britons: "England ... say[s] ... 'you ... should learn to read your mother tongue.'"[54] This, in encapsulated form, is the narrative address of *The Waves*. More than anything else, Percival is a linguistic signifier who draws attention to the fact that "from the start the nation was conceived in language."[55] Before we look more closely at how, and why, Percival embodies this function, the other characters' relation to linguistic agency and estrangement, particularly as it is expressed in terms of gender, requires consideration. Woolf gives us a spectrum of normative models of female identity in order to illustrate the social basis of women's inequitable – at times, adversarial – relation to symbolic discourse. Yet even as Woolf represents women's problematical relation to language, she simultaneously interrogates the ability of language to express the multitude of images, impressions, and reflections that comprise a life. For both the male and the female characters, access to language is dependent on their positions within empire, and for each national identity is conferred through language. Andrew Higson's observation that "[n]ationalism is about drawing boundaries, about marking an outside and an inside," speaks directly to what is each character's attempt to negotiate the limits of English national identity by grappling with language.[56]

Engendering the historical subject

Bernard's observation concerning the group's communal dynamic – "We rise, we disperse" (60) – is an obvious allusion to the interludes and reflects the two related tensions of the novel – between individuation and collectivity, and between the production and dissolution of the self. Despite the novel's intermittent focus on the desirability of collectivity and the blurring of individual boundaries, Woolf also exerts considerable energy to elucidate the differences among the six characters, differences which are stratified along traditional gender lines. The boys and the girls have disparate relations to history, education, and culture, which affect and even determine their sense of identity and their relations to language, and *The Waves* systematically exposes the masculine bias and privilege within these spheres. Yet the novel simultaneously demonstrates how male privilege is undermined by internal contradictions and instabilities. In particular, Woolf chooses male characters who are relatively marginal with respect to national ideals of masculinity. Bernard's androgyny, Louis's colonial status, and Neville's homosexuality marks each of them as liminal – a condition, I will argue, that links them to femininity. The liminal, furthermore, has a liberatory psychic potential, serving as the basis from which entrenched ideas of masculinity, and the imperial ambitions with which they are associated, might be disrupted. In this way, the male characters partially mirror Percival's own status as a split and feminized subject of empire.

Each of the male characters reveals an internalized Otherness, suggesting that a receptivity to the feminine exists at the heart of male privilege – even though they repeatedly resist that susceptibility. Both Louis and Neville in particular, who in many ways evince more egoistic versions of masculine identification than does Bernard, share the women's desire for social acceptance and inclusion; it is this impulse which largely unsettles their infatuation with singularity and underscores their most elemental identification, that of unsated children. Neville's homosexuality is the one area in his life which, like Louis's outsider status or Rhoda's visions, can neither be fully regulated nor contained; to that extent, homosexuality, foreignness, and uninterpellated femininity may be regarded as culturally liminal categories which are inherently dangerous because they threaten to encroach upon – and unsettle – the illusion of a unified transcendental group subjectivity. Both homosexuality and the *foreign* suggest that the self and the Other are not opposed, but coexist and are mutually constitutive. This repudiation of separateness, I'm suggesting, arises from the desire for cultural homogeneity, a homogeneity that is nationally bounded and heterosexually inflected. Although Neville exhibits a desire for some kind of integral wholeness, he has "no power of integrating [him]self" (70) with the assemblage of other lives. This fear of psychic incorporation is threatening precisely because it involves the confusion of ego boundaries that invariably results in the disintegration of the self. Even as a child Neville had recoiled from the ill-marked, from things that inhabited liminal territory, objects and experiences that were neither one thing nor another, but suspended somewhere in-between: "I hate dangling things; I hate dampish things. I hate wandering and mixing things together" (19). Even as the novel intimates the promise of intermediate states and category confusion, it shows individuals' antipathy toward them, compared with the group's desire for sameness: "We ... sedulously oppose any renegade (Neville, Louis, Rhoda) who sets up a separate existence" (246). Although the novel does not endorse Neville's self-reproach – "am I doomed to cause disgust? ... doomed always to cause repulsion" (88) – male homosexuality (in contrast to male homosocial ties) is not idealized by this text, nor is it used as a model for new social relations. At the same time, homosexuality functions, to borrow from Kristeva, as a sign of "the fascination and horror that a different being produces in us"; as such, it represents the possibility of escape from hegemonic culture by enabling the self to "recognize that … one is already a foreigner from within."[57]

The text's most marked example of the "foreigner" is Louis, who, like Neville, resists liminality though a fantasy of phallic mastery that fuels his investment in the repetitious re-inscription of the self: "I sign my name, I, I, and again I" (171). Yet Louis's status as a colonial subject from Australia positions him in stark contrast to the other male characters who, as he himself puts it, are ensured an insulated "continuance down the safe traditional ways" (67). Despite his scholarly aspirations as a boy, Louis is the only male who never goes on to college and instead proceeds directly into an uncertain labor force where, compelled to "go vaguely, to make money" (65), he is plagued by his "Australian accent" (201). Louis's cultural difference codes him as racially Other and keeps him on the periphery of the imperial center.[58] His difference, I'm suggesting, similarly threatens the cultural homogeneity of the group. Recalling the English denunciation of the Irish as racialized monkeys, Louis defines his actions as apelike mimicry: "I am the little ape who chatters over a nut," imitating English behavior – "I do these antics, smoothing my hair, concealing my accent" (128) – in an effort to disguise the fact that "[I am] an alien, external" (94). As he travels through the English countryside on a train, he experiences not tourism but exile: "I hang suspended without attachments. We are nowhere" (65). For Louis, the traversal of boundaries is not liberating, but merely evidence of his material displacement. His position is precarious because he is at once firmly entrenched within the exclusionary system of empire and simultaneously relegated to its periphery; his insistence that he is "ruthless" (219), when read alongside his lament, "I desire so much to be accepted" (170), alludes to the dual nature of his position, which constantly vacillates between incorporation and exile. It is that conflict, moreover, which ultimately dislodges Louis's fantasy of an indissoluble "I" by undermining his insistence on a universalized subjectivity.

All of the examples which confirm Louis's displacement also point to his status as Other and align him not only with Rhoda but with Neville, whose homosexuality similarly problematizes the illusion of a coherent self by casting him in an analogous role as *alien* within the text. Neville's undisclosed "secret told to nobody" (88) harbors the source of what ultimately fractures his otherwise cohesive surface of self-representation, much in the same way that Louis's private "attic room" (169) – the enclosure where he repeatedly takes refuge from the exigencies of public life, the place where he clandestinely meets Rhoda – works to conceal, through containment, the dissonance between his public and private selves. Both Neville and Louis colonize a private space (the closet, the attic room) that, within the world of the novel, cannot be imagined to exist inside the official realm of empire. The intimate attic dwelling functions as a kind of psychic meeting place for what Louis calls "the two discrepancies so hideously apparent to me" (53) for, like Neville's secret, Louis's room is a space of insularity that ultimately houses irreconcilable strains. For each, "opening a space" (88) where desire can circulate unimpeded means being situated at once inside and outside the imperial nation. These spaces of alterity are, in essence, places where self and Other meet and commune. This recognition, that identity is not only multifaceted – in Bernard's words, "many-sided" (116) – but is characterized by indeterminacy and irreconcilability, is most evident in the portrayal of Bernard himself, whose liminality aligns him most explicitly with the feminine. However, feminized men occupy a cultural position far from identical with that of actual women in the text. Liminality, Woolf intimates, can only be liberatory if one is already firmly entrenched (as are the men) within the national landscape, rather than categorically excluded from the start. Louis, in particular, exemplifies this dimension of male subjectivity: deeply identified with imperialism but internally alienated from it. Yet all of the male characters may be understood within this framework of mobile subjectivity. By showing how the male characters are internally divided and conflicted, Woolf tacitly asks: how can the subject coexist with Otherness? How can the nation?

Significantly, the first separation the six experience occurs when they are segregated by sex and sent to different schools; this moment signals a gendered split that will be recapitulated, in various ways, throughout the text. Neville's lament, "[t]his is our first night at school, apart from our sisters" (32), underscores their status as siblings and prefigures the text's later exploration of their familial relation to their 'mother', Percival. The contrast between the boys' and girls' responses to school is pronounced, not only in what they say but in the things that are not articulated. None of the girls ever voices anything comparable to Louis's self-assured declaration: "I am the best scholar in the school" (52); nor do they ever regard the academy with the kind of solemn reverence we see reflected in Neville: "I come, like a lord to his halls appointed … [a] noble Roman air hangs over these austere quadrangles" (31). In contrast, for the girls school is a place, at best, of distraction, and at worst, a source of extreme alienation. The girls experience neither the transformative influence of an intellectual model, nor instances of the kind of institutional identification that inform Neville's conviction that he "shall become a don … and lecture on the ruins of the Parthenon" (71). Unlike Neville, whose fate at only 18 is already indelibly inked within the academy's "ancient spaces" (86), Jinny sees her graduation from high-school as an embrace of adult sexuality, when she "shall leave school and wear long skirts" (55). Such examples effectively convey how educational contexts reflect polarized notions of masculinity and femininity. Louis's remark that he "would have been happier to have been born without a destiny, like Susan" (201) is patently disingenuous, but it epitomizes a certain accuracy about the imaginative impoverishment of the lives of all the women; not yet 20, Susan has already internalized a desire to replicate her mother's circumscribed life: "I shall have children … like my mother, silent in a blue apron" (99). This linkage of women and silence, though understated here, is, we will see, the most pronounced aspect of commonality among the three girls. Women's lives appear to be curiously suspended in an ahistorical elsewhere, informed only by the necessity to reproduce conventional forms of femininity.

Each of the males, to varying degrees, expresses a keen familiarity with ancient history, but also a self-confidence in his ability to invoke and personalize the past as a means of re-creating himself in the present. As Ruth Hoberman observes, an identification with the classics has long served to define the British ruling classes and to justify their position of "cultural superiority" and "national identity,"[59] and the boys display this connection. Neville, we see, is incredulous at the suggestion that he "should not be a great poet" (83). Bernard identifies with Hamlet and Shelley, and claims that he was "the hero ... of a novel by Dostoevsky; was ... Napoleon; but was Byron chiefly" (249). While it is true that each of the six characters undergoes a series of psychical and somatic transformations in which identities continually alter and blur, Susan speaks for all the girls when she says "[w]e change" (121), but offers no historical, literary, or cultural dimension for it beyond the body. Neville's identification with "Catullus, Horace, [and] Lucretius" (245), and Louis's affirmation, "I ... the companion of Plato, of Virgil" (95), have no female correlative. Such projections have no comparable expression in the lives of the three girls; nor do they affirm their own nobility or historical lineage, as does Louis, who envisions himself as "'a Duke – the last of an ancient race'" (119).

The boys and girls contrast also in terms of self-reflection, which is linked – for the male characters – to the centrality of historical narratives. Unlike Louis, the novel's chronicler of "human history" (66), the girls exhibit few traces of historical memory beyond the margins of their individual selves. Importantly, while Louis's invocation of "our history" transcends the particularities of gender, his compulsion to "unbury – to dig up" (127) the markers of civilization has everything to do with his identification with a masculine tradition. He functions not so much as a repository of historical knowledge, but rather as the actual embodiment of that paternal memory: "What you see ... this Louis, is only the cinders and refuse of something once splendid. I was an Arab prince ... a great poet in the time of Elizabeth ... a Duke at the court of Louis the Fourteenth" (127). We see him selectively evoke the past in order to trace his own place in a transhistorical continuum: "I ... mark ... the long, long history that began in Egypt, in the time of the Pharaohs ... I seem already to have lived many thousands of years" (66). Significantly, Louis traces his lineage back to Egypt, the country which had been under British occupation since 1882, though he does so as colonizer, not as colonized subject. Unlike Rhoda, who perceives herself to be spatially ostracized, Louis is fixed (albeit provisionally) within both British chronology and imperial space. The text frequently utilizes natural imagery – "My roots go down" (96) – in order to convey the magnitude of Louis's sense of longevity, and to essentialize his confidence in his own durability. The text's use of vegetative imagery to describe Louis naturalizes his insinuation into history and suggests the inevitability of his unique role as the excavator and bearer of civilization's multiple ethnic and racial strata. His identification with history and his reverence for "whatever our masters have had to give us" (57) ultimately do not result in a respect for all traditions, but rather degenerate into a universalized sense of masculine entitlement: "a vast inheritance of experience is packed in me" (167).

The text utilizes optical references to suggest a confluence between Louis's observation of historical events and the literal unfolding of human history, ironically signaling how, without his visual vigilance, the world itself would, in effect, desist: "if I shut my eyes ... human history is defrauded of a moment's vision" (66). In contrast to the girls, for whom vision functions primarily as a means of self-reflection, for Louis, *seeing* operates as a kind of generative social surveillance which works to animate and perpetuate the course of world events. Unlike Susan, whose eyes emit "green spurt[s]" (215) that exemplify her identification with nature, or

Jinny, whose preoccupation with mirrors signals her continual self-regard, Louis's disembodied gaze both deflects attention away from his individuality and underscores his sense of self-importance and control. It is precisely Louis's identification with Englishness that authorizes this visually devouring sense of global entitlement. As is the case with the other boys, Louis's sense of entitlement is culturally aligned with Britain's civilizing enterprise. His seemingly benign "I shall inherit" (169) betrays his interest in possession and recalls his childhood desire to be integrated into the military's regulated procession (47). The conflation that repeatedly occurs between "I" and "our" in Louis's speech is a sign of the narrative ease with which he constantly insinuates himself into the company of eminent men, so that his role as usurper invariably links him with an immortal English fraternity: "I roll the dark before me, spreading commerce where there was chaos ... If I press on, from chaos making order, I shall find myself where Chatham stood, and Pitt, Burke, and Sir Robert Peel" (168).

While all of the characters' experiences of identity fluctuate between singularity and diffuseness, Neville, Louis, and Bernard all project the belief in the primacy of a cohesive and independent self in ways which suggest that it is a feature of masculinity. The novel links their insistence on an autonomous "I," however momentary and illusory, with an ability to insert themselves into a larger national–historical framework. The male characters in general tend, more than do the girls, to be aligned with the nucleus of judgement that Kristeva calls the "thetic" position – the "positing of identity or difference."[60] To the extent that the boys are better able to posit the distinction between self and Other, each can be said to operate more as a *spokesman* for the symbolic than can any of the girls. Because each of the boys exhibits a greater tendency toward individuation, each is more likely to insist upon his autonomy than Susan, Jinny or Rhoda can, all of whom resist the impulse to differentiate. It is precisely the male characters' ability to conceptualize the self as distinct, separate, and integral that finally propels them into a space of symbolic enunciation – a space of language and articulation seemingly devoid of any maternal presence.

The boys' masculine identification has much to do with their "ceremonies" (59) – the communal reservoir of patrilineal rites – and illustrates James Donald's observation that national identity is constructed in and through representation: "A nation does not express itself through its culture: it is culture that produces 'the nation.'"[61] The boys' capacity for symbolic representation, their appropriative tendency to impose an arbitrary design and imbue it with some kind of seemingly inherent meaning, arises from their membership in what Neville refers to as a fraternity in which "Plato and Shakespeare are included" (179). Importantly, this consolidation of boundaries draws from a number of historical sources, but is coextensive with the construction of English national identity. Woolf's depiction of the male characters' "imagined linkage" recalls Anderson's argument that a deep sense of horizontal comradeship exists among men who perceive themselves to occupy a coherent national community.[62] Just as Louis had conceptualized his own imperial navigations in terms of the execution of an intelligible design – "We have laced the world together with our ships" (200) – what characterizes male comradeship in this novel is representation, their ability to "spin round [themselves] infinitely fine filaments and construct a system" (179). As the characters negotiate their relation to an imagined community, they mark the boundaries of national space. Bernard's and Neville's first words, "I see a ring" and "I see a globe" (9), respectively, speak directly to this desire to create unity and cohesion by marking the space between inside and outside, importantly, in order to consolidate the group's shared subjectivity. Even Louis, the colonial-born, perpetually attempts to forge a ring around the imperial center: his reference to shipping suggests that he is integral to the Colonial Service and is working to ensure the flow of empire products to a global market. Bernard, Neville, and Louis, particularly, use boundary markers to convey a sense of shared experience and shared geographical space, for they consolidate their Englishness through the symbolic construction of unity: "We are not single" (67). Although Neville adamantly claims at one point to "hate ceremonies" (179), it is precisely his familiarity with pageantry and spectacle, and, moreover, his ability to impose a certain kind of schematic arrangement, that largely distinguish his – and the boys' – experience from that of the girls. As Bernard puts it, "above all [Neville] desires order" (90).

For the girls, by contrast, the concept of systematic ordering and other acts of symbolization are largely elusive or idiosyncratically cryptic. Yet, when the girls do attempt some form of symbolic representation, they often recapitulate familiar Anglocentric tropes, which suggests the ideological intractability of the imperial myth. Thus, for example, Rhoda's exclusion from the world of signs is counter-balanced by a childhood moment in which she constructs an insular world of self-sufficiency, one that is animated by the imagery of colonization and conquest:

> I have a short space of freedom. I have picked all the fallen petals and made them swim … I will now rock the brown basin from side to side so that my ships may ride the waves … my ship … mounts the wave … and reaches the islands where the parrots chatter. (18–19)

Positioning herself as a autocratic figure who controls the destiny of her basin world, Rhoda imagines herself as a solitary traveler whose actions mimic those of British explorers who invaded foreign lands. Her acute interpersonal estrangement masks an alter-ego fueled by conceptions of imperial authority. As Rhoda bends over another "basin," this despotic persona emerges: "I will let the Russian Empress's veil flow about my shoulders. The diamonds of the Imperial crown blaze on my forehead … I am waving my fist at an infuriated mob. 'I am your Empress, people' … I am fearless. I conquer" (56). This is an extraordinary passage, for it exposes the degree to which even Rhoda – the most vulnerable character, who claims to have "no body" (22) and "no face" (33) – seeks to construct a cohesive self through recourse to the dominant discourse of empire. The "fearless" identity she appropriates in her imaginative attempt to create a self-contained universe demonstrates that colonialism – particularly the lasting power of the imperial myth – affects even those who are otherwise denied cultural agency. Yet while Rhoda's investment in an idealized self hinges on an English conception of expansion and cohesion – her "space of freedom" (18) – this enunciation of autonomy is only momentary. Like the other girls, Rhoda is unable to sustain or realize her acts of symbolization: her identification with the moral superiority of Englishness is primarily performative, and her attempts to "seal up, and make entire" (21) the boundaries of her world prove to be futile. Both undertakings are ultimately ineffectual exertions that function as signs of women's ambivalent cultural interpellation.

Significantly, it is in school that the children first exhibit either a resistance to or a facility for representation, an ability that testifies to the gendered nature of enculturation. Susan mocks what she perceives to be the inauthenticity of representations – either pictorial or written – in favor of what she calls "real things," that is, for example, the physical immediacy of "real cows, not school cows" (61). This perceived disparity between the *real* of the corporeal versus the *unreal* of the immaterial is an experiential divide that, for the most part, is overtly gendered throughout the novel; for the girls, it is primarily their preoccupation with the literal that most clearly characterizes their concerns, and problematizes their relation to language. In contrast to Susan, who insists on the primacy of the tangible, or Rhoda, for whom the abstraction of figures "mean[s] nothing" (21), the boys demonstrate a considerable facility for representation. The novel suggests socially constructed reasons for this difference. Meditating on their graduation, Louis's recollection of their academic success invokes the image of a select male enclave whose very existence is indebted to the generative potency of language: as the boys study within chambers on whose walls are "inscribed the names of men of war, of statesmen … men in black gowns," their teacher disseminates knowledge by circulating thick volumes of "Horace, Tennyson, the complete works of Keats and Matthew Arnold suitably inscribed" (58). The repetition of "inscription" here prefigures the link between the boys' identification with historical figures and their ability to inscribe themselves within that historical lineage, and it also suggests how language functions to bestow cultural privilege. Louis's conviction that, like those of other great men, his name will be indelibly etched into the walls of academe – "mine shall be among them" (58) – suggests a dynamic between subjectivity and the influence of ideological constructs that holds true even for the girls, although for them it is conceived in terms that emphasize embodiment.

Women, historical amnesia, and national narrative

While Woolf's portrayal of the boys delineates a model of identity whose subject position hinges on historical precedent, her depiction of the girls exposes the inherent limits on self-creation within what is, in effect, a historical vacuum. Bernard's assessment that for Jinny there existed "no past, no future … [but] merely the moment" (252) can be read as an elucidation of the girls' predicament of being suspended, in Kristeva's words, outside "the time of history": nebulously located within a continuous present, the girls seem to be positioned, as Rhoda puts it, "outside … the loop of time" (22).[63] The characterization of Jinny as one "who respected the moment with complete integrity" exemplifies the female preoccupation with the present, a static momentariness which ensures that she, like Susan and Rhoda, will not only be "without future, or speculation" (265), but without the ability to discern and establish boundaries. This limitation has troubling consequences for the girls' relations to language and national identity. While Anderson argues that the idea of "homogeneous, empty time" is integral to the imagined community of nationhood because it fosters a sense of simultaneity, in Woolf's novel that idea is no guarantee of either historical access or national consciousness. Anderson himself seems to acknowledge the gendered dimension of his understanding of temporal simultaneity when he links "fraternity, power and time meaningfully together", a conjunction that conspicuously omits femininity.[64] In contrast to the boys, who repeatedly posit the desirability of an indissoluble "I," the girls' formation of selfhood is never sufficiently fixed or stable to imagine itself in such discrete terms.

The girls' psychic landscapes, though varied, can be characterized by the way in which their 'selves' are frequently indistinguishable from, and continuous with, their surrounding world, rather than defined in opposition to it. Such permeable identities interfere with national identity because they fail to demarcate the boundary that is axiomatic of Englishness. Susan's identification with the natural landscape confirms her permeability, at the same time as it diminishes her specificity. Trading on the conventional trope of woman as landscape, Susan asserts: "I am not a woman, but the light that falls on this gate ... I am the seasons ... the mud, the mist, the dawn ... I am the field ... the barn ... the trees" (98, 97). Neither Susan's assertion of her omnipresence – "I cannot be divided, or kept apart" – nor Jinny's admission of her constant oscillation – "I do not settle long anywhere" – is utilized, at such moments, as a vehicle for egotism. Instead, Susan's identification with the natural world and Jinny's peripatetic self both work to obscure, rather than to amplify, a sense of the "self" as a singular entity. Rather than articulating an "I am" which sees itself as both singular and indelible, and is based upon individuation, the girls are more likely to substitute "I feel" as their mark of self-definition. Indeed, throughout the text the girls' focus is primarily on sensation, on that which is tangible, palpable, and immediate – in Jinny's words, "what one touches, what one tastes" (220). For them, identity is experienced largely through some relation to the body, even, as is the case with Rhoda, when that body seems to be barely present. Although both Susan, as the novel's earth-mother, and Jinny, as a heterosexually conceived coquette, embody different culturally constructed feminine selves, each visualizes her subjectivity through an intense identification with her own physicality. Identity, in each case, arises from the ability to reproduce conventional models of British womanhood – models which, whether generative or purely sexual, are dependent on some valorization of an essentialized female body. Bernard's claim, "[i]t was Susan who first became wholly woman, purely feminine" (247–8), underscores the way in which her compliance with the conventions of maternity recapitulates a recognizable model of femininity within the context of empire.

Susan is an exemplary model of the period's widespread belief that a British woman's primary role is that of "guardian of the race."[65] Although the novel does not explicitly invoke eugenicist discourse in conjunction with Susan, we know that her sole function is reproductive, and that she is linked with territory. Unlike the boys, who imagine their own continuation in terms of various inflated imaginative projections, Susan's only assurance of longevity is that her "children will carry [her] on" (132). The text repeatedly associates Susan with vegetable and animal imagery – "I shall eat nuts and peer for eggs through the brambles" (14) – the cumulative effect of which suggests that because "[a]ll the world is breeding" (100) Susan too is assured fertility: "I shall lie like a field bearing crops in rotation [...] more will come, more children; more cradles" (131, 173). We can begin to see an association between the female body and the motherland here, for Susan literalizes the genealogical principle that national identity is conferred through one's relation to territory. If Susan is, by virtue of her reproductive function, both body and land, she is also a space that has been colonized by an imperial masculinity. Like a British map whose places of conquest have been colored in with shades of red, Susan is a woman whose body has been marked as imperial territory: "life stands round me like glass round the imprisoned red" (192). Thus, although Susan gloats about Percival's territorial acquisitions – "He will come home, bringing me trophies to be laid at my feet. He will increase my possessions" (172) – she is a national signifier whose cultural agency is severely circumscribed; she is a symbol of the nation, but is not herself its legitimate heir. Despite Susan's fantasy of territorial increase, and her imaginative projection that, through Percival's intervention, she herself "shall see India" (172) and vicariously colonize foreign lands, the reader knows that she is forever fixed in place, denied geographical movement or autonomy.

Although *The Waves* idealizes the maternal through Percival, it simultaneously shows how, for women, literal motherhood is an impediment to selfhood. Determined by the demands of her procreative being, Susan is driven by "the bestial and beautiful passion of maternity" (132); at one point she exhibits a potential for maternal violence when, spinning round her child a protective "cocoon made of [her] own blood" (171), she threatens to attack any intruder who would dare approach her sleeping baby. This reference to blood evokes the notion of race preservation, reminding readers of the national significance of the maternal role. Through her representation of Susan, Woolf brings together a series of interrelated signifiers for Englishness: the ideology of the soil; the notion of blood-right; and the idea of racial purity. Like a maternal machine whose body is "used daily ... like a tool" (215), Susan's immersion in the physical precludes a familiarity with anything beyond her immediate sphere; as a result, when she speaks she conveys elemental emotions, "I love ... and I hate" (15). Although her impulses are naturalized throughout the text, there is a point of rupture in which she diverges from her alleged instinct by self-consciously remarking that she is "sick of natural happiness ... and children ... sick of the body" (191) and its relentless reproduction. This momentary recognition of her life's circumscription – "I am fenced in, planted here like one of my own trees" (190) – never translates into a full-scale retreat from an identification with maternity, but it does draw attention to the self's split subjectivity.

Ultimately, however, the text is interested not in Susan's evolution but in illustrating how she embodies cultural assumptions about British womanhood, namely, the idea that mothers and territory are guarantors of racial stability. *The Waves* suggests that women's corporeal identification is what characterizes their collaboration in the ideological work of empire: because they are seen only as bodies, in other words, they are implicitly incompatible with the spiritual aims of citizenship. The intensified image of the female body reiterated throughout the text – linked to sex (Jinny), childbirth (Susan), and death (Rhoda) – reminds one of the pervasive interwar-years' public discourses which argued that women's physiology made them unfit to enter public life. Jinny represents another version of the self realized in overtly physical terms: the novel frequently uses animal imagery to describe her and Susan, for, like animals, they are exclusively focused upon that which is immediately accessible. As Jinny puts it: "I see what is before me" (220). But where Susan often appears the model of physical tranquility, Jinny inhabits a kind of kinetic energy: she flutters through the novel, never static, always dancing, pirouetting, moving ceaselessly back and forth with a body that, by her own admission, "has a life of its own" (63). While Susan may be fertile to overflowing, Jinny is the only one whom we observe in moments of "heat and rapture" (63). Such moments of rapturous intensity indicate not merely Jinny's obsessive involvement with her body, but the broad limitations of women's imaginative scope, with negative implications for female forms of national belonging.

Jinny is the novel's most extreme example of woman's investment in a heterosexually conceived notion of British female beauty; her preoccupation with feminine artifice – "the infinite variety of women's dresses (I note all clothes always) delight me" (220) – is evidence of her collusion with masculinist, as well as racialized, imperial propaganda. Jinny is doubly situated, both as a woman who exerts control by deploying colonialist tropes, and as someone who is herself colonized by commodity culture. Aligning herself with the thrill of conquest, Jinny joins the "triumphant procession" through London, contrasting her "reddened lips and [her] finely pencilled eyebrows" with the image of "savages in loin cloths, women whose hair is dank, whose long breasts sag, with children tugging at their breasts" (194). While Woof links Jinny's use of cosmetics to sexual autonomy and self-legitimization, she simultaneously associates it with imperial imagery in order to foreground how the construction of a feminized mass cultural ideal is fueled by a dominant aesthetic of white racial beauty. Although she does not dwell on the racialized implications of cosmetic artifice, Woolf's portrayal of the female interest in powder and paint arguably alludes to this deeply embedded cultural stereotype concerning race. With her red lips and patent-leather shoes, Jinny strides through London's shopping thoroughfare – Piccadilly South, Piccadilly North, Regent Street, and the Haymarket – and re-imagines herself as a colonial invader, walking on "sanded paths of victory driven through the jungle" (194). Positioned as a stereotypical female consumer, Jinny's imperial imagination authorizes her entry into the public realm. Of course Jinny herself is sometimes positioned as the aggressively made-up exotic "native," petulantly powdering her face and reddening her lips as she "make[s] the angle of [her] eyebrows sharper than usual" (195), but this does not destabilize her identification with Englishness because her cosmetic savagery is really only a form of consumer tourism. Indeed, her encounter with consumer culture – she admiringly gazes upon "gauzes and silks illumined in glass cases and underclothes trimmed with a million close stitches of fine embroidery" (195) – is represented as a kind of debased ritual practice, the only legitimate outlet for the Englishwoman in search of transformation. Female subjectivity is consolidated, Woolf suggests, through cultural mirrors that reflect an image of imperial femininity.

All of the characters depend, to varying degrees, on physical reflection as a means by which to consolidate and maintain some notion of a cohesive identity, but the girls are unable to project themselves into the past or see themselves reflected in historical artifacts, as are the boys.[66] Although they too at times deploy metaphors of exploration and appear to access alternate geographical spaces – Rhoda, for example, "looks far away … beyond India" (139) – such moments of imagined self-amplification never result in literal transformation; nor are they conducive to their escape from masculinist notions of difference. Rather, for the women, reflection functions as a way of assembling the self, even when that self repeatedly resists consolidation, as is the case with Rhoda. Jinny provides the clearest example of the girls' repeated use of reflection as a means of self-identification; not surprisingly, she is also the only woman whose self-absorption is literalized through a preoccupation with actual and figurative mirrors. At one point she flirts with a stranger on a train and observes: "My body instantly of its own accord puts forth a frill under his gaze" (63). This man's gaze functions both as validation of her feminine allure and as a vehicle for her own self-involvement; whether through the gaze of men or that of literal mirrors, Jinny needs always a reflective surface. Her love of her own image seems at times pathological, and recalls Freud's largely female linkage of narcissism to the identificatory investment in another. At the same time, there is undeniably something exhilarating about Jinny's frenetic flutters and ripples, her unabated determination to "excite eagerness" at every moment (195), even though one senses something disconcerting about the way in which her kinetic energy appears to mask a contentless depth: "I can imagine nothing beyond the circle cast by my body" (129). Jinny's face in the mirror constitutes an attempt to see the self as organized and integrated, for she assembles herself primarily through the projection of an illusion: "I always prepare myself for the sight of myself" (193). It makes sense that Jinny should loathe the night, darkness, and even sleep, instead longing for the illumination of the day, because her self depends on the ubiquitous presence of reflection (54). More than self-involvement, Jinny's ritualistic self-regard has to do with her desire for some mark of identity coherence, of which the women appear to be categorically denied.

Nowhere is the construction of identity more problematical than in the text's representation of Rhoda, whose paralyzing inability to access the conventions of British womanhood and articulate a cohesive "I" together precipitate a kind of linguistic breakdown. Like both Susan and Jinny, Rhoda participates in mirroring as a way to establish some semblance of an integrated self; but where the others use inanimate objects or men, Rhoda uses other women. Her "hopeless desire to be Susan, to be Jinny" manifests itself in a relentless pantomime in which she is forever imitating their gestures, "copying what they do" in order to emulate appropriate feminine behavior (27, 43). Rhoda struggles to put on the masquerade of femininity, but her constant parody never inculcates in her an ability to authenticate her own experience. Jinny and Susan, models who embody traditional roles of womanliness, are ultimately inadequate prototypes for Rhoda, the only female character who does not define herself in terms of conventional femininity. At one point Rhoda even gazes into a mirror for congruence, but her countenance, "reflected mistily," immediately retreats from its amorphous image: "That is my face … in the looking-glass … But I will duck … to hide it, for … I have no face […] Susan and Jinny have faces … Their world is the real world" (138, 43). Rhoda regards herself as an internal exile, displaced from the "real world" that is England; like Louis, she laments her homelessness even though, like all the others, she is geographically fixed within the imperial center. Yet, in contrast to Louis, her spatial dislocation is not counterbalanced by moments of rootedness and stability. Without this conscious awareness of being part of an imagined national community, Rhoda is unable to construct a cohesive, historically generated, subjectivity. Because she has difficulty in demarcating the boundary between inside and outside, she has trouble not only in situating herself within the cultural space of England but in registering the limits of her own female body. Rhoda's refrain "I have no face" (33) arguably speaks to her realization that she has unsuccessfully put on the mask of imperial femininity, just as her confession that the "human face is hideous to me" (159) can be read as a critique of the travesty of feminine artifice within empire. Unable to situate herself within the geography of either the English imagination or female convention, Rhoda is truly culturally nowhere. Instead, she retreats into a private sphere in which her self-reflective "dreaming eyes" conjure amorphous, imaginary geographies: "I dream; I dream" (252; 45); thus, it comes as no surprise that she loathes reflecting surfaces that verify this absence: "I hate looking-glasses which show me my real face" (44).

Because female subjectivity is dependent upon at least limited access to the imperial narrative via bodily inscription, Rhoda has trouble consolidating a coherent self. Rhoda has a body, of course, but her body finds no place within the existing domestic ideology of empire as either a maternal or erotic site. Unlike Susan and Jinny, Rhoda personifies no apparent feminine or imperial norm – "no single body for me to follow" – upon which to establish such a correlation (130). As a result, the body never functions for Rhoda as an instrument, as it does for Susan, with which to establish a relation to the material world; nor does it operate as a catalyst for the kind of self-reflective involvement we see reified in Jinny. Her body, so transparent that it "lets the light through" (45), is diffuse to the point of ghostliness; Rhoda's need to "touch something hard" (159) shows her desire to establish some contact, albeit momentary, with her own corporeality. Rhoda's "ill-fitting body" (105), rather than anchoring her within the boundaries of the British empire, instead exiles her to a nebulous fringe space outside of the culture of conquest and domination: "Now I spread my body on this frail mattress and hang suspended. I am above the earth now" (27). But rather than liberating her from the confinement of an imperial identity, this moment illustrates only the terror of existing on the periphery of empire. Neville registers this when he observes Rhoda flying "with her neck outstretched and blind fanatic eyes, past us" (198), a spastic image that speaks to her disconsolate disembodiment, exiled to a space of cultural liminality. She frequently feels herself falling, sinking, being "rocked from side to side" (43), or "cast up and down, like a cork on a rough sea" (107), sensations that contrast sharply with her moment of imperial triumph, controlling her petals in a basin, Britannia-like, so that her "ships may ride the waves" (19). Rhoda's description of herself as dispersed: "I am the foam that sweeps and fills the uttermost rims of the rocks with whiteness; I am also a girl" (107), is the novel's most explicit evidence that identity is produced through one's relation to geographical location.

Rhoda's character illuminates the primary principle of Englishness, that identity is constructed through an identification with place; a citizen of nowhere,

Rhoda compensatorily deploys spatial and architectural metaphors in order to construct monuments of cultural belonging that reproduce the exclusionary and totalizing claims of empire. Her idealized image of home is a figure for the nation as well as for the maternal body, and marks her longing for national inclusion. Bernard's characterization of Rhoda as "the nymph of the fountain, always wet, obsessed with visions, dreaming" (274) speaks to her otherworldliness, but ignores the extent to which her private musings engage with narratives of Englishness. His depiction of her as "wild" (247) and "wandering vaguely" (252) would seem to consolidate the overall sense we have of her as not only fluid and diffuse, but disengaged from what Ian Baucom calls "the identity endowing properties of place" that are so fundamental to the formation of English selfhood.[67] The reappearance of the "cadaverous space of the puddle" (64) which Rhoda has difficulty crossing illustrates this spatial displacement. The puddle can be read as a figure for the erosion of identity, the dissolution of ego boundaries that constantly threaten to engulf her. Rhoda is forever negotiating the periphery of this conceptual puddle, whose spaciousness alludes not to the limitless possibilities of the English imagination but to the "enormous gulf" which severs her from her own body and the intimacy of other people (159). Even though she and Louis are both preoccupied with lodgement, it is finally only Rhoda who, as a woman who cannot successfully access the culturally prescribed feminine roles, remains unbound to place, "unattached, without anchorage anywhere, unconsolidated" (122). She constructs an alternative geographical sphere – "a world immune from change" (107) – in an attempt to counter her profound dislocation.

If Rhoda's attention to geometric shapes seems idiosyncratic, her rhetoric draws from domestic and imperial idioms that allude to the home as a metaphor for the nation: "A square is stood upon the oblong and we say, 'This is our dwelling place. The structure is now visible. Very little is left outside'" (228). Rhoda's promotion of insularity, her desire to construct a "house which contains us all" (205), and her erection of a boundary between internal and external spaces, recalls Gikandi's argument that Englishness is defined through "simultaneous acts of inclusion and exclusion."[68] Rhoda's colonization of space suggests a form of nation-building that mimics and reproduces the discourse of empire, even though her home seems to exist in a world apart; by staking a claim to "the house we have made" (205), she situates herself within an imagined collectivity of British subjects.[69] Although Rhoda is immersed in the details of her invented surroundings, she also recognizes that her visionary dwelling-place is a stark "consolation" (163) because it is, finally, a simulation. In contrast to the boys, whose structure-making accommodates them within the existing imperial order, Rhoda's architectural construction exiles her to the extreme periphery, to "the verge of [a] world" (205) that cannot literally incorporate her. If, as critics have argued, the female body is a figure for the bounded space of both home and nation, then Rhoda's fetishizing of the "perfect dwelling-place" (163) can be read as a desire for not only a place within England but for the inaccessible plentitude of the lost maternal body.[70] Makiko Minow-Pinkney reasonably reads Rhoda's dislocation to be a result of her unsuccessful repression of the mother, arguing that her problems stem from her failure to identify with the paternal symbolic order. Although one can certainly interpret

Rhoda's preoccupation with structure-building as a covert identification with the paternal, what is also true is that the idea of home, as many have argued, functions as a figure for the "originary birthplace" and "enigmatic homeland" of the maternal body, from which the subject has been "irrevocably exiled."[71] Rhoda has no father (20), but she also has no mother, provoking us to wonder if her dislocation is perhaps a sign of maternal absence rather than cathexis. All of Rhoda's references to "our dwelling-place" (228) would support a reading of the home as a figure for the maternal, for they occur, crucially, within the context of her invocation of Percival, the text's maternal figure. Recalling Gaston Bachelard's argument that the "maternal features of the house" are "enclosed, protected," and radiate "enveloping warmth," Rhoda recollects her paradisiacal "dwelling-place" in terms that suggest intrinsic satiation and comfort: "The sweetness of this content overflowing runs down the walls of my mind, and liberates understanding" (163).[72] In *The Waves*, this dwelling has a linguistic analogue in Percival, the maternal body through which the characters strive to colonize a new home in the symbolic order. Rhoda, however, is unable to participate in this narrative project for, suspended outside the sphere of time and rationality, she cannot satisfactorily access the disruptive potential of the maternal. Rather, Rhoda embodies the novel's most extreme example of what it means to be immersed in a non-symbolizable feminine space.[73]

Gender, language acquisition, and the imperial narrative

From the novel's opening pages, the boys' and girls' contrasting experiences confront us with the problem of language acquisition and its inextricable relation to identity and gender difference within empire. Although the girls, too, are educated under an imperial system – Jinny imagines sitting with the other girls "under a portrait of Queen Alexandra" (23), the wife of Edward VII – their exposure to language does not confer or solidify, as it does for the boys, a sense of national identification. Where the boys approach language as something to conquer and dominate, and are thereby bound together by a sense of common culture, the girls lack discursive facility on any terms, and consequently do not derive a similar sense of collective identification. In an early sequence suggestive of a classroom setting, Woolf demonstrates how each child's subjectivity is linked to his or her acquisition of language. This portrayal suggests that the children have already interpellated their culturally prescribed gender roles, recalling Raymond Williams's observation: "'Nation' as a term is radically connected with 'native.' We are born into relationships which are typically settled in a place."[74] In *The Waves*, that "place" reflects the interdependence of gender and imperial ideologies. We see Neville, like Louis, preoccupied with learning the specifics of sentence structure, focusing on conjugations and tenses, as a way of orienting and empowering himself in the world: "Each tense … means different. There is an order in this world" (21). Similarly, Louis's conviction that he can solidify his perceptions through language – "to fix in words, to forge in a ring of steel" – has to do with his expectation that discourse, like all experience, is subject to manipulation and control (40). In contrast to this approach to language as something that is both highly structured and controllable, Bernard's first encounter with words evokes an image of linguistic disruption according to which, as he articulates the sounds aloud, the words dynamically "flick their tails right and left … they move through the air in flocks … moving all together, now dividing, now coming together" (20). Yet even at this early stage of taking pleasure in a certain linguistic fluidity and autonomy, Bernard shows traces of a kinship with the regulatory impulses of Louis and Neville: like theirs, his self-perception is dependent on an organized system, for "when … there is no longer any sequence … he … falls silent, gaping as if about to burst into tears" (39). This vacillation anticipates Bernard's ambivalent relation to textuality, but what is important here is that he, like the other boys, evinces a facility for language that ultimately eludes each of the girls.

Nowhere in Jinny's, Susan's, or Rhoda's responses do we see evidence of a self-confidence like Louis's regarding the knowability of language, in which comprehension of the sentence confers a sense of encyclopedic access and global entitlement: "I know my cases and my genders; I could know everything in the world if I wished" (20). This linkage of the grammatical and the ontological, Julie Vandivere observes, not only puns on the words *gender* (as both sex and grammatical classification) and *case* (as both circumstance and grammatical category), but reveals the novel's most fundamental concern: "In making grammatical systems, one makes the world, and in making the world, one makes grammar."[75] Vandivere does not explore the imperial implications of this equation, but her observations are central to an understanding of how Woolf genders language acquisition and links it to cultural agency. Instead of linguistic fluency, the girls' responses to language range from distraction to antipathy. When Jinny does her lessons she responds aesthetically to the "yellow words … fiery words" (21), associating them with a tangible sensuality. Similarly, Susan literalizes the words, visualizing them in terms that are immediately accessible: "Those are white words … like stones one picks up by the seashore" (20). Although Susan uses a simile, she in general resists the figural and, even here, she employs it to foreground the materiality of language: what is important to her is that words are concrete entities, things that mark reality. In contrast to Bernard, whose love of metaphor and the slipperiness of language ensures that he will, according to Susan, ethereally "wander off … slip away … rise up higher, with words and words in phrases," she herself is weighed down by literalism, "tied down with single words" (16). What the girls lack is the potential for representational mastery, as well as a sense of language's malleability and play. They lack Bernard's tremendous faith in the transformative potential of language – his belief that "words … will break up this knot of hardness" (15) among people. Susan's repeated reference to "some hard thing" lodged within her body functions as material evidence of her sense of linguistic impediment; it is no coincidence that this undisclosed "something hard" first surfaces at school, with the introduction of language (54, 98). Jinny's disclosure crystallizes the girls' linguistic failure: "When I read, a purple rim runs round the black edge of the textbook. Yet I cannot follow any word through its changes. I cannot follow any thought from present to past" (42). The most extreme example of this temporal and linguistic blur is illustrated by Rhoda, whose anxious disregard for learning and language – "I flung words in fans like these the sower throws over the ploughed fields" (205) – sets her apart even from the other girls.

Unlike the boys, whose interest in narrative structure colludes with the processes of imperialism, the girls do not see language as an extension of the self's sovereignty and control. Woolf draws repeated parallels between the construction of a masculine ego and the discursive ramifications of empire-building. Bernard illustrates this when he refers to Louis's desire to unify the six of them through writing, invoking the color of imperial conquest: "How then ... would Louis roof us all in ... confine us, make us one, with his red ink ...?" (282). *The Waves* illustrates how masculine interest in the fixity of the self is tied to an investment in the laws of syntax and the logic of sequential momentum that conveys a sense of imperial mastery. For example, as Louis sits in an eating-shop reading a book that contains "forged rings," he positions himself as a linguistic conqueror: "I oppose to what is passing this ramrod of beaten steel ... I will not submit to ... the words that trail drearily without human meaning; I will reduce you to order" (95). Here, Louis utilizes language to regulate, to contain, and to demarcate that which is potentially knowable, much in the same way that he deployed ships to far corners of the earth in order to colonize native populations. Louis's pedagogical interest in the well-ordered sentence calls to mind Alastair Pennycook's discussion of the development of language policies under British colonialism: like colonial policy-makers who argued that English would "provide instruction in moral behaviour," Louis maintains that the "binding power" of language can "remove that degradation" that pervades the lives of the "cheap and the worthless" (95).[76] Echoing the British Bureau of Education in 1920, Louis sees English instruction as an ameliorative project, bringing enlightenment to backward peoples "in quest of civilisation" (95).[77] The cultural power of masculine privilege is not related merely to linguistic agency, but arises precisely from the boys' ability to inscribe themselves into being.

The Waves encodes culturally constructed definitions of difference in order to exaggerate the relation between linguistic privilege and gender identity. In doing so, it illustrates the arbitrariness of such binary oppositions, but also their decisive power to shape gendered subjects. Woolf's depiction of Neville as "the most slavish of students," surrounded by dictionaries and notebooks, who is willing to "follow the curve of a sentence wherever it might lead" (88), clearly signals the benefits of educational privilege. At one point, as Louis listens to Dr. Crane deliver a sermon, his tumescent response parodically materializes phallic privilege: "Now all is laid by his authority ... I feel come over me the sense of the earth under me, and my roots going down and down till they wrap themselves round some hardness at the center. I recover my continuity, as he reads. I become a figure in the procession, a spoke in the huge wheel that turning, at last erects me, here and now ... (as he reads) I rise" (35). The text here draws a parallel between narrative design and sexual trajectory, illustrating how male libidinal energy and linguistic control are interrelated; through Louis's arousal, Woolf suggests, the male engagement with texts solidifies the cultural power of homosocial ties by subordinating the feminine ("the sense of the earth under me"). The use of sexual imagery in conjunction with male linguistic potency is not confined to Louis, for we see instances in which both Neville and Bernard embody similar, although less emphatically masculine, literary–erotic impulses. Although the undulating motion of the waves is associated with each of the characters, and occurs repeatedly to signal the dialectic between identity and its inevitable loss, at one point Neville's use of that imagery draws attention to the ideological link between narrative and sexual conventions: "Now begins to rise in me the familiar rhythm; words that have lain dormant now lift, now toss their crests, and fall and rise, and fall and rise again. I am a poet, yes. Surely I am a great poet" (83). Instead of erecting himself as a definitive subject, Neville alternates between having a stable relationship with words and acknowledging them as "artificial, insincere" (83). It is not surprising that this revelation is accompanied by feelings of impotence and dissolution, in which some part of him "turns to foam and falsity" (83), for Neville's resistance to the totalizing claims of symbolic discourse are a consequence of his homosexuality. Although English linguistic values, the novel suggests, are sustained by homosocial relations between men, homosexuality itself threatens male supremacy.

The divided perspective on language that we see reflected in Neville is most pronounced in Bernard, whose belief in the sustaining power of English words is counterbalanced by a deep dissatisfaction with symbolic discourse. Of the three boys, Bernard most extremely exemplifies the continual vacillation between identity and dissolution, and, tellingly, the sexual imagery used to describe his linguistic fluency combines masculine and feminine elements. Bernard's meditation, as he expectantly awaits Percival's arrival at the group's communal dinner party, illustrates this androgynous lexical fecundity in which "[i]mages breed instantly" and he is "embarrassed by [his] own fertility" (117). Language here is realized in explicitly sexual terms as Bernard's autoerotic imagination generates a series of fertile images which first "breed" and then "explode" in an obviously phallic ("rocket") "explosion." Bernard's linguistic "joy of intercourse" (118) underscores his polymorphous experience, for what transpires here is a hermaphroditic scene of self-fertilization in which he functions as both agent and receptacle. There are several moments in the text that draw attention to Bernard's linguistic fertility, suggesting that ideas, like children, need to gestate before they can be produced. But whereas Bernard is depicted "[s]welling perpetually augmented … [with] … a vast accumulation of unrecorded matter in [his] head" waiting "some day to fructify," the novel's literal reproductive figure, Susan, never swells with a single idea that is then similarly realized in language (272, 157).

The girls' diffused ego boundaries are an impediment to their own linguistic fluency, although they facilitate the symbolic projects of men. Bernard's observation that Susan "was born to be the adored of poets, since poets require safety," crystallizes the novel's acknowledgement that traditional discourse is dependent upon both the silencing of female speech and the valorizing of conventional paradigms of femininity (248). Lacking the boys' linguistic agency and apprehension, Susan's relation to language is one of continual frustration. She recounts the way in which, even as a child, language eluded her grasp: "I jumped up and ran after the words that trailed like the dangling string from an air ball, up and up, from branch to branch escaping," while she stood fixed, like an "imprisoned reed," watching the words evaporate (192). In contrast to Bernard's words, which take "flight" with endless possibility, Susan's own words remain persistently earth-bound, unable to cohere, to form associative links. Powerless to discern or decipher her discursive universe, Susan understands only the language of elemental emotions: "The only sayings I understand are cries of love, hate, rage and pain" (131). The girls' identities, inexorably tied to the requirements of body, give rise to a language that reflects their engagement with the literal. Susan perceives her only defense against the indeterminacy of language to be the solidity of her own body, which, as she asserts to Neville, is capable of "quenching the silver-grey flickering moth-wing quiver of words with the green spurt of [her] clear eyes" (215).

Despite its potency, however, the materiality of the body never generates a liberatory discursive practice in *The Waves* along the lines which some proponents of feminine discourse have suggested is possible. The libidinal and elemental forces of their bodies never provide Susan, Jinny, or Rhoda with any collective resistance to symbolic discourse: they are able neither to inscribe themselves into language through the body, nor to deconstruct the dominant discourse of empire which excludes them. Susan and Jinny do at moments evince linguistic interest, but it remains subordinate to the possibility of a heterosexual union. This is most clearly reflected in Jinny, for whom body language is a way to create rapport with potential lovers; she is adept at reading the vocabulary of the body, deftly "decipher[ing] the hieroglyphs written on other people's faces" in order to secure intimacy (175). We see evidence of this desire for incorporation when Jinny converses at a party, flirtatiously engaged with a potential suitor. What transpires is an eroticized moment of linguistic consummation: "Words crowd and cluster ... jostle and mount ... We are together ... That is my moment of ecstasy" (104). In contrast to the boys, for whom sexual imagery suggests linguistic possibility, for Jinny language only paves the way to its own sexual foreclosure. Jinny admits that "it does not matter what I say" (104). Although the arbitrariness of the relation between signifier and signified will eventually be celebrated by Bernard, none of the girls registers this possibility of linguistic play as liberatory. For them, language has a utilitarian or performative, but never a subversive, function. Jinny puts out a "new unread book in case Bernard comes, or Neville or Louis," further signaling how language for her is both arbitrary and performative, a way to forge interpersonal connection rather than a vehicle for self-definition (195).

Significantly, it is Rhoda, the woman with the least conventional female role within British culture, who evinces the greatest alienation from language. Language neither confers an integrated identity nor situates Rhoda within the symbolic order: "I am not composed enough ... to make even one sentence ... I am interrupted" (106–7). Rhoda provides the text's clearest evidence that in order to speak and write, one must be able not only to conceptualize the self as a discrete entity, but to access and deploy the imperial narrative. The first indication we have of this is when she is in school, and feels the "terror" begin when her teacher draws figures on the blackboard and she has "no answer" (21). Rhoda fails at language, in Kristevan terms, precisely because she is unable to situate herself within historical, or linear, time. Importantly, it is *British* time and space from which Rhoda is estranged, a fact betrayed by her disclosure: "I ... draw a figure and the world is looped in it, and I myself am outside the loop" (21). Again, Rhoda tries to construct a boundary and thereby access the enabling narrative of empire. Despite her engagement with the discourse of inclusion and exclusion, Rhoda remains "outside the [imperial] loop" (21); Louis describes her as the one "who hung back and turned aside when the herd assembled and galloped with orderly, sleek backs over the rich pastures" (203). This inability, or refusal, to align herself with the cultural center of Englishness is a sign of her resistance to domination, but it is also the source of her deep alienation and despair. Although her silence appears at times to be a viable resistance to the normalizing strictures of symbolic discourse, Rhoda's profound incapacitation – her painful estrangements and eventual suicide – prevents us from celebrating her alleged "feminine way of knowing" as either liberatory or successfully subversive. [78]

While critics have read Rhoda's "strange communications" (98) as a site of resistance to the dominant discourse of empire, such an interpretation under-estimates the extent to which her visions themselves often rely upon Orientalist and primitivist imagery. Thus, for example, as she "float[s] suspended" (205) she imagines herself climbing a hill from whose top she is able to "see Africa" (206) – the last continent over which Britain vied for imperial control – while elsewhere she envisions "the drumming of naked men with assegais" (140). Such imaginative moments of colonial tourism, however, do not accompany or give rise to linguistic engagement or control. By contrast, Bernard's visualizing of "savages in Tahiti spearing fish ... or a naked man eating raw flesh" (187) – pictures similarly drawn from a colonial imaginary – results in his desire to "coax into words" (189) his myriad impressions so that he can unify them into a single overarching narrative. Although Rhoda's imagination is imbued with imperial signifiers, that imagery fails to authorize a writing practice, or any other "order in this world" (20). But, ironically, this failure may, in itself, amount to a form of redemption for Woolf. If, in exerting linguistic mastery one constructs the world, then the female characters are implicitly absolved from any responsibility for empire. This argument is very similar to one that Woolf makes in *Three Guineas*, where women are upheld as model "civilized human beings" (75) because they have been sequestered from the masculinized "world ... of public life" (18). But, paradoxically, in *The Waves*, where these two gendered worlds are linguistically configured, women's access to language is ultimately imagined precisely through those tropes of domination and conquest that, elsewhere, Woolf self-consciously eschews. In *The Waves*, perhaps more than in any other of her works, Woolf acknowledges that women's quest for linguistic inclusion is legitimized by and embedded in the doctrine of expansion and rule.

The imperial mother: Percival, eucharistic cannibalism, and national unity

As the characters struggle to acquire language, the previous sections have attempted to show, they simultaneously strive to access the dominant narrative of imperialism – the story that, as Gikandi argues, forms "the core of a common British identity."[79] In *The Waves*, language *thematically* confers this sense of national identity unevenly among the male and female characters, even as those linguistic disparities are *formally* dissolved. By intermittently blurring the six voices, Woolf seeks to draw attention to the nation as the effect of a collective rather than of an individual identification. Experientially, the six characters share many common bonds: their "rich legacy of memories"; their connection with an ancestral past; their "expressed desire to continue a common life"; and their shared longing for a collective identity.[80] Although the six voices retain, at intervals, the specificity of discrete entities, the multiple differences that characterize them diminish almost entirely when they are situated in relation to Percival, whom they collectively desire and with whom they experience momentary cohesion. This section demonstrates that Percival embodies the nation as "a soul, a spiritual principle"[81] around which the people cohere, though the exact meaning of that "principle" requires elaboration. As with the other male characters, Percival contains within him the potential to disrupt the dominance of symbolic structures; this liminality, Woolf suggests, holds the libera-tory potential to transform culture. Woolf's depiction of Percival as a character problematizes gender categories precisely because his covert structural function of signifying desire is at such odds with his overt masculinity. Woolf utilizes primarily militaristic imagery to describe him, so that from the idealized perspective of the other six, who remain mere "soldiers in the presence of their captain" (123), he embodies the chivalric aspect of a "medieval commander" who dominates "his faithful servants" (37).

Published during England's revival of medievalism, when Arthurian imagery – replete with knights, castles, armour, and heraldry – figured prominently in public discourse, *The Waves* incorporates elements of the Grail quest popularized by Jessie Weston's *From Ritual to Romance* (1920).[82] Also during this period the Round Table movement – a group of "British race patriots" – published *The Round Table* magazine and dedicated themselves to the maintenance of empire through "the world-wide ascendancy of the Anglo-Saxons."[83] By referring to Percival as a "medieval commander," Woolf borrows from the language of chivalry in order both to ironize Percival's imperial crusade, and to align her character with the super-natural forces of prehistoric England. Percival's name alludes to the mythological figure involved in fantastic feats who embarked, at the behest of King Arthur, on the quest for the sacred Grail, the cup that allegedly contained the blood of the crucified Christ.[84] Although *The Waves* features no sacred cup, Percival himself functions as a living Grail, embodying both Christian and pagan associations of rebirth that speak to Woolf's belief that the "exalted emotions" generated for this "one object in common" – the Grail – create a sense of "unity … which belong to the essence of our being."[85] Paul Rich demonstrates how the English preservation of the medieval chivalric code supported conservative notions of historical continuity that privileged the English gentleman as the racial survivor of an heroic age and celebrated behavior that re-inscribed patriarchy, heterosexuality, and nationalism.[86] Woolf deploys these associations, often ironically, to critique the view that mind-less obedience to a "general" is intrinsically "beautiful" (47), but at the same time she depicts Percival's metonymic association with the Grail – specifically, its nutritive aspect and its links with maternity, fertility, unification, and rebirth – to signal hope for England's cultural regeneration. Like the Grail itself, which is charac-terized by indeterminacy and absence, Percival is the abjected body which represents the loss of the mother/land, reminding us of Kristeva's contention that the "abject is the violence of mourning for an 'object' that has always already been lost."[87]

Percival's military engagement suggests not only patriarchal aggression – "brutal in the extreme" (39) – but also patriarchal language. Although Neville claims that Percival is incapable of reading (48), he remains allied with "Latin phrases" (36) through his dissemination of "the violent language [of the West] that is natural to him" (136). By connecting Percival with Latin, a language in which the British upper classes were schooled, and by showing him gazing upon an ancient "Roman wall" (71) situated within the English landscape, Woolf alludes to the late nineteenth–early twentieth-century identification of Britain and Rome that served to justify British imperialism as "the culmination of a natural, evolutionary progress."[88] Percival's identification with Rome signals an ardent hyper-masculine British nationalism. It comes as no surprise that Susan is the woman "whom he loves" (123), for she personifies the motherland and embodies the hope for territorial expansion. Woolf suggests a relation between linguistic aggressiveness and imperialism, aligning Percival's instinctive use of "violent language" with his colonizing impulses. A salient example is Bernard's imagining a "tortuous" colonial scene in India, where Percival circulates amid decaying "ramshackle pagodas" and "strange sour smells" as "innumerable natives in loin-cloths swarm" with an uninterrupted sense of human "uselessness" (136). Unable to realign a cart that sways "incompetently" on its wheels, the Indians sit passively awaiting Percival's intervention; by deploying the civilizing standards of empire, Percival ensures within minutes that "the bullock-cart is righted" (136). Here, Woolf ironizes the exploitation and repressiveness of British imperialism – Percival is ridiculously outfitted in a "sun-helmet," riding a "flea-bitten mare" – and simultaneously conveys the unspeakable horror of the colonial outpost. Progressive civilization depends on the cultural superiority of empire: Percival intervenes, and the "Oriental problem is solved" (136).

Percival's silence obstructs any immediate access to his interiority, but it has a still more significant function. His silence operates also as an interpretive repository, a blank, wordless screen which is able to reflect, without reconciling, the various contradictions which the six project on to him. Percival is, on one level, a model of the unexceptional man: unreflective, slovenly, aggressive, obsessed with winning at sport, his manner, even as a child – "[h]e should have a birch and beat little boys for misdemeanours" (36) – is imperious and disciplinary. Yet Percival's evident mediocrity or, as Neville baldly puts it, his "stupidity" (48), is counterbalanced by the repeated, if seemingly incongruous, references to his "magnificence" (37). The intermittent recognition of his ordinariness, from the perspective of the six voices, is superseded by their collective view that he is an exceptional being. Percival's commonness is significant, in part, because it speaks to Woolf's desire to disrupt the male canon of history; through Percival, one sees evidence of economic historian Eileen Power's argument, in *Medieval People* (1924) – which Woolf may well have read – that history is comprised of unexceptional deeds performed by ordinary people.[89] While the reader initially registers only Percival's conventionality, to the others he is from the outset a "figure ... robed in beauty" (159), a man of "great compassion" (156), with "extreme fineness" (243) of taste, and amazing gestures with which "one falls hopelessly in love for a lifetime" (36). Bernard's assessment of Percival's singularity – "He is conventional; he is a hero" (122) – neatly exposes the bifurcation that we, as readers, experience in attempting to reconcile Percival's seeming insubstantiality with his structural significance as the novel's nucleus, through which the six voices seek a sense of collective wholeness.

Percival's form as chivalric hero is at odds with his recognizably maternal function as the locus of desire; yet together, these two seemingly irreconcilable strains convey Percival's role as the conduit through which the other characters consolidate a desire for national unity. Although absent as a subject, Percival is overwhelmingly present as a body, a feature which underscores his maternal affiliation despite that body's evident masculinity. His frame is not only substantial but is frequently in motion – heavy, coarse, strong, and clumsy, yet so athletic that he can "feel the flight of the ball through [his] body" (48). That his anatomy characterizes him, however, is in itself to feminize him. Percival is described as being more animal than human, a mute, sensate creature who lounges in a "giant repose" and instinctively buffets distractions with a "blow of his paw" (82). The text's exclusive focus on his physicality also signals Percival's dissociation from consciousness, and is precisely what draws the other characters to him. His corporeal presence (both actual and recollected) provides the means through which each of the six voices is able, however briefly, to transcend, in Bernard's words, "the burden of individual life" (112), and to assume a sense of collectivity and wholeness – to scramble, like adoring "satellites" (82), to imitate Percival's "remarkable movements" (242). Yet even when the issue is not one of literal mimicry, and even when Percival himself is no longer visibly present, we see that he still functions, through the group's mediated desire, as a kind of mirroring surface for the six, propelling them beyond their individually fractured and splintered identities to see reflected in one another glimpses of a refracted totality.

The impulses of the six characters call to mind Anthony Easthope's characterization of national identity as an unconscious mirroring process, an imaginary identification through which collectivity is achieved.[90] In Woolf's novel, one of the most evocative images of this fantasy identification is the seven-sided red flower, which works metonymically not simply because of the numerical confluence between petals and people, but rather because the "single flower" transforms into a "whole flower" only through Percival's mediation, and only when it is "seen by many eyes simultaneously" (127). He consistently functions as such a projection screen – reflecting wholeness and stability – even, as at Hampton Court, when he is physically absent. Neville's mention of the maternal at the group's reunion dinner after Percival's death is an allusion to their desire for him, underscoring their communal yearning for his absent flesh: "we only wish to rejoin the body of our mother from whom we have been severed" (233). It is therefore not a surprise to witness the group's infantile regression at this Hampton Court gathering, when, after dinner, Louis declares: "we advance ... calling ourselves little children ... clasping hands, afraid of the dark" (228). This regression is, here as elsewhere, coincident with the erosion of identity and the confusion of ego boundaries that Percival's presence – or, in this case, absence – perpetually stimulates. That the group there seeks a collective identity is underscored by Bernard's observation, spoken within the context of a recollection of Percival: "laid out among us [is] the body of the complete human being whom we have failed to be ... our life, our identity" (276). These ephemeral yet stabilizing moments, in which the individual ego transcends its limitations and mutability, occur rarely in the text, and only – as at the two communal dinners – through the invocation, whether overt or inferred, of Percival's body.

In Woolf's portrayal of Percival's body at the two Hampton Court meals we see the influence of Harrison's work on the maternal and the primacy of ritual practice; we also find evidence of Weston's work on the Grail, particularly its nutritive and generative functions. In both English neo-medievalism and the modernist preoccupation with Hellenic primitivism, ritual practice is directly tied to the desire for community, wholeness, and a recuperation of the earth. Throughout *The Waves*, Percival's body is aligned with nature, which Woolf depicts as an archetypal feminine space: "not a piece of paper lies between him and the sun, between him and the rain, between him and the moon" (48). Even after his burial he remains fertile, "flowering with green leaves ... in the earth with all his branches still sighing in the summer wind" (203). Like his maternal predecessor Mrs. Ramsay, whom critics have read as a goddess of fertility, Percival is a vegetation deity; also like Mrs. Ramsay, his maternalism is linked to British imperialism.[91] That Hampton Court is the venue for the text's modern ritual also speaks to the nationalist impulses underpinning Percival's character, for that magnificent sixteenth-century palace is steeped in Englishness, with its connotations of male sovereignty and imperial control. Hampton Court is the nucleus that facilitates the group's "moments of purest exultation" in which, through Percival's mediation, they feel they are "masters of tranquillity and order; inheritors of proud tradition" (86). When Neville comments, on Percival's belated arrival at their first dinner, that "the reign of chaos is over" (122), the termination of "chaos" alludes to Percival's role as the guarantor of imperial redemption: "All oppression is relieved ... He has imposed order" (122). At the same time, this "chaos" characterizes the psychic disposition of the six, suggesting the kind of internalized division and rupture that Lacan and Kristeva theorize is a result of the originary loss of maternal unity. Percival's absence functions as such a gap for the six, propelling them to seek the fulfillment of this originary mother–child attachment – in Bernard's words, "the desire for some one not there" (274). Louis unequivocally affirms this longing for "order" when he states: "It is Percival ... sitting silent ... who makes us aware that these attempts to say, 'I am this, I am that' ... like separated parts of one body and soul, are false" (137). This representation of the mother's body as the imaginary source of gratification calls to mind Kristeva (following Lacan), but in *The Waves* Woolf reconfigures the structure of this symbiosis.[92] Her fictional rendering of such moments of plentitude or completion pre-empts conventional Lacanian logic by depicting the child's reconciliation with the maternal as explicitly multiple, rather than dyadic. As the indelible symbol of both empire and desire – signifying at once the body of the nation as well as the maternal body – Percival's integration of disparate elements ultimately suggests the possibility of some form of national unification.

The novel's clearest example of this multiple cohesion, and also the text's most emphatic correlation of Percival and the maternal, occurs during the group's first communal dinner, at which the language evokes both an image of liturgical ritual and an oral return to the maternal breast.[93] Eucharistically, Percival's "actual body" is represented as the basis for the communal sacrifice through which the "normal is abolished" (119) and the group is mystically "about to undergo an extraordinary transformation" (118). Jinny's disconsolate assertion that they shall perhaps never "make this moment out of one man again" (145) suggests the transubstantiation, which in turn reminds us that Percival is, in effect, the word made flesh. Weston has shown that the Grail has links to the eucharist, where each provides "a Sacred meal of Communion in which the worshipper ... partakes of, and becomes one with, his God."[94] Although in medieval legend God is perceived to be "the ultimate source of the Grail's ability to nourish," the mother is in fact "the only parent who may truly feed her children with her body." Rosalyn Rossingnol links the Grail's source of nourishment and perfect union with the "primal experiences arising from the original relationship with the mother," suggesting that the Grail, like Percival himself, is actually an androgynous signifier.[95] Caroline Walker Bynum's work on late medieval notions of the body of Christ provides a useful historical context for thinking about the significance of Percival's feminized corporeality. She demonstrates how, within medieval iconography, Christ's body was often depicted "as female, as lactating and giving birth," a constellation that points to the figure of "Jesus as mother."[96] Percival never lactates *per se*, but his body is clearly a nutritive and generative source of "spiritual milk."[97] The group's collective moment of "ravenous" convergence (143) at Hampton Court can be understood as a kind of fantasized return to the primal oral fusion with the mother, in which, through Percival's mediation, the group's "glutted" (143) contentment psychically replicates the satiety − as Bernard elsewhere articulates − of "[h]aving dropped off satisfied like a child from the breast" (112).

As the most intimate point of union and sustenance, the maternal breast may be identified with the eucharist, but it also suggests an association with nationalism − for Percival's breast, like the Grail itself, is clearly British.[98] The implications of Bernard's meditation concerning Percival, that people regard him "as if he were − what he is − a God" (123), are fully exploited in this 'last supper' (literally, Percival's final meal with them before India), consecrated to the "love of Percival" (126). The invocations of "God" and "love" inevitably signal the meal's sacramental nature, calling to mind Derrida's assertion that nationality is "mystical," as well as Easthope's observation that the communal feeling for the nation is "like falling in love."[99] In Woolf's text, the six characters repeatedly voice an irrational, obsessive devotion to their beloved imperialist, who puts them into a "trance of well-being ... [a] rapture of benignity" (136−7). But in contrast to the "stricken figure of Christ," Percival inhabits a "pagan universe" (36) within the context of empire; as such, he can be read as a vegetation god whose role is to counteract what Woolf perceived as the loss of organic community.[100] But the community in which Percival's restorative mediation is central is not the colonial outpost, where "many obscure Indians ... [are] dying of famine and disease" (243), but England, the heart of empire. While Woolf's depiction of Percival anticipates Weston's argument that the "mystic" food provided by the Grail and partaken of by the group is "a Food of Life,"[101] one realizes that this sacramental moment is staged for those already steeped in the ideology of Englishness. Although the identification of Percival with the Grail links him to the interwar association of Arthurian legend with fascism, Woolf does not aestheticize his militaristic patriotism; yet the nationalistic aspects of his character cannot be severed from his maternal function.[102]

Percival's position as the organizing principle at this ritualistic "communion"

(126) is constitutive of English identity for the group, recalling Harrison's argument that primitive ritual arises from an inchoate emotional impulse associated with nature, irrationality, and the feminine. For Harrison, as for Weston, communion is importantly linked to literal consumption.[103] We see all of these elements in play at Hampton Court, where Woolf stages a modern ritual that recalls Mrs. Ramsay's unifying and imperious influence at the dinner party in *To the Lighthouse*. There, as Mrs. Ramsay prepares the feast and feels a sense "at once freakish and tender, of celebrating a festival" (100), Woolf suggests that it is the maternal body itself that is being sacrificed for the satiation and nurturance of the group. As "every nerve of her body" creates an atmosphere of coherence and stability, Mrs. Ramsay ritual-istically feeds her guests a "specially tender piece, of eternity" (105). This language evokes Harrison's contention that the function of primitive ritual is "to restore by communion that complete unity" which people have lost through enculturation.[104] In both Woolf novels it is clearly maternal sustenance that facilitates this union, mitigating interpersonal tensions and solidifying the group. Just as Mrs. Ramsay's evening begins with conflict, before Percival's appearance the six are distracted and filled with "hostility" and "indifference" (118–19), but moments after his arrival "oppression is relieved" (122), and they begin to recount shared memories. The restaurant is transformed from a place of conflict, in which "everybody's interests are at variance" (123), to a confluent space where discord is resolved however fleetingly – through Percival's mediation: "sitting together now we love each other and believe in our own endurance" (123).

Although Percival's deification is improbable, implicitly functioning as a critique of colonialism's conversionary impulses, the text nonetheless invokes such discourse to summon reverence for Percival and capture the group's experience of emotional intensity and collectivity – both of which, Harrison argues, are crucial elements in primitive ritual. As Percival enters the restaurant, Louis and Rhoda hear "dancing and drumming" (140) and re-imagine themselves as modern celebrants of an orgiastic cannibal feast: "Like the dance of savages … They dance in a circle … The flames leap over their painted faces, over the leopard skins and the bleeding limbs which they have torn from the living body" (140).[105] This reference to blood invokes both the Eucharist and breast milk, which were linked in medieval understandings of physiology; at the same time, the primitivist iconography at work in this "Eucharistic cannibalism" reflects colonialist patterns of thought, if only in a revisionary way.[106] Woolf's use of racialized imagery does not destabilize the characters' national identity, but it does erase the distinction between the savage and the civilized: Percival is linked with the primitive, but only in order to recuperate an ancestral Englishness. While in general Woolf's use of "savage" is slippery and unstable, here it has a positive valence that is aligned with mysticism, irrationality, and femininity. Of course, the "living body" which the group symbolically dismembers (and consumes) is Percival's own, for his flesh has enabled the group to "make one thing" (127) by facilitating a ritual re-enactment for the collective which they describe as "our festival" (122). This imagery reminds us of Harrison's contention that the psychology and gestures of "the savage" are "based on instincts kindred to … our own"; this is precisely what the text suggests in staging a primitive ritual in Hampton Court, the national space which, according to Woolf, "might be marked blank [on a map] like certain districts of Africa" because it remains, for most English people, "unexplored land."[107] This equation of Africa with Hampton Court speaks to Woolf's desire to demonstrate how "pure primitive instinct" – embodied in Percival – can infiltrate and have a curative effect on the "collective conscience" of the nation.[108]

Although in *The Waves* the literal consumption of meat is tied to masculinity and British colonialism, the figurative eating of Percival is more complexly gendered, but it is still depicted as an act of conquest.[109] As Bernard puts it: "We have proved, sitting eating ... that ... [we] stride not into chaos, but into a world that our own force can subjugate" (146). Whereas meat-eating was during this period linked with national degeneration, due to the widespread consumption of low-quality beef,[110] the symbolic eating of Percival is associated with national redemption: to the extent that he is both mother and imperialist, he embodies the ideological assumption that good motherhood is an essential component in Britain's ideology of racial health. Although the discourse of maternalist imperialism remains buried, Woolf does convey that, like Mrs. Ramsay, Percival comes from Aryan stock – has a "straight nose" and "blue, oddly inexpressive eyes" (36) – and she repeatedly shows how his role is fundamental to the characters' ability to constitute themselves as national subjects. That eating functions as a means of consolidating national identification is seen in Neville's observation: "We are walled in here. But India lies outside ... as I eat ... delicious mouthfuls ... I feel ... gravity, control. All is solid now" (135, 138). Through consumption Neville both concretizes his identity and ingests the precepts of empire. Similarly, it is at the dinner that Rhoda envisions "India ... fetched up out of darkness ... muddy roads, twisted jungle, swarms of men," all part of the group's "proud and splendid province" (137) because of Percival's violent intervention. Again, we see evidence of Gikandi's argument that the consolidation of British identity depends on imperial possession. Rhoda further expresses this view by showing how the colonial space shapes the cognitive map of English identity: "The world that had been shrivelled, rounds itself" (137). It is no accident that the group's fleeting moments of communion occur at collective meals, for food stabilizes the body in the same way that Percival's imposing presence affects the group: in Bernard's words, food "blunt[s] the sharp tooth of egotism" (224). Percival's maternal body is offered and cannibalized; as the characters experience "the swelling and splendid moment created by us from Percival" (146), they symbolically ingest the domesticating injunction of empire, to "impose order" (161). Louis's phrasing in describing their experience at the meal is characteristic of his own obsession with order, but it also speaks to their communal fascination with Percival's status as their stabilizing central influence: "Before the chain breaks, before disorder returns, see us fixed ... held in a vice" (142). Rhoda's reference to Percival's imposing bearing as a "great stone" around which the others "undulate and eddy contentedly" (136) is indirectly echoed by Louis, who remarks: "I am like some vast sucker, some glutinous ... some insatiable mouth. I have tried to draw from the living flesh the stone lodged at the centre" (201). While Louis's self depiction here recalls his rapacious imperialist impulses, this image of him as an "insatiable mouth," gluttonously sucking at the "living flesh," also conveys that, in relation to Percival, he is more than anything a hungry child. Food's sensations instill the group's fragmented bodies with weight, substance, and a sense of inclusion, thereby warding off invasions of a disjunctive Othered self or nationality.

Eating, I'm arguing, is the means through which the group subjugates and regulates the non-English world at Hampton Court, constructing through collectivity a "globe whose walls are made of Percival" (145). It is the maternal–imperial body that nourishes and consolidates this English space, enabling the group to draw a boundary around itself through the mediation of Percival's flesh: "Happiness is in it ... and the quiet of ordinary things" (145). Neville's claim that without him they are "silhouettes, hollow phantoms moving mistily" (122) evokes an image of emaciation that is nourishable only through their nutritive communion with Percival. It is also no coincidence that Rhoda's migratory wanderings reflect her elusive desire to "replenish ... emptiness" (139), and always commence from the solidity of their "communal table" (139). That this meal is characterized by Bernard as a subjugation reminds us of Renan's observation that national unity is always effected through means of violence and brutality.[111] As the group consumes, it creates a new world, but this globe is made possible only through the familiar tropes of imperial conquest. Thus as Louis encourages the group to observe "the thing that we have made, that globes itself here," Rhoda contemplates the uncolonized portions of the planet unenclosed by Percival's body, "far countries on the other side of the world ... seas and jungles" (145). This imagery suggests that it is only his body that constructs a boundary for them, enabling the creation of a border against the threat of foreign encroachment. At the same time, Percival's body is the means through which the six are able to traverse boundaries and colonize imagined space. Yet this imaginary traversal inevitably affirms the imperative of English identity. Louis illustrates this when he remarks that, through Percival, "the circle in our blood ... closes in a ring ... do not ... cut to pieces the thing ... that globes itself here" (145). The language of blood-right and territorialism here recapitulates Anglocentric conceptions of national, cultural, and racial difference. Bernard insists that they are "not slaves" in relation to Percival, nor are they mindless "sheep ... following a master" (146); rather: "We are creators" (146). It is only through their appropriation of the narrative of empire that the characters are able to consolidate their British identities.

At the second communal meal at Hampton Court, Percival's physical absence makes the process of convergence more difficult, but again the group's ability to achieve coherence and stability – "being one, being indivisible" (235) – relies fully upon his mediation. Similarly, the rhetoric of territorialism and the use of the spatial metaphors invoked at the first meal are echoed here, within the "battlements of Hampton Court" (210), underscoring the constitutive power of the dominant discourses of Englishness. While both dinners progress from the group's resistance to cohesion to the blurring of individual identities, Percival's absence at the second gathering delays their willingness to be "dissolved utterly" (224). However, by the end of the meal, "[g]orged and replete" with both rich food and memories of Percival, the six see themselves as beings "scarcely to be distinguished from another" (224) – again experiencing a "momentary alleviation" (228) from their fragmentary selves. The ability of the group to accomplish this unity even in Percival's absence emphasizes the symbolic place he has always occupied, just as Bernard's

reiteration of the text's earlier premise, that unified national identification is constituted only through violence, demonstrates the sustaining power of the imperial
myth. We see the violent underpinnings of this imagined community, as well as the
liberatory aspect of an imperial identity, in Bernard's words: "We have destroyed
something by our presence … a world perhaps" (232). Echoing the moral superiority of Englishness, Neville asserts that collectively they have imposed order
against the "illimitable chaos" (226). Importantly, their moment of solidarity and
cohesion is perceived as a metaphorical mapping of territory – "We are landed; we
are on shore" (225) – and is contrasted with the "abysses of infinite space" (227) that
exist beyond the circumference of their bodies.

As elsewhere, Englishness is constituted through the demarcation of a boundary,
a corporeal border that is "made of six lives" (229) in which, as Bernard puts it, a
"flicker of light in us" (227) illuminates "this dark" (229). Although he intermittently mocks the concept of empire, like Neville, who imagines himself "a
subject of King George" (228), Bernard still constructs the group's collective
identity through recourse to an imperial narrative: "Our English past – one inch of
light" (227).[112] This rhetoric recalls the Bureau of Education's vehement support for
the teaching of English under British rule: "The true cure of darkness is the
introduction of the light."[113] Once again, through the invocation of Percival – or,
stated differently, through their imaginary relation to the mother's (absent) body –
they see reflected in one another the image of a unified national totality (232). Thus,
again, national desire is constituted as a "desire for what is missing."[114]

It is difficult, if not impossible, to ascribe a single *meaning* to Percival's
enigmatic status because of the conflict between his chivalric form and his maternal
function, but this excess of meanings is no hindrance to the group's adulation.
Woolf's representation of its idolatrous affection for Percival calls to mind Freud's
discussion of collective identity, in which he argues for the primacy of libidinal ties
to compel group attachment to its leader. Freud's identification of both the military
and the church as prime examples of this libidinal dynamic resonates with Percival's
sources of allure; Woolf borrows imagery from each in her portrayal of him as a
leader whose position is generated and maintained by group *eros*.[115] There is,
however, a constitutive tension between his function in the novel – as the unifying
signifier of desire – and the actual meaning of his interiority, which, because we
know it only by projection, remains unreadable. Neville's ambiguous observation
that Percival "sees nothing … hears nothing" (36) yet "understands everything" (71)
only confirms our perception of him as an inscrutable presence. Bernard makes
reference to Percival's "curious air of detachment," describing him as that which is
"abstract … eyeless … [and] blank" (154), thus confirming his anonymity and
alluding to his status as the novel's absent center, devoid of intrinsic meaning.
While the fact that Percival neither reads (48) nor speaks would seem to suggest his
estrangement from language, it is precisely this indeterminacy that most closely
aligns him with language in the text. The most salient features of Percival's
character are his absence and the arbitrariness of his significance, two pivotal
elements which suggest an equivalence in a linguistic register. As Lacan, among
others, has argued, language can operate only by designating an object as a presence
against a ground of absence. While Kristeva differs from Lacan in her attention to

maternity (for him, there is no semiotic), her theorization of language clearly builds on a Lacanian model. Although the emphasis for Lacan is on paternal prohibition rather than the maternal function, for both of them the loss of the mother propels the subject into language. Like language, Percival himself functions primarily in terms of absence in the novel. Moreover, if we understand language to be an arbitrary system with no intrinsic meaning, that *produces* meaning through the interrelations of signs, then Percival can be read as a floating signifier whose meaning remains both arbitrary and unstable. I want to suggest that, ultimately, Woolf represents Percival as a figure for language itself, an embodiment of what, in Kristeva's terms, is the dynamic of symbolic–semiotic processes; but his reincarnation as "the flesh become word" is fully legible only through Bernard's intervention.[116] As a signifier of empire, Percival represents the law, which, like language, serves a regulatory function as a symbolic discourse and may be deployed to subjugate and contain the Other. However, at the same time as he represents paternal law – as imperialist, chivalric hero, headmaster, and even God – he is also something else, something submerged and irreconcilable. Just as the repressed is aligned with the maternal semiotic, Percival's simultaneous alterity can be read as a signifier for what British culture seeks to exclude. Like the abject, he represents that which "cannot be assimilated" by the nation, nor entirely repudiated.[117]

Through her depiction of Percival, Woolf posits a "'splitting' of the national subject" in which the linguistic body of the masculinized imperial nation is infiltrated by the repressed, preoedipal drives of the maternal.[118] Kristeva's work on how to live with national difference, *Strangers to Ourselves*, provides us with a way of articulating Percival's problematic status, that of "being an other" to himself.[119] Kristeva argues that what we eradicate in order to cohere as a nation is actually a part of our own identity: "The other is [our] ... unconscious." On both an individual and a national level, Kristeva argues, it is our own unconscious that is projected on to those who we seek to exclude: alterity is not elsewhere, but within us. Kristeva suggests that psychoanalysis enables us to view the stranger, or "Other," as that part of ourselves that is repressed; by formulating a model "founded on the consciousness of the unconscious" we are better equipped to welcome "the strangeness of the other." The foreigner is in an analogous position to the subject's, for both have to leave their homeland, and submerge their "mother tongue," in order to form a stable identity; the exile, like the subject in language, has "lost his mother." Kristeva's theorizing of "the stranger" as that which exists internal to the self, and her contention that what one remembers is the resonance of the maternal body, can be used to understand what is arguably at stake in Percival's character in *The Waves*. To the extent that he embodies the imperialist–maternal split, Percival can be said to be Other to himself: culturally liminal, he is ultimately an ambivalent figure for the nation because Woolf uses him to critique the ideology that he represents, at the same time as she instills him – via Bernard – with the potential for cultural transformation.[120]

Feminizing national space: Elvedon's ancestral Englishness

It is precisely through the mediation of Percival, as archaic hero–mother, that Bernard is able ultimately to critique the dominance of symbolic discourse, and invoke the semiotic. What he finally comes to, in Kristevan terms, is a recognition of maternal presence: "I have not lost her ... I can recover her in language."[121] Like Percival, who sought to create order through violence, Bernard seeks linguistic order through recourse to the narrative of conquest and possession: "Let us again pretend that life is a solid substance, shaped like a globe, which we turn about in our fingers ... [to] make out a plain and logical story" (251). Yet as Bernard grows into language, he realizes that counternarratives of the nation disrupt this totalizing and homogeneous story: "the globe of life ... far from being hard and cold to the touch, has walls of thinnest air" (256). It is this spatial confusion, moreover, which ultimately results in his skepticism regarding the viability of the symbolic's sequential narratives. Bernard's embrace of the ego's multidimensionality is linked to his desire for a discursive practice that will replace the illusory conception of the unitary ego and keep faith with his discovery that, while there are countless stories to record, "none of them are true" (238). By the end of the novel, Bernard comes to denounce what he had earlier hoped to secure: he forgoes his dream of a precise symbolic discourse, now claiming that the "true order of things – this is our perpetual illusion" (271). We can read Bernard's final soliloquy as his most sustained opposition to the symbolic order, even though in terms of the language itself it is one of the most conventionally written parts of *The Waves*. The novel at the same time stages a critique of narrative, while suggesting that the potential for subversion is located within narrative itself. Although Bernard's countless stories are themselves conventionally rendered, they are also fragmentary, incomplete, and resistant to closure. It is the embrace of this linguistic instability and proliferation that characterizes Bernard's final movement in the novel: what he recognizes is that narrative consistency–coherence is "a convenience, a lie ... [because] ... always deep below it ... [is] a rushing stream of broken dreams, nursery rhymes, street cries ... half-finished sentences" (255). What Bernard discerns is that the symbolic – like national identity itself – is not monolithic and unitary, but rather is unstable and shifting, and perforated with semiotic residues – "cries, cracks, fissures" (263) – which have not been sublimated into a regulated and syntactically governed language. Yet while Bernard's claim that "what one needs is nothing consecutive but a bark, a groan" (251) is a desire for the dissonance of the semiotic – an invocation of the repressed feminine – it is crucial to recognize that his desire for that which is unsubsumable within rational discourse is overlaid with national meaning. This semiotic, I'm suggesting, is aligned also with Englishness, albeit differently than its symbolic counterpart, with its affiliation to imperial unity.

It is no accident that Bernard invokes music in order to describe his desire, for music conveys not only the "oral and glottal pleasure [which] combats the superego and its linear language," but a longing for the kind of ancestral national unity Woolf has privileged all along.[122] Bernard's wish for a "guttural, visceral ... pealing song" which might replace what he refers to as those "flagging, foolish transcripts" that are "much too deliberate ... too reasonable" (250) again recalls the rhythm of the maternal semiotic, in which libidinal drives are capable of resisting the demands of the symbolic order. Significantly, Bernard distances himself from the symbolic dimension of Percival represented by nationalistic anthems – "that wild hunting-song, Percival's music" – at the very moment when he implicitly invokes Percival in his semiotic aspect by insisting that "there should be music" of somatic proportions: "painful, guttural, visceral" (250). If the feeling for nation is like falling in love, then Bernard's desire for some kind of dissonant harmony that might describe that "moment of first love" (250) inevitably speaks to his desire for the maternal–imperial body – the first love – which Percival represents. The simple "concord" and "discord" (246) Bernard imagines – barks, cries, groans – express a foundational bodily music that recalls Percival in his most maternal and ancestral aspect. This representation reminds us of the argument, upheld by critics during the interwar period, that "the traditional songs of England" were "the soul of the nation" and should be reinstated in the popular consciousness in order to "refine and strengthen the national character."[123] Bernard's attention to music, and his linkage of it to Percival, suggests that the "pealing song" (250) he longs for has to do with the re-awakening of a buried national consciousness. It is thus not a surprise to see Bernard articulate a longing for "broken words, inarticulate words" (239), "words of one syllable such as children speak when they come into the room and find their mother sewing" (295), for what he seeks is the materiality of language, its rhythms and music prior to syntax.

This is a pivotal moment in the text, for although Bernard on the one hand rejects the master narrative of imperialism – "it is a mistake … this orderly and military progress" (255) – he simultaneously recuperates an imperial identity through the mediation of Percival, who embodies the space of English alterity. Louis's observation that Percival "inspires poetry" (40) is not fully realized until this climactic moment, when Bernard – by invoking Percival – articulates his desire for an overtly heterogeneous "poetic" (in Kristevan terms) discourse that reminds us of Woolf's contention: "Poetry ought to have a mother as well as a father" (*ROO*, 103).[124] Woolf's depiction of Percival as a Christ-like androgyne who is associated with poetry (the Word made flesh) recalls Eliot's depiction of Tiresias in *The Waste Land*, and reminds us of his argument that the primitive's "pre-logical mentality survives in civilized man, but becomes available only to or through the poet."[125] As the embodiment of the "power of the Word to contain opposites" who, arguably, is "tied to a prelapsarian vision of androgyny or double-sexedness," Percival – as Grail, as absent signifier – is a perfect example of what Marc Manganaro calls the "trace of that quest for the ultimate signified, a logos that is only fully felt by absence."[126] But in contrast to Eliot's use of sexual doubling, which reinforces the gender hierarchy, Woolf's portrayal of Percival's sexual amorphousness uncovers a peculiarly feminine consciousness.[127] Percival embodies a complex network of signifiers that ultimately promote a primitive, prelogical, and mystical conception of maternal discourse. Yet Bernard's disavowal of signification (and simultaneous inscription of Percival) cannot escape representation, even though it points to the inadequacy of language. Bernard's clamour for "a howl; a cry" (294) is not merely a full-scale retreat from the falsity of phrases, but signals his plunge into a kind of primal revelry in which an undomesticated primordial self emerges – "the savage"

(289). Significantly, this moment is coincident with his inability "to speak save in a child's words of one syllable" (287), a phenomenon that recalls both the Bloomsbury adulation of children as exemplary "primitive artist[s]" and the period's (as well as Bloomsbury's) characterization of the savage as child-like.[128] But whereas British social evolutionists sought to show parallels between the language of children and that of savages in order to document the childishness of the latter, Woolf arguably identifies the child with the primitive in order to rewrite the originary narrative of Englishness.[129]

If it is one's first language that confers a sense of national identification, then Bernard's devolution into a English child–savage revises his relation to national discourse, aligning him with a kind of ancestral preoedipal maternalism. It is, however, misleading to refer to this primitive entity as Bernard's "self," for the moment is preceded by his refusal to individuate. By insisting that there is no distinction between himself and his friends (276), Bernard becomes the spokesman for the group's common emotion, thereby personifying Harrison's contention that the "collective conscience" is primary.[130] Bernard addresses this collective alter-ego as "the savage, the hairy man who dabbles his fingers in ropes of entrails ... whose speech is guttural, visceral ... [and who] ape-like ... has led me [in] wild dances" (289–90). This ecstatic figure calls to mind Harrison's characterization of the savage as one who enjoys a totemic merging with nature, and it reminds us also of the earlier moment, at Hampton Court, when primitive discourse is invoked to convey the group's frenzied emotional response to Percival's bleeding and "living body" (140).[131] In both instances racialized discourse invokes the English association of apes and cannibals with Africans, but ultimately the text's use of primitivist discourse does not destabilize the characters' whiteness or Englishness.[132] Rather, the allusion to blackness is an integral means by which the characters are able to make sense of themselves as English subjects, connecting them with a prehistoric England.

Bernard appropriates the role of savage and re-imagines the Hampton Court scene of eucharistic cannibalism – "flesh being gashed and blood spurting, a joint suddenly twisted" (263) – but he remains white, middle-class, and identifiably British. Like Percival earlier, Bernard becomes an animal – his hand is a hairy "paw," he "gobbles and belches," he cannot control his bodily gestures (289–90) – and, as at the two communal meals, this moment is infused with imperial signifiers and religious imagery. There, as here, it is the visceral, primitive, physical body that is embraced – a momentary incorporation of the abject self whose permeability threatens the "clean and proper body."[133] Bernard's language – "altars," "incense," "transcendency," "my body rises" (290) – also suggests a kind of extra-corporeal divinity. But this poses no contradiction, for bodily exhibition conjoins with spiritual discourse, as Harrison reminds us, in ritual re-enactment. Bernard registers, finally, no distinction between human and non-human, nor between the primitive and the civilized, echoing Harrison's belief in a collective consciousness: "We are all of us members of one another," unified in a transhistorical cross-cultural time and space "in which all *our* past, and also the past out of which we sprang ... is rolled up, involved."[134] It is crucial here to recognize that Bernard's sense of spatial and temporal freedom is undergirded by an *English* conception of space and location. In referring to his life as a "globe, full of figures" (238), he shows how English identity is established through the demarcation of a boundary that is both exclusive and inclusive, as well as racially inflected. We see this vividly just moments before Bernard mutates into the ape-like being as he recollects the group's communal meal at Hampton Court: "we felt enlarge itself round us the huge blackness of what is outside us, of what we are not" (277). Perceptions of Anglo-Saxon supremacy, I'm arguing, necessarily underwrite Bernard's image of himself and the group as an autonomous globe, whose minds "expand, contract" (94), through investment in the narrative of empire. Bernard's invocation of "the savage" illustrates both his complicity in the imperialist enterprise and his immersion in a feminized space of psychic alterity based upon his recuperation of the maternal.

With the obliteration of the unitary self (239), we see Bernard invoke a series of immaterial and subterranean images, fragments lodged in the unconscious, in an effort to define his life-story: "things gone far, gone deep ... dreams ... ghosts ... unborn selves" (289). While earlier in the novel Bernard had claimed with certainty, "I am no mystic" (288), by the end of text he pointedly aligns himself with what he terms "the mystery of things" (291), which invokes Harrison's concept of "savage magic." For Bernard, as for Harrison, this "childlike power" is aligned with the irrational, femininity, and disrupts temporal and spatial boundaries. [135] For Bernard and the group, this "interference with the sense of time, of space" (263) is inseparable from the idea of "conquest" and is indelibly tied to the "freedom" and "exaltation" (264) that Percival's maternal imperialism represents. Bernard's invocation of mystical discourse can be read as Woolf's vehicle for constructing an alternative to Freud's virulent anti-mysticism by privileging the space of the mother's body, for his experience of this alterity is implicitly linked with Percival.[136] The language Bernard uses to describe his confrontation with the unknown closely parallels the way in which he recollects Percival: "what we cannot account for, what turns symmetry to nonsense – that comes suddenly to mind, thinking of him" (243). The implication of Bernard's statement here – turning symmetry to nonsense – has resonance only if we view Percival as a figure for language, embodying the potential for subversion, through which Bernard comes to privilege the transgressive over the conventional narrative. However, at the same time, the soliloquy itself indisputably demonstrates Bernard's discursive mastery. To that extent, the novel is finally less an enactment of the semiotic than a call for its implementation. Woolf's text suggests that Western culture has evolved at the expense of the maternal, which must be rediscovered on a national scale if culture is ever to move beyond the tyranny of the symbolic. This encapsuates and prefigures Kristeva's own utopian argument that motherhood can serve as a model for a new civic ideal – "an essential contribution to civilization."[137]

Bernard's final embrace of "this margin of unknown territory" (143), which I read as maternalized space, coincides with his loss of a discrete self and a desire for a semiotic signifying practice that has Percival as its source. Not surprisingly, Bernard's recollection of Percival's loss is formulated in terms that re-inscribe the centrality of the mother–child dyad: "No lullaby has ever occurred to me capable of singing him to rest" (243). By inverting the roles here and casting Bernard as a (deficient) mother figure, the text revisits Percival's loss and Bernard's limited capacity to sing the songs of national inscription, even as it suggests that the maternal is a mobile function. Significantly, the moment in which Bernard wanders without a self – without the impediment of an I/eye (294) – is also the only point at which he is completely without gender (288). This symbolic death of the self is, moreover, the only point at which the language of the interludes and that of the text merge indistinguishably. The words Bernard uses during this moment of selflessness recapitulate his own experience of androgyny: "Day rises; the girl lifts the watery fire-hearted jewels to her brow; the sun levels his beams ... What does the central shadow hold?" (291–2). Bernard's query about the contents of the mysterious "central shadow," framed within a context in which gender has no salience, inevitably invokes Percival's sexual indeterminacy and his affiliation with the unconscious. Although the interlude that begins this final section of the novel conveys that *"the sun had sunk"* (236), we here see the obverse, for Bernard experiences a "whitening of the sky; some sort of renewal" (296) in the midst of what logically should be darkness. Whereas the solar movement of the interludes indicates a geographical progression from sunrise in the East (the site of colonization) to sunset in the West (the motherland), this simulated dawn suggests that the narrative of empire is now focused on England.[138] By redirecting our gaze from the colonies to the territory at home, the novel alludes to the colonization of Elvedon, the English location that, from the text's opening pages, has been celebrated as a site of conquest.

It is precisely Bernard's own desire to rupture language, and his association of Percival with linguistic subversion and maternity, that link the two of them to Elvedon, a maternalized space in which an unnamed and silent "lady sits writing" (248). The language Bernard uses to describe Elvedon recalls Percival through a series of associations that have to do with the unknown, the transgressive, and the maternal. Bernard and Susan are the first explorers to espy Elvedon when, as children, they encounter what they perceive to be a "hostile country," enclosed by a ringed wood and silent except for the sound of "some primeval fir-cone falling" (17). Although there are signs pointing the way, Bernard claims that "[n]o one has been there" (17), a patently false statement for we immediately learn that there is an indigenous population: ladies and gardeners. Bernard mythologizes Elvedon through the discourse of imperial conquest, saying of himself and Susan: "We are the first to come here. We are the discoverers of an unknown land" (17). Both of them instinctively fear being shot for trespassing on this "foreign" soil, which is populated only by "those fabulous presences, men with brooms, women writing" (285). Although critics have reasonably argued that Elvedon is a mythical place, the name may allude to two, interrelated, English spaces: the aristocratic estate of Elveden Hall, in Suffolk, owned by the titled and territorial elite; and Avalon, the otherworldly island of Celtic myth that is associated with Arthurian legend and the Holy Grail.[139] Woolf's Elvedon is clearly modeled on the "great house" of the English aristocracy, with its servants, protective wall, "stable-boy," "gilt" clock, and "close-clipped hedge of the ladies' garden" (16), at the heart of which is the "lady [who] sits between two long windows, writing" (17).[140] That this anonymous woman is a "lady" indicates a crucial thing about Elvedon: the writing that occurs there is carried out by one of the cultural elite, perhaps someone who has gained (or purchased) a knighthood, a baronetcy, or a peerage.[141] At the same time, the name invokes the earthly paradise of "Avalon," conjuring images of the Grail quest, an association that

Bernard exploits when he describes Elvedon as a prehistoric English space: "It is as if one had woken in Stonehenge surrounded by a circle of great stones, these enemies, these presences" (240). The reference to Stonehenge, the ancient megalith, recalls not only Percival's incarnation as "a great stone" (136) – a "monolithic" (82) earthwork – but his phantasmatic status in the novel as someone who "sat there in the centre" (153) but is "not there" (274). Like Stonehenge, which represented the "organicist search for English origins" during the interwar period and is associated with nature worship, popular mysticism, and militarism, Percival is the means through which – to borrow the language of British ruralist H.J. Massingham – "we step upon ... [archaic] turf as aliens ... seeking once more the ancient mother of our race."[142] Elvedon's "ringed" (17) enclosure reminds us of the group's description of their bodies as a "circle" that "closes in a ring" (145), and both conjure images of Stonehenge, whose continuous ring of bluestone monoliths is interpreted as evidence of English racial survival.[143] Each in turn is linked with the nationalism that Percival represents. The language Bernard uses to recollect Elvedon invokes an image of Percival's mediating function – "that which is beyond and outside our own predicament ... that which is symbolic and thus perhaps permanent" (248–9).

An understanding of the symmetry between Percival and Elvedon hinges on the words "symbolic" and "permanent" here, for both evoke the maternal and linguistic in ways that remind us, in Bernard's words, of "things [that] happen in one second and last forever" (240). To register how this intersection works, one must consider a critical moment in the novel, following the group's communal meal with Percival, in which each of them recounts certain formative childhood experiences. In Bernard's case, what surfaces are three seemingly distinct, yet intimately related, memories: Mrs. Constable giving him a bath; the woman writing in Elvedon; and the initial separation from his mother. Here, the meaning of Elvedon merges with the image of Old Mrs. Constable, herself a maternal figure, who "lifted her sponge and warmth poured over" the children's naked bodies. What Bernard remembers is a child's fantasy of birth: "We became clothed in this ... garment of flesh" (124). Earlier in the novel, the actual bath itself is similarly linked with Elvedon; there, Bernard recounts how, as the water poured down his spine – "arrows of sensation shoot[ing] down on either side" – at the same time "[r]ich and heavy sensations form[ed] on the roof of [his] mind ... the woods; and Elvedon" (26–7). In each case, the language Bernard uses to render his memory – "I am covered with warm flesh" (26) – suggests not merely an imaginative re-experience of birth, but signals the pivotal moment in which the self becomes aware of itself as a distinct entity. Bernard's association of the bath and Elvedon with his account of the group's first departure to school as a "second severance from the body of our mother" (125) cumulatively suggests that what is at stake in the intertwinement of these three memories is not only the self's primal memories of coming into consciousness, but also of that self's relationship to language. At the start of Bernard's final soliloquy he again situates Mrs. Constable within the context of Elvedon – not named but invoked by his reference to "a woman ... a garden" – but here instead of bathing him she is a nanny figure who turns the pages of a picture-book and in effect initiates him into the symbolic: "That's a cow. That's a boat'" (239). This domestic vignette recurs at the end of the same soliloquy, after Bernard's embrace of the self's multiplicity, after his visionary rhetoric, and after his appeal for a child's discourse. Once again, the memory of this childhood scene is conflated with Elvedon: "for a moment I had [heard] the woods, had seen the house, the garden ... The old nurse who turns the pages of the picture-book had stopped and had said, 'Look. This is the truth'" (287). The "truth," finally, has to do with that which escapes the symbolic. What emerges from the accumulation of all these individual memories – Mrs. Constable, the bath, arrows of sensation, invisible enemies, a garden, a woman writing – is an image, at the center of Bernard's imaginative life, of a maternal figure and language.

Elvedon "records a vestigial memory" for Bernard to the extent that it harbors the traces and residue of a relation to maternity that then propels him toward Percival, and compels him to seek a discourse closer to the body – a discourse, in Kristevan terms, whose basis is "a reunion with the mother's body."[144] Both Percival and Elvedon are connected for Bernard with the recovery of that which has been lost, submerged, and buried in the unconscious by the process of attempting to become a unified subject. They are both also, crucially, associated with violence and the narrative of imperial conquest. When Bernard says of Elvedon, as a child, "[l]et us take possession of our secret territory" (22), and then imagines a "swamp ... a malarial jungle" (23), he demonstrates once again that English identity is constituted in relation to some colonial elsewhere. As the children come into consciousness as national subjects, they assume a place in language that is made possible only by the imperial myth. While Woolf is critical of this process of interpellation, she assents to its power, arguably because those are the cultural idioms available to her, and she is, finally, unable to see outside of her historical moment. Although Percival and Elvedon are each associated with that part of Bernard which longs to escape the symbolic, access to each, paradoxically, is associated with the doctrine of conquest and rule that is legitimized by the narrative of empire. By destabilizing both Percival's and Bernard's gender identification – each propagates certain hegemonic assumptions about men as the "inheritors" (86) of England – the novel demonstrates the necessity of feminizing British national culture. As the national subject splits, it seeks a return to an originary prehistoric English source; the effect of Bernard's liminality is thus to unearth this heterogeneous history through narrative: "I wish to go under; to visit the profound depths ... to explore; to hear vague, ancestral sounds of boughs creaking, of mammoths" (114). Geographically, Elvedon is described as "down there ever so far beneath us" (16), a spatial allusion to its link with the unconscious. What Woolf suggests through the triangulation of Percival, Bernard, and Elvedon is a reconfiguration of the nation by putting into language that which Western culture has silenced and repressed: the abjected maternal body. In this way, *The Waves* both confronts the problem of women's linguistic disinheritance through the portrayals of Jinny, Susan, and Rhoda, and re-imagines the cultural inclusion of real women through the depiction of Elvedon. Yet this elaboration of female authorship is conceivable only as a space of high culture, reminding us of Woolf's contention, elsewhere, that working-class women do not write literature.[145]

By feminizing Elvedon, and associating it with territory and English prehistory, Woolf naturalizes the lady's rights to a literary inheritance and, by extension, the rights of all women of a certain class. It is, moreover, through Elvedon's link with Percival – and hence, with medievalism – that we see further evidence that women's relation to empire is legitimized by their relation to territory, for in medieval times land was more commonly given to daughters throughout England.[146] Woolf never mentions this phenomenon *per se*, but she alludes to it through her association of the Elvedonian lady with conquest, territory, and the recuperation of the imperial narrative. The novel demonstrates that women's relation to empire is both collaborative and oppositional. To the extent that their geographical imaginary, like men's own, is infused with imperial referents that envision the body as "a whole universe, unconfined and capable of being everywhere" (292), the collaborative aspect appears to be the more prominent; however, this nostalgic fantasy of expansiveness is ultimately undermined by the prospect of the end of empire. Yet, even as the empire wanes, the lady's ubiquitous appearance suggests not only that women's writing cannot be eradicated or displaced, but that it is at the sacred heart of national culture; as Bernard says: "'I cannot interfere with ... the fixity of that woman writing' ... one cannot ... dislodge a woman. There they have remained all my life" (240–1). In Bernard's memory, Elvedon is a treacherous place: to be one of the "discoverers of [this] unknown land" will have unforeseeable consequences, and any transgression of its borders may mean sudden death (17). Elvedon is dangerous precisely because it represents the idea of women's literary colonization, their radical employment of the semiotic within a symbolic sphere. While this "language of signs" has not yet been realized, the lady functions as a living Baedeker who "carries the sign language ... into the sublime realms of art"; as such, she lets the reader know that this space – "'To Elvedon'" (17) – is already culturally marked as English.[147] We see this reflected in the fact that Elvedon is an *English* garden, a cultivated space that arguably inculcates "a sense of botanical nationalism."[148] While we can read Elvedon as the Englishwoman's "regained ... territory" (86), it is misleading to interpret it as "a utopia of feminine writing," for to idealize this phantom place in isolation from any relation to Bernard or Percival runs counter to the novel's implicit insistence on their integration, and it diminishes the text's recognition that women's access to language has a material basis.[149] Significantly, the lady writing has no counterpart in a female character: Elvedon remains only theoretically a signifying possibility that is legitimized by conquest. The novel sustains a tension between two seemingly irreconcilable positions, illustrating women's cultural and linguistic marginalization at the same time as it enshrines a mythical woman writer at the center of the text.

Elvedon, then, can be read as an image of Britain's cultural imaginary – "our universe ... our world" (22–3) – a maternalized space which functions as a kind of national unconscious in the novel, accessible only, as is true for Bernard, through the presumption that what language lacks is a maternal dimension. It is significant that Susan is the only female character who espies Elvedon, for her transgression signals the possibility of the cultural integration of the material and textual maternal bodies. Through the defamiliarizing of Percival, Woolf suggests that what is finally at stake for the nation is the recuperation of the maternal body, though, as I have argued, that body is inconceivable outside the parameters of empire. In colonizing a new and dangerous space through Percival's mediation,

Bernard reminds us of Woolf's admonition: "Words are dangerous things let us remember. A republic might be brought into being by a poem."[150] Elvedon is that "unsubstantial territory" (16), a republic presided over by Englishwomen – though only of a certain class – who reterritorialize the empire through language. Yet despite the text's formal iconoclasm and investment in what Woolf understands to be a progressive political vision for women, *The Waves* ultimately colludes with the conservative, albeit ideologically powerful, British feminist perspective that the mother is the moral guardian of the nation. Now that "civilisation is burnt out" (296); or, stated differently, now that symbolic discourse has ceased to tyrannize English culture, national consciousness can be revived through the redemptive mediation of Percival, in his archaic maternal aspect. Maternalist imperialism, Woolf suggests, is the civilizing mission that authorizes women's discursive entry into the public sphere, enabling them to embark on a "new world, never trodden" (287), through the trope of linguistic conquest.

Notes

1 Virginia Woolf, "The journal of Mistress Joan Martyn," *The Complete Shorter Fiction of Virginia Woolf*, ed. Susan Dick (New York: Harcourt Brace, 1985), 33; hereafter cited in the text.
2 Bonnie G. Smith discusses the centrality of the male gaze in her discussion of historical observation: *The Gender of History: Men, Women, and Historical Practice* (Cambridge, MA, and London: Harvard University Press, 1998), 140–1.
3 Ernest Renan, "What is a nation?" (1882) in Homi Bhabha ed. *Nation and Narration* (London: Routledge, 1990), 19.
4 Renato Rosaldo, "Imperialist nostalgia," *Representations*, 26 (spring, 1989): 108.
5 Simon Gikandi, *Maps of Englishness: Writing Identity in the Culture of Colonialism* (New York: Columbia University Press, 1996), 29.
6 Jane Marcus, "Britannia rules *The Waves*," *Decolonizing Tradition: New Views of Twentieth-Century "British" Literary Canons* (Urbana and Chicago, IL: University of Illinois Press, 1992), 144. Patrick McGee provides a trenchant critique of Marcus in "The politics of modernist form; or, who rules *The Waves*?" *Modern Fiction Studies*, 38 (1992).
7 Robert H. MacDonald discusses children as primary targets of imperial propaganda in his "Introduction" to *The Language of Empire: Myths and Metaphors of Popular Imperialism, 1880–1918* (Manchester and New York: Manchester University Press, 1994).
8 Anderson, *Imagined Communities*, 145, 154; Gikandi, *Maps of Englishness*, 27.
9 Virginia Woolf, *A Writer's Diary*, ed. Leonard Woolf (New York: Harcourt Brace & Co., 1954), 104. Recent critics who discuss the novel's engagement with history and politics include: Jessica Berman, *Modernist Fiction, Cosmopolitanism, and the Politics of Community* (Cambridge: Cambridge University Press, 2001); Jane Goldman, *The Feminist Aesthetics of Virginia Woolf: Modernism, Post-Impressionism and the Politics of the Visual* (Cambridge: Cambridge University Press, 1998); Judith Lee, "'This hideous shaping and moulding': war and *The Waves*" in Mark Hussey ed. *Virginia Woolf and War: Fiction, Reality, and Myth* (Syracuse, NY: Syracuse University Press, 1991); Marcus, "Britannia rules *The Waves*"; Kathy J. Phillips, *Virginia Woolf Against Empire* (Knoxville: University of Tennessee Press, 1994); Michael Tratner, *Modernism and Mass Politics: Joyce, Woolf, Eliot, Yeats* (Stanford, CA: Stanford University Press, 1995).
10 Like Harrison, who grounds her understanding of ancient Greek ritual practice in her Yorkshire familiarity with mysticism, Woolf at times collapses the distinctions between Greece and England. Recounting her experience at the Temple of Poseidon, Sunion, in 1932, Woolf writes: "I thought of Piccadilly ... This is England in the time of Chaucer ... So at Sunium ... all as in the time of Chaucer or Homer": *Dairy*, Vol. 4: 92.
11 Virginia Woolf, *The Waves* (New York: Harcourt Brace, 1978), 58; hereafter cited in the text.

12 Karen Kaivola, *All Contraries Confounded: The Lyrical Fiction of Virginia Woolf, Djuna Barnes, and Marguerite Duras* (Iowa City: University of Iowa Press, 1991), 26; Alex Zwerdling, *Virginia Woolf and the Real World* (Berkeley: University of California Press, 1986), 13.

13 Garrett Stewart discusses the alliterative structure of Woolf's sentences in "Catching the stylistic d/rift: sound defects in Woolf's *The Waves*," *English Literary History*, 54. 2 (summer, 1987).

14 From *The Teaching of English in England* (1921), reprinted in Judy Giles and Tim Middleton eds. *Writing Englishness 1900–1950: An Introductory Sourcebook on National Identity* (New York: Routledge, 1995), 157 and 155. Elsewhere, Woolf derides the idea of "a Society for Pure English" and revels instead in a fantasy of linguistic miscegenation: "Royal words mate with commoners. English words marry French words, German words, Indian words, Negro words … our dear Mother English … has gone a-roving": "Craftmanship," *Collected Essays*, Vol. 2: 250.

15 Arthur Mee, "Ourselves and the nation" in *The Children's Encyclopedia*, Vol. 9, reprinted in Giles and Middleton eds. *Writing Englishness 1900–1950*, 63–4.

16 Kathy Phillips observes that the six characters "project onto Percival their need for union, as with a mother," interpreting this desire for plentitude as a sign of Woolf's critique of "totalitarian politics": *Virginia Woolf Against Empire*, 157 and 156. Jessica Berman similarly links the novel's oceanic impulses with "the cult of Percival,"arguing that *The Waves* resists fascism precisely through its repudiation of Percival: *Modernist Fiction*, 147. Such readings, while persuasive, tell only one side of the story.

17 Woolf, *Letters*, Vol. 6: 354 and 460.

18 Marianne Hirsch, *The Mother/Daughter Plot: Narrative, Psychoanalysis, Feminism* (Bloomington: Indiana University Press, 1989), 96.

19 Laura Doyle, *Bordering on the Body: The Racial Matrix of Modern Fiction and Culture* (New York and Oxford: Oxford University Press, 1994), 4.

20 Julia Kristeva, *Crisis of the European Subject* (New York: Other Press, 2000), 105–9.

21 See Ruth Hoberman, *Gendering Classicism: The Ancient World in Twentieth-Century Women's Historical Fiction* (Albany: State University of New York Press, 1997). Critics who address Harrison's influence on Woolf include: Patricia Maika, *Virginia Woolf's "Between the Acts" and Jane Harrison's Con/spiracy* (Ann Arbor, MI: University Microfilms Research Press, 1987); Jane Marcus, *Virginia Woolf and the Languages of Patriarchy* (Bloomington: Indiana University Press, 1987); K.J. Phillips, *Dying Gods in Twentieth-Century Fiction* (Lewisburg, PA: Bucknell University Press, 1990), 17–92, and "Jane Harrison and modernism," *Journal of Modern Literature*, 17. 4 (1991): 465–576; Annabel Robinson, "Something odd at work: the influence of Jane Harrison on *A Room of One's Own*," *Wascana Review*, 22 (1987): 82–8; Sandra D. Shattuck, "The stage of scholarship: crossing the bridge from Harrison to Woolf" in Jane Marcus ed. *Virginia Woolf and Bloomsbury: A Centenary Celebration* (Indianapolis: Indiana University Press, 1987), 278–98.

22 Sigmund Freud, "Female sexuality," *Collected Papers: Volume 5*, ed. James Strachey (New York: Basic Books, 1959), 253–4.

23 *Ibid*. Carolyn Denver demonstrates the degree to which metaphors of nationalism and imperialism persistently emerge from psychoanalytic descriptions of the all-powerful mother in not only Freud, but Melanie Klein, whom Woolf also read: *Death and the Mother from Dickens to Freud* (Cambridge: Cambridge University Press, 1998).

24 Elizabeth Abel, *Virginia Woolf and the Fictions of Psychoanalysis* (Chicago, IL, and London: University of Chicago Press, 1989), xvi.

25 Jane Harrison, *Themis: A Study of the Social Origins of Greek Religion* (New York: University Books, 1962), 539.

26 *Ibid.*, 125.

27 Woolf, *Letters*, Vol. 3: 58; Vol. 2: 391.

28 Jane Harrison, *Alpha and Omega* (London: Sidgwick & Jackson, Ltd., 1915), 134–5.

29 For a fascinating overview of Harrison's life and work, see Mary Beard, *The Invention of Jane Harrison* (Cambridge, MA: Harvard Univeristy Press, 2000).

30 Emma Jung, *The Grail Legend* (Boston, MA: Sigo Press, 1980), 113.

31 Rosalyn Rossingnol, "The holiest vessel: maternal aspects of the Grail," *Arthuriana*, 5. 1 (1995): 53.

32 Shari Benstock, *Textualizing the Feminine: On the Limits of Genre* (Norman and London: University of Oklahoma Press, 1991), 37. Gillian Rose, *Feminism and Geography: The Limits of Geographical Knowledge* (Minneapolis: University of Minnesota Press, 1993), 60.

33 Luce Irigaray, "Sexual difference" in Toril Moi ed. *French Feminist Thought: A Reader* (Oxford: Blackwell, 1987), 123.

34 Makiko Minow-Pinkney reads *The Waves* through a Kristevan lens, but she does not historicize the novel's engagement with the maternal: *Virginia Woolf and the Problem of the Subject* (New Brunswick, NJ: Rutgers University Press, 1983), Ch. 6.

35 Julia Kristeva, *About Chinese Women* (New York and London: Marion Boyars, 1986), 34 and 29–30.

36 *Ibid.*, 30.

37 *Ibid.*

38 *Ibid.*, 41.

39 Julia Kristeva, "Psychoanalysis and the polis," *Critical Inquiry*, 9. 1 (1982): 84.

40 *Ibid.*

41 Julia Kristeva, *Desire in Language: A Semiotic Approach to Literature and Art* (New York: Columbia University Press, 1980), 157.

42 Marcia Ian explores the recurring centrality of "the phallic mother" within literary modernism in *Remembering the Phallic Mother: Psychoanalysis, Modernism, and the Fetish* (Ithaca, NY: Cornell University Press, 1993).

43 *Ibid.*, 240. Kelly Oliver discusses this dualistic model of maternity in *Reading Kristeva: Unraveling the Double-Bind* (Indianapolis: Indiana University Press, 1993), 1–17.

44 Julia Kristeva, *Powers of Horror: An Essay on Abjection* (New York: Columbia University Press, 1982), 4.

45 *Ibid.*, 167. Norma Claire Moruzzi, "National abjects: Julia Kristeva on the process of political self-identification" in Kelly Oliver ed. *Ethics, Politcs, and Difference in Julia Kristeva's Writing* (New York: Routledge, 1993), 144.

46 What we see throughout Woolf's analysis of the gendered implications of novelistic form and her discussion of women's political agency is the structural interdependence of the oblique, the deviant, and the skewed.

47 Woolf, "Women and fiction," 50–1. Linden Peach, "No longer a view: Virginia Woolf in the 1930s and the 1930s in Virginia Woolf" in Maroula Joannou ed. *Women Writers of the 1930s: Gender, Politics and History* (Edinburgh: Edinburgh University Press, 1999), 192–204.

48 Tamar Katz insightfully discusses Percival's "peculiarly double function" in *Impressionist Subjects: Gender, Interiority, and Modernist Fiction in England* (Urbana and Chicago, IL: University of Illinois Press, 2000), 189.

49 Kristeva, *Desire in Language*, 182. It is worth noting that Percival was modeled after Woolf's beloved brother Thoby, who died prematurely from typhoid. After she completed *The Waves*, Woolf wrote: "sitting these 15 minutes in a state of glory, & calm, & some tears, thinking of Thoby & if I could write Julian Thoby Stephen 1881–1906 on the first page": *Diary of Virginia Woolf*, Vol. 4: *1931–1935*: 10.

50 See Janet Winston, "'Something out of harmony': *To the Lighthouse* and the subject(s) of empire," *Woolf Studies Annual*, 2 (1996): 39–70; Doyle, *Bordering on the Body*, 139–73.

51 Antoinette Burton, "'The Indian woman,'1865–1915" in Nupur Chaudhuri and Margaret Strobel eds. *Western Women and Imperialism: Complicity and Resistance* (Bloomington and Indianapolis: Indiana University Press, 1992).

52 For references to the maternal, see *The Waves: The Two Holograph Drafts*, ed. J. W. Graham (Toronto: University of Toronto Press, 1976), 9–10, 44–5, 61–2.

53 Benedict Anderson, *Imagined Communities: Reflections on the Origin and Spread of Nationalism* (London and New York: Verso, 1983), 204. See also Renan, "What is a nation?," 11; Bhabha, *Nation and Narration*, 311.

54 Woolf, "The leaning tower," *Essays*, Vol. 2: 180. Bhabha, *Nation and Narration*, 294.

55 Anderson, *Imagined Communities*, 145.

56 Andrew Higson, *Waving the Flag: Constructing a National Cinema in Britain* (Oxford: Clarendon Press, 1995), 277.

57 Julia Kristeva, *Nations Without Nationalism* (New York: Columbia University Press, 1993), 30; also *Strangers to Ourselves* (New York: Columbia University Press, 1991), 14.

58 While Britons regarded Australia as a white colony whose climate enabled "British families [to] continue true to ancestral type," there was also considerable anxiety about maintaining the purity of "White Australia": Vaughan Cornish, *Geographical Essays* (London: Sifteon, Praed & Co.), 13–14.

59 Hoberman, *Gendering Classicism*, 103.

60 Julia Kristeva, *Revolution in Poetic Language*, trans. Margaret Waller (New York: Columbia University Press, 1984), 43.

61 James Donald, "How English is it? National culture and popular literature," *New Formations*, 6 (1988): 32.

62 Anderson, *Imagined Communities*, 33.

63 Julia Kristeva, "Women's time," *The Kristeva Reader* (New York: Columbia University Press, 1986), 192.

64 Anderson, *Imagined Communities*, 26, 36.

65 Jane Mackay and Pat Thane, "The Englishwoman" in Robert Colls and Philip Dodd eds. *Englishness: Politics and Culture 1880–1920* (London: Croom Helm, 1986), 199.

66 Eileen B. Sypher makes a similar observation about the girls'dependence on reflection in "*The Waves*: a utopia of androgyny?" in Elaine K. Ginsberg and Laura Moss Gottlieb eds. *Virginia Woolf: Centennial Essays* (New York: Whitston, 1983), 198–9.

67 Ian Baucom, *Out of Place: Englishness, Empire, and the Locations of Identity* (Princeton, NJ: Princeton University Press, 1999), 4.

68 Gikandi, *Maps of Englishness*, 8.

69 For a discussion of the links between architecture and Englishness, see Baucom, *Out of Place*, 41–74.

70 See Sue Best, "Sexualizing space" in Elizabeth Grosz and Elspeth Probyn eds. *Sexy Bodies: The Strange Carnalities of Feminism* (New York: Routledge 1995), 182.

71 Rita Felski, *The Gender of Modernity* (Cambridge, MA: Harvard University Press, 1995), 41.

72 Gaston Bachelard, *The Poetics of Space* (Boston, MA: Beacon Press, 1969), 7.

73 See Minow-Pinkney, *Virginia Woolf and the Problem of the Subject*, 187.

74 Raymond Williams, *Towards 2000* (London: Chatto & Windus, 1983), 180.

75 Julie Vandivere, "Waves and fragments: linguistic construction as subject formation in Virginia Woolf," *Twentieth-Century Literature*, 42. 2 (1996): 223.

76 Alastair Pennycook, *English and the Discourses of Colonialism* (London and New York: Routledge, 1998), 73.

77 *Ibid.*, 80.

78 Patricia Ondek Laurence, *The Reading of Silence: Virginia Woolf in the English Tradition* (Stanford, CA: Stanford University Press, 1991), 169.

79 Gikandi, *Maps of Englishness*, 29.

80 Renan, "What is a nation?" 19.

81 *Ibid.*

82 Jesse Weston, *From Ritual to Romance* (Princeton, NJ: Princeton University Press, 1993).

83 Kathryn Tidrick, *Empire and the English Character* (London: I.B. Tauris & Co., 1990), 231. A. Susan Williams, *Ladies of Influence: Women of the Elite in Interwar Britain* (London: Allen Lane, 2000), 70.

84 Christine Poulson provides an overview of the popularity of the Authurian myth during this period, linking it to the discourses of race, gender, and nationality: *The Quest for the Grail: Arthurian Legend in British Art 1840–1920* (Manchester and New York: Manchester University Press, 1999).

85 Woolf, "Impressions at Bayreuth," *Essays*, Vol. 1: 289.

86 Paul Rich, "The quest for Englishness," *History Today*, 37 (June, 1987): 25. See also Stephanie L. Barczewski, *Myth and National Identity in Nineteenth-Century Britain: The Legends of King Arthur and Robin Hood* (Oxford: Oxford University Press, 2000); Mark Girouard, *The*

Return to Camelot: Chivalry and the English Gentleman (New Haven, CT: Yale University Press, 1981); P. J. Cain and J. G. Hopkins, *British Imperialism 1688–2000* (London: Longman, 2002), 38, 56 n. 91, 646–7.

87 Kristeva, *Powers of Horror*, 15.

88 See Hoberman, *Gendering Classicism*, 104, 111, 103. Cain and Hopkins, *British Imperialism 1688–2000*, 45.

89 Power dined with Woolf in 1925. See Woolf, *Diary*, Vol. 3: 30.

90 Easthope, *Englishness and National Culture* (London and New York: Routledge, 1999), 46.

91 See Tina Barr, "Divine politics: Virginia Woolf's journey toward Eleusis in *To the Light-house*," *boundary 2*, 20. 1 (1993): 125–45. Woolf's portrayal of Percival's body as an analogue for nature further underscores his maternal role as a conduit for Englishness, for the country (and rural inhabitants) were widely regarded as "the essence of England, uncontaminated by racial degeneration." Alun Howkins, "The discovery of rural England," in *Englishness: Politics and Culture 1880–1920* (London and New Hampshire: Croom Helm, 1986), 69.

92 Kristeva, *Revolution in Poetic Language*, 47.

93 See Makiko Minow-Pinkney, "Virginia Woolf: 'seen from a foreign land'" in John Fletcher and Andrew Benjamin eds. *Abjection, Melancholia and Love: The Works of Julia Kristeva* (London and New York: Routledge, 1990), 170.

94 Weston, *From Ritual to Romance*, 141.

95 Rossingnol, "The holiest vessel," 53. See also Sherlyn Abdoo, "Woman as Grail in T.S. Eliot's *The Waste Land*," *Centennial Review*, 28 (1984): 48–60; Susan Aronstein, "Rewriting Percival's sister: eucharistic vision and typological destiny in the *Queste del San Graal*," *Women's Studies*, 21. 2 (1992): 211–30.

96 Caroline Walker Bynum, *Jesus as Mother: Studies in the Spirituality of the High Middle Ages* (Berkeley: University of California Press, 1982).

97 See Patricia Ann Quattrin, "The milk of Christ: Herzeloyde as spiritual symbol in Wolfram Von Eschenbach's *Parzival*" in John Carmi Parsons and Bonnie Wheeler eds. *Medieval Mothering* (New York and London: Garland, 1996), 25–38.

98 Christine Poulson discusses the long association between the Grail legend and British nationalism in *The Quest for the Grail*, Ch. 4.

99 See Anthony Easthope, *Englishness and National Culture* (London and New York: Routledge, 1999), 28 and 36.

100 Kathy Phillips reads Percival as a vegetation deity: *Dying Gods in Twentieth-Century Fiction*, 29–37.

101 Weston, *From Ritual to Romance*, 147.

102 Mary Baine Campbell. "Finding the Grail: fascist aesthetics and mysterious objects" in Debra N. Mancoff ed. *King Arthur's Modern Return* (New York: Garland, 1998), 213–25.

103 Harrison, *Ancient Art and Ritual*, 36 and 50; Weston, *From Ritual to Romance*, 146–7.

104 Harrison, *Epilegomena to the Study of Greek Religion and Themis: A Study of the Social Origins of Greek Religion* (New Hyde Park, NY: University Books, 1962), 125.

105 Bonnie G. Smith discusses Harrison's *Themis* as a text that privileges the eating of raw flesh as a means of imbibing cosmic power: *The Gender of History: Men, Women, and Historical Practice* (Cambridge, MA, and London: Harvard University Press, 1998), 237. Woolf's scene also recalls Harrison's focus on the centrality of dancing in *Ancient Art and Ritual* (30) and *Themis* (45–6).

106 Geraldine Heng, "Cannibalism, the First Crusade, and the genesis of medieval romance," *differences: A Journal of Feminist Cultural Studies*, 10. 1 (1998): 109.

107 Harrison, *Ancient Art and Ritual*, 29. For Woolf's remarks about Africa, see "An expedition to Hampton Court," *A Passionate Apprentice: The Early Journals, 1897–1909*, ed. Mitchell A Leaska (San Diego, CA: Harcourt Brace, 1990), 172.

108 Harrison, *Themis*, 27 and 485.

109 In *The Waves*, the literal eating of meat functions as an insidious, masculine tool of cultural imperialism. Woolf's attack on meat-eating is perhaps in part attributable to the fact that meat consumption during the interwar period was associated with national decay. See Sadie Ward and John Creasey, *The Countryside between the Wars, 1918–1940: A Photographic Record*

(London: B.T. Batsford, 1984), 9. In Woolf's novel, scenes that involve meat give suggestion of rottenness and grossness (109), male dominance (44), cultural assimilation (92–4), and the gluttonous aspects of empire. Because eating meat is linked to the ingestion of empire, we see ambivalence from the female characters. Rhoda, for example, is terrified that she will be "hung … like a joint of meat among other joints of meat" (162). Ultimately, Woolf suggests that beef consumption turns the body into slabs of meat – "gorged … torpid … swollen" (162) – or, ideologically speaking, turns citizens into unconscious subjects of empire. For a discussion of eating in Woolf, see: Harriet Blodgett, "Food for thought in Virginia Woolf's novels," *Woolf Studies Annual*, 3 (1997): 46–60; Allie Glennie, *Ravenous Identity: Eating and Eating Distress in the Life and Work of Virginia Woolf* (New York: Garland, 2000); Patricia Moran, *Word of Mouth: Body Language in Katherine Mansfield and Virginia Woolf* (Charlottesville: University of Virginia Press, 1996).

110 British agriculture was in distress during the interwar period, when economic stagnation and a governmental policy of importing imperial goods threatened domestic farmers. Rising beef prices by the early 1930s encouraged the livestock industry to supply low-quality cows to farmers, thus contributing to the beef industry's public image as unhealthful. Several people, for instance H.J. Massingham, promoted positive measures to ensure "the regeneration of rural life, necessary to 'regain our national health'": Ward and Creasey, *The Countryside Between the Wars, 1918–1940*, 9 and 13.

111 Renan, "What is a nation?" 11. The imperial imagery of the italicized interludes echoes this preoccupation with conquest. For example, in the interlude that frames the section devoted to the group's farewell dinner with Percival, "the waves rose like the tossing of lances and assegais … beat[ing] like a drum that raises a regiment of plumed and turbaned soldiers" (108–9). Linden Peach persuasively reads such references as a reflection of British anxiety over the demise of empire: see "No longer a view," 196–200.

112 Bernard ridicules empire – "Then people put teapots on their heads and say, 'I am a King!'" (227) – therein encapsulating the novel's larger tension between anti-imperialist parody and imperial nostalgia.

113 Pennycook, *English and the Discourses of Colonialism*, 78.

114 Easthope, *Englishness and National Culture*, 37.

115 Freud, *Group Psychology and the Analysis of the Ego*, trans. and ed. James Strachey (New York: Norton, 1959 [1922]), 92–6.

116 Kelly Oliver, *Reading Kristeva: Unraveling the Double-Bind* (Bloomington and Indianapolis: Indiana University Press, 1993), 53.

117 Kristeva, *Powers of Horror*, 1.

118 Bhabha, *Nation and Narration*, 298.

119 Kristeva, *Strangers to Ourselves*, 13.

120 Ibid., 183, 192, 182, 15, and 5.

121 Quoted by Kelly Oliver, *Reading Kristeva*, 62.

122 Kristeva, *Revolution in Poetic Language*, 153–4.

123 Alun Howkins, "The discovery of rural England" in Robert Colls and Philip Dodd eds. *Englishness: Politics and Culture 1880–1920* (London: Croom Helm, 1986). Georgina Boyes argues that the revival of English folk music in early twentieth-century England was in response to perceived threats to English racial and cultural superiority: *The Imagined Village: Culture, Ideology, and the English Folk Revival* (Manchester: Manchester University Press, 1993).

124 Neville conveys Percival's alignment with the semiotic: "For he cannot read. Yet … he understands … Not the words – but what are the words?" (48). Like Mrs. Ramsay (*TLH*, 115 and 119), Percival is associated with a pre-linguistic discourse that issues from the body.

125 Quoted by Marc Manganaro in *Myth, Rhetoric, and the Voice of Authority: A Critique of Frazer, Eliot, Frye, and Campbell* (New Haven, CT, and London: Yale University Press, 1992), 92.

126 Ibid., 85 and 88.

127 For a classic discussion of the male modernist appropriation of femininity, see Sandra Gilbert, "Costumes of the mind: transvestitism as metaphor in modern literature," *Critical Inquiry*, 7 (1980): 397–8.

128 Roger Fry, "Children's drawings," *A Roger Fry Reader*, ed. Christopher Reed (Chicago, IL, and London: University of Chicago Press, 1996), 267. See also Fry's "The art of the bushmen" and "Negro sculpture," *Vision and Design* (London: Chatto & Windus, 1925), 85–98, 99–103. Clive Bell draws similar analogies between the child and the artist in "Art and society," *Art* (New York: Capricorn Books, 1958), 186–7.

129 See Gustav Jahoda, *Images of Savages: Ancient Roots of Modern Prejudice* (London and New York: Routledge, 1999), 7–9; see also Ch. 10; Harrison, *Alpha and Omega*, 166–7. Bernard's embrace of "primitive" discourse reminds us of Woolf's insistence that what "we need" is "a new language ... primitive, subtle, sensual, obscene": "On being ill," *Essays*, Vol. 4: 319.

130 Harrison, *Themis*, 485.

131 Harrison, *Themis*, 125; Harrison, *Alpha and Omega*, 51.

132 Peter Fryer discusses this stereotype in *Staying Power: The History of Black People in Britain* (London and Sydney: Pluto Press, 1984), Ch. 7. For a discussion of racialized performance in the novel, see Genevieve Abravanel, "Woolf in blackface: identification across *The Waves*" in Jessica Berman and Jane Goldman eds. *Virginia Woolf Out of Bounds: Selected Papers from the Tenth Annual Conference on Virginia Woolf* (New York: Pace University Press, 2001), 113–19.

133 Kristeva, *Powers of Horror*, 72.

134 Harrison, *Themis*, 46; Harrison, *Alpha and Omega*, 48.

135 Harrison, *Alpha and Omega*, 166–7.

136 Alice Jardine argues that, for Freud, "any conceptual system that valorizes the maternal space, the Id, is mystical": *Gynesis: Configurations of Women and Modernity* (Ithaca, NY: Cornell University Press, 1985), 142–3.

137 Kristeva, *Crisis of the European Subject*, 105.

138 I am grateful to Renee Dickinson for this insight: "The language of empire: identity and the imperial narrative in Virginia Woolf's *The Waves*" (unpublished essay).

139 J. Mordaunt Crook discusses Elveden Hall in *The Rise of the Nouveaux Riches: Style and Status in Victorian and Edwardian Architecture* (North Pomfret, VT: Trafalgar Square, 1999). See also Sonya Rudikoff, *Ancestral Houses: Virginia Woolf and the Aristocracy* (Palo Alto, CA: Society for the Promotion of Science and Scholarship, 1999), 199–201.

140 I would also argue that Elvedon conflates several images from Woolf's recollection of her childhood summer home, Talland House, which she describes as "an old white country house" surrounded by a garden, with "[l]ong windows [which] open onto the lawn." At the center of this "poetical fairyland" is an image of her mother and the sound of a voice reading poetry. See Woolf, "A sketch of the past" in Jeanne Schulkind ed. *Moments of Being* (New York: Harcourt Brace, 1985), 86–8.

141 That the woman who writes in Elvedon is a "lady" suggests her connection with the British aristocracy, which was in decline during the half century before the First World War due to agricultural depression, the extension of the franchise, and the passage of the 1911 Parliament Bill which limited aristocratic power and attacked the peerage system. Woolf claims to be in favor of the older peerage (those lords and dukes and viscounts whose families can be traced back to time immemorial), while asserting that she is against those peers of more recent vintage, that is, those elevated because of political expediency. See *Letters*, Vol. 5: 131. Of course, the oldest peers were once given their titles out of political expediency. See *Debrett's Peerage and Baronetage*, ed. Patrick Montague-Smith (New York: Arco Publishing Co., 1977). Woolf's fictionalized Elvedon appeared during a period when the British Society for the Protection of Ancient Buildings urged patriotic respect for "old houses" and "primeval earthworks," maintaining that the beauty of England is a source of national distinction. Trevelyan, *Must England's Beauty Perish?* 18–20.

142 Quoted by David Matless, *Landscape and Englishness* (London: Reaktion Books, 1998), 117. Both Vaughan Cornish's *The Scenery of England: A Harmonious Grouping in Town and Country* (London: Council for the Preservation of Rural England, 1932) and H.V. Morton's *In Search of England* (New York: Dodd, Mead & Co., 1927) invoke the language of the Grail quest and focus upon the landscape of ancient Britain, seeing it as a space that reflects the essential racial and psychological character of England.

143 For an examination of the symbolic significance of Stonehenge, see Grahame Clark,

Prehistoric England (London and New York: B.T. Batsford, 1940), Ch. 9; Timothy Darville, *Prehistoric Britain* (New Haven, CT, and London: Yale University Press, 1987). The Ancient Monuments Act was passed in 1931, specifically to help safeguard the environs of places such as Stonehenge. Woolf's description of Stonehenge in 1903 anticipates her representation of Percival: see *A Passionate Apprentice*, 199–200.

144 Kristeva, *Revolution in Poetic Language*, 153. Joseph Allen Boone contends that the woman "writing at the core of Bernard's mind" is "an image of his mother": "The meaning of Elvedon in *The Waves*: a key to Bernard's experience and Woolf's vision," *Modern Fiction Studies*, 27. 4 (1981–82): 634.

145 See Woolf's "Introductory letter" to Margaret Llewelyn Davies ed. *Life As We Have Known It* (New York: Norton, 1975).

146 Eileen Power, *Medieval Women* (London: Methuen, 1924), 38.

147 Woolf, "Craftsmanship," *Collected Essays*, Vol. 2: 246.

148 Donald P. McCracken, *Gardens of Empire: Botanical Institutions of the Victorian British Empire* (London and Washington: Leicester University Press, 1997), 3.

149 Minow-Pinkney, *Virginia Woolf and the Problem of the Subject*, 179.

150 Virginia Woolf, "Royalty," *"The Moment" and Other Essays* (San Diego: Harcourt Brace Jovanovitch, 1974), 240.

Epilogue
Rebuilding the house
of England

Suddenly, from the loud-speakers, crashed the National Anthem ... They were singing with the whole kingdom, perhaps the empire. They were banded in the unity of mass emotion. Sarah could not remain immune ... "And the nations of them that are saved shall walk in the light." (Winifred Holtby, *South Riding*, 1936)

Well, then, when this loss of faith is getting a real hold ... that is the time the Evangelists of truth must start their mission ... I know one place from which, if we all have good luck, a messenger *will* come, and that is from England. (Katherine Burdekin, *Swastika Night*, 1937)

The idea of England as a new Jerusalem permeated British women's culture, making both literal and figurative appearances in the fictions which appeared throughout the interwar period. The two novels from which these epigraphs are drawn not only represent England in such a redemptive light, but depict it as a specifically *feminine* space that offers secularized salvation through a re-awakening of national consciousness. Like Richardson, Warner, Butts, and Woolf, the authors of these two novels are deeply critical of imperialism and nationalism at the same time as they evince a great love of nation and position themselves as transmitters of cultural renewal. Written during the 1930s, a decade of economic crisis, unemployment, poverty, protest, and impending war, the words of Holtby and Burdekin, like those of the other writers examined in this study, envision national revival not through the deployment of a crude chauvinism – "England ... the mistress of the globe" – but through a dissemination of feminine values that identify women, and feminized protagonists, as "moral leader[s] of civilisation."[1] We find evidence of this essentially domestic nationalism in Holtby's best-selling *South Riding*, in which the heroine, Sarah Burton, attends a Jubilee celebration (alluding to the Silver Jubilee marked by Britons on May 6, 1935) at which the narrator interweaves religious rhetoric with flag-waving and bombastic music. Sarah critiques overt patriotic fervor, but nonetheless experiences her most epiphanic moment amid this "demonstration of national unity" (482); as she contemplates her own "heretical" faith and overhears a minister's references to "the holy Jerusalem" and "salvation" (484), Sarah wonders what it means for the nation to play the role of redeemer. Alternating between a critique of the political system and a concern for the "citizens of the future" (488), Sarah succumbs to the "unity of mass emotion" that the Jubilee spectacle induces. Holtby demonstrates not only how powerful the conservative discourse of national redemption is – Sarah ultimately sees herself as a politically progressive "sav[ior]" (489) of an "everlasting Providence" (321) – but shows how that discourse facilitates women's emancipatory aims. Published the same year, Burdekin's widely read *Swastika Night* similarly plays with salvational and national rhetoric, vehemently critiquing nationalism, imperialism, and the doctrine of "racial-superiority" that fuels German fascism. At the same time, Burdekin locates cultural salvation in the English people, identifying them as potential "Evangelists of Truth" who will "not only ... deliver *England* from the Germans," but ultimately will "deliver the world" from mass destruction.[2] Like the other British women writers examined here, Burdekin and Holtby express complex, ambivalent, and bifurcated responses to the notion of national belonging, ultimately seeking a sacrosanct national space in which "we are members one of another" (*SR*, 490).

Despite the obvious temperamental and ideological differences among the British women writers of the interwar period, there are surprising areas of congruence in their thinking, such as their shared desire for a communal national space. These commonalities make it not only possible but crucial to begin to see these writers as a part of an articulable cultural formation: where women are concerned, a mystical union with England supersedes other kinds of political commitments. Their use of mystical discourse can be understood as part of a larger resurgence of mysticism during this period, when female and lesbian writers often used spiritual experience as a frame for questioning received notions of gender and sexuality.[3] For Richardson, Warner, Butts, and Woolf, this mystical state is accessible only through some form of mediation: thus, we see their repeated focus on women's dual perspective; on the use of metonymy to inscribe femininity; on allusions to mythic structures as a way of compensating for women's historical elision; and on a destabilizing of gender binaries even as femininity is enshrined as sacred. The fantasy of transnational unity informing these writers' varied strains of national allegiance appears, ironically, to be indebted to the very limitations imposed on female subjects by their curtailed citizenship rights. The "sudden splitting off of consciousness," as Woolf describes women's bifurcated sociopolitical position, translates women's cultural liminality into an asset by highlighting the female subject's multiperspectivalism – a shifting location which better equips her to fashion a universal perspective.[4] Due to this psychic splitting, British women of the interwar years invariably occupy a dual location – neither fully within nor completely outside of national culture. Women are "always ... bringing the world into different perspectives," that is, remapping public space in order to account for their "alien" (*ROO*, 97) viewpoint. We can see this attempt to suture the gap between women's real and imagined geographies echoed in Warner's description of "bi-location"; in Richardson's desire "to be perfectly in two places at once"; and in Butts's belief that women have the unique ability "to live in two worlds at once ... in time and out of it" (*CC*, 13).[5] Both Richardson and Butts represent female spectatorship as the way by which to access this realm of temporal simultaneity, though each ultimately values vision only because it facilitates another mode of perception – one that privileges the unseen. The female eye is a revelatory organ, for it can access what Richardson calls "the mystery of space" (*Pilgrimage*, 4: 648) that is distinctively English. It is in response to their problematic relations to habitable national space that these four writers reorganize temporal and spatial dimensions, to embrace what Warner calls the "secret place between two worlds … ambiguous territory."[6] As Woolf puts it in *Orlando*, "when we write of a woman, everything is out of place" (47).

Such acute spatial displacement may account both for British women's divided national loyalties *and* for why the four authors examined here privilege a logic of substitution as a way to mitigate the actual cultural marginality of the female body, with symbolic objects or the land itself typically standing in for the English nation. Thus, both Butts and Woolf metonymically link the Grail with the female – or, in the case of Woolf, the feminized – body in order to align that body with English- ness. Butts, furthermore, depicts both Scylla and Felicity as interchangeable with the land, as signs of their fecundity, while Woolf represents Percival as a maternal substitute who is similarly linked with territory and associated with cultural rebirth and renewal. Butts and Woolf construct novels that feature central characters who are largely absent (Felicity; Percival), and both conceptualize that absent nucleus as the driving force which compels the rest of the characters to search for what has been lost. In either case, the quest is about the search, ultimately, for national origins and unity. In Richardson and Warner, this desire for national affiliation entails the displacement and recontainment of the lesbian body, which is meto- nymically (and mystically) linked with territory – either the city or the country – in order to signal its inherent Englishness. If nationalism is conventionally reinforced through imagery that equates the female body with the land, and if British women themselves seek to see the feminine as coextensive with the nation, then it makes sense that they would trade on – even as they manipulate – these engrained asso- ciations as a way in which to stage their complex affiliations. Hence, Butts and Woolf subversively use the trope of the nation as *motherland* – in each case femininity is aligned with spiritual regeneration and racial preservation – while Richardson and Warner exploit the homoerotic possibilities of the female–female bond between woman and nation by representing England as not a mother but a lover. In doing so, these writers refute the contention that women have no place in the cultural imaginary by demonstrating how the nation can be accessed through nurture and/or eroticism.

Like Butts and Woolf, both Richardson and Warner rely on mythic structures and primitivist iconography (each relies upon a particular vision of the nation's prehistory) in order to make a case for women's national inclusion; in this way, they tacitly acknowledge that only a literary "supplement to history" (*ROO*, 45) can successfully chronicle the perspective of those who have been eclipsed by dominant culture. Where Butts and Woolf borrow from Arthurian legend and matriarchal prehistory, Warner alludes to sexological discourse that links homosexuality to the primitive to challenge her culture's assumptions about sexuality and convey a distinctly English mysticism. Although Richardson does not rely on identifiable mythic structures, such as those invoked by Butts or Woolf, like them – like Warner, too – she links the mystical with English territory in order to tap into a collective unconscious that is overtly femininized.[7] Indeed, the language Miriam uses to describe her joy in Quaker community – "togetherness on neutral territory" (*Pilgrimage*, 4: 634) – is not only resonant with imperial notions of transparent space, but is inextricably tied to her sexual and emotional intimacy with Jean, the transcendent signifier of "sacred place" (4: 609).[8] This shared preoccupation with mystic consciousness, or what Woolf calls the "ancient consciousness of women," appears to embrace a universalized–transnational subjectivity, but finds its expression through imagery steeped in the particularity of Englishness.[9] All four authors invert the hierarchy of the primitive and the civilized by representing the 'primitive' nature of femininity as a kind of moral compass through which the masculinized nation – overly mechanized, rational, detached, individualistic, and violent – can be repositioned and healed. To that extent, each echoes Willa Muir's 1926 contention that women are more closely aligned with "the processes of the unconscious." Each writer constructs her own fantasy out of the idea that "the really creative New Woman" can revitalize civilization through the construction of "a feminine State."[10] Although these authors concur that masculinity is the most intractable of the barriers to women's national inclusion, all four simultaneously complicate this critique by destabilizing gender binaries and representing their protagonists as androgynes and sexual outlaws, mediating the polarized social identities of male and female, and the sexual identities of heterosexual–homosexual, in order to convey those characters' cultural liminality. Thus, Richardson masculinizes Miriam, employing her phallic identification as a marker of her lesbianism; Woolf represents Bernard as androgynous and depicts Percival as a phallic mother; Warner portrays Lolly's "unladylike" passions and Satan's transgenderism as integral to their sexual identities; and Butts imbues both Scylla and Felicity with a castrating power that suggests their female monstrosity. These gender border-crossers become in effect new mythic heroes, grounded in but complicating the discourse of the primitive which gives rise to them. Cumulatively, these preoccupations suggest that, as British women modernists experience themselves as gendered and sexual subjects, they constantly negotiate a disorienting slippage between male and female identifications.

As these same women experience themselves as national subjects, they similarly negotiate a split identification – what Richardson calls the state of being at once "not-English as well as English" (*Pilgrimage*, 4: 632). The question of how this national liminality affects their status as English modernists is important, particularly given the classic male modernist fetishization of formal innovation and its simultaneous devaluation of femininity. We can see such disparagement reflected in T.S. Eliot's characterization of Katherine Mansfield's short story "Bliss," which he dismisses as "slight," "negligible," and lacking in "moral implication." Eliot's constrained praise of Mansfield's technical artistry is tempered by his disparagement of her content – the feelings of a disillusioned wife: "she has handled perfectly the *minimum* material – it is what I believe would be called feminine."[11] In using "feminine" Eliot effectively collapses the distinction between Mansfield's form and her content, leaving the reader to infer that her "skill" is severely "limited" by its debilitating focus on domestic life. To generalize that male modernists frequently characterize modernist form as essentially masculine – "the power of the spermatozoid is precisely the power of exteriorizing a form," in Pound's words – is to repeat a critical commonplace; but Eliot's characterization of Mansfield's work as inherently "feminine" is worth repeating because it exposes the belief that the particularity of the woman writer locates her outside the English literary tradition of "men of letters" whose gender is allegedly undetectable.[12] One might argue that the very selection of experimentalism should be read as a credentializing or legitimizing move, on the part of Richardson, Warner, Butts, and Woolf, given the period's opposition to traditional realism, its denigration of mass cultural forms as artistically impoverished, and its institutionalization of the Leavisite construction of English literature as an academic discipline. If British women's use of experimentalism can be read as an aim at literary legitimacy, it can furthermore be understood as an attempt to construct new cultural paradigms – paradigms that would challenge trivializing views such as Eliot's that "the moral and social ramifications [of women's fiction] are outside of the terms of reference."[13] British women modernists eschew that perspective by employing modernist formal experimentation both to critique the "Phalliculturists" and to position themselves as moral guardians of what Olive Moore calls the "[n]ationalisation of the emotions" – her biting observation that feminine values will become "universal only when raised to the dignity of an Act of Parliament."[14]

Moore's "[n]ationalisation of the emotions" unintentionally captures a central tenet shared by Richardson, Warner, Butts, and Woolf: namely, the desire to alter the course of British culture by taking that which is "psychically sick" (to borrow Butts's locution) and make it healthy through an infusion of femininity.[15] This restorative desire is part of a larger cultural paradigm that identifies women at the forefront of "the birth of a new social era," in feminist Dora Montefiore's words, that will shift consciousness "from the material to the spiritual plane."[16] We can see Butts's preoccupation with healing echoed by Richardson, Warner, and Woolf, each of whom seeks to gain access to a collective national unconscious as a way to restore awareness of the "holy beauty" of their "native heath" (*Pilgrimage*, 2: 187, 4: 635). This peculiarly English vision of collectivity is powerful enough to unite even such politically polarized writers as Warner and Butts in understanding that rural England is constitutive of English national identity. Even Richardson, who idealizes London, exhibits a nostalgia for the countryside by having Miriam eventually retreat to the "healing salve" (4: 414) of Sussex – a traditional community where change was protracted and oxen were still used for plowing as late as 1926.[17] Without homogenizing these four authors, it is still possible to note how a love of the land dominates their imagination of the nation. Indeed, the sanctity of the land arguably remains the dominant mobilizing myth of interwar Britons generally, even when that stance is ironized, as it is in Woolf's *Orlando*, as the "English disease, a love of Nature" (143). To regard the land in such a redemptive light, one might argue, in itself reflects a conservative attachment to the sacredness of place, one that in *Orlando*, for instance, mitigates that character's initial forsaking of England for apparently liberatory foreign territory. While it is true that Orlando's sex-change occurs in Constantinople, she does not ultimately reject English soil. On the contrary, Orlando's repatriation is motivated precisely by a longing for rural England, that imaginary landscape of crooning woods, gleaming fields, and manicured gardens which greets her at the end of the novel, when she flings herself on the ground and embraces the land as she would a body, attempting to bury her poem – "The Oak Tree" – as a tribute to the majestic land that gave rise to its conception.[18] In this way, conservative notions of what it means to be an English-woman may be said to inform the experimental aesthetic practices of Richardson, Warner, Butts, and Woolf, however much they are complicated by the simul-taneous presence of more progressive aims.

These authors convey their visions of the re-awakening of national conscious-ness, as I have argued, through a reconfiguration of spatial arrangements that privilege female embodiment – "the broad continent of a woman's life"[19] – and provide them with a global sense of place. By creating correspondences between the female body and "the world, the nation, regions, cities, and home," they constitute women as *national subjects* and invite a re-imagination of those spaces of human habitation.[20] Woolf's depiction of Eleanor Pargiter's spatial and temporal displace-ment in *The Years* captures this complicated topography, in which the female body metonymically stands in for the nation: "when will this New World come? When shall we be free? ... she felt not only a new space of time, but new powers, something unknown within her."[21] Although by the time Woolf writes *The Years* she is skeptical of the possibility for cultural renewal, the representation of Eleanor still illustrates how, for Englishwomen, the body remains *the* crucial site for theorizing national belonging. By depicting femininity as a constitutive element in the construction of new national fictions, female modernists ignore strictly historial characterizations of nationhood and suggest, instead, that "the nation is a tran-scendental entity," subject to myth-making, even though its imaginary borders correspond to actual political and geographical territories.[22] In doing so, British women modernists allude to the primordial vocabulary of kinship – "nation" is from the Latin root *nasci* (to be born) – and imaginatively position the female body itself as the ultimate dwelling-place, coterminous with nationalism.

The idea of the female body as a kind of home preoccupied interwar feminists such as Eleanor Rathbone and Jane Harrison, both of whom utilize architectural metaphors to conceive of the reconstruction of British culture during a period when architecture as a profession was male-dominated.[23] Several women's organ-izations worked to foreground the particular housing needs of women, arguing for more innovative designs on the grounds that a "[woman's] chief contribution to the work of the world is the management of her home."[24] Echoing this gendered concern, Rathbone argues that "women really do not invariably fit well into the ... structure of society ... because that structure has been built by and for the sex which has ... alone inhabited it."[25] This critique of the debilitating effect of masculine space is anticipated by Jane Harrison, who prefigures Rathbone's concern with the ways in which spatial arrangements reflect and reinforce gender inequities. Harrison argues that "the institution of the Man's House" rigidly excludes women from contact with the "outside world," and must therefore be rebuilt to privilege "the *racial* conscience" of women. By intertwining the discourse of the domestic with the idea of women's role as guardians of "the Human Race," Harrison effectively conveys the way in which the home, the place of belonging, functions as a microcosm of the nation. What Harrison proposes is a feminization of "virile" England so that domesticity, specifically "the woman's province" of the home, can function as the ground and justification for the reorganization of "the whole body politic."[26]

For both Harrison and Rathbone, as for Richardson, Warner, Butts, and Woolf, the house that is both England and the female body is racialized and nationalized. These women's imaginative preoccupation with architectural metaphors may owe something to the interwar housing boom, but more likely they derive from the idea, famously captured by E.M. Forster in *Howards End* (1910), that the home constitutes the genuine locus of national worth and, moreover, that inheritance of the home is synonymous with the inheritance of England. Harrison's observation that women "like to live spaciously" positions them as usurpers of male territory, pivotal architects in the restructuring of England: "*The Institution of the Man's House almost invariably breaks down*."[27] Like Rathbone, who critiques masculine space and ascribes a redemptive function to femininity, Harrison suggests that women's "consciousness may yet save" England from self-destruction.[28] If the home is an imagined collectivity that has national significance, and if, as several theorists have suggested, the home itself is a figure for woman, then we can begin to understand why, for British female modernists, the task of rebuilding the edifices constructed by the male imaginary is of paramount importance. Although Rathbone's remarks, quoted above, are not specifically about writing, her suggestion that women "must recondition the structure" until it has the "room" and "equipment" to meet the special needs of women, parallels, in a different register, Woolf's and Richardson's comments about female authorship. Likewise, Harrison's insistence that women "must adopt the method of experiment" in their usurping of masculine space speaks to women modernists' interest in troubling the ideological links between narrative and gender conventions.[29] Harrison's and Rathbone's spatial concerns find an analogue in Woolf's observation that women modernists' fiction will exhibit "marked differences of plot and incident," as well as "infinite differences in selection, method and style."[30] Such experimental literary methods are historically varied and overlaid with national meaning, providing an ideological critique of restrictive literary conventions as well as Englishwomen's spatial confinement. Woolf deploys spatial and architectural metaphors to critique masculine literary space as inhospitable and to suggest that women must rebuild the dwelling – despite a "scarcity and inadequacy of tools" (*ROO*, 77) – by carving a "home in the symbolic order" through experimentalism.[31]

The spatial image Woolf conjures as she urges women toward experimentalism – to "[make] something that is different" – is a kind of magisterial enclosure: "sentences built ... into arcades and domes" (*ROO*, 77–8). Although Woolf does not situate this literary home within a national context, her larger concern with Englishwomen's relation to literary culture, in *A Room* and elsewhere, indicates that it is an English house which women must refurbish. The use of architectural metaphors in *A Room* anticipates Woolf's focus on rebuilding in *Three Guineas*, where women are coaxed to construct an "experimental college" in order to restructure the "effect of education upon the race."[32] In this way Woolf echoes Edith Lees Ellis, who, in her discussion of women's moral and racial superiority, similarly utilizes metaphors of home to urge Englishwomen toward greater national responsibility: "woman ... wants to build [a home] under which she can walk upright ...

Experiments cannot dwarf or destroy her ... For a woman to crave a man's place ...
is to arrest progress."[33] This surprising image of the innovative female architect
inverts claims of women's mental inferiority by aligning men with the atavistic
practices that retard civilization. National progress depends on disseminating
women's redemptive impulses into the public sphere through the vehicle of
experimentalism, for British women, Woolf writes in 1937, are living in a "moment
of transition on the bridge [...] which connects the private house with the world of
public life" (*TG*, 18). Woolf elsewhere mocks the monumentalizing of "great men's
houses, bought for the nation and preserved entire" as mausoleum showcases of
masculine privilege, but here she suggests that the private home will be central to
the reconstitution of female citizens' relationship to the nation.[34] Indeed, by urging
women to refurbish and redecorate this "house hitherto exclusively owned by men,"
Woolf borrows from the pervasive cultural identification of women with houses
even as she subverts this association by figuratively recasting the art of decorating as
a literary form of "doing battle."[35] If the "door of the private house [is] thrown
open" (*TG*, 16), Woolf suggests, the world may then be claimed as women's
possession, for women's new ideas will transgress boundaries and will be "tenderly
enclosed, and expressed in a globe of exquisitely coloured words."[36]

Like conquest itself, this imaginative process of constructing a new world
through language necessitates some form of violence. Woolf's *The Voyage Out*
exemplifies the violent implications of this linguistic conquest, through Rachel
Vinrace's critique of "the masculine ... world" of spatial divisions and territorial
borders.[37] Rachel instead conjures a globe whose unification would facilitate limitless access: "Would there ever be a time when the world was one and indivisible?"
(296). Rachel's cognitive map is drawn through familiar Anglocentric tropes: she
sits in nature and reads a few pages of Gibbon's *History of the Decline and Fall of the
Roman Empire* that focus on how "unwarlike natives" (174) foil an imperial conquest;
and she imagines a primeval sphere, "back to the very beginning of the world,"
which enables her to access "all knowledge" from "the populations of all times"
(175). It is no coincidence that Rachel's reading about colonial invasion gives rise to
her fantasy of a transhistorical, cross-cultural, repository of "knowledge [that]
would be hers" (175). At the end of this appropriative reverie Rachel returns home,
"much as a soldier prepared for battle" (176). Here, as elsewhere, her private conquest
of "the imaginary world" (123) is coincident with appropriating transparent space, a
passage "away to unknown places" (302) as yet unmapped. Although in *A Room*
Woolf parodies the taxonomic gestures of colonial explorers – "One could not go to
the map and say Columbus discovered America and Columbus was a woman" (85)
– in *The Voyage Out* Rachel's cognitive map, not overtly aligned with the violence of
imperial conquest, is nonetheless cast in terms that recapitulate familiar tropes of
British expansionism. By the time Woolf writes *The Years* she is more self-
conscious of the violent underpinnings of such rhetoric. Here, Woolf both ironizes
the young Rose Pargiter and illustrates how powerfully her imagination has been
colonized by imperial tropes when we see her pack up her "ammunition" (a
latchkey), slip out of her night nursery on an "adventure" (26), and embark on a
"desperate mission to a besieged garrison" (a shop) (27). As Rose navigates the
London streets at night she rides through "the enemy's country," conjuring images

of a general and the British flag as she repeats her talisman: "I am Pargiter of Pargiter's Horse ... riding to the rescue" (27). *The Years*, like *Between the Acts*, no longer reflects a belief in the kind of communal national cohesiveness that Woolf was able to sustain in *The Waves*, where the rhetoric of conquest, unity, and wholeness was more nostalgically deployed. And yet, like both *The Voyage Out* and *The Waves*, *The Years* evinces a modernist longing "to enclose the present moment" (428) and make it "whole" (390) by constructing a "New World" (292) out of "fractured" (390) and "deformed" (380) cultural artifacts – what Woolf calls the "primeval swamp" (378) of contemporary life. Here, as elsewhere, the desire for national unity coincides with the female character's disdain for "her native land" (199) and a simultaneous nostalgia for that which is "pure English" (207).

That the female appropriation of space requires acts of violence is registered differently by colonial writers such as Rhys, Mansfield, and Marson: unlike Rachel Vinrace, who unselfconsciously deploys imperial imagery in order to constitute the self, these writers demonstrates the degree to which British women's emancipatory fantasies of spatial trespass rely on exclusionary notions of both Englishness and femininity. In *Voyage in the Dark*, Rhys intertwines her depiction of English space with a critique of whiteness, both of which produce an oppressive homogeneity: "hundreds of white people white people rushing along and the dark houses all alike."[38] Anna Morgan's attention to topography in London highlights the claustraphobia and uniformity of Englishness: hotel rooms, neighborhoods, and streets all appear to be undifferentiated, their invariability making Anna feel entombed – "like being in a small, dark box" (25). The novel's repeated focus on homogeneity and containment speaks to Anna's racial anxiety and her fear of assimilation. Although she herself is a white West Indian, it is not a whiteness that is interchangeable with Englishness; thus, her aunt urges her to pass for an Englishwoman – "to talk like a lady and behave like a lady and not like a nigger" (65) – while she repeatedly resists this interpellation by identifying with blackness. Anna's colonial liminality shapes her cognitive map of Englishness, enabling her to navigate through the infrastructure of empire without ever being legitimized by it. Rhys illustrates how, for the colonial subject, geographical knowledge is tied neither to the culture of exploration nor to imperial power, for Anna's familiarity with British cartography – "Lying between 15 10 and 15 40 N. and 61 14 and 61 30 W. 'A goodly island'" (17) – ultimately leads nowhere. While Anna is able to conjure a map of Great Britain, this image does not give rise to liberatory feelings of expansiveness; nor does it facilitate a spatial fantasy of coextensiveness with the nation. Rather, her inassimilable body remains trapped within English space, stuck "in a prison, wandering round and round in a circle" (76). And yet the novel does illustrate the seductiveness of colonizing tropes when, in her homeland, Anna imagines discovering a "forest where nobody had ever been – virgin forest" (83). By representing Anna's wishful appropriation of the cultural logic of empire even as she herself remains forever on the colonial periphery, Rhys illustrates how imperialism "messes with the identity of both the colonizer and the colonized."[39]

Ultimately, Rhys's colonial others experience the metropole as a claustraphobic space of confinement, best captured by Sasha Jenson in *Good Morning, Midnight*: "all the time I was in London, I felt as if I were being suffocated, as if a large derriere was sitting on me."[40] The difference between this spatial fantasy and those expressed by Richardson, Warner, Butts, and Woolf is crucial, for, however ambivalent these four writers are about Englishness, the repression of their cultural agency is never synonymous with self-annihilation. Indeed, while interwar British modernists may repudiate the nation's totalizing aims, they remain nonetheless invested in accessing the master narrative of empire in order to ensure their own national inclusion. Anything less than full citizenship, to borrow Vera Brittain's words, is "an example of national waste," for the "ability of women is nationally needed [now, in 1932] as never before."[41] For colonial writers such as Rhys, such rhetoric of national responsibility is of course problematized by the radical asymmetry between those inhabiting the metropole and its colonies. The appeal of mythic prehistories of the nation that we see operating in Richardson, Warner, Butts, and Woolf ultimately holds little allure for someone like Rhys, who, without access to the myths that are intrinsic to Englishness itself, has no basis on which to construct a fantasy of citizenship. By contrast, and despite their misgivings about the nation, Englishwomen remain convinced that women's moral authority is indispensable to national consciousness.

The national imaginary generated by Richardson, Warner, Butts, and Woolf echoes Cicely Hamilton's declaration, uttered in 1935: "I am ... but a poor internationalist; unable to feel anything like equal affection for all regions of the earth and all races of mankind ... I never step ashore on Dover Pier without the thought that here are my own folk ... and here is the place where I belong."[42] Even when such topophilia is counterbalanced by moments of acute cultural estrangement, British women modernists' imaginative appropriation of space – "a view of infinite possibilities ... no bound to the horizon" – still shapes their understanding of national belonging and remains a constitutive component of how each envisions "her sovereignty" in relation to home and world.[43]

Notes

1 Winifred Holtby, *South Riding* (London: Virago, 1988 [1936]), 404; hereafter cited in the text and abbreviated *SR*.

2 Katherine Burdekin, *Swastika Night* (New York: Feminist Press, 1987 [1937]), 21, 130, and 30.

3 Suzanne Raitt provides a fascinating account of lesbian mysticism in the period in *Vita and Virginia: The Work and Friendship of Vita Sackville-West and Virginia Woolf* (Oxford: Clarendon Press, 1998), 117–45.

4 Virginia Woolf, *A Room of One's Own* (New York: Harcourt Brace & Co., 1981), 97; hereafter cited in the text as *ROO*.

5 For a discussion of "bi-location," see Ch. 3, this volume. Dorothy Richardson, "Confessions," *Little Review*, 12 (May, 1929): 70.

6 Sylvia Townsend Warner, *The True Heart* (New York: Viking Press, 1929), 25.

7 The female modernist interest in the conjunction between landscape and mysticism may owe much to the pervasiveness of the "spiritual culture of landscape" – and its links to citizenship – during the interwar period. See David Matless, *Landscape and Englishness* (London: Reaktion Books, 1998), 84.

8 Joanne Winning discusses Richardson's representation of lesbian mysticism in *The Pilgrimage of Dorothy Richardson* (Madison: University of Wisconsin Press, 2000), 146–51 and 204 n. 36.

9 Woolf, "George Eliot," *Essays*, Vol 4: 178.

10 Willa Muir, *Women: An Inquiry* (New York: Alfred A. Knopf, 1926), 11, 49, 21.

11 T.S. Eliot, *After Strange Gods* (London: Faber, 1934), 35–6.

12 *Ibid.*, 49. See Ezra Pound, *Pavannes and Divagations* (New York: New Directions, 1958), 204.

13 Eliot, *After Strange Gods*, 36.

14 Olive Moore, *Collected Writings* (Elmwood Park, IL: Dalkey Archive Press, 1992), 352 and 353.

15 Robert H. Byington and Glen E. Morgan, "Mary Butts," *Art and Literature*, 7 (winter, 1965): 171.

16 Dora B. Montefiore, *From a Victorian to a Modern* (London: E. Archer, 1927), 222.

17 Michael Reed, *The Landscape of Britain from the Beginnings to 1914* (Savage, MD: Barnes & Noble, 1990), 281.

18 Susan Bazargan observes that the oak tree is a symbol of the British monarchy, arguing that in *Orlando* the tree functions as "an emblem of Orlando's vast estate and by extension, England and all of her dominions": "The uses of the land: Vita Sackville-West's pastoral writings and Virginia Woolf's *Orlando*," *Woolf Studies Annual*, 5 (1999): 34.

19 Virginia Woolf, "Harriette Wilson," *Essays*, Vol. 4: 255.

20 Sue Best, "Sexualizing space" in Elizabeth Grosz and Elsbeth Probyn eds. *Sexy Bodies: The Strange Carnalities of Feminism* (New York: Routledge, 1995), 181.

21 Virginia Woolf, *The Years* (New York: Harcourt Brace, 1965), 297; hereafter cited in the text.

22 Stathis Gourgouris, "Notes on the nation's dream-work," *Qui Parle*, 7. 1: (1993): 84.

23 Lynn Walker, "Women and architecture" in Jane Rendell, Barbara Penner and Iain Borden eds. *Gender, Space, Architecture* (London and New York: Routledge, 2000), 254.

24 David Jeremiah, *Architecture and Design for the Family in Britain, 1900–70* (Manchester: Manchester University Press, 2000), 40.

25 Eleanor Rathbone, "Victory – and after?" *The Woman's Leader*, March 8, 1929.

26 Jane Ellen Harrison, *Alpha and Omega* (London: Sidgwick & Jackson, 1915), 109, 135, 123, 127, 140, 128, 134. For a discussion of "home" as a woman's place, see Doreen Massey, *Space, Place, and Gender* (Minneapolis: University of Minnesota Press, 1994), 157–72.

27 Jane Ellen Harrison, *Reminiscences of a Student's Life* (London: Hogarth Press, 1925), 88; *Alpha and Omega*, 109.

28 Harrison, *Alpha and Omega*, 136.

29 *Ibid.*, 139.

30 Virginia Woolf, "Women novelists" in Michele Barrett ed. *Women and Writing* (New York: Harcourt Brace, 1979), 71.

31 Margaret Whitford, *Luce Irigaray: Philosophy in the Feminine* (London and New York: Routledge, 1991), 156.

32 Virginia Woolf, *Three Guineas* (New York: Harcourt Brace & Co., 1966), 33 and 38; hereafter cited in the text as *TG*.

33 Edith Lees Ellis, *The New Horizon in Love and Life* (London: A. & C. Black, 1921), 128 and 135.

34 Sonita Sarker, "Locating a native Englishness in Virginia Woolf's *The London Scene*," *National Women's Studies Association Journal*, 13. 2 (2001): 10.

35 Virginia Woolf, "Professions for women" in S.P. Rosensbaum ed. *A Bloomsbury Group Reader* (Oxford, and Cambridge, MA: Blackwell, 1993), 278. Adrian Forty discusses women's identification with houses in early twentieth-century British culture in *Objects of Desire: Design and Society since 1750* (London: Thames & Hudson, 1992), 104–7.

36 Woolf, *Letters*, Vol. 1: 320.

37 Woolf, *The Voyage Out* (New York: Harcourt Brace, 1948), 296; hereafter cited in the text. Several critics have observed structural and thematic similarities between Woolf's novel and *Heart of Darkness*. See, for example, Rosemary Pitt, "The exploration of the self in Conrad's *Heart of Darkness* and Woolf's *The Voyage Out*," *Conradiana*, 10 (1978): 141–54.

38 Jean Rhys, *Voyage in the Dark* (New York: W.W. Norton, 1982), 17; hereafter cited in the text.

39 Simon Gikandi, *Maps of Englishness: Writing Identity in the Culture of Colonialism* (New York: Columbia University Press, 1996), 31.

40 Jean Rhys, *Good Morning, Midnight* (New York: W.W. Norton, 1986), 98.

41 Paul Berry and Alan Bishop eds. *Testament of a Generation: The Journalism of Vera Brittain and Winifred Holtby* (London: Virago, 1985), 141 and 144.

42 Cicely Hamilton, *Life Errant* (London: J.M. Dent, 1935), 293–4. See also Hamilton's loving tribute to "my people, my English" in *The Englishwoman* (London: Longman, Green & Co., 1940), 11 and 12, where she enumerates "the Englishwoman's rights as a citizen" and tracks her role in public life.

43 Woolf, "Modern novels," *Essays*, Vol. 3: 36.

Bibliography

A.B.T. "A woman's place." *The Englishwoman* 123 (March, 1919): 113–17.

Abdoo, Sherlyn. "Woman as Grail in T.S. Eliot's *The Waste Land.*" *Centennial Review* 28 (1984): 48–60.

Abel, Elizabeth. *Virginia Woolf and the Fictions of Psychoanalysis.* Chicago, IL, and London: University of Chicago Press, 1989.

Abercrombie, Sir Patrick. *Town and Country Planning.* London: Thornton Butterworth, 1933.

Abraham, Julie. *Are Girls Necessary? Lesbian Writing and Modern Histories.* New York and London: Routledge, 1996.

Abravanel, Genevieve. "Woolf in blackface: identification across *The Waves.*" In Jessica Berman and Jane Goldman eds. *Virginia Woolf Out of Bounds: Selected Papers from the Tenth Annual Conference on Virginia Woolf.* New York: Pace University Press, 2001: 113–19.

Ackland, Valentine. *Country Conditions.* London: Lawrence & Wishart, 1936.

Anderson, Benedict. *Imagined Communities: Reflections on the Origin and Spread of Nationalism.* London and New York: Verso, 1983.

Anonymous. "The biological study of women." *Time and Tide* (September 24, 1926).

——. "The female mind!" *The Vote* (January 28, 1927): 30.

——. "'Literary surgery': a review of *Speed the Plough.*" *Liverpool Post* (April 11, 1923).

——. "Paint and powder." *Vogue* ([London] late January, 1921)

——. "Review of *Armed With Madness.*" *Manchester Guardian* (June 15, 1928).

——. "Review of *Armed With Madness.*" *Oklahoma City Times* (October 14, 1928).

——. "Summer days *en automobile.* " *Vogue* ([London] early June, 1919).

——. "Review of *Several Occasions.*" *Yorkshire Post* (March 16, 1932).

——. "When the world begins to fly." *Vogue* ([London] early March, 1920).

Armitage, David. *The Ideological Origins of the British Empire.* Cambridge and New York: Cambridge University Press, 2000.

Armstrong, Nancy. *Desire and Domestic Fiction: A Political History of the Novel.* Oxford: Oxford University Press, 1987.

Armstrong, Tim. *Modernism, Technology, and the Body.* Cambridge: Cambridge University Press, 1998.

Aronstein, Susan. "Rewriting Percival's sister: eucharistic vision and typological destiny in the *Queste del San Graal.*" *Women's Studies* 21. 2 (1992): 211–30.

Asian, Maroon Arrive, Jr. *The Rhetoric of Eugenics in Anglo-American Thought.* Athens, GA, and London: University of Georgia Press, 1996.

Atholl, Duchess of, MP. *Women and Politics*. London: Philip Allan, 1931.

Bachelard, Gaston. *The Poetics of Space*. Boston, MA: Beacon Press, 1969.

Backus, Margot Gayle. "Sexual orientation in the (post)imperial nation: celticism and inversion theory in Radclyffe Hall's *Well of Loneliness*." *Tulsa Studies in Women's Literature* 15. 2 (1996): 253–66.

Bamford, Kenneth. *Distorted Images: British National Identity and Film in the 1920s*. New York: St. Martin's Press, 1998.

Barczewski, Stephanie L. *Myth and National Identity in Nineteenth-Century Britain: The Legends of King Arthur and Robin Hood*. Oxford: Oxford University Press, 2000.

Barkan, Elazar and Ronald Bush. *Prehistories of the Future: The Primitivist Project and the Culture of Modernism*. Stanford, CA: Stanford University Press, 1995.

Barr, Tina. "Divine politics: Virginia Woolf's journey toward Eleusis in *To the Lighthouse*." *boundary 2* 20. 1 (1993): 125–45.

Barrett, Eileen. "Unmasking lesbian passion: the inverted world of *Mrs.Dalloway*." In Eileen Barrett and Patricia Cramer eds. *Virginia Woolf: Lesbian Readings*. New York and London: New York University Press, 1997: 146–64.

Barstow, Anne Llewellyn. *Witchcraze: A New History of the European Witch Hunts*. San Francisco, CA: Pandora, HarperCollins, 1994.

Baucom, Ian. *Out of Place: Englishness, Empire, and the Locations of Identity*. Princeton, NJ: Princeton University Press, 1999.

Bazargan, Susan. "The uses of the land: Vita Sackville-West's pastoral writings and Virginia Woolf's *Orlando*." *Woolf Studies Annual* 5 (1999): 25–55.

Beard, Mary. *The Invention of Jane Harrison*. Cambridge, MA: Harvard Univeristy Press, 2000.

Beauman, Nicola. *A Very Great Profession: The Woman's Novel 1914–39*. London: Virago, 1983.

Beer, Gillian. "Sylvia Townsend Warner: 'the centrifugal kick.'" In Maroula Joannou ed. *Women Writers of the 1930s: Gender, Politics, History*. Edinburgh: Edinburgh University Press, 1999: 76–86.

Bell, Clive. "Art and society." *Art*. New York: Capricorn Books, 1958: 181–90.

——. *Civilisation: An Essay*. New York: Harcourt Brace & Company, 1928.

——. "The Metaphysical Hypothesis." *Art*. New York: Capricorn Books, 1958. 13–55.

Benstock, Shari. "Expatriate sapphic modernism." In Lisa Rado ed. *Rereading Modernism*. Austin: University of Texas Press, 1986: 97–122.

——. *Textualizing the Feminine: On the Limits of Genre*. Norman and London: University of Oklahoma Press, 1991.

——. *Women of the Left Bank: Paris, 1900–1940*. Austin: University of Texas Press, 1986.

Berg, Maxine. *A Woman in History: Eileen Power 1889–1940*. Cambridge: Cambridge University Press, 1996.

Berman, Jessica. *Modernist Fiction, Cosmopolitanism, and the Politics of Community*. Cambridge: Cambridge University Press, 2001.

Berry, Paul and Alan Bishop eds. *Testament of a Generation: The Journalism of Vera Brittain and Winifred Holtby*. London: Virago, 1985.

Best, Sue. "Sexualizing space." In Elizabeth Grosz and Elspeth Probyn eds. *Sexy Bodies: The Strange Carnalities of Feminism*. New York: Routledge, 1995: 181–94.

Betts, Ernest. "Why 'talkies' are unsound," *Close Up* 4. 4 (1929): 22–4.

Bhabha, Homi K. ed. *Nation and Narration*. London: Routledge, 1990.

——. "Of mimicry and man: the ambivalence of colonial discourse." *October* 28 (1984): 126–8.

Binding, Paul. "Sylvia Townsend Warner and *Mr. Fortune's Maggot*." *Poetry National Review* 23 (special issue) (1981): 51–3.

Birt, Dan. "Be British." *Close Up* 8. 4 (December, 1931): 284–86.

Bivona, Daniel. *British Imperial Literature, 1870–1940: Writing and the Administration of Empire*. Cambridge: Cambridge University Press, 1998.

Bland, Lucy. *Banishing the Beast: Sexuality and the Early Feminists*. New York: New Press, 1995.

Blaser, Robin. "Here lies the woodpecker who was Zeus." In Christopher Wagstaff ed. *A Sacred Quest: The Life and Writings of Mary Butts*. Kingston, NY: McPherson & Co., 1995): 159–223.

Blodgett, Harriet. "Food for thought in Virginia Woolf's novels," *Woolf Studies Annual* 3 (1997): 46–60.

Blondel, Nathalie. *Mary Butts: Scenes from the Life*. Kingston, NY: McPherson & Co., 1998.

Bluemel, Kristin. *Experimenting on the Borders of Modernism: Dorothy Richardson's Pilgrimage*. Athens, GA, and London: University of Georgia Press, 1997.

——. "Missing sex in Dorothy Richardson's *Pilgrimage*." *English Literature in Transition, 1880–1920* 39. 1 (1996): 20–38.

Blunt, Alison and Gillian Rose eds. *Writing Women and Space: Colonial and Postcolonial Geographies*. New York and London: Guilford Press, 1994.

Bogle, Donald. *Toms, Coons, Mulattoes, Mammies, and Bucks: An Interpretive History of Blacks in American Films*. New York: Continuum, 1992.

Boone, Joseph Allen. "The meaning of Elvedon in *The Waves*: a key to Bernard's experience and Woolf's vision." *Modern Fiction Studies* 27. 4 (1981–82): 629–37.

Booth, Allyson. "Forgetful objects." *Postcards from the Trenches: Negotiating the Space between Modernism and the First World War*. New York and Oxford: Oxford University Press, 1996.

Booth, Howard J. and Nigel Rigby eds. *Modernism and Empire*. Manchester and New York: Manchester University Press, 2000.

Bourke, Joanna. *Working-Class Cultures in Britain, 1890–1960*. London and New York: Routledge, 1994.

Boyes, Georgina. *The Imagined Village: Culture, Ideology, and the English Folk Revival*. Manchester: Manchester University Press, 1993.

Brantlinger, Patrick. *Fictions of State: Culture and Credit in Britain 1694–1994*. Ithaca and London: Cornell University Press, 1996.

——. "Victorians and Africans: the genealogy of the myth of the dark continent." *Critical Inquiry* 12. 1 (1985): 166–203.

Bredbenner, Candice Lewis. *A Nationality of Her Own: Women, Marriage, and the Law of Citizenship*. Berkeley: University of California Press, 1998.

Brennan, Timothy. "The national longing for form." In Homi K. Bhabha ed. *Nation and Narration*. London and New York: Routledge, 1990: 44–70.

Briggs, Asa. *Mass Entertainment: The Origins of a Modern Industry*. Adelaide: Griffin Press, 1960.

Brimstone, Lyndie. "Towards a new cartography: Radclyffe Hall, Virginia Woolf and the workings of common land." In Elaine Hobby and Chris White eds. *What Lesbians Do in Books*. London: Women's Press, 1991: 86–108.

Brittain, Vera. "Married women and surname." *Time and Tide* (January 15, 1926).

——. *The Women at Oxford: A Fragment of History*. London: Harrap, 1960.

——. *Women's Work in Modern Britain*. London: Noel Douglas, 1928.

Broe, Mary Lynn and Angela Ingram eds. *Women's Writing in Exile*. Chapel Hill and London: University of North Carolina Press, 1989: 269–194.

Bronfen, Elizabeth. *Dorothy Richardson's Art of Memory: Space, Identity, Text*. Manchester: Manchester University Press, 1999.

Brothers, Barbara. "Flying the nets at Forty: *Lolly Willowes* as female bildungsroman." In Laura L. Doan ed. *Old Maids to Radical Spinsters: Unmarried Women in the Twentieth-Century Novel*. Urbana: University of Illinois Press, 1991: 195–212.

——. "Through 'The Pantry Window': Sylvia Townsend Warner and the Spanish Civil War." In Frieda S. Brown, Malcolm A. Compitello, and Victor M. Howard eds. *Rewriting the Good Fight: Critical Essays on the Literature of the Spanish Civil War*. East Lansing: Michigan State University Press, 1989: 161–73;

——. "Writing against the grain: Sylvia Townsend Warner and the Spanish Civil War." In Mary Lynn Broe and Angela Ingram eds. *Women's Writing in Exile*. Chapel Hill and London: University of North Carolina Press, 1989: 350–68.

Brotton, Jeffrey. "Terrestrial globalism: mapping the globe in early modern Europe." In Denis Cosgrove ed. *Mappings*. London: Reaktion, 1999: 71–89.

Browne, Stella F. W. "The feminine aspect of birth control." In Raymond Pierpoint ed. *Report of the Fifth International New-Malthusian and Birth Control Conference*. London: Heinemann, 1922: 40–3.

Bryher, Winifred. "Dawn's Left Hand," *Close Up* 8. 4 (1931): 337–8.

——. "Films for children." *Close Up* 3. 2 (August 1928): 22.

Bunce, Michael. *The Countryside Ideal: Anglo-American Images of Landscape*. London and New York: Routledge, 1994.

Burdekin, Katherine. *Sw astika Night*. New York: Feminist Press, 1985 (1937).

Burke, Carolyn. *Becoming Modern: The Life of Mina Loy*. Berkeley and Los Angeles: University of California Press, 1996.

Burton, Antoinette. *At the Heart of Empire: Indians and the Colonial Encounter in Late-Victorian Britain*. Berkeley: University of California Press, 1998.

——. *Burdens of History: British Feminists, Indian Women, and Imperial Culture, 1865–1915*. Chapel Hill: University of North Carolina Press, 1994.

——. "The feminist quest for identity: British imperial suffragism and 'global sisterhood,'1900–1915." *Journal of Women's History* 3. 2 (1991): 48

——. "'The Indian woman,' 1865–1915." In Chaudhuri Nupur and Margaret Strobel eds. *Western Women and Imperialism: Complicity and Resistance*. Bloomington: Indiana University Press, 1992: 137–57.

——. "Who needs the nation? Interrogating 'British' history." In Catherine Hall ed. *Cultures of Empire: Colonizers in Britain and the Empire in the Nineteenth and Twentieth Centuries*. New York: Routledge, 2000. 120–36.

Bush, Barbara. *Imperialism, Race and Resistance: Africa and Britain, 1919–1945*. London and New York: Routledge, 1999.

Bush, Julia. *Edwardian Ladies and Imperial Power*. London: Leicester University Press, 2000.

Butler, Judith. *Bodies that Matter: On the Discursive Limits of "Sex."* New York: Routledge, 1993.

——. "Imitation and gender insubordination." In Diana Fuss ed. *Inside/out: Lesbian Theories, Gay Theories*. New York and London: Routledge, 1991: 13–31.

Butts, Mary. *Armed With Madness*. Reissued in *The Taverner Novels*. Kingston, NY: McPherson & Co., 1992.

——. "A Russian prophet." *Time and Tide* (October 14, 1933): 1228, 1230.

——. "Bloomsbury," *Modernism/Modernity* 5. 2 (1998): 321–45.

——. *The Crystal Cabinet: My Childhood at Salterns*. Boston, MA: Beacon Press, 1988.

——. *Death of Felicity Taverner*. Reissued in *The Taverner Novels*. Kingston, NY: McPherson & Co., 1992.

——. "'England.' Review of *Week-Ends in England* by S.P.B. Mais." *The Bookman* 85 (December, 1933): 257–8.

——. "Ghosties and ghoulies: uses of the supernatural in English fiction." *Ashe of Rings and Other Writings*. Kingston, NY: McPherson & Co., 1998: 333–63.

——. "Green." *From Altar to Chimney-Piece*. Kingston, NY: McPherson & Co., 1992.

——. *Imaginary Letters*. Reprinted in *Ashe of Rings and Other Writings*. New York: McPherson & Co., 1998.

——. "The master's last dancing." *The New Yorker* (March 30, 1998): 109–13.

——. "Negro." *The Adelphi*, 3rd series, 9. 1 (1934): 185–7.

——. "Parzival." *Time and Tide* 17. 2 (January 11, 1936): 57–8.

——. "The Sanc Grail." *The Bookman* 84. 499 (1933): 72–4.

——. *Scenes from the Life of Cleopatra*. Reprinted in *The Classical Novels*. Kingston, NY: McPherson & Co., 1994.

——. "Selections from the journal." (Edited by Robert H. Byington and Glen E. Morgan.) *Art & Literature* 7 (winter 1965): 166–79.

——. *Traps for Unbelievers*. London: Desmond Harmsworth, 1932.

——. "Unpleasant court cases, facts of life, plea for rank and adequate knowledge" (interview). *Pall Mall Gazette* (December 20, 1922).

——. "Vision of Asia." *The Bookman* (December, 1932): 223–5.

——. *Warning to Hikers*. London: Wishart & Co., 1932.

Byington, Robert H. and Glen E. Morgan. "Mary Butts." *Art and Literature* 7 (winter 1965): 163–5.

Bynum, Caroline Walker. *Jesus as Mother: Studies in the Spirituality of the High Middle Ages*. Berkeley: University of California Press, 1982.

Cain, P.J. and J.G. Hopkins. *British Imperialism: Crisis and Deconstruction, 1919–1990*. London: Longman, 1993.

——. *British Imperialism 1688–2000*. London: Longman, 2002.

Caine, Barbara. *English Feminism 1780–1980*. Oxford: Oxford University Press, 1997.

Campbell, Mary Baine. "Finding the Grail: fascist aesthetics and mysterious objects." In Debra N. Mancoff ed. *King Arthur's Modern Return*. New York: Garland, 1998: 213–24.

Carpenter, Edward. *Intermediate Types Among Primitive Folk: A Study of Social Evolution*. London: George Allen & Co., 1914.

——. *Love's Coming of Age: A Series of Papers on the Relations of the Sexes*. New York and London: Mitchell Kennerly, 1922.

Carpentier, Martha C. *Ritual, Myth, and the Modernist Text: The Influence of Jane Ellen Harrison on Joyce, Eliot, and Woolf*. Amsterdam: Gordon & Breach, 1998.

Case, Sue-Ellen. "Tracking the vampire." *differences: A Journal of Feminist Cultural Studies* 3. 2 (1991): 1–20.

Caserio, Robert L. "Celibate sisters-in-revolution: towards reading Sylvia Townsend Warner." In Joseph A. Boone, and Michael Cadden eds. *Engendering Men: The Question of Male Feminist Criticism*. New York: Routledge, 1990: 254–74.

——. *The Novel in England, 1900–1950*. New York: Twayne, 1999.

Castle, Terry. *The Apparitional Lesbian: Female Homosexuality and Modern Culture*. New York: Columbia University Press, 1993.

Cather, Willa. "The novel démeublé." In Bonnie Kime Scott ed. *The Gender of Modernism: A Critical Anthology*. Bloomington and Indianapolis: Indiana University Press, 1990: 53–6.

Cavaliero, Glen. "The short stories." *Poetry National Review*, 8. 3 (1981): 45.

Chapman, Wayne K. and Jamet M. Manson eds. *Women in the Milieu of Leonard and Virginia Woolf: Peace, Politics, and Education*. New York: Pace University Press, 1998: III–24.

Chatterjee, Partha. *The Nation and its Fragments: Colonial and Postcolonial Histories.* Princeton, NJ: Princeton University Press, 1993.

Chaudhuri, Nupur, and Margaret Strobel eds. *Western Women and Imperialism: Complicity and Resistance.* Bloomington: Indiana University Press, 1992.

Cheng, Vincent J. *Joyce, Race, and Empire.* Cambridge: Cambridge University Press, 1995.

Cheyette, Bryan ed. *Between "Race" and Culture: Representations of "the Jew" in English and American Literature.* Stanford, CA: Stanford University Press, 1996.

——. *Constructions of "the Jew" in English Literature and Society: Racial Representations, 1875–1945.* Cambridge: Cambridge University Press, 1993.

——. "Neither black nor white: the figure of 'the Jew' in imperial British literature." In Linda Nochlin and Tamar Garb eds. *The Jew in the Text: Modernity and the Construction of Identity.* London: Thames & Hudson, 1995: 31–41.

Chinn, Sarah E. "'Something primitive and age-old as nature herself': lesbian sexuality and the permission of the exotic." In Laura Doan and Jay Prosser eds. *Palatable Poison: Critical Perspectives on* The Well of Loneliness. New York: Columbia University Press, 2001: 300–15.

Chrisman, Laura. "Imperial space, imperial place: theories of empire and culture in Fredric Jameson, Edward Said and Gayatri Spivak." *New Formations* 34 (1998): 53–69.

Clark, Grahame. *Prehistoric England.* London and New York: B.T. Batsford, 1940.

Clark, Suzanne. *Sentimental Modernism: Women Writers and the Revolution of the Word.* Bloomington: Indiana University Press, 1991.

Cliff, Michelle. "Virginia Woolf and the imperial gaze: a glance askance." In Mark Hussey and Vara Neverow eds. *Virginia Woolf: Emerging Perspectives: Selected Papers from the Third Annual Conference on Virginia Woolf.* New York: Pace University Press, 1994: 91–102.

Colls, Robert and Philip Dodd eds. *Englishness: Politics and Culture 1800–1920.* London: Croom Helm, 1986.

Conner, Randy P. *Blossom of Bone: Reclaiming the Connection between Homoeroticism and the Sacred.* San Francisco, CA: HarperCollins, 1993.

Connolly, Cyril. "The vulgarity of lesbianism." *New Statesman* (August 25, 1928): 614.

Conrad, Joseph. "Geography and some explorers." *Last Essays.* Ed. R. Curle. Garden City, NY: Doubleday, Page & Co., 1926: 1–21.

——. "Travel." *Last Essays.* Ed. R. Curle. Garden City, NY: Doubleday, Page Co., 1926. 121–34.

Constantine, Stephen. "'Bringing the empire alive': the Empire Marketing Board and imperial propaganda, 1926–33." In John M. Mackenzie ed. *Imperialism and Popular Culture.* Manchester: Manchester University Press, 1987.

——. "Migrants and settlers." In Judith M. Brown and William Roger Louis eds. *The Oxford History of the British Empire.* Oxford and New York: Oxford University Press, 1999. Vol. 4: *The Twentieth Century:* 163–87.

Coombes, Annie E. *Reinventing Africa: Museums, Material Culture and Popular Imagination in Late Victorian and Edwardian England.* New Haven, CT, and London: Yale University Press, 1994.

Cornish, Vaughan. *Geographical Essays.* London: Sifteon, Praed & Co., Ltd. 1923.

——. *A Geography of Imperial Defence.* London, 1922.

——. *The Scenery of England: A Harmonious Grouping in Town and Country.* London: Council for the Preservation of Rural England, 1932.

——. *Scenery and the Sense of Sight.* Cambridge: Cambridge University Press, 1935.

Coroneos, Con. *Space, Conrad, and Modernity.* Oxford: Oxford University Press, 2002.

Corrigan, Philip. "Film entertainment as ideology and pleasure: a preliminary approach to a history of audiences."In James Curran and Vincent Porter eds. *British Cinema History*. London: Weidenfeld and Nicolson, 1982: 24–35.

Cosgrove, Denis. *Apollo's Eye: A Cartographic Genealogy of the Earth in the Western Imagination*. Baltimore, MD, and London: Johns Hopkins University Press, 2001.

Crawford, O.G.S. *Said and Done: The Autobiography of an Archaeologist*. London: Weidenfeld & Nicolson, 1955.

Creasey, John. *The Countryside between the Wars, 1918–1940*. London: B.T. Batsford, 1984.

Crook, J. Mordaunt. *The Rise of the Nouveaux Riches: Style and Status in Victorian and Edwardian Architecture*. North Pomfret, VT: Trafalgar Square, 1999.

Crosland, Margaret. *Beyond the Lighthouse: English Women Novelists in the Twentieth Century*. New York: Taplinger Publishing, 1981.

Cuddy Keane, Melba. "Virginia Woolf and the varieties of historicist experience." In Beth Carole Rosenberg and Jeanne Dubino eds. *Virginia Woolf and the Essay*. New York: St. Martin's Press, 1997: 62–77.

Curtin, Philip D. *The Image of Africa: British Ideas and Action, 1780–1850*. Madison: University of Wisconsin Press, 1964.

Darville, Timothy. *Prehistoric Britain*. New Haven, CT, and London: Yale University Press, 1987.

David, Deirdre. *Rule Britannia: Women, Empire, and Victorian Writing*. Ithaca, NY, and London: Cornell University Press, 1995.

Davidson, Cathy. "No more separate spheres!" *American Literature* 70. 3 (1998): 443–63.

Davies, Margaret Llewelyn. *Life As We Have Known It*. New York: W.W. Norton, 1975.

Davies, Owen. *Witchcraft, Magic and Culture, 1736–1951*. Manchester and New York: Manchester University Press, 1999.

Davin, Anna. "Imperialism and motherhood." *History Workshop: A Journal of Socialist Historians* 5 (spring, 1978): 9–65.

Defries, Amelia. "Criticism from within," *Close Up* 1. 3 (1927): 48–56.

de Grazia, Edward. *Girls Lean Back Everywhere: The Law of Obscenity and the Assault on Genius*. New York: Random House, 1992.

de Lauretis, Teresa. "Eccentric subjects: feminist theory and historical consciousness." *Feminist Studies* 16. 1 (1990): 115–50.

——. "Upping the anti (*sic*) in Feminist Theory." In Marianne Hirsch and Evelyn Fox Keller eds. *Conflicts in Feminism*. New York: Routledge, 1990: 255–70.

DeKoven, Marianne. *Rich and Strange: Gender, History, Modernism*. Princeton, NJ: Princeton University Press, 1991.

Denver, Carolyn, *Death and the Mother from Dickens to Freud*, Cambridge: Cambridge University Press, 1998.

DeSalvo, Louise A. "Every woman is an island: Vita Sackville-West, the image of the city, and the pastoral idyll." In Susan M. Squier ed. *Women Writers and the City: Essays in Feminist Literary Criticism*. Knoxville: University of Tennessee Press, 1984: 97–113.

Dickinson, Renée. "The language of empire: identity and the imperial narrative in Virginia Woolf's *The Waves*." Unpublished manuscript. University of Colorado at Boulder, 1999.

Dismond, Geraldyn. "The negro actor and the American movies." *Close Up* 5. 2 (August 1929): 94.

Doan, Laura. "'Acts of female indecency': sexology's intervention in legislating lesbianism." In Lucy Bland and Laura Doan eds. *Sexology in Culture: Labelling Bodies and Desires*. Chicago: University of Chicago Press, 1998. 198–213.

—— *Fashioning Sapphism: The Origins of a Modern English Lesbian Culture* (New York: Columbia University Press, 2001), 95–125.

Doane, Mary Ann. "Dark continents: epistemologies of racial and sexual difference in psychoanalysis and the cinema" *Femmes Fatales*. New York and London: Routledge, 1991: 209–48.

——. *The Sexual Subject: A Screen Reader in Sexuality*. London and New York: Routledge, 1992.

Dodd, Philip. "Englishness and the national culture." In Robert Colls and Philip Dodd eds. *Englishness: Politics and Culture 1880–1920*. London: Croom Helm, 1986: 1–28.

Donald, James. "How English is it? National culture and popular literature." *New Formations* 6 (1988): 32.

Doyle, Laura. *Bordering on the Body: The Racial Matrix of Modern Fiction and Culture*. New York and Oxford: Oxford University Press, 1994.

Dresser, Madge. "Britannia." In Raphael Samuel ed. *Patriotism: The Making and Unmaking of British National Identity*. London and New York: Routledge, 1989, Vol. 3: *National Fictions*: 26–49.

Driver, Felix. *Geography Militant: Cultures of Exploration and Empire*. Oxford: Blackwell, 2001.

Driver, Felix and David Gilbert. "Heart of empire? Landscape, space and performance in imperial London." *Environment and Planning D: Society and Space* 16 (1998): 11–28.

Duncan, Nancy. *Body Space: Destabilizing Geographies of Gender and Sexuality*. London and New York: Routledge, 1996.

DuPlessis, Rachel Blau. *Writing Beyond the Ending: Narrative Strategies of Twentieth-Century Women Writers*. Bloomington: Indiana University Press, 1985.

Dutt, G.S. *A Woman of India: The Life of Saroj Nalini*. London: Hogarth Press, 1929.

Easthope, Anthony. *Englishness and National Culture*. London and New York: Routledge, 1999.

Eger, Elizabeth, Charlotte Grant, Clíona Ó Gallchoir, and Penny Warburton eds. *Women, Writing and the Public Sphere 1700–1830*. Cambridge: Cambridge University Press, 2001.

Egger, Rebecca. "Deaf ears and dark continents: Dorothy Richardson's cinematic epistemology." *Camera Obscura: A Journal of Feminism and Film Theory* 30 (May 1992): 4–33.

Eliot, T. S. *After Strange Gods*. London: Faber, 1934.

Elliott, Bridgett and Jo-Ann Wallace. *Women Artists and Writers: Modernist (Im)Positionings*. London and New York: Routledge, 1994.

Ellis, Edith Lees. *The New Horizon in Love and Life*. London: A.&C. Black, 1921.

Ellis, Havelock. "The school friendships of girls." *Studies in the Psychology of Sex*. New York: Random House, 1936, Vol. 2: 368–84.

——. *Man and Woman: A Study of Secondary Sexual Characteristics*. London: Walter Scott, 1894.

——. *Studies in the Psychology of Sex*, Vols. 1 (1901) and 2 (1910). Re-issued New York: Random House, 1936.

Ellis, Havelock and John Addington Symonds. *Sexual Inversion*. New York: Arno Press, 1975.

Emery, Mary Lou. *Jean Rhys at "World's End": Novels of Colonial and Sexual Exile*. Austin: Univeristy of Texas Press, 1990.

Erickson, Amy Louise. *Women and Property in Early Modern England*. London and New York: Routledge, 1993.

Evans, Arthur. *Witchcraft and the Gay Counterculture.* Boston: Fag Rag Books, 1978.

Faderman, Lillian. *Odd Girls and Twilight Lovers.* New York: Columbia University Press, 1991.

——. *Surpassing the Love of Men: Romantic Friendship and Love between Women from the Renaissance to the Present.* New York: William Morrow, 1991.

Fanon, Franz. *The Wretched of the Earth.* New York: Grove Press, 1963.

Farwell, Marilyn R. *Heterosexual Plots and Lesbian Narratives.* New York and London: New York University Press, 1996.

Felber, Lynette. *Gender and Genre in Novels Without End: The British Roman Fleuve.* Gainesville: University of Florida Press, 1995.

Feldman, David. "Jews in London, 1880–1940." In Raphael Samuel ed. *Patriotism: The Making and Unmaking of British National Identity.* London and New York: Routledge, 1989, Vol. 2: *Minorities and Outsiders*: 207–29.

Feldman, David and Gareth Stedman Jones eds. *Metropolis London: Histories and Representations since 1800.* London and New York: Routledge, 1989.

Felski, Rita. *The Gender of Modernity.* Cambridge, MA: Harvard University Press, 1995.

Fetterley, Judith. "My Antonia, Jim Burden, and the dilemma of the lesbian writer." In Karla Jay and Joanne Glasgow eds. *Lesbian Texts and Contexts: Radical Revisions.* New York: New York University Press, 1990. 145–63.

Ford, Elizabeth Madox. "Comment and review." *Close Up* 1. 3 (1927): 66–8.

Forster, E. M. "What I believe." In S. P. Rosenbaum ed. *A Bloomsbury Group Reader.* Oxford, UK, and Cambridge, MA: Blackwell, 1993: 165–72.

Forty, Adrian. *Objects of Desire: Design and Society since 1750.* London: Thames & Hudson, 1992.

Foy, Roslyn Reso. *Ritual, Myth, and Mysticism in the Work of Mary Butts: Between Feminism and Modernism.* Fayetteville: University of Arkansas Press, 2000.

Frank, Furedi. *The New Ideology of Imperialism: Renewing the Moral Imperative.* London and Boulder, CO: Pluto Press, 1994.

Frankenberg, Ruth ed. *Displacing Whiteness: Essays in Social and Cultural Criticism.* Durham, NC, and London: Duke University Press, 1997.

——. *White Women, Race Matters: The Social Construction of Whiteness.* Minneapolis: University of Minnesota Press, 1993.

Fraser, Nancy. "Rethinking the public sphere: a contribution to the critique of actually existing democracy." In Bruce Robbins ed. *The Phantom Public Sphere.* Minneapolis: University of Minnesota Press, 1993: 1–32.

——. "What's critical about critical theory? The case of Habermas and gender." *New German Critique* 35 (spring–summer 1985): 97–131.

Frazer, J.G. *The Golden Bough: A Study in Magic and Religion.* New York: Macmillan Co., 1900.

Freud, Sigmund. *Civilization and its Discontents.* New York: W.W. Norton, 1961.

——. "Female sexuality." *Collected Papers. Voume 5.* Ed. James Strachey. New York: Basic Books, 1959: 252–72.

——. "Femininity." *New Introductory Lectures on Psychoanalysis.* New York: W.W. Norton, 1965.

——. *Group Psychology and the Analysis of the Ego.* Trans. and ed. James Strachey. New York: W.W. Norton, 1959.

——. "The psychogenesis of a case of homosexuality in a woman." *Collected Papers. Volume 2.* Ed. Ernest Jones. New York: Basic Books, 1959: 202–31.

——. *Totem and Taboo.* Trans. James Strachey. New York: W.W. Norton, 1950.

——. "The 'uncanny'" (1919). *Collected Papers. Volume 4.* New York: Basic Books, 1959.

Friedberg, Anne. "Writing about Cinema: *Close Up* 1927–1933." Dissertation. New York University, 1983.

Friedman, Ellen G. and Miriam Fuchs. *Breaking the Sequence: Women's Experimental Fiction*. Princeton, NJ: Princeton University Press, 1989.

Friedman, Susan Stanford. "'Beyond' gynocriticism and gynesis: the geographics of identity and the future of feminist criticism." *Tulsa Studies in Women's Literature* 15. 1 (1996): 13–40.

——. *Mappings: Feminism and the Cultural Geographies of Encounter*. Princeton, NJ: Princeton University Press, 1998.

Fromm, Gloria G. *Dorothy Richardson: A Biography*. Athens, GA: Univeristy of Georgia Press, 1994.

—— ed. *Windows on Modernism: Selected Letters of Dorothy Richardson*. Athens, GA, and London: University of Georgia Press, 1995.

Fry, Roger. "The art of the bushmen." *Vision and Design*. London: Chatto & Windus, 1925. 85–98.

——. "Children's drawings." *A Roger Fry Reader*. Ed. Christopher Reed. Chicago, IL, and London: University of Chicago Press, 1996: 266–71.

——. "Negro sculpture." *Vision and Design*. London: Chatto & Windus, 1925: 99–103.

Fryer, Peter. *Staying Power: The History of Black People in Britain*. London and Sydney: Pluto Press, 1984.

Furedi, Frank. *The Silent War: Imperialism and the Changing Perception of Race*. New Brunswick, NJ: Rutgers University Press, 1998.

Garber, Eric and Lyn Paleo eds. *Uranian Worlds: A Reader's Guide to Alternative Sexuality in Science Fiction and Fantasy*. Boston, MA: G.K. Hall & Co., 1983.

Gariepy, Jennifer ed. "Mary Butts, 1890–1937," *Twentieth-Century Literary Criticism* 77 (1988): 69–109.

Garner, Shirley Nelson, Claire Kahane, and Medlon Sprengnethereds. *The (M)other Tongue: Feminist Essays in Psychoanalytic Interpretation*. Ithaca, NY: Cornell University Press, 1985.

Garrity, Jane. "Selling culture to the 'civilized': Bloomsbury, *Vogue*, and the marketing of national identity." *Modernism/Modernity* 6. 2 (1999): 29–58.

Gellner, Ernest. *Nations and Nationalism*. Oxford: Blackwell, 1983.

George, Rosemary Marangoly. *The Politics of Home: Postcolonial Relocations and Twentieth-Century Fiction*. Cambridge: Cambridge University Press, 1996.

Gerzina, Gretchen. *Black London: Life Before Emancipation*. New Brunswick, NJ: Rutgers University Press, 1995.

Gevirtz, Susan. *Narrative's Journey: The Fiction and Film Writing of Dorothy Richardson*. New York: Peter Lang, 1996.

Gikandi, Simon. *Maps of Englishness: Writing Identity in the Culture of Colonialism*. New York: Columbia University Press, 1996.

Gilbert, Paul. *The Philosophy of Nationalism*. Boulder, CO: Westview Press,1998.

Gilbert, Sandra M. "Costumes of the mind: transvestitism as metaphor in modern literature." *Critical Inquiry* 7. 2 (1980): 391–417.

Gilbert, Sandra M. and Susan Gubar. *No Man's Land: The Place of the Woman Writer in the Twentieth Century*. Vol. 1: *The War of the Words*. New Haven: Yale University Press, 1988.

——. *No Man's Land: The Place of the Woman Writer in the Twentieth Century*. Vol. 2: *Sexchanges*. New Haven, CT: Yale University Press, 1989.

——. *No Man's Land: The Place of the Woman Writer in Twentieth-Century*. Vol. 3: *Letters from the Front*. New Haven, CT: Yale University Press, 1994.

Giles, Judy and Tim Middleton eds. *Writing and Englishness 1900–1950: An Introductory Sourcebook on National Identity*. London and New York: Routledge, 1995.

Gilman, Sander L. *Creating Beauty to Cure the Soul: Race and Psychology in the Shaping of Aesthetic Surgery*. Durham, NC, and London: Duke University Press, 1998.

——. *Difference and Pathology: Stereotypes of Sexuality, Race, and Madness*. Ithaca, NY: Cornell University Press, 1985.

——. *The Jew's Body*. New York: Routledge, 1991.

Girouard, Mark. *The Return to Camelot: Chivalry and the English Gentleman*. New Haven, CT: Yale University Press, 1981.

Glennie, Allie. *Ravenous Identity: Eating and Eating Distress in the Life and Work of Virginia Woolf* (New York: Garland, 2000).

Gloversmith, Frank ed. *Class, Culture and Social Change: A New View of the 1930s*. Brighton, Sussex: Harvester Press, 1980.

GoGwilt, Chris. "The geographical image: imperialism, anarchism, and the hypothesis of culture in the formation of geopolitics." *Modernism/Modernity* 5. 3 (1998): 49–70.

Goldman, Jane. *The Feminist Aesthetics of Virginia Woolf: Modernism, Post-Impressionism and the Politics of the Visual*. Cambridge: Cambridge University Press, 1998.

Gorham, Deborah. *Vera Brittain: A Feminist Life*. Oxford: Blackwell, 1996.

Gothard, Janice. "The healthy, wholesome, British domestic girl: single female migration and the Empire Settlement Act, 1922–1930." In Stephen Constantine ed. *Emigrants and Empire: British Settlement in the Dominions between the Wars*. Manchester: Manchester University Press, 1990.

Gott, Richard. "Little Englanders." In Raphael Samuel ed. *Patriotism: The Making and Unmaking of British National Identity*. London and New York: Routledge, 1989, Vol. 1: *History and Politics*: 90–102.

Gottlieb, Julie V. *Feminine Fascism: Women in Britain's Fascist Movement, 1923–1945*. London and New York: I.B. Tauris, 2000.

Gourgouris, Stathis. "Notes on the nation's dream-work." *Qui Parle* 7. 1 (1993): 81–101.

Grainger, J.H. *Patriotisms: Britain 1900–1939*. London: Routledge & Kegan Paul, 1986.

Graves, Robert. *The White Goddess: A Historical Grammar of Poetic Myth*. New York: Creative Age Press, 1948.

Greenfield, Liah. *Nationalism: Five Roads to Modernity*. Cambridge, MA: Harvard University Press, 1992.

Grewel, Inderpal. *Home and Harem: Nation, Gender, Empire, and the Cultures of Travel*. Durham, NC, and London: Duke University Press, 1996.

H.D. *Trilogy*. New York: New Directions, 1973.

Halbot, Mrs. "Pro patria." *The Conservative Woman* (June 1921): 10.

Haldane, Charlotte. *Motherhood and its Enemies*. London: Chatto & Windus, 1927.

Hall, Catherine. *Civilising Subjects: Colony and Metropole in the English Imagation, 1830–1867*. Chicago, IL, and London: University of Chicago Press, 2002.

Hall, Lesley A. "Uniting science and sensibility: Marie Stopes and the narratives of marriage in the 1920s." In Angela Ingram and Daphne Patai eds. *Rediscovering Forgotten Radicals: British Women Writers, 1889–1939*. Chapel Hill: University of North Carolina Press, 1993.

Hall, Radclyffe. "Miss Ogilvy finds herself" (1934). *The Norton Anthology of Literature by Women*. Ed. Sandra M. Gilbert and Susan Gubar. New York, 1985: 1443–57.

——. *The Well of Loneliness*. New York: Anchor, 1990.

——. *Your John: The Love Letters of Radclyffe Hall*. Ed. Joanne Glasgow. New York and London: New York University Press, 1997.

Hamer, Emily. *Britannia's Glory: A History of Twentieth-Century Lesbians.* London: Cassell 1996.

Hamilton, Cicely. "The abolition of England." *Time and Tide* (September 3, 1926): 793.

——. *The Englishwoman.* London: Longman, Green & Co. 1940.

——. *Life Errant.* London: J.M. Dent, 1935.

——. "The return to femininity." *Time and Tide* (August 12, 1927): 737.

——. "The Women's Congress and the peace problem." *The Englishwoman* 140 (August 1920): 81–6.

Hamilton, Mary Agnes. "Changes in social life." In Ray Strachey ed. *Our Freedom and its Results.* London: Hogarth Press, 1936: 231–85.

Hanscombe, Gillian and Virginia L. Smyers. *Writing for their Lives: The Modernist Women 1910–1940.* Boston, MA: Northeastern University Press, 1987.

Haraway, Donna. "The persistence of vision." In Katie Conboy, Nadia Medina and Sarah Stanbury eds. *Writing on the Body: Female Embodiment and Feminist Theory.* New York: Columbia University Press, 1997: 283–95.

Harding, Esther. *The Way of All Women: A Psychological Interpretation.* London: Longman, 1933.

Harley, J.B. "Maps, knowledge, and power." In D. Cosgrove and S. Daniels eds. *The Iconography of Landscape: Essays on the Symbolic Representation, Design and Use of Past Environments.* Cambridge: Cambridge University Press, 1998: 277–312.

Harman, Claire ed. "Introduction" to "Sylvia Townsend Warner, 1893–1978: a celebration." *Poetry National Review* 23 (special issue) (1981): 30–1.

——. *Sylvia Townsend Warner: A Biography.* London: Chatto & Windus, 1989.

Harrison, Brian. *Separate Spheres: The Opposition to Women's Suffrage in Brittain.* New York: Holmes & Meier, 1978.

Harrison, Jane Ellen. *Alpha and Omega.* London: Sidgwick & Jackson, 1915.

——. *Ancient Art and Ritual.* New York: Holt, 1913.

——. *Epilegomena to the Study of Greek Religion and Themis: A Study of the Social Origins of Greek Religion.* New Hyde Park, NY: University Books, 1962.

——. *Mythology.* New York: Longmans, Green and Co., 1924.

——. *Prolegomena to the Study of Greek Religion.* Princeton, NJ: Princeton University Press, 1991.

——. *Reminiscences of a Student's Life.* London: Hogarth Press, 1925.

——. *Themis: A Study of the Social Origins of Greek Religion.* Cleveland and New York: World Publishing Co., 1912.

Haseler, Stephen. *The English Tribe: Identity, Nation and Europe.* New York: St. Martin's Press, 1996.

Haste, Cate. *Rules of Desire: Sex in Britain, World War I to the Present.* London: Chatto & Windus, 1992.

Heath, Stephen. "Writing for silence: Dorothy Richardson and the novel." In Sue Kappeler and Norman Bryson eds. *Teaching the Text.* New York: Routledge, 1983: 126–47.

Heng, Geraldine. "Cannibalism, the First Crusade, and the genesis of medieval romance." *differences: A Journal of Feminist Cultural Studies* 10. 1 (1998): 98–175.

Henry, Holly G. "Nebulous networks: Virginia Woolf and popular astronomy." Dissertation. Abstracts International (1999): 9937985.

Heywood, Leslie. *Dedication to Hunger: The Anorexic Aesthetic in Modern Culture.* Berkeley: University of California Press, 1996.

Higgins, Lesley and Marie-Christine Leps. "Passport, please": legal, literary, and critical fictions of identity." *College Literature* 25. 1 (1998): 94–138.

Higonnet, Margaret R. and Joan Templeton. *Reconfigured Spheres: Feminist Explorations of Literary Space*. Amherst: University of Massachusetts Press, 1994.

Higson, Andrew. *Waving the Flag: Constructing a National Cinema in Britain*. Oxford: Clarendon Press, 1995.

Hill, Christopher. *Milton and the English Revolution*. Harmondsworth, England: Penguin, 1979.

Hill, Margaret E. "Letter to the editor." *The Freewoman: A Weekly Feminist Review* 1. 2 (1911): 31.

Hill, Marylu. *Mothering Modernity: Feminism, Modernism, and the Maternal Muse*. New York: Garland, 1999.

Hill, Mike. *Whiteness: A Critical Reader*. New York and London: New York University Press, 1997.

Hirsch, Marianne. *The Mother/Daughter Plot: Narrative, Psychoanalysis, Feminism*. Bloomington: Indiana University Press, 1989.

Hoberman, Ruth. *Gendering Classicism: The Ancient World in Twentieth-Century Women's Historical Fiction*. Albany: State University of New York Press, 1997.

Hobsbawm, Eric. *The Age of Empire 1875–1914*. New York: Vintage, 1989.

——. *Nations and Nationalism since 1780: Programme, Myth, Reality*. Cambridge: Cambridge University Press, 1990.

Hobson, J.A. *Imperialism: A Study*. London: Allen & Unwin, 1938 [1902].

Hoffman, Donald L. "Percival's sister: Malory's 'rejected' masculinities." *Arthuriana* 6. 4 (1996): 72–83.

Hollis, Patricia. *Ladies Elect: Women in English Local Government 1865–1914*. Oxford: Clarendon Press, 1987.

Holt, Ann. "Hikers and ramblers: surviving a thirties' fashion." *International Journal of Sport* 4. 1 (May 1987): 56–67.

Holtby, Winifred. "Are spinsters frustrated?" *Women and a Changing Civilization*. London: John Lane–Bodley Head, 1934.

——. "Feminism divided." *Time and Tide* (August 6, 1926). 714–15.

——. "Notes on the way." *Time and Tide* (May 4, 1935): 647–8.

——. *South Riding* (1936). London: Virago, 1988.

——. *Virginia Woolf: A Critical Memoir*. Chicago, IL: Academy Press, 1978.

——. *Women and a Changing Civilization*. London: John Lane–Bodley Head, 1934.

Homans, Margaret. *Bearing the Word: Language and Female Experience in Nineteenth-Century Women's Writing*. Chicago, IL: University of Chicago Press, 1986

Howe, Stephen. *Anticolonialism in British Politics: The Left and the End of Empire, 1918–1964*. Oxford: Clarendon Press, 1993.

Howkins, Alun. "The discovery of rural England." In Robert Colls and Philip Dodd eds. *Englishness: Politics and Culture 1880–1920*. London: Croom Helm, 1986: 62–88.

Hutton, Isabel Emslie. *The Hygiene of Marriage*. London: Heinemann, 1923.

Hutton, Ronald. *The Stations of the Sun: A History of the Ritual Year in Britain*. Oxford: Oxford University Press, 1996.

Huxley, Aldous. *Beyond the Mexique Bay*. New York and London: Harper & Bros., 1934.

Hynes, Samuel. *A War Imagined: The First World War and English Culture*. London: Bodley Head, 1990.

Ian, Marcia. *Remembering the Phallic Mother: Psychoanalysis, Modernism, and the Fetish*. Ithaca, NY: Cornell Univeristy Press,1993.

Ingram, Heather. *Women's Fiction between the Wars: Mothers, Daughters and Writing*. New York: St. Martin's Press, 1998.

Irigaray, Luce. "Sexual difference." In Toril Moi ed. *French Feminist Thought: A Reader.* Oxford: Blackwell, 1987: 118–32.

——. *Speculum of the Other Woman.* Ithaca, NY: Cornell University Press, 1985.

Jacobs, Karen. *The Eye's Mind: Literary Modernism and Visual Culture.* Ithaca and London: Cornell University Press, 2001.

Jahoda, Gustav. *Images of Savages: Ancient Roots of Modern Prejudice.* London and New York: Routledge, 1999.

Jameson, Fredric. "Modernism and imperialism." *Nationalism, Colonialism, and Literature.* Minneapolis: University of Minnesota Press, 1990: 43–66.

——. *The Political Unconscious: Narrative as a Socially Symbolic Act* (Ithaca, NY: Cornell University Press, 1981.

Jardine, Alice. *Gynesis: Configurations of Women and Modernity.* Ithaca, NY: Cornell University Press, 1985.

Jarrett-Macauley, Delia. *The Life of Una Marson, 1905–65.* Manchester: Manchester University Press, 1998.

Jayawardena, Kumari. *Feminism and Nationalism in the Third World.* London: Zed Books, 1986.

——. *The White Woman's Other Burden: Western Women and South Asia During British Colonial Rule.* New York and London: Routledge, 1995.

Jeffreys, Sheila. *The Spinster and Her Enemies: Feminism and Sexuality 1880–1930.* London: Pandora, 1985.

——. *Women's History: Britain, 1850–1945.* New York: St. Martin's Press, 1995.

Jeremiah, David. *Architecture and Design for the Family in Britain, 1900–70.* Manchester: Manchester University Press, 2000.

Joannou, Maroula. *"Ladies, Please Don't Smash These Windows": Women's Writing, Feminist Consciousness and Social Change 1918–1938.* Oxford and Providence, RI: Berg, 1995.

——. "Sylvia Townsend Warner in the 1930s." In Andy Croft ed. *A Weapon in the Struggle: The Cultural History of the Communist Party in Britain.* London: Pluto Press, 1998: 89–105.

Jones, Stephen G. *Workers at Play: A Social and Economic History of Leisure 1918–1939.* London: Routledge & Kegan Paul, 1986.

Jung, Emma. *The Grail Legend.* Boston, MA: Sigo Press, 1980.

Kaivola, Karen. *All Contraries Confounded: The Lyrical Fiction of Virginia Woolf, Djuna Barnes, and Marguerite Duras.* Iowa City: University of Iowa Press, 1991.

Kaplan, Amy. "Manifest domesticity." *American Literature* 70. 3 (1998): 581–606.

Kaplan, Caren, *Questions of Travel: Postmodern Discourses of Displacement.* Durham, NC, and London: Duke University Press, 1996.

——. ed. *Scattered Hegemonies: Postmodernity and Transnational Feminist Practices.* Minneapolis: University of Minnesota Press, 1994.

Kaplan, Sydney Janet. *Feminine Consciousness in the Modern British Novel.* Chicago and Urbana: University of Illinois Press, 1975.

Kato, Megumi. "The milk problem in *To the Lighthouse.*" *Virginia Woolf Miscellany* 50 (1997): 5.

Katz, Tamar. *Impressionist Subjects: Gender, Interiority, and Modernist Fiction in England.* Urbana and Chicago: University of Illinois Press, 2000.

Kaye, Richard A. "'A splendid readiness for death': T.S. Eliot, the homosexual cult of St. Sebastian, and World War I." *Modernism/Modernity* 6. 2 (1999): 107–34.

Keane, Angela. *Women Writers and the English Nation in the 1790s.* Cambridge: Cambridge University Press, 2001.

Kellman, Steven G. "The cinematic novel: tracking a concept." *Modern Fiction Studies* 33. 3 (1987): 467–77.

Kenealy, Arabella. *Feminism and Sex Extinction*. London: T. Fisher Unwin, 1920.

Kennedy, Hubert. "Kark Heinrich Ulrichs: first theorist of homosexuality." In Vernon A. Rosario ed. *Science and Homosexualities*. New York: Routledge, 1997.

Kent, Susan Kingsley. "Gender reconstruction after the First World War." In Harold L. Smith ed. *British Feminism in the Twentieth Century*. London: University of Massachusetts Press, 1990.

——. *Making Peace: The Reconstruction of Gender in Interwar Britain*. Princeton, NJ: Princeton University Press, 1993.

——. *Sex and Suffrage in Britain 1860–1914*. Princeton, NJ: Princeton University Press, 1987.

Kessler, Jascha. "Mary Butts: lost ... and found." *Kenyan Review* 17. 3–4 (1995): 211.

Kranidis, Rita S. *The Victorian Spinster and Colonial Emigration: Contested Subjects*. New York: St. Martin's Press, 1999.

Kristeva, Julia. *About Chinese Women*. New York and London: Marion Boyars, 1986.

——. *Crisis of the European Subject*. New York: Other Press, LLC, 2000.

——. *Desire in Language: A Semiotic Approach to Literature and Art*. New York: Columbia University Press, 1980.

——. *Nations Without Nationalism*. New York: Columbia University Press, 1993.

——. *Powers of Horror: An Essay on Abjection*. New York: Columbia University Press, 1982.

——. "Psychoanalysis and the polis." *Critical Inquiry* 9. 1 (1982): 77–89.

——. *Revolution in Poetic Language*. Trans. Margaret Waller. New York: Columbia University Press, 1984.

——. *Strangers to Ourselves*. New York: Columbia University Press, 1991.

——. "Women's time." *The Kristeva Reader*. Ed. Toril Moi. New York: Columbia University Press, 1986: 187–213.

Kuhn, Annette. *Cinema, Censorship, and Sexuality, 1909–1925*. London and New York: Routledge, 1988.

Kuklick, Henrika. *The Savage Within: The Social History of British Anthropology, 1885–1945*. Cambridge: Cambridge University Press, 1991.

L.E. "Review of *Armed With Madness*." *Liverpool Post* (May 16, 1928).

Langlan, Mary and Bill Schwartz. *Crises in the British State 1880–1930*. London: Hutchison, 1985.

Langland, Elizabeth. "Nation and nationality: Queen Victoria in the developing narrative of Englishness." In Margaret Homans and Adrienne Munich eds. *Remaking Queen Victoria*. New York and London: Cambridge University Press, 1997: 13–32.

Laurence, Patricia Ondek. *The Reading of Silence: Virginia Woolf in the English Tradition*. Stanford, CA: Stanford University Press, 1991.

Lawrence, D.H. *Women in Love*. New York: Penguin, 1987.

Lawrence, Margaret. *We Write As Women*. London: Michael Joseph, 1937.

Lee, Judith. "'This hideous shaping and molding': war and *The Waves*." In Mark Hussey ed. *Virginia Woolf and War: Fiction, Reality, and Myth*. Syracuse, NY: Syracuse University Press, 1991: 180–202.

Lewis, Jane. *The Politics of Motherhood: Child and Maternal Welfare in England, 1900–1939*. London: Croom Helm, 1980.

Lewis, Pericles. *Modernism, Nationalism and the Novel*. Cambridge: Cambridge University Press, 2000.

Lewis, Reina. *Gendering Orientalism: Race, Femininity, and Representation*. London and New York: Routledge, 1996.

Light, Alison. *Forever England: Femininity, Literature and Conservatism between the Wars*. London and New York: Routledge, 1991.

Loewenstein, Andrea Freud. *Loathsome Jews and Engulfing Women: Metaphors of Projection in the Works of Wyndham Lewis, Charles Williams, and Graham Greene*. New York: New York University Press, 1993.

Looser, Devoney. *British Women Writers and the Writing of History, 1670–1820*. Baltimore, MD: Johns Hopkins University Press, 2000.

Louis, William Roger. "Introduction." In Judith M. Brown and William Roger Louis eds. *The Oxford History of the British Empire*. Oxford and New York: Oxford University Press, 1999. Vol. 4: *The Twentieth Century*: 1–46.

Low, Rachel. *The History of the British Film, 1918–1929*. London: Allen & Unwin, 1971.

Lowerson, John. "Battles for the countryside." In Frank Gloversmith ed. *Class, Culture and Social Change: A New View of the 1930s*. Brighton: Harvester Press, 1980: 258–80.

Lowndes, M. "Domestic service." *The Englishwoman* 123 (March 1919): 109–12.

Loy, Mina. *The Lost Lunar Baedeker*. Ed. Roger L. Conover. New York: Noonday Press, 1996.

Lucas, John. *The Radical Twenties: Writing, Politics, Culture*. Nottingham: Five Leaves, 1997.

Ludovici, Anthony M. *Lysistrata or Woman's Future and Future Woman*. New York: E. P. Dutton & Co., 1925.

Lynch, Deirdre. "At home with Jane Austen." In Deirdre Lynch and William B. Warner eds. *Cultural Institutions of the Novel*. Durham, NC, and London: Duke University Press, 1996: 159–92.

McClintock, Anne. "Family feuds, gender, nationalism and the family." *Feminist Review* 44 (summer, 1993): 61–80.

——. *Imperial Leather: Race, Gender and Sexuality in the Colonial Contest*. New York: Routledge, 1995.

——. "'No longer in a future heaven': gender, race and nationalism." In Anne McClintock, Aamir Mufti, and Ella Shohat eds. *Dangerous Liaisons: Gender, Nation, and Postcolonial Perspectives*. Minneapolis: University of Minnesota Press, 1997: 89–112.

McCracken, Donald P. *Gardens of Empire: Botanical Institutions of the Victorian British Empire*. London and Washington: Leicester University Press, 1997.

McCrone, David. *The Sociology of Nationalism*. London and New York: Routledge, 1998.

MacDonald, Robert H. *The Language of Empire: Myths and Metaphors of Popular Imperialism, 1880–1918*. Manchester and New York: Manchester University Press, 1994.

McDowell, Linda and Joanne P. Sharp. *Space, Gender, Knowledge: Feminist Readings*. New York: Arnold–Hodder Headline, 1997.

McGee, Patrick. "The politics of modernist form; or, who rules *The Waves*?" *Modern Fiction Studies* 38. 3 (1992): 631–50.

Mackay, Jane and Pat Thane. "The Englishwoman." In Robert Colls and Philip Dodd eds. *Englishness: Politics and Culture 1880–1920*. London: Croom Helm, 1986: 191–229.

MacKenzie, John M. ed. *Imperialism and Popular Culture*. Manchester: Manchester University Press, 1987.

——. *Propaganda and Empire: The Manipulation of British Public Opinion, 1880–1960*. Manchester: Manchester University Press, 1984.

Mackinder, H.J. *Britain and the British Seas*. Oxford: Clarendon Press, 1902.

——. *The Development of Geographical Teaching Out of Nature-Study*. London: George Philip, 1908.

McNaron, Toni A.H. "Mirrors and likeness: a lesbian aesthetic in the making." In Susan J. Wolfe and Julia Penelope eds. *Sexual Practice, Textual Theory: Lesbian Cultural Criticism*. Cambridge, MA, and Oxford: Blackwell, 1993: 291–306.

McNeillie, Andrew. "Virginia Woolf's America." *Dublin Review* 5 (winter, 2001–2): 41–55.

Macpherson, Kenneth. "As is." *Close Up* 1.3 (1927): 5–16.

——. "As is." *Close Up* 4. 3 (1929): 5–9.

——. "As is." *Close Up* 5. 2 (1929): 85–90.

Maguire, G. E. *Conservative Women: A History of Women and the Conservative Party, 1847–1997*. Oxford: St. Anthony's College, 1998.

Maika, Patricia. *Virginia Woolf's* Between the Acts *and Jane Harrison's* Con/spiracy. Ann Arbor: University of Michigan Research Press, 1987.

Malinowski, Bronislaw. *Sex, Culture, and Myth*. New York: Harcourt Brace Jovanovich, 1962.

——. *The Sexual Life of Savages: An Ethnographic Account of Courtship, Marriage, and Family Life Among the Natives of the Trobriand Islands, British New Guinea*. New York: Harcourt Brace, 1929.

Manganaro, Marc. *Myth, Rhetoric, and the Voice of Authority: A Critique of Frazer, Eliot, Frye, and Campbell*. New Haven, CT, and London: Yale University Press, 1992.

Mansfield, Katherine. *Journal of Katherine Mansfield*. Ed. John Middleton Murry. New York: Ecco Press, 1983.

Marcus, Jane. "Alibis and legends: the ethics of elsewhereness, gender and estrangement." In Broe and Ingram eds. *Women's Writing in Exile*.

——. "Britannia rules *The Waves*." In Karen R. Lawrence ed. *Decolonizing Tradition: New Views of Twentieth-Century "British" Literary Canons*. Urbana and Chicago, IL: University of Illinois Press, 1992: 136–162.

——. "Registering objections: grounding feminist alibis." In Margaret R. Higonnet and Joan Templeton. *Reconfigured Spheres: Feminist Explorations of Literary Space*. Amherst: University of Massachusetts Press, 1994: 33–63.

——. "Sapphistry: narration as lesbian seduction in *A Room of One's Own*." *Virginia Woolf and the Languages of Patriarchy*. Bloomington and Indianapolis: Indiana University Press, 1987.

——. "Sapphistry: the Woolf and the well." In Karla Jay and Joanne Glasgow eds. *Lesbian Texts and Contexts*. New York: New York University Press, 1990. 164–79.

——. *Virginia Woolf and the Languages of Patriarchy*. Bloomington: Indiana University Press, 1987.

——. "A wilderness of one's own: feminist fantasy novels of the twenties: Rebecca West and Sylvia Townsend Warner." In Susan Merrill Squier ed. *Women Writers and the City: Essays in Feminist Literary Criticism*. Knoxville: University of Tennessee Press, 1984: 134–60.

Marcus, Laura. "Mysterious Mary Butts." *Times Literary Supplement* (August 24, 2001): 3–4.

Marston, Jay. "My cook was an African." *Vogue* ([London] August 19, 1936).

Marcus, Laura. "Virginia Woolf and the Hogarth Press." In Ian Willison ed. *Modernist Writers and the Marketplace*. London: Macmillan, 1996: 124–150.

Marek, Jayne E. *Women Editing Modernism: "Little" Magazines and Literary History*. Louisville: University of Kentucky Press, 1995.

Marler, Regina. *Bloomsbury Pie: The Making of the Bloomsbury Boom*. New York: Henry Holt & Co., 1997.

Marshik, Celia. "Publication and 'public women': prostitution and censorship in three novels by Virginia Woolf." *Modern Fiction Studies* 45. 4 (1999): 853–86.

Marson, Una. *Towards the Stars*. Bickley, Kent: University of London Press, 1945.

Maslen, Elizabeth. *Political and Social Issues in British Women's Fiction, 1928–1968*. New York: Palgrave, 2001.

Massey, Doreen. *Space, Place, and Gender*. Minneapolis: University of Minnesota Press, 1994.

Matalene, Carolyn. "Women as witches." *International Journal of Women's Studies* 1. 6 (1978): 573–87.

Matless, David. "'The art of right living': landscape and citizenship, 1918–1939." In Steve Pile and Nigel Thrift eds. *Mapping the Subject: Geographies of Cultural Transformation*. London and New York: Routledge, 1995: 93–122.

——. *Landscape and Englishness*. London: Reaktion Books, 1998.

——. "Ordering the land: the 'preservation' of the English countryside, 1918–1939." Ph.D. thesis, University of Nottinhgam, 1990.

——. "Seeing England with Morton and Cornish: travel writing and a quest for order." In Mike Hiffernan and Pyrs Gruffudd eds. *A Land Fit for Heroes: Essays in the Human Geography of Inter-War Britain*. Loughborough: Loughborough University Department of Geography Occasional Paper No.14, 1988: 110–29.

Matthews, Jill Julius. "They had such a lot of fun: the Women's League of Health and Beauty." *History Workshop: A Journal of Socialist and Feminist Historians* 30 (autumn 1990): 22–54.

Mee, Arthur. "Ourselves and the nation." *The Children's Encyclopedia*, Vol. 9. Reprinted in Judy Giles and Tim Middleton eds. *Writing Englishness 1900–1950: An Introductory Sourcebook on National Identity*. New York: Routledge, 1995: 63–6.

Meese, Elizabeth A. *(Sem)Erotics: Theorizing Lesbian Writing*. New York and London: New York University Press, 1992.

Melman, Billie. *Borderlines: Genders and Identities in War and Peace 1870–1930*. New York and London: Routledge, 1998.

——. *Women and the Popular Imagination in the Twenties: Flappers and Nymphs*. New York: St. Martin's Press, 1988.

——. *Women's Orients: English Women and the Middle-East, 1718–1918: Sexuality, Religion, and Work*. Ann Arbor: University of Michigan Press, 1992.

Meyer, Susan. *Imperialism at Home: Race and Victorian Women's Fiction*. Ithaca, NY: Cornell University Press, 1996.

Miller, Tyrus. *Late Modernism: Politics, Fiction, and the Arts between the World Wars*. Berkeley and Los Angeles: University of California Press, 1999.

Minow-Pinkney, Makiko. "Virginia Woolf: 'seen from a foreign land.'" In John Fletcher and Andrew Benjamin eds. *Abjection, Melancholia and Love: The Works of Julia Kristeva*. London and New York: Routledge, 1990: 157–76.

——. *Virginia Woolf and the Problem of the Subject*. New Brunswick, NJ: Rutgers University Press, 1983.

Mitchell, J. Lawrence. "The secret country of her mind: aspects of the novels of Sylvia Townsend Warner." *Poetry National Review* 23 (special issue) (1981): 52–6

Mohanty, Chandra Talpade. "Under Western eyes: feminist scholarship and colonial discourses." In Patrick Williams and Laura Chrisman eds. *Colonial Discourses and Post-Colonial Theory: A Reader*. New York: Columbia University Press, 1994: 196–220.

Montague-Smith, Patrick ed. *Debrett's Peerage and Baronetage*. New York: Arco Publishing Co., 1977.

Montefiore, Dora B. *From a Victorian to a Modern*. London: E. Archer, 1927.

——. *Race Motherhood: Is Woman the Race?* London, 1920.

Moore, Olive. *Collected Writings*. Elmwood Park, IL: Dalkey Arhive Press, 1992.

Moran, Patricia. "'The flaw in the centre': writing as hymenal rupture in Virginia Woolf's work." *Tulsa Studies in Women's Literature* 17. 1 (1998): 101–21.

——. *Word of Mouth: Body Language in Katherine Mansfield and Virginia Woolf.* Charlottesville: University of Virginia Press, 1996.

Morton, H.V. *In Search of England.* New York: Dodd, Mead & Co., 1927.

Moruzzi, Norma Claire. "National abjects: Julia Kristeva on the process of political self-identification." In Kelly Oliver ed. *Ethics, Politcs, and Difference in Julia Kristeva's Writing.* New York: Routledge, 1993: 135–49.

Mosse, George L. *Nationalism and Sexuality: Middle-Class Morality and Sexual Norms in Modern Europe.* Madison: University of Wisconsin Press, 1985.

Muir, Willa. *Women: An Inquiry.* New York: Alfred A. Knopf, 1926.

Mulford, Wendy. *This Narrow Place: Sylvia Townsend Warner and Valentine Ackland: Life, Letters and Politics, 1930–1951.* London: Pandora, 1988.

Mulvey, Laura. "Visual pleasure and narrative cinema." In Constance Penley ed. *Feminism and Film Theory.* New York: Routledge, 1988: 57–68.

Munt, Sally. *Heroic Desire: Lesbian Identity and Cultural Space.* New York: New York University Press, 1998.

——. "The lesbian *flâneur*." In David Bell, and Gill Valentine eds. *Mapping Desire: Geographies of Sexualities.* London and New York: Routledge, 1995: 114–25.

—— ed. *New Lesbian Criticism: Literary and Cultural Readings.* New York: Columbia University Press, 1992.

Murray, Margaret Alice. *The God of the Witches.* London: Oxford University Press, 1931.

——. *The Witch Cult in Western Europe: A Study in Anthropology.* London: Oxford University Press, 1921.

Musolf, Karen J. *From Plymouth to Parliamen: A Rhetorical History of Nancy Astor's 1919 Campaign.* New York: St. Martin's Press, 1999.

Myers, Norma. *Reconstructing the Black Past: Blacks in Britain c. 1780–1830.* London: Frank Cass, 1996.

Nast, Heidi J. and Kobayashi, Audrey. "Re-corporealizing vision." In Nancy Duncan ed. *Bodyspace: Destabilizing Geographies of Gender and Sexuality.* London and New York: Routledge, 1996.

Newbigin, Marion I. *Aftermath: A Geographical Study of the Peace Terms.* Edinburgh: W. & A.K. Johnson, 1920.

——. "The origin and maintenance of diversity in man." *The Geographical Review* 6 (July–December, 1918): 411–20.

——. "Race and nationality." *The Geographical Journal* 1. 5 (1917): 313–28.

Noble, Peter. *The Negro in Films.* London: Skelton Robinson, 1948.

Nolan, Emer. *James Joyce and Nationalism.* London and New York: Routledge, 1995.

O'Brien, Sharon. "'The thing not named': Willa Cather as a lesbian writer." In Estelle B. Freedman, Barbara C. Gelpi, Susan L. Johnson, and Kathleen M. Weston eds. *The Lesbian Issues: Essays from Signs.* Chicago, IL, and London: University of Chicago Press, 1985: 67–90.

——. *Willa Cather: The Emerging Voice.* New York: Oxford University Press, 1987.

Oliver, Kelly ed. *Ethics, Politcs, and Difference in Julia Kristeva's Writing.* New York: Routledge, 1993.

——. *Reading Kristeva: Unraveling the Double-Bind.* Bloomington and Indianapolis: Indiana University Press, 1993.

Oram, Alison. "'Embittered, sexless or homosexual': attacks on spinster teachers 1918–39," *Not a Passing Phase: Reclaiming Lesbians in History 1840-1985.* London: Women's Press, 1989: 99–118.

——. "Repressed and thwarted, or bearer of the new world? The spinster in inter-war feminist discourses." *Women's History Review* 1. 3 (1992): 413–34.

Patterson, Ian. "'The plan behind the plan.' Russians, Jews and mythologies of change: the case of Mary Butts." In Bryan Cheyette and Laura Marcus eds. *Modernity, Culture, and "the Jew."* Palo Alto, CA: Stanford University Press, 1998: 126–42.

Peach, Linden. "No longer a view: Virginia Woolf in the 1930s and the 1930s in Virginia Woolf." In Maroula Joannou ed. *Women Writers of the 1930s: Gender, Politics and History.* Edinburgh: Edinburgh University Press, 1999: 192–204.

Pennycook, Alastair. *English and the Discourses of Colonialism.* London and New York Routledge, 1998.

Percy, W. *The Empire Comes Home.* London: William Collins, 1937.

Pertwee, B. *Promenades and Pierrots: One Hundred Years of Seaside Entertainment.* Taunton, Devon: Westbridge Books, 1979.

Phillips, K.J. *Dying Gods in Twentieth-Century Fiction.* Lewisville, PA: Bucknell University Press, 1990.

——. "Jane Harrison and modernism." *Journal of Modern Literature* 17. 4 (1991): 465–576.

——. *Virginia Woolf Against Empire.* Knoxville: Univeristy of Tennessee Press, 1994.

Pitt, Rosemary. "The exploration of the self in Conrad's *Heart of Darkness* and Woolf's *The Voyage Out.*" *Conradiana* 10 (1978): 141–54.

Playne, Caroline E. *The Neuroses of the Nations.* London: George Allen & Unwin, 1925.

——. *The Pre-War Mind in Britain: An Historical Review.* London: Allen & Unwin, 1928.

Ploszjska, Teresa. "Down to earth? Geography fieldwork in English schools, 1870–1944." *Environment and Planning D: Society and Space* 16. 6 (1998): 757–74.

——. *Geographical Education, Empire and Citizenship: Geographical Teaching and Learning in English Schools, 1870–1944.* Liverpool: University of Liverpool Department of Environmental and Biological Studies, 1999.

Poovey, Mary. *Uneven Developments: The Ideological Work of Gender in Mid-Victorian England.* Chicago, IL: University of Chicago Press, 1988.

Porter, B. *The Lion's Share: A Short History of British Imperialism 1850–1983.* London: Longman, 1984.

Potamkin, Harry Alan. "The Aframerican cinema." *Close Up* 5. 2 (1929): 107–17.

——. "The English cinema." *Close Up* 4. 3 (1929): 17–28.

Poulson, Christine. *The Quest for the Grail: Arthurian Legend in British Art 1840–1920.* Manchester and New York: Manchester University Press, 1999.

Pound, Ezra. *Pavannes and Divigations.* New York: New Directions, 1958.

Power, Eileen. *Medieval Women.* London: Methuen, 1924.

Prosser, Jay. *Second Skins: The Body Narratives of Transsexuality.* New York: Columbia University Press, 1998.

Pugh, Martin. *Women and the Women's Movement in Britain 1914–1959.* New York: Paragon, 1993.

Purkiss, Diane. *The Witch in History: Early Modern and Twentieth-Century Representations.* London and New York: Routledge, 1996.

Quattrin, Patricia Ann. "The milk of Christ: Herzeloyde as spiritual symbol in Wolfram Von Eschenbach's *Parzival.*" In John Carmi Parsons and Bonnie Wheeler eds. *Medieval Mothering.* New York and London: Garland, 1996: 25–38.

Radford, Jean. "Coming to terms: Dorothy Richardson, Modernism and women." In Peter Brooker ed. *Modernism/Postmodernism.* London and New York: Longman,

——. *Dorothy Richardson.* Bloomington and Indianapolis: Indiana University Press, 1991.

Ragussis, Michael. *Figures of Conversion: "The Jewish Question" and English National Identity*. Durham, NC, and London: Duke University Press, 1995.

Rainey, Lawrence. "Good things: pederasty and jazz and opium and research." *London Review of Books* (July 16, 1998): 14–17.

——. *Institutions of Modernism: Literary Elites and Public Culture*. New Haven, CT, and London: Yale University Press, 1998.

Raitt, Suzanne. *Vita and Virginia: The Work and Friendship of Vita Sackville-West and Virginia Woolf*. Oxford: Clarendon Press, 1993.

Ramdin, Ron. *Reimagining Britain: Five Hundred Years of Black and Asian History*. London: Pluto Press, 1999.

Ramusack, Barbara N. "Cultural missionaries, maternal imperialists, feminist allies: British women activists in India, 1865–1945." In Nupur Chaudhuri and Margaret Strobel eds. *Western Women and Imperialism: Complicity and Resistance*. Bloomington and Indianapolis: Indiana University Press, 1992: 119–36.

Rappaport, Erica D. *Shopping for Pleasure: Women in the Making of London's West End*. Princeton, NJ: Princeton University Press, 2000.

Rathbone, Eleanor. *The Disinherited Family: A Plea for the Endowment of the Family*. London: Edward Arnold, 1924.

——. "Victory – and after?" *The Woman's Leader* (March 8, 1929). 35–6.

Reed, Michael. *The Landscape of Britain from the Beginnings to 1914*. Savage, MD: Barnes & Noble, 1990.

Reiss, Erna. "Changes in law." In Ray Strachey ed. *Our Freedom and its Results*. London: Hogarth Press, 1936: 77–116.

——. *Rights and Duties of Englishwomen*. Manchester: Sherratt & Hughes, 1934.

Renan, Ernest. "What is a nation?" In Homi K. Bhabha ed. *Nation and Narration*. London and New York: Routledge, 1990: 8–22.

Rhondda, Viscountess (Margaret Haig). *Notes on the Way*. London: Macmillan & Co., 1937.

——. "Woman's place VI." *Time and Tide* (9 December, 1927).

Rhys, Jean. *Good Morning, Midnight*. New York: W.W. Norton, 1986.

——. *Voyage in the Dark*. New York and London: W.W. Norton, 1982.

——. *Wide Sargasso Sea*. New York: W.W. Norton, 1992.

Rich, Paul. "The quest for Englishness." *History Today* 37 (June, 1987): 24–30.

——. *Race and Empire in British Politics*. Cambridge and New York: Cambridge University Press, 1986.

Richards, Jeffrey. "'Patriotism with profit': British imperial cinema in the 1930s." In James Curran and Vincent Porter eds. *British Cinema History*. Weidenfeld & Nicolson, 1983: 245–56.

——. *The Age of the Dream Palace: Cinema and Society in Britain 1930–1939*. London and New York: Routledge, 1984.

Richardson, Dorothy. "Continuous performance." *Close Up* 1. 1 (1927): 34–7.

——. "Continuous performance: musical accompaniment." *Close Up* 1. 2 (1927): 58–62.

——. "Continuous performance III: captions." *Close Up* 1. 3 (1927): 52–6.

——. "Continuous performance IV: a thousand pities." *Close Up* 1. 4 (1927): 60–4.

——. "Continuous performance V: there's no place like home." *Close Up* 1. 5 (1927): 44–7.

——. "Continuous performance VI: the increasing congregation." *Close Up* 1. 6 (1927): 61–5.

——. "Continuous performance VIII [article untitled]." *Close Up* 2. 3 (1928): 51–5.

——. "Continuous performance IX: the thoroughly popular film." *Close Up* 2. 4 (1928): 44–50.

——. "Continuous performance: the cinema in the slums." *Close Up* 2. 5 (1928): 58–62.

——. "Continuous performance: the cinema in Arcady." *Close Up* 3. 1 (1928): 52–7.

——. "Films for children." *Close Up* 3. 2 (1928): 21–7.

——. "Continuous performance: pictures and films." *Close Up* 4. 1 (1929): 51–7.

——. "Continuous performance: almost persuaded." *Close Up* 4. 6 (1929): 31–7.

——. "Continuous performance: dialogue in Dixie." *Close Up* 5. 3 (1929): 211–18.

——. "Continuous performance: a tear for Lycidas." *Close Up* 7. 3 (1930): 196–202.

——. "Continuous performance: Narcissus." *Close Up* 8. 3 (1931): 182–5.

——. "Continuous performance: this spoon-fed generation?" *Close Up* 8. 4 (1931): 304–8.

——. "Continuous performance: the film gone male." *Close Up* 9. 1 (1932): 36–8.

——. "Leadership in marriage," *The New Adelphi*, 2. 4 (1929): 347.

——. "Novels." In Bonnie Kime Scott ed. *The Gender of Modernism: A Critical Anthology*. Bloomington and Indianapolis: Indiana University Press, 1990: 432–5.

——. *Pilgrimage*. London: Virago, 1979, 4 vols.

——. *The Quakers Past and Present*. London: Constable & Co., 1914.

——. "The reality of feminism." In Bonnie Kime Scott ed. *The Gender of Modernism: A Critical Anthology*. Bloomington and Indianapolis: Indiana University Press, 1990: 401–7.

——. "Women and the future." In Bonnie Kime Scott ed. *The Gender of Modernism: A Critical Anthology*. Bloomington and Indianapolis: Indiana University Press, 1990: 411.

——. *Windows on Modernism: Selected Letters of Dorothy Richardson*. Ed. Gloria G. Fromm. Athens, GA, and London: University of Georgia Press, 1995.

Rigby, Nigel. "'Not a good place for deacons': the South Seas, sexuality and modernism in Sylvia Townsend Warner's *Mr Fortune's Maggot*." In Howard J. Booth and Nigel Rigby eds. *Modernism and Empire*. Manchester: Manchester University Press, 2000: 224–48.

Riley, Denise. "*Am I That Name?*" *Feminism and the Category of "Women" in History*. Minneapolis: University of Minnesota Press, 1988.

Riviere, Joan. "Womanliness as a masquerade." In Victor Burgin, James Donald and Cora Kaplan eds. *Formations of Fantasy*. New York and London: Routledge, 1986: 74–88.

Robbins, Keith. *Great Britain: Identities, Institutions and the Idea of Britishness*. Harlow, Essex: Longman, 1998.

Roberts, Elizabeth Madox. "Comment and review." *Close Up* 1. 3 (1927): 66–8.

Robertson, Ritchie. "Historicizing Weininger: the nineteenth-century German image of the feminized Jew." In Bryan Cheyette and Laura Marcus eds. *Modernity, Culture, and "the Jew."* Palo Alto, CA: Stanford University Press, 1998: 23–39.

Robinson, Annabel. "Something odd at work: the influence of Jane Harrison on *A Room of One's Own*." *Wascana Review of Contemporary Poetry and Short Fiction* 22. 1 (1987): 82–8.

Rony, Fatimah Tobing. *The Third Eye: Race, Cinema, and Ethnographic Spectacle*. Durham, NC, and London: Duke University Press, 1996.

Rosaldo, Renato. "Imperialist nostalgia." *Representations* 26 (spring, 1989): 107–22.

Rose, Gillian. "As if the mirrors had bled: masculine dwelling, masculinist theory, and feminist masquerade." In Nancy Duncan ed. *Body Space: Destabilizing Geographies of Gender and Sexuality*. London and New York: Routledge, 1996: 56–74.

——. *Feminism and Geography: The Limits of Geographical Knowledge*. Minneapolis: University of Minnesota Press, 1993.

Rose, Jacqueline. "Dorothy Richardson and "the Jew," in Brian Cheyette ed. *Between "Race" and Culture: Representations of "the Jew" in English and American Literature*. Stanford, CA: Stanford University Press, 1996: 114–28.

Rosenberg, Carol Smith. *Disorderly Conduct: Visions of Gender in Victorian America.* New York and Oxford: Oxford University Press, 1985.

Ross, Ellen. *Love and Toil: Motherhood in Outcaste London, 1870–1918.* New York: Oxford Univeristy Press, 1993.

Rossingnol, Rosalyn. "The holiest vessel: maternal aspects of the Grail." *Arthuriana* 5. 1 (1995): 52–61.

Royden, Maude. *The Moral Standards of the Rising Generation.* London: League of the Church Militant, 1921.

——. "Women and the League of Nations." *The Englishwoman* 134 (February, 1920): 81–8.

Rubenstein, Helena. "On her dressing table." *Vogue* ([London] early November, 1922).

Rudikoff, Sonya. *Ancestral Houses: Virginia Woolf and the Aristocracy.* Palo Alto, CA: Society for the Promotion of Science and Scholarship, 1999.

Rutherford, Jonathan. *Forever England: Reflections on Masculinity and Empire.* London: Lawrence & Wishart, 1997.

Ryan, James R. *Picturing Empire: Photography and the Visualization of the British Empire.* Chicago, IL: University of Chicago Press, 1997.

Sackville-West, Vita. *All Passion Spent.* London: Virago, 1983.

Said, Edward. *Culture and Imperialism.* London: Chatto & Windus, 1992.

Samuel, Raphael, ed. *Patriotism: The Making and Unmaking of British National Identity.* London and New York: Routledge, 1989, 3 vols.

Sarker, Sonita. "Locating a native Englishness in Virginia Woolf's *The London Scene.*" *National Women's Studies' Association Journal* 13. 2 (2001): 1–30.

Scharlieb, Mary. *The Bachelor Woman and Her Problems.* London: Williams & Norgate, 1929.

——. *The Claims of the Coming Generation.* London: Kegan Paul, 1923.

——. *What it Means to Marry.* London: Cassell & Co., 1914.

Schenck, Celeste M. "Exiled by genre: modernism, canonicity, and the politics of exclusion." In Mary Lynn Broe and Angela Ingram eds. *Women's Writing in Exile.* Chapel Hill and London: University of North Carolina Press, 1989: 225–50.

Schlesier, Renate. "Prolegomena to Jane Harrison's interpretation of ancient Greek religion." In William M. Calder ed. *The Cambridge Ritualists Reconsidered.* Atlanta, GA: Scholar's Press, 1991: 185–226.

Schlueter, June and Paul Schlueter eds. *An Encyclopedia of British Women Writers.* New Brunswick, NJ: Rutgers University Press, 1998.

Schuster, Ernest J. "The effect of marriage on nationality." *International Law Association: Report of the Conference on Nationality and Naturalization.* London: ILA, 1923, Vol. 1–2: 9–51.

Schuyler, Sarah. "Double-dealing fictions." *Genders* 9 (autumn, 1990): 75–92.

Scobie, Edward. *Black Britannia: A History of Blacks in Britain.* Chicago, IL: Johnson Publishing Co., 1972.

Scott, Bonnie Kime ed. *The Gender of Modernism: A Critical Anthology.* Bloomington and Indianapolis: Indiana University Press, 1990.

——. *Refiguring Modernism.* Bloomington and Indianapolis: Indiana University Press, 1995, 2 vols.

Sedgwick, Eve Kosofsky. *Tendencies.* Durham, NC: Duke University Press, 1993.

Shakespeare, William. *The Merchant of Venice.* London: E. Bern, 1923.

Shattuck, Sandra D. "The stage of scholarship: crossing the bridge from Harrison to Woolf." In Jane Marcus ed. *Virginia Woolf and Bloomsbury: A Centenary Celebration.* Indianapolis: Indiana University Press, 1987: 278–98.

Shaw, Marion. "Winifred Holtby and the peace movement between the wars." In

Wayne K. Chapman and Janet M. Manson eds. *Women in the Milieu of Leonard and Virginia Woolf: Peace, Politics, and Education.* New York: Pace University Press, 1998: 111–24.

Sheal, John. *Rural Conservation in Inter-War Britian.* Oxford: Clarendon Press, 1981.

Showalter, Elaine. *The Female Malady: Women, Madness, and English Culture, 1830–1980.* London: Virago, 1987.

———. *A Literature of Their Own: British Women Novelists from Brönte to Lessing.* New Jersey, NJ: Princeton University Press, 1977.

———. *Sexual Anarchy: Gender and Culture at the* Fin de Siècle. New York: Viking, 1990.

Shyllon, Folarin. *Essays on the History of Blacks in Britain: From Roman Times to the Mid-Twentieth Century.* Ed. Jagdish S. Gundara and Ian Duffield. Aldershot: Ashgate, 1992.

Silver, Brenda. *Virginia Woolf Icon.* Chicago, IL, and London: University of Chicago Press, 1999.

Simpson, Anne B. "Architects of the erotic: H.G. Wells's 'new women.'" In Carroll M. Kaplan and Anne B. Simpson eds. *Seeing Double: Revisiting Edwardian and Modernist Literature.* New York: St. Martin's, 1996: 39–55.

Sinclair, May. "The novels of Dorothy Richardson." In Bonnie Kime Scott ed. *The Gender of Modernism: A Critical Anthology.* Bloomington and Indianapolis: Indiana University Press, 1990: 442–8.

Smith, Anthony. *Nations and Nationalism in a Global Era.* Cambridge: Polity Press, 1995.

Smith, Bonnie G. *The Gender of History: Men, Women, and Historical Practice.* Cambridge, MA, and London: Harvard University Press, 1998.

Smith, Harold L. "British feminism in the 1920s." *British Feminism in the Twentieth Century.* Amherst, MA: University of Massachusetts Press, 1990.

Smith, Patricia Juliana. *Lesbian Panic: Homoeroticism in Modern British Women's Fiction.* New York: Columbia University Press, 1997.

Smith, Rosaleen. "Movies and mandarins: the official film and British colonial Africa." In Curran and Porter eds. *British Cinema History.* London: Weidenfeld & Nicolson, 1982: 129–43.

Souhami, Diana. *The Trials of Radclyffe Hall.* London: Weidenfelt & Nicolson, 1998.

Spraggs, Gillian. "Exiled to home: the poetry of Sylvia Townsend Warner and Valentine Ackland." In Mark Lilly ed. *Lesbian and Gay Writing: An Anthology of Critical Essays.* Philadelphia, PA: Temple University Press, 1990. 109–250.

Sprengnether, Madelon. *The Spectral Mother: Freud, Feminism, and Psychoanalysis.* Ithaca, NY: Cornell University Press, 1990.

Squier, Susan M. *Babies in Bottles: Twentieth-Century Visions of Reproductive Technology.* New Brunswick: Rutgers University Press, 1994.

———. *Virginia Woolf and London: The Sexual Politics of the City.* Chapel Hill and London: University of North Carolina Press, 1985.

———. ed. *Women Writers and the City: Essays in Feminist Literary Criticism.* Knoxville: University of Tennessee Press, 1984.

Steen, Marguerite. "The glory that was Greece." *Everyman* (March, 1933).

Stella Browne. "The right to abortion." In Norman Haire ed. *World League for Sexual Reform. Proceedings of the Third Congress.* London: Kegan Paul, 1930: 13–50.

Stewart, Garrett. "Catching the stylistic d/rift: sound defects in Woolf's *The Waves,*" *English Literary History* 54. 2 (1987): 421–61.

Stinton, Judith. *Chaldon Herring: The Powys Circle in a Dorset Village.* Suffolk: Boydell Press, 1988.

Stoler, Ann Laura. "Carnal knowledge and imperial power: gender, race, and morality in colonial Asia." In Micaela di Leonardi ed. *Gender at the Crossroads of Knowledge: Feminist Anthropology in the Postmodern Era*. Berkeley: University of California Press, 1991: 51–101.

———. *Marriage in My Time*. London: Rich & Cowan, 1935.

———. *Married Love*. London: Trafalgar Square, 1918.

———. *Wise Parenthood*. London: Trafalgar Square, 1918.

Straayer, Chris. *Deviant Eyes, Deviant Bodies: Sexual Re-Orientations in Film and Video*. New York: Columbia University Press, 1996.

Strachey, Philippa. *Memorandum on the Position of English Women in Relation to that of English Men*. London: National Society for Women's Service, 1935.

Strachey, Ray. *Careers and Openings for Women: A Survey of Women's Employment and a Guide for Those Seeking Work*. London: Faber & Faber, 1934.

———. *Our Freedom and its Results*. Ed. Ray Strachey. London: Hogarth Press, 1936.

Strobel, Margaret. *European Women and the Second British Empire*. Bloomington and Indianapolis: Indiana University Press, 1992.

Swanwick, H.M. *The Roots of Peace*. London: Jonathan Cape, 1938.

Swiney, Frances. *The Awakening of Women*. London: William Reeves, 1899.

———. *The Cosmic Procession or the Feminine Principle in Evolution*. London: E. Bell, 1906.

Symonds, John. *The Great Beast: The Life and Magick of Aleister Crowley*. London: Mayflower Books, 1973.

Sypher, Eileen B. "*The Waves*: A utopia of androgyny?" In Elaine K. Ginsberg and Laura Moss Gottlieb eds. *Virginia Woolf: Centennial Essays*. New York: Whitston, 1983: 187–213.

Szreter, Simon. *Fertility, Class and Gender in Britain, 1860–1940*. Cambridge: Cambridge University Press, 1996.

Tabili, Laura. *"We Ask for British Justice": Workers and Racial Difference in Late Imperial Britain*. Ithaca, NY: Cornell University Press, 1994.

Tallents, Stephen G. *The Projection of England*. London: Faber & Faber, 1932.

Taylor, Harvey. *A Claim on the Countryside: A History of the British Outdoor Movement*. Edinburgh: Keele University Press, 1997.

Thomson, George H. *Notes on* Pilgrimage: *Dorothy Richardson Annotated*. Greensboro, NC: ELT Press, 1999.

———. *A Reader's Guide: Dorothy Richardson's* Pilgrimage. Greensboro, NC: ELT Press, 1996.

Tidrick, Kathryn. *Empire and the English Character*. London: I.B. Tauris & Co., 1990.

Todorov, Tzvetan. "The quest of narrative." *The Poetics of Prose*. Ithaca, NY: Cornell University Press, 1977: 120–42.

Torgovnick, Marianna. "Discovering Jane Harrison." In Corola M. Kaplan and Anne B. Simpson. *Seeing Double: Edwardian and Modernist Literature*. New York: St. Martin's Press, 1996: 131–48.

———. *Gone Primitive: Savage Intellects, Modern Lives*. Chicago, IL, and London: University of Chicago Press, 1990.

———. *Primitive Passions: Men, Women, and the Quest for Ecstasy*. New York: Alfred A. Knopf, 1997.

Torjesen, Karen Jo. *When Women Were Priests: Women's Leadership in the Early Church and the Scandal of their Subordination in the Rise of Christianity*. San Francisco, CA: Harper, 1994.

Tratner, Michael. *Modernism and Mass Politics: Joyce, Woolf, Eliot, Yeats*. Stanford, CA: Stanford University Press, 1995.

Tremayne, Sydney. "A career for women: being beautiful." *Vogue* ([London] early September, 1923)

Trentmann, Frank. "Civilization and its discontents: English neo-Romanticism and the transformation of anti-modernism in twentieth-century Western culture." *Journal of Contemporary History* 29. 4 (1994): 583–625.

Trevelyan, George Maucaulay. *Must England's Beauty Perish? A Plea on Behalf of the National Trust for Places of Historic Interest or Natural Beauty.* London: Farber & Gwyer, 1929.

Trumback, Randolph. "London's sapphists: from three sexes to four genders in the making of modern culture." In Gilbert Herdt ed. *Third Sex, Third Gender: Beyond Sexual Dimorphism in Culture and History.* New York: Zone Books, 1994: 111–36.

Tyler, Carole-Anne. "Boys will be girls: the politics of gay drag." In Diana Fuss ed. *Inside/out: Lesbian Theories, Gay Theories.* New York and London: Routledge, 1991: 32–70.

Van De Velde, Th.H. *Sex Hostility in Marriage: Its Origin, Prevention and Treatment.* London: Heinemann, 1931.

Van der Meer, Theo. "Sodomy and the pursuit of a third sex in the early modern period." In Gilbert Herdt ed. *Third Sex, Third Gender: Beyond Sexual Dimorphism in Culture and History.* New York: Zone Books, 1994: 137–212.

Vandivere, Julie. "Waves and fragments: linguistic construction as subject formation in Virginia Woolf." *Twentieth-Century Literature* 42. 2 (1996): 221–33.

Vernon, Frank. "Books we'd like to burn: writers' contorted view of morality." *John Bull* (April 28, 1923).

Vicinus, Martha. *Independent Women: Work and Community for Single Women, 1850–1920.* Chicago, IL, and London: University of Chicago Press, 1985.

Vishram, Rozina. *Ayahs, Lascars and Princes: The History of Indians in Britain, 1700–1947.* London: Pluto Press, 1986.

Wachman, Gay. *Lesbian Empire: Radical Crosswriting in the Twenties.* New Brunswick, NJ: Rutgers University Press, 2001.

Walker, Helen. "The popularization of the outdoor movement, 1900–1940." *British Journal of Sports History* 2. 2.(1985): 140–53.

Walker, Lynn. "Women and architecture." In Jane Rendell, Barbara Penner, and Iain Borden eds. *Gender, Space, Architecture.* London and New York: Routledge, 2000: 244–57.

Walkowitz, Judith. *City of Dreadful Delight: Narratives of Sexual Danger in Late-Victorian London.* Chicago, IL: University of Chicago Press, 1992.

Walton, Jean. "Re-placing race in (white) psychoanalytic discourse." In Elizabeth Abel, Barbara Christian, and Helene Moglen eds. *Female Subjects in Black and White: Race, Psychoanalysis, Feminism.* Berkeley: University of California Press, 1997. 223–51.

Walvin, James. *England, Slaves and Freedom.* Basingstoke: Macmillan, 1986.

Ware, Vron. *Beyond the Pale: White Women, Racism and History.* New York: Verso, 1992.

Warner, Maria. *Monuments and Maidens: The Allegory of the Female Form.* New York: Atheneum, 1985.

Warner, Sylvia Townsend. *Collected Poems.* Ed. Claire Harman. New York: Viking Press, 1982.

——. "The Green Valley." *Selected Poems.* New York: Viking Books, 1985.

——. *I'll Stand by You: The Letters of Sylvia Townsend Warner and Valentine Ackland.* Ed. Susanna Pinney. London: Pimlico, 1998.

——. *Letters.* Ed. William Maxwell. New York: Viking, 1982.

——. *Lolly Willowes or the Loving Huntsman.* Chicago: Academy, 1978.

——. *Mr. Fortune's Maggot*. London: Virago, 1978 [1927].

——. *Summer Will Show*. New York and London: Penguin Books, 1987.

——. *The True Heart*. New York: Viking Press, 1929.

——. "The way by which I have come." *The Countryman: A Quarterly Review and Miscellany of Rural Life and Progress* (July, 1939): 472–86.

——. "Women as writers." In Bonnie Kine Scott ed. *The Gender of Modernism: A Critical Anthology*. Bloomington and Indianapolis: Indiana University Press, 1990: 538–46.

Watson, Paul. "'Siamese twins': the verbal and the visual in Dorothy Richardson's *Pilgrimage*." *Trivium* 18 (May, 1983): 73–85.

Watts, Carol. *Dorothy Richardson*. Plymouth: Northcote House, 1995.

Webb, Virginia-Lee. "Manipulated images: European photographs of Pacific peoples." In Elazar Barkin and Ronald Bush eds. *Prehistories of the Future: The Primitivist Project and the Culture of Modernism*. Palo Alto, CA: Stanford University Press, 1996: 175–201.

Weber, Charlotte. "Unveiling Scheherazade: feminist Orientalism in the International Alliance of Women, 1911–1950," *Feminist Studies* 27. 1 (2001): 125–57.

Weeks, Jeffrey. *Sex, Politics and Society: The Regulation of Sexuality Since 1800*. New York: Longman, 1981.

Weininger, Otto. *Sex and Character*. New York and Chicago, IL: A.L. Burt, 1906.

West, Rebecca. *Black Lamb and Grey Falcon: A Journey Through Yugoslavia*. New York: Penguin, 1994.

——. "Equal pay for men and women teachers." *Time and Tide* (February 9, 1923): 147.

——. *Harriet Hume: A London Fantasy*. London: Virago, 1980.

——. *The Judge*. London: Virago, 1993.

——. *The Strange Necessity: Essays and Reviews*. London: Jonathan Cape, 1928.

West, Shearer ed. *The Victorians and Race*. Aldershot, UK: Scholar Press, 1996.

Westcott, Glenway. "The first book of Mary Butts." *The Dial* 75 (September, 1923): 282–4.

Weston, Jesse L. *From Ritual to Romance* (1920). Princeton, NJ: Princeton University Press, 1993.

Whitford, Margaret. *Luce Irigaray: Philosophy in the Feminine*. London and New York: Routledge, 1991.

Whittick, Arnold. *Woman into Citizen*. Santa Barbara, CA: Athenaeum Publishing, 1979.

Wier, Alison. *Britain's Royal Families: The Complete Genealogy*. London: Bodley Head, 1989.

Williams, A. Susan. *Ladies of Influence: Women of the Elite in Interwar Britain*. London: Allen Lane–Penguin, 2000.

Williams, Raymond. *Towards 2000*. London: Chatto & Windus, 1983.

Williams-Ellis, Clough. *England and the Octopus*. London: Geoffrey Bles, 1928.

Williamson, Hugh Ross. "A writer's childhood: the testament of Mary Butts." *John O'London's Weekly*. June 11, 1937.

Willis, H.H., Jr. *Leonard and Virginia Woolf as Publishers: The Hogarth Press 1917–1941*. Charlottesville and London: University Press of Virginia, 1992.

Wilson, Elizabeth. *The Sphinx in the City: Urban Life, the Control of Disorder, and Women*. Berkeley: University of California Press, 1991.

Wilson, Leslie. "Broom, broom." *The London Review of Books* (December 2, 1993): 26.

Winning, Joanne. *The Pilgrimage of Dorothy Richardson*. Madison: University of Wisconsin Press, 2000.

Winston, Janet. "'Something out of harmony': *To the Lighthouse* and the subject(s) of empire." *Woolf Studies Annual* 2 (1996): 39–70.

Wolfe, Humbert. "Turning over new leaves." *Vogue* ([London] September 21, 1927).

Wood, Elizabeth, "Sapphonics." In *Queering the Pitch: The New Gay and Lesbian Musicology* eds Philip Brett, Elizabeth Wood, and Gary Thomas. New York: Routledge, 1994, 27–66.

Woolf, Leonard. *Downhill All the Way: An Autobiography of the Years 1919 to 1939* (New York: Harcourt Brace Jovanovich, 1967.

———. *Imperialism and Civilization*. New York: Harcourt Brace, 1928.

Woolf, Virginia. "America, which I have never seen." *Dublin Review* 5 (winter, 2001–2): 56–60.

———. "American fiction." *The Moment and Other Essays*. San Diego, CA: Harcourt Brace, 1947: 113–27.

———. *Between the Acts*. New York: Harcourt Brace, 1969.

———. "Craftsmanship." *Collected Essays*, 4 vols. London: Hogarth Press and New York: Harcourt Brace Jovanovich, 1966–67, Vol. 2 (1966): 245–51.

———. "David Copperfield." *Collected Essays*, 4 vols. London: Hogarth Press and New York: Harcourt Brace Jovanovich, 1966–67, Vol. 1 (1967): 193.

———. *The Diary of Virginia Woolf*. Ed. Anne Olivier Bell. London: Hogarth Press, 5 Vols., 1977–84.

———. "The Elizabethan lumber room." *Collected Essays*. London: Hogarth Press, 1966, Vol. 1: 46–53.

———. *The Essays of Virginia Woolf*. 4 vols. Ed. Andrew McNeillie. London: Hogarth Press, 1986–94.

———. "An expedition to Hampton Court." *A Passionate Apprentice: The Early Journals, 1897–1909*. Ed. Mitchell A. Leaska. San Diego, CA: Harcourt Brace, 1990: 23–32.

———. "George Eliot." *The Essays of Virginia Woolf*. Vol. 4 (1994): 170–80.

———. "Harriette Wilson." *The Essays of Virginia Woolf*. Vol. 4 (1994): 254–59.

———. "Impressions at Bayreuth." *The Essays of Virginia Woolf*. Vol. 1 (1986): 288–92.

———. "Introductory letter." In Margaret Llewelyn Davies ed. *Life As We Have Known It*. New York: W.W. Norton, 1975.

———. "The journal of Mistress Joan Martyn." *The Complete Shorter Fiction of Virginia Woolf*. Ed. Susan Dick. New York: Harcourt Brace, 1985: 33–62.

———. "The leaning tower." *Collected Essays*. London: Hogarth Press, 1966, Vol. 2: 162–81.

———. *The Letters of Virginia Woolf*. 6 vols. Ed. Nigel Nicolson. London: Hogarth Press, 1975–80.

———. "Literary geography." *The Essays of Virginia Woolf*. Vol. 1 (1986): 32–6.

———. "The mark on the wall." *The Complete Shorter Fiction of Virginia Woolf*. Ed. Susan Dick. New York: Harcourt Brace, 1985: 83–9.

———. "Modern fiction." *Collected Essays*. London: Hogarth Press, 1966, Vol. 2: 103–10.

———. "Modern novels." *The Essays of Virginia Woolf*. Vol. 3 (1988): 30–6.

———. "Mr. Bennett and Mrs. Brown." In S.P. Rosenbaum ed. *A Bloomsbury Group Reader*. Oxford, UK, and Cambridge, MA: Blackwell, 1993: 238.

———. *Mrs. Dalloway*. New York: Harcourt Brace & Co., 1925.

———. "The narrow bridge of art." *Granite and Rainbow: Essays*. New York: Harcourt Brace & Co., 1958: 11.

———. *Night and Day*. New York: Penguin, 1992.

———. "On being ill." *The Essays of Virginia Woolf*. Vol. 4 (1994): 317–29.

———. *Orlando*. New York: Harcourt Brace & Co., 1956.

———. *A Passionate Apprentice: The Early Journals, 1897–1909*. Ed. Mitchell A. Leaska. San Diego, CA: Harcourt Brace, 1990.

———. "The Plumage Bill." *The Essays of Virginia Woolf*. Vol. 3 (1988): 241–5.

——. "Professions for women." In S.P. Rosensbaum ed. *A Bloomsbury Group Reader.* Oxford, UK, and Cambridge, MA: Blackwell, 1993: 274–279.

——. *Roger Fry: A Biography.* London: Hogarth Press, 1940.

——. "Romance and the heart." *The Essays of Virginia Woolf.* Vol. 3 (1988): 288–92.

——. *A Room of One's Own.* New York: Harcourt Brace & Co., 1981.

——. "Royalty." *The Moment and Other Essays.* San Diego, CA: Harcourt Brace Jovanovitch, 1974: 234–40.

——. "Sir Walter Raleigh." *The Essays of Virginia Woolf.* Vol. 2 (1987): 91–5.

——. "A sketch of the past." In Jeanne Schulkind ed. *Moments of Being.* New York: Harcourt Brace & Co., 1985: 86–8.

——. "A society." *Complete Shorter Fiction of Virginia Woolf.* Ed. Susan Dick. New York: Harcourt Brace & Co., 1985: 124–36.

——. *Three Guineas.* New York: Harcourt Brace & Co., 1966.

——. *To the Lighthouse.* New York: Harcourt Brace & Co., 1989.

——. "The tunnel." *The Essays of Virginia Woolf.* Vol. 3 (1988): 10–12.

——. *The Voyage Out.* New York: Harcourt Brace & Co., 1948.

——. *The Waves.* New York: Harcourt Brace & Co., 1978.

——. *The Waves: The Two Holograph Drafts.* Ed. J.W. Graham. Toronto: University of Toronto Press, 1976.

——. "Women and fiction." In Michele Barrett ed. *Women and Writing.* New York: Harcourt Brace & Co., 1979: 58–64.

——. "Women and fiction." *Collected Essays.* London: Hogarth Press, 1966, Vol. 2: 141–8.

——. "Women novelists." In Michele Barrett ed. *Women and Writing.* New York: Harcourt Brace & Co., 1979: 68–71.

——. *A Writer's Diary.* Ed. Leonard Woolf. New York: Harcourt Brace & Co., 1954.

——. *The Years.* New York: Harcourt Brace & Co., 1965.

Wood, Ruby Ross. "Blackamoors come back into fashion." *Vogue* ([London] May 17, 1933).

Woollacott, Angela. *To Try Her Fortune in London: Australian Women, Colonialism, and Modernity.* Oxford: Oxford University Press, 2001.

Wright, Patrick. *On Living in an Old Country: The National Past in Contemporary Britain.* London: Verso, 1985.

——. *The Village that Died for England: The Strange Story of Tyneham.* London: Vintage, 1996.

Yuval-Davis, Nira. *Gender and Nation.* London and Thousand Oaks, CA: Sage, 1997.

Zimmerman, Bonnie. "Perverse reading: the lesbian appropriation of literature." In Susan J. Wolfe and Julia Penelope eds. *Sexual Practice, Textual Theory: Lesbian Cultural Criticism.* Cambridge, MA, and Oxford: Blackwell, 1993: 135–49.

——. *The Safe Sea of Women: Lesbian Fiction 1969–1989.* Boston, MA: Beacon Press, 1989.

Zwerdling, Alex. *Virginia Woolf and the Real World.* Berkeley: University of California Press, 1986.

Index

Ackland, Valentine, 26, 143, 149
America, 16–17, 26, 34n. 68
Anderson, Benedict, 11–12, 21, 28, 245,
  257, 259–60
Anglo-Saxon, 22–3, 58, 107, 191, 285
anti-feminism, 44, 67
anti-Semitism, 51, 66, 113, 225, 228
  see also Jew, the
Arthurian legend, 189, 208, 272, 276, 286,
  300
Astor, Nancy, 76n. 2
Atholl, Duchess of, 6, 23, 50
autoeroticism, 163–4, 269

Bachelard, Gaston, 266
Baldwin, Stanley, 21
  "On England and the West," 59
Barnes, Djuna, 148
Bataille, Georges, 221
beauty culture, 57–63, 103, 262
Bhabha, Homi K., 110, 252
bi-location, 147, 149, 152, 176, 299–300
Biron, Sir Chartres, 142
birth control, 63, 67
blackness
  Englishness, 306
  Hearts in Dixie, 98–9
  homosexuality, 191, 212
  Otherness, 109–11
  Richardson and, 98–9, 136n. 121
  see also race
Bland, Lucy, 64
Bloomsbury Group, 19, 52, 188–9, 284
body, female
  agent of civilization, 15, 190

beauty culture, 54
chastity, 54
conquest, 264
disciplining of, 4
essentialized, 260
feminine discourse, 270–1
geography, 27–8, 190, 210, 218, 303
law, 56
lesbian, 118, 138n. 146, 300
London, 7
mass culture, 60
materiality, 270
maternity, 1, 251, 265–6, 283, 285, 288–9
medical experts on, 44
national life, 2, 26–7, 73, 90
nature, 275
race, 4, 22, 224, 304
reproduction, 260–1
visibility, 53, 63
witch, 167
Bowen, Elizabeth, 57
  The Death of the Heart, 60
breast, maternal, 276–9
Britannia, 31n. 22
Britishness, 22, 29n. 2
Browne, Stella, 55, 63, 67
Bryher, Winifred, 85–6, 97
Burdekin, Katherine, *Swastika Night*,
  299
Burton, Antoinette, 12, 66–7, 96
Bush, Barbara, 14
Butts, Mary
  Armed With Madness, 62, 189, 191–2,
    204, 207–10, 214, 231–2
  Ashe of Rings, 215–16